Curriculum-Based Evaluation

Curriculum-Based Evaluation
Teaching and Decision Making

Second Edition

Kenneth W. Howell
Western Washington University

Sheila L. Fox
Western Washington University

Mada Kay Morehead
Kyrene School District
Tempe, Arizona

Brooks/Cole Publishing Company
Pacific Grove, California

Sponsoring Editor: Vicki Knight
Marketing Representative: Karen Buttles
Editorial Assistant: Heather L. Graeve
Print Buyer: Vena M. Dyer
Production: Julie Kranhold, *Ex Libris*; Joan Marsh
Manuscript Editor: Judy Johnstone
Interior Design: Nancy Benedict
Interior Art: Lotus Art, Williams, Oregon
Photo Research: Dianne J. Rhudy, *Ex Libris*
Typesetting: Shepard Poorman Communications
Cover Printing: Phoenix Color Corporation
Printing and Binding: R.R. Donnelley at Crawfordsville
Cover Design: Roy Neuhaus
Cover Art: Ron Grauer

Brooks/Cole Publishing Company
A Division of Wadsworth, Inc.

Printed in the United States of America
10 9 8 7 6 5 4 3 2 1
Library of Congress Cataloging-in-Publication Data
Howell, Kenneth W.
    Curriculum-based assessment : teaching and decision making /
Kenneth W. Howell, Sheila L. Fox and Mada Kay Morehead. -- 2nd ed.
        p.   cm.
    Rev. ed. of: Curriculum-based evaluation for special and remedial
education. 1987.
    Includes bibliographical references (p.   ) and index.
    ISBN 0-534-16428-5 : $29.00
    1. Curriculum-based assessment--United States.   2. Educational
tests and measurements--United States.   I. Fox, Sheila L., 1945-
. II. Morehead, Mada Kay.   III. Howell, Kenneth W.   Curriculum
-based evaluation for special and remedial education.   IV. Title.
LB3060.32.C74H68   1993
371.2'7--dc20   92-43402
                                                          CIP

This text is dedicated to Alvin and Claire Howell.
The love they cast dissolved the years to give us continuity and comfort.

"Though we talk little here, I am never lonely; I am returned into myself."

Peter Matthiessen, *The Snow Leopard*

Photo Credits

Preface

This text represents an expansion and revision of several previous works on the topic of evaluation and teaching. Throughout this sequence, we have become increasingly aware of two things: the need to emphasize decision making over measurement, and the need to unite the functions of evaluation and instruction. Both are reflected in this volume.

The literature for practitioners is filled monthly with the business of assessment: journal articles with baseline and intervention data, task analyses, statistical operations of all sorts, and critiques and defenses of one or another of the seeming hundreds of tests used to identify, label, place, or program for children who need help in school. But mechanisms for distilling and coordinating this inventory of professional material are seldom provided. In fact, common practice in the classroom seems to continue in the same unproductive direction regardless of the literature.

This text was written in an attempt to break through the inertia of common practice by integrating the basic concepts of evaluation and instruction with the best current knowledge, in order to generate productive tools for classroom use. Not surprisingly, the goal of integration has dictated the plan of this book. Part One consists of five chapters that focus on the thought processes of teachers and the basic models of evaluation and teaching. Part Two consists of four chapters that explain, demonstrate, and encourage practice in functional evaluation. Part Three illustrates the application of material from the first two parts across academic and social-skills content. This part includes extensive material on the things teachers teach. It also provides exact directions for deciding which of these to teach a particular student. In a very real way Part Three of this text—in combination with the accompanying workbook—is more an assessment manual than a textbook.

The workbook, which complements this text, is not a supplement. It contains instructional activities designed to make the content of the text concrete, serviceable, and handy. This will be accomplished for the early chapters through the use of problem-solving exercises. The portion of the workbook aligned with Part Three of the text, in addition to containing testing and interpretation materials, contains practice items utilizing the works of real students. These items have been selected to provide the reader with relevant practice.

Finally, Appendix material is included in the text as a source of support for teachers who want a quick (and, we hope, understandable) guide to the statistical and instructional content referenced in the chapters.

Rationale for Our Approach

The majority of special/remedial students (sometimes called mildly disabled) require services because of their failure to learn the academic or social curriculum presented in school. These "exceptional" services may range from modifications by the general education teacher to placement and service in a separate program. The special programs developed to combat student failure (not only special and remedial education programs but also migrant education, bilingual education, and those for students disadvantaged by their living conditions) have many commonalties (Wang, Reynolds, & Walberg, 1986). For example, each program's primary goal is to raise the student's level of curricular performance. Regulatory intricacies and technical vocabulary aside, the nature of special/remedial education is easy to describe: Students who are behind in the curriculum are placed in special programs and those who catch up are (it is hoped) removed from them. Therefore, by its very nature, special/remedial education for the mildly disabled is *curriculum-based.*

Functional, classroom-based evaluation draws much of its strength from the *principle of alignment.* This principle states that greater learning will occur in programs that ensure that evaluation and instruction complement each other. The catalyst for this alignment is the curriculum (i.e., the body of things a student is expected to learn). In other words, students will learn more if teachers use materials and activities that target needed portions of the curriculum and make decisions from tests that measure those portions of the curriculum. This "test what you teach" and "teach what you test" orientation makes common sense and has been found to be very effective.

Curriculum-based evaluation is not new (Carroll, 1963). However, in the past it has lost the competition for coverage in journals and texts in special education and educational psychology. We blame this loss on a pervasive and misguided myth about special/remedial students. That is the myth that these students have fixed and unalterable defects that prevent typical learning. While the rest of education has been acutely interested in curriculum-based issues such as *mastery learning, outcome-based instruction* and *teacher effectiveness*, special/remedial education has often shown more interest in the characteristics of its students than in the activities of its teachers. It is important to understand that it is this failure to focus on curriculum and instruction, not the absence of functional technology, that has led to the inertia that clogs current practice. In short, we are where we are today because a lot of us have made mistakes in thinking. Unfortunately such mistakes are not corrected by writing new tests, rather, they are corrected by promoting new ways to solve problems. That is what this text attempts to do.

The most easily recognized label for the thought processes and techniques we will present in this text is "curriculum-based evaluation," however other terms such as "functional evaluation," "practical evaluation," "situation-centered evaluation" and even "direct evaluation" are all descriptive. Whatever the terminology, this approach to evaluation is no less complex, theoretical, or sophisticated than the traditional approach, which focuses on the incapacities of students. While it does involve some different procedures and techniques, its main distinction is one of focus. It focuses on what teachers and evaluators do— not on who they do it to.

From any perspective, educational decision making is a complex task. Many teachers and psychologists do not do it well. In this book, we have tried to say how it should be done, but we recognize that it frequently won't be done our way. In part this is because many teachers lack the time, the materials, or the support needed to employ the best classroom practices. The authors recognize that the efforts of schools and teachers are often vandalized by social failures beyond

the scope of this text. However, functional decision making, and the tools required to carry it out, are within the scope of this text. These procedures are also within the reach of most teachers.

Evaluation is a difficult, time-consuming business. We'd like to claim that our techniques will save you time and effort, but they probably won't. What we *can* offer you is a chance to feel good about time well spent. This book won't fix many of the things that prevent you from doing your best, but it can see to it that you are never prevented from using quality practice because you don't know how!

Notes on the Text

1. References to the gender of students and teachers are reversed in each chapter of this text. Therefore, in one chapter all references will be male and in the next they will be female. This pattern does not hold when specific case studies are provided. In those instances, references to the gender of the student involved is not changed.

2. To facilitate referral, all figures and tables in this text are called "exhibits." This will make Part Three of the text easier to use. A number of these exhibits will be followed by an asterisk (star), which stands for "application." This means that the exhibit in question will be put to use during the actual evaluation of students. We grant you permission to duplicate these starred exhibits for the purpose of working with students.

   Each starred exhibit will be duplicated in the accompanying workbook. Starred exhibits in the text may be smaller than those in the workbook. The ones in the workbook are the ones we expect you to duplicate and use. Finally, all starred exhibits are listed on page x of the text.

3. Throughout the text, notations like these will appear: (see Chapter 1, pp. 4–5). These notations are provided to help you find related information without having to refer to the index. In some cases, when the coverage of a topic is infused throughout a chapter, page numbers will not be supplied.

4. Each chapter begins with a quote. The first nine chapters also start with a map of the concepts presented in the chapter. We have selected the

map format because we believe that it illustrates the interrelation of ideas more accurately than an outline. We recommend that students use these maps when studying.

5. Sometimes we will refer to our clients as students, and at other times we will refer to them—as we do in our everyday conversations—as "kids." However, many of the practices explained in this text have utility for anyone, regardless of age, experiencing difficulty learning the content we address. Please do not assume that the use of "kid" is intended to preclude adult learners.

Acknowledgment

Much of the material presented here is drawn directly from the invaluable work of Joe Kaplan. Dr. Kaplan's orientations to education, and his conceptualization of evaluative practice are as much a part of this work as those of the current authors, and we thank him for his contribution. We also wish to thank those who reviewed and worked on the text, particularly Ange Evoy for his hours of attention, Austin Witter for her perseverance, Pam Hamilton for her unrestricted assistance, and Karna Nelson for her provision of reality checks. In addition, we are grateful to James Palmer, Teresa Howard, Rebecca Olson, John Freeman, and Bridget Karns for their efforts in preparing and organizing the manuscript. Our special thanks goes to Susan Bigelow for tolerance and alacrity. And finally, I wish to thank Kathy Lorson-Howell for her contributions of indulgence and mercy.

We would also like to acknowledge the assistance of the following reviewers: Leonard P. Haines, University of Saskatchewan at Saskatoon; Harry Dangel, Georgia State University at Atlanta; Sharon Raimondi and Richard Towne, State University College at Buffalo; Nancy L. Cooke, University of North Carolina at Charlotte; Tom Lovitt, University of Washington at Seattle; and Gregory Williams, Pacific Lutheran University, Tacoma, Washington.

KWH

Starred Exhibits Duplicated in the Workbook

Exhibit 10.1* Comprehension Status Sheet

Exhibit 10.8* Status Sheet for Awareness of the Reading Process

Exhibit 11.3* Passage Summary Sheet with Criteria for Acceptable Performance

Exhibit 11.5* Awareness of Print and Sound

Exhibit 11.6* Error Pattern Checklist: Specific-Level Procedure 5b

Exhibit 11.7* Decoding Content Checklist: Specific-Level Procedure 5c

Exhibit 11.8* Error Category Checklist for Meaning Violations: SLP 5a

Exhibit 12.4* A Table of Specifications for Language Syntactic Structures

Exhibit 12.8* Setting Observation

Exhibit 12.9* Table of Specifications for the Executive Function of Pragmatics

Exhibit 12.10* Table of Specifications for Communication Skills

Exhibit 13.4* Analytic Scales for Dimensions of Writing Using a Five-Point Anchors of Quality

Exhibit 13.6* Status Sheet for SLP 1: Interview/Observation of Writing Process and Product

Exhibit 13.9* A Modification of Isaacson's Syntax Scale

Exhibit 14.4* Writing Sample Summary

Exhibit 14.6* Handwriting errors.

Exhibit 14.11* Mechanics Error Summary

Exhibit 15.6* Asking Questions

Exhibit 15.10* Math Summary Checklist

Exhibit 15.14* Application Survey Answer Sheet

Exhibit 15.15* Applications Content Test

Exhibit 16.18* Social Skills Status Sheet

Exhibit 16.20* Thinking Error Summary

Exhibit 17.1* Status Sheet for Task Related Knowledge

Exhibit 17.4* Checklist for Study/Test Taking and Problem Solving/Self-Monitoring

Exhibit 17.5* Basic Learning Strategies and a Sequence of Assistance

Contents

Curriculum-Based Evaluation

Part 1 / Things to Think About

The relationships among evaluation, curriculum, and instruction, while difficult to influence, can be stated fairly simply:

Curriculum is what we teach;

Instruction is how we teach it; and

Evaluation guides the process.

Part 1 was written to provide the reader with the vocabulary and background knowledge needed to understand and carry out the processes presented in Parts 2 and 3. All of the chapters in Part 1, especially Chapters 1 and 5, supply definitions for evaluation, curriculum, and instruction. They also elaborate on the specifics of evaluation and decision making. Chapters 2, 3, and 4 supply mostly technical infor-

mation. Chapter 2 explains how different views of learners result in different views of teaching. Chapter 3 explains that the curriculum is a set of outcome expectations. These expectations, which are typically called objectives, are much more complex than most of us think. In Chapter 4 we explain how the various elements of objectives, and their subdivisions, can be addressed through instruction. We also explain how different thought processes (factual, strategic, and conceptual) can be promoted through different forms of teaching.

Part 1 is crowded with information. In order to make this information useful we have provided exercises in the accompanying workbook that reinforce the lessons in each chapter. We urge you to make use of them.

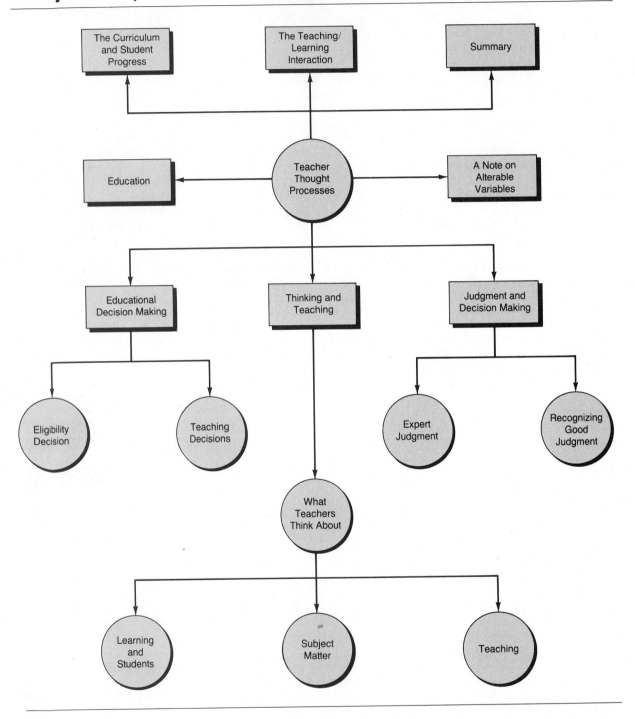

Situations, or tasks, rather than people, should be the basic units of analysis.

—E. Brunswick (1943)

Formal education is planned and carried out by our society at great public expense. If you ask people why we do this, you're apt to get a lot of different answers. One of the most common answers is "to help students learn." We now know that learning is a complex phenomenon, and rather than try to explain what it is, let's simply acknowledge its complexity and say that it is best indicated by changes in student performance (Ohlsson & Rees, 1991). That is, students have learned something if they leave class *doing* (overt behavior) or *thinking* (covert behavior) something different from when they entered.

The exact products of education—and their value—are frequently debated, but most of us would probably agree that they fall into the areas of (a) promotion of knowledge, (b) promotion of skill, (c) certification, and (d) custodial service (Boulding, 1972). Teachers focus on promotion of knowledge and skill, while certifications (in the form of grades, degrees, credentials, and transcripts) are supposed to document the students' acquired knowledge and skills. And, although it is a painful realization for many professional teachers, it is simply a fact of modern economic and social reality that schools also provide a custodial service by occupying student time (Glass, 1974a).

The Curriculum and Student Progress

Teachers tend to focus on the promotion of skills and knowledge. For them, the purpose of education is to prepare people to be socially competent. These "things" are the skills and knowledge formally articulated in a school's curriculum. A curriculum is a structured set of learning outcomes (objectives) result-

ing from instruction (Johnson, 1967). Curriculum is pivotal to all instructional activities, including evaluation. The curriculum indicates what we need to teach and when we need to teach it.

Because all the things in the curriculum cannot be taught at the same time, the curriculum must be subdivided so that different objectives can be assigned to different grades, classes, and times of the year. A complete curriculum specifies what will be learned and when it will be learned (for example, most school districts expect students to have learned multiplication facts by the end of third grade).

Exhibit 1.1 shows a line of expected student progress. The line is determined by noting the intersections of time spent in school and various levels of curriculum. This line indicates that a student is expected to have learned one year's worth of curriculum in one year's time. Students whose progress falls above the line are working above their expected level; students whose progress falls below the line are below expectation.

Special and remedial students are those who, for various reasons, have trouble moving through the curriculum at the expected rate. For example, the student shown in Exhibit 1.2 is not progressing as he should. The student was expected to learn 5 years' worth of objectives in 5 years of schooling. However, he has only learned about 2.5 years' worth of curriculum. Therefore, he is only progressing at 50% of the expected rate. This failure to progress typically prompts teachers or parents to seek special support for their students. This support commonly involves attempts to fix whatever is preventing the student from learning adequately in the general-education class, or to move the student through the curriculum faster in order to catch up. To accomplish these changes, a decision-making process must be set in motion.

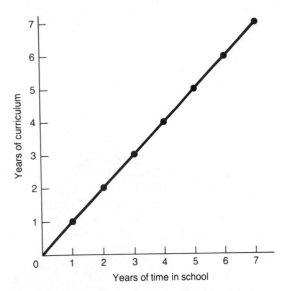

Exhibit 1.1   Expected course of student learning.

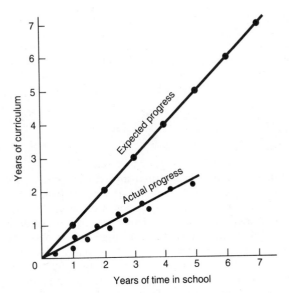

Exhibit 1.2   Actual course of learning of special student.

Educational Decision Making

To help students who are behind, we must make changes in their educational programs. For students with disabilities, these modifications are required by laws such as PL 101-476, the Individuals with Disabilities Act (IDEA), and PL 101-336, the Americans with Disabilities Act (ADA). But they should also represent best educational practice. Continuing to use techniques that have failed in the past shows poor judgment and is a waste of student and teacher time. Therefore, we must modify our instruction by applying exceptional evaluation and teaching techniques. In other words, we must do something different, or exceptional, to help the child catch up. We must decide which of many paths to take when selecting objectives, settings, facilities, groupings, materials, and staff. If we use good judgment, make the correct decisions and carry them out effectively, the student's progress and performance will be improved. Exhibit 1.3 shows the progress of a student before and after an educational decision was made. Before the decision was made, the student was not progressing adequately; after the decision was made, he was. It is important to know (and to believe strongly) that teaching can have this kind of positive effect on student

learning. You are more likely to have this sort of positive effect if your educational decisions are guided by appropriate evaluative information.

Let's take a quick look into the box in Exhibit 1.3 labeled Decision Making. Educational decisions serve two functions: to guide placement and to guide teaching.

Placement Decisions

Placement decisions deal with the assignment of the student to a particular category of students, resources, or services. Placement decisions concern grouping, grading, retention/promotion, screening, and the determination of eligibility for remedial or support programs (such as services for students needing to acquire English or those needing additional reading instruction).

The general heading of Placement Decisions also covers decisions about the duration of service, the service model to be employed, and the district, school, and program to be used. These placement decisions pertain to students' movement within the school system and their purpose is classification. That is, they involve sorting activity through which students are

The purpose of education is the promotion of knowledge and skills.

assigned into general categories (for example, "students needing summer school" versus "students not needing summer school").

Schools handle large numbers of students. As a result, they traditionally reserve support programs for those who need them most. Therefore, classificatory decisions are usually normative; that is, they are based on comparison of students to each other. Under current regulations these comparisons seem to require the use of measurement instruments, such as achievement tests, which are designed to identify the students, relative to others, most in need. By using a few items ranging from very easy to very hard, these normative instruments cover a range of content to highlight students' relative achievement. It is an error to assume that such tests say anything useful about how individual students should be taught.

Although the current literature reflects an interest in collaborative and integrated educational programs within schools (Baker & Zigmond, 1990; Nowacek, 1992; Ysseldyke, Algozzine & Thurlow, 1992), this orientation is still rarely applied to all students. Classification—particularly classification into various disabling conditions—remains more common than it is useful.

Teaching Decisions

Teaching decisions deal with two things: what will be taught and how it will be taught. These decisions include the specification of objectives, materials, time, instructors, and other instructional variables. Teaching decisions are based on different information than are placement decisions. The normative standards and global measures used in placement are not functional for guiding teaching. There are two reasons for this. First, the variables measured during placement evaluations (intelligence, general achievement, chronological age) are chosen because they are "unalterable" (that is, resistant to change through instruction; you might teach a kid for a month and see terrific academic progress but his score on an achievement test wouldn't

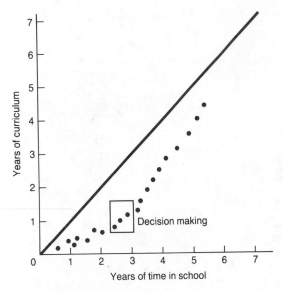

Exhibit 1.3   *Effect of decision making on educational progress.*

Special and remedial students are those who, for various reasons, have trouble moving through the curriculum at the expected rate.

change much—it isn't supposed to). Second, as mentioned above, the placement instruments used to classify students sample very large domains of curriculum. Consequently, they produce results that lack the specificity and focus needed to guide daily decision making. In other words, if somebody hands you a copy of a kid's scores on the California Achievement Test, or tells you his IQ is 85, or says he's in the bottom 10% of his grade, you still don't know what to teach him or how. To start teaching, you need different information.

For these reasons it is best to keep placement and teaching clearly separated in our thought and practice. The placement criteria developed to move students through the school system, and to hold the entire system accountable, reflect policies that vary from year to year, and district to district. These criteria, as will be explained in Chapter 9, are often determined as much by funding, political, and administrative trends as they are by sound educational practice. For example, in the mid-1960s, when learning disabilities (LD) was being defined as a condition excluding mental retardation (MR), the definition of retardation most commonly applied was an IQ below 80. Therefore, an LD student became anyone who could not learn and who scored

over 80 on an IQ test. Later many states changed the maximum IQ for MR to 70 but left the lower limit of LD at 80. This happened because two different committees set the two definitions. As a result, a large group of learners with IQ scores between 70 and 80 were left without any available category, a situation that still exists in some school districts. Because these non-LD and non-MR students need special/remedial instruction as much as their formally classified peers, they are often treated "under the table" by special/remedial teachers. This same process of redefinition is currently occurring relative to the groups of students called "seriously emotionally disturbed" and "socially maladjusted" and, once again, it is very political (Nelson, Rutherford, Center & Walker, 1991; Maag & Howell, 1992).

In contrast to placement criteria, the proficiency criteria for task performance and the prerequisite skills students must master to succeed in their work are determined, to a large extent, by the tasks making up the curriculum. A child labeled mentally retarded in New Jersey may not be labeled mentally retarded

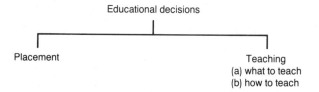

Exhibit 1.4   *Types of decisions.*

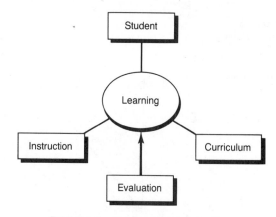

Exhibit 1.5   *The learning interaction.*

in California. But a child who knows her math facts in California will still know her math facts when she gets to New Jersey. These outcomes, which do not vary from district to district, are easily altered through instruction and should be reflected on the tests used to guide teaching.

As shown in Exhibit 1.4, teaching decisions fall into two categories: what to teach and how to teach. Both of these categories are directly tied to the curriculum, just as the whole concept of teaching is tied to moving the student through curriculum. The purpose of teaching is promotion of desired changes in the student's literacy, numeracy, social skills, language, or topical knowledge. When these desired changes do not take place, the student is not progressing. This lack of progress can be attributed to poor decision making or to ineffective implementation of decisions already made.

Before anyone gets nervous, let us be quick to assert that poor decision making does not necessarily mean bad teaching. Ineffective instruction simply means that the teaching is not producing the desired learning (change). There are many types of treatment, and the special/remedial teacher must select the best one for each student. This selection, when based on good evaluative information and a good decision-making model, can increase the student's progress.

The Learning Interaction

Learning is interactive. It arises from the interchange of many factors that can be grouped under the headings of Student, Curriculum, and Instruction (see Exhibit 1.5). Because it is interactive, learning will not take place if one of the factors is missing. A teacher with no material to present and no one to present it to will not produce learning, just as a student without instruction (of some sort) will not learn. Therefore,

when learning occurs, we must be willing to give some credit to each of the three elements: instruction (evaluation and teaching), student, and curriculum. Similarly, when learning fails to occur, we must consider each element. Most important, we must consider each element not in isolation but in interaction with the others.

All of us have encountered material that was easy for us to learn but proved difficult for someone else— or teachers under whose instruction we seemed to learn easily while the person next to us sweated out the course in near despair. These different interactions resulted from the relative influences of various student, instruction, and task characteristics. These interactions cannot occur if one of the elements is isolated. A student's reading problem, for example, cannot be identified if he is not given something to read, and the kind of reading problem he appears to have will depend in large part on the kind of material we ask him to read.

The interactive nature of learning, illustrated in Exhibit 1.5, means that evaluations designed to guide instruction must focus on interactions themselves, not on individual components of interactions (Eisner, 1982). This focus is represented by the placement of the calipers in Exhibit 1.5. The point of all this is simple. The solution for a student's failure to learn will not be found by looking just at the kid. It is critical that this point be understood because the traditional procedure for evaluating special/remedial students has been, and unfortunately continues to be, to examine unalterable personal characteristics such as IQ, learn-

**Exhibit 1.6
Effects of early
decision
making on
progress of
students.**

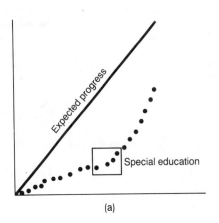

(a)

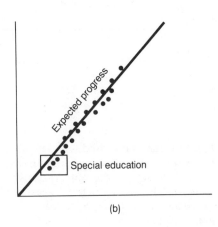

(b)

ing style, cerebral dominance, perceptual ability, preferred mode of information processing, and family/home variables. This tendency to blame the student for the failure has a long history and is deeply entrenched in our thinking about success and failure in school and life.

Obviously we are proposing a shift away from our preoccupation with unalterable student characteristics. This is hardly a new proposal, but it remains timely. Consider the following example, which is a logical extension of our discussion of progress and decision making. In Exhibit 1.2, data were presented showing the learning of a student who was falling behind in school. Does this mean that there was something wrong with the student? Consider for a moment that the whole idea behind special/remedial education is that instruction can alter the rate at which students learn. This premise is basic to the entire teaching profession. What it means can be seen in Exhibits 1.6a and 1.6b. In Exhibit 1.6a the student is moving across time but is functioning below expected levels. Then, as a result of the decision making and instruction that takes place, the student progresses faster.

Even if every child does not make that much progress, it is imperative that educators think they will (Clark & Peterson, 1986). This is the most basic premise of all formal education: *Instruction matters.*

The solution in Exhibit 1.6b is only slightly different. In this case the student has received appropriate instruction all along, and as a result has never fallen behind. This illustration is not intended to build a case for early intervention. Instead, it is intended to make

the point that if a student can catch up with special instruction, then the lack of it can make a student fall behind. We can't have it both ways. *If the pupil has not learned, the teacher has not taught.*

Once again, if instruction can help a student change, the student has failed to change because instruction has been inappropriate. It is interesting to note that talking about inappropriate instruction tends to alienate some teachers much faster than talking about the problems of students. And it is true that while a teacher may reassure parents that the substandard performance of their child isn't anything to feel angry or guilty about, the same teacher will probably feel guilty and ashamed if the source of the substandard performance is somehow traced back to the teacher.

But inappropriate instruction, as pointed out earlier, is not synonymous with bad teaching. *Inappropriate instruction* is instruction that didn't work. It means that, for some reason, the decisions made to influence learning were not arranged to that student's benefit. Today these decisions may be made through a shared process of collaboration and consultation. However, the teacher still has primary responsibility.

A Note on Alterable Variables

Throughout this chapter we use terms like *alterable variables, unalterable variables, prior knowledge,* and *student characteristics.* These terms deserve some clarification. A *variable* is an environmental or student characteristic. ("Student height" is a variable and so is "intensity of room lighting.") *Alterable variables* are things that can be changed through reasonable efforts. *Unalterable variables* cannot be changed, or require unreasonable efforts to change. Because we are talking about instructional efforts here, when we say something is unalterable, we mean that thing can't be changed through reasonable instructional effort.

Here are some variables that, in this sense, we consider to be unalterable: IQ, race (student or teacher), gender (student or teacher), family poverty, parental drug use, ethnicity, teachers' education, teachers' caring, class size, birth order, various student abilities (cerebral dominance, sequential processing, IQ), and student disability category. While we consider these to be unalterable because they cannot be changed through reasonable instruction, they are not unimportant; they are simply beyond the influence of effective instruction. Certainly parental drug use, class size, and family poverty can be changed—and they should be! In fact, all of these variables can be altered at some level, but that alteration won't come about through classroom instruction. That is why, in spite of their importance, we have called them unalterable.

What are *alterable variables*? They are the things related to instruction that teachers can control or change. Here are some alterable kid variables: knowledge of vowel sounds, appreciation of literature, desire to learn spelling, attention to critical passage content, memory skills, analysis of social settings, and addition rate. All of these variables are the result of a student's previous learning (Snow & Lohman, 1984) and reside in what we call the student's "prior knowledge" (see Chapter 2).

Here are some alterable teacher variables: use of wait time, review of classroom rules, focus on objectives, and organization. These teaching variables, as you will discover in Chapter 4, can be controlled. It is also reasonable to expect teachers to control them. We believe these changes will be effective only if teachers make judicious decisions. We also believe that the quality of teacher decision making can be altered.

Thinking About Teaching

Variables that influence instructional practice produce what Bloom (1976) referred to as *quality of instruction*. Instructional quality variables, rather than

unalterable student traits, are the focus of a substantial portion of the current teaching research (Northwest Regional Laboratory, 1990; Nowacek, McKinney & Hallahan, 1990; Wang, Haertel & Walberg, 1990). Originally, instructional quality research focused on the interaction of what teachers do and how students respond (Anania, 1983). This research resulted in the recognition of sets of teacher actions (how they use questions, review previous lessons, explain new material) that promote student learning (Christenson, Ysseldyke & Thurlow, 1989; Rosenshine & Stevens, 1986). These investigations into the things teachers do have now been followed by examinations of what teachers think (Carter, Cushing, Sabers, Stein & Berliner, 1988; Shavelson, 1983). The critical assumptions behind this research are that: teacher thought processes determine teacher actions, the thought processes of effective teachers differ, and the thought processes teachers employ can be changed in ways that will improve their classroom effectiveness (Berliner, 1989; Clark & Peterson, 1986; Gersten, 1990; Shavelson & Stern, 1981).

Special and remedial support programs are based on the belief that well-trained teachers working through collaboration can more effectively solve problems (Lloyd, Crowley, Kohler & Strain, 1988; Pugach & Johnson, 1988; Idol and West, 1987). The idea is that teachers selected and trained to solve classroom problems will think of things that other teachers won't. A basic impediment to this collaborative approach is that different teachers think different things (Gersten, 1990). Special/remedial educators for example, often approach problems through a "deficit model" (see Chapter 3).

Teachers make a lot of decisions. By some estimates they may make as many as one decision every two minutes (Clark & Peterson, 1986). These decisions are products of the teacher's thought processes. They are determined by the way a teacher thinks about the elements of learning, students, curriculum, and instruction illustrated in Exhibit 1.5.

Learning and Students

What teachers believe about the way students learn affects the way they teach (Fuchs, Fuchs, Hamlett & Ferguson, 1992; Pugach & Johnson, 1988; Shulman, 1986). Given the major changes that have occurred in the field of learning theory in the last two decades, particularly with respect to problem learners (Wang & Peverly, 1987), it can be expected that not all teachers share a common view of the learning process (Gersten, 1990). This is why learning will be discussed in some detail in Chapter 2.

What teachers think about their students as individuals can also have a profound impact on the way they interact with them in class. This has been shown within the broad context of teacher-expectation literature (Good & Brophy, 1986) and the more specific content of student evaluation (Cadwell & Jenkins, 1986; Hemingway, Hemingway, Hutchinson & Kuhns, 1987).

The way teachers think about students is so important that its impact goes beyond lesson and classroom effects to the school level. High teacher expectations, and an unwillingness to write off students who have trouble, are listed as primary determinants of school effectiveness (Good & Brophy, 1986; Teddlie, Kirby & Stringfield, 1989).

Considerable research has examined the role of teacher thoughts about students. This research has found that teachers' problem-solving skills are limited by their own stereotyping and value judgments (Shavelson & Stern, 1981). It appears that teachers' judgments about students hinge as much on their own theories of learning as they do on observations of individual students (Cadwell & Jenkins, 1986; Clark & Peterson, 1986). Teacher beliefs about students are addressed further in Chapter 2.

Teaching

Leinhardt and Greeno (1986) say that teaching skill resides within two systems: knowledge of the lesson structure, and knowledge of the subject matter being taught. A skilled teacher's knowledge of lesson structure is composed in large part of "routines" that allow the teacher to carry out relatively low-level classroom tasks efficiently while allocating most of their attention and energy to important goals.

Knowledge of lesson structure includes certain teacher actions, or functions, that have been found to be necessary for effective instruction (Rosenshine & Stevens, 1986). These include lesson preview, explanation, demonstration, guided practice, correction, and independent practice. As will be explained in Chapter 4, part of effective teaching includes being proficient

in accessing routines for accomplishing each of these functions, while another aspect of effective teaching involves deciding which action to implement. What is unclear is how much of the decision-making process involved in the delivery of any given lesson can be planned ahead of time and how much must be based on information picked up during the lesson (Leinhardt & Greeno, 1986). Certainly a teacher who doesn't have a readily implemented routine for using guided practice won't use it. This is true even if there is knowledge that guided practice is needed.

Subject Matter

Peterson, Fennema, Carpenter, and Loef (1989) cite Shulman's (1986) observation that the failure to consider a teacher's knowledge of the content being taught is a major blind spot in investigations of teaching. Teacher beliefs about the content they teach have simply not received the attention given their beliefs about students or about the teaching process itself.

Teachers vary widely in their beliefs about content—the endless debates about the importance of phonics in reading (McGee & Lomax, 1990; Schickedanz, 1990; Stahl, 1990) is an example. What teachers believe about the task being taught interacts with how they teach it. Therefore, in order to influence teaching, we must offer information about content as well as instruction. Chapters 9–16 present information about the specific content typically taught to special and remedial students. Chapters 4 and 8 cover general information about instruction.

Judgment and Decision Making

In order to examine judgment, let's try a quick exercise. Respond to each of the following situations by selecting one of the three choices offered with each. Don't bother looking ahead for the correct answer because there isn't one (although we will discuss your responses later). Do commit to an answer in spite of the limited information, as it will help you understand the discussion that follows. This text is intended to be of use to educators, so we encourage you to use it. Go ahead and circle your answers.

Two students, Carl and Jim, are in a sixth-grade teacher's class. Carl has lived in the district for 4 years. Carl is not particularly interested in the things in which Jim is interested. He is tall, needs glasses, and doesn't get along well with some of his peers. In this teacher's class there is a 15% chance that any given student will be hard to teach.

Is the chance that Carl will be hard to teach

a. less than 15%

b. greater than 15%

c. 15%

You are a special education teacher without a lot of spare time. Two new students, Sara and Pam, have been sent to you but you don't have time to work with them both. You could decide which one to work with by flipping a coin (which would give each student a 50/50 chance of getting your attention), but that seems silly. You notice that on Sara's referral the teacher has warned that Sara is in great need of help and is actually "suffering" her way through school.

Is the chance that you'll see Sara

a. less than 50%

b. greater than 50%

c. 50%

In the school where you work, there are two school psychologists. You need to get a student evaluated. Psychologist 1 typically administers tests of general knowledge sampling several grade levels of academic skills, and consults summaries of what teachers and parents think about referred students. Psychologist 2 uses an adaptive behavior scale, IQ test, and an achievement test.

Which psychologist do you want to test your student?

a. 1 more than 2

b. 2 more than 1

c. either one

The heading for this portion of Chapter 1 is "Judgment and Decision Making." Before debriefing your responses to these simulations, maybe the first thing to figure out is whether or not that heading is redundant. Certainly the two words are sometimes used inter-

changeably, but experience tells us that lots of decisions don't necessarily represent good judgment. In an effort to clarify the distinction between these two terms, we turned to the Classics, and found Dante. He said, "Wherever there can be contention, there judgment should exist . . . " Well, that certainly cleared it up for us!

Decision making is the process of resolving contention. If the contention gets resolved to our satisfaction, we think it was done with good judgment. If the resolution is not so positive, then the judgment seems bad. Leader (1983) reported on an incident that happened during World War II. Admiral Karel Doorman, of the Royal Netherlands Navy, decided to engage a stronger force of the Japanese Navy. He signaled "Follow me" to his ships, got half of them sunk, himself killed, and didn't sink a single enemy vessel. Doorman was decisive, and brave, but in retrospect his judgment has been questioned.

Decision making seems to refer simply to the making of decisions, not to their outcome, and there are numerous models of decision making available. For example:

1. What are my possible courses of action?

2. What are the events that might follow from these actions?

3. What is the likelihood of each event?

4. What is the value of each event to me?

(Arkes & Hammond, 1986)

Judgment is not easily outlined, and, according to Edwards and Neumann (1986), there are at least three reasons for this.

1. Judgment makes use of data, which can be seen, to draw conclusions about things that can't be seen (because they are absent or in the future).

2. The conclusions drawn in situations requiring judgment only have a *probability* of being correct (when there is no risk of error, judgment is not necessary).

3. The correctness of a judgment is defined by how well it matches the setting and how well it works. (Joking about your boss in front of your boss's best friend is probably never good judgment—even when nothing goes wrong. It is clearly bad judgment when something does.)

The last two points combine to give us a basic

Effective instruction includes lesson preview, explanation, guided practice, correction, and independent practice.

truth about judgment: *Decisions based on the best possible judgment aren't always correct.* This truth results from the fact that outcomes often depend on more than our decisions. Take Admiral Doorman's unfortunate Naval battle. Was it bad judgment that the Admiral went after 17 Japanese ships with only 15 Allied ships? Well, as Leader (1983) pointed out, in 1797 Horatio Nelson violated British battle protocol and took on 18 enemy ships with his *single* ship. He captured two Spanish vessels, turned back the enemy fleet, and as a result, was promoted to Admiral. Yet on the face of it, Nelson's decision seems like worse judgment than Doorman's.

The definition of good judgment, then, does not hinge on good results. However, the probability of good results should increase whenever good judgment is used. Good judgment diminishes the risk of failure, but it does not guarantee success.

Expert Judgment

Experts are thought to be experts because they make the best decisions, or go about making decisions very well (regardless of outcome). Experts are not always correct, because it is not possible always to be correct. However, many of us think we are experts because, as a result of our knowledge, we are often right and because our work is judicious and polished.

Experts, regardless of their field, tend to work in certain characteristic ways. As has already been pointed out, expert teachers make good use of routines, which allows them to accomplish some classroom tasks without giving them much individual consideration. This tendency to make the "small stuff" routine in order to save energy for the "big stuff" is one characteristic of experts. Experts also tend to see patterns, or themes, where novices may only see unrelated events (Carter et al. 1986; Sabers, Cushing & Berliner, 1991).

A person can learn to be an expert. This is usually accomplished by finding out how someone who is already an expert works. It may also be accomplished by reflecting on experience. This is the way most things are learned. When teaching a student to solve problems, teachers, acting as experts, first demonstrate and explain how one should go about solving the problem, and then ask the students to practice, using feedback. That is the format we hope to use later in this text, as we teach you to make teaching decisions.

Our goal is to teach you to be an expert educational problem solver. We want you to learn what is and isn't good practice so that you will utilize good judgment when you make teaching decisions about students. To accomplish this goal we will use the text, and much of the accompanying workbook, to ask you to make decisions. Next, we will explain how we (a selected group of experts, or teachers in tune with the prevailing literature) would go about making the same decisions. This is sometimes called "making the thought process public" (Englert, Raphael, Anderson, Anthony & Stevens, 1991; Serapiglia, 1992). It is important to understand that it is the thought process—or judgment—that we will be trying to develop. This means you must try to focus on the way the problems were solved, and not whether your decisions seemed right or wrong.

To get a feel for the way these simulations work, let's try one.

CASE STUDY / Dayna Jo 1

Dayna Jo's teacher is trying to decide what spelling book Dayna Jo should be using. He gives Dayna Jo a spelling test. She scores at the fourth-grade level, so the teacher decides to put her in the fourth-grade book.

Write yes or no for each of these questions:

1. Do you agree with the decision as long as the teacher monitors Dayna Jo and is willing to change books later?
2. Do you think this is as good a decision as the teacher can make considering the data available?
3. Do you think the decision is likely to be correct?
4. Do you think the decision is probably correct?
5. Do you think the decision is correct?
6. Are you sure the decision is correct?
7. Would you bet $100 that the decision is correct?

CASE STUDY / Dayna Jo 2

Dayna Jo is given a spelling test. Only 5% of the words on the test are found in the fourth-grade spelling book used at her school. Only 15% of the words on the test are found in any fourth-grade book. Twenty-five percent are third-grade words and 30% are fifth-grade words. Dayna Jo's handwriting is poor, and in fact about 10% of the mistakes the teacher scores as spelling errors are actually the result of unclosed loops and out-of-proportion letter parts. Also, as it turns out, 10 of the 60 words on the spelling test appeared in an essay on the meaning of life that Dayna Jo had correctly copied just this morning for her humanities class. Dayna Jo's dog was hit by a car this morning. Her pencil broke during the test. But her mother has promised to give her a trip to Wally World if she improves her spelling grades this year. She scores at the fourth-grade level, so the teacher decides to put her in the fourth-grade book.

Answer yes or no for each of these questions:

1. Do you agree with the decision as long as the teacher monitors Dayna Jo and is willing to change books later?
2. Do you think this is as good a decision as the teacher can make considering the data available?
3. Do you think the decision is likely to be correct?
4. Do you think the decision is probably correct?
5. Do you think the decision is correct?
6. Are you sure the decision is correct?
7. Would you bet $100 that the decision is correct?

Exhibit 1.7   Percent Saying Yes

| | Dayna Jo 1 | | Dayna Jo 2 | |
| | Preservice students (n=65) | Experienced teachers (n=102) | Preservice students (n=65) | Experienced teachers (n=102) |
Item				
1	42%	18%	25%	16%
2	45%	18%	23%	10%
3	40%	16%	17%	5%
4	38%	9%	14%	0%
5	36%	6%	9%	0%
6	27%	5%	1%	0%
7	15%	0%	1%	0%

Did your answers differ on the two sets of questions? Exhibit 1.7 shows the answers given by a group of students learning to be teachers and a group of expert teachers. As you can see from those answers (and probably from your own), the additional information supplied in 2 changed the students' answers, but it didn't change the experienced teachers' answers as much. Why? Because the teachers already know that factors like those reported in Dayna Jo 2 influence test scores, and that tests and textbook are often misaligned. This knowledge of testing caused the expert teachers to think the same way about Dayna Jo 1 as the novices thought about Dayna Jo 2.

Recognizing Good Judgment

Because judgment is complex, it is easier to produce a model for messing it up than it is to produce one for creating it. The threats to good judgment given on the next page are taken largely from the work of Adams (1979), Tversky & Kahneman (1986) and Margolis (1987).

Before summarizing the chapter, let's return to the three problem situations presented on page 11. For comparison to your own answers, Exhibit 1.8 presents the results we obtained when these situations were given to expert teachers and preservice education students. (We called the expert teachers *expert* because they were experienced, in graduate training programs, and trained in functional assessment.)

Carl and Jim.   Because of the limited information and noninteractive format of these situations, *any* decision raises "problem definition," "premature resolution," and "sample size" risks. But all of the experienced teachers selected C. Why? Because the information about Carl had nothing to do with how easily he

Exhibit 1.8   A Comparison of Preservice Students and Expert Teachers

	Preservice students (n=78)	Expert teachers (n=15)
Carl and Jim		
(a)	5%	0%
(b)	47%	0%
(c)	48%	100%
Sara and Pam		
(a)	1%	0%
(b)	86%	22%
(c)	13%	78%
Dueling Psychologists		
(a)	37%	27%
(b)	45%	2%
(c)	18%	71%

might be taught. If you selected either A or B you may have made a "misconception of chance," "correlational relationship" or "unwarranted confidence" error. (You may also have a stereotype about students wearing glasses.)

Sara and Pam. Again, most of the expert teachers picked C. (Some of them noted that they would *never* flip a coin.) Why? Because the intensity of concern expressed by Sara's teacher has nothing to do with Pam's needs. To act as if it does is to make an "unwarranted confidence" error. Those experienced teachers who selected B said that they did so because they believed that if Sara's teacher was that worried her teacher would push until Sara was eventually seen by someone, even if it wasn't necessary.

Threat	Explanation/Example
Lack of the knowledge needed to make a judgment	Working on things you don't know about (e.g., trying to teach about the role of minority cultures in U.S. history—when that wasn't taught to you when you were in school).
Stereotyping	Working with someone's label and not their characteristics (e.g., ignoring Ralph and only attending to the fact that he is labeled LD).
Failure to define the problem	Not knowing what it is you are trying to do (e.g., deciding to have students work lessons without giving them a pretest).
Defining the problem too trivially or narrowly	Concentrating on a trivial aspect of a larger problem (e.g., thinking about the haircut of a student who has no friends).
Lack of perspective	Only seeing things one way (e.g., not seeing the problem from the parents' point of view).
Fear	Of failure, risk, notoriety, success, responsibility or nearly anything else.
Premature resolution	Stopping work too early—failing to be comprehensive (e.g., picking the first solution recommended).
Insensitivity to probabilities	Not considering that some things are already more or less likely to work (e.g., adopting specialized reading materials when the general-education class materials haven't been tried).
Sample size	Drawing conclusions from too few experiences or examples (e.g., concluding that a student can add because he works four problems correctly).
Misconceptions of chance	Thinking that unrelated events can affect each other (e.g., believing that flipping three heads in a row somehow alters the 50/50 chance of flipping a head with a fourth coin—it doesn't!).
Unwarranted confidence	Deciding to do something on the basis of evidence, or advocacy, that doesn't have anything to do with the problem at hand (e.g., deciding a student will have trouble in math because she is bad at reading).
Selective or incomplete search	Only considering one category of options (e.g., only considering the use of teaching methods advocated by your friends).
Mistaking a correlational relationship for cause and effect	Just because two things happen at the same time doesn't mean one causes the other (e.g., thinking that a student threw up in class for attention because everyone looked at her when she did).
Lack of a supportive environment	Not having a chance to observe others use good judgment or have that use encouraged (e.g., working in a school where everyone routinely makes all of these errors).

Dueling Psychologists. The expert choice was C again! Why? Because the expert teachers recognized that the two psychologists are actually doing the same things: IQ tests *are* tests of general knowledge; achievement tests *are* measures of academic skills across grade levels; and, adaptive-behavior scales *are* summaries of what teachers and parents think about referred students. Most experienced teachers knew that. Novice teachers made "lack of knowledge" errors when picking either A or B. Interestingly, the words "IQ test" made some teachers (both experts and novices) either like, or not like, psychologist 2. A similar biasing effect was not found for achievement testing or adaptive-behavior scales (very few preservice teachers had even heard of adaptive behavior). It seems that some teachers were dazzled by psychologist 2's use of the all-powerful IQ measure while others were offended by its use. It occurred to the authors that this demonstrates, once again, the prejudicial nature of the IQ (fixed capacity) concept. If the simple use of the test can bias teachers for or against a psychologist, imagine what a low score does to a student!

Summary

Expert teachers use good judgment when they make decisions. This expert decision-making skill can be learned. The use of good judgment depends on knowledge (of curriculum, students, learning, and instruction). It also depends on freedom from certain threats to good judgment, and on the availability of quality options.

Chapter 2 / Thinking About Learning and Students

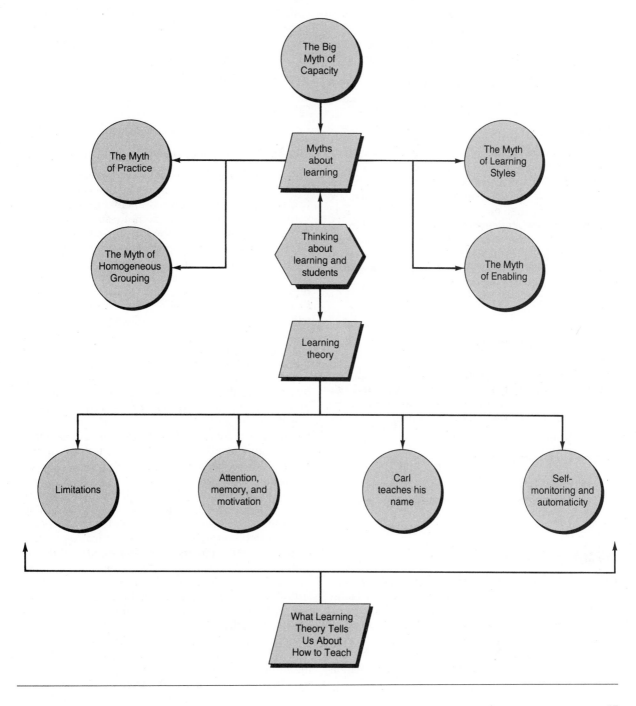

The cause of disease, Paracelsus insisted, was not the maladjustment of the bodily humours within a person, but some specific cause outside the body . . . Paracelsus' faith led him to believe that there were no incurable diseases, only ignorant physicians.

—D. J. Boorstin (1983)

What teachers do is influenced by what they think about instruction, the tasks they are teaching, and the ways students learn (Clark & Peterson, 1986; Shavelson, 1983). We believe some ways of thinking are more productive than others. The goal of this unit is to convince you that students who haven't learned in the past *can* learn in the future. This is important because without that belief, remedial and special educators can be thought of as nothing more than babysitters supplying custodial care for "defective" children—and that's incorrect.

Myths About Learning

To illustrate the relationship of teacher thoughts to teacher actions, and to set up the rest of the unit, let's examine this series of myths about learning and the instructional actions that follow from them:

The myth of practice

The myth of learning styles

The myth of enabling

The myth of homogeneous grouping

The myth of ability

The Myth of Practice

This is the belief that learning occurs gradually. Learning doesn't occur gradually, it occurs almost instantaneously. *Proficiency* (how well you use what you've learned) often occurs gradually and therefore requires lots of practice. But practice does *not* produce learning. Learning is assisted through explanation or demonstration that helps the student link new information with what is already known (Walberg, 1988).

The Myth of Learning Styles

This is the belief that people have unique and stable (constant over time) learning styles that can be identified through testing and used to enhance instruction.

Obviously, all students do not respond to instruction in the same way. In the learning-styles view, the blame for these inconsistencies has often been laid on the influence of one or more personological variables (variables within the person). These variables are referred to as "styles," "aptitudes," or "abilities." Some educators have claimed that instruction can be adjusted to account for the influence of these styles (Carbo, 1992; Dunn, 1983; Dunn, Dunn & Price, 1981; Willis, 1985). The principle thrust of these claims is that certain types of students will learn more efficiently if they are treated in ways indicated by their scores on aptitude measures. Learning-styles instruction is not to be confused with selecting different objectives for students at different skill levels or with assuming that some treatments are more efficient than other treatments. But when educators test for an individual's ability strengths and weaknesses, they are attempting to use learning styles.

Some authors, such as Waugh (1975), were early critics of learning styles. However, the use of learning-styles instruction flourished through the seventies and into the eighties under the tutelage of teacher trainers who apparently ignored the absence of validation. Today the use of learning styles, while clearly refuted by authors such as Arter and Jenkins (1979), Kavale (1981), Glass (1983), Lloyd (1984), Ulman and Rosenberg (1986), and Snider (1992) continues to be advocated by teachers and psychologists who attempt to tailor instruction to left or right brains, avoid deficits in simultaneous processing ability, or continue the search for auditory and visual learners.

The frustration many educators feel over this continuing distraction from more legitimate instructional concerns was well articulated over a decade ago by Lakin (1983):

> It is a professional disgrace, given the wealth of evidence made available in the past decade, that . . . [this] position still may be seen as controversial in some quarters. Not only has the . . . approach lacked substantiated effectiveness in teaching children but, also, its general acceptance in special education circles has encouraged the creation of many essentially worthless, though profitable, enterprises of psychometry and "treatment." Its demise as an educational paradigm is long overdue as the research cited so clearly shows . . . it is outrageous that these essentially useless "professional" practices are allowed to persist. (p. 237)

The Myth of Enabling

This is the belief that motivation can be developed by giving students easy things to do.

Motivation does not come with success alone—it comes with the sense of control and accomplishment. These are not always promoted by success. They are promoted by the student's adaptive interpretation of *both* successes and failures. These adaptive interpretations are themselves promoted by the way teachers and parents handle and explain the successes and failures in students' lives. Students who have been taught that positive outcomes are the result of external factors like luck, easy tasks, or pampering teachers don't become motivated. Neither do students who believe positive outcomes are the result of unalterable, internal factors like fixed intelligence. Motivated students are those who learn to see a relationship between their efforts and their accomplishments (Seligman, 1990; Dweck, 1986; Landfried, 1989).

The Myth of Homogeneous Grouping

It seems at times that human beings have a natural predisposition to sort and label (Carnine, 1990). That is how, particularly in the so-called western cultures, we have traditionally handled our information and our schooling. This Aristotelian approach may be fine for cataloging and investigating bodies of information, but it doesn't work too well on individuals (Korzybski, 1948).

The myth of homogeneous grouping, which is closely aligned with assumptions about learning styles,

is education's Holy Grail. This myth has led us into an exhausting and fruitless search for educationally relevant ways to group students. It stems from the belief that students who are different from each other can't be taught together. This belief has caused teachers to focus on ways to reduce the variability in their classrooms, rather than ways to accommodate student variability. (This focus has led to tracking, leveling, referral, pull-out, and categorical funding. With the exception of short-term skill groupings, which are based on highly specific objectives, these efforts at grouping have not worked.)

- The teacher who believes the myth of practice may drill students when he should be explaining things to them.
- The teacher who believes the myth of learning styles may avoid tasks she thinks conflict with the student's preferred mode of learning.
- The teacher who accepts the myth of enabling may not allow students to experience the personal satisfaction of overcoming challenge.
- The teacher who believes the myth of homogeneous grouping may try to sort students instead of teaching them.

Each of the myths already presented (there are others, such as the grade-level myth) carry the risk that, through their application, teachers will be less effective. However, there is one learning myth—the Big Myth—that can outdo all others. That is because the Big Myth encourages teachers not to teach at all.

The Big Myth

The Big Myth is the myth of ability. It says that what a student learns, and how a student learns, is controlled by a fixed capacity to learn. This was called a nonalterable variable in Chapter 1. Capacity, or potential, is conceptualized by many teachers as being unalterable. To these teachers, failure indicates that the limits of capacity have been reached and that no more learning can occur. As a result, when a student starts having trouble, such teachers do not respond by teaching (Greenwood, 1991; Teddlie, Kirby & Stringfield, 1989). In the case of most remedial/special students this is wrong because, as we'll try to explain in the rest of this chapter, the idea that things like capacity, potential, ability, or intelligence are fixed is inconsistent with

Motivated students are those who learn to see a relationship between their efforts and their accomplishments.

current theory. In spite of this, as Ysseldyke, Algozzine, and Thurlow (1992) point out, studies have found that only 5% of teachers blame themselves or the schools for the widespread occurrence of student failure. The rest of the teachers attribute failure to factors that cannot be routinely influenced by instruction.

Learning Theory

Learning is influenced by teaching, tasks, and students. The student characteristics of greatest importance to a teacher are those that are alterable (Bloom, 1980). These are the skills, strategies, perceptions, expectations, and beliefs that the student has already learned. (This includes things like motivation, attention, and memory, which are discussed in Chapter 17.) All of these are lumped under the heading "prior knowledge." A student's prior knowledge (what he already knows) is the primary personal limitation on his learning.

In order to understand how prior knowledge functions, it is important to know something about the way learning seems to occur. According to current theory, learning occurs primarily through the process of categorization. The brain does not simply store new information, it processes and amplifies it by linking it to prior knowledge through elaborate networks of organization. (These networks are often referred to as *schema* and are explained in greater detail in Chapter 17.) As Carnine (1990, p. 372) puts it, "Categorization and recategorization might be viewed as the overriding activity of the brain . . . ". The act of categorization will be explained in the following, admittedly simplistic, review of the information-processing model of learning (Reed, 1992).

The information-processing model is illustrated in Exhibit 2.1. As can be seen, information (a flash card requiring the student to add 2 + 2) comes into the system through the receiving sensory organs (eyes, ears) and then flows through the system. Information that arrives from the environment (anything outside of the information-processing system—including a growling stomach or itchy foot) is combined with what is already in there (prior knowledge). If this information requires action, then the system implements the action by using muscles (speech mechanisms, hand movement) to affect the environment. Researchers can see what is put into this system and what comes out of it. The rest is carefully and tenuously assembled supposition.

Once an environmental stimulus has arrived, it is translated from its sensory language (light waves or sound waves) into something the rest of the system

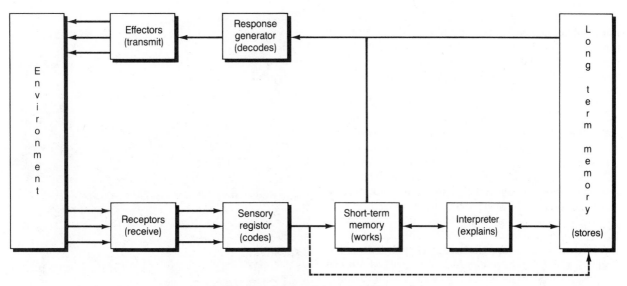

Exhibit 2.1 *Information processing model.*

can understand. We'll call this "brainese." Sensory images do not exist within the system per se. Instead there is an *analog* replicated by the processing system. This is something like the conversion from a live concert to a CD. There are no musicians in the CD, nor any live music, only a digital record. That record, if properly retranslated, can be converted to sound.

In the "old days" (still being experienced in some classrooms) learning theorists hadn't thought of the sensory register. In the 1960s and early 1970s it was widely believed that messages maintained their sensory definition after entering the information-processing system. At that time it was thought the information that a person saw, heard, smelled, or felt was either treated independently, or integrated with other information through a series of sensory-specific channels or processes. These sensory channels were called *modalities* according to the mode of information they handled (auditory mode, visual mode, tactile mode). People discussing learning at that time would refer to things like "visual memory" or "auditory attention deficits." The model that spawned this modality-based terminology is now out of vogue among researchers, although it is popular among educators who believe in the myth of learning styles.

Once the environmental stimuli has been translated into "brainese," the message goes into the net-

work of short-term memory, interpreter, and long-term memory. Short-term memory is very limited. It can only hold a few items (six or seven) for a few seconds. So it isn't just short, it is sort of narrow too. By the way, the length of stay in short-term memory is generally described in terms of milliseconds or seconds—at most a couple of minutes.

When someone says "I told him the answer yesterday, but he missed the item today. He has a short-term memory problem" they aren't using the information-processing definition of short-term. Long-term memory, in distinction, apparently lasts longer than we do (that is, we die of old age before our memories erode). Therefore, while there is some speculation about the electrochemical decay of memories, once it's in there, it's there for good.

Notice that in Exhibit 2.1 the arrows connecting the interpreter and long- and short-term memory have two heads. This means information may move back and forth among these components. That's critical.

Short-term memory is typically described as working memory. According to the theory, we are only aware, or conscious, of things that are currently in short-term memory. (We use the term *conscious* here to mean awake or tuned in, not necessarily deliberate or insightful.) Long-term memory is more like a file cabinet. We have stuff in there, but we can't use it until we open the drawer, find the file, and take it out. (It's kind of like income-tax preparation—it doesn't matter that you kept the receipt from last September, what matters is that you can find it by April 15th.) As a result, the phenomenon we call memory is probably better described as *recall*.

Information can get into, and out of, long-term memory without going through short-term memory. This allows a person to function without overloading his or her limited short-term memory. For example, when reading this text, you use your prior knowledge of reading to decode and comprehend without consciously reflecting on vowel sounds and vocabulary (unless you come to a word you don't know).

The interpreter is a relatively recent addition to the information-processing model. The component received its name from Gazzaniga (1989). Gazzaniga and his associates have conducted a series of studies on patients with brain dissections which seem to document the existence of a specialized cognitive subsystem for unifying prior knowledge and current experience. The interpreter "explains" what is happening to the rest of the system, which then stores the explanation and/or acts upon it. As the world flows toward us, the interpreter "makes sense" of it by attempting to fit data into previously developed categories. If data is found to be inconsistent with the categories that already exist, the interpreter develops new schemes for categorizing it. The interpreter may also recategorize information previously stored. Therefore, things coming in have potential. What they ultimately mean to us is determined by the connections established between this new experience and our prior knowledge. This is one reason why two people in the same geographic environment may have different thoughts and engage in different behaviors. They are interpreting the environment in terms of their unique histories and behaving, not in direct response to the geographic environment, but in response to their explanations of it (Kaplan, 1990; Mahoney, 1977).

Some messages require a behavioral reaction. Commands to carry out these reactions are sent from long- or short-term memory to the response generator, which performs the reverse function of the sensory register. The response generator takes the brainese command and translates it into muscular movement. This results in the conversion of covert thought into overt action. The recollection of the calculation of 2 + 2 is therefore expressed as the spoken word "four."

The idea that things like capacity, potential, skill, and/or intelligence are static characteristics is inconsistent with current theory.

Limitations

There are several cautions that need to be applied to the theory illustrated in Exhibit 2.1.

1. We must remember that theories are temporary and, like the modality theory that preceded it, this one will be modified.

2. Theories have multiple purposes. Primarily, they are developed and presented to help people understand things, as well as to coordinate investigations of them. While they may be helpful for guiding practice, they need not and will not

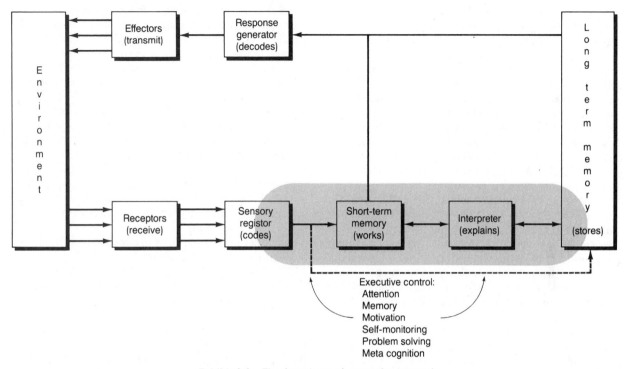

Exhibit 2.2   The functions of executive control.

always have immediate instructional implications. (It is better to judge the quality of teaching by the positive effect it has on a student than by its congruence with a theory.)

3. The only things in Exhibit 2.1 that have any *physical* reality (or specific location) are the receptors and effectors. You can be poked in the eye. You cannot be poked in the short-term memory.

4. The shapes and lines in the exhibit are better thought of as functions than components. These are things our minds get done, not pieces of our minds. They cannot be isolated from each other physically or through testing. Short-term memory, whatever it is, cannot exist on its own. Therefore it is unlikely that it can have anything wrong with it.

5. Even though it has been described as one, it is probably better not to insist on conceptualizing the information-processing system as a computer,

because that encourages us to think of job-specific components and permanent circuits. Thinking is more fluid than that.

Now look at Exhibit 2.2. Here a new element has been added. This element, executive control, influences the way the system functions. In this sense—and this is a risky metaphor—the mind works like a college. It has a dean. While deans don't schedule classes, teach students, advise, or type tests, they do influence how these things are done. They monitor activity, allocate resources, evaluate outcomes, and tell people what to do. That's what executives are for. But while two deans may have equivalent faculties to work with, these capacities (absolute potentials) may not be equally productive. Some executives are more effective than others. Let's consider an example.

If a researcher, Carl, takes an average-OK-general-education 6-year-old and tells him "Hi! My name is Carl. In 5 minutes I'm going to ask you what my name is. If you remember my name I'll give you a Porsche. If you forget it, I'll break your legs." (We're joking, of course.) That average-OK-general-education 6-year-old will immediately begin to do something. He will start saying "Carl, Carl, Carl" over and over. This is called *rehearsal*, and it is an executive-control strategy for holding something in short-term memory by simply updating the memory every second or two. It is an efficient way to retain a few items of information (usually no more than six or seven) in short-term memory as long as the person using it doesn't want to think about anything else. Therefore, 5 minutes later, the average-OK-general-education 6-year-old will tell the researcher that his name is Carl and will get a new sports car. (This is one reason research is so expensive!)

Next, the researcher selects an at-risk LD-remedial 6-year-old. He tells him "Hi! My name is Carl. In 5 minutes I'm going to ask you what my name is. If you remember my name I'll give you a Porsche. If you forget it I'll break your legs." That at-risk LD-remedial 6-year-old will probably look at the researcher, smile, and say OK. He will not use rehearsal and will not remember the researcher's name. (We hope he has a ride home.)

Now for the important part of this example. Suppose the researcher selects another at-risk LD-remedial 6-year-old and says "Hi! My name is Carl. I want you to say my name to yourself over and over for 5 minutes. Then if you remember it I'll give you a Porsche. If you forget it I'll break your legs." The 6-year-old will start saying "Carl, Carl, Carl," and 5 minutes later will remember the name.

The punch line here is that, if the original difference in memory between the general-education kid and the remedial kid were a matter of absolute memory potential (if the general-education kid was born with ten pounds of memory but the remedial kid was only born with three), the use of the rehearsal strategy would *not* have helped. But it did! This kind of study has shown us that special students don't always fail because they haven't got the potential to learn. They fail because they don't use their potential effectively. *They lack effective executive-control strategies.* And, most important, *executive-control strategies are learned* (Brown, 1987; Palincsar, 1990; Paris & Winograd, 1990; Wong, 1991a; Wong 1991b).

Attention, Memory, and Motivation

When learning does not occur, the problem is often traced to deficits in attention, memory, or motivation.

According to current theory, these are housed within the body of prior knowledge called executive control. To illustrate these basic strategies, we must discuss them in terms of some area of curriculum because they do not exist in the absence of a task. Without something to attend to, there isn't any attention, and the way a student attends to one thing will differ from the way that student attends to another. For purposes of this discussion we'll use reading comprehension.

Attention seems to float somewhere between the sensory register and long-term memory. It functions like a screen, allowing only certain environmental input inside for processing while keeping other stuff out. Probably the easiest reading strategy for illustrating this phenomenon is the use of pre-reading questions. Students who are given questions about a passage before they read it are more apt to find the answers than those who aren't (Reynolds & Anderson, 1982). Therefore, teaching students to develop their own pre-reading questions is an excellent way to get them to focus on the important aspects of a passage (Gillespie, 1991; Ryder, 1991).

The key term here is *focus*. Attention, as we are using the term, refers to the selective allocation of processing. The successful student focuses on what is important and ignores what is not. (Of course, to do this the student must categorize the messages in the passage as "important" or "nonimportant.") The development of prereading questions allows for this by providing the interpreter with criteria for judging the relevance of different parts of a passage. Without selective attention, the student wishing to remember something wouldn't be able to figure out what to remember.

Memory, as previously explained, is not the simple storage of information. Memory, as we experience it, is the recall or use of what has been stored. Both storage and recall can be facilitated through the use of strategies like rehearsal. However, rehearsal is a fairly limited strategy, as it can only be used for simple information, and only for short periods of time.

Effective readers utilize a variety of strategies to help them comprehend what they read. Some of these seem clearly related to memory. For example, students who score high on comprehension tests are more likely to underline or hi-lite than students who score low. They are also more likely to write notes in the margin of a text, or to write notes that summarize what they have read (Thornton, Bohlmeyer, Dickson & Kulhavy,

1990; Wade, Trathen & Schraw, 1990). Teaching students to engage in these activities will improve their comprehension scores.

Motivation is the last of the big three information-processing functions. Interestingly, it is very hard for some teachers to accept that motivation is learned. To these teachers, attention and memory may seem alterable but motivation is a different story. Still, how else can one account for a junior-high student's comprehension scores improving whenever he or she is placed at the same table with a particular junior-high student of the opposite sex?

To understand motivation we need to define it. Motivation can be operationally defined as persevering at a task (Dweck, 1986; Katzell & Thompson, 1990). The student who works on something the longest, particularly in the face of difficulty or negative feedback, seems the most motivated. Some students work harder in the face of difficulty, while others with equal skills give up. Why?

Many researchers believe that students fail to persevere on tasks they are sufficiently skilled to complete because they suffer from something called *learned helplessness* (Seligman, 1990). According to motivational theory, learned helplessness is rooted in the acquired erroneous belief that success and failure are determined by external events (luck, teacher decisions, task difficulty) or internal incapacities (stupidity) over which the student has no control (see Chapter 16).

When a kid believes these things cause failure, and that he can't control them, the onset of difficulty is used by the interpreter as a signal to quit working. In contrast, students who believe that success is related to things they can control (for example, how much effort they put into work) view the same difficulty as a cue to work harder. On reading-comprehension tasks, a student who believes he is helpless will skip over a passage that is difficult to understand. Conversely, a student who believes he has control over his own success, upon encountering a difficult passage, will slow his reading rate, reread the passage, or consult needed resources. These different approaches are learned.

How effectively a person works is determined in part by his beliefs about himself, his skills, and the tasks on which he is working. These beliefs, which reside with the executive-control function, may be motivationally adaptive or destructive. For example, students who have developed learned helplessness

often believe that getting things done is more important than learning.

Dweck (1986) draws a distinction between learning and performance orientations. According to her theory, a student with a learning orientation believes that success comes with improvement and a student with a performance orientation believes success comes with completing tasks. The learning orientation represents a more adaptive motivational pattern because it allows students to find success on challenging tasks even when they don't correctly complete them. Remember that learning is change. Learning isn't getting things done, or completing work. Accomplishments (completed products) are only artifacts of learning. For example, suppose you have asked a student to read a passage and write a summary statement. The written statement merely shows what was learned; if you burn it up, the learning does not disappear.

Teachers can promote a learning orientation by praising and documenting improvement (Palincsar, 1990). They should not overemphasize task completion. If task completion is overemphasized ("You must get this done by recess" or "Good, you finished several pages today") some students come to believe that success is synonymous with task completion, not improvement. The danger in this belief is that it may cause the student to avoid difficult tasks. It may even cause the student to seek out easy tasks in order to stack up accomplishments. This nonadaptive motivational pattern will cause students to avoid new material and, therefore, learning will suffer (Dweck, 1986).

Self-Monitoring and Automaticity

Self-Monitoring. Attention, memory, and motivation are familiar concepts to most of us. Another important executive-control function is self-monitoring. According to Rigney (1980), a competent learner is always confronting questions like these:

- What is the problem?
- What should I do about it?
- How am I doing so far?
- Am I finished yet?

While we don't consciously ask ourselves these questions, we do get alarmed if we can't answer one or

Exhibit 2.3
Task difficulty
and
information
processing.

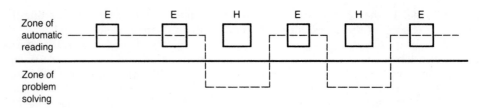

more of them. During reading comprehension, for example, a student must monitor the meaning of a passage in order to recognize when attention, memory, or motivational strategies should be applied (Gillespie, 1991; Ryder, 1991). It is self-monitoring that alerts us to the need for extra effort or the application of problem-solving strategies. The form of self-monitoring varies dramatically with the nature of each task. In general it is promoted by encouraging students to ask questions, to judge the difficulty of tasks, and to check their own work, and by holding them accountable for their decisions (Paris & Winograd, 1990). Self-monitoring will be stressed throughout the topic-specific chapters in Part 3.

Automaticity.   To drive a car you have to know both how the car works and the rules of the road. Driving to work is a major task composed of many smaller tasks like starting the car, using the turn signals, stopping at traffic signals, and changing lanes. The subtasks of traffic signals include color recognition, recall of color meaning, use of brakes, and knowing where and when to stop. In order to drive one must watch for lights, check color, determine meaning of color, judge time and distance to the stopping point, determine the need to stop according to duration of a signal, and determine the braking pressure required. Recall the last time you drove a car. Were you aware of thinking about any of those things? Probably not. That's because you have become highly proficient at driving. If you had to consider all the subtasks and strategies of driving while driving, you would probably end up stopping several blocks past the traffic signal, or sooner—if something solid got in the way!

When you first learned to drive you occupied your short-term memory with the task of driving. You may even have talked to yourself as a device for recalling what to do when you got in difficult situations. But, you don't do that now because driving has become automatic. Achieving automaticity allows us to employ

strategies without allocating any of our awareness to them. If we encounter very different tasks, we may have to resort to conscious problem solving again.

The shift from automaticity to problem solving is illustrated with a reading example in Exhibit 2.3. In this exhibit (based on a model by Holdaway, 1979), the boxes are words labeled E for easy or H for hard. As you'll learn in Chapter 3, the difficulty of any word may be the result of novelty, related to the person's background, so what is hard for one person may be easy for another (Chi & Glaser, 1985; Fisher & Hiebert, 1990; Frederiksen, 1984). The reader in Exhibit 2.3 (dotted line) is doing fine (not thinking about reading) until hitting the first hard word. At that point self-monitoring says that meaning has been lost. As a result, the reader drops out of automatic reading and into a zone of problem solving. In the zone of problem solving, the reader has to think (be aware) of the act of reading and solving problems. Once the problem is solved, the reader can return to the automatic zone until the next hard word comes along.

One important ramification of this is that conscious problem solving occupies the reader's awareness and competes with the meaning of the passage. For readers with limited prior knowledge of a topic, or of decoding itself, many words seem difficult. Thus much of their awareness must be allocated to problem solving rather than to the meaning of a passage. Of course, students who lack knowledge of problem-solving strategies as well as task-specific reading strategies are even worse off. They may have to allocate all of their awareness to simple decoding. These students will understand little of what they read. Another equally disabling problem occurs when a student's self-monitoring skills are so poor that he fails to notice the loss of meaning and simply misreads difficult words without trying to solve the problems they present. This student may appear to be impulsive to an observer.

The model of task performance presented in

Self-monitoring alerts students to the need for extra effort or the application of problem-solving strategies.

Exhibit 2.3 is a reasonable analogy for many tasks. The squares can represent arithmetic problems, social situations, ideas to verbalize, or words to spell. In each case success depends on the proficient use of skills. High levels of proficiency are necessary for students to achieve automaticity. A person who works automatically maintains accuracy and fluency in the presence of distractors.

The short-term memory function allows us to solve problems with consideration and intent. It allows us to work. However, it is so limited that we can't consciously work on too many things at one time, or even on one thing for too long. Therefore, in order to protect the space in our working memory, we must move certain routine activities out of it. This is done by

raising proficiency on these activities to automaticity. Here's another example. As you read this passage you are making use of various decoding, comprehension, and study skills. You aren't "thinking" about them—you are using them automatically from within the executive and long-term memory functions. If you had to allocate short-term memory to these skills, the result would be a reduction in the allocation available for dealing with the message of the passage.

Automaticity is developed through practice. This practice must move the student's proficiency beyond accuracy to mastery (fluency), and it must occur across a variety of situations and problem types. This last point is critical. While drill on subtraction flash cards may help students become automatic at looking at problems and writing answers, it may not help them use the subtraction strategy to balance a checkbook. It will prepare the student for checkbooks, but checkbook instruction, including practice, will probably still be required. This need to transfer learning across situations cannot be stressed enough. Automaticity comes about through fluency instruction *and* application instruction (see Chapter 4).

A kid's automatic strategy use depends on skill and on the task the kid is facing. For now, it is only important to understand that every learner eventually encounters a task that can't be accomplished on automatic. The question, therefore, is not whether automaticity is always available, but whether it is available for the routine demands placed on the learner. (Remember that automaticity is only needed to free us from those routine acts we don't want or need to think about. Therefore, a fourth-grade student should spell automatically in order to write, just as an airplane pilot should respond automatically to engine failure. Automaticity is important to both the kid and the pilot, but the kid doesn't need to practice handling engine failures.)

Time spent taking students to automaticity on skills they will use infrequently, or those not critically important, is wasted. Therefore, teachers must set priorities when they teach students to work automatically. Students need to do the same thing themselves; they must self-monitor. That's because automatic use of a strategy isn't always such a great idea (automatically reading a passage you don't understand is a mistake).

Have you ever walked out of a room and switched off the lights when someone else was still in the room? Have you ever underlined a passage in a book you borrowed? How about automatically locking your car door when your keys were inside? In each of these cases automaticity was actually working against you. Similarly, some students will automatically read passages they don't comprehend, or they'll resort to violence when it isn't needed. In such cases the students are failing to be mindful of their behavior. Self-monitoring must always be emphasized when attempting to build a student's automaticity because, from an information-processing view, it is just as easy to become automatic at doing things wrong as it is to become automatic at doing them right (Spiro, Coulson, Feltovich & Anderson, 1988). In fact, that is exactly what has happened to many special and remedial students.

Learning Theory and Teaching

While learning theory may not provide direct clues to daily instruction, or instruction on specific objectives, it does have something to say about instruction (Carnine, 1990; Palincsar, 1990). Here are some statements based on learning theory and a brief explanation of their coverage in this text.

1. *Prior knowledge is the most important variable in learning.* Coverage: We have divided prior knowledge into two broad categories—topical knowledge and task-related knowledge. Topical knowledge refers to what a student knows about an area of subject matter (computation, social behavior, written expression). Techniques for assessing and teaching prior knowledge in topic areas are discussed in Chapters 10–16. Task-related behavior (study skills, memory, attention, and motivation) are discussed in Chapter 17.

2. *Special/remedial students do not make good use of executive-control strategies.* Coverage: In Part 3, each chapter (10–17) will identify important strategies and provide information about how to teach them. In addition, techniques for defining strategies will be presented in Chapter 3 and techniques for teaching them will be presented in Chapters 4 and 8.

3. *Prior knowledge, and use of strategies, can both be altered through careful evaluation and focused instruction.* Coverage: Chapters 4 and 8 will emphasize a set of functions critical for appropriate instruction. These generic recommendations are referred to throughout the subject-matter chapters in order to reduce redundancy. Chapters 5–8 will outline procedures that must be carried out to assure that instruction and the curriculum are aligned.

Summary

According to current learning theory, mildly disabled students fail to learn because they do not make adequate use of executive-control strategies. They do not fail because they lack the capacity, or ability, to learn. Failure by the teaching profession, and its associates, to acknowledge this important change has had a negative impact on teaching and learning (McGill-Franzen & Allington, 1991).

Chapter 3 / Thinking About the Curriculum*

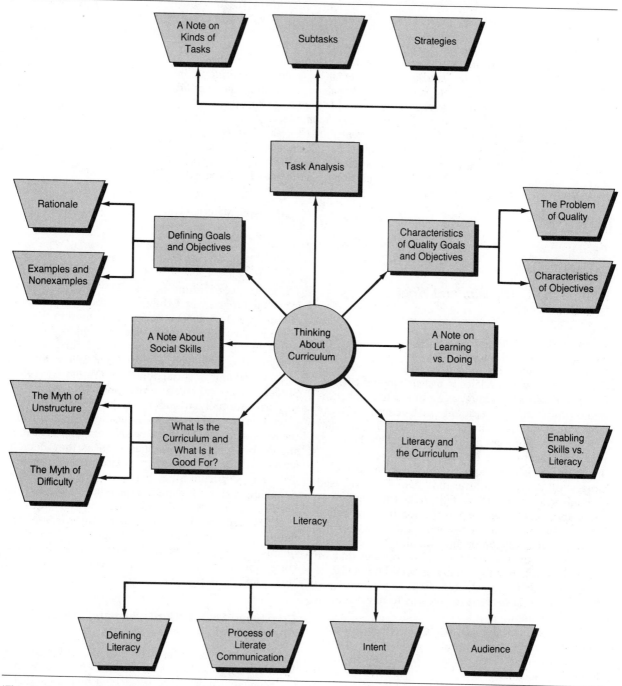

*This chapter was prepared with the assistance of Karna Nelson, Western Washington University.

If we consider the whole arguement to this point, we are easily led . . . to see language, reasoning, and culture as things that evolve together, each reinforcing the others. . . . Reasoning depends on language; but the evolution of language must be contingent on the existence of important things to talk to each other about. . . . Anyone who has had occasion to visit a country in which he does not know the language must have discovered that a good deal of human discourse can be handled using no more than a grammarless handful of nouns and verbs, supplemented by shrugs, points, facial expressions, etc. . . . Language apparently developed because human beings had something more to say to each other. The most stiking candidate for the "something more" is that human groups thrived that were able to explicitly plan and coordinate activities tailored to novel contingencies.

—H. Margolis (1987)

What Is the Curriculum and What Is It Good For?

This chapter is about curriculum. It is about the stuff teachers should be teaching and students should be learning. In Chapter 1 we briefly outlined the role of decision making as it relates to instruction and curriculum and described learning as an interactive phenomenon (involving the student, instruction, and the curriculum) that is indicated by changes in behavior. Teaching decisions are intended to improve the progress and performance of special/remedial students. Teaching decisions require educators to focus on causes of student failure that can be addressed through instruction. These fall under the heading of prior knowledge. Deciding which of the curriculum tasks a student should be taught, and which of the many instructional approaches will allow us to teach it best, requires the use of evaluative procedures that are themselves sensitive to a student's prior knowledge of the curriculum. Obviously this sort of *curriculum-based assessment* (Tucker, 1985) requires us to pay attention to the curriculum.

Knowledge of the curriculum is an absolute for successful test construction, evaluation, decision making, and teaching (Fuchs & Fuchs, 1986; Howell, 1986; Shinn & Hubbard, 1992; Shulman, 1986). One can't evaluate a student's reading without first finding out what reading is and what portions of it are essential.

These are curriculum issues. The illustrations of expected progress in Exhibits 1.2 and 1.3 present a picture of a student who had fallen behind in the curriculum. This picture represents the majority of special/remedial students, most of whom are only considered disabled because of their failure to meet certain academic or social objectives (Ysseldyke, 1987). Students who can read, write, spell, do math, and socialize normally would never be referred for and placed in special/remedial education. Additionally, the ones who are placed in special/remedial education should be removed from it as soon as they demonstrate adequate curriculum performance/progress. Therefore, curriculum has both definitional and functional implications for special/remedial education. The term *curriculum-based* describes this relationship well. This chapter will deal with generic information pertaining to the curriculum. The chapters in Part Three of this text focus on specific topics such as decoding, comprehension, language, and social behavior. But first, some more myths!

Curriculum Myth 1: Curriculum and Instruction Are the Same

It is a mistake to confuse curriculum and instruction. *What* is taught isn't the same thing as *how* it's taught.

Some educators act as if teaching method and curriculum are synonymous. You can tell this is happening when you ask teachers what they are teaching and the response is the name of a program (DISTAR, Scott, Foresman, Spalding, SRA, Merrill, or Addison-Wesley) rather than a skill (saying vowel sounds, solving multiplication problems, writing prime factors, or comparing economic systems).

The curriculum is a structured set of learning outcomes, or tasks, that educators usually call objectives (Johnson, 1967). The curriculum is intended to prepare students to succeed in society. Consequently, the material in the curriculum comes from someone's analysis of what society requires for success. The curriculum should include not only static bits of skill and knowledge but also the dynamic principles of how to learn. These will be needed for material not in the curriculum when the student is in school. All students (including special and remedial ones) need to learn the things specified in the curriculum.

To accommodate students, the sequence of the curriculum may be shuffled, its tasks may be broken into small pieces or combined into larger ones, its organizational structure may be altered, and it may be reassigned to different instructors, but the substance of the curriculum is not changed. The idea that special/remedial students need individualized programs pertains to the way the curriculum is delivered, not to the curriculum itself. Objectives are matched to society's requirements and are written into curriculum guides before the student even shows up for class. The substance of the curriculum shouldn't be altered as long as we believe that all students deserve a competitive shot at life.

Once again, curriculum and instruction are *not* the same. While they should be compatible and complementary, it is important to remember that (1) the value of instruction is determined by how well it teaches the curriculum, and (2) the value of the curriculum is determined by examining how well it promotes social competence. Therefore, when learning does not occur, it is the instruction that should be changed.

Curriculum Myth 2: Difficulty Resides with the Task

To most of us, driving a car is no harder than fixing lunch, and reading this page is no harder than cleaning up after lunch. That is because we are adequately skilled to do all of these things. However, not every one is. Tasks become difficult when we don't have adequate prior knowledge and skill to do them. Because we all have different prior knowledge, some tasks are harder for us than for others. In general, tasks are difficult if they have ambiguous cues, missing information, and a lack of predictability (Fisher & Hiebert, 1990; Kotovsky & Simon, 1990; Siegler, 1983). However, as you probably have discovered, the things that seem ambiguous to a novice are often quite clear to an expert. That is because difficulty is defined by the interaction of the task and the person. This has several implications for instruction.

The first implication of the interaction between a person's skills and the demands of the task is that students with the fewest skills have the hardest time in school. On the face of it, this seems pretty obvious. Unfortunately, educators often attribute difficulty in school to deficits in a student's capacity to learn—not to missing prior knowledge (see Chapter 2, page 20). Failure to learn a skill, particularly one of the so-called basic skills, can have a profound cumulative impact on a student. It makes *everything* hard.

The second implication is that the primary predictor of success in a lesson is knowledge of the lesson before it started (Bloom, 1980; Kulik, Kulik & Bangert-Drowns, 1990).

The last implication builds from the first two. It is that, when a student has trouble learning new material, teachers should check to find out what the student does and doesn't know. These elements of prerequisite knowledge are typically found at earlier levels of the curriculum, but they often must be identified through processes called concept analysis, task analysis, and error analysis. These will be covered shortly.

Literacy

Children's success in school depends on behaviors that most of us associate with literacy (which includes numeracy). Literate communication and language are the means by which we engage in extended thinking. Because language and thought are related, language influences and interacts with processes such as perceiving, understanding, remembering, feeling, and reasoning. As the cognitive demands of tasks become more complex and more abstract, communication and language play an increasingly important role. Consequently, deficiencies in communication skill will impair the way a child functions within complex and interactive settings—such as schools. An illiterate child may have difficulty gaining information from verbal and printed messages, have problems displaying what she knows, and often may not be sufficiently skilled to express specific needs for help.

The failure to develop literacy may prove devastating and isolating. Communicating lets us participate in society, and with ourselves. It is the means by which we are able to label our wants and needs, to express our feelings and emotions, and to form our social interactions. That is why schools should teach students to be literate. Literacy is at the heart of any socially relevant curriculum. But what *is* literacy?

Defining Literacy

Literacy is one of those things that is easier to describe than to define. This is a problem because description, by its nature, says as much about the person who is giving the description as it does about the thing described. The prior knowledge of speakers differ. Therefore, their descriptions must be interpreted within the context of what they believe and know. This little blurb on existential truth is more relevant here than it might seem. Literacy, as described or defined within the current literature, is tightly linked to context.

Consider a couple of examples. First, imagine that you have spent years learning to speak Spanish and are now fluent. You have a friend, also a teacher, who is just as fluent at speaking Pohnpeian (used to conduct government business in the Federated States of Micronesia). You and your friend are certified to teach in both elementary education and special education. You have decided to apply for jobs in California. In that state there are many thousands of Spanish-speaking students (see Chapter 12, page 263) and almost none who speak Pohnpeian. Which one, you or your friend, is most likely to get a job?

Let's try another example. This one was suggested by Langer (1991). You are touring a local junior high school. First, you go to a social studies class where students are working on an assignment. They have each silently read a passage about life in the Middle East and are answering questions at the end of the unit. They are quietly writing out their work. As you walk around the room you note that the students are all answering correctly, and that their spelling and handwriting is excellent.

After leaving the social studies class, you walk by the room used for in-school suspension of problem students. You are interested in this group of students because you have been told they are almost all nonreaders. When you walk in you find the students engaged in an argument. You are surprised to find that the argument is also about the Middle East. It was sparked by a TV show that two of the students watched the night before while eating their dinner. Much of what the students are saying is poorly worded, but their ideas seem considered and they are trying hard to get the rest of the students to understand the intricacies of the particular territorial dispute presented in the broadcast. The other students seem to be trying especially hard to understand.

Now the question: In which setting, the social studies class or the detention class, did you find students engaging in the most literate exercise? And, more direct to this illustration, in which class did the students seem to be learning important curricular skills?

Whatever literacy is, it is clearly culturally defined. Dictionaries typically define a literate person as one who is "cultured." This means that the form and quality of literacy are linked to the context in which it occurs (Valencia, McGinley & Pearson, 1992). What is literate behavior in one setting may be less than literate in another. Similarly, illiteracy may be a function of misalignment, not inaccuracy. (Your Pohnpeian speaking friend, while technically skilled, may seem less cultured to a class of Latino students in Modesto, California, than will you, the Spanish-speaker.)

So to understand a definition, or description, of literacy one has to understand the ways individuals communicate within a cultural context. The key term here may not even be literacy—or culture— it may be communication. Literacy is the efficient exchange of messages within a particular cultural context, and the analogy of a dialogue is useful when trying to understand it.

The General Process of Literate Communication

Communication seems to have four stages: planning, transcribing, reviewing, and revising (Isaacson, 1985) as shown in Exhibit 3.1. What is done in these stages

Exhibit 3.1   The General Process of Literate Communication

When Formulating and Sending a Message the Writer/Speaker:			
Plans	Transcribes	Reviews	Revises
• establishes intent • organizes resources • researches content • develops message • selects style	• speaks • writes • follows conventions • supplies material • reveals message	• judges integrity of plan • compares transcription to plan • checks accuracy of mechanics	• modifies plan • modifies message • modifies style
When Receiving and Understanding a Message the Writer/Speaker:			
Investigates	Recognizes	Monitors	Reforms
• asks questions • selects sources • chooses material • studies	• listens • reads • responds to intent • recognizes plan • utilizes structure • decodes message	• checks message for internal consistency • compares message to prior knowledge • compensates for errors in presentation	• seeks clarification • finds solutions • personalizes message by integrating it with prior knowledge

depends, of course, on whether one is formulating/sending or receiving/understanding.

It also depends on whether the communication is being carried out through speaking or writing. These variations will receive elaboration in the topical chapters, 10–17. However, there are two other factors that determine how literate communication functions that need to be explained here: intent and audience.

As you can see in Exhibit 3.1, sending and receiving literate messages are both complex activities. While it is probably true that most people who are good at one of these activities will also be good at the other, there is no guarantee. (One wonders if good listeners will ever get elected to public office!) However, most of the time people send and receive messages without even considering the mechanisms they are using. We don't work at it, we just do it—*unless* we are put under stress. Under stress, even the most sophisticated thinker can be jarred out of automatic functioning by tasks that appear difficult, ambiguous, or unclear.

Here is an exercise to help you understand the complexities facing an illiterate individual. Imagine that you have been assigned to make a major presentation in a university class, and 50% of your grade depends on your performance. However, you know very little about the topic and even less about what your instructor (a principal in the highest paying

school district in the area) thinks of as a good presentation. What do you do? Think about it before you continue reading.

Most of us would seek clarification about the purpose and intent of the assignment. We would also try to find out as much as we could about the topic. Having done those things, we would begin to plan the presentation, to formulate the message we want to deliver. In doing so, we would consider various factors, including the intent of the message and the nature of the receiving audience.

Intent

Wiig and Semel (1984) have provided a general organizing structure for intent (function). It is shown in Exhibit 3.2. According to these authors, messages can be categorized by their function. Wiig and Semel were writing about the pragmatic use of oral language. Other authors provide similar structures when they talk about the differences between descriptive, narrative, expository, and persuasive writing, or expressive, poetic, and transactive intent (Britton, 1978) as illustrated in Exhibit 3.3 (also see Chapter 13). (Any, or all, of these various systems may be appropriate for guiding instruction or evaluation. They are all logically derived but not empirically validated.)

The various functions in Exhibits 3.2 and 3.3

Exhibit 3.2   *Framework for Organizing Pragmatics*

Function	Uses	Examples
Ritualizing	Greetings, farewells, regulation of turn taking, etc.	''Hello'' ''How are you?'' ''See you later''
Informing	Give or request information	''This chapter is about language.'' ''What is the definition of pragmatics?''
Controlling	Commanding, warning, giving permission, threatening, refusing, offering	''Summarize what you have read before you continue''
Feeling	Express attitudes/feelings. Respond to attitudes/feelings. Monitor attitudes/feelings of self and others	''I believe thoughtful teachers can make a difference''
Imagining	Storytelling, lieing, speculating, fantasizing	The authors are excellent spellers

Source: Reprinted with permission of Merrill, an imprint of Macmillan Publishing Company, from *Language Assessment & Intervention for The Learning Disabled, Second Edition,* by E.H. Wiig and E. Semel. Copyright © 1984, 1980 by Bell and Howell Company.

should not be thought of as mutually exclusive. Let's assume that your intent (the class presentation) is to (1) inform, and (2) do so in a narrative fashion.

Audience

Evaluators cannot judge whether a communication is literate if they don't know the intent and the conventional form. It is also useful to know what effect the communication has on the recipient. Does your teacher expect you to present as if your audience is made up of adults or of the students you might rou-

tinely teach? If you are presenting to 8-year-olds, you will do different things than you would do with adults—even if the intent is the same. (Actions that amuse adults may not please 8-year-olds—you can think up your own examples.)

Literacy has a social framework or context (Gaffney & Anderson, 1991; Miller-Jones, 1989). In a social framework, communication initiates and sustains interaction. A kid's development requires that the people around her are willing to communicate with her, respond to what she says, encourage her by their understanding, and allow her to modify and expand her communication skills. Family members, other adults, and peers are important in the child's social environment. So are teachers.

We are neither just speakers nor just listeners. We do both things. Frequently the audience is as important as the speaker to the context of literate exchange. How well a child receives the messages of others depends on that child's intent and how receptive he is. The quality of one's listening/reading is not fixed; it varies according to things like interest, prior knowledge, and intent. If a speaker intends to control (for example, give a warning), but the listener only wants to be informed, someone will be disappointed. Similarly, a listener who speaks with one accent may seem illiterate to a speaker who uses a different accent, or the speaker may seem illiterate to the listener.

Exhibit 3.3   *Writing Purposes*

Function	Attributes
Expressive	Close to the self Addressing speaker's consciousness May be relatively unstructured
Poetic	Patterned verbalization of feelings and ideas Not restricted to poems
Transactive	Instructs Performs Persuades

Literacy is present when a person has the skill to both understand and respond to the demands of academic and social contexts.

A Note About Social Skills

The child's understanding of social rules and the range of her familiarity with social contexts are important aspects of literacy. This will be explained in Chapter 16. Students who do not know the social rules may appear rude or insubordinate (Iglesias, 1985; Larson & Gerber, 1987; Martens & Witt, 1988; Saville-Troike, 1976). For example, when the teacher asks "Would you like to do your spelling now?" the child who understands the sociolinguistic rules of classrooms, but does not want to do the assignment, may say "Can I do it later?" or just sharpen her pencil a lot. A child who does not understand the sociolinguistic rules might just say no, and be considered unresponsive or rude.

Children often communicate poorly because the social conditions to which they are accustomed are missing (Philips, 1970). Not only are there sociolinguistic rules for turn-taking or following directions, there are also different rules for the structure of discourse. In some cultures, stories and messages are not organized around a main idea and a sequence of events. They may be organized as associated topics. When a child's discourse style is different from the majority, she may have trouble understanding both oral and written messages. Research indicates that directly teaching children about different classroom interaction styles will improve learning (see Chapter 17) (Kawakami & Hupei Au, 1986).

Literacy and the Curriculum

All students need to learn the literacy strategies outlined in Exhibit 3.1. They need to learn to plan, transcribe, review, revise, investigate, recognize, monitor, and reform. Obviously if that is what they need to learn, then that is what should be taught. However, there is one problem with doing that. Some students lack the necessary prior knowledge, and so these literacy strategies are currently too difficult.

Literacy strategies are "enabled" by underlying skills (Valencia et al., 1992). If students do not have those enabling skills, they cannot efficiently employ the complex strategic operations we associate with literate communication. Similarly, if they have the enabling skills but lack the strategies for using them, they will not behave in a literate fashion.

The relationship between enabling skills and literacy strategies is easiest to see in terms of transcribing and recognizing (Exhibit 3.1). A person can have wonderful penmanship, but have nothing to say. Therefore vocabulary and grammar skills enable, but do not assure, literate transcription and recognition of messages.

Exhibit 3.4 shows the relationships among the literacy strategies found in Exhibit 3.1, enabling skills, and the title traditionally used to refer to these enabling skills in schools. Exhibit 3.4 will serve as an organizer for each of the topical chapters (10–17) found in Part 3 of this text.

Enabling Skills vs. Literacy

This section is going to sound a bit defensive. That's because it touches on a major controversy that runs through much of education today. It is a controversy best illustrated through the topic of reading.

For decades, arguments about reading have focused on whether reading is a top down (whole-language) or a bottom up (skill-based) process (Samuels & Kamil, 1984). Proponents of the top-down theories focus attention on the meaning-driven integrated process of reading, while bottom-up advocates note that reading is comprised of many teachable skills

(such as phonics). Top-down teachers argue that you cannot break reading into subtasks, while bottom-up teachers teach students to read by focusing on specific skill acquisition. In short, top-down advocates target literacy strategies, and bottom-up advocates target enabling skills.

Discussions about reading practice, and comprehension in particular, often seem to be more political than empirical (Adams, 1991). This is due to the fact that such discussions often center on controversies introduced, not by contradictory data, but by contradictory interpretation and speculation. Much of this represents a classic confusion of curriculum and instruction. This confusion is particularly apparent within discussions about the relative merits of whole-language and direct-instruction approaches to reading. Basically, whole-language proponents argue that reading is most effectively taught as a holistic process and that its reduction to a sequence of subskills destroys the language-based cohesion that defines it. Because they are committed to the belief that language acquisition is an appropriate model for initial reading acquisition, they propose that reading be taught through the same sorts of experiential and enriching activities associated with optimal language development (Ensminger & Dangel, 1992; Heshusius, 1991; McGee & Lomax, 1990). In contrast, proponents of direct instruction maintain that reading is most effectively taught through highly focused, outcome-oriented lessons that emphasize enabling skills.

An excellent analysis of reading instruction conducted by Stahl and Miller (1989) highlights the confusion over curriculum and instruction so typical of this debate. These authors concluded, in part, that while the direct-instruction people and the whole-language people think they are contrasting forms of *instruction*, they are actually contrasting *curriculums*. Therefore, the issues of instructional superiority can't really be addressed. Typically, whole-language instruction focuses on literate communication, whereas direct instruction tends to focus on enabling skills like phonics, morphology, and vocabulary. It's sort of like arguing about whether or not the best way to ski downhill is with scuba tanks or golf clubs.

The authors of this text believe that, as a group, proponents of direct instruction have erred by ignoring the important conceptual and strategic components of literacy (an error they are rapidly correcting) (Dixon & Carnine, 1992). In addition, direct-instruction propo-

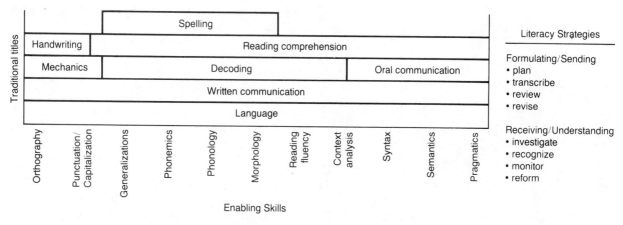

Exhibit 3.4   Skills that enable literacy and their traditional titles.

nents have often isolated enabling skills like phonics. This is probably wrong (Adams, 1991), but that doesn't necessarily mean direct instruction is wrong—it means it has been applied to the wrong outcomes. We also think that proponents of a literacy approach make their own errors when they ignore the importance of enabling skills and, sometimes, fail to use hands-on instruction to direct the learning of students (this is clearly not the case in literacy programs, like Reading Recovery, in which teachers actively use instruction) (Gaffney, 1991).

We hardly think the total debate will be influenced by these few pages. However, for you to understand this text, it is important to understand the premises upon which it was developed. We are proponents of direct (hands-on) instruction because we are working in a deficit model. This text is not about initial instruction. The student addressed in this text has already had some sort of instruction—and it has failed. The goal of remedial and special education is to overcome this initial failure by accelerating the student through the curriculum. This may require elements of many instructional approaches. However, the goal can only be accomplished through highly focused and intentional interventions (Palincsar, 1990). It is up to the teacher to arrange this focus. It is also up to the teacher to make sure the object of this focus, the curriculum, is worth the student's attention.

One last note. Remember the myth that curriculum and instruction are the same? Understanding that confusion is important to understanding this particular discus-

sion, because our advocacy of intentional and focused instruction does not preclude advocacy for student involvement, and even generative (that is, student-directed) instruction (see Chapter 4, pp. 56–57). Any teaching technique that excludes the student will fail.

Defining Goals and Objectives

Rationale

The curriculum is operationally defined as a set of goals and objectives. Goals and objectives are specified for students in special/remedial education for three reasons: It is necessary in order to maintain curriculum focus; various regulations and laws say we must (for compliance); and because it's a good thing to do, (for accountability, monitoring of progress, and motivation).

The Education for All Handicapped Children Act (PL 94–142), has recently been extended by the Individuals with Disabilities Education Act of 1990 (IDEA). These legislative actions require that each child with a disability receive a free and appropriate public education. An important part of this law is the individual education plan (IEP) which must include the specification of goals and objectives. These are drawn from an analysis of each child's unique needs as identified and described through a process of comprehensive evaluation. While IEPs are required by law for students with disabilities, for remedial and at-risk

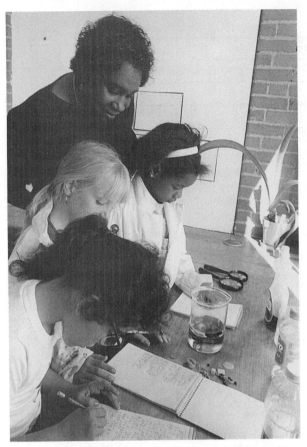

Hands-on instruction is used with special and remedial students because they have already demonstrated that they have not responded adequately to initial instruction.

students (for whom IEPs are not a legal requirement), the preparation of an IEP-type plan is considered to be good practice.

If we look at the history of special education and the court cases that led to the passage of PL 94–142 and IDEA, it is clear that these laws were written in part because students with school difficulties were sometimes forced into alternate programs that were neither appropriate nor particularly beneficial in meeting their educational needs. And one of the reasons that due process provisions were specifically included in the law is that when we remove a student from general education we are limiting her freedom. For these reasons, we have a particular legal duty in spe-

cial/remedial education to be accountable to students and their parents.

We also have a professional obligation to provide students with the best possible education. To advance this aim we must demonstrate that students are benefiting from their individualized education program. This accountability is accomplished by establishing present levels of performance and developing goals and objectives that detail where the student is and where she needs to go.

There are other important, related reasons for having goals and objectives. One is that it is impossible to efficiently monitor a student's progress without them. Special/remedial students have fallen behind in the curriculum. As their advocates it is our job to find the programs that will catch them up. However, the selection of programs, methods, and materials always involves guesswork. Without goals and objectives there is nothing against which progress can be judged and, therefore, no basis for evaluating instruction.

Establishing goals and objectives that allow us to be accountable to students and their parents and to monitor progress also facilitates motivation. Students, particularly those who have trouble in school, learn more when sequences of curriculum are specified (Gleason, Carnine & Vala, 1991; Kulik et al., 1990) and teachers are able to feel a sense of competence when they see their students reach these objectives. In summary, by writing goals and objectives we not only comply with the law but also benefit our students and ourselves (Sulzer-Azaroff & Mayer, 1991).

Examples and Nonexamples

One mechanism widely used to teach concepts like "appropriate" is to present examples and nonexamples of the concept (Arends, 1991) (see Chapter 8, p. 157). We will use this device over the following pages to present the concept of "good" goals and objectives. But first, here is some performance information about a student, because appropriate goals and objectives are derived from assessment data.

Present Levels of Performance Statement

Kim is a fourth-grade girl with good attendance and appropriate social skills who is having difficulty in math. She scored second grade, second month on a math test. She indicated a good understanding of how to tell time and of metric measurement, but does not understand money value or computations in addition or subtraction when problems yield answers greater than ten. Through testing and teacher interview, it was determined that her skills in other academic areas are average or above. Her vision, hearing, speech, and health are normal according to records.

Example: Here is an example of an appropriate goal written for one area of need identified in the present levels of performance statement (addition with regrouping). Other goals and objectives could also be required for those other areas of concern noted in the evaluation results (additional goals and objectives for covering money and subtraction would also need to be added for Kim).

Goal: Kim will improve her accuracy and rate at writing answers to addition problems.

Objectives:

1. Kim will write answers to addition fact problems with sums 11 to 18 (for example, 6 + 5) on a worksheet with 100% accuracy.
2. Kim will write answers to addition fact problems with sums from 0 to 20 (1 + 1 or 10 + 10) on a worksheet at a rate of 40 problems correct per minute with no errors.
3. Kim will write answers to two-digit plus one-digit without regrouping addition problems on a worksheet at a rate of 40 problems correct per minute with no errors.
4. Kim will write answers to two-digit plus one-digit with regrouping addition problems on a worksheet with 100% accuracy.
5. Kim will write answers to two-digit plus two-digit without regrouping addition problems on a worksheet with 100% accuracy.
6. Kim will balance her checkbook without making errors in two-digit addition. She will work the two-digit addition problems in the context of her checkbook, with 100% accuracy.

Nonexample: Once again, when explaining a concept, it is sometimes as helpful to show incorrect (nonexamples) as it is to show correct examples. The following statements, also drawn from Kim's present level of performance statement, are not appropriate goals or objectives. The reasons they are inappropriate are presented in brackets after each objective. These will be explained shortly.

Goal 1: Kim will draw the geometric shapes: line, circle, square, triangle, and rectangle when the shape name is given. [unrelated to present level of performance statement]

Objectives:

a. Kim will recognize geometric shapes on paper when the shape name is given.
   [no behavior and no criteria]
b. Kim will point to geometric shapes in the classroom when the shape names are given.
   [no criteria]
   [both objectives a and b call for identification responses, while the goal calls for production]

Goal 2: Kim will write answers to subtraction fact problems 10–20 with 75% accuracy. [criteria too low]

Objective: Kim will say answers to subtraction fact problems when shown flashcards. [no criteria and only one objective for goal]

Goal 3: Kim will understand the importance of doing homework. [goal too vague]

Objective: [only one objective for goal] Kim will write down her homework assignments with 100% accuracy. [no condition specified]

Characteristics of Quality Goals and Objectives

The Problem of Quality

Widely accepted standards for goals and objectives do not currently exist. This is partly because different states and educational agencies are allowed the freedom to adopt their own formats. More important, the goals and objectives are intended to reflect the individual needs of the student and the individual thought processes of the professionals writing the IEP. However, the concept of individualization can only be carried so far. Goals and objectives are statements of curricular expectation. They tell us what students will do after instruction has taken place. Therefore, they must ultimately reflect the tasks, skills, content, behaviors, and thought processes that make up curriculum domains.

For students placed in special education programs, some additional guidance on the issue of quality is available from the Federal Government's Compliance Guidelines (what a comfort!). As pointed out under Rationale, one of the reasons we write goals and objectives is to comply with the law. Consider the following guidelines from the Office of Special Education and Rehabilitation Services, Education, Pt. 300, App. C:

1. The statutory requirements for including annual goals and short term objectives . . . provide a mechanism for determining, (1) whether the anticipated outcomes for the child are being met . . . and (2) whether the placement and the services are appropriate to the child's special learning needs.

2. . . . there should be a direct relationship between the annual goals and the present levels of educational performance.

3. The annual goals in the IEP are statements which describe what a handicapped child can reasonably be expected to accomplish within a twelve month period. . . .

4. Short term instructional objectives . . . are measurable, intermediate steps between a handicapped child's present levels of educational performance and the annual goals that are established for the child.
   The objectives are developed based on a logical breakdown of the major components of the annual goals, and can serve as milestones for measuring progress toward meeting the goals.

5. There should be a direct relationship between the IEP goals and objectives for a given handicapped child and the goals and objectives that are in the special education instructional plans for the child . . . The IEP, through its goals and objectives, (1) sets the general direction to be taken by those who will implement the IEP, and (2) serves as the basis for developing a detailed instructional plan for the child.

6. IEP goals and objectives are concerned primarily with meeting a handicapped child's need for special education and related services, and are not required to cover other areas of the child's education.

7. . . . the goals and objectives in the IEP are not intended to be as specific as the goals and objectives that are normally found in daily, weekly or monthly instructional plans.

8. IEP objectives must be written before placement [and cannot] be changed without initiating another IEP meeting.

9. The goals and objectives in the IEP should be helpful both to parents and to school personnel, in a general way, in checking on a child's progress in the special education program.

These guidelines can be changed into a series of questions one might ask when attempting to discriminate between examples and nonexamples of appropriate goals and objectives.

1. Do the goals and/or objectives represent an important learning outcome that is a priority for this student?

2. Is there a goal written for each area of need stated in the present levels of performance?

3. Are the goals realistic one-year accomplishments?

4. Are the goals and objectives easily measured?

5. Are there multiple objectives, representing intermediate steps to each goal?

6. Are the goals and objectives appropriately calibrated (sliced neither too broadly nor too narrowly)?

7. Are the goals and objectives useful for planning and evaluating instructional programs?

These seven questions reflect at least three primary concerns: measurement, calibration, and utility. These concerns interact with each other and, while we will discuss them separately, they can't exist without each other.

Measurement.   Goals and objectives, as emphasized by question 4, must be measurable so that their status can be monitored. This does *not* mean that they need to be derived from, or linked to, published tests. However, basic measurement principles such as reliability do apply (see Chapter 6). Probably the simplest way to judge if a goal or objective can be reliably measured is to apply the stranger test (Kaplan, 1990).

If the goals and objectives pass the stranger test, someone not involved in developing the statements—a stranger—could still use them to write appropriate instructional plans and evaluate student progress. Obviously, a stranger could not reliably do so unless the goals and objectives were written in a sufficiently observable and specific form.

Utility. Questions 1, 2, and 7 address the utility or validity of the goals and objectives. Just as the stranger test is synonymous with reliability, the so-what test embodies validity. As stated earlier, a well developed curriculum reflects the idea that the purpose of education is to prepare people to be socially competent. The so-what test looks at the relationship between the present performance of the child and the school's curriculum. The so-what test asks whether the goals and objectives are important. This is a more difficult test than the stranger test, because it involves value judgments about the curriculum and speculation about the child's long-term needs.

Good objectives specify outcomes that will benefit students by teaching them things that are socially significant (Ensminger & Dangel, 1992), and not simply make life easier for parents and teachers (although these are not always mutually exclusive). If an objective is to pass the so-what test, it should act to develop, rather than suppress, behavior. In cases where behaviors need to be suppressed (because they are dangerous), goals or objectives should include alternate positive behaviors (Sulzer-Azaroff & Mayer, 1991).

Calibration: How Short Is a Short-Term Objective?

Part of the curriculum development process in any school involves apportioning lessons. Typically this is handled by designating which topics will be covered at which depth at each grade level. After this grade-level allocation has occurred, individual teachers will also plan to cover particular lessons at particular times. In most classrooms these planning decisions are based on ideas about the expected progress of nondisabled students. This process of lesson time allocation is different in special/remedial education programs because, while the character of the objectives remains the same, the amount of material covered per time unit (day, week, month) is adjusted to match the individual progress expectations of each student. *Calibration* is a technical term referring to the process of setting values, gradations, positions, and segments. Starlin (1982) addressed the problems of educational calibration in a publication from the Iowa Monograph Series. In the monograph, Starlin explained the need to gauge carefully the amount of curriculum presented to students. He pointed out, for example, that the material in lessons on written communication could be "sliced" to target any of the following outcomes:

Write a letter or theme

Write a paragraph

Write a sentence

Write a phrase

Write a word

The appropriate scale for establishing the size (caliber) of each slice is the student's own need.

When it comes to the topics of goals and objectives, two of the most confusing questions are "Just exactly how long is a long-term goal?" and "How short are short-term objectives?" These are calibration questions and, while not as imposing as the so-what test, they are equally problematic. Questions 3, 5, and 6 all address this troublesome issue of objective size.

There is considerable controversy about how detailed the goals and objectives should be. The special education regulations say goals should be annual. Strickland and Turnbull (1990) state that it is *very* important that each teacher and planning committee resolve this question. They point out that many teachers find that objectives only set the general direction (Guideline 5 above) and are not helpful for specific lesson planning. However, other teachers complain that they do not have time to develop specific objectives. The secret, it seems to us, is to keep the needs of the individual student in mind when gauging progress expectations. And, in all cases, our recommendation is to err in the direction of specificity. If teachers find that the annual goals and objectives in IEPs or curriculum manuals are too broad to be helpful in planning, these objectives will come to be seen as unrelated to teaching—and teachers will stick them in a file drawer somewhere.

Selecting Objectives

Special and remedial students are supposed to receive an "individualized" education. Let's discuss what individualization is and what it is not:

- Individualization is *not* one-to-one teaching.
- Individualization is *not* unique objectives.
- Individualization is *not* necessarily different instruction.
- Individualization *is* a process of decision making.

When we talk about individualization we are talking about a thought process, not a product. Picture this. Chip overhears Norma being praised for the fantastic objectives she wrote for her student. Chip borrows this IEP, copies it, and puts his student's name on it. Then Chip is shocked when he is criticized for writing terrible objectives. What happened? Chip didn't individualize; he mistakenly believed that the product of someone else's efforts was more important than going through the process of individualization. The best IEP is not necessarily the one that includes the most creative objectives or the most esoteric methods. It is the one resulting from the most careful consideration of the individual student.

The curriculum is a sequence of objectives or tasks. So the decisions here seem straightforward. We look at the curriculum, decide what the student already knows, what he needs to know, and what he is ready to learn. For example, here is an analysis of critical reading (Carnine, Silbert & Kameenui, 1990):

- recognize author bias through critical reading
  —recognize author's purpose
  —distinguish evidence from opinion
  —judge quality of evidence
  —judge author's expertise

Given this task analysis, the teacher can use the student's assessment data and parental input to find out which critical reading tasks the student can already perform and which she can't, and then select those she is ready to learn (because the evaluation indicates she can do some essential subtasks). These will become goals and objectives in the IEP.

While the substance of the curriculum should not be changed, its form can be modified. Teachers can break it into small pieces, combine parts of it into

Exhibit 3.5   Elements of Objectives/Tasks

Content—What the student learns
Behavior—What the student does with the content
Criteria—How well the student does it
Conditions—Under what circumstances the student does it

larger pieces, or reorder the parts. The parts we do this to are the same as the parts of an objective that all teachers have heard about: content, behavior, conditions, and criteria. The purpose of each of these elements is stated in Exhibit 3.5.

Content.   We aren't going to spend much time on the content element because it is the most familiar and the most obvious. An objective covering "multiplication" is clearly different than one covering "context dependent vocabulary" or "dressing oneself." A typical content sequence is shown in Exhibit 3.6.

Content can be categorized in a variety of ways. One way it is routinely categorized is by the kind of knowledge which it seems to reflect. The kinds of knowledge we refer to in this text are factual (rote), strategic (procedural), and conceptual. Procedures for evaluating and teaching to each of these content types will be explained in Chapters 4 and 8.

Behavior.   The behavior statement is put in an objective for two reasons. First, it is there because it makes the objective more reliably measurable. "Knowing" is hard to measure (it is a construct) but "writing the answer" is easy to measure because it is a behavior. Second, different types of behavior can indicate different levels of competence. Two familiar behavior domains that seem to do this are "identify" and "produce."

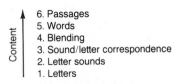

Exhibit 3.6   Decoding content.

We can test a student's knowledge of vocabulary by asking her to *identify* pictures of the objects we name, or by asking her to *produce* the names of objects in pictures that we show. As a domain, identifying (recognition) is typically easier for the student than producing (recall). If asked to name all of the states and capitals, you might have trouble. But if given a list of states and capitals and asked to match them, you'd probably get them right. If a student is tested on his identification skill (pointing, circling, crossing out) we can't leap to the conclusion that he can produce (say, write). Sometimes it is important that the student be able to identify before we ask him to produce and sometimes it isn't. It depends on the task. (In general, identification formats are only appropriate for objectives with accuracy criteria.)

The critical thing to remember is that identification and production are different domains of behavior and that "write the correct answer" is a different objective than "circle the correct answer," no matter what the content of the objective is. If a student can't produce answers, practice at identifying them may not even be a useful instructional activity.

Conditions. There are many conditions under which students may work. They may work in small groups or large groups, on worksheets or at the board, with assistance or on their own. Two condition domains that are useful for individualizing are "isolation" and "context." Something done in isolation is separated from all contextual clues and distractions. Something done in context is embedded within a larger frame of reference.

If a student needs to learn to read CVC words (hot, lip), we have to decide whether she needs to learn them in isolation (on flashcards) or in context (within sentences or stories). Ordinarily doing tasks in context is preferable because it has more meaning and involves the application of skills or knowledge. Typically, evaluators and teachers need only isolate specific skills in their own thinking. This is necessary to provide focus and assure curriculum alignment. They should *not* teach skills in isolation unless it is absolutely necessary.

The decision to teach a skill in isolation is typically based on assessment data indicating that the student can't handle the distractions imposed by context. Therefore, in order to teach the student, it is natural to reduce the distractions in the hope that the student will learn

more easily. However, it is important to remember that *it is the distractions that the student needs to learn to handle.* This is obvious within the domain of social behavior when, presented with a student who has difficulty communicating appropriately in a general-education fourth grade (if there is such a thing), we remove the student to a smaller special class and find, as a result of instruction in prosocial skills, that the student is communicating appropriately in the special class. This *doesn't* necessarily mean that the student will communicate well when back in the fourth-grade classroom. In many cases, particularly with social behavior and language skills, objectives can be written to specify movement along a sequence of conditions, rather than of content. For example:

1. Initiate contact with peers during role playing
2. Initiate contact with peers in unstructured activities
3. Initiate contact with strangers in familiar situations
4. Initiate contact with strangers in unfamiliar situations

The conditions specified in the objective have direct implications for assessment. The need for alignment, therefore, dictates that objective 4 must be assessed outside the classroom.

Criteria. A *criterion* is a standard. Like the behavior element, criteria are needed in an objective to allow evaluation to take place. Criterion statements also are in objectives to specify different levels of competence. Three commonly utilized proficiency levels are accuracy, mastery, and automaticity. Look back at the section where we talked about two types of performance in objectives: to identify and to produce. We can further individualize these objectives by specifying the proficiency levels at which we want students to identify or produce. This is shown in Exhibit 3.7. For example, we could say that a student needs to identify or produce answers to addition fact problems with 100% accuracy. We can add another dimension by saying that the student will produce answers to addition fact problems with 100% accuracy and at a rate of 40 per minute. Doing a task accurately and quickly represents a higher level of knowledge and is called *mastery* (fluency). The third level of proficiency involves doing a task accurately, quickly, and in context. For example,

Exhibit 3.7 *Parameters of Proficiency*

	Behavior →		
	Produce		
	Accuracy	Mastery	Automatic
Content: Addition facts	The student will supply the correct answer at a predetermined percentage level	The student will supply the correct answer at a predetermined rate	The student will supply the correct answer at a predetermined rate or percentage level in the presence of distractors
	The student will produce the correct answer to addition problems 100% of the time	The student will produce the correct answer to addition problems at a rate of 40 per minute	The student will balance a checkbook, making no errors in addition

"student will produce answers to addition fact problems within a checkbook" or "at the grocery store when buying ingredients for a recipe that needs to be quadrupled." This is called the automatic level, or automaticity. (Because they only indicate low levels of proficiency, identification tasks should include accuracy, not rate, criteria.)

It is important that we not establish proficiency levels or standards arbitrarily. Establishing a standard of 80% accuracy, for every objective, which is common practice, is not appropriate. Would a standard of 80% accuracy on multiplication facts mean that we think 8×7 or 4×5 are not particularly important or useful? Will we hope that quadrupling that recipe will not require knowing 4×5? Appropriate mastery levels are very important too. The chances are slim of getting through a page of long-division problems if your rate on multiplication facts is only 5 per minute. Appropriate standards of accuracy and fluency for basic skills in reading, writing and math are available in various research studies and in the topical chapters of this text. (Some examples of locally established standards can also be found in Chapter 9.)

It is also important that the distractors we include in automatic level objectives be relevant—that they have a real world application. We shouldn't write an objective that says "student will read sight words while standing on her head." More appropriate might be "reading sight words in job notices at the crowded and noisy Employment Security Office."

Exhibit 3.8 presents what is called a table of speci-

fications. Tables of specifications can be used to plan tests (Gronlund, 1973). In Exhibit 3.8 there are four columns. Each of these represents a separate objective that may or may not be relevant to an individual student. If the expected outcome is to have the student balance her checkbook (Objective D.1) then Objectives A.1, B.1, and C.1 represent a sequence of reasonable enabling objectives leading to that goal.

To summarize, examine the following objective as it is modified in (1) content, (2) behavior, (3) conditions, and (4) criteria.

Original objective:
Pam will write the answers to *addition facts* on a worksheet at a rate of 40 correct per minute.

Content modification:
Pam will write the answers to *subtraction facts* on a worksheet at a rate of 40 correct per minute.

Modification of behavior:
Pam will *say the answers* to addition facts on a worksheet at a rate of 40 correct per minute.

Condition modification:
Pam will write the answers to addition facts *in a checkbook* at a rate of 40 correct per minute.

Criteria modification:
Pam will write the answers to addition facts on a worksheet *with 100% accuracy.*

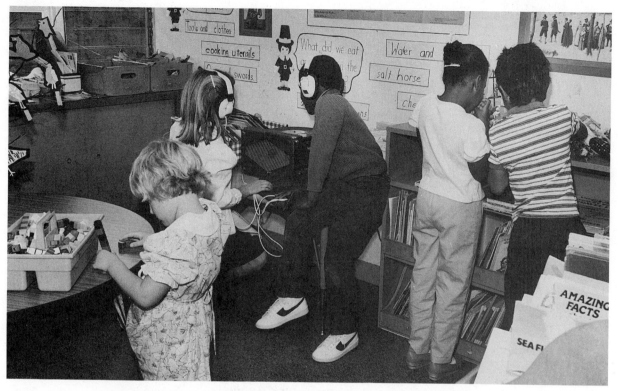

Individualization is a process that bases goals on the specific needs of each particular student.

Progress Objectives.   Up until now all of the objective modifications we have discussed have been defined by their unique elements: content, behavior, conditions, or criteria. Using that strategy, we have seen that it is possible to devise intermediate steps (leading to an annual goal) by establishing a sequence of objectives each of which states a particular task the student will perform. However, there is another strategy that can be used to specify intermediate steps.

It is possible to slice (recalibrate) any performance objective by adding time to the decision-making process. For example, look at Objective C.1 in Exhibit 3.8. It says a student will "write the answers to 2-place addition problems without regrouping at the mastery level." This objective can be sliced by generating a sequence of aim dates specifying different proficiency levels. For example ". . . rate of 5 problems a minute by November 1st," ". . . rate of 10 problems a minute

by December 1st," and ". . . rate of 20 problems a minute by January 1st."

The use of a sequence of aim dates to adjust objectives for individuals can be applied to any of the objective elements. Here is another example using the addition facts objective but focusing on the content dimension. "Will write answers to problems including the numbers 0–5 by November 1st" and "will write answers to problems involving the numbers 6–9 by December 1st."

To slice objectives by writing them in terms of expected progress, pick a task and set intermediate aims along a single element (content, behavior, condition or criteria). This works best for skills like oral reading that reflect the use of multiple skills and processes. For example, if our objective is that the student read orally from a passage in the fourth-grade reading book at a rate of 140 words correct per minute, we can set intermediate aims such as 50 correct per min-

Exhibit 3.8   Table of Specifications for Two-Place Addition

	Behavior ➤			
	Identify Accuracy	Produce Accuracy	Produce Mastery	Produce Automatic
	A.1	B.1	C.1	D.1
Content: Two-place addition facts	"Point to the answer for this problem": 10 + 1 (a) 6 (b) 7 (c) 11 (d) 15	"Write the answers to two-place addition problems without regrouping accurately"	"Write the answers to two-place addition problems without regrouping at a rate of 20 problems per minute"	"Quickly balance a checkbook and make no errors in two-place addition without regrouping"

ute by November 15 and 75 correct per minute by December 15.

A Quick Review

This is a big chapter so let's quickly review the relationship between all this slicing and our need to write annual goals and objectives that comply with legal guidelines *and* represent best practice: (1) Goals must be directly related to present levels of performance, that is, assessment data, that tell us what the student knows and how well she knows it; for example, "says regular one-syllable words accurately, but slowly, in isolation." (2) Annual goals reflect an IEP committee's or teacher's decisions about what the student needs to know and will know as a result of one year of special education; for example, "Will decode one syllable words accurately." (3) Objectives represent milestones or intermediate aims on the way to that goal.

Goals need to be measurable so that we can determine if they have been met; however, the actual measurement procedure need not be specified in each goal. Additionally, there need to be *multiple* objectives so we know if we are getting there. We don't want to wait a year to find out that our plan didn't work. We don't even want to wait 3 months to find out that it isn't working. A student who is already behind can't afford that. Developing annual goals and objectives is

extremely important. We don't individualize by leaving out important content or lowering standards (student will cross busy street with 80% accuracy), but by setting realistic goals and objectives that are specific enough to be useful.

Task Analysis

Few teachers will ever need to develop curriculum from scratch. However, we do know that the decision making of expert teachers is based, in part, on the process of task analysis (Berliner, 1989; Shavelson, 1983).

The idea behind task analysis is that a student must learn the components of a task in order to learn the task. Teachers using task analysis attempt to identify these components and to test the student's knowledge of them in order to decide what a student needs to be taught. (Once again, just because specific subcomponents have been identified it does *not* follow that they should be taught in isolation.)

Task analysis is the process defining all of the essential components of a task (Bateman, 1971). Any job or activity that a student engages in during the school day may be referred to as a task. Any behavior, or set of behaviors, that a child must engage in to demonstrate skill or knowledge is a task. A task, as we've defined it, always includes an element of application.

Kinds of Tasks

Tasks (objectives) are often categorized in an effort to coordinate the curriculum. Typically they will be categorized by content ("This is a *language* task"). Sometimes, however, authors attempt to categorize tasks according to the demands they place on the student's information-processing system. In such cases, the tasks may be referred to by titles like "higher level," "meaningful," "abstract," "concrete," "rational," "symbolic," "rule-governed," "synthetic," "cognitive," or "affective" (Simmons & Kameenui, 1990).

In this text we will consistently refer to three sorts of knowledge/task amalgamations: facts, concepts, and strategies. We picked the term *amalgamation* because it describes the relationship of task demand and information-processing response that seems to us to be most realistic. You see, task demands do not reside exclusively within the tasks themselves, but within the linkage of the task to the thought processes of the learner. Therefore, because learners each have different prior knowledge, the demands of a particular task vary from person to person (just as task difficulty varies) (see Chapter 2, p. 20).

What does all of this mean? It means we think that conceptual knowledge, factual knowledge, and strategic knowledge exist. However, we don't really believe that certain tasks are conceptual, factual, or strategic. Instead, we believe it is possible—and probably even ideal—to have all three types of knowledge whenever we can. Therefore, we recommend teaching all three kinds of knowledge, which means we must be prepared to evaluate all three types as well.

Factual knowledge involves the simple awareness of links. For example: "Increased education typically leads to increased earnings" or "6×8 is 48." These are things a person can know without knowing how to figure them out or what they mean. *Conceptual knowledge*, in distinction, involves the awareness of meaning. With conceptual knowledge the person understands the implications and underlying ideas associated with "increased learning" and "6×8." *Strategic knowledge* relates to a person's knowledge of the procedures you could use to figure out what happens to people's income as they become more educated or what the product of 6×8 is. It is impossible to determine which of the three types of knowledge a person possesses by simply having them tell you that $6 \times 8 = 48$.

Obviously, which of these types of knowledge a person does or doesn't have depends a lot on the lessons the person has or hasn't received. All or none of these types of knowledge may be present as a result of the approach taken during instruction. This will be explained in greater detail in Chapter 4.

Subtasks

Tasks (objectives) have two components: subtasks and strategies. A student must have knowledge of both components to work a task. Subtasks are simply smaller, or more elementary, tasks required for the performance of an objective. Subtasks and tasks are exactly the same except for their relative positions in some skill sequence. If counting is required for addition, then counting is a subtask of addition. If addition is required for multiplication, then addition is a subtask of multiplication. (We suppose this means that one task's subtask is another subtasks's task—bet that cleared it up for you!) Subtasks must have all the same elements (content, behavior, criteria, and conditions) or they aren't complete. Subtasks can be viewed as the stuff (knowledge, facts, vocabulary, skills) students use whenever they try to do something.

Strategies

Strategies are the rules, procedures, and algorithms students follow to combine subtasks into larger tasks. There can be several different strategies for combining a set of subtasks, because there is often more than one way to do something correctly (and there are definitely many ways to do things incorrectly). If two students with the same subskill competency follow different strategies, one may succeed at the task whereas the other might fail.

The term *strategy* is currently very trendy in the educational literature. While it has yet to be clearly defined (Larson & Gerber, 1987; de Bettencourt, 1987), it seems the term is used most widely to characterize the process of work, as opposed to its products (Weinstein & Mayer, 1983). A strategy, once again, is the procedure, plan, or rule one uses to arrive at a product, and not the product itself. A strategy is what a teacher says to a student when explaining how to do a task. Telling answers or giving feedback on the accuracy of answers, while common, are not examples of strategy-focused teacher talk (Anderson, 1985; Anderson, Ste-

Exhibit 3.9   Task Analysis of Fractions

Task	Example
Add or subtract fractions without common denominators that *do not* have common factors between denominators. Convert to simplest form.	$\dfrac{2}{7} + \dfrac{3}{4} = 1\dfrac{1}{28}$
Task strategy	
(a) Decide if denominators are the same.	
(b) Find the least common denominator.	
(c) Produce the equivalent fractions.	
(d) Decide what operation (add or subtract) is called for.	
(e) Carry out the operation.	
(f) Decide if the answer is in simplest form. If it isn't,	
(g) Convert it.	
Essential subtasks	
5 Converting fractions to simplest form	$\dfrac{29}{28} = 1\dfrac{1}{28}$
4 Adding and subtracting fractions that do have common factors	$\dfrac{8}{28} + \dfrac{21}{28} = \dfrac{29}{28}$
3 Multiplication and division facts	$7\,\overline{\smash{\big)}\,28}^{\;4}\quad 4 \times 2 = 8$ $4\,\overline{\smash{\big)}\,28}^{\;7}\quad 7 \times 3 = 21$
2 Finding least common denominators	⑦14, 21, *28* ④8, 12, 16, 20, 24, *28*
1 Addition facts	$2 + 3 = 5$

vens, Prawat & Nickerson, 1988). For example, if a teacher is trying to promote the use of a "count-by strategy" in multiplication, and the student correctly says that $2 \times 4 = 8$, the teacher should respond by saying "Good! You counted by 2 four times!" This has the effect of reinforcing the use of the targeted strategy, whereas simply saying "Good, you got the correct answer!" does not.

Computation is one of the easiest domains for illustrating strategies because mathematics instruction is based on the presentation of algorithms. Algorithms are step-by-step procedures for arriving at the answers to computational problems. Look at the fraction example in Exhibit 3.9, where the task (adding $2/7 + 3/4$) is presented at the top and the subtasks are presented at the bottom. The strategy for combining the subtasks is also presented. As you read the strategy, you will notice that it isn't particularly sophisticated; it simply tells what to do first, second, third, and so on. As you can see, a student who can't multiply and divide accu-

rately (subtask 3) will be unable to succeed at this task even if the student has memorized the strategy and writes it on the board 50 times every day. That student will fail at the task because there is a lack of the necessary (prerequisite) enabling skills. This student needs work on multiplication prior to, or along with, work on fractions.

Ensuring that a student can do all subtasks still does not assure success. A student must also know the strategy. Sticking with the problem in Exhibit 3.9, imagine that a student writes this answer:

$$2/7 + 3/4 = 29/28$$

This answer is wrong because it is not converted to simplest form, which does not necessarily mean the student doesn't know how to convert fractions (subskill 5). It could mean the student forgot the last step in the strategy (step g). If that is the case, having this student memorize the strategy might be a good instructional technique (we'd pass on writing it 50 times a day), but working on multiplication would be a waste of time.

Students will frequently attempt to solve a new problem by using a strategy that has worked in the past. For example, a student who writes

$$2/7 + 3/4 = 5/11$$

has not gotten the "add-unlike-fraction strategy" wrong—it hasn't been used at all. Errors are not always the result of a flawed strategy. Rather, they are often the result of a correct strategy incorrectly applied. In the $2/7 + 3/4$ example, the student applied the addition strategy for whole numbers to a fraction problem. In one sense, what the student did was right (added correctly). Unfortunately that wasn't what was needed. When students apply strategies they have already learned to new tasks, the errors they produce are not the result of missing subskill information.

Fitting Strategies into the Curriculum. The belief that problem learners lack the basic capacity, or ability to learn, has been replaced by a belief that these students do not make effective use of the capacity they have (Palincsar & Brown, 1987) (see Chapter 2). The importance of this change lies in the idea that a student's use of cognitive strategies, unlike her capacity, can be altered through instruction. This characterization of mildly disabled students as "strategy deficient" has been followed by the recommendation that strategies be taught (Derry & Murphy, 1986; Herrmann, 1988). As is often the case, such calls for change in instructional practice have not been accompanied by complementary calls for change in the practice of curriculum development and evaluation. This isn't good.

Calls to include strategies in instruction are, by implication, calls to include them in the curriculum. Exactly how this inclusion should take place is not clear, although at least three alternatives are available. The first is to focus on strategies that facilitate skill acquisition and application (Palincsar & Brown, 1987). Under this alternative, the strategies required to succeed in the current curriculum are identified and stated as part of existing objectives. This has been referred to as Embedded Strategy Training (Derry & Murphy, 1986). The second alternative is to place within the existing curriculum a new area of content—thinking. Examples of this second alternative can be seen in the work of Feuerstein (1980) and Sternberg (1982). The third alternative, of course, is to do both.

So far the evidence on teaching general thinking skills to special/remedial students, while interesting, isn't setting the world on fire (McKeachie, 1987a; McKeachie, 1987b; Sweller, 1990). This seems to be because the general thinking skills are not being generalized to specific academic and social tasks. This means that, at present, the idea of embedding strategies within the existing curriculum is probably the best idea. (Teaching thinking skills is not a bad idea, it simply isn't sufficient).

In an embedded strategy curriculum, the outcomes (objectives) are not simply conceptualized as things a person will do—the objectives also specify *how* the student will do them. An embedded strategy objective, therefore, combines orthodox product statements ("student will write the answers to multiplication fact problems with 100% accuracy") with process statements ("count by the larger number as many times as indicated by the small number.") This would yield objectives that sound like this: "The student will solve multiplication fact problems by counting by the larger number as many times as the smaller number indicates and write the answers with 100% accuracy." A student who recalls these facts by rote, copies them from the kid across the aisle, or uses a calculator to get multiplication facts correct would *not* have met this objective even if every answer was right.

There are some problems with the concept of embedded strategy objectives. First, they are more complex. Therefore, they require more time for teachers to produce (most teachers are not burdened with excess time). Second, there is the considerable risk that a student might be penalized for doing something correctly, but in the "wrong" way. This could happen if the *process* portion of the objective is given a higher priority than the *product* portion. But it shouldn't. *Adherence to the process should never be elevated over completion of the product.*

Remember that this text deals with special/remedial teaching. The material in it is directed at students who have problems. Students who have problems, according to current theory, don't use strategies well. Exceptional teachers must fix that. One way to do this is to ensure appropriate strategy use by including strategic statements in objectives. This is not necessary if the student isn't having problems. In short, if a student is already multiplying with 100% accuracy, leave him alone!

Kinds of Strategies. There may be several different strategies for any one task. The fraction strategy presented in Exhibit 3.9 is one way to arrive at the answer; another way is to ask the teacher. The first strategy (adding fractions without common denominator) is *specific* to fractions. The second strategy (seeking assistance) is a *general* strategy, and may be used in many situations.

Specific strategies apply to only a limited range of tasks while general strategies may be used across several content domains (Frederiksen, 1984; Rigney, 1980; Wagner & Sternberg, 1984). The fraction algorithm in Exhibit 3.9 is a specific strategy that is good for solving only one type of fraction problem. It won't help do long division, it won't help you get a date, and it won't help you find words in a dictionary. Asking

for assistance, in contrast, is a strategy that may help you succeed at all of those tasks and many more. Exhibit 3.10 shows the steps of a general strategy and how it might be applied to three problems.

A Note on Learning vs. Doing

We often begin a task analysis by observing an expert working the task, or by doing it ourselves. This is to help recognize the components of task completion that may be considered essential subtasks or strategy steps. There is one thing wrong here: Learning to do something differs from doing it once learned (Howell, 1983).

Learning to spell in one instructional program, in one teacher's class, is a different task from learning to spell in another program or class. We are all familiar

Exhibit 3.10   Three Problems

General Strategy	27 $\overline{/84}$	Arrange a Date	Define "Strategy"
Recognize problem	I have to figure this out and I don't know the answer.	If I don't get a date I'll be the only one watching *Star Trek* Saturday night.	I still don't know what a strategy is.
Generate options	I could use a calculator. I could copy off Jennifer. I could ask the teacher. I could look for help in my math book.	I could ask Jennifer or Tammy and go to a movie, dinner, or skiing.	I could look it up in the dictionary. I could reread this chapter. I could check the glossary.
Consider resources	I don't have a calculator, Jennifer is worse at math than I am, I can't read the math book, and I hate the teacher.	Tammy has a 230-lb boyfriend who eats nails. I don't know how to ski.	I've read this chapter already and don't have time to waste.
Anticipate consequences	If I do copy off Jennifer I'll owe her a favor and that's the *last* thing I want.	If I ask Jennifer she'll owe me a favor. If I ask Tammy she'll say no or her boyfriend will kill me.	The dictionary and glossary will be too simplified for my needs.
Solve problem	I'll ask the teacher for help.	I think I'll ask Jennifer.	I'll check the index to see if there is more information on strategies somewhere else in the text.
Check work	Asking worked out OK and the teacher put me in a work group with Tammy.	It didn't work. Jennifer is busy Saturday. I hope I've only seen this episode ten times.	There is a lot of stuff on strategies in Chapters 2, 7, and 8.

with nonreading students who fail subject-area courses because they cannot read history or science books. Reading is not a subskill of knowing the causes of the Civil War, but if the instruction a student receives from the history teacher involves reading assignments, then reading is a subskill of learning to know the causes of the Civil War *in that teacher's classroom.*

Suppose you have a teacher teaching a student to locate words in a dictionary. If the teacher decides to use a computer to teach them, computer-control subtasks are added to the dictionary subtasks to form the task of using a computer to learn to locate words in a dictionary, as shown in Exhibit 3.11. While the subtasks of locating words are the same for all students (because they are determined by the task), the subtasks of learning to locate words vary from class to class (because they are determined in part by the teachers' instruction). This is the final reason that task analysis is such an important skill.

The subtasks and strategies introduced by various materials and classroom techniques need to be examined carefully and probably deserve the same attention we typically give to content (Gersten, Woodward & Darch, 1986; Lloyd & Loper, 1986; Shulman, 1986). However, some general advice will have to do for now. The advice is to consider carefully what a student needs to be able to do to benefit from the lesson you are giving. This may include the needed vocabulary, basic skills, study skills, and knowledge of other tasks imposed by the correction routines, mode, and pace of your presentation. Because some students may

learn more efficiently if you select a different procedure (requiring different skills and strategies) task analysis gives us guidance in deciding both "how to teach" and "what to teach." It is remarkable how many hours teachers have spent analyzing the demands of tasks like spelling and multiplication without paying similar attention to the demands imposed by their own instructional approach. A task analysis of "how to learn in my class" would represent time well spent by any teacher, as it would be relevant to all areas of the curriculum.

Holistic vs. Reductionistic Approaches to Curriculum

We know that tasks have various elements of content, behavior, conditions, and proficiency. These elements are considered when articulating the objectives that make up a curriculum. Typically, objectives specify fairly narrow behavioral outcomes. For example, an objective may call for a student to "write the correct answers to multiplication problems 0–9," or to "initiate verbal contact with a peer during recess." This narrow approach makes a great deal of sense because it exactly defines the outcome. Therefore, it also allows the clarity needed for intentional instruction. Further, it is entirely consistent with the various federal guidelines for IEP development presented earlier. However, it has its problems.

The primary problem of a reductionistic approach to curriculum is that many teachers seem to assume that it automatically leads to a supplantive (teacher-dominated) (Smith, 1992) approach to instruction. This is a mistaken assumption and highlights the danger in confusing *what* one is teaching with *how* one should teach it. A second problem with a reductionistic approach to curriculum is that, as will be pointed out over and over throughout this text, tasks are often more than the sum of their parts. In other words, a teacher may, by dissecting a task, miss its most important elements. This can be stated yet another way by quoting a bit of verse:

> Sweet is the lore that Nature brings;
> Our meddling intellect
> Mis-shapes the beauteous forms of things:—
> We murder to dissect.
>
> —Wordsworth, *The Tables Turned*

Exhibit 3.11 Subtasks for "Using a Computer to Learn to Locate Words in a Dictionary"

Subtask: Locate words in dictionary
 Match words
 Alphabetize words
 Estimate location in dictionary
 Use guide words
 Use base words
Subtask: Use computer to learn
 Turn on computer
 Select diskette
 Load diskette
 Follow commands
 Use Function keys

Holistic vs. Hierarchical Domains

The specification of narrowly drawn behavioral objectives is only advisable within domains of curriculum that are incremental or hierarchical. These domains, and the factual and strategic aspects of computation, are the easiest examples to present, because they can be reduced to isolated components through the decomposition of larger tasks into smaller ones. This isolation allows teachers to plan highly targeted teaching interventions that are aligned with the narrowly drawn objectives. The process of dissection can then be reversed by instruction. In other words, the teacher reassembles the pieces of the curriculum by teaching them in a carefully determined sequence.

All curriculum domains are not hierarchical. Therefore, the decomposition of tasks within these domains, while possible, will not necessarily lead to instructionally relevant progressions of objectives. Nonincremental domains are popularly termed *holistic*. These domains, for example, and the conceptual aspects of computation (Ohlsson & Rees, 1991), are often complex, in that they contain tasks which are interactive and compensatory. In holistic domains a student who is unskilled in one area, but who has the cognitive flexibility to compensate by using another skill very well, will produce an acceptable total product (Spiro et al., 1988). Teaching is another domain that contains many holistic elements.

When working with holistic tasks, it is often more important to describe the total product adequately than to isolate its parts. This is typically accomplished by carefully selecting exemplars. *Exemplars* are prototypes, or examples, of the desired product. In creative writing, an exemplar might be a work by John Steinbeck, Ann Tyler, Alice Walker, or John Updike. Evaluators use exemplars as standards to which they compare the work of students. (In Chapter 7's discussion of Formative Evaluation and Assisted Assessment, a student's previous work is used as the exemplar. In these cases new work is compared to the old work to see if improvement has been made.)

If the strength of holistic analysis is its recognition of the whole, its weakness is its lack of specificity. Anyone who has read works by Steinbeck, Tyler, Walker, and Updike can tell you that they are vastly different. Therefore, the selection of exemplars must be made carefully. That is because, once the exemplars are identified (remember we are talking about works, not people), they become the definition of the curriculum.

In the holistic domains we don't say "I want you to do these things." Rather, we say "I want you to do something like this." The goal, therefore, is to teach the student to approximate the exemplary work. *In order for this approach to have instructional utility, the exemplar must have been the result of the instruction you are using.* Therefore, the exemplar must be selected from works completed on the basis of the same resources (including prior knowledge), and the same instruction that you will be supplying to your students.

How to Recognize a Holistic Domain

Considering that we have been using the term *domain* for some time, maybe it would be a good idea to look at the word. Our dictionary defines a domain as a distinctly marked territory. Some synonyms for *domain* on our word processor are zone, area, sphere, jurisdiction, and province. A domain, therefore, has boundaries—something surrounds it, or ties it together. In the case of curriculum domains, they may be consolidated by many kinds of boundaries. But the ones we are most interested in in this text are those that have something to do with instruction. These boundaries can be constructed by attending to the kinds of knowledge: facts, concepts, and strategies. This is a generalization, but for the most part hierarchical domains are consolidated by strategies, whereas holistic domains are consolidated by concepts.

A hierarchical domain contains a group of tasks that share common strategic components. Learning is facilitated by presenting these tasks together, because the solution for any one item points the way to solving the others. If a domain is sufficiently consolidated by strategies, a student may learn how to solve problems in it without ever actually being asked to do so. For example, it is completely possible that you have never faced the division problem 10101/333333 but you can work it (relax, you don't have to) because you have learned the strategy for dealing with items in the domain—division—from which it was drawn. The most rapid learning can be expected in those domains in which the most items can be approached with the fewest common strategic steps.

Holistic domains tend to be consolidated by concepts. Therefore, the items in the domain can be classified as either instances or noninstances of the concept, according to how well they approximate the critical attributes illustrated in exemplars of the concept. Let's try the example "polite conversation." Polite conversation, whatever it is, is easier to recognize than it is to subdivide. That is because it's definition is controlled by the social context in which it occurs (that is, it is holistic). This means a statement like "Boy, you're the last person I want to see today!" might be polite in one context (two old friends meeting by surprise) but not in another. As soon as the context is removed, the concept "polite," which is contextually dependent, is destroyed. That is why it may be an error to attempt to reduce conceptual material to isolated subparts. The hierarchical approach is indicated if the domain being taught is highly consolidated by strategies. A guide for determining if a curriculum domain is holistic or hierarchical is presented in Exhibit 3.12.

Any major curriculum category (reading, math, social skills) will contain tasks that are holistic as well as tasks that are incremental. Therefore, a combined (holistic and hierarchical) approach to the curriculum will be best. It is important to remember that there isn't a clear boundary between these types of domains.

From Curriculum to Instruction.   As pointed out above, it is an error to confuse the process by which you analyze the curriculum with the process by which you teach it. That is because there are many ways to teach anything, and the effectiveness of these efforts will vary according to the characteristics of the stu-

Exhibit 3.12   *Guidelines for Judging Curriculum Consolidation*

| Hierarchical Curriculum | | |
What It Looks Like	What Is Typically Taught/Tested	How It Is Typically Evaluated
• Many operations can be carried out by following a few similar procedures. • Operations called for in objectives are obviously rule-governed. • Learning the rules for using content will allow the student to succeed on unfamiliar related tasks. • Learning one item prepares you to learn the next one. • Students do problems to practice strategies. • Problems may have more than one correct answer.	Strategy content—procedures, rules, algorithms. ↓	Measure how to carry out operations and complete tasks. ↓
Holistic Curriculum		
• Many operations with unique rules. • Items share common attributes. • Each concept must be studied if it is to be learned. • Generalization between items is based on attribute recognition. • Students do problems to learn answers. • Answers depend on context	Conceptual content examples, nonexamples, vocabulary. ↓	Contrast student work with that of exemplars ↓

dent. A reductionistic approach to the curriculum does **not** automatically imply the need for reductionistic instruction (instruction that targets decontextualized subskills and attempts to teach them through isolated rote-type instruction). Similarly, constructivist (generative) instruction is not synonymous with hands-off instruction (Harris & Pressley, 1991).

Today there is a major debate, if not a war, going on between advocates of *generative* instruction and advocates of a *supplantive* approach (neither side really has a name so we picked these out of a couple of articles on the topic). The holistic people are associated with the ''discovery learning'' approach, while the behavioral types are associated with ''direct instruction'' (see Chapters 10 and 11). If you want to get a quick overview of the competition, check out Heshusius (1991) and Dixon and Carnine (1992). We will present our own position more thoroughly in Chapter 8. However, to give you some idea of where we stand, relative to instruction, we have selected the following quotes. One of them is from the generative camp and the other is from the supplantive (direct instruction) camp. We agree with both of them:

> The holistic/constructivist orientation recognizes that learning is dependent on prior learning experiences. Of great importance to holistic or experiential learning is that skill and process instruction is integrated with information that matches the student's desires, interests, and experiences . . . (Ensminger & Dangel, 1992, p. 3)

> The direct instruction tradition relies on two pillars: an empathy for students' desire for success and an understanding of students' need for clarity, especially when confronted with new or demanding material. The artful modulation of intellectual challenge with success and clarity represents the core of direct instruction. (Gersten, 1992, p. 464)

Summary

This has been a crowded chapter and a final review is definitely in order. The curriculum is an ordered set of learning outcomes. Typically, these outcomes are called objectives or tasks. Objectives are derived from an analysis of the demand for literacy that society places on its members. Literacy, which can be viewed as communication within a cultural context, demands the use of effective strategies for sending and receiving messages. These literacy strategies in turn depend on the use of certain enabling skills.

Tasks have subtask and strategy components. Subtasks (like tasks) are composed of elements of content, behavior, conditions, and criteria. Each of these elements must be present, or the task has not been truly defined. If a change is made in any of the four elements, a new objective is produced. By systematically varying the four elements, a sequence of objectives or tasks can be produced for the purpose of planning instruction or evaluation.

Content sequences should be relevant, complete, free of trivial material, composed of necessary material, and free of redundancy.

Behavior sequences should correspond to the real-world demands of tasks and allow the designation of meaningful proficiency levels.

Conditions should also reflect the real world, while criteria must accurately indicate functional levels of performance.

The knowledge reflected in objectives is of three types: factual, conceptual, and strategic. All of these are important, however they can exist independently of each other. Different instructional and measurement procedures are used to address facts, concepts, and strategies.

There are two kinds of strategies: task-specific and general. Task-specific strategies apply to a particular domain. General strategies apply to many domains. Strategy use depends on prior knowledge, self-monitoring, and problem solving.

Task analysis is a process applied to well-defined tasks. Through task analysis, the essential components of the task can be identified. The process of task analysis is different for tasks in hierarchical and holistic domains. When a student is unable to work a task, the student should be taught any missing subtask and/or strategy components. This is true even for a domain such as ''how to survive in my class.''

Chapter 4 / Thinking About Instruction

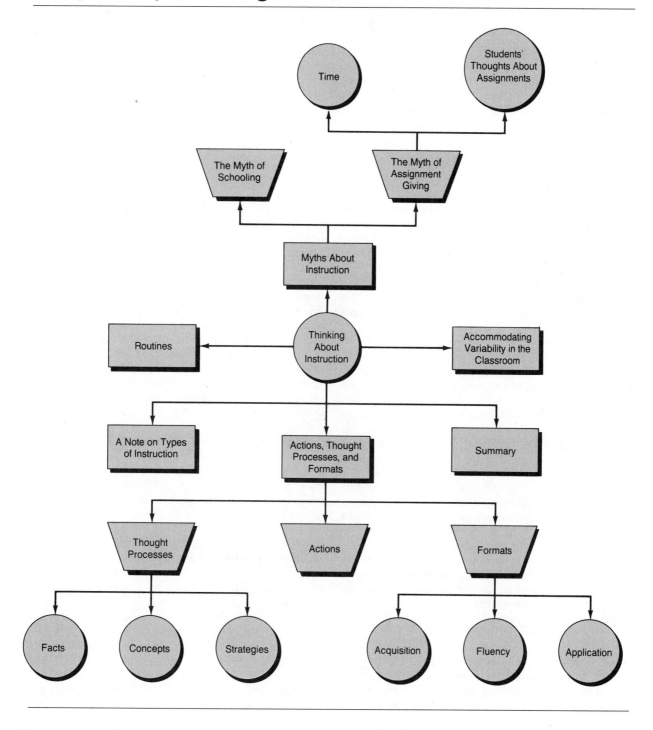

Education is about opportunity and enfranchisement. It is about knowledge, economic potential, self-determination, perspective, and power. Education is inherently political. However, the political issues are those of how committed one is to education and for whom. Given full commitment, questions of how best to achieve it are issues that belong, not to politics, but to science and pedagogy.

—M.J. Adams (1991)

The topical chapters (10–17) each contain instructional recommendations. To avoid repetition across topic chapters, the key elements of the recommendations are explained here and in Chapter 8. This means that in the language chapter (Chapter 12) we will only explain instructional recommendations specific to language. Therefore, you will need clear recall of the information in this chapter to benefit from the recommendations in the topical chapters.

Just as beliefs about learning have changed, so have beliefs about teaching—and the shifts in these beliefs have been intriguingly similar. Early research on teaching focused almost exclusively on the personal characteristics of teachers. These characteristics included things like their form of dress, gender, sense of humor, race, and voice. The assumption driving this research was that certain types of people make good teachers. Researchers working from this assumption concentrated on identifying this type of person. The resulting work was kind of silly, and easier to understand in terms of public relations than instruction. In addition, because the things being studied were almost impossible to alter, the research results were nearly useless to teacher trainers (Bloom, 1980).

In the mid-1970s, and accelerating through the 1980s, research on teaching changed dramatically as it shifted from an emphasis on the personal characteristics of teachers to the quality of their teaching. Using simple methods of observation and testing, researchers began to map out correlational relationships between certain teacher actions and student learning. The resulting body of literature has come to be known by several terms including Teacher Effectiveness Literature, Essential Elements of Instruction, Instructional Theory into Practice, and Critical Delivery Skills.

The effective-instruction literature is expanding at an incredible rate. In fact, it has grown so fast that it has become unconsolidated and, therefore, hard to summarize. (In part this is because it is almost exclusively empirical and has yet to evolve a theoretical frame of reference.) It has also been marketed with unprecedented energy. It reached the classroom primarily through teacher in-service (purchased by states and school districts) rather than pre-service teacher training (which tends to be university-based).

The resulting combination of rapid change and uncoordinated implementation led to teachers hearing about this stuff in different ways. A new era of technical vocabulary (just what we needed) flourished along with anxiety about teacher evaluation, and, finally, resistance (Skrtic, 1991).

We (you remember us—Sheila, Mada Kay, and Ken—the authors) think the effective instruction literature is great stuff. We like it because, for the first time, it focuses on what we (teachers) do, not on whom we do it to (the kids). And we like it because it is useful.

A Note on Types of Instruction

When talking about instruction, it is necessary to use terms like *type, approach, program, method,* and *style.* These are used to differentiate among the various ways of teaching. In some content areas, most notably reading, there seems to be an almost endless debate about the relative superiority of the so-called meaning-based and direct approaches to instruction (see the February, 1991, issue of *The Reading Teacher*). These debates are often made so bewildering by the confusion of curriculum and instruction that it is impossible to tell if the authors are arguing about *what* should be taught, or about *how* it should be taught. When the debate finally does come down to the question of superior method (instruction), the main contestants usually end up being the supplantive approach and the generative approach.

When using a supplantive approach, the teacher attempts to promote learning by actively supporting the student. In some instances this support is provided in the form of "scaffolds" (Gaffney & Anderson, 1991) that the teacher erects to help the student understand the lesson. Scaffolds are described in detail in Chapter 17; for now we'll just define them as structures composed of linkages between the current lesson and things the student already knows. In other words, they are *clues*. In other cases, the teacher provides support by giving the student explicit directions and explanations regarding how to do the task.

In the generative approach the teacher provides opportunities for the student to make his own linkages to prior knowledge, and to devise his own strategies for work. This emphasis on student-generated understanding places the teacher in more of a collaborative role and less of an expert role (Ensminger & Dangel, 1992).

The supplantive approach is popularly referred to as "direct instruction," while the generative approach is often called "student-centered." Neither of these labels are satisfactory because both are confused with particular published programs and particular curriculum. However, one defining characteristic of the orientations represented by these labels is the role of the teacher. Some educators, usually the ones who think they are doing direct instruction, believe that the teacher brings the agenda to the room and provides the focus. Others, who think of themselves as student-centered, believe that the teacher's role is to facilitate the agenda set by the kid. These are two radically different beliefs.

In order to avoid the surplus meaning that comes with terms like direct instruction, we are going to try to stick to *hands on* and *hands off* (this is done in the fine educational tradition of responding to excess terminology by creating more of it). In this book we advocate instruction that is teacher-directed. Hands-on instruction is curriculum-based, meaning that what the teacher does is intentionally aligned with the intended outcomes of the lesson (English, 1987; Palincsar, 1990; Spady, 1988). However, the fact that this book advocates a hands-on approach does not mean we are proponents of nonmeaning-based or half-language

instruction. In fact, we aren't always against a hands-off approach. The issue really isn't *whether* teachers should use an approach, but *when*. Smith (1992) has offered guidelines for deciding which approach may be best for any particular lesson. Her work served as the basis for the decision-making guidelines in Exhibit 4.1. Many of the descriptors in that exhibit are explained elsewhere in this text (for example, "motivation" is in Chapters 2 and 17). As you can see from the exhibit, students requiring a hands-on/supplantive approach are those who are experiencing difficulty and are working on critical skills.

Our rationale for advocating hands-on instruction for special/remedial students grows out of Exhibit 4.1 and the presentation in Chapter 1. In that chapter we asserted that the primary defining characteristic of students requiring support services is their failure to progress through the curriculum. This argues strongly for the need to facilitate the movement of these students through the curriculum, and, by implication, the need for teacher direction. The debate about the relative merits of telling students answers vs. having them discover answers is interesting. However, if the student has failed to discover what he needs to know for so long that the system is about to call him "disabled," the situation requires that teachers give him a break and tell him what he needs to know.

While two-factor models lend themselves nicely to comparative discussions, they also tend to exaggerate differences. We don't believe that the generative and supplantive methods must always be in strict opposition. Just as a good amplifier allows someone to adjust bass with one knob and treble with another, a good teacher can fine-tune instruction by adding a splash of support without overriding the student's interest in inquiry or joy of discovery. Hands-off instruction, as we are defining it, is not synonymous with concern about literacy or recognition of the student's role in learning. These things are necessary. However, it is often synonymous with the teacher's failure to focus the lesson and it is difficult to justify a lack of direction when the student is lost.

Myths About Instruction

Just as there are certain myths about learning that can threaten a teacher's judgment, there are also misconceptions about instruction. How a person views his

Exhibit 4.1   Selecting the Instructional Approach

Select the Generative Approach When	Select the Supplantive Approach When
the student:	
• has adaptive motivational patterns.	• has nonadaptive motivational patterns.
• has considerable prior knowledge of the task.	• has little prior knowledge of the task.
• experiences initial success on the task.	• experiences failure on the task.
the task:	
• is simple.	• is complex.
• is well-defined.	• is ill-defined.
• is conceptual.	• requires the use of a task-specific strategy.
• can be completed using a general problem-solving strategy.	• is factual.
	• is pivotal to the learning of subsequent tasks.
	• must be used with a high level of proficiency.
	• is hazardous.
the setting:	
• allows plenty of time for instruction.	• allows limited time.
• places priority on "learning to learn."	• places priority on task mastery.

role as a teacher, and the act of teaching, determines the kind of instruction he will deliver. Much of this falls legitimately into the domain of educational philosophy and, while it should be clear by now that the authors are willing to let their preferences go public, we'd rather only write one book at a time. So, we are going to try to keep this section under control by limiting ourselves to the three threats to instructional thought ("myths") that we find to be most harmful.

The Myth of Schooling

This myth asserts that going to school is the same thing as receiving instruction. But that isn't true. The clearest evidence of this can be found in the fact that perfect attendance at an ineffective school doesn't assure perfect learning. Schools are institutions, and anyone who has been a patient in a hospital, a student at a university, a passenger on an airline, or an applicant for a teaching credential knows that institutions don't behave like people. Teachers are people, and schools are institutions. It's a mistake to confuse the two because one gets into trouble whenever one insists that institutions behave like people (for example, by considering our personal wishes and not the corporate

policy), or that people behave like institutions (for example, by acting consistently). Here is an example.

In the entryway of a school that one of us visited, there was a plaque that read "We believe all students can learn." However, in a meeting that day, many of the teachers seemed to be spending time trying to convince the visitor that a student named Rocko couldn't learn. Finally, in a desperate effort to stop the negative talk about Rocko, the author made a sign that said "except Rocko" and taped it under the entryway plaque where every visiting parent and civic leader would see it. No one seemed amused by this juxtaposition of school policy and teacher expectation (except maybe Rocko).

The key to institution/person conflict is to understand that institutions are developed to carry out specific functions for specific populations. They do not respond well when something is needed that they are not organized to provide (try telling a theater manager to stop a movie while you go to buy popcorn), and they do not respond well when the audience they are designed to work with is changed.

Special/remedial students often need things that differ from what schools commonly provide. The treatments selected for special/remedial students should be defined by students' needs—not those of the schools. It is extremely hard for schools to provide this sort of accommodation because, as institutions, they are designed to make changes through long-term administrative action that affects everyone at the school (English, 1988; Skrtic, 1991). This conflicts with exceptional teaching. Exceptional teaching can only be accomplished through the sort of flexible, immediate, contextual, ambiguous—almost organic—activity institutions are ill-prepared to provide.

Quality instruction is intimate, personal, and interactive, so how do you select correct objectives and treatments when the demands of quality instruction are at odds with the limitations of the institutions designed to provide it? The answer, in terms of thought processes, is simple to state. Expert teachers remember that the institution (the school) was developed for a purpose: to deliver quality instruction to students. If the student needs something that it is not the school's policy to provide, the policy should change!

The Myth of Assignment Giving

One of the biggest threats to good instruction is the belief that the core of teaching is assignment giving. Working within this erroneous belief system a teacher will make decisions about the number and kind of assignments a student should do, not what the student needs to learn. To appreciate how this sort of error can make an impact on classroom practice it is necessary, just as it was in the learning chapter, to review what is known about the way things work on the inside. This time we aren't talking about the way things happen inside a kid's head; we are talking about the way things happen inside some classrooms.

Time. Haynes and Jenkins (1986) studied the instruction that students receive in special education pull-out programs. One of their findings was that, among the classes they observed, students in one class received an average of 57.79 minutes of reading instruction a day. In another class the students only received 16.67 minutes a day. They also found that (and this will be a big surprise) students in the 57.79 class learned more about reading than students in the 16.67 class.

How much time a person works greatly influences how good they become at whatever it is they are working on. Time, and how it is spent in classrooms, is important. Researchers have defined different types of

classroom time. One type of time is "engaged time." It is that portion of the day during which a student is working. We know that the larger the proportion of engaged time in a class, the more students will learn. We also know that students are more engaged when teachers are using hands-on instruction (Chow, 1981; Murphy, Weil & McGreal, 1986).

Academic learning time (ALT) is that time when a student is working on something directly related to the intended learning outcome (Berliner, 1987; Walberg, 1988). Engaged time and ALT are not the same. A student can be intensely engaged in activities that have nothing to do with what the student needs to learn.

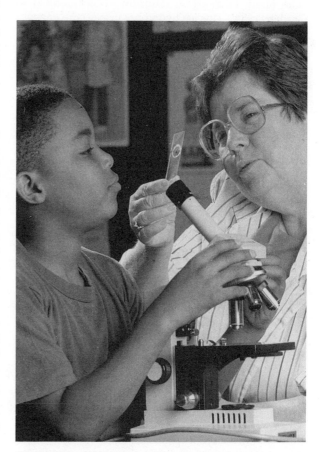

Completing assignments is less important than learning. Effective teachers use explanation, demonstration, guided practice, timely correction, and task-specific feedback to encourage learning.

(This may occur during hands-off instruction.) ALT controls how much students learn and, like engaged time, increases with teacher direction (Cohen, 1987). ALT is increased by assuring that the curriculum and instruction are aligned. One way to do this is to make sure that instructional decisions are made from curriculum-based evaluation (Shinn & Hubbard, 1992).

Observations of general education classroom practice have found that students spend from 50% to 70% of the time allocated to instruction doing independent, nonteacher-directed (hands-off) activities (Borg, 1980; Doyle & Carter, 1987). This finding has been noted in both elementary and secondary classrooms (Everston, Anderson, Anderson & Brophy, 1980), and in special classrooms (Ysseldyke, Thurlow, Mecklenburg & Graden, 1984). This isn't good because (a) the engagement ratios of hands-off instruction are so low, and (b) the stuff the students are doing (we are talking dittos, copies, and workbooks here) is frequently unrelated to what they are supposed to learn.

Without teacher direction, students often spend time working on tasks that are inappropriate. This might mean that the task covers an irrelevant topic. It may also mean that the student is working on something that is too hard, or something that is too easy. As a result, even if engagement were to be high, ALT would be low. During hands-off instruction teachers apparently do not accurately match students to activities (Anderson, 1985; Bennett and Desforges, 1988; Bennett, Roth & Dunn, 1987; McIntyre, Copenhauer, Byrd & Norris, 1983). Worse yet (from the perspective of this text) they do the poorest job with low-achieving students (Chow, 1981; Fisher et al., 1980).

There are several possible explanations for the failure of teachers to select appropriate assignments. One explanation is that they don't know how to recognize appropriate tasks. Another explanation is that they don't know how to recognize appropriate learning outcomes. But both of these explanations assume that the teacher is actively trying to make decisions. This, sadly, is not even the case in some hands-off classrooms. There is a substantial body of literature on teacher planning that indicates that many teachers simply give the same assignment to everyone, and they pick the assignment because it is the next lesson in whatever published series they are using (Borko, Livingston & Shavelson, 1990).

In a classroom such as the one described above, students spend time working on things that have been selected, not on the basis of student need, but on the day of the school year (they do lesson 27 because they are 27 days into the year). The decision-making system in such classes is driven by the need to finish lessons—not the need to learn—and that constitutes bad judgment. It also represents the ultimate in hands-off instruction, because the teacher relinquishes all delivery of information, selection of curriculum, and placement of students to the published materials. Teachers may even convey this elevation of the assignments' value over learning to their students.

Students' Thoughts About Assignments. As we learned in Chapter 2, human beings seem just naturally to want to know what is going on. This leads us to interpret events in our lives and to attribute them to some kind of cause. In hands-off classrooms, in which the teacher does not provide a learning focus, the students make up their own attributions from whatever information they have. Usually this will be what the teacher says.

When teachers emphasize assignment completion over learning, students come to believe that the purpose of doing assignments is to get them done—*not* to learn anything from them. This misunderstanding is supported in part by the teacher's talk, and in part by the general confusion most low-achieving students experience in school. Therefore, the students who can least afford to misunderstand the purpose of an assignment are the ones who are most apt to misunderstand (Bennett & Desforges, 1988). When asked why they are doing assignments, these low-achieving students report that their teachers "want the assignments done" (Anderson, 1984; Doyle, 1983). Often, they will even add "by recess" to their explanations. Special/remedial students tend to develop strategies for finishing assignments (such as copying from other students), not for understanding them. While they realize they don't understand what they are doing, they see no reason to change. That's because they don't think understanding has anything to do with the assignment (Anderson, Brubaker, Alleman-Brooks & Duffy, 1985; Englert, 1987).

How can this misunderstanding occur? Often it's simply that the assignment is meaningless to remedial students. In such a case, getting the work finished in order to make it to recess reflects good judgment. In addition, students think about what teachers talk about. A variety of researchers have noted that teacher talk is often compatible with the "getting it done" mentality (Anderson, 1982; Anderson, 1984; Doyle, 1986; Mergendoller, Marchman, Mitman & Parker, 1988). These authors observed that teachers emphasize completion, persistence, and effort, while seldom addressing the need to think, or what to think about. They also noted that many teachers only comment about how busy students are, not how accurately they are working.

At some point every teacher has had the experience of a student's absence for a family trip. It usually goes like this. The mother or father calls to say little Betsy will be away at Wally World all of next week. "Oh?" reacts the teacher with concern. "Don't worry!" responds the parent, "I'll come by and *pick up her work*." When this happens expert teachers think the parent has completely misunderstood what teachers do for a living. "Pick up the work!" they think, "What about the instruction? Do they think teaching is just giving out work?" Yes! That is exactly what they think. And it is exactly what Betsy thinks, too.

Anderson (1984) listened to students working in classrooms. She found that their talk centered on getting things done, and very little of it dealt with the content of the lesson. (This does not seem to be true in correctly managed cooperative learning lessons.) She also recognized a category of student talk she referred to as "expressions of relief." Here is a quote from that category: [following a long sigh] "There!" [as student stacks up his papers] "I didn't understand it, but I got it done!" (Anderson, 1984, p. 98).

The biggest myth in instruction, we believe, is that assignments need to get done. Assignments do not need to get done. Students need to learn. And getting assignments done does not ensure learning.

What does ensure learning? Learning is ensured by explanation, demonstration, guided practice, timely correction, and task-specific feedback. These make up the substance of the effective-teaching literature.

The Myth of the Calendar

This one is easy to explain. In most classrooms teachers plan instruction according to the calendar. They do this by allocating fixed periods of time to teach a particular objective (for example, 4 weeks to work on "developing story outlines"). At the end of the scheduled time the teacher stops instruction on that task and moves to another *regardless* of student performance.

While the number of sessions is fixed, the learning of the students in class may be quite different. No rationale for this prevailing practice exists within the learning literature.

When a teacher uses exceptional teaching practices he or she must be willing to vary the length of lessons, and the number of sessions, in order to guarantee that all students learn what they need to learn. Therefore the variability in student learning is replaced with variability in days of instruction. This is one of the basic principles of mastery learning (Kulik, Kulik & Bangert-Drowns, 1990) and the Carroll Model (Clark, 1987). The authors think it is safe to say that, if teachers are unwilling to employ flexible scheduling according to student needs, all other discussions of program or method superiority are silly.

Actions, Thought Processes, and Formats

When teaching a lesson, the instructor must consider several factors. In order to discuss all of these, and to give a sense of how they interact, we are going to categorize and label them. The categories we'll use are based on information already presented in this chapter and in Chapter 3. It is important for you to understand that these various subdivisions are presented to clarify, and not to dazzle or confuse.

Look at Exhibit 4.2. This exhibit is meant to illustrate some of the factors that influence how a lesson is delivered. This exhibit could be used to plan a lesson, but we doubt that anyone would ever want to use it for that purpose. However, we do think it is important to understand the variables listed along each axis and how they interact with each other.

Perhaps the greatest advantage of the effective teaching literature is that it clarified the set of teacher *actions* utilized during the delivery of instruction. These are generic, meaning they can be applied across content, types of students, and approaches to instruction. This is important, because teachers sometimes have preferred published programs or methods of instruction. Because effective practices are not method-specific, any teacher should be able to accommodate most of these actions within their teaching.

For these actions to produce desired learning outcomes they must be aligned with the objectives of the lesson (just as the evaluation procedures must be

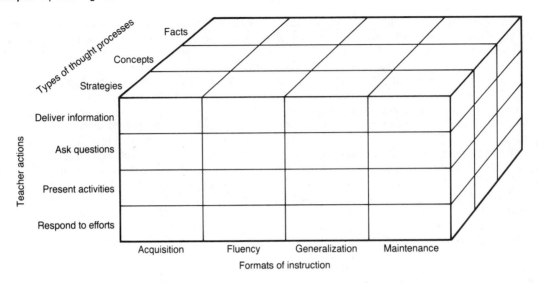

Exhibit 4.2   Actions, thought processes, and formats.

aligned) (Spady, 1988). This means that the teacher delivers information about the objective, asks questions about that information, uses activities to emphasize or practice using the information, and monitors the student in order to give objective-specific feedback and praise (Englert, 1984). Specific teacher actions associated with increased learning are presented in Exhibit 4.2 along with a brief explanation. The four categories of teacher action in Exhibit 4.2 represent the primary functions teachers must accomplish during instruction. These actions are linked to the specific teacher behaviors that have been shown, through research, to be related to improvements in student achievement (see also Chapter 8).

Thought processes (facts, concepts, and strategies) were explained in Chapter 3. In that chapter, we explained that a student can have three kinds of knowledge (thought processes) to use when solving problems. The three kinds of knowledge are factual, conceptual, and strategic.

Factual knowledge, sometimes called rote learning, is taught by presenting items and answers. It is the least sophisticated but most rapidly employed kind of knowledge. *Facts* are typically taught through drill and practice and require little, if any, explanation. A student who only has factual knowledge will know that $8 \times 6 = 48$. But that student may not have any idea what that means or how the answer was derived.

Conceptual knowledge relates to the meaning of a task. It is often ignored in lessons directed at remedial students and this is undoubtably an error. A student with conceptual knowledge will understand the message conveyed by a number sentence like $8 \times 6 = 48$. He will be aware of the relationships, ideas, and meaning of this statement (Spiro et al., 1988).

Concepts are taught by presenting students with information that will allow them to categorize items. In other words, if a student understands the concept of fairness, he will be able to sort examples of behavior into fair and unfair categories. As explained in Chapter 3, this sorting is possible if the student knows about the so-called attributes of the concept. Relevant (or critical) attributes are those that are present in all examples of the concept. Irrelevant (noncritical) attributes may or may not be present. Because critical attributes must be present for the concept to exist, they are the defining characteristics of the concept (Carnine, 1983; Thiagarajan, Semmel & Semmel, 1974). Let's take an easy example. The concept is "square." Think about both the critical attributes and a few noncritical attributes. Answers are shown in Exhibit 4.3. As you can see, the four different examples of squares shown in Exhibit 4.3 are all instances of the concept. The four nonexamples are not squares. By comparing the examples and nonexamples, you can discover the critical and noncritical attributes. Attribute *d*, for instance, is

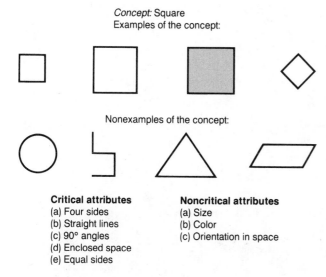

Concept: Square
Examples of the concept:

Nonexamples of the concept:

Critical attributes	**Noncritical attributes**
(a) Four sides	(a) Size
(b) Straight lines	(b) Color
(c) 90° angles	(c) Orientation in space
(d) Enclosed space	
(e) Equal sides	

Exhibit 4.3   Analysis of the concept "square."

the only thing preventing our second nonexample from being a square.

Strategies were covered extensively in Chapter 2, and their importance was highlighted again in Chapter 3. Having strategic knowledge allows a student to direct his actions and to solve problems. Sticking with 8 × 6, a student with relevant strategic knowledge will be able to figure out the answer—without relying on rote information and without even understanding what the answer means (although, obviously, this isn't a good idea).

The first critical attribute of strategy instruction is that, through it, *the student is taught procedures for utilizing previously learned skills.* Therefore, it is essential that a teacher check to make sure these skills have in fact been learned. For example, teaching a student to multiply by repetitive addition (8 + 8 + 8 + 8 + 8 + 8) won't work if the student can't add. Similarly, telling a student how to read a passage critically won't work if the student has not been taught what the vocabulary in the passage means.

A second attribute of strategy instruction is that *the emphasis is on the process of doing the task, not on product that is completed.* Strategy instruction does not teach answers, it teaches *how* to arrive at answers. Therefore, the emphasis on product completion common in many lessons is inappropriate. For example, if

a student given 8 × 6 were to write the answer 48, the traditional feedback would be something like "Good, you got the right answer—it's 48." However, in a lesson teaching the repeat-addition strategy feedback would not emphasize the answer. Instead, it might include a statement like "Good, you remembered to add the largest number to itself as many times as the smaller number indicated."

Teachers teach strategies by making them visible to the student. This is a third critical attribute of strategy instruction, and it is most effectively accomplished by demonstrating the act of problem solving (as opposed to showing a model of a problem that is already completed). In strategic terminology this is called "making your thought process public" (Englert et al., 1991; Serapiglia, 1992). Some teachers find this difficult because they believe good teachers should have all the answers. In this model, as explained, answers don't matter. In fact, the best teachers are the ones who show the effort, procedures, and even the revision, of work.

The fourth attribute of strategy instruction is closely tied to the third. It is called *verbal mediation.* When using verbal mediation, teachers teach the process of talking through a solution while carrying out the steps (Gerber, 1987). During initial acquisition of a strategic thought process, students are encouraged to repeat the explanation as they work. In this way they learn to coach themselves through different tasks. However, while this verbal mediation of the strategy is important, remember that the goal is *not* to get students to list steps. Application of the strategy—not the listing of its elements—is the goal.

A fifth important thing to remember about strategy instruction is that it seems to be most successful in classrooms where the teacher promotes a *"strategic environment"* (Schumaker, Deshler & McKnight, 1991). As mentioned earlier, one way to do this is to emphasize the quality of work over merely getting things done. This is complemented by efforts to guarantee that students know why they are doing assignments. It is not necessary for students to work 8 × 6 to find the answer (we have already done that and know that it is 48). In strategy instruction, students do items to practice the procedures, not to find the answers, and they should be told this.

The final critical attribute of strategy instruction (and this is really part of maintaining a strategic environment) is an *emphasis on personal accountability in*

Strategy instruction teaches procedures for using previously learned skills.

the form of self-monitoring. For example, in a strategic classroom those students who turn in math pages with errors are told to go back and fix them (as long as they know how). In fact, the errors are not even marked. This means that the teacher doesn't say "Oh look, you missed number 17—go fix it" but instead says "I see a mistake on this page, see if you can find it and fix it." Under the second condition the student is required to self-check his work, and is held accountable for doing so.

Sometimes this emphasis on self-monitoring and accountability may seem harsh. But it doesn't need to be. In the example, it will take the student longer to find the item 17 error and fix it than it would have taken him if the teacher had marked item 17. However, because this teacher understands the importance

of developing self-monitoring strategies, and the irrelevance of getting pages done, he will allow the student to do fewer total problems.

We know a teacher named Karla in western Washington State who works with students who have fairly severe skill deficits. It rains a lot in western Washington, and before recess Karla's students always used to ask her if they needed to wear a coat. Last year she started telling them to open the window, stick their hand out, look at the sky, and decide for themselves about the coat. Occasionally a student made a wrong decision and went outside without a coat when it was cold, wet, or both. The first couple of times this happened other teachers returned the kid and asked for a coat. Karla refused, saying "She decided she didn't need one." The other teachers probably thought Karla wasn't all that nice, but now her students make the decisions and dress appropriately on their own.

Lessons fall into various types, or *formats*, regardless of the objectives they teach or the thought processes they advance. The format of a lesson should be selected to match the phase of learning in which the student is currently involved (Shuell, 1990). For example, if the student lacks knowledge of the task, he is in the initial phase of learning. In this phase, sometimes called *acquisition*, the teacher should provide that knowledge to make the student accurate. If the student has the knowledge to work accurately, but is so deliberate that he does not complete the work in time, the teacher should provide practice opportunities so that the student will become fluent. Instruction that builds accuracy is different from instruction that builds fluency.

Formats of instruction, which complement the various phases of learning, have been described under different names, but the labels *acquisition, fluency,* and *application* (generalization and maintenance) seem most descriptive (Haring & Eaton, 1978).

Acquisition lessons teach the student to be accurate. They are designed to take a student through the novice phases of task performance. Because students in this phase make frequent errors, they should never be allowed to work without carefully arranged monitoring and feedback procedures (cooperative learning, peer tutoring, choral responding). These initial lessons are characterized by elaborate explanations, extensive use of models, correction procedures that focus on accuracy and deemphasize rate, and reinforcement for accurate performance. For example, suppose you have decided to teach a student "to display knowledge of punctuation by inserting necessary commas in a series or list. Accuracy CAP—100%." In your efforts to teach this skill to accuracy you will need to emphasize procedures for forming commas, the purpose of commas, steps for identifying a list, and how to check work. Some of these might be appropriate for one student but not for another. During acquisition, it is best to emphasize the strategic thought processes a student must apply to arrive at an answer, rather than the answer itself. An acquisition strategy might address the steps to be followed when writing a list, or forming a comma, simply by asking the student to verbalize each step as it is carried out.

Feedback and error correction are important parts of the acquisition format. If a student makes important errors, instruction should be designed to build accuracy.

This recommendation is also justified when a student seems to be accurate but is *very* slow (less than 25% of appropriate rate criterion). Students who are extremely slow are often inaccurate, though they don't display their errors. These students make errors, catch them, and correct them before making an overt response. They may also avoid errors by skipping items or using functional but inefficient strategies (such as counting on their fingers or repeating the whole alphabet in sequence to recall a particular letter).

If you find a student who is inaccurate, you should check less complex skills (the subtasks) to find out what accounts for the current failure. When a point is reached at which the student is inaccurate at a task, but accurate at its subtasks, stop testing and teach the task strategy.

Fluency lessons take accurate students and provide them the intense drill and practice they need to add speed to the skills at which they have already become accurate. Fluency formats are characterized by drill and practice, repetition, minimal teacher talk, heavy external reinforcement (if needed), and feedback without correction. (No correction is needed because the student is already accurate and errors are viewed as rate-induced.) The need for fluency building is indicated when the student is accurate but slow at the task. (Note the discussion of inaccuracy and rate in the last section.) How accurate a student has to be at something before moving into rate-building instruction is debatable, but estimates range from 80% to 100%, with most authors settling for something around 90% (Berliner, 1984; Liberty, Haring & White, 1980; Rosenshine, 1983; White, 1986).

As you can imagine, placing a student who is inaccurate into a fluency format would be a mistake, because it would allow the student to practice being inaccurate without any correction procedures. Similarly, an acquisition lesson plan would never allow an accurate student to become fluent, because the student would receive constant explanations about how to do things he already can do (this might bore the student and actually produce *decreases* in performance).

The ultimate goal of instruction is *application*. The lessons are all over when the student can use a skill and maintain competence over time.

Generalization formats teach students to apply skills in a larger context. They involve presentations of novel situations (those including distractions as well as the transfer and modification of knowledge) and an emphasis on self-regulation and adaptive task-related beliefs (see Chapter 17) rather than teacher control (Weed, Ryan & Day, 1990). *Maintenance* lessons do not involve any active teaching and are usually limited to periodic reviews and monitoring.

Sometimes an evaluator will find that a student can succeed at a task when it is presented in isolation, even though he cannot apply the same skill within other, more complex, tasks. For example, the student may be able to read vowel teams when presented by themselves on flash cards but be unable to use them in words. Another student may accurately work addition and subtraction fact problems on worksheets but make errors on the same facts during long division.

There are four explanations for the failure to generalize the use of a skill to a larger task: (1) failure to recognize when to use the behavior, (2) inadequate skill (automaticity) on the task to be generalized, (3) inadequate knowledge of the other skills with which the task must be combined to perform larger tasks, or (4) uncertainty about how to do the larger task (which can result from teaching skills in isolation). To find out which of these applies (they could all apply), the evaluator must check each one. You check for lack of automaticity by examining the effect of realistic distractions on the student's accuracy and rate. Realistic distractions are those imposed by the context in which a skill would normally be used. For example, suppose you are testing a student's skill at driving a car. You could test this skill in an empty parking lot or on a freeway in the middle of high-speed traffic. The freeway is a good test of automaticity at driving as it supplies realistic distractors (in this case we'd advise seatbelts). Testing a student's recall of history vocabulary in the middle of a freeway would not provide a good test of automaticity for vocabulary. The same distractors, speeding trucks and occasional highway-patrol cars, that provide realistic distractions for the driving test do not provide realistic distractions for testing historical vocabulary.

A Note on Isolation.   Application instruction typically involves the combination of the targeted skill with other skills. This means that the skill is not taught in isolation.

Isolation has the advantage of focusing all attention on the skill in question, but it has the disadvantage of making the skill seem meaningless. Things are meaningful as a function of their context (snorkles have more meaning by the pool than they do on a ski slope; reading skill has more meaning in the context of a library than it does in a game of soccer). It is safe to say that the more meaning a student perceives in a task the easier it will be for him to learn it. This is largely because meaning tends to motivate, activate the storage and retrieval mechanisms of memory, and promote early application of skills (Paris & Winograd, 1990; Torgesen & Kail, 1980). These advantages justify an initial bias towards teaching all skills within a context that will make them appear meaningful. However, some tasks seem more naturally meaningful than others, probably because they are immediately useful or easily related to a variety of contexts.

Learning key phrases in a foreign language is a good example of a task best approached from an applied orientation. Learning your social-security number is a good example of a task that is not. The former may be more efficiently taught by using the setting in which the phrase will be used to provide context (learning how to order dinner by going to a French restaurant). The latter won't be any easier to learn in the social-security office than it will be at home. Explaining the social-security system and what it will supposedly do for you may raise your interest but will not provide clues to your particular number.

There are, however, at least two situations where isolation "makes sense." In some cases, students may lack the prior knowledge of the context needed to draw meaning from it. For example, just as a student who doesn't understand basketball wouldn't benefit from a lesson linked to the sport, a student who doesn't understand consonant sounds may not learn vowels surrounded by them. In these cases, which usually occur very early in a sequence of instruction, a teacher may wish to isolate a particular task element because its context only distracts or confuses the student. (As an alternative, the teacher can leave the element in context and assist the student by supplying the unknown information. For example, the teacher can read the words in a sentence that the student doesn't know, then pause and cue the student to read the words he is currently studying.)

There are cases where students are so unskilled that they are unable even to appreciate the context. In those cases intense isolated practice (drill) may be justified. Whenever a skill is taught in isolation, or without application, the teacher should take extra steps to make the exercise seem meaningful and to provide motivation, until the skill can be gradually shifted

Exhibit 4.4 Instructional Formats and Learning Outcomes

Format Type	Prerequisite	Lesson	Goal
Acquisition	Knowledge of subskills and prerequisite strategies	Elaborate explanation and feedback on strategies for getting correct answers	Accurate behavior
Fluency	Accurate behavior	Drill, practice, and minimal correction to fade conscious use of strategies	Mastery behavior
Application	Knowledge of subskills and prerequisite strategies	Novel context, self-management, and problem-solving strategies	Automatic behavior
Maintenance	Automatic behavior	Periodic review and monitoring	Retention of automatic behavior

from isolation into its functional context. This external approach to motivation may be handled through efforts to link the task to favorite activities, point systems, or other rewards.

Exhibit 4.4 outlines the prerequisites for each instructional format and its goal. Note that application instruction can and should begin early. This is usually accomplished by *showing* the student how the skill being studied will be useful (showing is emphasized because promises like "studying this now will lead to a happy and fulfilling life in eighth grade" usually don't cut it).

Routines

Expert teachers use fixed routines for carrying out common classroom functions (Borko, Livingston & Shavelson, 1990; Schumaker, Deshler & McKnight, 1991). There are many advantages to developing such routines. They decrease student uncertainty, save instructional time, and support academic focus. However, their primary advantage is that, by adopting and practicing routines, teachers are able to deal with recurring instructional demands automatically. This means, as we explained in Chapter 2, that the teacher is able to employ various devices for delivering information, asking questions, utilizing activities and monitoring/responding to students without awareness. Automaticity frees the teacher to think about the curriculum and student.

Schumaker and colleagues (1991) list five criteria for useful instructional routines:

* They must be straightforward and easy to master.
* They must be practical and easy to use.
* They must be effective with typical and hard-to-teach students.
* They must improve student performance.
* They must complement current teaching practices. (pp. 479–80)

Here is an example of a routine for monitoring students that seems to meet these five criteria. It was developed by Kaplan (1972) as part of a peer tutoring program and can be utilized whenever students are expected to follow along while another student reads. We'll call it the "point-to-place routine."

In order to use the point-to-place routine, a teacher teaches students that he will occasionally tap them on the shoulder. When this happens the student who has been tapped is expected to point in the book to the word currently being read. This simple routine replaces a lot of coaxing and dramatically increases the participation of the class (Howell & Kaplan, 1978).

Routines must be taught to students—and practiced. They must also be periodically reviewed. Expert teachers set aside time early in the school year to teach routines so that active learning time will be increased later.

Accommodating Variability in the Classroom

There is an old joke in education that says if you ask any teacher what they think is the perfect class size

Expert teachers use fixed routines for carrying out common classroom functions.

they will reply "The number of students I have right now minus one—that kid over there!"

There has been a major shift in special/remedial education. The shift is away from efforts to reduce the range of students in the general education classroom by sending them to special programs. Today, the emphasis is on increasing general education class accommodation of students with learning problems (Jenkins, Pious & Jewell, 1990; Stainback, Stainback & Forest, 1989).

This accommodation of student variability depends on a number of system modifications which, while beyond the scope of this text, are clearly needed in education. These include programs of teacher consultation and prereferral (Fuchs, Fuchs, Hamlett & Ferguson, 1992; Hoover & Collier, 1991; Johnson & Pugach, 1991; Showers, 1990). However, accommodation also depends on the wide-scale adoption, by general education, of effective proce-

dures for group instruction. These include: teacher-assistance teams (Carter & Sugai, 1989; Nolet, Tindal & Howell, 1992), direct instruction (Gersten, 1992), peer tutoring (Jenkins & Jenkins, 1988; Warger, 1992), cooperative learning (Tateyama-Sniezek, 1990), cognitive strategy instruction (Harris & Pressley, 1991), instruction in task-related behavior (Chapter 17), and curriculum-based measurement (Shinn & Hubbard, 1992; Ysseldyke, 1987). The critical elements of each of these procedures will be presented in Chapters 7 and 8.

Summary

Take another look at Exhibit 4.2. All of the lines in that cube imply boundaries that don't really exist. They are more a convenience of text writing than they are a representation of instruction. This means that eventually a teacher must take *all* of the actions, promote *all* of the thought processes, and utilize *all* of the formats. Here's how that might look.

In the context of a daily lesson, a teacher can cover a topic in many ways. The teacher may utilize routines for explanation, demonstration and correction that provide drill and independent practice. A complete lesson should never be *all* explanation or *all* activities.

During a lesson, each action should be utilized and each thought process addressed.

In the topical chapters that follow (10–17) the emphasis is on deciding what students need to be taught. Each chapter will begin with strategies and conclude with teaching recommendations for enabling skills. These recommendations will refer to material found in this chapter and in Chapter 8.

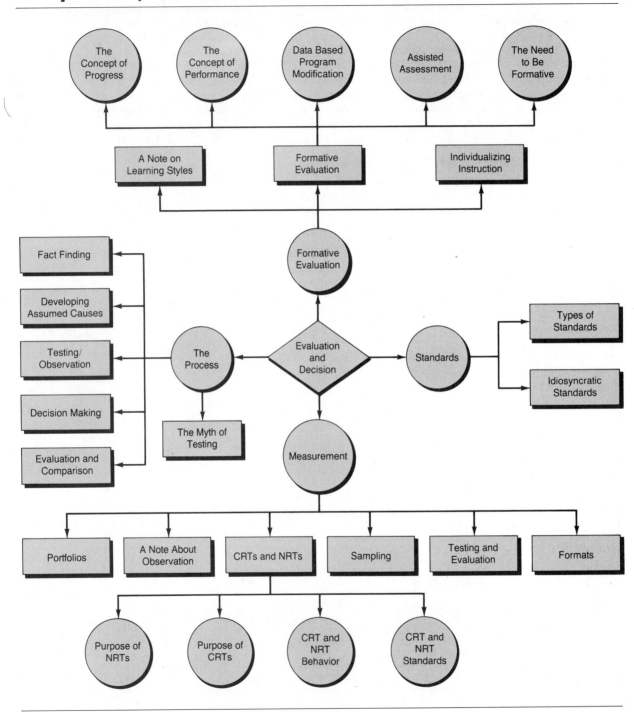

When it's said that something means *something, what's meant by that?*

—R.M. Pirsig (1974)

When a student fails to learn, it is a signal that the interaction of curriculum, instruction, and student has somehow broken down. In order to correct this problem, educators need to make good decisions and carry them out effectively. Good decisions are grounded in good judgment and based on good information. Both of these are part of good evaluation. Chapter 1 presented a general discussion of expected educational progress and the effect decision making can have on actual progress. In this chapter we will present some background information about evaluation and some basic schemes for employing it. But first, a myth!

Myth

Evaluation is the same thing as testing.

Evaluation is *not* the same thing as testing. Testing is simply a procedure that is used to sample behavior. Evaluation is a thoughtful process involving the comparison of the way things are to the way they should be. Therefore, while evaluation requires good measures of the way things are, it also requires good estimates of the way they should be. It requires active decision making on the part of the evaluator (Shinn & Hubbard, 1992).

The Process of Evaluation

The process of decision making can be broken down into the steps illustrated in this model:

Fact   Assumed Cause   Test   Decide

The F.A.C.T. format (we left the D out because it doesn't spell anything, not because it's unimportant) should be followed regardless of the type of student or content with which you are working. The format, as expanded in Exhibit 5.1, has four steps.

Fact Finding

When following the format, you first collect some information about the student, usually through something called a survey procedure. The purpose of a survey procedure is to determine the student's general status. This survey procedure may include the use of general outcome measures such as achievement tests, interviews, or collections of class assignments (portfolios). Survey procedures uncover "facts" about the student. These facts are hardly the equivalent of universal truths. More often they are simply lists of things the student can do, can't do, or fails to display in terms of academics, language, or social behavior. For example, a survey-level reading test may require the student to read several passages out loud so that success on particular skills can be noted.

Developing Assumed Causes

The next step, developing assumed causes, requires the evaluator carefully to consider the facts revealed by the survey test. The goal of this step is to develop an explanation for the facts. At this point, the explanations are only assumed causes or hypotheses to be validated or rejected during testing. During the assumed-cause step, the evaluator sits back in the chair and looks at the collected facts and tries to figure out why these facts exist. This step is often done in consultation with other teachers or reference materials.

The interesting thing about the assumed-cause step is that there can be different assumed causes for the same facts. Which assumed causes a person lists and later attempts to validate will depend on what that person, as an evaluator, thinks. This is a good news/bad news situation. The good news is that our judgment as teachers and psychologists is essential. The bad news is that most of us have been trained to think incorrectly about the causes of student behavior. While the issue is complex, we can sum it up briefly by

Exhibit 5.1   F.A.C.T. Format

Fact	Assumed Cause (Thinking Required)	Test	Decide (Thinking Required)
Find out what it is about the student that is problematic.	Develop a hypothesis that can explain why the fact (problem) exists.	Test your hypothesis (through additional observation or testing) to see if it is correct.	Reach conclusions about the problem based on your attempt to validate the assumed cause.

saying that some people seem to think student errors are the result of various student illnesses, insults, or unalterable variables associated with cognitive or perceptual weaknesses; others think errors simply indicate missing prior knowledge. Therefore, given the

During the evaluation process, teachers survey the student's skills, develop a hypothesis about their skills, test that assumed cause, and then decide what the teaching goals should be.

same fact—a reversed letter B, for example—one evaluator might assume "failure to exercise directionality due to poorly established cerebral dominance," while a second evaluator might assume "lack of knowledge about the formation of B's" (Howell, 1991).

Obviously two different assumed causes such as these will lead to the selection of very different tests and the eventual formation of very different conclusions. Because *we* are doing the evaluation, our results will say as much about the way *we* think as they will about our client's skills. Again, the way evaluators think about their clients determines the outcome of their evaluations, and not everyone in education thinks the same way. Attention to evaluator thought is critical. (In fact, it's what Chapter 7 is all about.)

Testing/Observation

After developing an explanation for the student's problem, the evaluator must test the hypothesis to see if it is correct. This means that we must select or produce whatever instrumentation is needed to resolve the question. Obviously the resolution will be clearest if the instrument used is a direct measure of the factor suspected of causing the problem. That's why this step is referred to as specific-level–testing/observation (sometimes called probing). Where survey-testing/observation may have covered a wide range of material, the specific-level probing procedures are narrowly focused. Ideally, specific-level "tests" are in the evaluator's head and are delivered through brief questions or simple tasks. When traditional testing does occur at the specific level, the evaluator will use a criterion-referenced test that is based on an objective which, if not passed by the student, will be listed as an instructional objective. These tests/observations may take only a minute or less to administer.

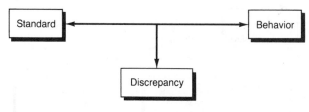

Exhibit 5.2   The comparison model.

Decision Making

Now the evaluator compares the results obtained through specific level probing to the assumed causes and then decides. If she decides that the assumed cause was correct, then it is listed on the student's plan as an objective. If it was incorrect, or the results are inconclusive, then a new assumed cause is developed and the whole procedure starts again. By repeating the testing cycle, the number of student-specific explanations for failure is gradually pared down to an instructionally manageable set. (We'll get to explanations external to the student later.) You see that the entire process goes well beyond the simple act of testing.

Evaluation and Comparison

If evaluation isn't testing, then what is it? Evaluation is a thoughtful process. We use it to help us understand things. Evaluation has been defined in a variety of ways, all of which have at their core the idea of *comparison*. When we evaluate, we make comparisons between things, note any differences, summarize our findings, and draw conclusions about our results.

A basic model can be used to represent the evaluation process. This model is shown in Exhibit 5.2. In the model, a sample of student behavior is compared to a performance standard and the discrepancy (difference) between the two is noted (Deno & Mirkin, 1977; Yavorsky, 1977). The behavior represents what the student is doing; the discrepancy represents how much the student's behavior must change to match the performance standard. If, for example, a student is expected to read 140 wpm but only reads 35 wpm, there is a 105 wpm discrepancy in reading behavior. (Progress standards, such as "the student will improve by 25% per week" can also be specified.)

The comparison of a student's behavior to a standard is central to the process of evaluation. The process is complete when the evaluator makes a judgment about the significance of any discrepancy and, based on that judgment, decides how to treat the student. Therefore, to understand evaluation, we must know about taking behavior samples, establishing standards, summarizing discrepancies, and judging significance. All of these depend upon the use of measurement.

Measurement

Measurement has been defined as the assignment of numerical values to objects or events according to rules (Campbell, 1940). Measurement is a tool used to summarize the behavior of a student in manageable terms (scores) so that comparison can take place. (It is critical for evaluators to understand that scores don't just reflect information about the student, they also reflect the measurement rules used to derive the scores.) Measurement is limited to the characteristics of things. People have both physical and behavioral characteristics that are investigated and measured for any number of reasons. However, you should never assume that scores based on even the most thorough measurement procedure can actually summarize the total person. We are making this point at the outset to promote a realistic understanding of the limitations of all evaluation, not simply to document a commitment to human individuality (the same statement applies equally well to trout and to car transmissions). What it means is that the results of every measurement should be interpreted not only in terms of what is summarized, but also in terms of what is *not* summarized. Educational evaluators measure the behaviors, states, and critical effects that *indicate* learning. They don't measure learning itself.

Thorndike and Hagan (1969) have outlined three steps common to all types of measurement:

1. Identify the characteristic to be measured.

2. Devise a procedure to make the characteristic observable.

3. Devise a system (numerical or visual) for summarizing the observations.

Davies (1973) has suggested another essential step. If the results of educational measurement are to be of practical use, this fourth step should be included.

Exhibit 5.3
Various item formats

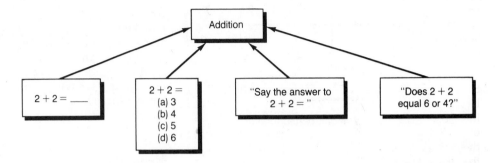

4. Ensure that the measurement procedure corresponds to reality.

These four steps must be followed no matter what is measured. For example, suppose a teacher wants to measure a student's computational skills. The heading Computation includes a number of operations, so the teacher must first identify which ones to measure (step 1). If the teacher identifies writing multiplication facts as the characteristic to be measured, the teacher must next think of a way to observe the student multiplying. The obvious procedure is to supply the student with a sheet of multiplication problems and a pencil. The student's behavior on the task can be observed by checking the written responses on the worksheet (step 2). The student's work can be kept in a portfolio for reexamination (Reif, 1990; Valencia, 1990), or responses completed correctly and incorrectly can be counted to summarize numerically the work done (step 3). A teacher uses curriculum-based measurement when she ensures that the problems on the worksheet are similar to multiplication problems found on class assignments (Deno, 1989; Fuchs, 1992). The results of curriculum-based measurement can be applied in the classroom (step 4).

Educational evaluators are primarily interested in measuring children's prior knowledge (skills, thought processes, and attitudes). Although none of these is directly observable, we can draw inferences about them from the way students behave. Many behaviors are overt (observable) and are assumed to be brought about by thought processes that are covert. Because we depend on observed behavior to make these inferences, our conclusions will always be threatened by the imperfect correspondence between overt behavior, actual knowledge, and the occasional reluctance of

students to display what they know (Fuchs, Fuchs, Dailey & Power, 1985).

Knowledge is more than behavior. This can be seen by noting that many different behaviors may indicate the same thought process. For example, Exhibit 5.3 shows that a student's knowledge of addition may be indicated by several behaviors: writing answers, selecting answers, saying answers aloud, or circling answers. While a student who can only perform one of these responses is assumed to know less than a student who can carry out all four, that student has still indicated some knowledge of addition.

Just as many behaviors can indicate the same thought process, many thought processes can result in the same behavior. This means that there is more than one way to get the correct or incorrect answer on a test. For example, suppose a test requires two students to solve this problem:

$$50 \\ + 43$$

One student might work the problem by following the standard addition algorithm ($0 + 3 = 3$, $5 + 4 = 9$, so $50 + 43 = 93$). The other, realizing that both numbers together will approach 100, could solve it this way: 43 is 7 less than 50, $50 + 50 = 100$, $100 - 7 = 93$. These two students both have the same answer and will engage in the same "writes 97" behavior, but they have arrived at the answer by applying very different computation strategies. While both students probably know the addition algorithm, it is possible that only the second student knows how to solve problems by rounding and subtracting. Because there are different ways to arrive at answers, scores from the same tests do not always summarize the same thought processes and may not mean that the students know the same things (Frederiksen, 1986).

Sampling

Some domains of knowledge, ability, or attitude are so large that it is impossible to pick every behavior that indicates the student's status. For example, the domain of reading has so many elements (words and stories) that any attempt to test all of them would take so long that the student would die of old age long before the measurement was complete. For this reason, it is necessary to sample.

Sampling involves selecting a few items from the domain of interest. The procedure used to select these items influences the usefulness of a measure. The items selected must represent the domain about which conclusions will be drawn. However, while several items may indicate knowledge in an area, some are better indicators of that knowledge than others. For example, supplying the names of coins and stating their value are both indicators of knowing about money. However, stating value is probably a more meaningful behavior than supplying names. There are two ways to get a sample of a student's behavior. First is to *test* the behavior and second is to *observe* it.

Observations of behavior should be made when the behavior occurs freely in the environment. Testing, in contrast, elicits behavior under artificial conditions (this includes role playing, interviewing, and simulations). So, all things being equal, observation is superior to testing because it supplies information about behavior that may be less influenced by the evaluator or the evaluation process itself. Some things are not conveniently observed.

A teacher who is interested in a student's knowledge of the Civil War, for example, might observe the student for some time before the student happens to chat spontaneously with friends about the Civil War. If the teacher needed to judge that knowledge at a particular time, say the end of a history unit, then he would probably be forced to elicit the behaviors that indicate Civil War knowledge. This procedure of manipulating the environment to elicit behaviors at particular times, or under particular conditions, is called *testing*.

Tests are constructed by developing items that sample behaviors reflecting the things of interest to the evaluator. As already mentioned, test items must

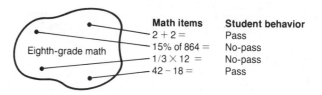

Exhibit 5.4   Sampling.

be representative of the targeted domain to be useful. Observations sample time intervals as well as particular behaviors. If these time intervals are not representative, the usefulness of the observation is decreased.

Think about times during your typical day and imagine the different conclusions an evaluator might reach if you were observed for only one 10-minute period. If you happen to be arguing with someone during that period, you might complain that the 10-minute sample wasn't really representative of your whole day and puts you in a negative light. This misalignment could be corrected by lengthening the observational interval to allow measurement of a wider range of behavior or by breaking the interval into ten 1-minute samples taken at ten different times. Either technique, or both, would make the observation more representative of your typical day.

If a student does well on a test or during an observation, the evaluator infers that the student will do well within the domain from which the sample was taken. For example, in Exhibit 5.4 four items have been sampled and an eighth-grade student has passed only two. This leads to the inference that the student knows only half of what she should know about math. To accept that this conclusion, based on four items, applies to the thousands of math items an eighth grader is expected to have learned, but which are not on the test, is to place great faith in the representativeness of the four items. However, educators do this sort of thing all of the time when they interpret scores from published achievement tests that include only a few items at each grade level (Shinn & Hubbard, 1992).

The number of items (remember we are not just talking about written test items, we are also describing interview questions and simulations) required to adequately sample a domain depends in part on the cohesiveness, or consolidation, of the domain from which the sample is taken. If the domain is composed of items that are very dissimilar from one another (for

Exhibit 5.5   Example Test Item Formats

Addition		Geometry	
(a) $\begin{array}{r} 2 \\ +\,2 \\ \hline \end{array}$	(b) $2 + 2 =$	(a) Define the term *triangle*	(b) Which of the following is *not* a triangle? □ ◺ △
Spelling		**Phonics**	
(a) Spell the word *analytical*	(b) Circle the misspelled word: —antilytical —sequences —computation —components	(a) What sound do these letters make? *oo*	(b) Circle the word that rhymes with *oo* —dome —run —some —tune

example, capital cities of states), the student's response on one item will say little about the likely response on another. However, if the items in the domain share many stimulus and response properties, or if completion of the items depends on a common set of underlying strategies or rules, these generalizations are easier to draw. In cases where the domain is consolidated by rules (such as multiplication) fewer items are needed as a basis for making an inference. If, however, the domain is filled with dissimilar materials, many items will be necessary to obtain a representative sample and make accurate predictions from a test. This point was elaborated on in Chapter 3.

A Note About Observation

The difference between testing and observation is that, in testing, we elicit responses, and in observation we deal with whatever occurs freely. That sounds simple enough, but there's one little hang-up: Whenever we measure something we change it. This doesn't just mean we interpret it in some novel way or misrepresent it in our summary (though that happens too). It means we actually change it. This line of discussion quickly gets metaphysical. If a child miscues in the forest where no one can hear, is there an error? (In physics this is called "Schrodinger's cat" dilemma. It states that nothing is resolved until we measure it [Zukav, 1979].) Once the evaluator enters the scene,

things are changed. In fact everything is changed. Of course, this is just as true of achievement testing as it is of observing, yet in schools today people seem to accept the impact of 16–page computer-response forms more easily than the effect of strange adults with clip boards and stop watches lurking in the back of classrooms.

Test Item Formats

The term *item format* refers to the way a question is presented. The best item formats for collecting behavior are those that are most realistic. In other words, the best test doesn't just sample what a person knows, it samples it the way a person will use it in real life. While the content of two items may be the same, the format or conditions imposed by the items may vary. Exhibit 5.5 shows items with different formats for four domains of content.

There are many different types of item formats and each has its particular disadvantages. Frederiksen (1962) has ranked item types according to their "fidelity," or degree of realism. These levels are shown in Exhibit 5.6. The least generalizable item format calls for the teacher to solicit the student's opinion about her own skill (while difficult to interpret, these reports are essential when the goal of instruction is self-control). The next calls for assessment of the student's attitude toward the task in question, and the third calls

Exhibit 5.6 *Formats of Measurement*

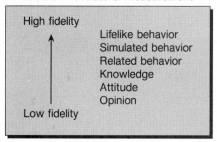

High fidelity

↑

Lifelike behavior
Simulated behavior
Related behavior
Knowledge
Attitude
Opinion

Low fidelity

for a measure of the student's knowledge. The third format is the most commonly used in schools; it typically comes in the form of an objective test. Unfortunately item formats that call for the performance of related behavior, the use of simulations, and lifelike behavior (the highest fidelity category) are seldom used. This is probably because these formats, while more realistic, are often difficult to arrange and score. (You will see examples of this problem in Chapter 10's section on reading comprehension. In that chapter a variety of procedures that are difficult to produce, score, and interpret will be presented in an effort to address the complexity of reading comprehension.) The interest in curriculum-based evaluation has led to the development of efficient scoring and decision-making procedures that can be applied to these "general task outcomes" and that have higher fidelity than the narrowly defined behavior samples found in some tests (Fuchs & Deno, 1991).

Many evaluators have an almost intuitive loathing of the seemingly absurd item formats that test authors must use to sample the behavior of large groups and for the insensitivity these formats have to local curriculum. This is one of the main reasons educators are so dissatisfied with traditional tests (Miller-Jones, 1989; Reif, 1990) and are drawn to alternatives, like *portfolio assessment*, which will be explained in a minute.

The need to use item formats of higher fidelity increases as the importance of the measurement increases. A low-fidelity format may be adequate for spot checking a student's learning, but higher-fidelity formats must be used before making important teaching decisions such as movement to a new objective or assignment to a particular skill group.

Exhibit 5.7 presents a series of operations that students may be expected to carry out when displaying skill or knowledge. This series is drawn from Tindal and Marston (1990) and is based on work by Roid & Haladyna (1982). As you can see when you read through the descriptions of these operations, some seem to require more sophisticated applications of knowledge than others. Tindal and Marston suggest that these various operations may be uniquely suited to different categories of content or thought process. For example, only Reiteration and Summarization may be used to display factual knowledge, whereas all of the operations may be used for conceptual and strategic knowledge.

While test items can be categorized in many ways, it is common to group them by formats such as Identify (select the answer) and Produce (provide the answer) (Exhibit 5.8). While Identify and Produce items both indicate knowledge, they too have certain

Exhibit 5.7 *Student Operations*

Operation	Manner in Which Content Is Used or Manipulated
Reiteration	A verbatim reproduction of material that was taught
Summarization	Generation or identification of a paraphrase, rewording, or condensation of content presented during instruction
Illustration	Generation or identification of an example not used during instruction
Prediction	Description or selection of a likely outcome, given a set of circumstances or conditions
Evaluation	Using appropriate criteria to make a decision when presented with a situation
Application	Description of the circumstances or condition that would be necessary to bring about a particular outcome

Exhibit 5.8   Item Formats

Identify Formats	Produce Formats
True/false	Fill in the blank
Multiple choice	Short answer
Matching	Essay
Select procedure	Apply procedure

advantages and disadvantages. For example, Produce items, such as fill-in-the-blank or short-answer, are better for gaining insight into a student's thought processes. Identify items, such as matching and multiple choice, are easier to score and are less ambiguous, because the responses are limited to the alternatives supplied. This is why group tests are almost invariably composed of Identify items while individual "diagnostic" tests are commonly composed of Produce items. The need to trade ease of scoring for usefulness of results is a constant problem for test authors and users. (*Diagnosis* is a medical term that means a description of an individual's physical status. Educators have adopted the term for their own use, but have changed its meaning. Typically educators call a procedure *diagnostic* when it has some teaching implications. Probably the best way to clarify the term *diagnosis* would be to give it back to the medical profession.)

Portfolios

Frequently the best samples of behavior are not collected through testing, but through the analysis of classroom work assignments. This has recently become known as portfolio assessment (Wolf, 1989; Flood & Lapp, 1989). Using portfolio assessment, teachers/evaluators carefully collect and catalog the work students do on routine assignments and projects. These can be examined, and compared across time, to support decisions about skill and progress (Hall & Tindal, 1991). The portfolio approach applies what Fuchs & Deno (1991) refer to as observational assessment methodology. This combination of testing technology and observational procedures "grounds" the evaluation procedures to the classroom by replacing externally developed tests with classroom-generated work

samples. In order for portfolio assessment to have utility, the portfolio must meet the same standards of fidelity, sampling, scoring, and comparison that any test or observation procedure must meet.

CRTs and NRTs

Teaching evaluation requires the use of criterion-referenced measures. To understand what a criterion-referenced test/observation (CRT) is, you must know how it differs from a normative test/observation (NRT). We will compare these two types of testing with regard to purpose, construction, and standardization. But first we need a new term: probe. A *probe* is a criterion-referenced test or observation procedure. It is the material or time interval used to sample behavior during criterion-referenced sampling (White & Haring, 1982). The term *probe* will often be used in place of criterion-referenced test/observation from now on.

Purpose of NRTs.   The major purpose of the norm-referenced test/observation (NRT) is to help educators see how a student compares with other students of the same age or class placement. Use of NRTs is limited primarily to the determination of program eligibility (see Chapter 9). This is accomplished by comparing the student's performance on an NRT to the performance of a peer group (which has been summarized in the form of norms). Sufficiently low scores on NRTs may be used as evidence that a student needs support services.

Purpose of CRTs.   To find out why a student is not performing as well as required in reading, or to find out exactly on what skill he needs to be working, it is necessary to do some further testing. This is where the criterion-referenced test/observation (CRT) becomes useful. The purpose of the CRT (probe) is to help you discern the particular skills or knowledge the student lacks. Using CRTs, you can compare a student's skills to those specified in the curriculum and find out which skills are missing. Once you determine what the student should be taught, you can begin instruction. Some probes can also be readministered in order to carry out assisted assessment or formative evaluation. These will be explained shortly.

CRT and NRT Behavior Samples.   Tests and observations are constructed according to the purposes for

Exhibit 5.9   *Computation Survey*

1. (A1,1)	2. (S1,1)	3. (A3,2)	4. (A5,2)	5. (S2,2)	6. (S6,3)
2	8	3	39	46	51
$+3$	-6	6	$+\ 4$	$-\ 3$	-28
$\overline{5}$	$\overline{2}$	$+\ 2$	$\overline{43}$	$\overline{43}$	$\overline{23}$
		$\overline{11}$			

27. (A8,3)	8. (S7,4)	9. (M1,4)	10. (M3,4)	11. (D2,4)	12. (D3,4)
601	9062	8	47	6	.63
39	$-\ 4185$	$\times\ 9$	$\times\ 5$	$4\ \overline{)\ 24}$	$4r5$
$+\ 427$	$\overline{4877}$	$\overline{72}$	$\overline{235}$		$8\ \overline{)\ 37}$
$\overline{1067}$					

13. (M7,5)	14. (D6,5)	15. (DR% 11,5)	16. (F11,5)	17. (F16,6)	18. (F20,6)
3075	.36	$\dfrac{4}{20} = \dfrac{1}{5}$	$\dfrac{3}{11} + \dfrac{2}{11} = \dfrac{5}{11}$	$\dfrac{1}{2} - \dfrac{5}{18} = \dfrac{2}{9}$	$2\dfrac{3}{4} \times 5\dfrac{1}{3} = 14\dfrac{2}{3}$
$\times\ \ 62$	$4r27$				
$\overline{190650}$	$74\ \overline{)\ 3061}$				

19. (F24,6)	20. (DR% 8,7)	21. (DR% 9,7)	22. (M8,8)	23. (D7,8)	24. (DR% 6,8)
$6\dfrac{3}{4} \div 3\dfrac{1}{6} = 2\dfrac{5}{38}$	2.43	16.26	$7^2 = 49$	12	$\dfrac{7}{8} = 87.5\%$
	$\times\ \ 2.5$	$1.5\ \overline{)\ 24.39}$		$\sqrt{144}$	
	$\overline{6.075}$				

Source: From K. W. Howell, S. H. Zucker & M. K. Morehead (1982) *Multilevel Academic Skills Inventory.* H & Z Publications, 6544 E. Meadowlark, Paradise Valley, AZ 85253. Reprinted with permission.

which they are designed. Because the norm-referenced achievement test is used to determine how one student compares with age-mates (or in some cases grade-mates), it is important that the test contain items from across a wide range of curriculum. Imagine you have been working with a student named Kathy. Kathy is a third-grader working well below her expected level. Because the achievement test given Kathy included items taught at the third-grade level, she missed them all. As a result, we know from her performance that her scores are below the average score of other third-graders.

To discriminate among large groups of students, it is necessary to include items that cover the range of curriculum from preschool to high school. Exhibit 5.9, which is the survey computation test of the Multilevel Academic Survey Test (Howell, Zucker & Morehead, 1985), provides an example of the types of progressively difficult items found on typical NRTs. There are a few items in Exhibit 5.9 that ''average'' third-graders would be working on, but most of the items—probably as many as 80% of them—are either too hard or too easy for a third-grader. As a result, a score representing how a student does on the test will not reflect

how she is doing on third-grade math. This is why NRT scores aren't of much interest to teachers trying to find instructional guidance. Remember that the normed achievement test was designed this way on purpose. Its purpose is to measure a student's academic functioning in relation to peers—not to measure actual skill.

The criterion-referenced test, in contrast, is designed to measure only one objective and is composed of items that are all at the same level of difficulty. Because this results in less variation in performance, you would not use a CRT to see how Kathy's performance compares with her age-mates. The CRT is used to determine whether a student has a particular skill or piece of knowledge. So it includes only those items that measure the skill or knowledge in question. Between-student performance will not vary greatly on the CRT because the item difficulty does not vary. Students either have a sufficient amount of the skill or knowledge being measured or they do not. Exhibit 5.10 provides an example of a CRT. Notice that they are addition problems involving one- and two-digit numbers. This happens to be first-grade material. If a student passes this test (sometimes

Exhibit 5.10   Addition Objective 5m

							45	28	94	76	
							+ 7	+ 6	+ 8	+ 4	
					Practice Items		52	34	*102*	80	

											Digit Count
28	53	16	94	87	63	60	32	42	51		
+ 4	+ 9	+ 8	+ 8	+ 7	+ 9	+ 8	+ 9	+ 2	+ 9		
32	62	24	102	94	72	68	41	44	60		
										1s	(21)
31	58	13	26	74	69	83	49	22	93		
+ 5	+ 2	+ 7	+ 4	+ 7	+ 9	+ 7	+ 0	+ 8	+ 3		
36	60	20	30	81	78	90	49	30	96	non-instance	(41)
39	62	78	43	56	24	18	73	83	92		
+ 9	+ 4	+ 3	+ 8	+ 5	+ 9	+ 8	+ 8	+ 5	+ 9		
48	66	81	51	61	33	26	81	88	101		
										2s	(62)
28	49	93	98	15	85	34	45	63	71		
+ 1	+ 6	+ 6	+ 5	+ 7	+ 9	+ 6	+ 5	+ 9	+ 4		
29	55	99	103	22	94	40	50	72	75	non-instance	(83)
31	97	19	70	48	65	95	84	36	83		
+ 9	+ 2	+ 5	+ 9	+ 8	+ 8	+ 6	+ 8	+ 6	+ 8		
40	99	24	79	56	73	101	92	42	91		
1s	non-instance	9s	non-instance	8s	3s 5s	6s 5s	4s	number added to itself		3s	(104)

An addition probe sheet *Source:* From K. W. Howell, S. H. Zucker & M. K. Morehead (1982) *Multilevel Accademic Skills Inventory.* H & Z Publications, 6544 E. Meadowlark, Paradise Valley, AZ 85253. Reprinted with permission.

called a probe sheet), it doesn't necessarily mean that she is working on a first-grade level in arithmetic. There are many other math objectives in first grade not represented on this CRT. It does tell us, however, that she has the single skill being measured. If this is all we wanted to know, it is not necessary to include any other items on the test.

CRT and NRT Standards.   To use an NRT to determine how a student compares with her peers, you obviously need a measure of both the student and the peers' behavior. The way to obtain these measures is to gather a representative group of the student's peers, test them, and then summarize the performance of the group. This group is called the *standardization sample.* This process of testing and summarizing group scores is called *norming.* Given this summary of the group's

behavior, you can see how any individual's performance compares with the group. In discussions of sampling, the key concept is *representative*, because it is the selection of the standardization sample that definitionally separates NRTs and CRTs.

A representative sample used in the standardization of an NRT should include a relatively large number of individuals at each age or grade level. To ensure that the sample is representative, it may be carefully controlled to include the appropriate proportions of male/female, majority/minority, high/low socioeconomic status, and urban/rural students. These individuals are selected with no prior attention paid to their skill or knowledge. With regard to skill, the standardization group for the NRT is chosen at random from the population to ensure an even distribution of skills. For example, if you wanted to standardize a math test for use with students applying to college, you would not go to the Massachusetts Institute of Technology for your norming sample. Average MIT freshmen might have superior interest and training in math. They are a select group (having already been screened by the university admittance process) and are not representative of the population who would be taking the test. If your test were standardized on this group, it would have limited value because the norms would describe a special group of students (engineering, math, and science majors).

In direct contrast, the criterion-referenced sample need only include a small number of individuals with no attention to minority status, socioeconomic status, or home setting. These individuals may differ widely according to age or grade. However, they all would have one thing in common—the very thing the NRT tried to avoid. All the people in the CRT sample should have the skill or knowledge being tested. This is important, because a probe is used to assess whether a student has a particular skill. A random sample can't be used here because students picked by chance might not have the skill. For example, if we wanted to find out how well a student must know consonant sounds, we would construct a consonant-sound probe and then give it to a group of students skilled at reading consonants. Only skilled readers should be included in the sample. If we chose students at random, we would probably include some who do not know consonants. Therefore their performance on consonant sounds would lower the score we eventually came up with. The middle (median) score of this skilled standardization group would become the "criterion for acceptable performance" (CAP). This CAP is the standard, or criterion, in a CRT.

If students score at least as well as the CRT standard they are thought to have the skill being measured. If not, they are thought to need instruction in the skill. Notice the difference between the standardization samples in the two types of measures. On the norm-referenced math test for all college applicants, we didn't want to pick a select group of successful math students. We were looking for the typical college freshman. On the criterion-referenced consonant test, we wanted to pick a select group of students who had the skill being measured. Remember this, because it is the essential difference between the two types of tests: *NRTs reference student behavior to norms for the purpose of comparison to a group, while*

CRTs reference student behavior to behavioral criteria to guide teaching.

Testing and Evaluation

Once again:

- Evaluation is not the same as testing.
- Testing is simply collecting behavior.
- Evaluation is comparing a behavior to a standard and rendering a judgment based on that comparison.

Once a student's behavior has been summarized, it must be compared to a standard before evaluation can take place. This is an important point. Testing (assessment) and observing are only efforts to see what a person is doing. Behavior samples mean little without an authentic expectation, or standard, for comparison. This is true whether the behavior sample is taken from an achievement test or a classroom portfolio.

Testing should never be piecemeal. Unfortunately, this is often the case in special education. As Deno (1971) pointed out, some educators judge the quality of a testing program by the number of tests routinely given. It is not uncommon to find special education programs that subject all referred students to a standard battery of tests regardless of their needs. This is not evaluation—it is called fishing (or, as one of our text reviewers has observed, child abuse).

Standards

It is not enough to know a person's current status; we must know how to determine if that status is adequate. To make this determination we must compare the individual's status to a performance or progress standard. These standards are extremely important because an inappropriate standard can lead to inappropriate decisions. Just as a testing format that inaccurately represents a student's knowledge is also of limited value, a standard that inaccurately represents what that student's knowledge should be is of limited value. In general, the standards used in education are in such poor shape that they deserve cynicism. Because of this, whenever someone tells you that they know of a student who is unusual, or special, you should get in the habit of responding "As compared to what?"

Norm-referenced standards are used when we are interested in the way one student's status compares to that of other students. Criterion-referenced standards compare a student's performance to the requirements of a particular task.

Types of Standards

Most of us are familiar with two types of standards: norms and performance criteria. Normative standards are used when we are interested in the way a student's status compares to that of other students (above aver-

age, below average, way below average). Performance criteria are used when we are interested in the way a student's status compares to the requirements of a particular task (can she read the directions well enough to assemble the class's new computer?). These standards are called *criteria*. Norm-referenced (NRT) and criterion-referenced (CRT) tests compare (reference) scores to either norms or criteria. If norms or criteria are not available, there is nothing to which the scores can be referenced and they are essentially meaningless. In such a case, evaluation is impossible. Criteria and norms must be formally established and their relationship to decision making validated for them to be useful. This process is called *standardization.*

The term *standardized test* can have two meanings. One is that the test was developed to be administered in a standard fashion. This means a manual with administration guidelines *must* be available. The second meaning is that standards have been established following some type of standardization activity. In this case, technical information *must* be available describing the procedures followed to set the standards. There is a tendency to use the term *standardized test* as if it were synonymous with published or norm-referenced tests. This is a mistake. Criterion-referenced tests also need to be standardized.

Idiosyncratic Standards

There is one last type of standard that is particularly important in special/remedial education. However, this type of standard is so unfamiliar to most people it doesn't even have a widely accepted name. We're going to call it the idiosyncratic standard. *Idiosyncratic* means individual. Whereas norms compare students to groups, and criteria to tasks, the idiosyncratic standard compares a student to him- or herself. Exhibits 1.2 and 1.3 presented idiosyncratic data illustrating a student's progress while learning a task. This kind of data can be used to decide if one approach to instruction is superior to another, by comparing the student's progress under one teaching technique to her progress under different teaching. In this case, the issue is not "kid vs. group" or "kid vs. task." Rather, it is idiosyncratic—it is kid vs. kid. This will be mentioned again when we talk about assisted assessment. This approach applies what Fuchs and Deno (1991) refer to as *observational assessment methodology* to general task outcomes.

Formative Evaluation

Have you ever had trouble learning something in school? (If not, we'd rather not hear about it.) If so, who noticed the problem first—you, or the teacher?

One of the authors has asked that question of hundreds of adults and children. In almost every case the answer was that they, as the student, were aware of the problem long before the teacher. In fact, many people reported that they were the ones who first reported the problem. That may be understandable, but it isn't ideal.

There are two general types of evaluation, summative and formative, that educators can use to guide decision making (Bloom, Madaus & Hastings, 1981). All of the ideas discussed so far about measurement and sampling apply equally to both. While many of the same tests can be used for either function, the traditional measures (most classroom, achievement, and aptitude tests) are used almost exclusively for summative evaluation. *Summative evaluation* occurs after teaching and learning have taken place. Summative evaluation is employed to measure the end result (product) of instruction. It is typically carried out to grade students, or to identify the students who have and have not met the objectives of instruction. In contrast, *formative evaluation* attempts to examine learning as skills are being formed. Where summative evaluation is used to describe the current condition of the student, formative evaluation is used to illustrate the process of learning. The best measurement procedure in the world, when used in a summative way, will not necessarily improve a student's learning. To use an analogy (which we heard somewhere but can't attribute), "A thermometer never changed anyone's temperature."

When you went to school, the odds are that every test you took was used as a summative measure. The term *formative evaluation* is unfamiliar to most teachers. Nevertheless, the authors believe the formative function is critical to evaluation in special/remedial education. Because of this importance, and an unfortunate lack of interest in it, we have decided to infuse information about how to do it throughout the text. However, we are going to provide the rationale for its use here.

Individualizing Instruction

Many educators believe the skill to modify instruction at the appropriate time is the mark of true teaching. This "feel" (sometimes called "with-it-ness") for when a student is being frustrated or bored allows some teachers to pick the most effective technique at the right time. While the same techniques are available to everyone, only certain teachers seem to use them at the critical instant.

Let's go back to the problem you had in school. Most likely you knew that you didn't understand the material but you waited, hoping for Divine intervention, until after the first test. You took the test and failed. What happened next? Did the teacher take you aside and reteach the material, or simply write your failing score in the grade book? If the teacher retaught the material, or provided some sort of assistance, then the teacher was using the test as a formative measure (and you probably ended up appreciating that teacher).

Because exceptional teaching means modifying instruction, special and remedial teachers must have skills in at least two areas: instructional modification and decision making. Instructional modification skills allow them to adjust and implement a wide range of teaching methods, programs, and techniques. Decision-making skills allow them to decide when these adjustments are needed for individual students. One set of these skills is of limited use without the other. Obviously, there is no advantage to knowing that it is time to switch methods if you only know how to use one method. (You may have had that teacher too—the one you went to for help and who said "I don't know what to do about it" or "It wouldn't be fair to the other students if I gave you extra help." You probably *didn't* end up appreciating that teacher.) Similarly, knowing different ways to teach isn't particularly valuable if you can't decide which way to use. Formative evaluation is used to recognize which instructional techniques are most effective for particular students.

Curriculum-based, formative evaluation procedures can make your teaching many times more effective (Fuchs, Deno & Mirkin, 1985; Shinn & Hubbard, 1992; White, 1986). In our opinion formative procedures, most notably Data-Based Program Modification (DBPM) (Giek, 1992; Deno & Mirkin, 1977), and assisted assessment (Campione & Brown, 1985), provide the most promising solutions to the problem of selecting effective treatments for students.

A Note on Learning Styles

Educators have long acknowledged the idiographic (individual) nature of learning. For example:

> The best method for one cannot be the best for all. There is not one mind reproduced in millions of copies, for all of which one rule will suffice; there are many differing minds, each of which needs, for its adequate education, to be considered to some extent by itself. (Thorndike, 1917, p. 67)

The problem is finding the best way to teach. Once an evaluator/teacher has decided *what* a student needs to be taught (through the appropriate use of a summative approach), she must decide *how* to teach it (a function for which summative procedures are inadequate). As explained in Chapter 4, there are many different approaches, programs, techniques, and methods available for presenting any objective, and it is widely recognized that students vary in how well they respond to these treatments. Therefore, teachers must make selections.

Many educators have elected to base teaching selections on summative measures of student abilities or aptitudes. Historically, the line of research associated with these efforts has been called Aptitude Treatment Interaction (Bracht, 1970; Cronbach, 1957; Lloyd, 1984). This research deals with attempts to describe types of learners, as defined by various cognitive or perceptual aptitude measures, and to match these learners to complementary types of instructional programs. Today this is more commonly called *learning styles instruction* (LSI) (Carbo, 1992) and it is one of the most popular approaches to individualizing instruction. However, as popular as the idea of LSI may be, it has been invalidated and is probably fallacious (Snider, 1992). In fact, as you may recall, we listed it as a myth in Chapter 2.

In the opinion of the authors, the LSI approach to treatment selection isn't simply ineffective—it is dangerous. Here are some reasons we think it so:

1. It is based on the use of cognitive/perceptual measures that are: (a) time consuming to give, (b) poorly validated, (c) generally unreliable, and (d) not curriculum-based.

2. By emphasizing summative measures of the student over formative measures that can illustrate the learning interaction, LSI focuses teacher attention on various hypothesized student abilities/aptitudes and distracts from the curriculum and instruction.

3. LSI advocates disregard easily altered factors that cause treatments to vary in effectiveness, such as

the teacher's actions and the student's prior knowledge.

4. LSI doesn't work (Arter & Jenkins, 1979; Kavale & Forness, 1987; Snider, 1992).

The ultimate problem with LSI is that it is a summative procedure. Efforts to identify student learning styles have always been tied to the administration of some sort of test or questionnaire, the results of which are used to make predictive statements about the student's future response to instruction. For LSI to work, these measures would need to have spectacular predictive strength, yet no summative test has ever demonstrated such strength (Fuchs, Fuchs, Benowitz & Barringer, 1987; Ysseldyke et al., 1983). Summative evaluation, at its best, only tells us what a student can do now. That's it. It may be powerful enough to predict outcomes significantly for large groups of students on globally defined tasks, but those of us interested in selecting treatments for individuals, particularly individuals experiencing difficulty in school, will always be disappointed by the summative approach.

Educators have become bogged down in attempts to use tests of learning style to predict which students will do best in which programs. In many cases, these predictions have far surpassed the reliability of existing testing instruments and the validity of learning theories. As the science of instruction evolves, it is possible that both the reliability and validity of prediction will improve. In the meantime, educators should be asking if there is an alternative strategy for deciding how to teach. There is.

At present, the best way to decide how to teach is to pick one technique (this initial selection should be based on empirical support for a technique; however, it can be argued that a good way to make this initial treatment selection is simply to ask the student [Elliott, 1986]), place the student in it, and see how she does. In the past, this technique was not used because the tools were not available to evaluate quickly the effectiveness of the placement. The risk of misplacing a student for months or even weeks wasn't acceptable. Due to advances in formative evaluation, applied behavioral analysis, and curriculum-based measurement, this is no longer the case. It is now possible to place a student in a program and evaluate the validity of the placement in a matter of days. Essentially, this procedure is LSI backwards. Instead of looking for styles to interact with treatments, the teacher looks for

Exhibit 5.11   A student's progress compared to his aim.

treatments to interact with styles. The result is a movement away from attempts to measure and define abilities and toward the exact measurement of student behavior, tasks, and teaching (Deno & Espin, 1991).

The Concept of Progress

Recall the Chapter 1 description of special education. In that chapter, special/remedial education was characterized as the application of exceptional decision making and teaching techniques for the purpose of increasing the rate of student learning (as illustrated in Exhibit 5.11). Special/remedial students were shown to be less skilled than others because of their lower rates of learning, or progress, through the curriculum.

If the special/remedial student's chief problem is inadequate progress, then instructional interventions that improve progress should solve that problem. Because student progress through the curriculum is directly determined by the instruction received, information about progress, and the impact of various program modifications on it, is essential to the teacher. The procedures for collecting this information are more easily understood if the distinction between performance and progress is clear.

The Concept of Performance

Performance is how well a person does something. A person's current performance on a task can be shown by his position on the vertical (behavior) axis of charts like the ones shown in the exhibits this chapter. A performance level can be determined with as little as one summative measurement of the target behavior. The performance level is noted by simply giving a test (or taking an observation) and recording the student's score. For example, in Exhibit 5.12, the score reported is 40. (Note that the vertical axis always represents

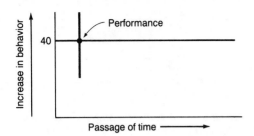

Exhibit 5.12 *A performance summary.*

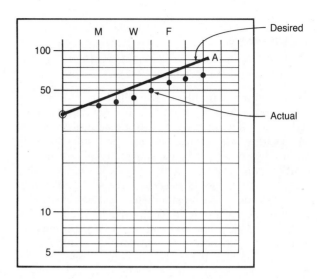

Exhibit 5.14 *A progress discrepancy.*

descriptions of skill or behavior, while the horizontal axis always represents the passage of time.)

If a performance standard (criterion) is 80 correct per minute, and the student works at a rate of 40 per minute, her level of performance relative to the standard can be displayed as shown in Exhibit 5.13. In this case, there is a discrepancy between the performance and the standard that can be summed up by saying "The kid is 40 behind and needs to move along the behavioral axis by going from 40 to 80."

A performance discrepancy tells both where the student is (40) and where she should be (80). It tells us what to teach. Unfortunately, this sort of summative statement gives no information about where the student is actually going, so an evaluator can't tell if the

student is getting better, worse, or staying the same. Performance data can only tell us that instruction is needed. For this reason, performance data are sometimes referred to as *static data*, meaning they do not show movement. These are the kinds of data educators are most familiar with, as they are derived from single administrations of a test.

Progress (Learning). A student's progress on a task is determined by simultaneously summarizing changes along both the vertical (behavior) and horizontal (time) axes of the chart. It is not possible to note progress without also noting performance, because progress is a change in performance over time. Therefore progress cannot be determined with a single datum. Several data points are needed to determine progress adequately and, while no fixed number is required, the validity of progress statements increases with both the number and quality of the data points upon which they are based.

Exhibit 5.14 shows several data points. Each data point represents a performance score obtained by giving the same probe at different times. Because identical, or equivalent, curriculum-based tests/observations were repeated daily, the differences in performance from day to day can be attributed to learning. As seen in Exhibit 5.14, there is clearly acceleration up the chart. This progression in a particular direction (it

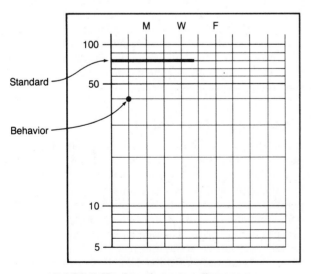

Exhibit 5.13 *A performance discrepancy.*

When teachers gather formative information during the teaching/learning process, growth patterns are visible to the student as well as to the teacher.

could be up, down, or flat) is called *trend*. Students with different trends are learning (progressing) at different rates.

Like performance, progress has little meaning without an aim or standard. If the standard is an increase of 40 per minute in one week (five instructional days) and the student only increases 20, then she is progressing at a lower rate than desired. As seen in Exhibit 5.13, this unacceptable rate of progress produces a performance deficit of 20 per minute in only one week. If the student's behavior remains at 40 for the entire week, no progress (change in behavior) is noted. If the student's behavior decreases, then she is

"progressing" away (decelerating) from the standard. In this context, progress only means change; it does not necessarily mean improvement.

Because learning is indicated by a change in behavior across time, it can be seen in the progress of the student toward a performance objective. This is formative information, and it is important because progress data are uniquely suited to deciding how to teach. Progress data tell you where the student is and, more important, where she is going. This type of data is fluid, or dynamic, showing both the direction and magnitude of change.

Educators are not especially familiar with progress (formative) data and in the past have been forced informally to judge the quality of progress. This is bad, malignant, menacing, and evil! (The authors have strong feelings on this issue.) There are many reasons why this is true, but one of the most important was provided in the Chapter 2 discussion of motivation. There you read about Dweck's theory that students who acquire a performance orientation instead of a learning (progress) orientation are more apt to have motivation problems in school (Dweck, 1986). You also read evidence that both adaptive and nonadaptive motivational patterns are learned. Obviously, a student is unlikely to pick up a learning orientation from a teacher who doesn't have that learning orientation. The student, however, is very likely to pick up a learning orientation from a teacher who thinks about, collects, displays, and talks about formative information.

Data-Based Program Modification (DBPM). Once you have decided what a student should be taught, you must decide how to teach it. This means sorting your way through the complex of instructional formats, teacher actions, and student thought processes illustrated in Exhibit 4.2. For reasons already explained, attempts to predict preferred treatments from measures of student learning style appear to be successful only about 25% of the time (Arter & Jenkins, 1979; Ulman & Rosenberg, 1986). What can be done to ensure that students are learning the most material in the least amount of time? The answer lies in the application of DBPM and assisted assessment procedures.

DBPM employs the repeated administration of specific tests in order to monitor the student's progress in treatments. Look again at the chart in Exhibit 5.14. If you are the teacher, the dots in that exhibit represent

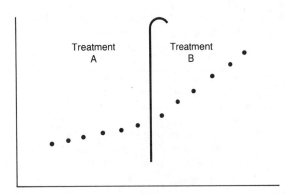

Exhibit 5.15   Teaching effect.

measures of a skill you want the student to learn, while the line represents how fast the student should be learning the skill. Would you continue to use the same treatment or would you change? Decide now.

If you said you would change, you made a correct Data-Based Program Modification decision (Howell & McCollum-Gahley, 1986). DBPM requires accurate, continual measurement of important student behaviors. The resulting data can be analyzed for evidence of acceptable or unacceptable growth (progress) toward a specific objective, and comparisons can easily be made between a student's growth in different teaching techniques.

Exhibit 5.15 shows changes in a student's oral reading rate under two teaching approaches. Each dot represents a timed oral reading from the student's classroom reader. In this case, the student is in each treatment for one week. The superiority of treatment B over treatment A is obvious, because the trend in the data is steeper. Because, when using DBPM, teachers base decisions on progress data, it is important to understand the concept of trend.

In Exhibit 5.16a, the score for one test is supplied. Whether the student is improving or getting worse can't be determined from this one summation of her total performance.

In Exhibit 5.16b, three possible posttest scores have been added. As a teacher, if you obtained posttest A, you would no doubt be pleased; posttests B and C would not cause you to celebrate.

Exhibit 5.16c contains a score as low as score C in Exhibit 5.16b. However, the low score in Exhibit 5.16c isn't particularly disturbing because the overall trend illustrated in that exhibit is positive. Given the data in Exhibit 5.16c and a progress standard, you could make decisions on the overall movement of the behavior, and not on a single point of datum. This is called trend analysis.

Assisted Assessment.   In DBPM, decisions are made by testing the student, teaching the student, and then interpreting the trend of scores. This teach-test, teach-test cycle is basic to all applications of formative evaluation including precision teaching (Howell & Lorson-Howell, 1990), and diagnostic teaching (Valencia & Wixson, 1991).

Assisted assessment is a procedure employed to determine the amount of aid a student must be given in order to learn. It is carried out by testing until the student fails on a task. The evaluator then supplies the student with carefully sequenced clues or explanations before retesting. This is done in the hope of determining the level of support the student requires for continued learning (Campione & Brown, 1985).

Conceptually, assisted assessment and DBPM are the same. Both of them rely on repeated measures of the same skill or strategy, and alterations in instruction. The primary difference is that proponents of DBPM focus almost exclusively on the development of

**Exhibit 5.16
Determining
trend.**

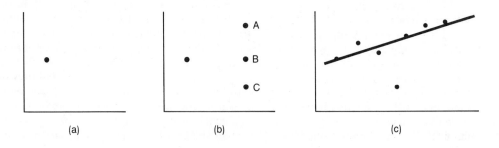

(a)   (b)   (c)

Exhibit 5.17   A Summary of Assisted Behavior*

		Original Test		A Prompt		B Demonstrate		C Reteach	
				Assistance Sequence					
		S1	S2	S1	S2	S1	S2	S1	S2
		5NP	NP						
		4NP	NP	NP	P	NP		P	
Skill Sequence		3P	P						
		2P	P						
		1P	P						

*P=pass; NP=no pass.

curriculum sequences and the application of direct curriculum-based measures (Fuchs & Deno, 1991). In distinction, proponents of assisted assessment tend to accept currently available measures while focusing their attention on the development of instructional intervention sequences.

Exhibit 5.17 provides a summary of assisted assessment for two students designated S1 and S2. During initial testing on a skill sequence, both of these students got items 1–3 correct. They both failed items 4 and 5. The evaluator then gave each student a skill-related prompt (intervention A) and tested item 4 again. As can be seen in the exhibit, student S1 failed this retest, but S2 passed it. Next, the evaluator tried demonstrating how to work item 4 to S1, but S1 failed the second retest. Finally, after having skill 4 completely retaught, S1 passed a third retest.

The results in Exhibit 5.17 are interesting in a formative sense. Note that on the original test—and after the entire procedure is over—both students apparently know exactly the same thing. Yet students 1 and 2 are different. S1 appears to require considerably more assistance (levels A, B and C) than S2 (S2 only requires level-A assistance). Exhibit 5.17, therefore, does not simply map out what these students know, it also maps out the assistance they require in order to learn. That is exactly what was illustrated for a single student in Exhibit 5.15. The only difference here is that repeated measures were given to recognize the necessary assistance (teaching approach). (This could be a

major weakness if the tests used for repeated measures aren't any good.) Assisted-assessment procedures will be recommended in several of the topical chapters in Part 3 of this book.

The Need for Formative Evaluation

The key to any formative evaluation system is frequent and direct data collection. Educators interested in making decisions about student programs should be able to see that the more frequently they test/observe, the more often they can make data-based decisions. If we schedule our data collection daily, then we can make daily decisions. If we only monitor learning on a monthly basis, we can only make informed decisions once a month. The best data decisions will be made from systems that include frequent curriculum-based monitoring because they will produce data that are sensitive to learning.

Formative evaluation can be particularly effective when it is combined with guidelines for systematic interpretation. These guidelines, called data decision rules, tell what to do when certain patterns in data occur. Many teachers are used to applying some set of decision-making rules to their instruction. These rules are seldom absolute, but they do provide guidance. An example of a data-based rule with which most teachers are familiar is the "three times in 3 days" rule attributed to Fernald (1943). This rule says if a kid works a task correctly three times a day for 3 days in a

Careful analysis of formative data allows teachers to make timely and appropriate instructional decisions.

row, she has learned the task and should move on to something new.

Another familiar rule is the instructional-level rule—often used to select readers for students. While designated levels vary, it is common to hear that if a student reads from material in which he is above 90% accurate it is too easy for instruction, and if he is below 80% it is too hard. Therefore, the interval from 80% to 90% represents the instructional level that falls between the so-called independent and frustration levels.

There are many other decision rules around, and each one depends on some type of data. In the examples above, the data required for the first rule illustrate "correct and incorrect behavior each day," while the data required for the second rule illustrate "accuracy of passage reading." As one might expect, the more sophisticated the data collection system, the more sophisticated the decisions that can be made with that system. Because the highest level of sophistication is characteristically reserved for the most problematic

students, educators may use data collection and interpretation procedures for some students that would seem needlessly complex for others.

If, every time teachers taught, students learned as quickly and as thoroughly as possible, then there would be no need for collecting formative data and making data decisions. However this is not the case. The techniques used for one student at one time on one task may not work as well at another time for another student. Even the same student may respond differently across tasks or time. The whole idea behind individualized instruction is that instruction can and should be altered to produce better results. These changes should not be made in objectives or criteria (the curriculum), but in the way the student is taught.

How Well Formative Evaluation Works

Formative evaluation is sort of like peer tutoring, it gets rediscovered every few years and every few years it is found to be effective. Research clearly demonstrates that teachers who periodically review formative data and base treatment decisions on this review are more effective (Shinn & Hubbard, 1992; White, 1986). For example, Haring, Liberty, and White (1980) found that a group of teachers using formative data were 2.2 times more successful at selecting appropriate teaching modifications than teachers who did not. Fuchs, Deno, and Mirkin (1985) found that teachers who employed formative evaluation and data-based program evaluation produced statistically and educationally superior student progress.

Fuchs and Fuchs (1986), in a meta-analysis, reviewed 21 studies and concluded that cumulative effects are obtained when formative data display, decision rules, and behavior modification are combined during teaching. In this case, the average performance of students receiving data display, decision rules, and behavior modification was 37% higher than that of students who weren't. This study looked at 3835 student programs, 83% of which involved learners with disabilities. Of these, 38% focused on reading, 19% on reading and math, 14% on math, and the remainder on areas such as preschool skills, spelling, and high-school content.

There is little doubt in our minds that formative evaluation is one of the most powerful tools currently available to teachers. That is why a section on monitoring procedures will be included in each content chapter, and information on data recording and interpretation is included in the workbook that accompanies this text. DBPM and assisted assessment are the sort of decision-making tools that make special education truly special. We also recognize that it is time consuming. In part, this is because researchers and publishers have failed to popularize the tools required to use it and teachers attempting to do so must therefore be prepared to develop some of their own (Wesson, King & Deno, 1984). However, this situation is improving with the increased availability of DBPM computer programs (Fuchs, Fuchs & Hamlett, 1989). We would like to say that formative evaluation provides a quick and easy way to individualize, but we can't, because we have found that in education, just as in any other field, the hardest problems necessitate the greatest effort.

Summary

This chapter was meant to serve as a bridge linking Part 1 with Parts 2 and 3 of the text. It began with some comments about the nature of evaluation, including explanations of the role of comparison and standards, and then went on to contrast the formative and summative functions of evaluation.

Part 2 / Things to Know About

Part 2 supplies extensive coverage of the processes of assessment and teaching. Chapter 6 covers the basic tools of measurement and comparison. Even if you are already knowlegeable in the area of measurement, you may want to read Chapter 6 to find out what we think about it.

Chapter 7 may well be the pivotal chapter in this text. In it we present guidelines for functional decision making. These guidelines come in the form of a set of *rules* for evaluator thought and *actions* for evaluation activity. The rules and actions in Chapter 7 are fundamental to expert problem solving and decison making. They were developed through an analysis of related literature, interviews with evaluators, and field testing by the authors. In Chapter 5 we made the statement that "Evaluation is not testing." That's because evaluation is a more sophisticated, judgment-driven endeavor than testing. Chapter 7 explains how we engage in that endeavor.

Chapter 8 provides specifics about instruction. The presentation is organized around certain *functions* of teaching and *formats* of delivery in order to establish sets of recommendations that can be used throughout Part 3. Just as evaluation is more than testing, teaching is more than the presentation of lessons. Teaching is also a sophisticated, judgment-driven activity. And, as anyone who has tried it knows, teaching goes well beyond the simple presentation of assignments. The process of instruction is influenced by many things.

These include the demands of the task being taught, the characteristics of the individual learner, and the skills of the teacher. Chapter 8 addresses these factors within each of the following catagories of teacher action: preparation, delivery of information, questioning, responding to students, and evaluation of outcomes.

Chapter 9 breaks the flow of Part 2—and of the book—by addressing the topic of *eligibility*. Because this text is almost exclusively about teaching, the presentation in Chapter 9 contrasts sharply with almost everything else you'll read here. However, the simple truth is that, because our society is not yet willing to provide a free and appropriate education to all students, schools must decide which students will and will not be provided with support services. This decision-making activity is carried out by groups of professionals including those who are reading this text.

There is another, less businesslike, explanation for the inclusion of Chapter 9 in this text. Eligibility determination has become almost an obsession within special education and school psychology. Unfortunately, the practices emerging from this obsession seldom have instructional utility. That's because these practices are rooted in the thinking of the early 1970s, when most of the regulations relative to eligibility were first developed. In preparing our chapter, we decided to discuss eligibility as it would have been established had today's thinking been available in 1970.

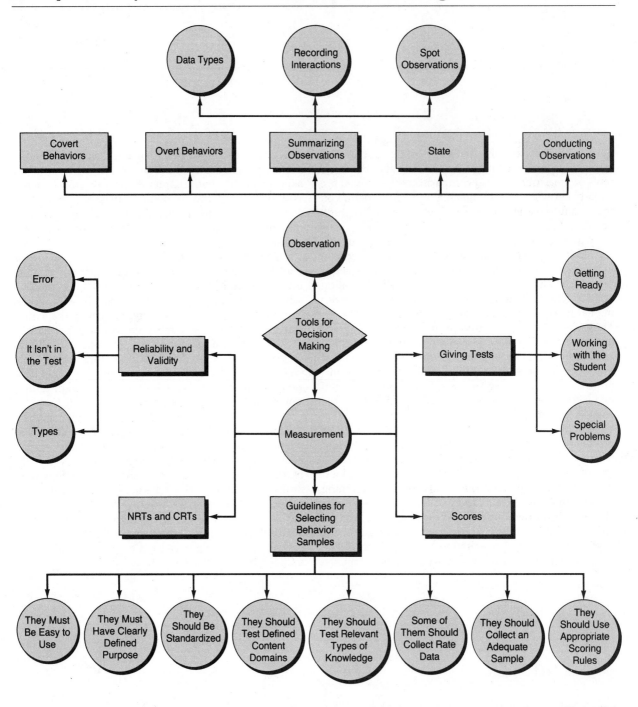

Knowledge in isolation is a sterile, lifeless thing. As a repertory of behavior, it is one of the tools we need to achieve competence, but it is not competence itself. All the knowledge of the world does not reveal the least bit of competence until we marry it to accomplishments. We may worship knowledge "for itself," just as we worship other valuable tools; but this is a totemism that is only superstitiously related to our survival, or to our achievement of excellence.

—T.F. Gilbert (1978)

Good judgment requires access to good data. While the first five chapters were oriented toward the purpose of, and rationale for, evaluation and instruction, Chapter 6 turns toward their more technical aspects. This shift is necessary as we approach the parts of this book that detail how to go about actually evaluating and teaching. Some of this material, particularly the discussion of statistics, has been placed in Appendix A to preserve the flow of the text. If you're not current on basic statistics, we encourage you to read Appendix A, as the tools associated with measurement and comparison are central to an understanding of informed decision making.

Because there is so much content in this chapter, we have broken it into three units: measurement, observation, and working with students.

Unit 1: Measurement

Recall that measurement has been defined as "the assignments of numerals to objects or events according to rules" (Campbell, 1940). As mentioned in the last chapter, any useful measurement procedure has four components: the definition of the quantity to be measured; a device for making that quantity observable; a mechanism (rule) for assigning different numerals to different magnitudes of the targeted quantity; and a mechanism (numerical or visual) for summarizing the whole activity (Thorndike & Hagan, 1969). Tests (NRTs and CRTs), observations, and portfolios all share these four essential components, though they may satisfy them in different ways.

In the case of CRTs, the first measurement com-

ponent, definition, is taken care of by the objective. A criterion-referenced probe is composed of two elements: a behaviorally stated objective and a procedure for measuring the student's behavior. This procedure may include the time, materials, and techniques needed to define, observe, and summarize the value of the objective. As we already know, a behavioral objective is composed of four components: content, behavior, conditions, and criteria for acceptable performance (CAP). All four of these components must be present for an objective to be useful in describing what is being taught and measured (refer to Exhibit 3.5).

The CRT objective is a behavioral statement. When the student carries out the specified behavior, the evaluator uses this action to infer that the student has knowledge of some particular fact, concept, or strategy. CRTs should be based on short-term instructional objectives. These objectives are either obtained directly from the school district's curriculum or from a task analysis of an objective found in the district curriculum. Obviously, if the results of the test are to be used to guide instruction, there should be no difference between the elements measured and those that will be taught. This assures alignment between testing and teaching. A typical CRT for computation is shown in Exhibit 6.1. The CRT objective and instructional objective are one and the same; we are interested in testing what we teach and teaching what we test. The more specific and behavioral the objective is, the more clearly it defines some quantity of the concept, strategy, or fact it represents, thereby making the conceptual, strategic, or factual knowledge more "observable."

Exhibit 6.1   An Addition Probe Sheet

						45	28	94	76	
Objective: Student will write answers to addition problems having one-digit addend to two digits with regrouping. CAP: 70 digits correct per minute.				Practice Items		+7	+6	+8	+4	
						52	34	102	80	

28 +4 32	53 +9 62	16 +8 24	94 +8 102	87 +7 94	63 +9 72	60 +8 68	32 +9 41	42 +2 44	51 +9 60	Digit Count
										1s (21)
31 +5 36	58 +2 60	13 +7 20	26 +4 30	74 +7 81	69 +9 78	83 +7 90	49 +0 49	22 +8 30	93 +3 96	Non- (41) instance
39 +9 48	62 +4 66	78 +3 81	43 +8 51	56 +5 61	24 +9 33	18 +8 26	73 +8 81	83 +5 88	92 +9 101	2s (62)
28 +1 29	49 +6 55	93 +6 99	98 +5 103	15 +7 22	85 +9 94	34 +6 40	45 +5 50	63 +9 72	71 +4 75	Non- (83) instance
31 +9 40	97 +2 99	19 +5 24	70 +9 79	48 +8 56	65 +8 73	95 +6 101	84 +8 92	36 +6 42	83 +8 91	3s (104)
1s	Non- instance	9s	Non- instance	8s	3s 5s	5s	6s	4s	Number added to itself	

Source: From K. W. Howell, S. H. Zucker, & M. K. Morehead (1982). *Mutilevel Academic Skills Inventory.* H & Z Publications, 6544 E. Meadowlark, Paradise Valley, AZ 85253. Reprinted with permission.

Scores

A *score* is a numerical summation of the student's overt behavior, covert behavior, state, or critical effects. That testing summarizes behavior is obviously true of pencil-and-paper tests, but the intricacy and expression of ice-skating routines are also reduced to scores by Olympic judges. Scores are useful because they help us compare people to other people, to task criteria, or to their own previous performance. Inherent in the use of scores is the idea that something can be segmented and then represented by a number value. In educational testing, however, scores seldom represent true units of knowledge because knowledge itself cannot truly be segmented.

Remember that measurement involves assigning numerals to objects and events according to rules. It is

important to know the rule of assignment because different rules applied to the same event can produce different scores. For example, a math test may have two addition problems, as in Exhibit 6.2. If a student gets both problems correct, he or she would usually get a score of 2, though in reality, problem b contains five times as much addition behavior as problem a. In Exhibit 6.2 the same problems and student behaviors have been scored according to a different measurement rule. In this case a point is given each time the student adds one number to another. This measurement (scoring) rule is more sensitive to what the teacher is teaching. The resulting score of 6 describes the kid's addition behavior better than the score of 2 in Exhibit 6.2. But when it comes to scores, all CRTs should use criterion-related measurement rules, while all NRTs must follow normative rules. The exact nature of these measure-

Exhibit 6.2   Two Scoring Procedures

Item Scoring	

(a)   3
       + 2
       5
	(b) 838
	       + 282
	       1120
	       Score = 2

Addition Scoring	

(a)   3
       + 2
       5
	(b) 838
	       + 282
	       1120
	       Score = 6

Exhibit 6.3   The Effect of Error

	True Score	Error Score		Truth in Obtained Score
Test A	.75	.25	=	.50–.75
Test B	.60	.40	=	.20–.60

ment rules, along with a discussion of how to treat them, is presented in Appendix A. You may want to read Appendix A now if you are unfamiliar with the following terms and concepts: score, distribution, mean, standard deviation, standard score, percentile, gain score, and grade equivalence score.

Reliability and Validity

Whenever we select a tool we are interested in its quality: If we buy a car we want to know about its security and economy; if we buy a radio we want to know about its reception and sound; if we buy a measure of student behavior we want to know about its reliability and validity. In measurement terms, reliability means consistency. Knowing that a test is reliable means knowing that it will work the same way every time it is given or on every student to whom it is given. In distinction, validity means goodness. A valid test can be used to benefit students.

Given these definitions, it should be clear that reliability is easier to document than validity. Proving reliability only requires the test writer to show consistency, not goodness. An automobile that never starts is reliable. It may not take you anywhere but it's consistent. Documenting validity, however, requires the test author to establish a relationship between the test and some other indicator of what the student needs. This "reality," of course, is difficult to pin down. Validating a test can be like interviewing people leaving an Arnold Schwarzenegger movie. Opinions vary.

It is possible for a measure to be reliable but not valid (using a bathroom scale to measure knowledge of reading); however, it is not possible to have validity without reliability. Therefore reliability is necessary but not sufficient for validity. Many educational and psychological tests are reliable because they produce consistent scores, but in some cases these scores are of limited use and therefore of limited validity.

Error

To understand reliability and validity you must understand what makes a measure unreliable, or invalid: error. Because it is not possible to measure knowledge directly, evaluators are forced to make inferences from behaviors they can measure. Reading comprehension, for example, cannot be seen or weighed. Its presence is inferred from behaviors such as defining words, solving problems, or recalling details. This need to infer introduces error into the measurement. Things that are easy to observe are easier to measure, because inferences about them are easier to make. However, because all measurement requires some level of inference, and contains some degree of imprecision, it is unreasonable to expect any measure to be 100% error-free.

Reliability and validity are desirable qualities that can be contrasted to the undesirable quality known as error. All obtained scores are composed of two components: truth and error. Exhibit 6.3 illustrates the relationship of truth and error in the form of two equations. For the equations to balance, any increase in error must be offset by a decrease in our vision of truth. Error is anything that affects a score **other** than the quality targeted for measurement. Error may arise from many sources, but labeling a thing as error does not mean it is bad or even unimportant. It only means it is not what the item in question was designed to measure. For example, suppose a teacher has designed a history test that includes the following item:

Circle the correct letter:

1. The first man on the moon was
   a. John Glenn
   b. Glenn Ford
   c. Neil Bush
   d. Neil Armstrong

This item would seem to be a valid measure of the student's recall of history. However, it also measures the student's skill at reading, following directions, and drawing circles. To the extent that a student does not perform these tasks, requiring their use during measurement becomes a potential source of error. Does a student need to know how to read to know who the first man on the moon was? No. Therefore, even though reading is an important skill, the dependence of this item on reading is a possible source of error.

If an evaluative instrument is sufficiently valid, it correctly describes reality well enough for us to accomplish what we need to do. As we have already indicated, validity may be hard to establish when opinions about "truth" vary. Validity is even harder to establish when truth itself varies. (What is really happening can change, just as our opinions about what is happening can change.) When reality fluctuates rapidly due to natural changes, or the intrusion of observers, validity is very hard to pin down. This is frequently the case when educational evaluators are attempting to get a look at a student's status on a short-term instructional objective. A student's skill and knowledge may vary quickly in the presence of good instruction. One of the biggest problems in educational and psychological measurement is recognizing when changes in a score signal the intrusion of error or an important alteration in the student's actual status.

It Isn't in the Test

Before going any further with this discussion of reliability and validity, an important point needs to be made. People talk about the reliability and validity of tests as if those things are characteristics of the instruments themselves. When you hear things like "the test is valid" or "the test-retest reliability is .89," you can almost imagine that at some critical point in the publishing process someone yells "OK, bring in the validity" and in response someone else (probably a reliable worker) comes running in from the next room with a bucket of validity and pours it into the ink. It isn't that way.

Both reliability and validity are determined by having students or experts interact with the tests. Reliability, for example, may be established by having a group of students take the same test twice to see if they get the same score both times (this type of reliability is known as *test-retest reliability*). Validity may be established by asking experts to examine the test to see if it is measuring important material. Therefore, our impressions of reliability and validity come from an analysis of how these students or experts behave. The important point (often forgotten) is that the resulting statements about reliability and validity say as much about those people as they say about the tests. The results of a validation study done on 8-year-old students may have little similarity to the results of a study using the same test on 18-year-old students. We must always remember that conclusions about reliability and validity, especially for NRTs, cannot be safely generalized (applied) to populations that differ along important variables from those populations used in the validation studies. Some of the variables we should be aware of are disability, age, sex, language status, socioeconomic status, geographic location, and especially differences in educational background that may have influenced prior knowledge of the task.

The terms *reliability* and *validity* refer to certain types of relationships. To summarize these relationships, statistical tools, called correlational procedures, have been developed. If you are unfamiliar with correlation, read about it in Appendix A.

Types of Reliability and Validity

Most discussions of reliability and validity describe various *types*. These include: content validity, concurrent validity, predictive validity, construct validity, alternative form reliability, test-retest reliability, and internal consistency. These various types are all related to the purpose for which the test is given. Everything in evaluation depends on a thorough understanding of purpose. In the absence of validity data (or even in their presence), a teacher/evaluator should sit down with the test and carefully analyze it in terms of the purpose for which it will be used. Some guidelines for judging a test's quality will be given in a minute. But ultimately you must look at the items and ask yourself "Does this test do what I need it to do?"

We aren't going to go into the various types of validity, but there is one type we will mention. This is *cash validity*.

Differences in educational background, race, disabilities, language status, age, and gender may affect prior knowledge of the task being tested, which in turn may influence the generalizability of test results.

Tests that sell well have high cash validity (Dick & Hagerty, 1971). It is possible to have cash validity in the absence of any other type of validity. Bestselling tests are *not* necessarily the most reliable or valid (Reschly, Genshaft & Binder, 1986). Therefore one cannot assume that because a test sells well, it is sufficiently valid for your purpose. It is just as likely that a bestselling test has been marketed well or happens to be in style. It is important, as consumers, for educators to critically examine the specifications of the tools they use. Cash validity, by the way, is the only kind that can exist in the absence of reliability.

Guidelines for Selecting/Writing Tests and Observations

The basic principle of curriculum-based assessment is "test what you teach and teach what you test." As explained in Chapter 3, this means that the curriculum

must be thoroughly defined. It also means that authentic behavior-sampling devices (tests and observations) must be constructed, or selected, to complement the various aspects of the curriculum and instruction. Devices sensitive to content, behavior, conditions, criteria, and strategies must be used. This can be accomplished by assuring that the following eight guidelines, summarized in Exhibit 6.4, are met.

Ease of Use

At the very least the test/observation should:

1. Be easy for the teacher to administer

2. Be easy for the student to take

3. Have consistent, clearly described directions and scoring procedures

4. Be easily transportable

5. Be easy to interpret

Exhibit 6.4   Guidelines for Selecting/Writing Behavior Samples

Guidelines	Explanation	Guidelines	Explanation
1. Tests must be easy to use.	Make sure there are directions and scoring procedures. Make the test easy to follow, transport, and interpret.	5. They should test relevant types of knowledge.	Decide if fact and concept evaluation is sufficient. If not, devise a way to make the strategy observable.
2. Tests must have clearly defined purposes.	Know the purpose and limitations of the instrument being used. Determine whether it is a placement or a treatment test and whether it is a norm- or criterion-referenced test.	6. Some tests should collect rate data.	Design tests which do not inhibit rate by assuring the random distribution of difficulty, adequate sample size, and opportunity to respond.
3. Tests should be standardized.	Decide on the appropriate type of data (accuracy or rate) for the content to be tested. Set standards by reviewing the literature, asking experts, or sampling a standardization population.	7. Tests should collect an adequate sample.	Decide how consolidated the content is. Write adequate items (usually 10) for each strategic element of highly consolidated content or for each instance of unconsolidated content.
4. They should test clearly defined content domains.	Be able to cross-reference items and procedures to content and behavioral domains.	8. Tests should use appropriate scoring rules.	Use measurement rules that assign points to the smallest educationally relevant unit.

6. Make the trouble of giving it and taking it worthwhile by providing reliable and valid results that can be used to make educationally relevant decisions

If a procedure is valid, but too cumbersome to be used, it won't be used—unless it is *really* needed. Concerns about ease of use must be balanced against the principle of maximum effort for maximum problems, meaning that it is just plain harder to evaluate the most problematic students. You have to be prepared to spend more time and effort with more complex instruments if you intend to help the kids that need the most help.

Clearly Defined Purposes

As stated in Chapter 1, the reason we evaluate is to make decisions. As a quick review:

1. Educational decisions can be roughly categorized as teaching decisions (about objectives, materials, lessons, and assignments) and eligibility decisions (about labeling, grading, retention, grouping, and placement).

2. Placement decision tools are usually normative; they sample global domains of achievement or ability.

3. Teaching decision tools are typically criterion-referenced and sample specific domains of achievement or ability.

4. It is a mistake to confuse placement and teaching or to try to use placement data for teaching decisions.

The best clue to a test/observation's purpose

should be the statement of purpose found in the manual, but these are often vague—and sometimes even self-contradictory. Besides, it is your purpose that needs to be specified most clearly. If you know what you are trying to do it is easier to figure what will help you get the job done.

Clearly Defined Content and Behavioral Domains

In Chapter 3 we stated that a task is more than a statement of content. We introduced response domains (identify, produce) and proficiency domains (accuracy, mastery, automaticity) to make the point that solving a multiple-choice untimed test item of 6×25 is very different from deciding how much six video-game tokens will cost before the kid in line behind you steps on your Achilles' tendon.

To relate the results of a test to the curriculum, you must have a test that allows the scores on items or subtests to be directly keyed to the curriculum. For example, if a student scores low on the addition subtest of a math inventory, it might be interesting to know that several of the items involved addition of fractions and decimals. Without that knowledge a teacher could erroneously conclude that the student wasn't skilled in addition when the real problem was fractions. The point isn't that fractions don't belong, but that their presence should be clearly acknowledged.

Teaching decision tests should link items, or groups of items, directly to objectives. Exhibit 6.5 is a table of specifications for multiplication. Below the table, the accuracy production objectives have been written out. Like most tables, this one is a grid defined by content, behavior, and proficiency dimensions. Exhibit 6.6 shows the key to a test composed of items from the accuracy column (the test is from the workbook that accompanies this text). The number in parentheses above each item can be found in the table of specifications (Exhibit 6.5) and the full objective found below the table. This clear cross-referencing of each item to an objective allows teachers to see immediately in which domains of content or behavior an error has occurred and to select an appropriate objective for the student.

Exhibit 6.1 presented a specific-level CRT designed to measure a student's rate at addition with regrouping. In this case the diagonal lines, which would not appear on the student's copy, are used to point out items that follow from the same subtask. When a test will be used repeatedly for collecting rate data, it is important to arrange items according to their difficulty so as not to distort the student's rate of production. The diagonal grouping technique shown in Exhibit 6.1 allowed an even distribution of items by difficulty, with item types (problems with 8s, addition of a number to itself, regrouping) identified to allow easy recognition of subtasks that are troubling the student (White & Haring, 1982). The diagonal pattern has the additional advantage of being hard to figure out, so that the test retains reliability over repeated administrations.

All objectives in a curriculum should be numbered and all test items that measure those objectives given the same numbers. In this way the curriculum-test match (alignment) is assured. It would be even better if applicable instructional materials could also be labeled with the same numbers. This is illustrated in Exhibit 6.7.

In Exhibit 6.7 objectives taken from the Addison-Wesley math program have been cross-referenced to test-item numbers, lessons in the Addison-Wesley series, and pages in the text *Direct Instruction Mathematics* (Silbert, Carnine & Stein, 1990). Using Exhibit 6.7 (which was prepared by Mark Jewell and teachers at Washington Elementary School in Mt. Vernon, Washington), a teacher can test his class and select lessons from the math series as they are needed for individual students. If those lessons don't seem sufficient, the teacher can then look in *Direct Instruction Mathematics* for additional help. Therefore, missing an item(s) would not only key recognition of an objective but selection of a teaching approach as well. Obviously such arrangements make a test easier to use.

Standardization Necessary

While all components are important to a well-written CRT, the criterion is so important that it is definitional. A criterion-referenced test uses a testing procedure to sample behavior and then contrasts, or references, that behavior to a performance criterion (CAP). Obviously, a criterion-referenced test is worthless if the criterion is arbitrarily established or completely missing. Unfortunately, this is the case for many published tests that claim to be criterion-referenced. Tests that are only keyed to content should be called *content-referenced*, not criterion-referenced. (The source of CAP and its validity should be supplied in the technical chapter

Exhibit 6.5   Table of Specifications for Multiplication

	Identify	Accuracy	Mastery	Automatic	MASI curriculum level	Local curriculum level
Placement test Mixed multiplication problems				9p		
Squaring Squares of numbers (0-12)	8i	8a	8m	9p	8	
Regrouping and no regrouping Two or more digits by two or more digits		7a		9p	4-5	
Two-digit numbers by a two-digit number		4a	4m	9p	4	
Place value Multidigit problems with zeros		6a		9p	4	
Multiply by 1, 10, 100, 1000		5a		9p	5	
Regrouping Two-digit number by a one-digit number		3a	3m	9p	4	
No regrouping Two-digit number by a one-digit number		2a	2m	9p	4	
Facts Multiplication facts (0-10)	1i	1a	1m	9p	4	

Accuracy Production Objectives

8a—Squaring	Produce squares of numbers (0–12). Accuracy CAP 100%.
7a—Regrouping and no regrouping	Multiply a number containing two or more digits by another number containing two or more digits with or without regrouping. Accuracy CAP 100%.
6a—Place value	Multiply multidigit problems with zeros as place holders. Accuracy CAP 100%.
5a—Place value	Multiply 1, 10, 100, 1000. Accuracy CAP 100%.
4a—Regrouping and no regrouping	Multiply a two-digit number by a two-digit number with or without regrouping. Accuracy CAP 100%
3a—Regrouping	Multiply a two-digit number by a one-digit number with regrouping. Accuracy CAP 100%.
2a—No regrouping	Multiply a two-digit number by a one-digit number without regrouping. Accuracy CAP 100%.
1a—Facts	Multiplication facts (0–10). Accuracy CAP 100%.

Source: From K. W. Howell, S. H. Zucker, & M. K. Morehead (1982). *Multilevel Academic Skills Inventory.* H & Z Publications, 6544 E. Meadowlark, Paradise Valley, AZ 85253. Reprinted with permission.

Exhibit 6.6   Test Key: Multiplication Accuracy Production

1. (1a)	2. (1a)	3. (1a)	4. (2a)	5. (2a)
2	9	8	64	24
$\times\ 6$	$\times\ 5$	$\times\ 3$	$\times\ 7$	$\times\ 3$
12	*45*	*24*	*448*	*72*

6. (2a)	7. (3a)	8. (4a)	9. (4a)	10. (5a)
91	18	22	85	$194 \times 10 =$ *1940*
$\times\ 1$	$\times\ 9$	$\times 86$	$\times 63$	
91	*162*	*1892*	*5355*	

11. (5a)	12. (5a)	13. (6a)	14. (6a)	15. (6a)
$3 \times 1000 =$ *3000*	$100 \times 74 =$ *7400*	102	40	7005
		$\times\ 20$	$\times 31$	$\times\ 26$
		4080	*1240*	*182130*

16. (7a)	17. (7a)	18. (7a)	19. (8a)	20. (8a)
87	215	5684	$5^2 =$ *25*	$12^2 =$ *144*
$\times 25$	$\times\ 48$	$\times\ 39$		
2175	*10320*	*221676*		

Source: From K. W. Howell, S. H. Zucker, & M. K. Morehead (1982). *Multilevel Academic Skills Inventory.* H & Z Publications, 6544 E. Meadowlark, Paradise Valley, AZ 85253. Reprinted with permission.

of the test manual. The criteria presented in this text were drawn from research findings and/or studies of successful students.)

CAP can be determined several ways. Most commonly it is determined by guessing (the worst way). For some reason, almost everyone guesses 80% accuracy. If asked to write any objective most teachers will write "Given _____, the student will _____, with 80% accuracy." We're not sure, but we think 80% became popular because Gronlund (1973) used it as an example in one of the first books on the subject. It is a nice enough number, but it cannot be equally relevant to all areas of curriculum: 80% add facts, 80% spell words, 80% adjust brakes, 80% land airplane? We once read an objective for a high-school math class that said "The student will write and read checks with 80% accuracy." That is not a reasonable criterion! Personal experience has taught us that anything less than 100% accuracy in checking can have a profound impact on one's standard of living.

Test of Relevant Types of Knowledge

Chapters 3 and 4 presented the idea that different kinds of knowledge might be applied to the same task. These kinds of knowledge were called factual, concep-

tual, and strategic. If these exist, and have instructional implications, then it follows that different evaluative procedures should be used to collect information about them.

Facts.   Facts are simple statements. To test them, we check to see if the student makes these statements correctly. For example, if $2 + 2 = 4$, then you show the student $2 + 2$ and ask "What does this equal?" It is easy to both test and teach factual knowledge. Unfortunately, it is so easy to do this that many tests ignore conceptual and strategic formats in favor of facts.

Concepts.   Conceptual knowledge is most conveniently evaluated by using categorization activities. These formats require the student to sort items into "example" and "nonexample" groupings (or "always," "sometimes," and "never") (see Chapter 4). Easy conceptual items ask the student to discriminate between obvious examples and nonexamples, while difficult items require fine discriminations. This is illustrated in Exhibit 6.8.

Sometimes it is convenient to ask students directly about the relevant ("always" or "never") attributes of a concept. For example: "What are the characteristics of a professional teacher?" (It may also be appropriate

Exhibit 6.7   Mount Vernon Project: Active Mathematics Teaching Cross References, Grade 4

Addison-Wesley objective number	Descriptor	Assessment probe item numbers	Direct-instruction reference
17.3	Add up to four-digit numbers with regrouping	1, 2	p. 150
17.4	Subtract up to four-digit numbers with regrouping	3, 4,	p. 173
23.3	Subtract whole numbers with or without regrouping; regroup and subtract across a middle zero	5, 6	p. 178
26.4	Name space figures and count faces, edges, and vertices	29, 30, 31, 32, 33, 34, 35	p. 482
15.1	Multiply by 10 and 100; multiply multiples of 10 and 100 by one-digit numbers	7, 8, 9, 10	
19.2	Multiply by one-digit factors	11, 12, 13, 14	p. 193

to ask them to role-play the concept; for example, "Act like a professional.") You can also ask the student to define the concept. The answers for characteristics and definitions should be the same, although asking for characteristics is more apt to avoid the possibility of a rote (factual) response. This is important, because it is often very hard to tell the difference between an answer reflecting understanding and a memorized conceptual statement.

Suppose, for example, that a student responded to the professional-teacher question by saying "A professional teacher works for the benefit of the student *and* the profession. But if the needs of the student are at odds with the needs of the profession, the teacher goes with the student." That would probably impress you as the answer of a student who has a conceptual understanding of the term *professional*. However, your view might change if it turned out the student had simply memorized that definition and couldn't think of a single example to illustrate it. Look again at Exhibit 6.1. Notice that while the objective of the test is "Add one-digit addend to two-digit with regrouping," some items (labeled "noninstances") do not require regrouping. This is to test the student's skill at deciding what to do, as well as his skill at doing it. Deciding what to do is one step in all problem-solving exercises, and it hinges on conceptual knowledge.

Have you ever seen a student borrow when it wasn't necessary, convert a vowel to the long or short sound without reason, or raise a hand for permission to speak when the situation was too informal? Those students knew what to do but they didn't know when to do it. The inclusion of noninstances (items of a different type than the type being tested) on tests allows the evaluator to know when students do not have the knowledge needed for deciding when to do something.

Exhibit 6.8   Items Testing: Conceptual Knowledge

Easy Item
Which of the following is most clearly a "type of knowledge"?   (a) red   (b) fish   (c) conceptual   (d) eating

Difficult Item
Which of the following is most clearly a "type of knowledge"?   (a) understanding   (b) relevant formats   (c) conceptual   (d) evaluation

Teachers who listen to a student explain the process used to arrive at an answer are obtaining information about the student's use of strategy.

Strategies. Tasks have various elements of content, behavior, conditions, and proficiency. These elements are considered when articulating curriculum or test objectives. Frequently, the objectives specify fairly narrow behavioral outcomes rather than the underlying processes students must follow to achieve these outcomes. For example, an objective may call for a student to write the correct answers to multiplication problems without really specifying the procedure he should follow to arrive at the answers, even though there may be several ways to do so. Obviously, if strategies are important things to teach, they are also important things to evaluate. There are three ways to do this: (1) ask, (2) use product analysis, and (3) use strategy-based items.

One very efficient way to find out how someone is doing something is to *ask*. This usually means encouraging the student to work through a task slowly while he verbalizes each step. Sometimes asking a student to teach you how to do the task will yield the same result. When compared with the elaborate alternatives about to be explained, this technique makes not only good evaluative sense, but good common sense as well (Elliott, 1986).

Incorrect procedures will eventually lead to incorrect products. Patterns in these incorrect products may reveal the flawed processes that produced them. This is known as error analysis or rule assessment (Siegler, 1983). The idea that *product analysis* can be used to determine what to teach is common in most basic skills

Exhibit 6.9   Test of Mathematics Strategies

5. There are 40 students. 25% of the students have blue eyes. How many have blue eyes?

(a) $\begin{array}{r} 40 \\ +\ .25 \\ \hline \end{array}$

(b) $.25\ )\overline{\ 40}$

(c) $\begin{array}{r} 40 \\ -\ .25 \\ \hline \end{array}$

(d) $\begin{array}{r} 40 \\ \times\ .25 \\ \hline \end{array}$

6. Colleen has 2 crayfish and Gary has 4 crayfish for the science project. On Tuesday, Albert brings them 3 more. On Wednesday, Robin brings them 5. How many crayfish do they have?

(a) $\begin{array}{r} 2 \\ +\ 4 \end{array} \quad \begin{array}{r} 6 \\ +\ 5 \end{array}$

(b) $\begin{array}{r} 4 \\ \times\ 2 \end{array} \quad \begin{array}{r} 8 \\ \times\ 5 \end{array} \quad 3\ )\overline{\ 40}$

(c) $\begin{array}{r} 4 \\ +\ 2 \end{array} \quad \begin{array}{r} 6 \\ -\ 5 \end{array}$

(d) $\begin{array}{r} 2 \\ +\ 4 \end{array} \quad \begin{array}{r} 6 \\ +\ 3 \end{array} \quad \begin{array}{r} 9 \\ +\ 5 \end{array}$

7. There are 40 desks in the fourth-grade classroom. 2 desks are loaned to the third-grade classroom, 5 desks are loaned to the sixth-grade classroom. How many desks are left in the fourth-grade classroom?

(a) $\begin{array}{r} 40 \\ -\ 2 \end{array} \quad \begin{array}{r} 38 \\ -\ 5 \end{array}$

(b) $\begin{array}{r} 40 \\ +\ 2 \end{array} \quad \begin{array}{r} 42 \\ +\ 5 \end{array}$

(c) $\begin{array}{r} 40 \\ -\ 4 \end{array} \quad \begin{array}{r} 36 \\ -\ 2 \end{array} \quad \begin{array}{r} 34 \\ -\ 3 \end{array} \quad \begin{array}{r} 29 \\ -\ 5 \end{array} \quad \begin{array}{r} 24 \\ -\ 6 \end{array}$

(d) $\begin{array}{r} 40 \\ -\ 4 \end{array} \quad \begin{array}{r} 36 \\ -\ 3 \end{array} \quad \begin{array}{r} 33 \\ -\ 6 \end{array}$

8. There are 4 packages of pencils. Each package contains 5 pencils. There are 8 students, and three are boys. The pencils are to be divided equally among the girls. How many pencils will each girl get?

(a) $\begin{array}{r} 4 \\ \times\ 5 \end{array} \quad \begin{array}{r} 8 \\ \times\ 3 \end{array} \quad 20\ )\overline{\ 24}$

(b) $\begin{array}{r} 4 \\ \times\ 5 \end{array} \quad \begin{array}{r} 8 \\ -\ 3 \end{array} \quad 5\ )\overline{\ 20}$

(c) $\begin{array}{r} 5 \\ -\ 4 \end{array} \quad \begin{array}{r} 8 \\ +\ 3 \end{array} \quad 1\ )\overline{\ 11}$

(d) $\begin{array}{r} 5 \\ \times\ 4 \end{array} \quad 8\ )\overline{\ 20}$

9. There are 30 pairs of scissors in the box. 10 are broken. Fifteen new pairs are given to the class. There are 5 art tables in the room. How many pairs of scissors that are not broken will each table get?

(a) $\begin{array}{r} 15 \\ -\ 10 \end{array} \quad \begin{array}{r} 30 \\ +\ 15 \end{array} \quad \begin{array}{r} 5 \\ +\ 45 \end{array} \quad 5\ )\overline{\ 50}$

(b) $\begin{array}{r} 30 \\ +\ 10 \end{array} \quad 5\ )\overline{\ 40}$

(c) $\begin{array}{r} 30 \\ -\ 10 \end{array} \quad \begin{array}{r} 20 \\ +\ 15 \end{array} \quad \begin{array}{r} 35 \\ \times\ 5 \end{array}$

(d) $\begin{array}{r} 30 \\ -\ 10 \end{array} \quad \begin{array}{r} 20 \\ +\ 15 \end{array} \quad 5\ )\overline{\ 35}$

10. 2% of the students were absent on Tuesday. 20% of those present brought a sack lunch and 75% of those present bought a hot lunch. The rest of the students fixed a lunch in their classroom. What percent of the students in school fixed a lunch in their classroom?

(a) $\begin{array}{r} 20\% \\ +\ 75\% \end{array} \quad \begin{array}{r} 100\% \\ -\ 95\% \end{array}$

(b) $\begin{array}{r} 2\% \\ 20\% \\ +\ 75\% \end{array} \quad \begin{array}{r} 100\% \\ -\ 97\% \end{array}$

(c) $\begin{array}{r} .20 \\ \times\ .02 \end{array} \quad \begin{array}{r} .20 \\ \times\ .75 \end{array} \quad .040\ )\overline{\ .1500}$

(d) $\begin{array}{r} 75\% \\ \times\ 20\% \end{array} \quad \begin{array}{r} 100\% \\ -\ 15\% \end{array}$

Source: From K. W. Howell, S. H. Zucker, & M. K. Morehead (1982). *Multilevel Academic Skills Inventory.* H & Z Publications, 6544 E. Meadowlark, Paradise Valley, AZ 85253. Reprinted with permission.

including reading, where it is sometimes called miscue analysis. (The diagonal item pattern illustrated in Exhibit 6.1 is one device a teacher might use to recognize error patterns.)

One disadvantage of product analysis is that some products won't occur if you don't happen to promote them. A student who has trouble spelling words with double consonants won't ever display that problem if you don't put double-consonant words on the spelling test. Similarly, a student who doesn't use past tense could speak correctly throughout an entire conversation conducted in the present tense.

Test items can be strategy-based-designed to sample the student's use of the process as well as the construction of a product. One procedure for testing strategy use is to present items that require the student to show how he would work the task. Several of these items are shown in Exhibit 6.9. Notice that these

Exhibit 6.10   Procedures for Different Types of Knowledge

Questions to Ask	Typical Methods for Finding the Answers
About Facts:	
1. Is the student accurate?	Administer an untimed test to see if the student can identify and/or produce the answer.
2. Is the student accurate and fast?	Administer a rate formatted test requiring fluent production of answers.
3. Is the student automatic?	Check to see if accuracy and fluency are maintained across higher levels of content and/or application.
About Concepts:	
1. Can the student recognize the concept?	Ask the student to sort instances and non-instances of the concept.
2. Can the student talk about the concept?	Check for adequate use of relevant vocabulary.
3. Can the student define the concept?	Ask.
4. Does the student apply conceptual knowledge?	Watch for misapplication of tools and/or vocabulary across topics, applications, and settings.
About Strategies:	
1. Does the student exhibit patterns of errors?	Give a test which provides adequate opportunities for relevant errors to occur.
2. Can the student explain the rule or procedure?	Ask.
3. Is the student ready to learn the strategy?	Check status of all essential subskills. If these subskills are adequate assume the strategy is missing.

items sample the student's knowledge of the process for finding answers and do not even ask the student for the answers. Exhibit 6.10 summarizes evaluation procedures commonly employed for examining a student's factual, conceptual, and/or strategic knowledge.

Collection of Rate Data

Time is an important concept for educators. How much time it takes to learn something is often used to determine how difficult it is to learn, just as how long something is remembered, or how quickly it can be completed, indicates how well it has been learned.

Rate is performance divided by time. It is how quickly we use the strategies that combine the subtasks to assemble appropriate behaviors. Rate has functional implications. If two firefighters both put on their uniforms with 100% accuracy, but one does

it in 1 minute and the other does it in 10 minutes, which one do you want working in your neighborhood? Rate also seems related to generalization, in that it is hard to assemble tasks into a more complex response if you are slow at all the pieces. If we encouraged our students to disregard any of the other dimensions, like height or width, they would leave school and walk into walls. Similarly, students who are not prepared to work within certain time constraints will not be able to function in the real world. Slower workers are actually less proficient workers, because rate is a proficiency dimension, just like accuracy.

But most important, rate is related to automaticity (see Chapter 2, p. 26). Everything we do without awareness we are doing automatically. Automaticity is the level of task performance above which doing the task does not require the use of working (short-term)

Exhibit 6.11   A Rate Probe

> Objective: Student will write answers to subtraction problems having one digit from two
> digits with borrowing. CAP: 40 problems per minute
>
> Noninstance
>
> | 94 | 61 | 79 | 53 | 27 | 60 |
> | − 8 | − 7 | − 5 | − 9 | − 8 | − 8 |
>
> | 71 | 47 | 94 | 28 | 35 | 53 |
> | − 7 | − 9 | − 6 | − 4 | − 8 | − 4 |
>
> | 63 | 84 | 42 | 51 | 16 | 75 |
> | − 3 | − 7 | − 6 | − 5 | − 3 | − 7 |
>
> | 91 | 52 | 65 | 82 | 94 | 42 |
> | − 8 | − 2 | − 7 | − 9 | − 9 | − 1 |
>
> Non-instance
>
> | 49 | 23 | 85 | 61 | 55 | 25 |
> | − 8 | − 7 | − 5 | − 9 | − 6 | − 9 |
>
> | 32 | 27 | 42 | 94 | 83 | 56 |
> | − 4 | − 6 | − 5 | − 4 | − 7 | − 8 |
>
> *Source:* From K. W. Howell, S. H. Zucker, & M. K. Morehead (1982). *Multilevel Academic Skills Inventory.*
> H & Z Publications, 6544 E. Meadowlark, Paradise Valley, AZ 85253. Reprinted with permission.

memory. Without automaticity, our thoughts would be so crowded with minutia that our thinking would become paralyzed.

A timed test is not a rate test. Timing is typically added to tests so that administration will be uniform; as a result, reliability will be inflated. But the data derived from timed tests are still accuracy data. A rate test yields data by timing the student's response to a single item or a series of related items. The count (number of items completed) is then divided by the time (traditionally in minutes) to obtain the rate. If one item is finished in 15 seconds, then the rate is 1/0.25 = 4 per minute. If 80 items are completed in 5 minutes, the rate is 80/5 = 16 per minute.

Rate could be used to develop norms for classification purposes (see Chapter 9) but seldom is. More often rate is used to illustrate proficiency on a single skill. As a result, it is used almost exclusively for CRTs.

If we still haven't convinced you that rate is

important, try to remember the last time everyone else in class finished a test while you were only halfway through. And if that doesn't do it, consider this story. A parent came in to a special education classroom we know of and complained "Why are you always testing my child with stop watches and telling him to work faster?" The teacher, Linda Levett, looked at the parent a moment and replied "Do you remember why your child is in this class? He's a slow learner. The cure for slow is fast."

Because so few tests are designed for collecting rate data or for use in continuous monitoring (which requires giving the same test over and over again), some of us have never seen a rate-formatted test. However, rate data and continual monitoring are very important when curriculum-based evaluation is employed. Exhibit 6.11 shows another rate-formatted CRT and its objective. Notice that there is adequate space to write the answers and that, while the items are organized diagonally by multipliers, they are randomized by difficulty.

Collection of an Adequate Sample

To collect an adequate sample, a test must accommodate sufficient items, the need for rate data, demands for repeated use, and various item formats.

Number of Items.   Many tests have a student work only one or two items per objective or domain. This leaves the evaluator with too limited a sample of the student's behavior to allow for interpretation. Tests with only a few items may also be memorized after several sessions. Once, one of us was giving a popular short-form achievement test to some students in a correctional institution. When he paused too long between spelling words, one of the kids in the group supplied the next word—and the exact sample sentence in the manual—from memory!

In general, fewer items are needed when the domain being sampled is fairly consolidated and transfer is expected between items. Remember that a curriculum domain is said to be consolidated if it is tied together by a common set of strategies (or rules) that can be successfully applied to most items within the domain. If a large number of examples can be dealt with reliably by a smaller number of strategic steps, the domain is consolidated. Phonics is a good example of a consolidated domain. A surprisingly large number of phonetically regular words can be written and decoded by using a small (about 40) set of fairly reliable phonetic units. This means that, when a student decodes a few regular words, the evaluator can assume that he can decode the many others not found on the test.

Rate Revisited.   When tests are used to collect rate data, students are often told to skip items they do not know so that their rate of response will not become distorted. For example, suppose a student was reading a selection in which the one word he did not know occurred 10 words into the passage. The student might read the passage at a rate of 100 wpm up to the tenth word and then stare at it for the rest of the allowed time. His rate would then seem to be 10 words per minute rather than the more representative 100 wpm. To avoid this problem, an adequate number of items is provided to allow skipping (usually 50% more than the criterion).

Repeated Measures.   If a test is to be used for repeated administration, enough items must be provided to avoid ceiling effects and prevent rote memorization of the test. Ceiling effects occur when there aren't enough items to allow improvement. If a test has only one item per objective and a student gets it right the first time he takes the test, he can't do any better no matter how much more is learned about the objective (unless the time required to do the item is recorded; in that case, decreases in time can be seen as improvement).

Item Format.   Occasionally, there is a disparity between the behavior required on a test and the behavior expected of the child in the classroom. We can best describe this with a hypothetical case. Billy was a third-grader who, after taking a norm-referenced achievement test, scored at the 3.6 level in spelling. At first glance, there was nothing unusual about this, except that Billy had failed every spelling test given by the teacher that year. Every Friday he brought home an F on his spelling paper. When his parents heard about his achievement scores, they were dumbfounded at first, and then became angry. They complained to the principal that Billy's teacher wasn't motivating him in school and that was why he wasn't "working up to his potential." His teacher's confusion and frustration were evidenced by remarks that Billy was both lazy (in class) and lucky (on the test).

Who was right? Billy's parents, or his teacher? In this case, neither. Billy's teacher was doing everything he could to motivate Billy in school. So it wasn't his fault. But neither was it Billy's. In fact, Billy should have gotten a medal for persevering in the face of failure (see Chapter 17). However, his teacher was right about his being lucky on the test. You see, the behavior expected of Billy on the spelling section of the achievement test was different from the behavior expected of him on his Friday quizzes. As part of the achievement test, Billy was given a page with rows of words on it. In each row were four words, one of which was the correct spelling of a word dictated to him. The teacher said "In the first row, underline the correct spelling of the word *enough*." Billy looked at each of the four words in the row and underlined one of them. The same procedure was used for the other items on the page. Sometimes Billy actually recognized the correct word and sometimes he just guessed. Since there was always a 25% chance of guessing the correct answer on this test, it was conceivable that Billy's high score in spelling was as much a result of his guessing skill as his spelling skill.

In this case the test format was in marked contrast to the format of the Friday quiz, when his teacher dictated a word and Billy had to write it from memory. Essentially, the teacher was testing spelling while the achievement test was testing proofreading. These are two different tasks. Needless to say, this disparity caused a great deal of confusion, not to mention friction, between school and home, with the child caught in the middle. The confusion was the result of poor curriculum-test alignment induced by the inadequate sample test format.

Appropriate Scoring Rules

Measurement is a crucial part of evaluation. As previously explained, measurement is the assignment of numerals to objects or events according to rules. These measurement rules guide our assignment of numerical values to student behaviors.

If the purpose of the evaluation is to guide instruction and facilitate learning, the results of the evaluation must be sensitive to learning. This means measurement rules must be established that will lead to the best scores. Remember that our purpose for evaluating is to affect educational decision making; therefore the best scores are those that reflect the curriculum and the student's learning of it: These are the things about which our decisions are made. Because learning is operationally defined as behavior change, measurement rules that result in scores sensitive to changes in behavior are the best rules to use. This sensitivity is usually obtained by assigning a number to the smallest educationally meaningful unit of behavior on the test. (However, this does *not* mean that instruction needs to target this small and isolated unit. Remember most things are best taught in a larger context.)

Unit 2: Observation

Some of the limitations of observation were discussed in Chapter 5. The biggest ones are: (a) Observations aren't any good for behaviors that don't occur spontaneously (spontaneous in this case meaning elicited by the kid or environment rather than the teacher); (b) observations of the kid are meaningless without including observations of the environmental context in which behaviors occur (test items and interview questions provide the context for tests, but observing that a student is "out of seat" without also noting if the behavior occurred during history class or swimming is nonsense); (c) limitation b is compounded by the reality that geographic environments often have less to do with student behavior than the student's personal psychological environment (see Chapter 16) (that is, we don't behave according to what is going on around us, but rather according to what we *think* is going on); and, finally, (d) when we observe things we change them. These considerations, along with the need to collect adequate samples of time and behavior, dictate the structure of a good observation.

The first thing to do when planning an observation is the first thing to do in any educational assessment activity: Define what will be measured by finding or writing an objective. This need for a clearly defined definiton of the thing being observed is linked to the need to count and describe. To count anything you must be able to recognize its beginning and end (White & Haring, 1982). For example, the behavior "writes digit" begins when the student puts pencil to paper and ends when the student stops writing the digit required. The status, or state, of "in seat" begins when the kid's rear hits the seat of the chair and ends when it leaves (most teachers don't think standing on the chair qualifies as "in seat"). These starting and stopping points must be recognizable.

Things to Observe

When conducting observations we may collect data from one of four categories: overt behavior, covert behavior, state, and/or critical effect. These four simply represent different approximations of our main focus, which is always the student's skill or knowledge. In some cases one of these categories may be more convenient to use, or may seem more clearly aligned with the essential nature of the knowledge we are attempting to summarize.

Overt Behaviors

These are the things we think of when we think of behaviors. Overt behaviors involve muscular movement. Overt behaviors are things like "say name" or "throw ball." They are best measured through frequency counts to determine their rate of occurrence within a time interval.

Recognition of overt behavior is made easier by applying the concept of a "movement cycle" (White, 1986). The criteria commonly used to define a movement cycle are:

1. The dead man test. Can a dead man do it? It isn't a movement cycle if the answer is yes.
2. Repeatability. Can you tell when the behavior starts and stops? You need to in order to count.

Here are some examples.

"Student will not interrupt."
1. Can a dead man do it? Yes. They seldom bother anyone.
2. Is it repeatable? Not clearly.
Conclusion: It's not a movement cycle as it lacks movement and fails the dead man test.

"Student out of seat."
1. Can a dead man be out of seat? Yes.
2. Is it repeatable? Yes.
Conclusion: It's not a movement cycle because it has no movement.

"Leaves seat."
1. Can a dead man do it? No.
2. Is it repeatable? Yes. (It ends when the student's rear no longer touches the seat.)
Conclusion: It is a movement cycle.

"Raises hand."
1. Can a dead man do it? No.
2. Is it repeatable? Yes.
Conclusion: It is a movement cycle.

(The "stranger" and "so-what" tests discussed in Chapter 3 should be applied to anything one counts.)

Covert Behaviors

Covert behaviors are thoughts and feelings. They are called covert because they can't be directly observed. In traditional behavioral or operant circles, concepts such as the movement cycle are considered to be absolute. This means that if it doesn't move, it can't be counted. The advantage of this approach is that it makes our observations reliable by excluding data on

things that can't be "seen." However, what people see is determined totally by what they are able to see. For example, sometimes teachers get concerned if students move their lips when they read, so they work to have them stop these movements. Actually, all people move their lips when they read; electrical sensing devices have found minute contractions of the throat and facial muscles during reading. These contractions can be "seen" by the electrical sensors but not by the human eye. Our point is that what one can see is influenced by our observational equipment. While some teachers may think they "stopped lip movement," all they really have done is reduce it to a level where detection with the human eye is impossible. This may not represent a significant change.

In Chapter 16, which concerns the evaluation of social behavior, we will discuss the idea of covert pinpoints. Covert pinpoints cannot be "seen" by observers but can be counted by the students themselves. These pinpoints include such things as having a thought about food, experiencing a concern about failure, or having a feeling of happiness. These covert responses can be self-recorded by students because they (and only they) are in a position to "see" and count them. When collecting such behavior, it is helpful to explain both the dead man test and the repeatability test to the student (the stranger test is not applicable to covert behaviors). Obviously, counting covert behaviors raises a variety of measurement and ethical issues. Some of these are covered in Chapter 16; they deserve your attention.

State

The state of a person is not a behavior, but his condition or location. Teachers often act as if a student's state were a behavior, but it is important not to confuse the two. A person's state is the condition (physical or psychological) in which the person resides. "In seat" is a declaration of student state like "in San Francisco" or "in a good mood." "Getting in seat," "going to beach," or "going to meet a friend" are behaviors. We may target overt state (in seat, paying attention, asleep, on time for class) or covert state (happy, angry, depressed, compliant) for observation.

To take data on someone's state, the best procedure is to use duration (length of time) or percentage data. To collect duration data, time how long the person is in the targeted state. When using state, it is a good idea to develop a clear definition of the state and

**Exhibit 6.12
Interval-
sampling
formats.**

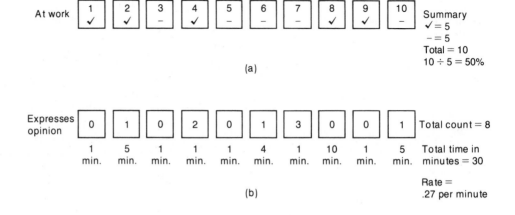

Summarizing Observations

Data Types

If you are interested in changing a student's behavior, you will want to assess the student's fluency by collecting rate data and counting how many times he engages in the covert or overt target during some time interval (50 times in 10 minutes is a rate of 5 per minute). If you are interested in changing or maintaining a student's state, you will want to collect duration data by timing how long he remains in the condition about which you are concerned. If you are interested in the critical effect of knowledge or skill, you will probably count the resulting products, or note the degree of impact the knowledge seems to have had on the student (for example, how highly you will rate the student's work).

All types of data can be collected continuously or at certain intervals. If a behavior is very disruptive and overt ("throws chair through window"), you might as well count it continuously because you're going to know about it every time it happens anyway. If it is more subtle (makes eye contact with peer), you will want to set aside a certain time (or times) to watch for it so you don't have to try to observe the kid's eyes all day. This is called interval sampling. Two interval-sampling forms are shown in Exhibit 6.12. In the first case, the "at work" state of the student is observed at certain times; for example, when the signal from a kitchen timer goes off. If the student is in the target state, the teacher records a check; if not, a dash. In this example, no time is spent waiting for the behavior to occur. A check is made only if the student is in the

to share that definition with the student. For example, "at work" might always mean "no talk, work materials out, appearance of attention to materials."

It is also possible to check in on the student at various intervals and to note if the student is in the targeted state. This information can be converted to percentage data by noting the proportion of intervals the student is in the targeted state.

Critical Effect

The critical effect is the product left after a behavior has occurred. For example, "problems completed" is the critical effect of the overt behavior "writes answers." Once we heard about a teacher who, when he left his classroom, would put tape over the outside edge of the door. If the tape was broken when he returned, he knew that someone had left their seat to peek down the hall. The broken tape was the critical effect of the state "out of seat."

Critical effect data are usually summarized as frequency counts. However, there are times when the essence of the information you are attempting to summarize can be captured more precisely through the use of rating scales. This is particularly true when you are concerned about either the intensity or quality of the representation (for example, rating a student's written expression) (see Chapter 13).

Remember that any, or all, of the observation categories can be used to indicate a student's knowledge. However, overt behaviors deserve at least an initial preference, as they are easier to count, and changes in them lead to changes in state as well as production of critical effects.

*Exhibit 6.13
Recording
interactions.*

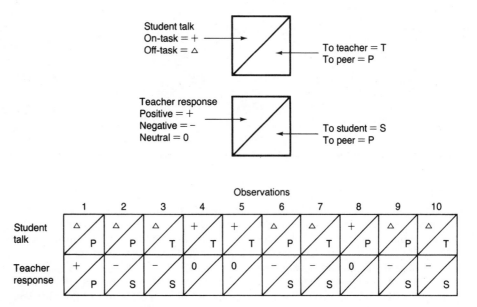

Student talk
On-task = +
Off-task = △
To teacher = T
To peer = P

Teacher response
Positive = +
Negative = −
Neutral = 0
To student = S
To peer = P

target state at the instant the timer signals the teacher to look up. In other cases the check would be made if the student maintained the state throughout the interval. Both cases would be examples of interval sampling, though the interval shown in Exhibit 6.12a is only an instant in length. This procedure is often called time sampling (Wolery, Bailey & Sugai, 1989).

"Expresses opinion" (Exhibit 6.12b) is counted every time it occurs during the time the evaluator watches for it. In this example, the evaluator has watched for a total of 30 minutes over ten separate intervals. During the 30 minutes of actual observation the behavior occurred eight times, for a rate of .26 (8/30) times per minute. The conversion to rate per minute puts the score on a common scale, so that the teacher can compare rates across days even if a different amount of observation time was used. Converting the "at-work" data into a percentage (occurrence/opportunity) accomplishes the same thing. Of course, as is the nature of sampling, the percentage listed is the percentage of intervals—not necessarily the actual percentage of time the student works.

Recording Interactions

Exhibit 6.13 shows a recording device in which the student's behavior is compared to the teacher's response. Every time the student says something, it is

coded as + (on task), − (off task), and T (to teacher) or P (to peer). The teacher's responses are coded as + (positive), − (negative), or 0 (ignore). Positive and negative responses are coded as S (to student) or P (to peer). The data in Exhibit 6.13 show a pattern in which off-task student talk is preceded and followed by negative teacher comments to the student. Additionally, on-task student talk is always ignored (observations 4, 5, and 8). The implications of these data for teaching (encourage the teacher to attend positively to on-task student talk), while clear, would be completely missing if the only data available were on the student.

Spot Observations

Spot observation (Rogoff, 1978) is similar to devices used in functional analysis (O'Neil, Horner, Albin, Storey & Sprague, 1989) and a sort of time-sampling procedure. With it the observer takes a mental snapshot of a moment in the classroom and later follows up on the snapshot with questions. The spot observation begins as the observer briefly notes an event, being sure to include the surrounding circumstances and people. He then turns away and writes down everything he can think of to explain what was seen. Sometimes this is done by "framing" the moment with a brief description of its antecedents and consequences.

Exhibit 6.14   A Snapshot

Antecedents	Events	Consequences
History lesson—large group—on Civil War. Many other students confused; Scott asking lots of advanced questions. Teacher responding to all questions.	Scott asks the teacher a question and the other students make fun of him.	Teacher ignores the reaction of the other students and answers Scott's question.

Exhibit 6.14 shows a single example, or frame. As you can see, it is hard to reach many conclusions from one frame, but if several are used a better image of interaction may become clear. This procedure is wordier than the recording systems usually recommended in educational texts, but it allows the observer to capture a moment so thoroughly that he can later ask the participants (teacher, student, peers) questions about it. This allows the evaluator to compare what appeared to be going on with what the participants thought was going on. The differences in perceptions of the event (such as may be illuminated by asking "Why did Scott ask questions?") can provide useful evaluative information (see Chapter 16). Such descriptive data will often be more important than "counts" obtained by scoring.

Conducting Observations

Nothing is more obvious than an unfamiliar adult lurking around the back of a classroom trying to observe a kid. If the student targeted for observation isn't one of your students, you may want to prepare the least bothersome observation system you can and then try to get the current teacher to use it. If that doesn't work, walk boldly into the room and get to know everyone (not just the target kid). It may be best to become involved before you start collecting data. This is better than trying to be sneaky.

One of the authors once asked a teacher what the target kid was wearing so he'd be able to spot her from a distance at recess. He then went out the back way and walked around the building to make a casual approach from the parking lot. As soon as he leaned against the flagpole and started making notes, one of the other students yelled "Hey, Bridget! Someone's watching you!" Everybody on the playground froze as

Bridget (an 8-year-old) walked timidly over to the evaluator and asked "Why are you watching me?" "It's OK," he told her, "I'm paid to do it." Satisfied with that, she shrugged and went back to "punching others" as if he weren't even there.

One-way mirrors have their pluses and minuses, depending on which side you are on. Videotaping is excellent after the kids have a day or so to get used to it. You do have to leave the TV monitor turned off. One favorite technique for unobtrusive counting is to fill one pocket with coins and then to shift a coin to an empty pocket every time the target behavior occurs. At the end of the day you just count the coins shifted and mark the number in your records. (Of course, with some behaviors, some kids, and some teacher salaries, this technique will be impractical!) As a rule, it is better to observe for several short periods spread over the day than for one long period.

Observation tends to be used for language and social behaviors, both of which are highly sensitive to changes in context. To capture the context, use interactive observation or spot observation. Both involve collecting data on others and therefore both raise some ethical concerns. Primary among these is the idea of consent. If an evaluator must obtain parental permission to observe a student, we can assume you should obtain teacher permission to observe a teacher.

To capture the context in which a behavior occurs, it is sometimes necessary to take data on the student's behavior and the behavior of other important people around him. This is done to try to find things that prompt the targeted behavior or reactions that support it. The most important people will be the teacher, close friends, and arch-enemies. In this case, if you are an outside evaluator, you can quickly find yourself on shaky ground. Some teachers who refer a student for evaluation won't take kindly to it if they think you're evaluating them. Unfortunately, if you explain what you are doing and why, they may change their teaching behavior when you're in the room. This is a real problem, as nothing will imperil your position as quickly as the suspicion that you are an undercover agent for the administration.

The real secret to conducting a classroom observation is to *not* be an outsider. If you work in a context of collaboration and teamwork this won't be a problem (Jenkins & Leicester, 1992). However, it is our experience that the tone of partnership needed to support collaboration isn't developed quickly and can only be established through active administrative support. Therefore, if you already have a collaborative environment—use it. If you don't, you must still proceed in your attempts to help the student. We are reluctant to advise you to take data secretly on teachers, as teachers have the same rights to informed consent that kids have. But consider this. Because behavior is interactive, if data are collected on the student only, the interaction is ignored and the essence of behavior avoided.

When testing academics, the other components of the learning interaction may be test items, books, and worksheets. Obviously these items can be examined closely without a great deal of ethical concern. In the case of language and social behavior, the interactive context includes teachers and peers (see Chapters 16 and 17). To ignore these components of the context during data collection is to ignore the heart of the interaction. To change the targeted student's behavior, modifications will have to be employed that affect both the teacher and peers. Therefore, a teacher who refers a student for help, particularly in social or language areas, is referring the whole room . . . including himself (Ysseldyke & Christenson, 1987). These are important things to talk over with teachers, and the talking should be done *before* anyone is evaluated.

Status Sheets

In a minute we will change focus from this preoccupation with the properties of tests/observations to the processes of using them. But first we need to introduce a final tool, the status sheet. Status sheets are used to summarize what is currently known about the student in order to *avoid* testing and observation. They are composed of a list of curriculum-related assumed causes for the student's failure and a set of questions. A status sheet is shown in Exhibit 6.15.

The status sheet isn't a test and it isn't really an observation procedure. It is a devise for aligning what is currently known about the student with the steps of the total evaluation process. We'll explain this by using a social behavior example. (You'll be asked to return to this example when you get to Chapter 16.)

Jay was a 7-year-old repeating the first grade. According to his teacher, he was "always hurting somebody." She tried a number of interventions, including removing Jay from the classroom (to stand in the hall or sit in the office) and making phone calls to Jay's parents. The calls home were stopped when Jay came to school with a bruised face the next day. She suspected that these bruises were inflicted by one of Jay's parents and that such abuse was not unusual. (Such suspicions should always be reported to authorities.)

Jay's physically aggressive behavior had been a problem since he first entered school. He was constantly being separated from the other children to keep him from hitting, biting, pushing, or squeezing them. His academic performance suffered as a consequence of the behavior, which continued into his second year in first grade. Jay was eventually referred for testing to determine his eligibility for a self-contained class of behavior-disordered (BD) students (see Chapter 9). He met the criteria and was immediately placed in the BD program. This solved the general education classroom teacher's problem, but it didn't help Jay. It also created a problem for the BD teacher, because Jay's hitting didn't stop in the new surroundings. So the BD teacher attempted to solve Jay's problem.

The solution to Jay's difficulty did not reside in the discovery of a particular test or observation procedure. There was enough behavioral data available from Jay's three years in school to simplify any assessment. The maladaptive pinpoint ("hits peers") was easy to select and count, and everyone (especially the peers) agreed that it passed the so-what test. Jay's new teacher decided that the target pinpoint should be "interact positively with his peers." To satisfy the stranger test, this was defined as (a) the absence of unprovoked physical acts inflicting pain, and (b) the presence of socially acceptable physical interactions, for example, touching without inflicting pain. These target pinpoints were then task-analyzed by Jay's new teacher. She listed all of the prerequisites on a status sheet, as seen in Exhibit 6.15.

Jay's new teacher, his parents, and his former

Exhibit 6.15   A Status Sheet

Status Sheet

Behaver: _Jay_   Manager: _Rice_
Diagnostician: _Kaplan_   Date: _November 1992_
Target Behavior: _Jay will interact positively with peers (no unprovoked hitting or other acts of physically aggressive behavior; instead, he will touch, pat, hold peer without inflicting pain)._

Prerequisites of Target Behavior	Available Evidence	Status: Yes = No need to test No = List as objective Unsure = Need to test
1. Knows how to engage in positive interactions with peers (knows that you are supposed to touch peers without hurting them).	1. This is really the target behavior; everything he does indicates he doesn't know this. And considering suspected corporal punishment at home plus considerable amount of time separated from appropriately behaving peers, it's likely Jay may not have learned how to interact positively with peers.	No
2. Knows difference between positive and negative interactions (able to recognize when he is hurting peer and when he isn't).	2. When he's interacting with peers, even if he's not hitting or squeezing, he's always rough— uses more force than necessary—has never been observed interacting in gentle, soft, or even neutral way.	Unsure
3. Knows and recognizes the consequences of engaging in positive and negative behaviors.	3. Knows what happens when he misbehaves but since he seldom, if ever, behaves properly with his peers, no one knows.	Unsure
4. Knows that it is more acceptable to interact positively with peers than negatively.	4. No information.	Unsure
5. Controls his own behavior.	5. The teacher reports no problems with nonsocial behaviors such as motor tasks or self-care. Interestingly, Jay interacts fairly well with adults by avoiding them or being passive around them.	Yes
6. Is not simply doing what the other kids do.	6. Jay's negative interactions are six times higher than the average in his special class!	No
7. Wants to interact positively with peers.	7. Current teacher says he clearly wishes he had friends—previous teacher assumes he does.	Yes
8. Considers the consequences of positive interactions rewarding and those of negative interactions aversive.	8. Since previously applied consequences for negative interactions do not appear to have any effect on his behavior, maybe Jay does not consider them aversive. No information about positive consequences since teacher has had little occasion to use any.	Unsure

teacher met to discuss each of the listed prerequisites. At first, Jay's former teacher was reluctant to meet. She protested "If I knew what Jay's problem was, I wouldn't have asked for somebody else to work with him!" She was told that her setback modifying Jay's behavior didn't mean she had nothing to contribute toward his program. She was an "expert" on Jay's behavior and so could provide valuable data to others.

By the end of the meeting, she tended to view Jay in a different light. She no longer saw him as a "bad seed" in need of exorcism, and it was largely through her cooperation that each prerequisite was evaluated.

During the meeting (held in Jay's old classroom), the prerequisites of the *target* behavior were listed on the status sheet and each one was discussed by the group. From this discussion, the status of all the prerequisites were determined and marked on the sheet. If Jay clearly did not meet a prerequisite (as was the case for prerequisites 1 and 6) it was marked no. A prerequisite marked no is automatically converted into an objective and placed in the teaching plan. When a student clearly meets a prerequisite, it is marked yes and, because the student has already learned this skill, it is *not* listed on the teaching plan. In some cases, however, the team reviewing a student's status will be "unsure" about a prerequisite. In such cases it will be necessary for the evaluator to select or develop a procedure for collecting more information.

Status sheets, if they have appropriate assumed causes written on them, are valuable tools for streamlining the evaluation process. Example status sheets will appear in each of the topical chapters in this text. Incidentally, it was determined that: Jay did not categorize examples of behavior as "positive" or "negative," so prerequisite 2 would become an objective; he did not know the consequences of specific behaviors, so prerequisite 3 became an objective; he did not say what others thought of his behavior—only how they acted around him (prerequisite 4); and it was not clear if he wanted to avoid negative contingencies, so prerequisite 8 also became an objective.

Given those determinations, it was obvious that Jay needed to be *taught* the concept of appropriate and inappropriate behavior. As things were, the consequences teachers were delivering in response to his misbehavior probably made little sense to him. Social reinforcers such as the attention of peers weren't making any sense at all. Jay did not know how to interact positively with his peers, nor did he know that it's more socially acceptable to interact positively with peers than to interact negatively. Therefore, he did not benefit from feedback about his behavior. These findings were converted into objectives (which can be found in Chapter 16). Programs designed to teach these objectives were developed by the BD teacher. After considerable time and effort, Jay learned to interact positively with his peers. Negative interactions were kept at a minimum and eventually disappeared altogether. Today Jay is a pillar of his community, has two normal children, drives a BMW, and owns a summer cabin near Estes Park!

Unit 3: Working with Students

There is much more to administering a test than reading questions from a manual. You must remember that you are interacting with a person. The kid you're working with might be scared or angry, or both. He probably hasn't had much success in school, isn't very good at answering questions, and is wondering why he has to take the 65th assessment of his young life. At its best, evaluation is anxiety-producing. At its worst, it can be a devastating experience for the kid as well as the examiner. So if you don't want to be devastating—or devastated—we suggest you pay close attention to this section. It is based upon years of experience in education, during which time the authors have worked with subjects ranging from 6 months to 60 years old, from severely disabled to precocious, from cooperative to noncompliant—and even physically aggressive. Over the years we've acquired a few tricks of the trade and, while you probably have seen or used some of them before, we hope there is something in this unit you haven't thought about.

Getting Ready

Let's start with the obvious. Know how to give the test or observation. This means that you should be able to administer the test/observation in a reasonable amount of time without any administrative errors that would invalidate the results. To accomplish this, study the directions carefully and practice using them on as many people as possible before using it "for real" (this is what friends and their children are for!).

A word of caution before going on: Most of the published procedures you will give have been designed to be used with average students (Fuchs et al., 1987). The typical test manual doesn't tell you what to do if a student refuses to answer a question or tells you to stuff the test up your nose (or what to do if she tries to stuff it herself). Later we'll discuss some problems you may encounter, provide some insight into why they occur, and offer some suggestions for dealing with them. In the meantime, here are some general rules.

1. Don't try to commit everything to memory. It is perfectly legitimate to make notations in the margins of the manual, to use index tabs, or to highlight certain parts for reference during administration. You should do the same with this text. If necessary, use 3×5 cards with pertinent data (time, basal, ceiling limits) on them. Be careful that you make these notations in such a way that reference to them will not interrupt the flow of evaluation. There is nothing so disconcerting to both student and examiner as those long pauses during a test when the examiner fumbles through the material trying to find out what to do next.

2. Have all of the materials (observation sheets, pencils, scratch paper, test booklets, manual, stopwatch) ready before the test. If you know that erasures are not permitted on a particular test, or you would like to have errors left intact for subsequent error analysis, use pencils without erasers. (Don't always use those fat primary pencils; tear the erasers off the narrow ones that students prefer.) The student has been conditioned to use an eraser and, no matter how many times you tell her not to, she will probably keep on erasing. This behavior is easier to stop if there is no eraser on the pencil to begin with.

   If you are giving a test, use a pencil that will facilitate, rather than inhibit, writing. Have a number of pencils of assorted sizes available and let the student choose the one she's most comfortable with. Try not to sharpen the pencils too finely. The anxious student may push down so hard when writing that she either breaks the point or tears a hole in the paper. This will only add to her anxiety. If the pencil supply is limited and there is no pencil sharpener in the room, have a pocket sharpener handy just in case.

   Provide the student with scratch paper if the test you are giving permits its use. Write her name or initials along with the date and any other pertinent information on each sheet. This is particularly important when you are testing more than one student during a given day. We would also suggest that you staple or clip each student's test materials, including the scratch paper, when the test is finished. Don't stuff little bits of paper inside pockets or purse and expect to remember later to whom they belong. Also fill in *all* pertinent data regarding the student on the cover of the test. Do this immediately or you may forget it. If you don't know things like dates of birth or age, don't be sure the kid does. On several occasions we've asked students their ages and found out later they were wrong.

3. Get the materials organized. Aside from having all necessary materials available, you should also make sure they are appropriately placed. Place your materials (remember all of those pencils) out of reach, or be prepared to spend the entire testing session taking things away from the kid. It might be wise to place the test materials on a table behind you with the student seated across from you.

   Also consider your own needs in the arrangement of materials. Try to have them placed so that they are easily accessible to you and in the proper order for use during testing. If they are laid out on a table, arrange them in sequence of use; if you don't have the table space, pile them in order of use from top to bottom.

   If you are planning to use a stopwatch or tape recorder, make sure it works. If it isn't electric, remember to wind the watch even if it appears to be working. Stopwatches are notorious for stopping by themselves in the middle of timed tests. Stay away from recorders with built-in microphones, because they will pick up everything in the room you don't want to record (buzzing lights or the blowing of a nose). Use a directional microphone and tape it to the table to lessen vibration and inhibit the student from picking it up. Our experience has been that kids are seldom neutral when it comes to tape recorders. Put a mike in front of one and he'll either run and hide, or begin to perform. Bring along an extra cassette in case the first one breaks or you'll discover at the last minute that it contains the concert you attended last summer. Also make sure that the outlet in the room works. If you are using batteries, have extras available. (By the way—check on your district's view of tapes. In some jurisdictions it is legally dangerous to retain them.)

4. Get the setting organized. Consider which side of the student you'll sit on if you are not going to sit opposite her. For instance, if she is right-handed, you will need to be on her left side so that you can easily observe her written responses. Arrange the environment so that it is comfortable for both of you. Make sure that the lighting and the room temperature are adequate: too warm, and you'll both nod off during the test; too cold, and you'll each be distracted by the clicking of teeth. Make sure that both seats are the right size: too small, and you'll be distracted by cramped muscles; too high, and you'll have a kid falling (or diving) off. Physical discomforts of any kind can be very distracting and tend to invalidate a student's performance.

Noise may also threaten test results. Extraneous auditory stimuli (the psychological term for noise) coming either from within the room, the room next door, or from outside, can be masked with a little gadget called a white noise machine. Available from specialty houses for around $50, it is worth every penny if you are required to do your testing across the hall from the gym or next to the cafeteria. If you can't afford one, tune a radio to a nonstation and adjust the volume for low level static. Recorded instrumental music (especially classical) or electric room-air purifiers will also effectively mask noise.

You should be aware of potential visual distractions and limit them before the student arrives. Try to have him facing in a neutral direction. Never seat him opposite a door, open or shut. If possible, neither should he be facing any of the windows. As soon as he walks into the testing area, show him where you want him to sit. You sure don't want to make any adjustments afterward. This doesn't mean that you shouldn't make adjustments during the testing session as they are needed. It means that, if you do your homework, you probably won't have to. If others are to be present in the room during testing, try to obscure any sight of movement. Post a sign on the door of the testing room that reads:

STOP   TESTING   DO NOT DISTURB

Most people will respect your privacy. If some curious or inconsiderate souls ignore the sign,

pay no attention to them and neither will your student. One last bit of trivia: If you can, sit between the student and the door.

5. Use a checklist. Many of these preliminary details (chair size, room temperature, pencil points, white noise machines, and the rest) may seem like so much minutiae to the novice. We're serious about all this. If you want to get valid test results and continue to remain on speaking terms with your students, we urge you to pay attention to as many of these "minor" details as possible. To make sure you don't forget any, use a checklist.

6. Modify normed measures. Normative measures are designed to inform eligibility and classification decisions. Sometimes, however, you may want to use a normed sample to help with teaching decisions. In this case you will be primarily interested in observing and recording the student's behavior, not the student's normative test scores. This means you may not want to follow all of the rules of administration exactly as stated in the manual. However, it is bad practice—and unethical—to report scores derived from the nonstandard administration of *any* standardized test. While modifications in test administration are permissible to get behavior samples, remember that your interpretations cannot follow the standardization guidelines. We recommend that any reference to nonstandard administration be accompanied by this statement: "These results were obtained through nonstandard test administration."

Modifications may be made during the testing session as the need arises, but it is better to prepare for them ahead of time so that you can put together all of the materials you may need (flashcards, occluders, large-print test forms, counting beads); this is where knowledge of the student's characteristics becomes so important. All it takes is a 10-minute question-answer session with the student's current teacher, a brief look at some student work, and a classroom observation to compile a list. (While you're in the room, say hello to the kid too, so he will have met you before the testing.) Using this information, take a look at the test you are going to use and make any modifications you think necessary.

If these modifications are too drastic or excessive, you would probably be better off either using or designing a different test.

Checking, Timing, and Taping

Make sure the student can't see you recording responses. If you must use a screen or a clipboard on your lap to hide your recording, explain why you are doing so. If you are sitting next to the kid, sit a little in back so that she can't easily look at the recording sheet.

If timing, do not leave the stopwatch where the student can see it, or he will pay more attention to the watch than to the test. (Don't take your latest microprocessor watch into the room and let it beep at the kid every half hour either—it's bad enough listening to them go off at the movies.) You could tape the watch to a clipboard so that you don't have to look back and forth from the test material. This way you can glance quickly at the watch without moving your head.

Some teachers report that their students get upset by stopwatches. We find this surprising, because every time we turn our backs the kids take the watches and play with them. If the student is upset by the watch, you must either time covertly (put a clock with a sweep hand where only you can see it), or desensitize the kid to the watch. One teacher we know had some students complain that a minute was too short a time to do any work. So the teacher started the stopwatch and asked the students to raise their hands when they thought a minute had passed. Most of them had their hands up within 30 seconds. This is a good exercise for kids who are nervous about running out of time.

Whenever possible, tape-record verbal responses that are lengthy or complex so that you can double check the student's work, at your leisure, after he has gone. This technique is good to use with tests requiring verbal responses that you must score or record during, instead of after, testing. It is especially helpful with reading tests where the student is required to read aloud and you have to score responses before deciding to move on to the next level. If you feel that you missed an item or two while the student was reading, all you have to do is replay the tape. You probably won't lose his attention during this time because most kids like to listen to their own voice. It is improper to have a student reread material because you didn't hear it the first time or he was moving too fast for you to score. It's tiring to have to reread this material, and it also may falsely cue the student. He may think you want him to change response(s). Besides, the behavior should be controlled by the student's skill at reading, and not by your skill at scoring.

Feedback

Try to limit all movement (marking or looking up from the test material) unless you are consistent in your behavior. Otherwise, besides distracting the student, you may also cue correct and incorrect responses. If you need to mark test items, mark *all* of them (not just correct or incorrect ones). By seeing you mark every item, all the kid knows is that the pencil moves when he responds. Because he can't see what you actually write, he doesn't know when he's correct or incorrect. Do the same thing with verbal responses. If you say "good" or "OK" for correct items and nothing for incorrect items, the student will soon know when he is right or wrong. You could say nothing at all or simply repeat the student's response, which, being noncommittal, doesn't cue him. You should also be careful not to cue with tone of voice or facial expression.

Sometimes it may be necessary to encourage the kid if he's reluctant to respond. Even here, try to make your encouragement as noncommittal as possible, because you want to reinforce working on the test rather than correct performance. Encourage with phrases such as "You're working hard," "Keep up the good work," "Let's try this one," "Do your best," "I like the way you are paying attention," and so on. Once again the idea is to reinforce work on the test, not correct or incorrect responses.

Sometimes students will begin to give themselves feedback on the test. They'll say things such as "I blew that one" or "That's another one wrong." This self-defeating feedback can become a vicious circle, particularly if their feedback is incorrect. If you see such a pattern beginning, you may want to break the no-feedback rule and tell the kid that he got the item correct (if he did). It is difficult to decide when this should be done. The purpose is to correct erroneous feedback, not to reinforce correct behavior. This distinction is very subtle. One clue that you can use is the student's statements. "I blew that one!" is an assertion; "I blew that one?" is a question. As a rule you should ignore the questions and correct false assertions if they seem to be part of a nonadaptive motivational pattern (See Chapter 16).

Rapport between a student and an evaluator contributes to the student's ability to perform well. Establishing rapport reduces the student's state of anxiety to the point where it no longer interferes with test performance.

Rapport

Every evaluation text tells you to establish rapport. While rapport building is one of the most important aspects of testing, it is also the most difficult to teach. Some say it can't be taught, but we'll give it a try. We have found from our experience that the keys to building rapport between student and examiner are empathy, honesty, and shared membership. Always try to put yourself in the student's place. Think about how you would feel if you were being asked to do things you weren't particularly good at, in front of an adult who may be a total stranger or, worse yet, someone you know and like.

Establishing rapport simply means reducing the student's state of anxiety (or hostility) to the point where it no longer interferes with the display of knowledge. It doesn't mean you have to love each other. There are a number of general things you can

do to facilitate rapport building. After discussing these, we'll go into the specific behavioral problems we've encountered during testing and describe some interventions we've used successfully.

The first thing you can do to establish rapport is to ask the student questions that don't relate to school. Try to find something you and the student share. Show the kid that you have a sincere interest in him as a person as well as a student. Begin with open-ended questions like "What do you have to say for yourself?" or "What's new?" If this doesn't elicit any spontaneous chatter, ask questions about what he likes to do after school, what his family is like, whom he plays with, or what shows he likes to watch on TV. If nothing else works, talk about pets or his brothers and sisters.

Depending on the student, we recommend that you discuss what's going on and why he's being evaluated. First, ask why he thinks he's being tested. If he is misinformed, tell him the truth. We usually try to get across the idea that we hope the testing will help him in school, because it will tell us what he needs to be taught. We tell him that we expect mistakes and that this is nothing to feel bad about. If he's afraid to try an item because he thinks he might be wrong, the test won't help him as much because we'll have less of his work to look at. Some of our older subjects tell us that they already know what they can't do. "I can't read, that's what I can't do. I don't need to take a test to know what I can't do." Good point. We reply that we also know that he's having trouble with reading and that our test should help tell us why. We explain each step of the procedure. We ask the student if he has any questions about anything we are doing. If he does, we answer them quickly and in language he can understand. We also explain that eventually he may be exposed to test items that will be too difficult for him. We explain about discontinue rules, so that he understands why we might continue to ask questions after he's reached material that may be too difficult for him. Students tend to trust you more if you are open with them and encourage them to ask you questions. After a while you'll begin to get "feelings" about some kids, and you'll act accordingly. We have spent upwards of an hour sitting and talking about whatever the kid wanted to discuss when we had a feeling that this was not the right time to push testing. At the end of this rapport-building session, we made a date to come back, and in most cases conducted our testing with no problems at all.

This emphasis on honesty can, however, promote its own problems. Some students are apt to react defensively to direct questions and others may attempt to tailor their answers to your questions. Rapport building is especially important when there are socio-cultural differences between the examiner and student (Tharp, 1989). This is particularly true where upper- to middle-class Anglo examiners and low-socioeconomic-status (SES) or minority-group subjects are concerned. Many of these students have learned to expect the worst from social institutions such as the schools, police, and child protective services. They expect to fail at all academic-related activities, including testing. Often they believe their failure is completely beyond their control and, ultimately, in the testing situation, they are correct. How do you establish rapport with a student who has learned to resent and distrust what you represent?

Initially you need to spend a moment actually considering the problem. When we first encountered this situation we were surprised that the student was hostile and uncooperative. Since we thought we were such nice, unbiased folks, we couldn't figure out the problem. Then we asked him, and he told us. "You people always ask me questions I can't answer. You always ask me to do things I can't do. You're trying to make me feel dumb!" In our narrowmindedness we had been focusing on racial and cultural differences as the cause of the problem when it was actually the things *we* (or previous educators) were doing. The fact that the student's discomfort was based on what we did and not who we were had never entered our minds. But once he informed us, we decided to try giving him questions he could answer and asking him to do things that he cared about and could do. We devoted an entire test period to this.

We gave him lots of verbal praise for effort, while being careful never to tie his personal worth to what he did. We made statements like "You're a good reader" only if they were true. If it wasn't the truth and he knew it (and was aware that we knew it), he wouldn't trust us. So we simply said "That was a good try" or "You did a good job." We weren't lying when we said this. He knew it and appreciated hearing it. After one or two of these confidence-massaging sessions, we began using "heavier" test material with which we knew he would have trouble. At this point we found him more willing to try some difficult items. He knew he wasn't dumb, and he knew that we knew it too.

Differences in ethnicity, race, language, and sex are important. However, the literature on evaluator/student interactions is mixed. It does seem to indicate that evaluators of the same race or sex elicit superior performance from students. However, the critical factor does not really seem to be race or sex. The critical factor is something called shared membership. The clue to rapport building seems to lie in this idea.

Shared membership refers to the student's perception that he and the evaluator both belong to the same "club." Race and sex, while important categories, are simply the most immediately obvious affiliations. Time spent before the evaluation begins provides an opportunity for you and the student to find something else in common. (In fact, this is important even if you *are* the same ethnicity, race, and/or sex).

Finally, the aim of the rapport building session

should not be to become buddies. It should be to establish a common affiliation—and *any* affiliation may do. Maybe you both like dogs—enjoy fishing—or even hate education. If so, you need to find this commonality and to use it as the basis for a functional relationship.

Special Problems

Here are some special problems you may encounter when you test problem learners. To our knowledge they are not discussed in any test manual you might use.

Acting-Out

The first problem that comes to mind is everybody's nemesis, the acting-out student. He may call you names, use profanity, throw the test materials on the floor, scream, or run out of the room. He may attempt to eat the test booklet or make you eat it! This behavior may serve two purposes: first, as a release for the tremendous pressure and tension he feels as a result of the testing; second, as an escape-avoidance strategy. A kid who is asked to read out loud in class may have learned that all he has to do is scream or throw something and most adults will make him stand in the hall. Kids don't have to read when they're in the hall.

Make sure you do not let the student's behavior lead to a payoff by removing him from the testing situation. If you do, you will only reinforce the behavior, and in the future it will be harder to test him. His behavior may be incompatible with testing, but that doesn't mean he can't stay in the room with you. If he runs away, get him and bring him back. Tell him that you will bring him back again if he runs away again.

When you are only going to be with a student for a short while, it is best to state your expectations clearly, and simply ignore it when they aren't met. Don't try to be a teacher. You aren't going to make any permanent change in someone's behavior during a brief testing session, so insisting on your view of appropriate behavior is a bit presumptuous. Understand that it usually gets worse before it gets better. You know you've got the student when he goes from acting-out to quiet noncompliance. At this point, and not before, move down to material that has already been mastered and positively reinforce effort. If none of this works, take the student back to his room when he is calm and

behaving politely toward you. Tomorrow is another day!

Anxious

Some students either ask the same questions over and over again,—"Is that the answer?" "Was I right?"—or they just plain cry. They are fearful of being wrong, probably because someone has taught them that being wrong is followed by rejection and ridicule. Once again, it is unlikely that anyone can reverse this sort of pattern during the short duration of evaluation. However, this anxiety reaction often subsides once a student sees that people are not going to make fun of him or send him away every time he makes a mistake. Try to be as encouraging as you can without committing yourself as to the correctness of responses. Don't reinforce the victim role the student may have negotiated with other adults. Like the rest of us, students usually know when they are right or wrong. What they may really be asking is "Do you still like me?" or "Are you mad at me?"

Unresponsive

Students who are withdrawn can be more frustrating than acting-out students. They do not speak unless they are spoken to, seldom speak in complete sentences, and then often speak only in barely audible tones. Our suggestion is initially to avoid tests with supply-response items unless the responses are written. Nonverbal tests with select-response items may get them working and can be followed with supply-response items. Another good idea is to bring a friend of the withdrawn student to the session and give extra items to the friend.

Inattentive

Students who lack attention skills may have difficulty following directions and remembering the test material you present to them. You may wish to give directions and then ask questions about the directions themselves. After asking a test question, have the student repeat it for you before asking for an answer.

Fidgeting

Some students engage in constant and excessive movement such as rocking in place or repeatedly getting in and out of their seats. The most effective way to deal with this so-called hyperactive behavior during the test is to ignore it. Try to introduce frequent breaks into the testing session so that the kid has the opportunity to move about freely. Do not force him to sit perfectly still with his hands folded in his lap.

Impulsivity

Some students tend to respond before they get all of the information they need to make a correct response. They answer questions before the examiner is finished asking them. An effective technique for dealing with such behavior is to require the student to repeat the stimulus (directions or question) before he is allowed to respond to it. This forces him to listen to everything you say and tells you whether or not he was paying attention. It also clarifies the task. If you are using a select-response format, do not expose any of the choices until you've finished presenting the stimulus and the subject has repeated it to your satisfaction. A modification of this technique is to expose only one of the possible answers at a time and repeat the stimulus ("Is this the letter P?") for each exposure as you point to the choices. This requires the student to stop and look at each possible choice before responding.

Summary

This chapter defined measurement, scores, reliability, and validity. It also pointed out problems with existing behavior samples and elaborated on eight requirements for good tests. It is particularly important to assure that tests and observations sample what is taught, are adequately sensitive to learning, and reflect meaningful conditions and criteria. As you will see in the following chapters, it is not possible to arrive at certain conclusions, or to make certain teaching recommendations, without adequate behavior samples.

In closing, one other point needs to be made. Threats to data are not limited to problems with tests. Tester/observer bias and behavior also influence scores. The student-evaluator interaction must be carefully and thoughtfully controlled in order to obtain useful information in a humane and respectful fashion.

Chapter 7 / Fundamentals of Evaluation

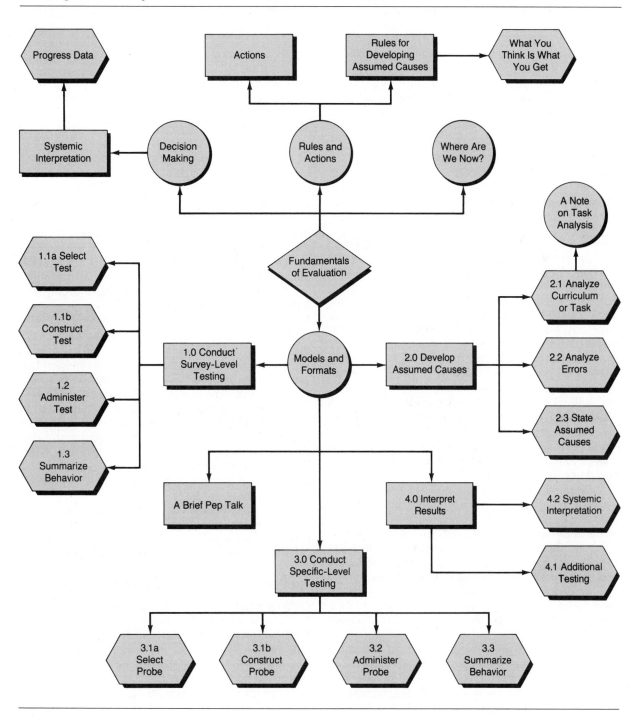

"A Trouble is a circumstance, a situation, that leaves one upset and at loose ends; one knows that things aren't going very well. It is a source of vague but persistent discomfort. A *puzzle* has a nice tight form, clear structure, and a neat solution. A *problem* then, is what you get if you can find a puzzle form to lay on top of a trouble."

—L. S. Shulman (1985)

Models and Formats

This chapter explains the process of conducting a curriculum-based evaluation for the purpose of making teaching decisions. This is a process that is considerably easier to demonstrate than it is to explain. That is why you will find that as you go through the topical chapters (10–17) the process will become not only clear, but also fairly intuitive. However, we need to lay out the entire process now so that we can present in those topical chapters the things you will need to know with minimal redundancy. In this chapter we will go into great detail describing steps that, in practice, will take only seconds to complete. As you read this chapter, try to focus on the flow of the process so you can learn how the various skills of evaluation fit with one another. This will allow you to return to this chapter if you should happen to get lost during an actual evaluation.

The purpose of a teaching-oriented evaluation (as opposed to a placement-oriented evaluation) is to provide the evaluator with information regarding what students should be taught, and how it can best be taught to them. The model we present here includes four stages: fact finding, hypothesizing, validation, and decision making. The entire process is graphically displayed in Exhibit 7.1*. Exhibits with asterisks are used for evaluation activities and are replicated in the workbook. They are also listed on page xii of the front matter of the book.

We have used this format throughout the book: circles are questions, rectangles are things the evaluator may or may not do, and decisions (Teaching Recommendations) are given in numbered rectangles. Flowcharts like the one in Exhibit 7.1* seem to drive

some people out of their minds. However, they seem to help other people. If you suffer from the dreaded "disflowchartia," just ignore the image and focus on the words that follow. To simplify this discussion, we are going to use the term *test* to include observations and portfolios.

The process of functional evaluation displayed in Exhibit 7.1* includes two kinds of assessment: survey-level and specific-level. Survey-level assessment relies most heavily on the use of interviews, class assignments, portfolios, NRTs, achievement tests, and published materials. The purpose of the survey-level is to get information from which explanations (assumed causes) for student failure may be generated. Usually survey testing is only done once, and it may not be needed at all if you are already sufficiently informed about the student's skills to generate appropriate explanations. Specific-level assessment is employed to determine which (if any) of the explanations are valid. Specific-level probing may be repeated to monitor student progress.

The competencies required to conduct survey-level assessment include: (1) select tests, (2) construct tests, (3) administer tests, (4) describe student behavior, and (5) make decisions. Here is a brief explanation of each.

1.0 Conduct Survey-Level Testing

Question 1A: Is survey testing/observation required?
Key consideration: How much you already know.
Explanation: For the purpose of this presentation, we will assume that you (in the role of evaluator) have never seen the kid before and have only the most superficial referral from which to start working. That's the most difficult situation for an evaluator. The need to test/observe depends on your familiarity with the

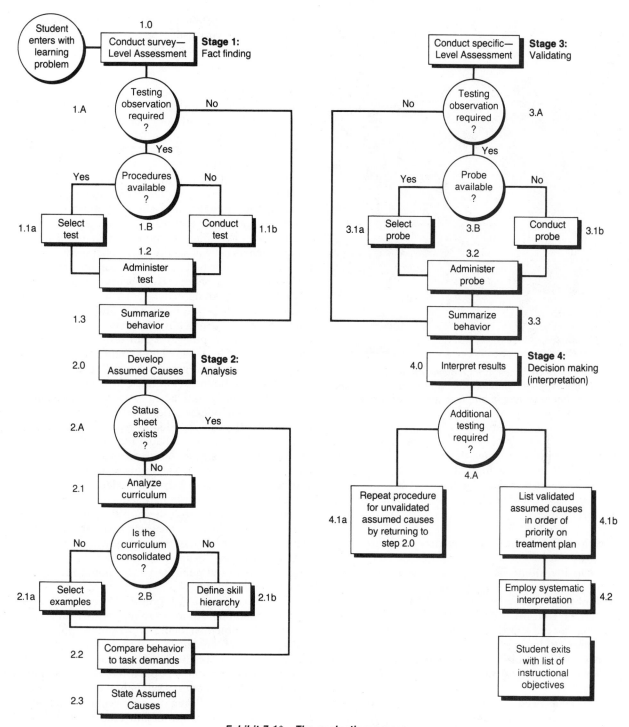

Exhibit 7.1*   The evaluation process.

The purpose of treatment-oriented evaluation is to provide the evaluator with information regarding what the students should be taught and how it can best be taught to them.

student. The less you know, the more you will need to find out and the more you will need to test/observe. Survey-level assessment might just as accurately be called fishing. It is a process of casting around for hidden information.

Question 1B: Is a testing/observation procedure available?

Key consideration: Coverage of problematic curriculum.

Explanation: Any referral should at least state a domain of concern. Usually these will be academic (reading, math, written communication), task-related (attention, study skills), or social (peer relations, assertiveness, self-control). There are more test/observation procedures available for academics than for social behavior.

The main need here is that you adequately cover the curricular area of concern. To do this you may

wish to use existing portfolio information, parts of several tests, modified existing tests, or a status sheet to interview teachers who are more familiar with the student.

1.1a Select Test

This activity, along with "construct test" and "summarize behavior," is found under both survey- and specific-level assessment, but we will describe it here. As just stated, the idea is to select a test that covers the curriculum area of concern.

While we did say that published standardized tests need not be used in survey-level assessment, we know from experience that many school administrators and classroom teachers prefer their use over teacher-made instruments or simple classroom observation. For one thing, teachers (as well as the lay public) seem to have more faith in published material than in anything they could design themselves. They believe that the only good test is a copyrighted test. (After all, don't we always call published tests "formal" and teacher-made ones "informal"?) Somehow they have gotten the idea that it is illegal to publish a bad test. The reasoning goes something like this: "How could it be as bad as you say it is and still get published?" The answer is simple. It's on the market because it makes money.

Another reason published tests are so popular is that many classroom teachers feel they have neither the time nor the skills needed to produce valid tests. If there already is a test available that is valid and will suit your purposes, it is foolish to spend time writing another. But remember, validity is related to purpose, and your purpose is to help the student in your class. Therefore, you are the ultimate judge of a test's validity. For the iconoclast or do-it-yourselfer, we have provided material on test construction in the teacher's manual that accompanies this text. Ask your instructor to supply it to you. Meanwhile, you traditionalists who wish to stick to the published tests should review the material in Chapter 6.

Whenever you use a published test, you must choose a good one. All tests are not created equal. Get rid of the notion that being copyrighted, published, and marketed automatically makes everything written a worthwhile investment. Educators must become better consumers. While it is popular to criticize test publishers, remember that they sell only what *we* continue to buy. Years ago, Postman and Weingartner (1969) stated that schools should prepare students to become experts at "crap" detecting. One way teachers can do this is to start detecting some themselves.

1.1b Construct Test

There are so many published achievement tests, end-of-unit tests, program placement tests, and district skill-level tests that it is unlikely you will ever have to construct a survey test in any basic skill area. If you need a test in an area of undeveloped curriculum, the best thing to do is to drop back and organize the curriculum (as described in Chapter 3). This means:

1. Recognizing the content to be taught or tested

2. Sequencing the content

3. Selecting behavior domains appropriate to the content

4. Recognizing appropriate conditions for the behaviors

5. Locating or establishing CAP

6. Arranging the content, behavior, conditions, and criteria into a table of specifications (test plan)

7. Selecting a relevant item format

8. Writing items for the most complex squares in the table of specifications (see Chapter 3).

It's a long process but a valuable one for material you frequently find yourself teaching. You can't expect to make a survey test that adequately covers curriculum that is a mystery. Today, this type of work is needed most of all at the high-school level and in the areas of social and task-related behaviors.

1.2 Administer Test

The procedures for collecting samples of student behavior were explained in some detail in the last chapter. When you get to Part 3 of this text, please remember there is more to administering a test than reading questions from our chapters. You are interacting with a person.

1.3 Summarize Behavior

Survey-level testing collects a general behavior sample. This sample is needed to narrow the range of curriculum so that specific-level testing can follow. The range is narrowed by identifying curriculum areas in which you will need to test further, as well as those in

Published achievement tests, end-of-unit tests, program placement tests, and district skill-level tests are often used as survey-level tests, but teachers can create their own.

which the student is clearly adequate or clearly inadequate. If you are using a status sheet (see Chapter 6, p. 115), mark the objectives "passed" that are clearly adequate and set them aside with a sigh of relief. Clearly inadequate areas are listed for future instruction. (Some may be far too advanced for current presentation, so priorities will still have to be set among these unlearned skills.) Areas marked as uncertain will require additional specific-level testing, but to guide this testing you need a set of assumed causes, or hypotheses, about why the student is having problems. The survey-level exercise is carried out to develop a sufficient curriculum-specific context for the hypothesizing step to follow. (Once again, if you are sufficiently familiar with the student's current performance, the survey-level testing may not even be necessary).

2.0 Develop Assumed Causes

Once you have some information about what the student is doing, you must pause and try to figure out why she is doing it. This is done by developing ideas about what skills or strategies the student is missing. This takes place during the hypothesizing stage of the evaluation. In that stage, possible explanations for the student's poor performance are developed. These explanations, or assumed causes, will be treated as hypotheses to be accepted or rejected through the process of specific-level testing. This stage is either very easy or very hard depending on your own knowledge of the curriculum and the degree to which the curriculum has already been adequately described. The workbook has material explaining what to do in the worst case (unorganized curriculum and little prior knowledge). You may wish to look at that now. In the next section of this chapter, Rules and Actions, we will elaborate on the process of developing assumed causes.

Question 2A: Does a status sheet exist?

Key consideration: Do you already know the essential subtask and strategy components of the task?

Explanation: If you already have identified a functional set of curriculum-based prerequisites for the target skill, then you can use this list as a status sheet. If a status sheet does not exist, you will need to develop one by analyzing the curriculum (steps 2.1a and 2.1b).

2.1a and 2.1b Analyze the Curriculum

In order to think from a curriculum-based orientation, it is necessary to have a curriculum. Hopefully, one will already exist in most of the domains you approach. However, if curriculum descriptions do not exist, you will have to develop them.

Question 2B: Is the curriculum consolidated?

Key consideration: Can you identify topics within the domain that can be approached from a hierarchical orientation? If yes, are there also topics that should be approached from a holistic orientation?

Explanation: If the domain in which you are working is primarily holistic (see Chapter 3), the items within it do not share a common set of strategies. As a result, transfer of learning within the domain is less likely to occur and generalizations about student knowledge based on a few items are not going to be sound. Within holistic curricula, items vary in complexity but cannot be easily arranged in order (because their difficulty is conceptual). In such cases, the material is typically arranged according to an imposed theme such as importance, chronology, or development. Therefore the domains must be evaluated according to the structure of that theme. For example, if you were testing a student's knowledge of state capitals, and the capitals were being introduced by region (northeast, midwest) then only the states in those regions that have been covered should be on the test. Additionally, because generalization among items is not likely, an item for each state should be included.

It is important to remember that conceptual content, even in a consolidated domain like multiplication, may not be related to the factual or strategic information in that same domain. In other words, it isn't necessary for a student to know all multiplication fact answers in order to "understand" the concept of square roots. Therefore, *teaching of a concept should never be delayed until the facts have been learned.* This is not an easy idea to grasp or to put into operation. Therefore, we encourage you to reread the portion of Chapter 3 that addresses types of curriculum (see Chapter 3, page 51).

2.1a Select Exemplars.

Tasks from holistic domains are analyzed by clearly describing the total task to obtain an image of it. Once this image is available, it can be used as an exemplar against which the student's work is to be compared (Gilbert, 1978). For example, the quality of a student's written expression might be judged by directly contrasting it with the work of an accomplished peer. Similarly, the student's current work can be judged against previously obtained samples of her own work in order to note improvement. The principle advantage of this approach is that it avoids the reductionist and often decontextualized flavor commonly associated with task analysis. Its principle disadvantage lies in the need to recognize exemplars that truly represent quality. Because written expression, to continue with that example, is often subjectively defined, it is necessary to rely on judges to select the exemplar. Because the judges themselves will sometimes disagree, it makes the curriculum ill-defined. This lack of definition is inconsistent with the need for alignment and focus needed for special and remedial instruction (see Chapters 3, 4, and 8).

So what does one do when faced with the need to task-analyze a holistic domain?

1. Take a deep breath and relax.

2. Locate authorities, in the form of people or research, that talk functionally about the domain in which you are going to teach.

3. Decide (a) which topics within the domain are consolidated by unifying skill sequences and/or strategic processes, and (b) which topics are best represented by holistic examination of exemplars.

4. If a holistic approach seems appropriate, find functional exemplars and use them as the standard for comparison.

5. Evaluate each item the student works by comparing it to the exemplar and describing any differences you recognize. Be particularly aware of the conceptual elements of the item.

2.1b Define Skill Hierarchies. If the curriculum is already consolidated (see Chapter 3), well-organized, and sequenced, you can skip this step. If not, you have a lot of work to do (although you'll only have to do it once).

When the curriculum in which the student is failing is not organized, you need to employ the process of task analysis. Task sequences such as the one in Exhibit 7.2* do not always exist (particularly for holistic tasks), and there will always be breaks in content sequences, or poorly defined behaviors, that produce holes in the curriculum. In addition, the calibration of curriculum isn't constant; the ideal distance between tasks varies from student to student. Therefore, it is up to each teacher to slice the tasks into smaller pieces or combine them into larger ones for optimal learning.

Task analysis was already covered in Chapter 3, but we will now present the steps to be followed while using task analysis to clarify curriculum.

Focus on the Target. The target behavior is what you want the student to do. The target isn't what the student is doing wrong—that is called the "maladaptive behavior" (Chapter 16). Often the referral, or errors on a test, will lead you to focus on maladaptive behaviors. This is a mistake. In functional evaluation it is assumed the kid engages in maladaptive behavior because she lacks the essential prerequisites of appropriate (correct) behavior. To find these prerequisites you must identify and focus on a target behavior that

is incompatible with the error. This is equally true for holistic and hierarchical domains. Here is an example:

Maladaptive	Target
Makes reading errors.	Reads accurately.
Talks out in class.	Raises hand to speak.
Omits operation signs.	Includes operation signs.
Writes vaguely.	Expresses message clearly.

Always focus on and analyze the target task, not the maladaptive behavior.

Specify the Main Task. Task analysis will be easiest and most useful if the target behavior (main task) can be stated very clearly in behavioral terms. At the very least, the statement must include the elements of content, behavior, conditions, and criteria that define instructional objectives (see Exhibit 3.5). In the case of a holistic task (express message clearly) include the exemplar in the description "will express messages as clearly as Susan expresses them."

Identify Concept Attributes. This process, which is particularly important for holistic tasks, was illustrated back in Chapter 4, in Exhibit 4.3.

1. Find or produce several clearly correct instances (exemplars) of the target task.

2. Find or produce several clearly incorrect instances (nonexamples) of the task.

3. Identify attributes (characteristics) of the concept that are present in *all* instances.

4. Identify attributes which, if present, will change an example into a nonexample (a square can never have a curved side).

5. List the attributes found in steps 3 and 4 as critical (essential) attributes. These are the things that define the concept and that students should include in their work.

6. List attributes that are found in some instances but not in others as noncritical (not essential).

These will be used as distractors for test items, and to teach generalization of the concept.

Identify Subtasks.

1. Ask "What must a student do to complete this task?"

2. State each subtask in the same behavioral format used for the main task.

3. Keep the distance between subtasks small. As a rule, if the subtasks you list will take more than a week or two to learn, you are dealing with oversized chunks of material.

4. List subtasks close to the main task. This is very important. If you find yourself listing subtasks that underpin many tasks (not just the targeted main task), you may want to consider that the main task is stated too generally.

5. Don't list motivation, attention, memory, intelligence, perception, or information-processing abilities as subtasks.

Identify Strategies.

1. Determine rules for task completion.

2. State the simplest procedure for task completion. (The simplest procedure is the one with the fewest steps.)

3. Determine if a formal algorithm (widely agreed upon step-by-step procedure) is commonly employed by experts for completion of this task.

4. Consider that a general study or test-taking strategy (see Chapter 17) may be required. General strategies often include:
   a. Deciding what needs to be done
   b. Evaluating resources
   c. Selecting a procedure to follow
   d. Carrying out all steps in a procedure
   e. Monitoring work
   f. Checking work
   g. Self-correcting work

5. Anticipate errors, or examine the kid's incorrect responses, to recognize where a procedural step is needed for accurate performance.

Terminate.

1. Do not overanalyze, as there is some risk of becoming trivial. A good instructor/evaluator

Exhibit 7.2   Sequence of Division and Status Sheet

	Status:	
	Pass	No Pass
Placement Test Mixed division problems		

Square Root
  Square root of a number in
  which the answer is 0–12		

Place Value
  Two- or more-digit number
  with zero		

Two- or more-digit number by 1, 10, 100, 1000		

Remainder and No Remainder
  Two- or more-digit number
  by a one- or two-digit
  number		

Remainder
  Two-digit number by a one-
  digit number (one- or two-
  digit answer)
		✓

No Remainder
  Two-digit number by a one-
  digit number (two-digit
  answer)
	✓	

Facts Division facts (0–10)	✓	

constantly balances the need for specificity against the need for authenticity. Most skills are learned best in context.

2. Initially recognize no more than five subtasks or attributes close to the main task.

3. If specific testing indicates that the student can handle (learn) the least complex of these subtasks, then the analysis has been sufficient and can be terminated.

2.2 Compare Behavior to Task Demands

Exhibit 7.2 is a status sheet based on a table of specifications for division. Because on the survey test, the student missed a problem that required her to quickly divide a two-digit number by a one-digit number and get a remainder. It has been marked with a no-pass (NP). The assumed cause of this failure is that a more basic objective, found below, has not been learned. To check this out, you will have to give specific tests of these objectives but, once the lower objectives have been identified, step 2.2 is over.

One trick to using a status sheet is to employ error analysis. Error analysis can be a real shortcut. It was explained in some depth in Chapter 6. Unfortunately, error analysis is hard to do on many survey tests, especially the ones that use multiple-choice items.

To analyze errors, follow these steps:

1. Select a test that provides an opportunity for a variety of errors to occur (items requiring borrowing are necessary to find borrowing errors).

2. Have the student work the items on the test. Encourage her to attempt everything and to show all of her work ("think out loud").

3. Try to get as many examples of errors as possible.

4. Try to gain insight into the student's thought processes by asking "How did you arrive at this answer?"

5. Note patterns, or consistencies, in the errors.

6. Note categories of errors or corrects. (This will be explained shortly under the heading Actions.)

A physical status sheet isn't always needed. Expert teachers seem to have status sheets stamped into their thought processes. This familiarity with the tasks they teach develops through experience and reflection. Using the information obtained through survey-level assessment, they consider each component on the status sheet and decide if the student appears skilled at that component. Then they answer yes, no, or "unsure."

2.3 State Assumed Causes

Any missing concept, fact, or strategy component (those marked no or "unsure" on a status sheet) is a likely cause of student failure. In step 2.3, the evaluator hypothesizes about the missing prior knowledge that is the student's most likely problem (*hypothesize* sounds so much nicer than "guess"). Rules for doing this will be presented shortly.

A Brief Pep Talk

Take a moment to think about where we are in the evaluative process. The format itself is very simple. It has four steps:

1. Find out what the student is doing now.

2. Think of explanations for what she is doing.

3. Check to see if these explanations are correct.

4. Decide what to teach.

To explain these steps, we have produced the flowchart in Exhibit 7.1* and are covering topics like error analysis, curriculum development, and test construction. These discussions are presented to ensure that you will have the extensive prerequisite knowledge required for intentional and meaningful evaluation.

While the explanations of how, why, and when to carry out each of these steps may get tedious, it is always important to remember that they can be implemented quickly. So hang in there!

3.0 Conduct Specific-Level Testing

The purpose of specific-level assessment is to verify assumptions formed at the survey level. The boundary between the specific and the survey levels is not always distinct, so let's talk about it for a minute. Stage 2 produces task-specific explanations for student failure. Because these explanations may or may not be correct, they are referred to as "assumed causes." The third stage, validating, is intended to find out if the assumptions are correct. This is done through specific-level assessment.

We do specific-level assessment to verify the assumptions made after survey-level assessment and we repeat it frequently to monitor the effectiveness of our teaching.

A specific-level test is always a criterion-referenced test. As mentioned in Chapter 6, a criterion-referenced test is composed of two things: (a) a behavioral objective, and (b) the materials necessary to implement the objective. Of course these objectives must have statements of content, behavior, conditions, and CAP. They must also be calibrated so that they cover about the same amount of curriculum that the teacher is going to teach. This is true because specific-level test objectives are the same as

Making decisions about what to teach is based on gathering a sample of student behavior and comparing it to a standard, generating assumed causes for any problems, and testing those assumptions.

short-term instructional objectives. By "the same" we don't mean similar—we mean they are the *exact* objectives. No difference. This is why failing the test/observation means instruction is needed and why instruction continues (assuming progress is adequate) until the test/observation is passed. It is also why data from readministration of the test (or a form of it) can be used to monitor student learning. However, while the objectives may be identical, the items on the tests don't need to be. We "teach to the test" by addressing objectives and student thought processes, not by having students memorize the answers to items.

We can repeat specific tests frequently because their finer calibration makes them sensitive to small increments in learning. At the specific level, instruction and evaluation become so tightly meshed that they are difficult to separate—and that's the way it should be.

Question 3A: Is specific-level testing/observation required?
Key consideration: Do you already have sufficient information to arrive at decisions about what to teach?
Explanation: Sometimes the survey procedures and your prior knowledge of the student will provide enough information to begin instruction, so you can go past specific-level assessment directly to interpretation. The status sheet may be helpful here. The only immediate standard for making this decision is your satisfaction that the data you already have provide adequate insight into the student's knowledge of the curriculum. If you are wrong, that will be apparent later when you monitor instruction.
Question 3B: Is a specific-level test available?
Key consideration: Correctly calibrated CRT that matches hypothesis.
Explanation: In the analysis stage, objectives were written or identified to correspond to each hypothesis.

If a probe (CRT) that matches these objectives is available, it can be selected and used; if not, it will have to be made.

3.1a Select Probe
Selecting a specific-level CRT is like selecting any other good test or observation procedure. First you make sure it matches your objective and then you check to be sure that it meets the eight criteria discussed in Chapter 6 (p. 100).

3.1b Construct Probe
It is considerably easier to select probes than it is to write them for every short-term objective in every content area. However, because the curriculum isn't individualized, once a probe is correctly written it's good for life.

The steps to probe construction are:

1. *Calibrate curriculum* to select the slice of material to be covered on the test.
2. *Plan probe* by recognizing content, behaviors, and conditions—sequencing them, and arranging them into a table of specifications (test plan).
3. *Select or write items* for the squares in the table of specifications.
4. *Establish criteria* by standardizing the test through a search of the professional literature or a sampling study of skilled students.

These four steps are explained in some detail, and practice is provided, in the workbook accompanying this text.

3.2 Administer Probe
Tips for administration were covered in the last chapter and are not significantly different at the specific level.

3.3 Summarize Behavior
Behavior summary was also discussed in Chapter 6, but aspects of it need to be repeated here. The most important thing to remember is that the summaries of behavior must be reported in relation to the assumed cause (or objective) for which the specific-level test was given.

There are three ways to summarize behavior:

1. Keep the actual behavior in a portfolio. This only works if (1) classroom assignments are relevant, (2) a permanent product has been produced, and (3) it is manageable to keep the product.

2. Report scores. At the specific level the scores reported are always direct summaries of accuracy or rate behavior, not normative derivations such as percentiles or grade equivalencies. Therefore, raw scores are often useful. If the CAP is 40 per minute and the kid did 20 per minute, then that may be all that is needed.

3. Note discrepancies between the student's work and the expected levels of performance noted in the objective. For example, if the standard was 80 and the kid did 40, the discrepancy is −40, or or ÷ 2.

4. Reporting status on objectives. This process is very useful and, once again, is simply an extension of a process introduced in Chapter 6. Take a sequence of objectives (or a status sheet) and after noting any discrepancies, simply mark the status of each assumed cause as pass (adequate), no-pass (inadequate), or ? (uncertain).

4.0 Interpret Results

This is the final stage of evaluation: decision making. The following steps are used to convert the information gathered into teaching recommendations.

Question 4A: Is additional testing required?
Key consideration: Have you found explanations for the student's failure that can be used to guide teaching?

4.1 Additional Testing
Compare the assumed causes for failure stated in step 2.3 to the summary of specific-level behavior in step 3.3. If the original assumed causes do not prove to be correct, you must return to step 2 and develop new ones. This means additional testing may also be required (4.1a). For example, if you suspected that a student could not comprehend a reading passage due to poor vocabulary skills, but specific-level testing revealed that the student's vocabulary was adequate, you would have to come up with a new assumed cause for the failure.

In most cases some of the assumed causes you developed will prove to have been accurate while others will not. Using Exhibit 7.3, we can see that, of the content areas originally assumed to be problematic (marked with an X), several specific tests were failed, several passed, and two remain uncertain. These results indicate that all objectives (assumed causes) marked yes should be dropped from active instruction and simply monitored for maintenance. Assumed causes marked no should be listed as short-term instructional objectives (step 4.1b). Those marked with ? (fluency of r-controlled vowels and vowel teams) will require additional testing (Step 4.1a).

4.2 Systematic Interpretation

As you may recall, teaching decisions pertain either to curriculum (what will be taught) or instruction (how it will be taught). To decide what to teach, look at the test results to determine the student's status. If there are discrepancies between expected and actual performance, then select those objectives. For example, assume that you have conducted a reading-comprehension evaluation and obtained the following results:

FACT: Student referred for poor comprehension of science book.

Assumed cause	Test	CAP	Behavior on test
1. Slow decoding	Timed reading of grade-level passage	140c 5–7e	148c 5e
Absolute discrepancy = +8.			

STATUS: Adequate (at performance aim)

RECOMMENDATION: Decoding instruction isn't needed

Assumed cause	Test	CAP	Behavior on test
2. Poor passage-dependent vocabulary	Select appropriate word definition for a given passage	90%	40%
Absolute discrepancy = −50%.			

STATUS: no-pass (There is a 50% point discrepancy between expected and actual performance.)

RECOMMENDATION: Because the student's score of 40% is less than it should be, you will need to get rid of the discrepancy by teaching to this objective: "Given a passage with underlined words and four possible definitions per word, the student will select the definition that matches the passages content, with at least 90% accuracy."

Given these results, it is clear that the student does not need to work on decoding rate, but does need instruction on vocabulary. Because she is partially proficient (40%) at using passage content, it is not necessary to search for additional subskills of that task, but rather to teach the student to use passage clues more efficiently to decide what words mean.

By examining the status of each validated assumed cause, you will be able to make recommendations about what the student should be taught. By readministering specific tests for each objective, you will also be able to monitor the effectiveness of teaching through noting if the discrepancy is decreasing. This process, called data-based program modification, is addressed primarily in your workbook and in the monitoring sections of each topical chapter (see Chapter 5, p. 87).

Where Are We Now?

So far, we have outlined and described a curriculum-based system of evaluation. Descriptions of each activity in the system have been presented and are summarized one last time in Exhibit 7.4*. At times these descriptions have been elaborate, giving the impression that the system is complex; of course, in some ways it is. To use curriculum-based evaluation, you must clarify the curriculum. If content recognition, specification of behavior/conditions, and development of criteria have not been completed prior to the evaluation, the job of doing them falls—by default—on the evaluator.

Attempting curriculum-based evaluation in the absence of a well-defined curriculum can be like assembling a piece of complicated equipment for the first time without any directions. You may know how to use all the tools but be frustrated by the need to puzzle each step out on your own. We have explained each step to help the first-time evaluator, but we

Exhibit 7.3
Behavior
summary

Assumed causes	Content subskills	Accuracy test	Fluency test
	Paragraph reading	*N P*	*N P*
	Polysyllabic words	*No test*	*No test*
	Contractions	*No test*	*No test*
	Compound words	*No test*	*No test*
X	Sight words	*P*	*N P*
X	Silent letters	*N P*	*N P*
	Modifications		
X	Endings (suffixes)	*P*	*N P*
X	Clusters	*N P*	*N P*
X	r-controlled vowels	*N P*	*?*
	Teams		
X	Vowel teams	*P*	*?*
X	Consonant digraphs	*P*	*N P*
X	Consonant teams	*P*	*N P*
	Conversions		
X	Vowel conversions	*P*	*P*
X	Vowel + e conversions	*P*	*P*
	Sounds		
	CVC words	*No test*	*No test*
	Vowels	*No test*	*No test*
	Consonants	*No test*	*No test*
	Sequence	*No test*	*No test*
	Sounds	*No test*	*No test*
	Symbols	*No test*	*No test*

strongly recommend that you study the relevant sections of the workbook for more detail.

Once the steps have been followed a few times, these directions may no longer be needed. However, when a particularly difficult student comes along, you may want to return to Exhibit 7.1* and Exhibit 7.4* and their explanations. You may also need to seek help in certain curriculum areas. The third part of this text provides information needed to conduct evaluations in both academic and social-skill curricula. In the second part of this chapter we will elaborate on a set of procedures that can be followed to assure that your evaluations are valid.

Rules and Actions

Rules for Developing Assumed Causes

What you think is what you get. Evaluation is a thoughtful process. As already mentioned, this is a good news/bad news situation. It is good news because it makes evaluation a professionally challenging activity that can be improved as our thinking matures. Conversely, it is bad news because the results obtained illustrate our flaws—not just those of our clients.

Here is an example. Dr. Howell was once asked to review the special educational program in a large school. In preparation, he pulled the teaching plans on several students and noticed something interesting. While about two thirds of the plans had various recommendations, in one third of the cases the teaching recommendations were essentially the same. Dr. Howell, being a fairly cynical sort of guy, doubted that one third of the remedial students at this school all needed the same interventions. So, he checked the scores reported in the evaluation section of the teaching plan. The scores were *not* all the same. In fact, there were only two portions of these student's plans that were similar—the teaching recommendations and the name of the person who wrote up the plans. This was getting interesting!

Exhibit 7.4*   The Task-Analytical Model of Assessment

Stage 1: Fact Finding

1.1 Purpose: To find out what the student is doing now.

1.2 Materials: Classroom work or published tests. A stimulus/response worksheet.

1.3 Procedure: Stimulus and response information is collected on each error.

1.4 Result: The stimulus and response columns of a worksheet are filled out and typical errors are listed.

Stage 2: Hypothesizing

2.1 Purpose: To think of explanations for what the student is doing.

2.2 Materials: Survey-level stimuli and responses.

2.3 Procedure: Each stimulus (task) is analyzed through task analysis or each student response is analyzed through error analysis. *NOTE: An existing table of specifications can be used to replace this step.*

2.4 Result: The subtasks required for successful completion of the survey material are listed. All comments are then reviewed, and general areas of difficulty are recognized and listed as assumed causes for the student's behavior.

Stage 3: Validating

3.1 Purpose: To see if the explanations are correct.

3.2 Materials: Specific-level assessment materials.

3.3 Procedure: Each assumed cause is reworded into a behavioral objective and the student is tested/observed to see if he or she passes or does not pass the objective.

3.4 Results: Conclusions about which task-related subskills the student has or does not have are reached.

Stage 4: Decision Making

4.1 Purpose: To decide what to teach.

4.2 Materials: Specific test results and guidelines for systematic interpretation.

4.3 Procedure: Compare test results to hypotheses and employ interpretation guidelines.

4.4 Results: Recognition of areas where additional testing/observing is required. Statements about what to teach and tentative statements about how to teach it.

Suspecting a major violation of the Federal Civil Rights Act and complicity among high officials in the government, our hero (that would be Howell) sought out one of the teachers at the school and asked "How come all of these kids, regardless of their test scores, have the same recommendations?"

"That's easy," the teacher replied, "Bob wrote them."

"So?" Howell queried.

"Bob thinks the solution to all social behavior problems can be answered by using Dreikurs," the teacher explained, "And that all reading problems are best dealt with through oral reading drills. So if it's a behavior problem he always says 'redirect' and if it's reading he always says 'do timings.'"

"That doesn't seem too functional."

"Oh, we don't expect Bob to be functional. We rely on the other two evaluators to do the really hard kids."

So what is to be gained from this story? First of all, if you are a teacher in a school that only has one evaluator—you'd better hope it isn't Bob! Second, if you are in a program that separates its staff into "evaluators" and "teachers" you are about a decade out of date. This is the nineties—*collaborate*! And finally, Bob was making a mistake. He was confusing curriculum with instruction and recommending only those objectives conveniently taught with *his* favorite instructional approaches. He was elevating his commitment to particular instructional procedures above the individual needs of his students. This error in Bob's thinking altered the results of his evaluations because evaluation is a thought-controlled process.

At the end of Chapter 1 (p. 15), we listed threats to good judgment. You might want to look back and review those now.

Bob's judgment seemed to have succumbed to several of these threats:

- Lack of perspective
- Premature resolution
- Unwarranted confidence
- Selective or incomplete search

Now Bob, for all of his problems, was not evil (in fact, after chatting with him, Howell decided that all of his problems evolved from lack of the knowledge needed to make a judgment). We all make the errors listed in Chapter 1 many times a day. That's because these errors are all completely human and even serve a useful function—they allow us to work on trivial tasks with great efficiency. What Bob, and the rest of us, need are two things: first, we need to recognize when our jobs call for work that is professional, focused, and reflective; second, we need a set of guidelines to follow when we do that kind of work.

A set of rules for developing assumed causes is presented in Exhibit 7.5*. These rules focus on the hypothesizing step of the evaluation format, because that is the step that most dramatically determines the quality of an evaluation (Howell, 1991; 1992). For example, look at Exhibit 7.6. In Exhibit 7.6 we see that two evaluators, working with the same student, have arrived at completely different teaching recommendations because of differences at the assumed-cause step. Whereas Bob's thinking made several different kids look the same, the thinking of these evaluators has made the same kid look like two different people.

The thinking of evaluator A in Exhibit 7.6 was curriculum-based. The thinking of evaluator B was not.

Obviously the text authors think evaluator A has done better than B. However, leaving that issue aside for a moment, can we teach evaluator B to think like evaluator A? Of course we can. All we have to do is recognize what A is thinking and train B to imitate A. B doesn't even have to agree with A, or the authors, to arrive at the same results.

This text was written to teach you the skills and thought processes associated with curriculum-based evaluation. First, carefully review the rules, explanations, and example errors found in Exhibit 7.5*. Then, look at the statements made by teachers in Exhibit 7.8. All of these statements represent one or more rule violations. We want you to categorize the type of error by writing the number of the error(s) next to each statement. Make your decisions and write the number of the error(s) next to each assumed cause.

Actions

We have identified 15 actions that we believe are critical to a functional evaluation. They are each listed in Exhibit 7.7*. Exhibit 7.7* is designed for use as a checksheet for reviewing assessment results prior to their interpretation. It begins with a column of questions that must *all* be answered Yes prior to decision making. If, in reviewing the assessment processes you have followed with a student, you cannot answer yes to a question, it means you have failed to carry out one or more of the actions.

Let's try a couple of identification-level exercises to be sure you understand these actions. For each of the examples in Exhibit 7.8 write the number of the action(s) which the evaluator most clearly has failed to carry out. Do it now.

Look quickly at the errors made by the evaluators in Exhibit 7.8.

A. Ted forgot actions 1 and 11. He made decisions without expecting the student to display knowledge in a critical area. In the case of sixth-graders, this would include computation with multiplication.

B. Margie is making recommendations about how to teach without information about the impact of instruction. She forgot actions 14 and 15.

C. Jim has confused what Andrew knows how to do with what he demonstrates in writing. It's a

Exhibit 7.5*   **Rules for Developing Assumed Causes**

Rule	Explanation	Example Error(s)
1. Don't evaluate if there isn't a problem (or if you haven't decided what the problem is).	You need to know what you are looking for before you start specific testing; vague concerns and ambiguous survey test results are useless.	• Trying to figure out why a referred students gets out of his seat when all the other students get out of their seats just as often.
2. Think about your purpose.	Are you evaluating to make classification decisions? If you are interested in treatment decisions, are you trying to decide "what to teach" or "how to teach"?	• Trying to draw treatment information from a norm-reference achievement test score. • Recommending "how to teach" without any information about what treatments have already been tried.
3. Think about the curriculum: (a) Stay close to the main task.	Because the student's major problem is being behind in the curriculum, it is important to avoid retreating to lower levels. Don't automatically take every student back to the first grade and basic skills.	• Deciding to test a junior-high student with reading comprehension problems on her vowel sounds before testing her knowledge of comprehension strategies.
(b) Think about what can be taught *right now*.	It is important to consider tasks within the so-called correct level of difficulty. Don't think about things that are obviously too hard (given the student's current knowledge), or things that are obviously too easy.	• Testing the vowel sound accuracy of an accurate reader. • Checking to see how a student who can't add does on long division problems.
(c) Stick to the essential.	Don't spent time thinking about things the student doesn't need to learn.	• Roman numerals. • Drawing lines between syllables in words. • Educational terminology (i.e., "diagraph" or "the levels of Bloom's taxonomy").
(d) Set priority.	When a student doesn't seem to know about a lot of things, you must decide which to test/teach first.	• Documenting lists of stuff a kid can't do and nothing that she can do. • Ignoring what he wants to learn first. • Checking on skills that have limited immediate utility.
4. Don't confuse the curriculum with instruction.	What a student needs to know is determined by the curriculum—not by the way the curriculum is taught.	• Thinking that a student who fails history has to learn to read to succeed in history. • Only checking for skills taught by your favorite instructional technique (remember Bob?). • Giving tests for "learning style."

Exhibit 7.5*   Rules for Developing Assumed Causes (continued)

Rule	Explanation	Example Error(s)
5. Don't confuse testing with evaluation.	There are many important things that are not sampled by certain tests. These must be checked.	• Ignoring a content area because it isn't sampled by the tests you happen to have available. • Ignoring skill fluency because you haven't got a rate test.
6. Think about *all* elements of the task.	Tasks are composed of content behavior, conditions, and criteria. You should develop assumed causes for each of these domains.	• Arranging to observe a student who gets into fights at recess during her lunch period. (You forgot about conditions!) • Deciding to check the counting skills of a student who doesn't produce answers to addition facts. (You forgot to see if she could identify the answers first!)
7. Consider *both* knowledge and display.	When we test and observe we only see behavior. Don't assume that all behavior indicates knowledge—or that the absence of behavior always means the absence of knowledge.	• Assuming that a student who skips the word *that* while reading a passage doesn't know how to read it. • Assuming that a student who can't do addition facts quickly—because of poor handwriting—doesn't know how to add.
8. Think about what can be taught.	Stick to alterable variables! Don't spend time thinking about things that can't be influenced through instruction.	• Beginning the evaluation by assuming that the student's problem is the result of things like: a poor family, low IQ, or attention deficit disorder. • Deciding to check task-related explanations for failure (attention, motivation, study skills) before topic specific explanations (reading skills).
9. Think about something else.	Be comprehensive. Students seldom have only one missing prerequisite so it isn't safe to assume that the first thing they can't do is the only, or most important, thing they need to be taught.	• Beginning testing without sufficient analysis of the curriculum and/or survey level results. • Prematurely finishing the evaluation. • Failure to ask for assistance, or use reference material.
10. Remember the breakout rule.	Breakout rules (White, 1984) tell a person when to ignore the rest of the rules. In this case we suggest that, if, after doing things our way three times, the student still hasn't improved significantly—try something else!	• Assuming that a student's failure to learn documents the severity of her disability, rather than the limits of your procedures.

Exhibit 7.6   Thought Processes of Two Evaluators

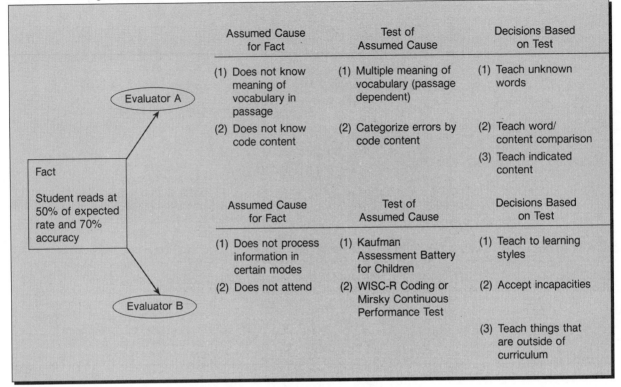

	Assumed Cause for Fact	Test of Assumed Cause	Decisions Based on Test
Evaluator A	(1) Does not know meaning of vocabulary in passage	(1) Multiple meaning of vocabulary (passage dependent)	(1) Teach unknown words
	(2) Does not know code content	(2) Categorize errors by code content	(2) Teach word/content comparison
			(3) Teach indicated content

Fact

Student reads at 50% of expected rate and 70% accuracy

	Assumed Cause for Fact	Test of Assumed Cause	Decisions Based on Test
Evaluator B	(1) Does not process information in certain modes	(1) Kaufman Assessment Battery for Children	(1) Teach to learning styles
	(2) Does not attend	(2) WISC-R Coding or Mirsky Continuous Performance Test	(2) Accept incapacities
			(3) Teach things that are outside of curriculum

pretty silly error (confusing writing legibility with spelling skill) but very common. Refer Jim to action 2.

D. Mark needs to carry out action 3. The student may know how to summarize, but he may not have been taught to list the five steps.

E. Stan knows that Alice is accurate at addition facts. But that doesn't mean she knows everything she needs to know about them. He should carry out actions 9 and 10.

Decision Making

To make decisions based on an evaluation, you have to conduct an evaluation first. This means taking a sample of student behavior and comparing it to a standard, noting the direction and magnitude of any discrepancies, generating assumed causes for any problems, and testing those assumptions. Now what?

Now you get to make decisions.

Again, keep in mind that special/remedial educators make two general types of decisions: placement decisions (to be covered in Chapter 9) and teaching decisions. Teaching decisions also come in two types: decisions about what to teach, and decisions about how to teach. A guide to making teaching decisions is provided in Exhibit 7.9*. This exhibit provides a structure for interpreting the results of evaluations that employed the rules in Exhibit 7.5* and the actions in Exhibit 7.7*.

Exhibit 7.9* refers to many of the major concepts presented in Parts 1 and 2 of this text. For example, it includes terms like fluency, automaticity, strategy, and context. These will not be reexplained here. Therefore, a thorough understanding of that material is necessary in order to understand the exhibit.

Exhibit 7.7*   **Fifteen Evaluation Actions**

Before interpreting the results of any test and/or observation, ask yourself *each* of these questions. If the answer is no (or "unsure") take the specified action(s).

Question	Action	Explanation/Example
Are you sure you got an instructionally relevant sample of behavior?	1. Continue the evaluation until you find the correct instructional level.	To guide instruction on evaluation must cover the things a student is currently prepared to learn. This means mapping out *both* those things a student can do and those he or she cannot do. An evaluation that yields all "pass" "no-pass" is worthless.
Did the student's work represent the student's skills?	2. Try to separate knowledge from display.	Remember that a student may know something but be unable to demonstrate this knowledge (due to a missing skill). A student may also fail to demonstrate knowledge because of conflicts with the testing situation. Be sure the work represents the student's best efforts. Try giving a pep talk, using preferred tasks, or having a friend present during testing.
Has the student received instruction on the skills missed?	3. Check to see if a pass is expected.	Don't be concerned when students fail at things they haven't been taught. Ask "Did you ever know how to do that?" or "Has this always been hard?" or "Is it new?" Check with teachers to see if the skill has been taught.
Have you attempted to categorize the errors?	4. Look for patterns of content errors.	Indicated by incorrect responses whenever particular content is involved (two-place addition, vowel sounds, on biology vocabulary).
	5. Look for patterns of concept errors.	Indicated by failure to recognize cues (borrows when it isn't necessary) and/or use vocabulary (says "reliable" when talking about "validity").
	6. Look for patterns of strategy errors.	Indicated by predictable error patterns and/or incorrect explanation of process.
	7. Look for patterns of fact errors.	Indicated by incorrect statements ("a = eeee" or "2 + 2 = 5").
Does the student's skill maintain across different response formats?	8. Switch from identify to produce or from produce to identify.	If the student can't produce a correct answer check to see if the answer can be identified. If you know something can be identified, check to see if it can be produced.
Does the student's skill maintain across different levels of proficiency?	9. Switch from fluency to accuracy or accuracy to fluency.	If the student cannot do something quickly ask that it be done accurately. If something is done accurately ask that it can be quickly.
Does the student's skill maintain across different situations and context?	10. Check the effect of context.	If a student can't do something in context (add in a story problem) check to see if it can be done in isolation. If a student can do something in isolation (add on a work sheet), check to see if it can be done in context.
Have you missed any important skills?	11. Check skills *not* displayed.	Don't concentrate exclusively on errors. Consider content the student avoids (if the student never tried to spell words with double consonants, you should check that area).

Exhibit 7.7*   Fifteen Evaluation Actions (continued)

Before interpreting the results of any test and/or observation, ask yourself *each* of these questions. If the answer is no (or "unsure") take the specified action(s).

Question	Action	Explanation/Example
Does the student know and understand self-skills?	12. Ask the student to judge the difficulty of the task or to predict success.	Ask "Will this be easy for you or will it be hard?" or "Which things are you good at and which need improving?" or "Why do other kids get these problems done faster?"
	13. Ask the student to explain how to do the task.	Say "Pretend that you are the teacher. Tell me how to do this."
Do you want to make decisions about how to teach (not just about what to teach)?	14. Check how the student responds to instruction.	Use assisted assessment. Take something the student has failed and try teaching it to him. Observe the student's learning and task-related behaviors.
	15. Summarize changes in the student's skill.	Use instructionally sensitive repeated measures of the skill and monitor progress over time. Compare progress obtained through different instructional approaches.

Systematic Interpretation

Evaluation is a thoughtful process. It is during the final step of this process that an evaluator's most sophisticated thinking should take place. After testing/observing, the evaluator either takes the available information and converts it into interpretations or, if not feeling adequately prepared to do that yet, sets it aside and continues testing/observing. The move to decision making follows the sequence illustrated in Exhibit 7.10. In this sequence, questions are asked, behavior summaries are collected, and decisions are made.

We believe that most evaluators can arrive at good functional teaching recommendations if they can confidently answer these questions:

1. Is the objective the student is trying to learn the right one?
2. Would the task be better learned by isolating it or by presenting it in context?

Exhibit 7.8   Evaluator Errors

A. While constructing a computation evaluation of a sixth-grader, Ted uses a test containing no multiplication items. Ted bases his instructional decisions on this test.

B. Margie has tested a student and found that she can't read vowel sounds. Margie recommends using small-group reading instruction.

C. Jim has concluded that Andrew can't spell because he has counted Andrew's handwriting errors as spelling errors.

D. A new student has arrived at Mark's school. Mark tests this student's knowledge of study skills by asking the student to list the five components of a good summary statement. When the student can't do it, Mark concludes the student can't make summary statements.

E. Stan tests Alice's knowledge of addition facts by asking her to take an untimed test composed of addition problems. She passes it and he concludes instruction on addition is not needed.

Exhibit 7.9*   Decision Making

Directions: Ask *each* question (more than one may be applicable to any student). Include in your considerations the kind of data (performance or progress) that is available to you *(behavior indicated by progress data listed in italics)*.

Questions	Behavior	Decisions
1. Am I working on the correct objective?	Student is at or above CAP.	No instruction is required on this objective. Monitor for retention.
	Student is not at CAP but has the necessary prerequisites to learn the skill.	Teach this objective.
	Student is not at CAP but *is making some correct responses.*	Stay with current objective.
	Student is below CAP and *has made no progress after several sessions.*	Confirm that the student has the necessary prerequisites: • If yes, change instruction; • If no, move back to a less complex objective.
2. Should I teach this skill in content or in isolation?	Student has the necessary background information to derive meaning for the context (knows what a checkbook is and what it is used for).	Teach the skill in the context of larger tasks. Explain the relevance of the task. Make the lesson "applied" (have him do subtraction in a checkbook).
	Student is lacking prior knowledge necessary to use context, or is confused by context.	Teach the largest manageable portion of the objective in isolation. Use "fact" instruction. If student is accurate, employ fast-paced repetitive drill. Set daily performance aims and reinforce improvement. Put the skill in context as soon as possible.
3. Should I use an acquisition or fluency format? (Application/ automaticity should *always* be emphasized.)	Student is inaccurate. Typically this means that the student is making meaningful errors, is less than 85% accurate, or is *very* slow.	Use acquisition instruction, including extensive explanations, models, demonstration, guided practice with correction and feedback. Allow little independent work.
	Student is accurate (85% or better), errors are not meaningful, and/or rate is low.	Use fluency instruction. Emphasize rate. Give extensive drill and practice. Make sure accuracy is maintained.
4. Am I emphasizing the correct thought processes? (Facts, concepts, and strategies are all important.)	Student's errors often reflect incorrect use of basic facts (thinks $8 + 7 = 14$ or that whales breathe under water).	Teach factual content through presentation of problems and answers.
	Students errors often reflect incorrect understanding of the meaning of the task (thinks $8 + 7$ is the same as 87, or that whales are fish).	Teach conceptual content by presenting critical attributes and requiring the student to discriminate between examples and non-examples of the concept.

Exhibit 7.9*   Decision Making (continued)

Directions: Ask *each* question (more than one may be applicable to any student). Include in your considerations the kind of data (performance or progress) that is available to you *(behavior indicated by progress data listed in italics)*.

Questions	Behavior	Decisions
	Student errors, or explanations, reflect incorrect knowledge of the procedures to follow when working on an item (thinks the solution to 8 + 7 can be found by counting backwards from 8, or thinks you can tell if something is a fish simply by determining if it lives in the water).	Teach strategic content by demonstrating the processes of task completion while talking through each step.
5. Am I employing the correct teacher actions when presenting the lesson?	Below CAP but making adequate progress.	Stay with current presentation.
	Below CAP but seems to have prerequisite skills. *Is making inadequate progress in spite of appropriate objective, emphasis, format, and incentive.*	Change setting, materials or delivery—variables such as: • Questioning • Feedback • Pace • Explanations • Length of lessons • Size of group • Lesson sequence • Type of practice
6. Should the lesson be made to seem more interesting?	Student *is improving*, seems interested in lessons, participates, and is nondisruptive.	Stay with current presentation.
	Student was improving, but is now getting worse. Student is beginning to resist lessons. Student is not participating (is bored!).	Provide meaning. Explain relevance of task. Work skills in the context of higher level skills. Begin and end lessons by explaining how the skill can be used. Allow student's input into the kind of instruction they receive. Allow them to chart their own progress. Make lessons "applied." *or* Change type or schedule of reinforcement. Use preferred activities or student-selected rewards. Consider increasing or decreasing the frequency of reinforcement. Change when reinforcement is delivered to make it more or less predictable. Change type of reinforcer.
7. Do I need more information?	You can't answer the first six questions.	Keep evaluating!

Exhibit 7.10 Systematic interpretation.

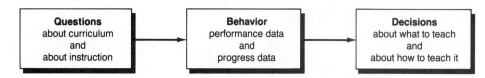

3. Should I emphasize accuracy, fluency, or automaticity?

4. Do I need to emphasize facts, concepts and/or strategies?

5. Should I modify the setting, materials, or instruction?

6. Should I do something to make the lesson more interesting?

7. Do I need more information to answer these questions?

Notice that we said you have to be able to answer these questions confidently. Among other things, this requires the recognition that some of the questions require the use of progress data.

Progress Data

The collection and analysis of progress data (sometimes called *formative* data) was discussed in Chapter 5. The term *progress* refers to changes in behavior during instruction. Performance data, the kind collected by giving a test once, tell us where a student is on a skill at the time the test is given. Progress data, which are collected by monitoring a skill over a period of time, tell us how the student's behavior is changing. Because instruction is designed to produce changes in behavior, only progress data can tell us if instruction is effective. Consider this example. A teacher gives Elena and Alan a spelling test and they both get scores of 45.

This means they are both performing at the same level. However, a week later when the teacher gives the test again, Alan only gets 50 while Elena gets 75. This means Elena is progressing faster than Alan. It also means that the instruction being used is more effective for Elena than it is for Alan. When using Exhibit 7.9* , remember that information about progress (change) is needed to make how-to-teach decisions.

We suggest that you read through Exhibit 7.9* carefully. Be sure to note any terms that seem unfamiliar and look them up in the glossary or index. If the exhibit seems unclear, it must be because we've explained it poorly or you've missed something. In either case, because we aren't around, it is up to you to clarify this very important information by recognizing topics you need to review.

Summary

This chapter has more stuff, in fewer pages, than the previous chapters. It's got flowcharts, multi-columned exhibits, and cross-referencing. It doesn't have as much explanation. That is because this chapter should be used as a reference. It outlines the various generic rules, formats, and actions you need to follow to conduct a functional teaching-oriented evaluation. You'll want to refer to this chapter while reading Part 3 of the text—or when you get hung up while conducting an evaluation.

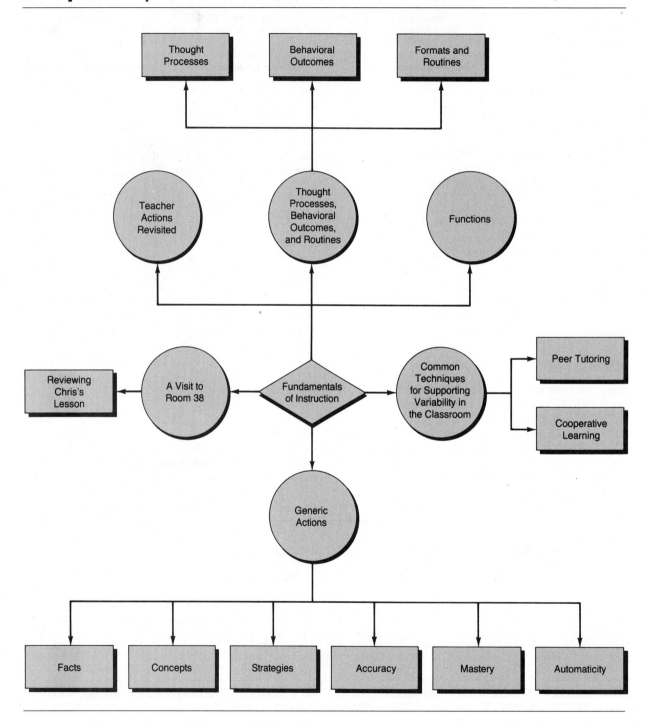

. . . the great teacher should care as much as any man for his subject and be able to convey his pleasure in it far better than most.

—N. Maclean (1974)

I hear and I forget. I see and I remember. I do and I understand.

—Chinese proverb

The first five chapters (Part 1) of this text covered a variety of ideas about students, curriculum, and instruction. One of the most powerful of these was something called the *principle of alignment* (see Chapter 3). In simplest terms, this principle says that teachers should test what they teach, teach what they test, and only teach/test essential aspects of the curriculum. Chapters 6 and 7 of this part (Part 2) have described generic procedures for defining the curriculum and for deciding which parts of it a student needs to be taught. This chapter will supply generic information about how that instruction should take place. It will also outline the "curriculum" of teaching so that, in later chapters (16 and 17), you will be prepared to evaluate the quality of instruction.

Teacher Actions Revisited

Chapter 4 presented information on instruction. In that chapter, a distinction was made among six categories of teacher action: preparing instruction, delivery of information, asking questions, responding to efforts, conducting activities, and evaluating instruction. In hands-on teaching these actions are carried out to complement the behavioral outcomes and thought processes targeted for learning.

Look at Exhibit 8.1. The teacher actions are displayed at the top of that figure and the thought processes and outcomes are listed down the left side. This exhibit illustrates, by generating an array of 36 squares, the complexity of teaching. The authors believe that each of these squares can be related to specific teacher actions (which themselves result from specific teacher decisions).

Our goal in this chapter is to illustrate the teaching represented in Exhibit 8.1. To do that, we will rely on a series of exhibits. The content in these exhibits was drawn directly from *The Instructional Environment Scale (TIES)* (Ysseldyke & Christenson, 1987). The content in TIES was itself drawn from a comprehensive review of teacher-effectiveness literature. The exhibits outline a set of guidelines for effective teaching and, as such, may be used for purposes of evaluating classroom instruction (as will be explained in Chapters 16 and 17). In order to cross-reference the TIES content directly to this chapter, we have listed it, by Ysseldyke and Christenson's headings, in six additional exhibits in Appendix B.

Turn to Appendix B and read through the six Exhibits at this time. They are provided in an attempt to define appropriate instruction which, as pointed out in Chapter 3, is a holistic domain. The material in Appendix B presents a vivid impression of exemplary teaching.

Thought Processes, Behavioral Outcomes, and Routines

Thought processes have been mentioned in almost every chapter. They were referred to in some depth in Chapter 3. The principle categories of thought referenced in this text are facts, concepts, and strategies.

As to *behavioral outcomes*, in order to determine if someone has learned something we have to get them to do something. Evaluators draw conclusions about a student's knowledge (use of thought processes) from the student's behavior. Three broad categories of behavior—accuracy, mastery, and automaticity—were also presented in Chapter 3.

Expert teachers employ *routines* (formats) for accomplishing many classroom tasks. These routines for fulfilling particular teacher functions are employed automatically. They allow the teacher to allocate needed attention to the decision making aspects of teaching.

Exhibit 8.1   Categories of Teacher Actions

		Teacher Actions					
		Prepare Instruction (B.2.1)	Deliver Information (B.2.2)	Ask Questions (B.2.3)	Respond to Efforts (B.2.4)	Use Activities (B.2.5)	Evaluate Instruction (B.2.6)
Thought Process	Facts	1	2	3	4	5	6
	Concepts	7	8	9	10	11	12
	Strategies	13	14	15	16	17	18
Behavioral Outcomes	Accuracy	19	20	21	22	23	24
	Mastery	25	26	27	28	29	30
	Automaticity	31	32	33	34	35	36

Functions

Exhibit 8.1 illustrates generic instructional formats (routines) that will be referred to throughout the topical chapters (Part 3) of the text. This will considerably reduce redundancy in Part 3. As you can see in Exhibit 8.1, teacher actions have been imposed across the categories of behavioral and thinking outcomes. This has the effect of generating the set of 36 teacher functions illustrated by the six columns and rows. For example, the grid tells us that teachers need to have activities for promoting strategic knowledge as well as information to deliver when trying to build mastery. The TIES content of Appendix B will be used to fill in each of the squares in Exhibit 8.1.

We present the generic routines in two ways. First, we illustrate their application by describing a typical hands-on lesson. The word **[marker]** will be inserted throughout this description and used to debrief the lesson. Second, the chapter will provide a set of tables presenting actions for each of the student thought processes and behavioral outcomes listed down the left side of Exhibit 8.1.

A Visit to Room 38

When you enter the room, the teacher, Chris Peterson, is working with a group of six students clustered in front of the board. Two students are working alone at their desks, while four others work with an aide. The board says:

Want
Water
Wall
Wasp
Watch
Wash
Wand
Walrus

Kathie would—
play with him.
Teach him tricks.
eat with him.
give him a name.
give him a home.
buy him a fish.

Walrus
Soft body
Silly face

Ad ver tise
Advertisement ———→ commercial
try to sell something

In the corner is a sign that says, "Be friendly with classmates." The room has five clusters of tables. Student folders sit on each table. There are fabric-covered room dividers and a large set of free-standing bookshelves to break up the space. Signs hang from the ceiling with words like *exit* and *tomorrow* printed on them. Everything is covered with posters, signs, and student art work. The space above your head is busy with the gently rotating signs.

Chris is introducing vocabulary for an upcoming story.

[marker 1] "Before we read I want to make sure

A well-structured classroom establishes routines for common activities, freeing teachers for meaningful instructional tasks.

everyone is familiar with some of the words in this story. Why should I care about that . . . Mark?"

"Well, if we don't know what the words mean it's not going to make any sense."

[marker 2] "That's right. Vocabulary is important for comprehension."

"**Plan**." She writes it on the board. "Who can give me a sentence?" [marker 3]

"I have a plan," dictates a girl with pink yarn bows in her hair. Chris writes it out and underlines the target word.

"What's the underlined word?" she asks.

"**Plan**," they all respond at once.

"Everyone read the sentence."

They read aloud in unison. No one misses a beat. [marker 4]

Chris writes **plum** on the board below **plan**.

"Who can give me a sentence?"

John, a thin boy, replies, "I have a plum on my thumb," with a smile to the side of his face.

She hesitates. " . . . on my thumb? Can you have a plum on your thumb?" She glances at you and then at the ceiling. "I guess . . . "

"Stuck in my thumb," John reminds.

"Oh!" she comments to herself. "Good sentence— it just took Ms. Peterson a second to realize what it meant. You have to know what the sentence means to know what each word means." [marker 5] She finishes the drill, then tells the students to open their books.

"I want you to read the first paragraph to yourselves and tell me what Dad was going to do." As they read, she clears off the board. When they've finished, Chris asks "Who can tell me?" [marker 6]

Someone raises a hand and tells the group, "He was going to dig a pit next to the kitchen."

Chris looks around the group and gets nods of agreement. She writes **Dig a pit next to the kitchen** on the board. She is left-handed and writes with her right hand on her hip.

"What was he going to do with the pit?" she asks.

No one knows. "OK—read the next paragraph and find out." [marker 7]

The lesson proceeds in steps. Each reading is preceded by questioning and is followed by the answer and an extension of the answer into a question for the next paragraph. Each answer is written on the board so that by the end, an outline of the story has been recorded. Chris uses the outline to summarize. It's a nice, tight lesson. It has clear purpose, is easy to understand, consistent, and has a natural summary. Lots of teachers don't summarize well, you realize. [marker 8]

Other students are working alone at their desks. They get up and move around to get materials and Kleenex without asking permission. They are on-task and well behaved without any attention or direction from Chris or her aide. You sit at a table and sneak a look at someone's folder. It's a basic plastic spiral folder with pockets in the front and back. An assignment calendar is taped to the inside cover. The front pocket holds work that needs to be done, while the back one has stuff that's finished. [marker 9] The student's name is on the spine and it's been personalized with stickers of animals and hearts.

Some of the pages seem to have schedules or directions for working on them, as opposed to actual work. For example, there is a page of spelling with dittoed directions and spelling words handwritten in like this: [marker 10]

Words to learn

1. sand
2. band
3. flags
4. play
5. ask
6. land
7. rake
8. slat
9. aunt
10. want

Monday—read words, define, make up sentences, copy words
Tuesday—write each word *five* times
Wednesday—write a sentence with each word
Thursday—trial test: write misspelled words *ten* times each
Friday—final test

An hourly bell rings, and there is a brief buzz of excitement as the girls line up and leave with the aide.

"Every spring the girls get to go see a movie on menstruation," Chris explains to your quizzical glance. "It's a real big deal."

With the girls gone, the room is nearly empty. Chris takes three boys to a table and begins to work with them. You examine one wall and find photos of a field trip and drawings of each student's family. All characters are labeled.

There are also pictures. One of them shows a cat-like dog with empty, pointed ears surrounded by birds. Under the picture some printing explains:

My dog. She eats birds. She eats food. She is big, too.
She is a good dog. Sometimes she jumps on people.
She has a cage, too, she sleeps in a big box sometimes.
Her name is Ginger.

Along the shelves you find: organized workbooks, a puzzle of the United States, a school menu, *Multiplication Self-teaching Flashcards*, and a book titled *The Bird Feeder*. There is a bulletin board titled *Responsibilities* that has a sink, shelves, dust, chairs, chalkboard, tables, and materials listed on it. Next to each responsibility are tacked cut-out hands with student names. There are bright birds and fish proceeding up one wall.

Chris is sitting with three boys—John, Manuel, and Bill. All three are working on math but are doing different assignments. Bill works almost exclusively by himself on a worksheet requiring him to identify ones, tens, and hundreds places in multidigit numbers while adding and subtracting. Chris glances at his work. He is adding 224 to 432.

"What did you just do?" she asks.

"Added 4 plus 2."

"When you add tens and ones, which column do you add first?"

"Ones."

"Very good. Point to the ones column." He points. "Very good. Tell me what you do first." She asks for a rule. [marker 11]

"Add the numbers in the ones column," he replies. [marker 12]

Manuel has worked a sheet of problems and submits it for her approval. She looks at it and informs him "I can see mistakes. If you don't know how to find an answer, what are you going to do?"

"Ask?" he wonders.

"That's right," she nods, "and to find out if you don't know the answer, you must work the problem, then check it twice. [marker 13] I can see errors in the very first row. I want you to check all the problems on this page." She hands it back to Manuel and turns to John. [marker 14]

John is subtracting 4 from 7. He's gotten 11 for an answer. "You started with what, John?"

"Seven."

"And then?"

"Plussed it to 4."

"Look at the problem and read it to me. She leans back and quickly writes 7 − 4 on the board.

Chris points to the 7 as John says, "Seven," then to the subtraction sign as he hesitates and says, "Take away 4."

"First you must decide what to do," she reminds. "What are you doing in this problem?" [marker 15]

"Subtracting."

"When you do a take-away, do the numbers get bigger or smaller?" [marker 16]

"Smaller."

"Good for you. Now try again."

Turning back to Manuel she says, "After you write an answer, check it, then check it again. What are you going to do?"

"Check it twice."

"Excellent."

Her hand drifts across the table toward Bill as if to let him know she is aware of his continued work while she returns to John, who's looking really confused.

Chris produces a set of seven blocks and has him take four away. "Did the number get smaller?"

"Yes."

"Now show me what you did with your fingers."

He holds up his hands and quickly counts out seven fingers. When he has them identified to his satisfaction, he folds down four. As he folds them down, he says "one—two—three—four." Then he counts the leftovers, "one—two—three" and says "three" with a mix of confusion and what looks like welcome resolution. [marker 17]

John's confusion is suddenly obvious. He is subtracting. Subtraction is the inverse of addition. Addition is counting forward; therefore, subtraction should be counting backward. Given seven fingers, he should be folding four of them down and saying, "Seven, six, five, four." But he isn't. As he tries to solve the subtraction problem, he employs the exact technique he uses on addition—counting forward. [marker 18]

The girls come back in the room and, with the other boys, move quickly to their business. Several of them group around Susan, the aide, and work on an alphabetizing drill. Other students work quietly by themselves from their folders. Susan corrects and praises the students' fluency with exactly the same phrases and inflection that Chris uses. She also arranges for the students working independently to check each other's work periodically. [marker 19]

Back at the table, one girl has joined the group. Chris is repeating the subtraction strategy once more as a summary of the lesson. "When you do 'take away,' do the numbers get bigger or smaller?"

"Smaller." [marker 20]

Chris turns to Manuel, who has been diligently checking his work. Manuel has taken an extra sheet of paper and used it to mask his previous answers.

"Good, Manuel, that's a good idea—covering up the old answers." It *is* a good idea. [marker 21]

Reviewing Chris' Lesson

Now let's look at the lesson for evidence that Chris seems to be using effective instruction. There are markers scattered throughout the description and we'll explain them in sequence. Within each explanation you will find a number, or numbers, in bold print. These tell you which of the squares in Exhibit 8.1 are illustrated by this example.

Marker 1: Chris is giving the purpose for the lesson, explaining what she will be doing, and activating the student's prior knowledge gained in earlier lessons **2, 8, 14**. Her question is conceptual **9**. Note that she calls a student's name *after* she has asked the question and paused to be sure all students are thinking about it **21**.

Marker 2: Here Chris gives feedback on the accuracy of Mark's answer **22**. The feedback rephrases his answer into the terminology associated with the lesson. This is a conceptual follow-up to her conceptual question **10**.

Marker 3: Generating sentences for each word is a vocabulary-building activity. Hearing/reviewing the sentences is a technique for automaticity because it promotes generalization **35**. From a decoding perspective, the words are being taught as facts (Chris shows each word and tells what it is **2**), but this lesson isn't really about decoding.

Marker 4: Choral responses are an excellent way to increase the active participation of a small group. By

Through the use of cooperative learning groups, teachers can arrange activities with varying degrees of difficulty to particular students within the group, thereby individualizing practice.

training the students to respond simultaneously, the risk of mimicking answers is removed, and it is easy to hear errors. When a teacher works with only one student at a time, the available class time is divided. Techniques that allow group responses make the whole hour available for each student **4, 10, 16, 22, 28, 34**.

Marker 5: Nice recovery! She took her own confusion and converted it into a little illustration of the strategy for figuring out context-dependent vocabulary **14**. She also made her thought processes public and, therefore, modeled use of self-monitoring and the context-vocabulary strategy **14**.

Marker 6: This is another strategic exercise. Asking questions about the story prior to reading is an excellent technique for enhancing reading comprehension **15, 17**. Many published programs seem to expect the

student to read the story and incidentally remember all of it in order to answer questions at the end. This assumes that the student thinks that what the author (teacher) believes to be important is worth remembering. The technique Chris is using develops the students' search skills. It causes them to become active readers who must judge the relevance or irrelevance of the passage components by comparing them to the given question **17**. By using it on various passages, she is building mastery and ultimately automaticity **29, 35**.

Marker 7: Delivery of information about the strategy for finding answers **14**.

Marker 8: Chris is leaving a tangible model of the process she is demonstrating **2, 8, 14, 20**. Additionally, her instruction is sequenced and consistent.

Marker 9: Whereas the group exercises are building

accuracy on various strategies **14**, **20**, the independent practice—on which the student must be 90% accurate—is designed to promote mastery **17**, **29**. Therefore, the aide is reinforcing rate.

Marker 10: This kind of routine serves three purposes: (a) it teaches spelling; (b) it relieves the teacher of the time-consuming task of explaining to each student what he is to do each day, and (c) it teaches the students a strategy for studying that they may learn along with the words and use on their own when they wish to study other material **5**, **11**, **17**.

Marker 11: Throughout all of her lessons, Chris is consistently teaching problem-solving strategies and procedures for learning **14**, in addition to isolated bits of information **2**. By teaching the strategies, Chris teaches the students how to learn and how to take control over their own learning. Additionally, the strategies tend to tie together bits of material that may seem unrelated and nonsensical to a student who is experiencing problems.

Marker 12: Notice that, throughout her lessons, Chris asks the students to articulate what they should do to work a problem, get help, locate an answer, or check one. She does not merely say these things to the student. She expects the student to be able to say them back **17**. Once the students are able to verbalize the procedure, they are able to literally talk their way through a situation to its solution. This is verbal mediation.

Marker 13: This is a nice, clear accuracy—format—response to Manuel's efforts **22**.

Marker 14: Chris is creating a strategic environment by emphasizing self-monitoring. Watch as she continues in the next few exchanges with Manuel **14**, **15**, **16**, **17**.

Marker 15: Here Chris is teaching a general problem-solving strategy.

Marker 16: Here she is addressing the conceptual aspects of the problem by having John sort problems into those yielding answers that are bigger or smaller.

Marker 17: Chris has an excellent correction procedure. She begins by having John say the strategy that he will follow to arrive at the answer **16**. Next, he works it concretely first with blocks, then with his fingers, and eventually in writing **23**. Each time he repeats the strategy aloud as he works. But he lacks one subskill necessary to carry out the strategy.

Marker 18: Error correction is often the most sophisticated portion of a lesson **4**, **10**, **16**, **22**, **28**, **34**. Sometimes it is best to introduce a lesson and its key strategies briefly and then use elaborate correction procedures to teach them. In order to do this, certain preconditions must be met.

First, the student must not view the error as a failure. Many students have learned to become upset when they make errors. Others have learned that errors signal that the task is too hard or beyond their ability, so they simply stop working. These students have learned counterproductive ways to respond from their past teachers—often through attempts at comfort. Students who constantly hear, "Don't worry about the mistake—this is a really hard task," may eventually learn that their success or failure is entirely determined by task difficulty and has nothing to do with how hard or well they work. If you are interested in this phenomenon reread the material on "learned helplessness" (see Chapter 2, p. 155).

A second precondition for error correction is that the student knows when a correction is taking place. A correction procedure relates to a past event (the production of the error). If a student believes you are presenting new material, she may become confused. The way to handle this is to use consistent correction techniques, including physical or verbal cues to signal when a correction begins and ends. Here is an extreme example of this confusion.

A common language-correction procedure involves "expansion" by the teacher of an incorrect utterance. If a student were to say "She gonna sleep there?" the teacher would expand and say "Is she going to sleep there?"

We once saw a child ask "I go ba-eroom," to which the teacher replied "Can I go to the bathroom?" After the teacher's response, the student stood in obvious confusion and eventually shrugged and nodded at the teacher as if she were an idiot. The kid was thinking "Of course *you* can go to the bathroom—you're the teacher. But what about *my* problem?"

This confusion could have been avoided if the teacher preceded all corrections with a cue (say, a hand on the shoulder) and followed the correction by responding to the meaning of the incorrect utterance. Then the whole exchange would have gone like this:

KID: "I go ba-eroom."

TEACHER: (placing hand on kid's shoulder) "May I go to the bathroom?" (Removing hand): "Yes, you may."

Exhibit 8.2   Teaching Facts

Deliver information	Ask questions	Respond to efforts	Use activities
• Review relevant prior knowledge • Show items and answers • Encourage use of memory strategies such as rehearsal and categorization • Keep delivery of information short • Separate the presentation of commonly confused items • Encourage rapid responses	• Ask a lot of direct questions • Ask for the simplest answers • Ask questions at a fast pace • Ask questions requiring identification of the answer *and* questions requiring production of the answer • Vary the presentation of stimulus items along realistic dimensions to encourage generalization	*Correct:* • Give frequent feedback on accuracy and rate • Give minimal praise required to maintain motivation *Error:* • Give immediate feedback on errors or slow responses • Do not employ elaborate correction procedures • Repeat items which have been missed	• Use drill and practice • Use several short sessions rather than one long one • Make practice as realistic as possible • Vary the conditions/settings of the practice • Provide practice to mastery

Marker 19: By using student checkers, the seatwork is made interactive and becomes much more effective. One way to handle this is to pair students, with one of the students having answers to all even-numbered items while the other has answers to all odd-numbered items. Then both students work problems and check each other.

Marker 20: Again this is a straightforward concept building exercise. Chris is having the student sort problems into two categories—those that produce bigger answers and those that do not.

Marker 21: Ten or fifteen years ago, this room might have looked very different. At that time, the analysis of curriculum tasks, problem-solving strategies, subskills, correction procedures, and verbal mediators were almost unheard of in special education. More frequent was the analysis of psycholinguistic abilities, visual perception, hemispheric dominance, and perceptual/intellectual function. In those days, Chris' room would have been dull green and segmented into cubicles to isolate the student from distractions. The lessons would have been very different. Balance beams, pattern boards, block-design drills, and pages of geometric shapes for tracing would have filled the shelves that hold reading and math books today. Today Chris trains academic skills, whereas yesterday she might have tried to train brain patterns.

There is a Down's syndrome student in the class who reads, spells, and does math and social studies as the other students do. The reason is that Chris's focus is on reading, spelling, math, and social studies. Her focus is not on IQ scores and fixed ability deficits. The Down's syndrome girl has just returned from watching a film on menstruation with the other girls in the school.

Manuel is correct. It's a good idea to cover up the old answers, so we don't drag yesterday's errors into today.

Generic Actions

All efforts at alignment begin with the specification of a learning outcome (objective). That's why we have spent so much time talking about exactly what objectives are, and about the fact that they have multiple elements. Obviously, if instruction is going to be aligned with a punctuation objective, it will supply information about punctuation (the content element of the objective will be addressed). However, each of the other aspects of tasks must also be addressed. These include not only the objective elements (content,

Exhibit 8.3   *Teaching Concepts*

Deliver information	Ask questions	Respond to efforts	Use activities
• Review relevant prior knowledge. • Name the concept and use the same name during all initial lessons (use synonyms later). • Show multiple examples of the concept and point out the critical and non-critical attributes in each example. • Use clear examples in early lessons and ambiguous examples in later lessons. • Take your time. • Emphasize reflection and accurate responding. • Work with the student to prepare a diagram (map) of the concept. • Encourage discussions and questions about the concept. • Demonstrate how an example can be changed to a non-example (and vice versa).	• Ask the student why something is or isn't an example of the concept. • Ask the student to identify things which are "always," "sometimes," or "never" attributes of the concept. • Ask the student to identify which things are, or are not, examples of the concept. • Ask the student to define the concept. • Ask the student to supply examples and attributes. • Intersperse questions throughout the delivery of information. • Ask a lot of questions but do not "drill" the student. • Ask the student to tell you how he knows an answer is correct.	*Correct:* • Give specific feedback by telling the student exactly what discrimination he made that was correct, or what information he recalled. • Periodically challenge correct answers by asking the student to support his response. *Incorrect:* • Use elaborate correction procedures during early lessons. • Explain exactly why a response is wrong. • Watch for, and label, examples of overgeneralization. • Encourage the student to judge his own work and to self-correct.	• Have the student sort items into categories. • Have the student convert nonexamples into examples by changing the necessary attributes. • Have the student "compare and contrast" examples and nonexamples. • Use clear examples and nonexamples in early lessons and subtle ones in later lessons. • Use activities that illustrate the range of concept.

behavior, conditions, and criteria) but the thought processes (factual, conceptual, strategic) that are being promoted.

As we saw in Chris's lessons, these functions are not necessarily allocated to different time periods during a lesson. They may come in and out according to the flow of the lesson. However, some students—John was an example—may require a particular emphasis. In John's case that emphasis was on the strategic and conceptual aspects of subtraction.

Exhibits 8.2 to 8.4 provide in-depth explanations of the sort of instruction that can be used to emphasize a particular thought process. Exhibit 8.5 provides information on procedures needed to promote differ-

ent behavioral outcomes. We realize that these are giant exhibits, but there is no reason to dilute this content with verbiage.

Supporting Effective Instruction

Exhibits 8.2 to 8.5 outline principles of effective instruction. This instruction can occur 1:1 or 1:100, but the techniques a teacher must employ with large groups obviously differ from those used with small groups.

Today, an increasing proportion of disabled and remedial students are being served within the general

Exhibit 8.4   Teaching Strategies

Deliver information	Ask questions	Respond to efforts	Use activities

• Review relevant prior knowledge.
• Name the strategy.
• Demonstrate use of the strategy.
  A. Work while talking aloud.
  B. Show recognition of problem.
  C. Show recognition of alternative strategies and selection of target strategy.
  D. Show self monitoring and decision making.
  E. Show limits of the strategy and rules for its use.
  F. Leave a model if possible.
• Encourage the student to work through difficult items.
• Encourage the student to monitor his work and to decide how things are going *before* an item as finished.
• Emphasize the process of work—not the completion of tasks.
• Point out the necessary prerequisite skills/ knowledge to use a strategy.
• Give elaborate explanations and demonstrations.
• Don't supply answers, only supply ways to get answers.
	• Ask student to supply rules, steps and procedures.
	• Ask questions about how things are done— deemphasize finding answers.
	• Ask the student how he got an answer.
	• Ask the student to predict the effect of an omitted or incorrect step.
	• Ask, "what is the first thing you will do? What will you do next?"
	• Use lead questions to prompt a strategy (e.g. is there an "e" on the end of that word? Then what sound will the vowel make?).
		Correct Effort:
		• Say, "good, you did it correctly," not "good you got the right answer."
		• Review the procedure the student has just finished.
		• Say, "that's correct— now tell me how you got it."
		
		Incorrect Effort:
		• Be sure the student has the skills needed to do the task.
		• Ask the student to recognize and correct his own errors.
		• Ask the student what went wrong.
		• Tell the student what went wrong.
		• Repeat the item.
			• Use guided practice (student thinks aloud, and teacher provides feedback).
			• Have student act as teacher.
			• Have student work alone and check own work.
			• Provide practice to automaticity.
			• Ask the student to recognize missing steps.
			• Ask the student to "think aloud" while working.
			• Ask the student to "work correctly." Do *not* emphasize getting answers or finishing pages.
			• Have the student practice recognizing problems.
			• Have the student practice generating and evaluating alternative solutions.
			• Have the student practice recognizing when a strategy will or will not work.

education classroom (United States Department of Education, 1991). This is true, in part, because of dissatisfaction with pull-out programs that have attempted to reduce the range of student skills within classrooms. These efforts have been based on erroneous assumptions about the possibility, and availability, of homogeneous grouping (see Chapter 4).

While it is common to contrast various delivery

Exhibit 8.5 *Teaching for Accuracy, Mastery and Automaticity*

	Deliver information	Ask questions	Respond to efforts	Use activities
Accuracy (Acquisition Instruction)	• Extensive explanation • Modeling and demonstration	• Ask about strategies and concepts • Do not emphasize answers	• Praise accurate responses • Use elaborate correction procedures	• Use only guided and controlled practice • Have student complete partially worked items
Mastery (Fluency Instruction)	• Review	• Emphasize answers • Ask many questions	• Praise fluent work • Do not use correction procedures	• Drill and practice • Independent practice
Automaticity (Generalization and transfer Instruction)	• Explain how existing skills can be generalized • Teach related vocabulary	• Ask how existing skills can be modified	• Use elaborate corrections when generalization or transfer fails to occur	• Use "real world" examples • Deemphasize classroom specific tasks

models (resource, self-contained, transition classes, tracking systems, and consultation), we believe that student learning hinges most directly on the teacher's use of the actions in Exhibits 8.2 to 8.5, *regardless* of the model in which the student is served. Therefore, a special education pull-out teacher working 1:1 who fails to employ these actions will facilitate less learning than a general education teacher who does. The question is "Can a general education teacher do all that stuff in a room with 30 students?" The answer is yes. It isn't necessarily easy, but it can be done.

First of all, it is important to remember that the level of support specified in this chapter really won't need to be supplied to all 30 of the general education class. However, it may need to be supplied to as many as ten of them. Regardless of the number, however, it is likely that the teacher will need some sort of support in order to provide the service while maintaining sanity. Many schools are currently supplying support to classroom teachers through the use of *teacher assistance teams*. These teams, which vary in composition, are intended to help students by providing staff development to their teachers (Carter & Sugai, 1989; Fuchs et al., 1992; Idol & West, 1987). In some cases, this consultation promotes the use of special education technology within the general education classroom. In other cases, the consultation promotes user-friendly whole-class instruction (Jenkins & Leicester, 1992).

The exact nature of user-friendly instruction varies according to the age of the students and the content being taught. However, peer-mediated instruction (peer tutoring) and cooperative learning are two of the most commonly employed ways of increasing the range of general education class instruction (Lloyd et al., 1988). Both of these techniques have long histories of successful application.

The provision of in-depth coverage on cooperative learning and peer tutoring is well beyond the scope of this chapter. However, we can provide what we believe to be excellent direction for readers interested in pursuing these topics, along with another topic of particular concern these days: instruction of remedial students at the junior and senior levels.

Information on **peer tutoring**:

Jenkins, J.R. & Jenkins, L.M. (1988). *Cross-age and peer tutoring: Help for children with learning problems.* Reston, VA: The Council for Exceptional Children.

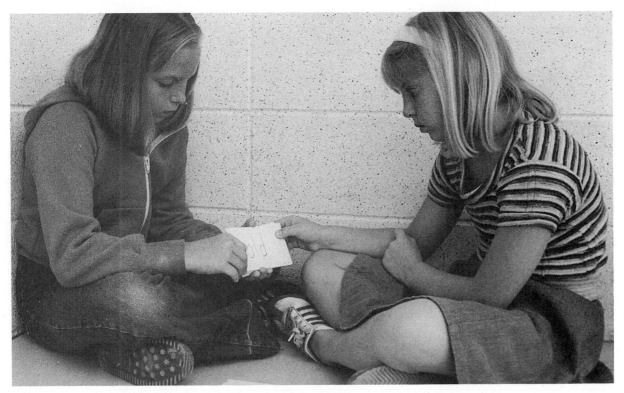

Peer tutoring helps students strengthen what they know while helping another student.

Warger, C.L. (1992). *Peer Tutoring: When working together is better than working alone.* Reston, VA: The Council for Exceptional Children.

Information on **cooperative learning**:

Stevens, R.J., Madden, N.A., Slavin, R.E., & Farnish, A.M. (1987). Cooperative integrated reading and composition: Two field experiments. *Reading Research Quarterly, 22,* 433–54.

Information on **teaching older students**:

Lovitt, T. & Horton, S.V. (1991). Adapting textbooks for mildly handicapped adolescents. In G. Stoner, M. Shinn, & H. Walker (Eds.), *Interventions for achievement and behavior problems* (pp. 439–72). National Association of School Psychologists.

Schumaker, J.C., Deshler, D.D., & McKnight, P.C. (1991). Teaching routines for content areas at the secondary level. In G. Stoner, M. Shinn, & H. Walker

(Eds.), *Interventions for achievement and behavior problems* (pp. 473–94). National Association of School Psychologists.

Summary

This very brief chapter has combined material from the first two parts of the text to provide information about effective instruction. It also painted an image of effective instruction by paying a visit to a special education classroom. The techniques employed by Chris in room 38 are not exclusive to pull-out programs. That is why we also discussed, and referenced, instructional approaches that can be used within general education.

Chapter 9 / Eligibility Decisions

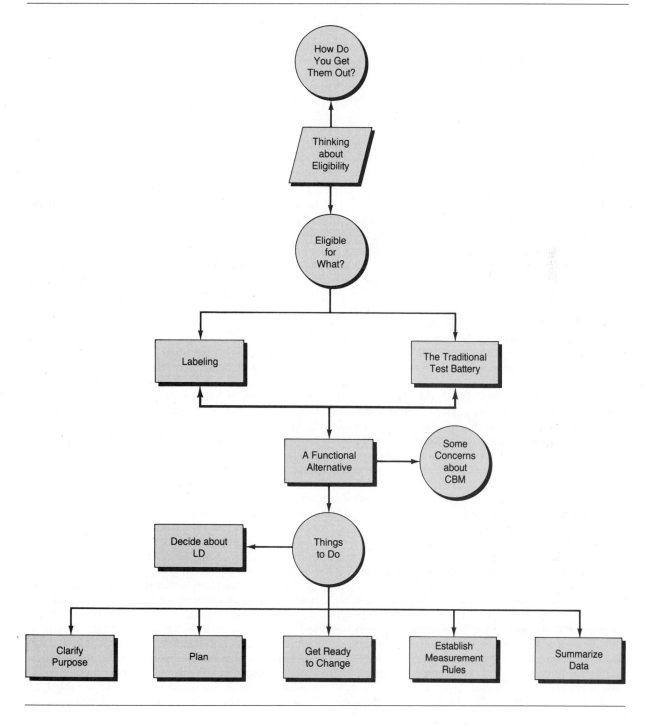

*. . . If nobody ever lifted a finger until people were deserving, the whole world would go
to hell. We better deal with each other out of need and forget merit, because none of us
have too much of that. Not me. Not you. Not anybody.*

—Barbara Rush, in the 1967 movie *Hombre*

*This chapter was prepared with the assistance of Petrea Hagen-Gilden
M.A., and Carol Sadler, Ph.D., Tigard-Tualatin School District No. 23J,
Tigard, Oregon.*

Thinking About Eligibility

Educators make two broad categories of decisions: eligibility decisions and teaching decisions. While this text deals almost exclusively with the topic of teaching, it is hard to imagine a book dealing with special or remedial education that doesn't spend some time addressing eligibility.

This discussion is important because very few schools allow all students the consideration granted to certain "types" of students by litigation and legislation. They could, but they don't. Therefore, while some students are guaranteed an "appropriate education," others are not.

Imagine this situation. Two students, Sara and Brian, are both in the fourth grade. According to their teacher, Ms. Buck, neither one of them can read adequately. Because Ms. Buck is concerned about Sara and Brian, she refers them for an evaluation in the hope of getting special or remedial support services. The evaluation reveals that both students have identical reading scores and both apparently need exactly the same level of support if they are ever going to read at grade level. However, Sara was schooled at home for the first three years by her father, who chose to attempt reading instruction exclusively through the use of lectures on the value of literacy. Brian, in distinction, received a more typical education.

After several meetings and considerable expense, Ms. Buck is informed that Brian will receive support services in the area of reading. Conversely, because her low scores seem to be the result of poor educational decision making by her father, Sara does not qualify for any of the special reading programs available at her particular school.

In a case such as this, two students *with the same
need for help* do not get the same support. Why? Because one of them is eligible for support and the other isn't. In order to understand how this could happen and to examine some procedures for preventing it, we must briefly examine the issues of labeling, causation, regulation, and funding. Often these issues, not the needs of students, determine the processes of eligibility decision making in schools.

Eligible for What?

Eligibility decisions are intended to help professionals place failing students in federal- or state-funded support programs. Exhibit 9.1 provides a very brief overview of some of these support programs and whom they are supposed to support. One assumption underlying the existence of these programs is that only certain students "deserve" support beyond that allocated to all students. These students fall roughly into two types—those with a personal disability and those who are members of a group that has been granted compensation on the basis of cultural, linguistic, or economic characteristics. It is assumed that these characteristics have had the effect of hindering their educational opportunity. Sara lost out on support services because "misdirecting father" is neither a recognized disability nor a protected group.

Because schools are social institutions, their structure is often determined through the political and quasi-political processes of elected government (Maag & Howell, 1992). These include lobbying. Groups of voters—interested in what they perceive to be the special needs of a particular group—will approach governing agencies ranging from the local school board to the United States Senate and argue for special help. If their lobbying efforts are successful, help is supplied in

Exhibit 9.1   Categorical Support Programs

Program Title	Function	Services Provided	Qualifying Criteria
Chapter 1	Meets needs of educationally deprived students, many of whom are impoverished	Primarily remedial math and reading pullout program	Parent or teacher referral, previous enrollment, low test scores
Chapter 2	Helps local education agencies meet needs of at-risk students; also supports school programs	Student support services, library/media resources, and staff development	Established at state level
Indian Education Act	Provides direct services to Native American children in public schools; also provides university fellowships	Curriculum development, dropout/drug-abuse prevention programs; also gifted and talented programs	Must be Native American
Bilingual education (ESL)	Transitional program to teach functional English to students with limited English proficiency (LEP)	English immersion program, Chapter 1–type pullout for small groups	Staff judgment, English oral/reading/writing proficiency tests
Migrant education	Meets special needs of children of migratory agricultural or fisheries workers	Chapter 1–type pullout program for small groups. May contain ESL component; also outreach/recruitment services	Parent must be migrant agricultural or fisheries worker
Special education	Provides free and appropriate education to all handicapped students in the least-restrictive environment	Resource rooms, self-contained classrooms, consultant services for special ed. students in the regular classroom; separate services for particular disabilities	Definitions and evaluation procedures are specified in federal and state regulations

the form of funds designated for the targeted group. This is called "categorical funding." It is categorical funding that drives the practice of labelling students (Ysseldyke et al., 1992). To guarantee that funds are actually spent on the targeted group of students, federally funded support programs typically have mandated eligibility criteria and selection procedures. Unfortunately these procedures, like the group definition they are meant to clarify, often have little to do with the actual teaching needs of the students falling within the group.

Eligibility procedures for some remedial programs, such as Chapter 1, have been aligned with the school curriculum. These programs characteristically rely on teacher referrals or cutoff scores on achievement tests to identify students in need of assistance. In contrast, eligibility criteria established for special education by the Individuals with Disabilities Education Act (IDEA) require that evaluations substantiate the presence in the child of a disability (which presumably exists under any educational condition). This, as you will read shortly, has created some major problems.

A Note on Labeling

Classification, when properly used, is a process that aids the development of theory by promoting understanding between interested parties. Researchers are

Two students with identical learning needs may not both qualify for special or remedial services. Eligibility for service is determined by matching personal characteristics to established definitions of disability or protected class.

able to classify according to any number or combination of variables. In education, students are routinely classified according to *source variables*, student characteristics that supposedly explain why a child isn't learning (Reynolds & Balow, 1972). Traditional source variables correspond to the current funding categories (learning disabled, seriously behaviorally disordered, low income, bilingual). These variables are thought of as the sources of educational failure because those who believe in them are working under the assumption that failures to learn can be traced to "problems" with the learner (see Chapter 2, p. 19).

The use of student source variables for classification is supported in part by the fact that, with certain severe conditions, classification and treatment are nearly synonymous. Because the field of special education grew out of treating severely handicapped individuals, the confusion may have been with us from the start (Quay, 1973). When the problem is the academic deficiency of a mildly disabled student, however, the variables for classification are less specific.

There is no one variable that explains reading failure. In fact, there is no one definition of reading.

Educational labels are far from precise; a "gifted" child in one school district may be "average" in another. This is because the categories of exceptionality, while based on theories of causation, are almost always defined with normative tests that compare students to each other rather than to a functional standard. Anyone who performs differently in the group looks exceptional when compared to a norm.

Labeling through normative comparison was initially acceptable because of the widely held belief that North American culture is a "melting pot" in which diverse individuals mix (Skrtic, 1991; Ysseldyke et al., 1992). Mercer (1973) spoke to this analogy when she observed that "clinical assessment has reinforced the 'melting pot' process by defining persons who have not 'melted' as subnormal" (p. 9). Normative comparison tends to isolate, and eventually stigmatize, any subgroup that is truly different from the norm. Two obvious ways in which people may differ from the norm are by race and wealth. Because both race and wealth have been viewed by the Supreme Court as discriminatory methods of classification, the courts have held that the use of norms that overrepresent members of certain races or classes is inappropriate for making educational placement decisions (*Larry P. v. Riles*, 1979; *Diana v. State Board of Education*, 1970, 1973; *Hobson v. Hanson*, 1967). In 1979, Howell, Kaplan, and O'Connell observed that:

> The legal, social, and educational price being paid for the use of traditional normative testing for the purpose of classification will almost certainly continue to rise. As it does, it will be interesting to see at what point this use is simply discontinued because of the confusion and misunderstanding this practice breeds. (p. 22)

Rueda, Figueroa, Mercado, and Cardoza (1985) have reported that this point was apparently reached in the State of California (which is not to imply that there is no confusion left in that state), where *Larry P. v. Riles* has curtailed the use of IQ testing (Galagan, 1985). As a result of that litigation, the proportion of students classified as educable mentally retarded has dropped by nearly 30%. (In the same time, the number of students served as learning disabled has increased by 140%.)

Saying Too Much and Too Little at the Same Time.
While there are legitimate reasons to classify and label students, there are also numerous problems with the practice. The main problem is that labels can mean different things to different people. Classifications and labels may lack meaning, or worse yet, have more meaning than they should. Korzybski (1948) described a kind of word game in which the players attempt to supply the meaning for words by first giving a definition and then defining the words in the definition without repeating key words. In a short time the players find their vocabularies exhausted as they reach a level at which they "know" but can't "tell" the definition. Korzybski says the game takes from 10 to 15 minutes. If the game is played by educators using labels such as *at-risk, mentally retarded, learning disabled,* or *disadvantaged,* it takes about 5 minutes.

Ironically, at the other extreme and at the same time, a label may have too much meaning. This is referred to as *surplus meaning* (Cromwell, Blashfield & Strauss, 1975), and it is produced when a term is used to describe too many things. A vague term can be applied to many situations and a person who hears it may not know to which situation it refers.

The term *mental retardation* (or even *retardation*) is the classic example of a term with both too little and too much meaning. The term has various definitions. Most include the key words *permanent limitation, intelligence (intellectual capacity), central nervous system,* and *incompetence.* The circularity of the term can be seen by playing Korzybski's (1948) game with a dictionary: the term *mental* relates to the term *intelligence,* and *intelligence* relates to the term *ability.* The term *retardation* relates to the term *limitation,* which relates to a lack of *capacity. Capacity,* by referring to *ability,* completes the circle back to *mental.*

The surplus meaning of a term like *retarded* is also obvious. It means *slow to develop* but, as explained in Chapter 2, it carries with it the image of incurable incompetence. We once sat in on a staffing in which the school psychologist's report contained the unfortunate comment that the child under review was "retarded in the area of reading." The parent, seeing that comment, never got beyond the word *retarded,* and reacted to the statement as if his child was unalterably mentally defective.

To special education teachers, who may spend hours each week in placement meetings, it often seems that education has become so focused on describing the disabilities of students that educating them is forgotten. Indeed, despite wording in the federal law (IDEA Reg. 300.533), which clearly separates the issues of eligibility and treatment, it has been found that the category of disability often influences the content of the Individual Education Plan (IEP). Because current disability definitions mix educational and medical models, evaluation activities conducted to determine eligibility lack educational focus. Since evaluations are very costly and educational resources are shrinking, reform is in order.

Costs in Time and Money.
A comprehensive evaluation utilizes significant economic and human resources. While estimates vary, the cost is often said to be somewhere between $3000 and $5000, and 40–60 hours of student time. (When one considers that most students are referred for poor reading skills, one wonders if the problem couldn't be solved more efficiently by telling the student "I'll give you $3000 if you'll learn to read.")

Since students with mild disabilities vary in their learning characteristics, so should the assigned goals, tasks, and strategies used to teach and motivate them.

The Traditional Test Battery

In many schools, when a student is referred for support services, she is given a standard battery of tests. This standard group of tests is often given to every student who is referred—regardless of need. There are at least two reasons why this is a mistake: first, it requires students to take tests they may not need; second, the standard battery is usually composed of norm-referenced ability and achievement measures.

In a recent audit of special education files, one of the authors pulled 25 student folders at random from the referral list of a large school district. Here are the tests that were given, and the number (out of 25) of students to whom they were given.

6   Memory for Designs

8   Bender Visual Motor Gestalt Test

10   Kaufman Assessment Battery for Children

10   Woodcock Reading Mastery

13   KeyMath Inventory

14   Woodcock Johnson Psycho-Educational Battery—Revised: Cognitive

15   Peabody Picture Vocabulary Test—Revised

18   Peabody Individual Achievement Test—Revised

22   Wechsler Intelligence Scale for Children—Revised

23   Woodcock-Johnson Psycho-Educational Battery—Revised Achievement

25   Wide Range Achievement Test—Revised

Many of the students were given almost all of the tests (one got 10 out of the 11). That represents roughly 8 hours of student time and 20 hours of administrator scoring and interpretation. Yet many of these tests are redundant—especially the achievement measures such as the Woodcock-Johnson Psycho-Educational Achievement, Wide Range Achievement, Peabody Achievement, Woodcock Reading, and KeyMath. The weaknesses of these global achievement measures is not addressed by giving more of them; that only wastes more kid time.

A Functional Alternative

Changes in the way remedial and special education programs are conceptualized have contributed to a shift in thinking about testing for eligibility (Ysseldyke, Algozzine & Thurlow, 1992). The roles of support personnel in schools are changing as the educational community has gradually become aware that there really isn't a separate instructional technology unique to "special" kids (Semmel, Abernathy, Butera & Lesar, 1991). This awareness has encouraged educators to bring resources to general education classrooms, emphasizing a collaborative relationship between general education and support services (Self, Benning, Marston & Magnusson, 1991). As pointed out in Chapter 4, the current trend in support service is toward addressing student variability within the general education classroom through teacher-assistance teams, consulting teacher models, collaborative teaching arrangements, and prereferral intervention programs (Jenkins & Leicester, 1992). These approaches require *functional* information about both the student and the environment, and the effects of instruction on skills. They also require the use of language that is easily understood by any professional involved in the education of the child.

In Chapter 5, Exhibit 5.2, evaluation was described as a process of comparison between student behavior samples and performance standards. When these comparisons reveal discrepancies in performance, it is assumed that the students need help. If the students can't get this help without someone first determining eligibility, then efforts must be made to efficiently determine eligibility. One way to assure that an evaluation is both efficient and functional is to use curriculum-based measures (Shinn & Hubbard, 1992). Curriculum-based measures (CBM), such as those described in this text, ensure that discrepancies are derived from meaningful behavior samples and standards. Additionally, CBM can provide a local referent for judging the significance of a student's achievement discrepancy. For example, when school districts have wide variability in student achievement from school to school, school-level CBM norms offer teams a better comparison than national, or even district, norms (Shinn, 1989).

From the teaching perspective, CBM has the additional advantage of curriculum relevance. Because it is drawn from the curriculum, it pinpoints skill deficits and contributes to instructional planning. Instructional plans developed from an analysis of the student's skills can also be monitored for effectiveness by using CBM measures (Tindal & Marston, 1990). As a result, curriculum-based evaluation methods are practical and flexible, and they focus professionals on issues that are educationally relevant. They are also cheaper (Marston & Magnusson, 1988). Curriculum-based tests are simple to administer and summarize, and are of equal utility to the remedial reading teacher, the classroom teacher, or the special educator.

When using CBM measures, evaluators develop tests from whatever objectives are in place in their local districts and test students as many times as necessary to allow confidence in eligibility and treatment decisions. These measures produce information that is relevant, such as the content the child needs to learn, the rate at which the child works, and the conditions under which the child is able to complete the task.

A CBM Example

Because so many students are referred for reading problems, let's examine how CBM might be used to decide if a student is eligible for service because of poor reading. Consider Suzy, a poor reader, who comes to the attention of a school support team while she's in third grade. Before the referral, Suzy will have already been given tests and assignments by her teacher. Because her school is committed to the use of functional evaluations, many of these measures (or their results) will have been stored in her classroom portfolio. This significantly reduces the amount of new testing required to decide what help Suzy needs. The portfolio, containing what is already known about

Suzy as a reader, comes with the initial request for help from her classroom teacher. It describes Suzy's reading in quantitative terms based on classwide CBM progress monitoring that the teacher routinely employs.

A typical CBM reading probe, administered three or more times, produces a score that can be used in identification, and also serves as the first- (or survey) level measure for a reading skills assessment. The same data is useful as a baseline of the student's achievement against which the effects of instructional interventions can be judged. CBMs are also flexible enough to be tailored to the individual needs of the student. For example, a problem frequently encountered in administering norm-referenced tests is that of the student who was ill, unhappy, or uncooperative on the day of the test. Because alternative normed test forms are a rarity, evaluators either have to use the questionable data obtained that day or administer a second test that may differ substantially from the first measure with respect to its construction and content. CBM probes, on the other hand, are suitable for repeated administration and may be given until a teacher or team feels the child's achievement has been accurately represented.

When the support team provides Suzy's teacher with some teaching ideas, the CBM monitoring procedure will be used to track her reading growth. When the Chapter 1 teacher supplements the classroom reading program with small-group instruction, CBM progress monitoring is used again to demonstrate the effectiveness of the Chapter 1 instruction. Finally, curriculum-based specific-level testing is used to identify missing prior knowledge related to reading.

The CBM procedures, therefore, replace the various achievement measures routinely given to referred students. However, CBM will not necessarily provide all of the information about Suzy that the regulations require for eligibility. Nor will CBM answer every question a team may have about the resources Suzy brings to the learning situation. It is expected that school teams will still have occasion to use tools such as nationally normed achievement, language, or intelligence tests. Nevertheless, in a functional assessment, discretion is exercised in the decision to use such tools. Tests that produce potentially stigmatizing and biasing scores are used only when they are absolutely required by regulations, or when they provide teams with information that cannot be obtained in any other way. For example, if an IQ test is required to document retardation for special education eligibility, then it is used. However, because the score is generated only to meet a specific legal purpose, it is used for that purpose only and then ignored when instructional decisions are being made. In a functional evaluation, explanations of student failure based on unalterable variables, such as IQ or dysfunctional home environment, are avoided. These variables are placed on the sidelines of decision making and are seen as sometimes required, perhaps interesting, but largely irrelevant to teaching.

Special Concerns About CBM

The remainder of this chapter focuses on using CBM to meet assessment requirements of categorically funded general education, remedial, and special education programs. Professionals need to consider the legal and practical issues that follow when planning to use CBM to meet eligibility criteria. However, it is our experience that many people believe that certain tools (for example, IQ tests) are mandated for use by law when actually they are not. It is often an error to assume that common practice is the result of best practice or legal requirements. More often we have found it to be the result of tradition.

Parent Permission

Because CBM probes appear informal, educators may not realize that these measures, like published achievement tests, can be individually administered, normed, and standardized. Any time information is obtained in order to make a special education eligibility decision, parents need to be informed of their rights under IDEA. Moreover, any state or local policy governing the administration of individual assessments must by followed. These include efforts to obtain written parental consent (IDEA Reg. 300.504). This means that if a classroom teacher is generally using CBMs to track total class progress or assign students to instructional groups, no parental consent is required. However, if CBMs are given to an individual child in order to plan a prereferral or special education intervention, written parental consent (or its legal alternative) would be required.

Reliability and Validity

Special education eligibility mandates typically are the most specific of categorical eligibility requirements. These mandates are the result of state interpretations of IDEA, and as a result, eligibility criteria vary widely from state to state (Ysseldyke et al., 1992), with some states leaving specific eligibility criteria to the local education agency. However, all states and local agencies are required by federal guidelines to use reliable and valid measures. Appropriately developed and normed CBMs meet this requirement (Shinn & Hubbard, 1992).

CBMs *can* be used whenever standardized, norm-referenced academic achievement measures are mandated. Nevertheless, limitations of CBM tests must be acknowledged. For example, most measures that have been fully developed and researched only target basic skills. They may not sample domains of more complex content. This point is well illustrated by mathematics probes that often only sample computation; skills in problem solving or mathematics application cannot be inferred from these computation scores. Furthermore, many CBMs are singularly useful at the elementary level, since little research has been conducted into their use *for making eligibility decisions* with older students. (The use of these measures for making teaching decisions is well established.)

Summative and Formative Data

Like any measure given at a single time, CBMs can provide summative data. Additionally, CBMs may be used for progress monitoring, offering evaluators a dynamic view of the learner that is unavailable through the use of traditional measures. Marston (1988) has demonstrated that CBM probes are more sensitive to student learning than traditional academic achievement tests. According to Marston, their simple format and brief administration time makes it possible to test in key areas up to three times weekly. These formative procedures, as described in Chapter 5 and the text workbook, allow teams to monitor student progress during prereferral interventions or assisted assessment. Thus a team can differentiate the student who has simply missed instruction from a student who is truly an atypical learner.

Consider the case of a second grader, Lindy. Lindy was brought to a building referral team due to her low reading achievement. To find out about Lindy's problem, the team had her reading assessed by administer-

ing 1-minute timed samples from the second-grade basal reader. She was given three reading probes for three consecutive days (9 probes in all) and each day's median score was charted. The median of these three days was used to represent her reading performance, at 35 words per minute. This score (35) was divided into the median score of her grade-level peers (79.5), producing a discrepancy ratio of ÷2.27 (meaning her performance would have to increase by a factor of 2.27 to meet the 79.5 standard). This placed her reading achievement at approximately 50% of her peers.

In Lindy's state and school district, any ratio ÷2.0 or greater would have qualified her for further assessment as learning disabled. However, Lindy was young and had frequently been ill during first grade, so the team elected to conduct a prereferral intervention in order to assess the effect intensified instruction would have on her progress. An intervention was designed that increased her practice in word attack skills by 10 minutes daily and included nightly reading practice. As part of the intervention design the team also determined that if Lindy doubled her performance in 10 weeks, and maintained that rate of growth, she would easily catch up with her peers.

Lindy was tested weekly with CBM probes from the second-grade curriculum and her scores were charted (see Exhibit 9.2). After eight weeks, it was clear from her trendline that she was making good progress and therefore did not qualify as disabled.

Training

CBM offers many appealing features to the educator who wants an alternative to the traditional battery of tests. It requires, however, different involvement with the eligibility process. Evaluators can no longer pull a test off a shelf, sit down with a kid for an hour and a half, enter scores into a computer, and let a formula decide whether the kid is disabled. Test materials must be developed, and class, school, or district norms must be obtained on the CBMs. Because the process of conducting individualized assessments with materials drawn from the curriculum must be mastered, and because it has not generally been taught (the fact that you are reading this text probably means that you are lucky enough to be in a class where it is being taught), a school district may need to undertake extensive staff-development activities prior to implementing a change to CBM.

Teachers may use Curriculum Based Measurement information from a student's portfolio to monitor learning progress.

Things to Do

This section describes tasks that must be accomplished in order to use CBM when making eligibility decisions.

Clarify Your Purpose

CBM can serve a number of basic evaluation functions including *screening, identification or eligibility, progress monitoring, and program evaluation*. Prior to implementing CBM in your school district, *decide what functions you expect CBM to fulfill*. A display of evaluation questions and the type of curriculum-based evaluations that best answer those questions is presented in Exhibit 9.3. Explanation of the CBM terms used in the exhibit follow.

1. *District-normed CBMs*. District norms are used when a high level of confidence is required for

decision making. For example, if a school or district would like to evaluate the progress of a group of students in an at-risk program and make efficacy decisions based on the data, district norms are preferred. Special education eligibility determination also requires district norms. District norming is typically completed on 15% to 20% of the population of a district at fall, winter and spring intervals using samples of the adopted reading, spelling, written language, and arithmetic curricula. District norms usually produce sufficient data to develop mean scores, medians, percentiles, and standard deviations.

2. *School norms*. Depending on the size of your school, school norms can offer a high level of confidence for decision making. When there is substantial achievement variability between schools in a district, school norms offer teams the best method of determining the least restrictive environment for a student. School norms are obtained similarly to district norms—sampling 20% of the students at each grade level. Interpretation of school level norms is limited to the local school, and the limited sample size available probably eliminates the use of school norms for making eligibility decisions.

3. *Class norms*. In the absence of support to develop district or school norms, a teacher may undertake the norming of a single classroom. In this procedure a total class is normed. Median scores may be produced and used to evaluate student performance and progress within that teacher's class.

The norms presented in Exhibit 9.4 are the result of a two-year, district-wide project involving approximately 4550 elementary students. In the first year, norming was piloted on two elementary schools. Approximately 1000 first- through sixth-graders were tested using probes from the adopted curriculum in reading, spelling, written language, and mathematics calculation. Testing procedures and sample probes are presented in the topical chapters (10–17). The second norming was completed a year later by repeating the process with 20% of the remaining elementary population. Scores from years one and two were then aggregated. School psychologists, special education teachers and assistants, and Chapter 1 teachers administered the probes. Assistants were hired to score the probes and prepare data for computer entry.

Student: *Lindy M.*   Grade/Age: *2*   School: *Tigard*   Teacher: *Clausson/Agevine*

Baseline Data:

Long Range Goal: *In 10 weeks Lindy will read 70 WPM from a randomly selected Macmillan Passage.*

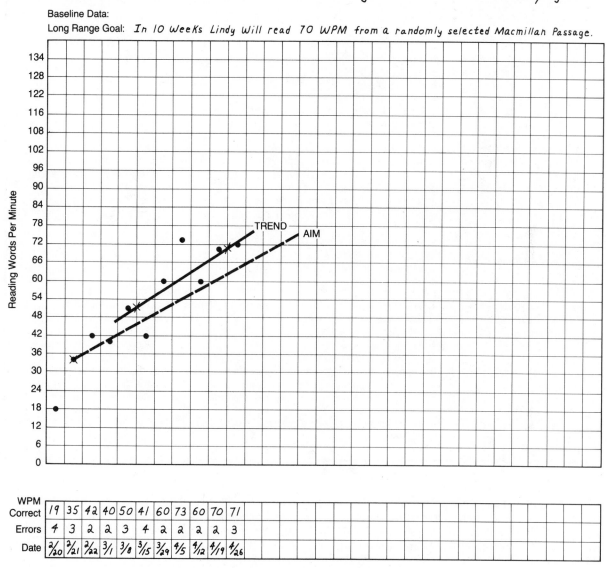

WPM Correct	19	35	42	40	50	41	60	73	60	70	71															
Errors	4	3	2	2	3	4	2	2	2	2	3															
Date	2/20	2/21	2/22	3/1	3/8	3/15	3/29	4/5	4/12	4/19	4/26															

Exhibit 9.2   A student's progress

Plan

District- and school-level standardization and norming of curriculum-based measures is an effort that requires substantial planning and preparation. The curriculum must be analyzed and probes developed; testers must be trained and checked for reliability; a calendar of norming activities must be produced; and cooperation must be obtained from school administrators and teachers so that students are available for individual and group testing. As with any large effort, it will be important to get additional assistance for things like

Exhibit 9.3   Utilization of CBE Techniques

Evaluation Category	Sample Evaluation Questions	Types of CBE
School-wide student program for evaluation, monitoring, and screening	1. Is one school's whole-language program more effective in reading-skill development than another school's basal program? 2. Are the students we retained now progressing at expected rates? 3. What are reasonable cutoff scores for referral to Chapter 1 reading services?	District- or school-level norms
Class-wide student monitoring and screening	1. How are my students progressing? 2. Who needs extra help in reading, math, spelling, or writing? What do they need to learn and how much practice do they need? 3. Are the low-achieving students in my class improving at a rate that will close their achievement gap? 4. With which kids in my class do I need help from the consulting teacher? 5. Who needs referral to remedial or special education programs?	District-, school-, or class-level norms Progress monitoring using CBMs Individual survey- and specific-level assessment (CBA)
Individual eligibility assessment and programming	1. Is a student's achievement low enough to warrant special education assessment? 2. Is this student really a different learner, or has she simply not been taught? 3. Are the student's scores sufficiently discrepant from peers to meet eligibility requirements? 4. What does the student need to learn? 5. What kind of teaching and practice does the student need? 6. Are there students with similar skills that I might group with this student?	District-level norms Progress monitoring using CBMs School-level CBMs to use for identification of LRE Individual survey- and specific-level assessment (CBA)

test scoring, data management, and statistical analysis. Shinn (1989) describes procedures for developing scoring and norming probes. Instructions for developing individual-classroom–level norms are also included in Shinn's work.

Establish Measurement Rules

In order to facilitate the use of CBM as part of formal academic evaluations, standard methods of recording and presenting student data should be developed. The use of tables like the ones in Exhibit 9.4 encourages standardization of procedures for reporting scores that

may be used for eligibility decision making. The tables also provide aesthetic support to satisfy the concerns of parents and uninformed professionals who believe that CBMs aren't as "real" as published norm-referenced measures.

Establish Procedures for Summarizing Data

It is a good idea to develop a graphic display of a student's CBM scores, as this will help teams to understand and interpret the student's academic achievement relative to the achievement of her peers. Exhibit 9.5 is a sample of a display that plots a student's read-

Exhibit 9.4   Curriculum-based Measurement—Spring Norms—1991 Tigard-Tualatin School District

| Grade | Reading-Words Correct: 1 minute | | | | | | | | |
	÷3.0	÷2.5	÷2.0	÷1.5	Median	×1.5	×2.0	×2.5	×3.0
1	21.2	25.4	31.8	42.3	63.5	95.3	127.0	158.8	190.5
2	32.7	39.2	49.0	65.3	98.0	147.0	196.0	245.0	294.0
3			46.0	61.3	92.0	138.0	184.0		
4			62.0	82.7	124.0	186.0	248.0		
5			63.0	84.0	126.0	189.0	252.0		
6			70.5	94.0	141.0	211.5	282.0		

Median Errors: Gr. 1: 3; Gr. 2: 1; Gr. 3: 3; Gr's 4–6: 2

| | Spelling-Words Correct: 2 minutes | | | | | | | | |
	÷3.0	÷2.5	÷2.0	÷1.5	Median	×1.5	×2.0	×2.5	×3.0
1	4.0	4.8	6.0	8.0	12.0	18.0	24.0	30.0	36.0
2	5.3	6.4	8.0	10.7	16.0	24.0	32.0	40.0	48.0
3			7.0	9.3	14.0	21.0	28.0		
4			7.5	10.0	15.0	22.5	30.0		
5			7.5	10.0	15.0	22.5	30.0		
6			7.5	10.0	15.0	22.5	30.0		

| | Spelling-Correct Letter Sequences: 2 minutes | | | | | | | | |
	÷3.0	÷2.5	÷2.0	÷1.5	Median	×1.5	×2.0	×2.5	×3.0
1	20.7	24.8	31.0	41.3	62.0	93.0	124.0	155.0	186.0
2	27.3	32.8	41.0	54.7	82.0	123.0	164.0	205.0	246.0
3			50.5	67.3	101.0	151.5	202.0		
4			53.0	70.7	106.0	159.0	212.0		
5			57.0	76.0	114.0	171.0	228.0		
6			63.5	84.7	127.0	190.5	254.0		

| | Writing-Total Words: 3 minutes | | | | | | | | |
	÷3.0	÷2.5	÷2.0	÷1.5	Median	×1.5	×2.0	×2.5	×3.0
1	5.7	6.8	8.5	11.3	17.0	25.5	34.0	42.5	51.0
2	8.7	10.4	13.0	17.3	26.0	39.0	52.0	65.0	78.0
3			19.5	26.0	39.0	58.5	78.0		
4			24.5	32.7	49.0	73.5	98.0		
5			26.0	34.7	52.0	78.0	104.0		
6			27.5	36.7	55.0	82.5	110.0		

(continued)

Exhibit 9.4   Curriculum-based Measurement—Spring Norms—1991 Tigard-Tualatin School District (continued)

Grade	÷3.0	÷2.5	÷2.0	÷1.5	Median	×1.5	×2.0	×2.5	×3.0
				Writing-Correct Word Sequences: 3 minutes				
1	2.0	2.4	3.0	4.0	6.0	9.0	12.0	15.0	18.0
2	5.3	6.4	8.0	10.7	16.0	24.0	32.0	40.0	48.0
3			15.0	20.0	30.0	45.0	60.0		
4			21.5	28.7	43.0	64.5	86.0		
5			23.0	30.7	46.0	69.0	92.0		
6			25.3	33.7	50.5	75.8	101.0		
				Math-Mixed Problems: 2 minutes				
	÷3.0	÷2.5	÷2.0	÷1.5	Median	×1.5	×2.0	×2.5	×3.0
1	3.0	3.6	4.5	6.0	9.0	13.5	18.0	22.5	27.0
2	6.0	7.2	9.0	12.0	18.0	27.0	36.0	45.0	54.0
3			8.0	10.7	16.0	24.0	32.0		
4			11.0	14.7	22.0	33.0	44.0		
5			11.0	14.7	22.0	33.0	44.0		
6			20.0	26.7	40.0	60.0	80.0		
				Math-Facts 1: 2 minutes				
	÷3.0	÷2.5	÷2.0	÷1.5	Median	×1.5	×2.0	×2.5	×3.0
1	5.3	6.4	8.0	10.7	16.0	24.0	32.0	40.0	48.0
2	14.7	17.6	22.0	29.3	44.0	66.0	88.0	110.0	132.0
3			25.0	33.3	50.0	75.0	100.0		
4			19.5	26.0	39.0	58.5	78.0		
5			44.0	58.7	88.0	132.0	176.0		
6			57.8	77.0	115.5	173.3	231.0		
				Math-Facts 2: 2 minutes				
	÷3.0	÷2.5	÷2.0	÷1.5	Median	×1.5	×2.0	×2.5	×3.0
1	2.7	3.2	4.0	5.3	8.0	12.0	16.0	20.0	24.0
2	8.0	9.6	12.0	16.0	24.0	36.0	48.0	60.0	72.0
3			14.5	19.3	29.0	43.5	58.0		
4			32.8	43.7	65.5	98.3	131.0		
5			22.0	29.3	44.0	66.0	88.0		
6			28.5	38.0	57.0	85.5	114.0		

Grade	Facts 1	Facts 2
1	Add	Sub
2	"	"
3	"	"
4	Sub	Mult
5	Mult	Div
6	"	"

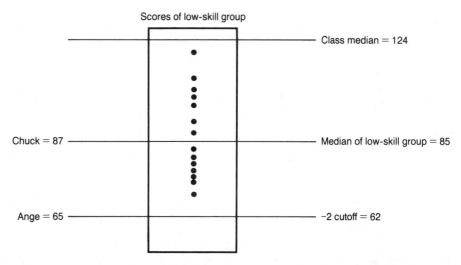

**Exhibit 9.5
Comparing
student scores
to class norms**

ing achievement by grade level relative to the mean and percentile rankings for the district. This display has been used to present student data for learning-disabilities evaluations because the school system required that the student's scores fall outside of the average range (below the local 16th percentile) at 2 years below the student's grade placement (Marston & Magnusson, 1988). The long bars represent average district achievement in the area of reading for grade levels 1 to 6. The dots represent individual student achievement and provide graphic representation of the individual's relative standing. (Other methods for determining learning-disability eligibility are discussed in the following.) It is also recommended that a standard method of charting and progress monitoring be developed so that data are easy to interpret. Our experience is that teachers initially prefer equal-interval charts, like the one in Exhibit 9.2, because they are easy to read.

Get Ready to Change

You will need to plan a period of transition as educators are introduced to new evaluation techniques and begin to use them in place of traditional methods. As mentioned above, CBM skills are often not taught in preservice training programs, and their mastery requires ample field experience. Successful implementation of a functional model demands a well-developed, continuing inservice program. CBM skills of specialists in the Tigard-Tualatin District were developed through intensive group training and general education commitment of team-planning time to

analysis of CBM information and progress monitoring charts. Such activities are most apt to succeed in an environment that is free of threat and rich in support.

Make a Decision About Your School's Position on Learning-Disabilities Evaluations

This is probably the area where the most controversy will be generated regarding the use of curriculum-based measurement. The field of learning disabilities has been largely responsible for the reification of psychoeducational testing, and proponents of this kind of evaluation may challenge the use of approaches that do not delve into a child's psychological processes.

One element of the learning-disabilities definition that has promoted considerable confusion is the wording that calls for educators to document a "significant" discrepancy between the student's "ability" and "achievement." This wording has been used as the rationale for extensive IQ testing in special education, because the IQ test is considered an ability measure. However, IQ tests are only considered to be ability measures because they predict achievement. Therefore, measures of achievement can be substituted for IQ tests to document high or low ability. Either of the following two approaches for comparing ability and achievement are compatible with the functional assessment model.

The achievement/expectancy approach identifies a student as learning disabled when the student falls significantly below average for his grade placement. This model defines a disability in terms of the discrepancy between what the student has achieved and what the system expects of the student. Expectancy levels are determined by the typical achievement of the student's peers. For screening purposes, students are identified as needing further assessment when their achievement is less than 50% of their peers. Using discrepancy ratios (see Appendix A), this achievement level is described as 2 ÷ (divide by 2) discrepant. This approach has been applied by the Minneapolis Public Schools (Marston & Magnusson, 1988). When discrepancy ratios are used, scores of ÷ 2.0 and greater have been found to identify approximately 7.5% of the student population in grades 3 to 6, but unacceptably large percentages of students in grades 1 and 2 (Marston, Tindal & Deno, 1984). Therefore, if discrepancy ratios are used, additional criteria must be developed for the lower grades. Additional criteria that are in keeping with a functional focus would include (1) required prereferral interventions and assessment of progress during the interventions, (2) extensive specific-level testing, and (3) the use of published tests that are chosen because they relate directly to the perceived deficits in the child's skills. It is imperative that fishing expeditions, which use a broad net of language achievement and processing tests, not constitute the additional criteria. Such approaches will result in nearly every referred child being found "disabled" (Ysseldyke et al., 1992).

Some of the shortcomings of discrepancy ratios can be avoided by using percentiles, which identify the same number of students regardless of grade level. Shinn, Habedank, Rodden-Nord and Knutson (1993, in press) recommend use of a 10-percentile cutoff score. Under either method, additional academic evaluation to describe skill deficits fully should be conducted using CRT measures.

The more traditional *aptitude/achievement discrepancy approach* to learning disabilities may be revisited with a functional orientation. This involves substantiating normal ability by documenting adequate achievement in some skill area unrelated to the referral problem. In this system, average scores on CBM probes in other academic areas, or scores on tests of adaptive skills, can be used to infer average ability. The reasoning goes like this: "If Ralph is intelligent enough to have learned math, his poor reading can't be the result of low intelligence." Again, discretion is required in this approach. It is probably not a good idea to infer "average ability" from a single math facts probe. An acceptable alternative might be the probe in combination with a good published test of mathemati-

cal application skills, or the probe in combination with work samples demonstrating good progress in mathematics application.

Following the reasoning above, ability measures (IQ tests) are only used when there is no clear indication of at least average achievement in some skill area. Percentiles or discrepancy ratios are used to describe the level of academic achievement that may be considered severe enough to require further special education evaluation. Additional academic evaluation to describe the student's skill deficits fully is conducted using CBM or CRT measures. This approach requires that evaluators are discriminating in their choice of published NRT language and achievement measures, and report and use such scores with discretion.

Now That We've Gotten Them In, How Do We Get Them Out?

If we wanted to search the literature on eligibility, we'd guess there have been 5000 pages written on how to decide who qualifies for special services for every single page written about how to decide when someone should leave. This emphasis on the "head hunting" aspect of evaluation raises serious questions about education's commitment to ideals like "reintegration," "transition," "mainstreaming" and "the least restrictive environment." The truth is, almost everyone referred goes in (Ysseldyke et al., 1983) and almost no one comes out (Greenburg, 1984; Kauffman, 1989).

Reintegration decisions are currently made two ways: by repeating the costly and flawed traditional eligibility process already criticized in this chapter, or by sampling the opinions of teachers relating to a student's potential for success in the mainstream (Shinn, Habedank, Rodden-Nord & Knutson (1993, in press). This last approach, which is almost certainly superior, also has its problems. Among other things, it depends on the general education teacher, who might have originally referred the student, reversing his or her opinion about the need for special services. The goal is further impaired by the implication of fixed pathology in traditional eligibility schemas. The bias of fixed pathology results from the fact that everyone at school had to work really hard and use lots of resources to prove that the student "had something wrong" with her.

Work by Shinn and colleagues (1993, in press), and Rodden-Nord and Shinn (1991), has shown that CBM data can have a significant impact on the willingness of general education teachers to accept or reaccept students. In fact, in a direct comparison of CBM and norm-reference data (from the Woodcock-Johnson Psychoeducational Battery), Rodden and Shinn found that CBM data significantly increased teacher willingness to reintegrate, while the norm-referenced data did not. This means that CBM data can be used to inform, and improve, the judgment of teachers who are reviewing reintegration decisions. The procedures for collecting and reporting these data are simple:

- CBM measures covering the target areas are administered to special students.

- These same measures are administered to students who are having difficulty, but who *are* being served within the general education class (general education students in a low reading group would be tested—not those in the highest group).

- Scores are displayed to illustrate the skills of reintegration candidates relative to current general education class members.

This process was illustrated in Exhibit 9.5. The candidates for reintegration have been tested on "words read per minute" from the general education classroom reader (both students were originally referred for reading problems). General education class students were also tested. As can be seen in Exhibit 9.5, student A's reading score is well within the range of students currently served by the general education teacher. Student B's scores are not in the general education class range. This display clearly indicates that student A is a good candidate for reintegration. This is the kind of data that Shinn and his associates have shown significantly alters the willingness of general education teachers to accept reintegration. Once again, similar alterations do not result from the presentation of traditional norm-referenced achievement data.

Summary

This chapter has described an alternative to traditional psychoeducational assessment for identifying students who may be eligible for remedial or special education programs. It has also discussed how CBM can be used to get students out of these programs. This alternative, curriculum-based measurement emphasizes the identification of alterable variables such as a student's academic skills, instructional needs, and rate of learning. CBM requires evaluator expertise in both curriculum-based evaluation and assessment. It has the potential to provide information for the full range of educational decisions that school teams make, including screening, identification and eligibility, student progress monitoring, instructional planning, and program effectiveness. The applicability of CBM depends on the extent to which school districts decide to norm student performance on measures taken from the local curriculum. The use of CBM is currently limited to the basic academic areas of reading, spelling, written language, and math computation that account for the majority of referrals to support services. Efforts to expand the measures to other curricular areas, and to higher grade levels, are in progress.

Schools wishing to employ a functional assessment approach need to provide a program of training and support so that each evaluator becomes an expert in the development and analysis of curriculum-based tests. Rote administration and interpretation of tests is not possible in curriculum-based evaluation. Resources must be made available for the development and updating of testing materials and methods of presenting information. These limitations require school districts that adopt CBM to plan for a period of transition as professionals practice new assessment skills.

A Final Point

One of the authors once received a phone call from a parent in a nearby community. The mother was concerned about her eighth-grade son who was only sufficiently skilled to read fourth-grade books. The author asked if she had referred her son for help to the school district and the mother replied that she had.

"So what happened?" the author asked.

"They said there isn't anything wrong with him."

The author thought about that for a moment.

"I can't believe they said it was all right for eighth-graders to only read fourth-grade books. My guess is that they said he isn't eligible for services. They didn't say 'there isn't anything wrong with him.' "

"What's the difference?" asked the mother.

It is difficult to understand, let alone explain, the current policies and regulations that determine who is and who is not eligible for special services. However, it is important *not* to confuse eligibility with need. Many students—like that eighth-grader reading from a fourth-grade book—need help. It is our job to find ways to respond to people who need help, regardless of funding procedures and administrative regulations.

Part 3 / Things to Do

Part 3 of this text, Chapters 10 to 17, contains detailed information about how to conduct evaluations within critical content areas. Each chapter presents highly specific procedures for evaluating student skills. They are presented in a linear fashion, even though most of the content isn't really linear. Therefore, knowing the process as it was explained in Chapter 7 is essential. You might want to go back and review Chapter 7 as soon as you finish this introduction.

These content-specific chapters will be very complex (because they deal with the application of a complex operation—evaluation—to sets of complex curriculum domains). The best situation would be for you to have already taken courses in reading, for example, before attempting to understand the process of reading evaluation. However, because we doubt if that will have happened, each topical chapter begins with a general discussion of the content area (comprehension, decoding, language, math) aimed at defining the content and addressing important topics relative to its evaluation and instruction.

The opening discussion of each content domain is followed by specific techniques for evaluation. This second part of each chapter should be viewed, and read, in much the way one would approach a test manual. These parts contain highly content-specific descriptions of evaluator actions and the materials required to carry out these actions. This is not the stuff that one curls up to read for enjoyment, nor is it the stuff anyone (including the authors) can easily recall from memory.

The *Evaluation Procedures* section of each topical chapter is most accurately viewed as reference material. We hope that once you enter the classroom you will use these procedures in conjunction with the testing materials in the accompanying workbook to conduct functional evaluations. However, in order to allow you the flexibility of selecting testing materials not in the workbook, each required behavior-sampling technique is explained in sufficient detail to allow you to make, or select, alternative tests. We like the testing materials we have put in the workbook, but we recognize that they are not sufficient.

In addition to evaluation techniques, the second part of each topical chapter includes instructional objectives and teaching recommendations. The *Teaching Recommendation* sections contain explicit objectives. These are the objectives that, according to student need, you would put on the IEP or the lesson plan. The objectives are then followed by the teaching recommendations and monitoring suggestions. These evaluation actions, objectives, teaching recommendations and monitoring suggestions are coordinated through the directions and interpretation guidelines.

Text Cues   In order to help you through the maze of directions and guidelines (check out Exhibit 10.6* as an example), we are introducing three text-structure devices: $\triangledown$, $\approx$, $\bigcirc$. These sections will have related vertical rules bracketing the text. Chapter wording that explains concepts and provides rationale will appear as it has throughout the rest of the text. However, wording that directs you to take a specific action or to think about a particular variable will be set off. If the text is describing a *direction*, it will have a ▸▸▸▸ rule. If the wording directs you to *interpret* something, or to make a decision, it will have a ∿∿ rule. If the wording presents an objective, it will be designated by a ••••• rule.

In addition to the margin lines and logos, Part 3 will continue to distinguish between informational and applied exhibits. Remember that some exhibits are followed by a designator asterisk that stands for "application." This means that the exhibit in question will be put to use during the actual evaluation of students. We grant you permission to copy these application exhibits for the purpose of working with students.

Also remember that the application exhibits are

duplicated in the accompanying workbook. *Exhibits in the text may be smaller than those in the workbook, because the ones in the workbook are the ones we expect you to copy and use with students. Finally, all * exhibits are listed on the inside front cover of the text to make them easier to find.

Teaching recommendations It is imperative that you remember that all teaching recommendations are simply "first guesses," and that monitoring of student progress will always be necessary in order to confirm the utility of these recommendations for individual students. That is why *Monitoring Procedures* are supplied in the workbook. In our opinion, an evaluation is not complete until the student has received instruction and you have documented progress toward the objectives specified. "How-to-teach" decisions can never be truly resolved until this important step of formative evaluation has been taken. For this reason, a thorough description of data-based program modification techniques has been included in the workbook.

Chapter 10 / Reading Comprehension

The Content of Comprehension

Comprehension Stategies
  Active and Thoughtful Reading
  Monitor for Meaning and Self-Correct
  Adjust for Text Difficulty
  Merge Text with Prior Knowledge
  Clarify

Enabling Skills
  Prior Knowledge
  Decoding
  Semantics (Vocabulary)
  Syntax (Grammar)

Commonly Used Comprehension Testing Techniques
  Portfolio Analysis
  Oral Reading Fluency
  Cloze or Maze Plus Questions

Evaluation Procedures

Survey-Level Testing

Specific-Level Testing
  Assisted Monitoring
  Retell
  Awareness of Reading
  Assisted Activation of Prior Knowledge
  Make Predictions
  Assisted Search
  Referent Knowledge

Teaching Recommendations

I took a course in speed reading, learning to read straight down the middle of the page, and was able to read War and Peace *in twenty minutes. It's about Russia.*

—Woody Allen

The Content of Comprehension

Reading comprehension is an interactive process through which the reader uses code, context analysis, prior knowledge, vocabulary, and language, along with executive-control strategies, to understand text (Adams, 1990). It is a multidimensional construct and, as such, not easily observed. In order to talk about something that cannot be seen, we must rely on inference and on theories—and to evaluate anything we must compare it to a standard (see Chapter 5, p. 81). In the case of comprehension, the latest reading theory often becomes that standard (Stanovich, 1991). Therefore, a student's behavior may seem either typical or atypical, depending on the theoretical standard used. Tindal and Marston (1990) have proposed one way to avoid the problems of definition that come with the term *comprehension*. Instead of talking about *decoding* and *comprehension*, they talk about *reading* and *reacting*.

Use of the term *reacting* shifts the focus from psychological processes, which cannot be observed, to behaviors and products that can. For example, students may react to what they read by answering questions, retelling, paraphrasing, or completing cloze passages. Each of these techniques can be used to illustrate a student's comprehension—but few people would agree that any of them are pure measures of it.

The prototypical "diagnostic reading inventory," for example, is made up of passages followed by questions. The student reads each passage and then answers questions before reading the next passage. In these cases, the interval between reading the passage and answering the questions is a minute or two. What if you waited 30 minutes before asking the questions? What if you waited a week? If you did wait longer, the student's score would almost certainly be different (probably lower), because what was once "comprehended" may no longer be recalled. Therefore, a student's score on post-passage

questions depends not only on what he understands but on what he remembers. Many educators seem to accept this confusion, though few of them would agree that memory and comprehension are synonymous.

We think that comprehension is the act of combining information in passages with prior knowledge in order to construct meaning. Comprehension, therefore, takes place *as a person is reading* and comprises the set of skills that lets him find information and understand it in terms of what is already known. It is a process that is influenced by a number of variables. The interactive nature of comprehension requires that these variables combine and at times compensate for each other.

Comprehension Strategies

Competent readers use vocabulary, decoding, prior knowledge, and other skills to react to print—but these things only enable the reaction. The reaction itself, which we call comprehension, is carried out through the application of comprehension strategies. These strategies are used to accomplish certain functions for the reader.

Exhibit 10.1* lists five strategy categories including active and reflective reading, connecting the text with prior knowledge (to produce meaning), monitoring and evaluating meaning, and regaining meaning when it is lost.

Part of the complexity of comprehension can be traced to the likelihood that the five functions presented in Exhibit 10.1* are not really separate. Even if they were separate, it is just as likely that they are "compensatory." This means that a reader who is temporarily unsuited (probably because of missing prior knowledge) to distinguish relevant from irrelevant information in text may compensate by relying on other comprehension strategies (Rauenbusch & Bereiter, 1991), such as seeking clarification. This compensatory feature, combined with the

Exhibit 10.1   Comprehension Status Sheet

Purpose: To limit the scope of the comprehension evaluation.
Directions: Consider the indicators for each of the strategy and enabling skill categories.
Consult with anyone who may have comprehension-specific knowledge of the student.
Mark the status of each category:
"Yes" means the skill is adequate.
"No" means it should be taught.
"Unsure" means additional testing is required.

Category	Indicators	Status			Specific-level procedure (SLP)
Comprehension strategies					
1. Active reading	1.1 Monitors meaning	Yes	No	Unsure	Select from 1–7 using this
	1.2 Adjusts for text difficulty				Status Sheet—or administer
	1.3 Connects text with prior knowledge				all 7 procedures
	1.4 Clarifies				
	1.5 Previews text				
	1.6 Develops and answers questions				
	1.7 Takes notes and/or highlights				
	1.8 Reviews				
2. Monitors meaning	2.1 Self-corrects reading errors which violate the meaning of the passage (such as non-meaningful insertions)	Yes	No	Unsure	1—Assisted monitoring
2—Retell
	2.2 Rereads confusing portions of material, or adjusts reading rate on difficult sections				
	2.3 Can predict upcoming events in the passage				
	2.4 Identifies when additional information is needed, or specifically what kind of information is needed to answer questions				
	2.5 Reads with expression and/or automation				
3. Adjusts for task difficulty	3.1 Utilizes study skills appropriately	Yes	No	Unsure	3—Awareness of reading
	3.2 Allocates study time according to passage difficulty				
	3.3 States purpose for reading				
	3.4 Accurately estimates success on passage				
	3.5 Adjusts reading rate appropriately				
4 Connects text to prior knowledge	4.1 Answers "best title" and main idea questions accurately	Yes	No	Unsure	4—Assisted Activation of Prior Knowledge
5—Prediction
6—Assisted Search
	4.2 Retells story with emphasis on major points				
	4.3 Describes author's purpose for writing				
	4.4 Can locate information in the passage which answers assigned questions				
	4.5 Can accurately apply stated criteria to the story to judge its value as entertainment or as an information source				
	4.6 Uses information gained from reading the passage to focus on subsequent topics/information in the passage				
5. Clarifies	5.1 Adjusts reading rate for material which is not understood	Yes	No	Unsure	3—Awareness of Reading
7—Referent Knowledge
	5.2 Is more likely to recall important passage details, not trivial ones				
	5.3 Answers comprehension questions in terms of stated information in passage, not necessarily prior knowledge				
	5.4 Uses multiple strategies to determine passage meaning				
	5.5 Uses multiple strategies to decode words				
	5.6 Self-corrects errors which violate meaning				
	5.7 Asks for assistance				
Enabling skills					
6. Decoding	6.1 Reads passages with 90% accuracy	Yes	No	Unsure	1—Assisted Monitoring and/or go to Chapter 11
	6.2 Reads passages at 75% of expected rate				
	6.3 Makes few errors that violate meaning				

(continued)

Exhibit 10.1 **Comprehension Status Sheet (continued)**

Category	Indicators	Status			Specific-level procedure
Enabling skills *cont'd*					
7. Vocabulary	7.1 Can define words in passage	Yes	No	Unsure	Go to Chapter 12
	7.2 Can modify the definition of words in passage according to context (does not miss context-dependent vocabulary questions)				
	7.3 Balance of errors on maze exercise does not show excessive semantic errors				
	7.4 Comprehension does not increase dramatically and/or decoding errors do not decrease when key words are introduced prior to reading				
	7.5 Makes few nonmeaningful substitutions				
	7.6 Uses pronouns and tenses correctly				
8. Syntax	8.1 Balance of errors on maze exercise does not show excessive syntax errors	Yes	No	Unsure	Go to Chapter 12
	8.2 Primary language is same as texts				
	8.3 Oral language adequate (does not contain excessive syntax errors which violate the standard of adult speech) particularly in the use of subject-verb agreement, tense, and pronouns				
9. Prior knowledge	9.1 Comprehension does not vary dramatically according to familiarity with the passage topic	Yes	No	Unsure	Go to Chapter 17
	9.2 Can correctly define words in passage				
	9.3 Can relate information in passage to personal experience or to other sources of information (other passages, books, authors, classes, etc.)				
	9.4 Comprehension does not improve dramatically when a passage is previewed and unstated ideas are explained prior to reading				
	9.5 Can discuss unstated ideas accurately				

fact that passage difficulty is determined in large part by the reader's prior knowledge (so that the same passage is difficult for some readers but not for others), makes the evaluation of comprehension *really tough*.

When a teacher teaches comprehension (as opposed to its enabling skills) he teaches comprehension strategies (Dole, Duffy, Roehler & Pearson, 1991). The content of comprehension is not factual or conceptual (those things are found in the topics being understood)—it is strategic (see Chapter 3). Therefore, when evaluators attempt to explain why a student is failing to react appropriately to text, they either focus on enabling skills or skill at using the comprehension strategies. When the target is strategic knowledge, an evaluator must use error analysis, assisted assessment, or interviews (to get the student to make his thinking public) (see Exhibit 7.7). Here is a brief description of the major categories of comprehension strategy knowledge and enabling skills necessary for effective

reaction to text. Each category can be found in Exhibit 10.1*.

Strategy 1: Active and Thoughtful Reading

Successful readers approach passages vigorously. Unlike less efficient readers, they are energetic and almost aggressive in their pursuit of meaning (Kletzien, 1991; Paris & Oka, 1989). Successful readers are also thoughtful and reflective (Pearson, Roehler, Dole & Duffy, 1990). Often they will preview the passage, formulate their own pre-reading questions, make comments in the margins, underline and highlight text. In addition, these readers review what they have read and may even seek clarification if passages don't seem to make sense.

Both Kletzien (1991) and Andrews and Mason (1991) present lists of tactics used by active readers and quotes from interviews that indicate which readers use them. Here are some examples:

Tactic	Student explanation
1. Use of background knowledge	''It sounds right'' ''From books before'' ''I've seen 'em''
2. Reread	''I'm reading it over'' ''I've read it again''
3. Look back	''I've looked up 6 and 7'' ''Found answer in 1''
4. Look ahead	''And then it says . . .''
5. Contextual clues	''June is after May'' ''Because it says juicy''

Andrews and Mason (1991, p. 541)

Strategy 2: Monitor for Meaning and Self-Correct

Competent readers monitor what they are reading, and if they find that they have lost meaning, they do something about it. Kids who don't read well will often go right on reading even though the passage makes no sense to them. Often they make no effort to correct errors. For example, here is a sentence as originally written and as it was read by a student in Portland, Oregon:

> **Original:** Stories of dragons are part of folk tales from almost every land.
> **Student reading:** Stories of danger are part of the followed from almost all the lands.

This student's errors, which generally would be categorized as ''whole-word substitutions, having the correct initial sound, that violate meaning,'' represent a *very* common error pattern (sometimes referred to as reading the white portions of the page [Bishop, 1992]). These errors destroy the meaning of the message (errors that do not violate meaning should generally be ignored).

Some readers don't self-monitor and, as a result, never attempt to correct their errors. These students may not even realize that errors have been made. Other students, who do self-monitor, realize when they have lost meaning and stop to try and fix it. If they have the necessary enabling skills (decoding, vocabulary, syntax, prior knowledge) and comprehension strategies (active reading, adjust for task difficulty, connect to prior knowledge and clarify) to reckon out the original wording, they self-correct and regain understanding of the passage.

Strategy 3: Adjust for Text Difficulty

Any reader, regardless of skill, will eventually encounter material that is challenging. (This ''difficulty'' may be the result of a missing enabling skill such as reader prior knowledge. However, it may also be the result of a poorly written text.) When use of the comprehension monitoring strategy (comprehension strategy 2) tells the student that a passage is difficult, a competent reader will make adjustments for this difficulty. To adjust for text difficulty, the reader will employ tactics such as reduction in reading rate, rereading of passages, or the use of highlighting and note taking (Paris & Jacobs, 1984) (see Chapter 8).

Strategy 4: Merge Text with Prior Knowledge

The use of selective attention (see Chapters 2 and 17) is a critical part of reading comprehension. As the student reads, he combines what he already knows about the topic with the message in the text. Obviously, this requires the student to have the enabling skill we call prior knowledge. However, it also requires strategies for combining prior knowledge and text message. A student merges text message with prior knowledge by considering both what the text says and what he already knows. A competent reader will not automatically replace prior knowledge or disregard text messages simply because they conflict with, or contradict, each other (Carnine, 1992).

Selective attention is important to this particular strategy because it is prior knowledge (what the student already believes or knows) that allows the student to pick portions of the message for reflection and storage (Stahl, Jacobson, Davis & Davis, 1991). Unfortunately, people often disagree about what is critical and what isn't.

Strategy 5: Clarify

When a student fails to understand what he is reading and is aware of the failure, he can attempt clarification. If he has the necessary enabling skills (decoding, vocabulary, syntax, prior knowledge) and comprehension strategies to figure out the original wording, he'll self-correct and fix the mistake. If he does not have these task-specific strategies, he may fall back on a general strategy like asking for help.

Enabling Skills

Comprehension strategies like clarification, self-monitoring, and prediction depend on competence in certain domains of enabling skill. When these enabling skills are missing comprehension may not occur. However, there is no reason to assume that a student who has these enabling skills will be qualified to comprehend anything intuitively. The following discussion explains briefly how one's reaction to print depends upon skills other than those we have decided to call "comprehension strategies." These enabling skills have been placed into categories that correspond to the other topical chapters in Part 3. We'll explain them here, and provide keys to reaching those other chapters, but testing approaches will not be included in this chapter. This means you'll have to go to Chapter 12 to find out how to confirm a vocabulary problem.

Enabling Skill 1: Prior Knowledge

Because comprehension involves the interaction of text information with what the student already knows, the student has to know something for it to take place (Valencia, Stallman, Commeyras, Pearson & Hartman, 1990; Palincsar & Brown, 1984). Prior knowledge of the passage topic is necessary for appropriate reaction to print. The stronger this non-strategic knowledge base is, the better prepared a student is to comprehend new material about a topic (Roller, 1990; Stahl, Jacobson, Davis & Davis, 1991). A student who doesn't have some basic core of information about the topic of the passage will not be suited to comprehend the passage. Steps for evaluating the adequacy of a student's general knowledge will be presented in Chapter 17.

Enabling Skill 2: Decoding

Decoding includes phonemics, phonology, phonetic generalizations, morphology (see Chapter 12), reading, fluency, and context analysis.

Proficient decoding is necessary for efficient comprehension; however, comprehension instruction should not be delayed until decoding is mastered. Automaticity in decoding frees the student's working (short-term) memory so that it may focus on the meaning of the text (Adams, 1991; Samuels, 1983). One indication of automaticity (see Chapter 2) is the speed at which the student decodes passages through oral or silent reading (Carver, 1992).

In general, speeding up or slowing down a student will not alter the quality of comprehension (only the number of ideas encountered). The real problem occurs when the student falls below a critical threshold of reading fluency (Carver, 1992; Samuels & Kamil, 1984). Then the student must attend so closely to the task of decoding that he cannot attend to the meaning of the passage. Estimates of this critical decoding threshold vary, but 140 to 200 words per minute is probably a good minimal rate after the third grade (Biemiller, 1978; Tenenbaum, 1983; Carnine et al., 1990).

It is impossible to set a fixed fluency aim for all reading because rate may vary according to the difficulty of the material. And, of course, difficulty depends upon the reader's own knowledge base, and his purpose for reading. Flexibility, having the option to speed up or slow down according to the demands of the material, is more important than simple speed. Decoding assessment will be described in Chapter 11.

Enabling Skill 3: Semantics (Vocabulary)

If a student fails to demonstrate comprehension but passes tests of decoding (including phonics, fluency and context analysis) as well as prior knowledge, the next most likely cause of the failure is vocabulary. Word meaning may account for up to 70% of the variability between students who do and do not score well on published comprehension tests (Waugh, 1978; Carnine et al., 1990).

There are two critical elements of vocabulary knowledge that can interact with comprehension (and decoding):

1. Knowledge of word definitions
2. Determination of word meaning from context

The first of these, definitions, is totally word-based. It is the sort of knowledge one would gain from looking in a dictionary. The second has to do with the contextual nature of vocabulary. Although context can influence word meaning at the story level, it is most conveniently tested at the phrase level.

To find out if a comprehension problem is the result of poor vocabulary, an evaluator must check the student's knowledge of the meaning of the words *in the paragraph* he did not comprehend. The use of published vocabulary tests is not likely to aid in this evaluation. Such tests are composed of words that may or may not be representative of the words in the passage that is giving the student trouble. The average child enters school with a vocabulary of from 5000 to 10,000 words. By high school, the vocabulary may be 10 times that size as he adds approximately 5000 new words per year (Nagy & Scott, 1990). Given all those words to choose from, a standard vocabulary test is not likely to be relevant to any individual passage. Evaluation of semantics will be explained in Chapter 12.

Enabling Skill 4: Syntax (Grammar)

Assume now that you have a student who was given a paragraph he didn't comprehend (react to satisfactorily). You have tested his decoding (procedures to be described shortly) and determined that he decodes the paragraph fluently. You have also checked his prior knowledge of the content and knowledge of the meaning of the words in the paragraph. You found no problems. What's left?

Reading comprehension cannot be observed directly, but may be monitored through reactions to what was read. Reactions may include answering questions, retelling, paraphrasing, and completing close passages.

First, a kid who doesn't tell you what a passage said but (1) can decode the passage, (2) has adequate background information, and (3) knows the meaning of all the words in it, is rare. The most likely explanation is a difference between the child's language and the language (discourse style) of the passage. Students who have oral language deficits or bilingual interference (see Chapter 12) generally have difficulty understanding mainstream text (Edwards, Beasley & Thompson 1991; Hoffer, 1983; Kintsch & Greene, 1978; Pritchard, 1990). Both vocabulary and syntax are discussed in some detail in Chapter 12.

A Note on Text Variables

Text variables can influence understanding. They reside in the book, therefore they are neither enabling skills nor comprehension strategies. Text variables include both general organizers and overall structure. Examples of general organizers **are** abstracts, focus questions, headings, and summaries. Overall structure is the way the ideas in the text **are** related to convey a message to the reader (Carnine, 1992; Duffy et al., 1989; Meyer & Rice, 1984). The organization of written material can signal a reader as to what is relevant. It can either provide cohesion or interrupt and mislead the reader (Armbruster, 1984a; Meyer & Rice, 1984). (An illustration of the disruptive effect may have occurred earlier when you encountered the word *are* in boldface type.) Text structure influences the quality of the reactions we elicit from students during evaluation and contributes to, or interferes with, the way they react to text (Gerber, 1992).

Any evaluation of a student's reading skills should include an evaluation of text readability. Readability cannot be estimated with a formula of word frequency, word length, and sentence length alone. Those who want to become more conversant with text structure should read Armbruster (1984b) and MacGinitie (1984). Those who are interested in developing criteria for evaluating text should read Anderson and Armbruster (1984) and Armbruster (1984a).

Commonly Used Comprehension Testing Techniques

In attempting to assess reading comprehension, an evaluator asks the student to react to printed messages. He decides that the student "comprehended" the message if the kid reacts appropriately to it (Tindal & Marston, 1990). Unfortunately, different testing formats require different types of responses, depend on different enabling skills, and reflect different comprehension strategies or enabling skills. Therefore, as we outline the actions that should be employed during the evaluation process in the second part of this chapter, we will have to refer to a variety of testing/interview formats. While these will be explained in the text, they are condensed in Exhibit 10.2.

The purposes of survey-level assessment are (1) to decide if the student needs help, (2) to determine if additional testing/analysis is necessary, and (3) to obtain direction for this additional analysis (see Chapter 7, p. 126). Not all reaction formats are equally suited for the survey-level purpose. In some cases this is because the format is too hard to control, as in the case of questioning. In other cases the format is relevant, but too difficult to prepare and score, as in the case of retell. Best practice is probably to combine the two or three procedures that are easiest to use and match your purpose.

The survey procedure you use should be selected on the basis of the questions you need to answer, and your familiarity with the student. If you only want to screen for students in need of additional help in comprehension, you can do this by using *oral reading fluency*. If such a limited sample makes you uncomfortable, you can also use *cloze or maze plus questions*. If you want to make teaching decisions about comprehension, and you (or your colleagues) know lots about the student, then use *portfolio analysis*. If you want to make teaching decisions but know very little about the student, then use a combination of *oral reading fluency, portfolio analysis, and cloze or maze plus questions*.

Portfolio Analysis

Portfolio analysis is not listed in Exhibit 10.2 because it really isn't a testing procedure. But sometimes a test isn't needed. Sometimes it is possible to arrive at resolution of a student's problem without any additional test at all. When you, or an available colleague, think you already have plenty of information about the student, but need to coordinate this information, you can do this by using portfolio assessment. In all cases, the use of portfolio analysis is limited by the quantity and quality of the relevant material in a student's portfolio. If you have routinely collected student work related to comprehension, the analysis of that material is possible. If the student has just arrived at the school, it isn't possible.

Reading comprehension problems are indicated by a variety of behaviors. Many of these are listed on the status sheet in Exhibit 10.1*. Unfortunately, many of these indicators do not take the form of permanent products (for example, "reads with expression"). As a result, there won't be any evidence of these behaviors that can be picked up and filed away in a portfolio (unless you routinely make notations about such things). This doesn't mean that there isn't any evidence; it just means that the evidence is not the sort

Exhibit 10.2   Comprehension Testing Procedures

Procedure	Example	Advantages	Disadvantages	Type of Data	Criteria	Comprehension SLP	Other Assumed Causes for Failure
1. Questioning	S*: "Who was Ambrose?" R*: "A Civil War author"	(1) The teacher can focus on information of particular interest (2) Attempts to test levels of comprehension	(1) Hard to score (2) Only a few questions can be written for each paragraph (3) Levels of comprehension may not match types of questions (or even exist) (4) Risk of poorly written questions (5) The student's answer is determined by the question asked	Percent correct	Undetermined	SLP 4: prior knowledge	Lack of general knowledge Go to Chapter 17 (SLPs 1 and 2)
2. Paraphrasing	S*: "... was fascinated with the human aspect of war ..." R*: "... he wanted to know why people decide to fight ..."	(1) Student responses aren't influenced by the way the questions are asked (2) Supplies an overall impression of the student's understanding (3) Can be used in daily lessons so has fidelity	(1) Hard to score (2) Difficult to control sudden responses without questioning, which in turn would negate advantage 1	Percent correct	Undetermined	SLP4: prior knowledge	Poor vocabulary, lack of familiarity with procedure Go to Chapters 12 (SLP6) and 17 (SLPs 1 and 2)
3. Story retelling	S*: "... was fascinated with the human aspect of war ..." R*: "... was fascinated with the human aspect of war ..."	(1) Student responses are not influenced by the way questions are asked (2) Indicates overall number of idea units the student recalls (3) Can be used as a component of daily lessons and therefore has fidelity to real life (4) Can be analyzed for match to text structure or story map	(1) Cumbersome to transcribe student responses (2) Analysis of idea units in text to enhance scoring is time consuming (3) May not sample understanding; may only tap recall	Percent correct	Undetermined	SLP 2	Lack of familiarity with procedure

(continued)

Exhibit 10.2   Comprehension Testing Procedures (continued)

Procedure	Example	Advantages	Disadvantages	Type of Data	Criteria	Comprehension SLP	Other Assumed Causes for Failure
4. Cloze	S*: ". . . was fascinated with the _____ of war . . ." R*: ". . . was fascinated with the human aspect of war . . ."	(1) Easy to score (2) Success depends on all types of passage clues (3) Item difficulty is random (4) Large sample of behavior	(1) Does not directly test understanding of what you think is the most important part of the passage (2) Can only be used with redundant texts	Percent correct	Instructional level 30–45%; below 30% is no-pass	Follow qualitative interpretation guidelines for maze and cloze	Discrepancy between student language and text language Go to Chapter 12—oral language sample
5. Maze	S*: ". . . was fascinated with the technical, geographic _____ human aspect . . ." R*: ". . . was fascinated with the technical, geographic _____ human	(1) Easy to score (2) Success depends on all types of passage clues (3) Distractors can be used to alter the test difficulty or the focus of the test (4) Large sample of behavior	(1) Risk of poorly selected distractors	Percent correct	Instructional level is 60–80%; below 60% is no-pass	Follow qualitative interpretation guidelines for maze/cloze	Discrepancy between student language and text language Go to Chapter 12—oral language sample
6. Oral reading rate	One-minute timing of passage reading	(1) Easy to give (2) Easy to score (3) Excellent screening devise (4) Large sample of behavior (5) Excellent for monitoring progress	(1) Little "diagnostic" information	Rate per minute	1st grade, 50 wpm 2nd grade, 100 wpm +3rd grade, 140 wpm	SLP 1	Poor decoding accuracy and/or fluency. Go to Chapter 11

one can file, photocopy, drop, or spill coffee over. The evidence is usually in a teacher's head!

The conduct of portfolio assessment for comprehension is more akin to a staff meeting than to a testing session. In fact, in many instances the student won't even be in attendance. The assessment involves going through the available hard evidence, and professional observations, that have accumulated through contact with the student. This body of evidence and observations is compared to a rubric like the one represented by the status sheet in Exhibit 10.1*.

The trouble with this system is that it may not be employed the same way with all students or when different teachers are participating in it. The challenge of all portfolio-assessment procedures is to retain professional judgment while eliminating personal bias. One way to do this is to use the Rules for Developing Assumed Causes and the 15 Evaluator Actions (see Chapter 7, pp. 140–146) to guide the group discussion. The advantage of the system is that the judgments produced are developed by teachers who are actually working with the student. Therefore, the results can have a high degree of instructional utility.

Oral Reading Fluency

There is a certain amount of perverse pleasure in presenting something that we know many people will hate. This is one of those presentations. "Reading fluency" was listed as an enabling skill for comprehension. It is also a way people react to print. Students who react to a passage by reading it quickly understand it better than students who react by reading it slowly aloud (Carnine et al., 1990; Tindal & Marston,

1990; Shinn, 1989; Shinn, Good, Knutson, Tilly & Collins, 1992; Fuchs, Fuchs & Maxwell, 1988). Therefore, using oral-reading rate to identify students who may have a comprehension problem is a good idea. The trouble is that the oral-reading score does not give much beneficial information. It tells the evaluator that there is a problem (because the student is reading slowly), but it does not provide abundant insight into the nature of that problem. As a result, oral-reading rate has somewhat limited utility. However, it is excellent for screening/identification, for eligibility decision making (see Chapter 9), and for monitoring teaching effectiveness. Fluency tests are quick to give and easily developed, scored, and summarized. Therefore, they were the only procedure in Exhibit 10.2 that can conveniently be repeated for progress monitoring. If you suspect a comprehension problem because a student's reading rate is slower than expected, you should always do two things: (1) confirm the problem by following up with another survey procedure, and (2) if the problem is confirmed, check the student's decoding skills.

Cloze or Maze Plus Questions

The *cloze* technique has received attention both as a comprehension measure and as a system for selecting instructional-level reading material (Baker & Brown, 1984; Baldauf, 1982; Berk, 1979; DeSanti & Sullivan, 1984). The basic cloze system starts with choosing a 250-word selection. The first and last sentences of the passage are left intact, while every fifth word in the remaining sentences is blanked out (the blanks should be of equal length regardless of the word removed or you'll end up testing the student's skill at interpreting blanks). The students are asked to read the passage orally and to say (or write) the word that goes in the blank (they do *not* read the unmodified passage first). Most authors require that the students supply the exact missing word. This may seem hard but the CAP is fairly low. If a student supplies more than 50% of the missing words, the material is considered too easy for instruction. If he gets between 40% and 50% of the words correct, the material is said to be "at the instructional level." A score of below 40% indicates the material is too hard (Pikulski & Pikulski, 1977). Exhibit 10.3 provides portions of two cloze passages (they are not complete, as they don't contain enough words and the first and last sentences are not intact).

Cloze is an interesting technique because it seems to challenge the student's skill at using all types of passage information. Cloze performance is closely related to the redundancy of the text as well as to the similarity between the language of the student and the language of the text. One disadvantage, therefore, is that it can't be used with passages that aren't redundant (ruling out particularly descriptive material). Also, students with language problems, or a primary language other than English, may do poorly on cloze regardless of their comprehension; unfortunately, these same students may do even worse on questions and paraphrasing (Propst & Baldauf, 1981).

The foremost advantage of cloze is that it is easy to score (unlike the questioning, paraphrasing, and retelling techniques) because corrects and errors are easy to recognize. The cloze procedure for blanking out words distributes item difficulty randomly, which permits the blanks to be treated equally and to be added together without weighting or conversion.

The *maze* procedure is similar to the cloze procedure, but the behavior of the student is quite different. In cloze, the student recalls and produces the correct response. In maze, the student identifies and indicates it. Again, the procedure requires the selection of a 250-word passage. The first and last sentences of the passage are left intact. Next a group of words is inserted for every fifth word. The student is asked to select the original word (usually by circling it) from among these three to five distractors. Therefore, *maze is to multiple choice as cloze is to fill in the blank*. Because identification of a correct word is easier than production of a correct word, the criterion for passing is higher. Eighty percent correct can be considered instructional level, with scores above 85% indicating easy material and scores below 60% material that is too hard. Just as with all cutting scores (scores used as boundaries for certain decisions), the 85% maze criterion is not absolute. However, in a study using 237 students of grades 2 through 8, working on the maze tests supplied in your workbook, the average score was 94% and the average standard deviation was 2.39 items (roughly 6%). These students were randomly selected and included both high and low achievers. This means that most of the normal and high achieving students actually topped out on the maze passages with scores at or near 100%. Incidentally, the internal consistency, averaged across

Exhibit 10.3   Cloze paragraphs—Text Difficulty and Prior Knowledge

Passage 1	Answers to Passage 1
"As the teacher _____ the option of limiting _____ vocabulary, but your students _____ necessarily have the option _____ expanding theirs. In addition _____ of remedial tests, or _____ reading texts, will intentionally _____ the vocabulary to well _____ the student's speaking vocabulary _____ will seldom include adequate _____ for teaching necessary words. _____ failure to provide for adequate _____ instruction is also _____ of most basal programs . . ."	"As the teacher have the option of limiting your vocabulary, but your students don't necessarily have the option of expanding theirs. In addition authors of remedial tests, or corrective reading texts, will intentionally limit the vocabulary to well below the student's speaking vocabulary and will seldom include adequate procedures for teaching necessary words. This failure to provide for adequate vocabulary instruction is also typical of most basal programs . . ."

Passage 1 blank numbering: 1, 2, 3, 4, 5, 6, 7, 8, 9, 10, 11, 12, 13.

Passage 2	Answers to Passage 2
"Thus if the critical _____ for galactic confinement of _____ protons is 2.6×10^{19} electron _____ according to certain _____, the critical energy for _____ of cosmic-ray iron nuclei _____ to the same model _____ be 26 times less, _____ only 10^{18} electron volts. _____ therefore makes a great _____ of difference whether on _____ one hand the highest-energy _____ rays are protons or _____ nuclei or on the _____ hand they have a composition unlike either of those alternatives."	"Thus if the critical energy for galactic confinement of cosmic-ray protons is 2.6×10^{19} electron volts according to certain model, the critical energy for confinement of cosmic-ray iron nuclei according to the same model will be 26 times less, or only 10^{18} electron volts. It therefore makes a great deal of difference whether on the one hand the highest-energy cosmic rays are protons or iron nuclei or on the other hand they have a composition unlike either of those alternatives."

(*Source:* Passage 2 drawn from J. Linsley, "The Highest-Energy Cosmic Rays," *Scientific American*, 1978, *239* (1), p. 67.)

all passages and grade levels (an indicator of reliability), was .83 (see Appendix A).

The difficulty of maze will vary not only according to the difficulty of the passage but also according to the difficulty of the distractors selected. For example, in Exhibit 10.4, item A is easier than item B because the distractors (incorrect choices) are more clearly incorrect. Because you can choose easy or hard distractors, maze is more flexible than cloze. Of course, this also makes it easier to produce an invalid test.

One way of controlling for the difficulty of the distractors is to have one word that is syntactically correct but semantically incorrect and to have another word that is both syntactically and semantically incorrect. A passage modified in this manner would appear as follows (the choices are categorized under the sample) (Howell, Zucker & Morehead, 1982).

They felt a soft wind 1. _____ (little, pass, walk) them by. Then standing 2. _____ (until, little, in) the darkness beside them, a strange little man appeared.

	Correct word	Semantic distractor	Syntactic distractor
Item 1	pass	walk	little
Item 2	in	until	little

The distractors should be drawn from the passage itself to control for complexity and assure that they are words typically taught and used at the passage's reading level. Guthrie (1973) has suggested that distractors also be systematically drawn from categories of word types: noun, verb, modifier, and function. Nouns may include nouns and pronouns; the verbs may include transitives, intransitives, and auxiliaries; the modifier group may include adjectives and adverbs; and the function group may include prepositions, articles, and conjunctions. In item 1 above, "walk" and "pass" are verbs and are syntactically correct. "Little" is a modifier and is both syntactically and semantically incorrect (see Chapter 12). Only "pass" is both syntactically and semantically correct.

While some research has suggested that the maze format does not sample comprehension beyond sentence boundaries, the careful selection of distractors appears to influence these findings (Cziko, 1983; Parker, Hasbrouck & Tindal, 1992). The passages included in the student workbook that accompanies this text were written following these rules.

Both cloze and maze formats let the evaluator

Exhibit 10.4   Maze Formats with Choices of Varying Difficulty

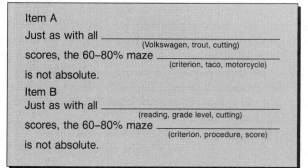

sample about 40 responses in a single 250-word passage. This is certainly is a larger sample than would be obtained using a question format, and this contributes to the reliability of the scores. In addition, some theorists believe that cloze and maze have superior validity for comprehension because both permit readers to look ahead as well as back to previous text to confirm or disconfirm their responses. (Both cloze and maze are worked in much the same way that a crossword puzzle is worked. Finding one answer may cause the student to go back and change another.) The use of text lookbacks and lookaheads seems to be a key self-monitoring tactic used by comprehending readers (Baker & Brown, 1984; Hosseini & Ferrell, 1982). Maze, like cloze, is also easy to score.

Because the maze format lets students select a response rather than produce one, it is especially appropriate for students with language-production problems or students who are acquiring a new language. Even though they may not comprehend well in the second language, the maze format permits them to demonstrate what they do understand (Bensoussan & Ramraz, 1984). This means that content teachers can maze portions of their textbooks and use the tests to determine if the student has sufficient language proficiency to comprehend the reading assignments.

One additional advantage of cloze and maze is that the same passage can be used to screen for both comprehension and decoding problems. Scores from these formats appear to be as useful as the graded passages found in reading inventories for selecting instructional-level material.

As shown in Exhibit 10.2, questioning, in spite of its frequent use, is one of the worst ways to measure reaction to reading text. However, questioning can be used in conjunction with the cloze and maze procedures. Questions should be limited to things like "What would be the best title?" or "Can you tell me what the passage was about?" Such questions will not yield pass/no pass data, but will augment the cloze/maze by giving some information about the student's overall understanding of the passage.

Evaluation Procedures

Note: If for some reason you did not read the introduction to Part 3 (p. 181), read it now.

Exhibit 10.5
Process of
comprehension
evaluation

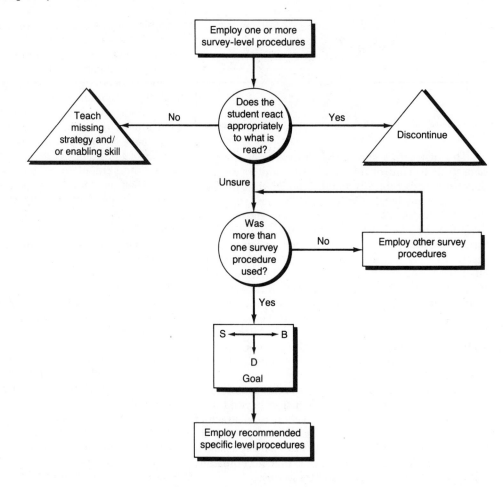

Survey-Level Testing

Survey-level testing is used to answer this question: Does the student adequately comprehend text? This section describes how the survey-level procedures work. The overall process is reviewed in Exhibit 10.5*.

Directions and interpretation guidelines are provided for portfolio, reading rate, cloze/maze, and question. While CAP will be presented in the guidelines, often it is only a recommendation, because CAP will vary according to the text structure and the student's prior knowledge. We have set the CAP high because it is probably safer to give the student an extra test than it is to risk missing a problem. Also, you should be aware that if the student is extremely slow

at any of the survey-level formats, decoding should be tested.

Portfolio Directions

1. Ask anyone with direct knowledge of the student's skills to a meeting. Individuals who have worked on reading with the student are particularly valuable.

2. Explain the purpose of the portfolio analysis to everyone (it is to limit the field of inquiry by ruling out things we already know the student does or doesn't do).

3. Using the status sheet in Exhibit 10.1*, go through each of the primary categories and mark the appropriate status (yes, no, unsure). The

indicators are only there to help define the categories—*it is the category you are rating.* Therefore, you can still mark yes when an indicator is missing, or no when an indicator is present.

Qualitative Interpretation

Question: How were the categories marked?

If a category is marked YES, then it is assumed the student has this skill. No other action (other than monitoring for maintenance and generalization) is required.

If a category is marked NO (a clear no-pass), then the student needs instruction in this area and the category and its indicators become instructional objectives. Specific-level testing may still be required to guide this or to monitor progress.

If a category is marked UNSURE, additional information is needed. Employ the specific-level procedures (SLPs) indicated for each category marked "unsure."

Reading Rate Directions

1. Select three 250-word passages at the student's expected reading level (the grade he should be in). Make a copy for yourself. You may want to use one of the reading passages provided in the workbook (for primary grades 1 and 2, 100 to 200 words is adequate).

2. For each passage say to the student "I want you to read part of this story out loud. Read it as quickly and carefully as you can. If you come to a word you do not know then skip it. Please begin." Time the student for 1 minute and make a slash (/) after the last word read in the 1-minute time limit. As the student reads, mark all errors on your copy of the passage. It is not necessary to recognize different types of errors when determining rate and accuracy (that will come later, in the decoding chapter).

3. To establish the student's oral reading rate, count the number of words read correctly *and* the number of words read incorrectly during each minute (up to your slash mark). Number correct and number incorrect are always reported separately (added together they will yield the total number of words read). Omissions are not errors. To obtain the student's passage accuracy, find the

percentage correct on the entire passage. Divide the number of words correct by the total number of words read. Report the median scores of the three passages.

Score Interpretation

Grade	Pass	Marginal	No Pass
		Fluency	
early 1	+ 40wpm	30–40wpm	−30wpm
late 1	+ 50wpm	40–50wpm	−40wpm
early 2	+ 80wpm	50–80wpm	−50wpm
late 2	+120wpm	90–120wpm	−90wpm
3 and above	+140wpm	100–140wpm	−90wpm
		Accuracy	
	+95	90–95%	−90%

Qualitative Interpretation

Question: Did the student score in the pass range?

If YES, then he should be understanding the passage. Discontinue.

If MARGINAL, use an additional survey procedure.

If NO, assume he has a decoding problem *and* a comprehension problem. As explained earlier, oral reading fluency separates those students who comprehend well from those who do not. However, the score has little interpretive value. Obviously, a no-pass score strongly indicates the need for a decoding test. So, you should use Comprehension SLP 1, and/or go to Chapter 11. Also, if you haven't already done so, use maze/close and portfolio analysis to determine what other additional testing may be needed.

Cloze and Maze Directions

Cloze

1. Remember, cloze is difficult for poor decoders and young (first- and second-grade) students. If the student falls into these categories, use maze.

2. Collect passages of varying difficulty from texts used in the classroom or from published tests. The passages should be about 250 words in length (for primary grades 1 and 2, 100–200 words is adequate). It is best to use the type of passages (expository or narrative) to which you

will generalize the test results. Also, they must be roughly equivalent in topic complexity.

3. Leave the first and last sentence intact and omit every fifth word. Leave blanks of equal length for all omitted words.

4. Tell the student that you are going to have him read a passage in which some words have been omitted. Tell him to fill in each blank with the word he thinks is missing. Have him practice with a sentence such as "Twinkle, twinkle, little _____," or "Old MacDonald had a _____." Tell him he need not fill in the blanks, so that he may go back and change answers if he thinks of a better word. If he can't write or spell, fill in the blanks for him.

5. Allow 10 minutes per passage.

6. After the student has answered for each blank (remember, it is not necessary that the student write out the answer) ask him the questions.

7. Score the cloze responses. We use "exact word only" for ease of scoring. Our criteria are based on this procedure.

Maze

1. Use the set of maze tests in the workbook. If you want to prepare you own, follow the directions provided earlier on page 191.

2. Tell the student that he is going to select the correct word for each blank. Provide a practice example such as "Old MacDonald had a _____ (farm, bike, running)." Tell him that he need not do the items in sequence, and may go back and change them.

3. Allow 10 minutes per passage.

4. Score responses.

5. Compare the student's score to the criterion you have established (see Chapter 6) or use ours. Criteria do vary as a function of the difficulty of the distractors so, *if you create your own passages, we encourage you to validate your own criteria.*

Score Interpretation for Expected Level

	Criteria	
	Maze	Cloze
Pass	85% or better	50% or better
Marginal no-pass (instructional level)	80–85%	40–50%
No-pass	80% or less	40% or less

Pass. If the student scores in the pass range, then he should be skillful enough to understand the material in this passage. If you have other information to indicate a comprehension problem, you should repeat the survey test on other material (to rule out the possibility that the student was simply familiar with the topic of this passage).

If your concern about comprehension was prompted by poor grades, then consider that the problem may actually be the result of poor study skills, or even compliance with homework assignments, and not comprehension (see Chapter 17).

Marginal Pass at Expected Level. If the student falls into the marginal-pass range, he is having some trouble with passages at that level of difficulty. However, that is probably the best level of material for him during comprehension lessons. If you want additional guidance to begin this instruction, follow the no-pass guidelines below.

No-pass at Expected Level. If you gave the cloze test and the student is in the first or second grade (or reads inaccurately or slowly), give a maze test to confirm the problem. Otherwise follow the qualitative interpretations.

Qualitative Interpretation

Question: Did the student make some effort on the task and have some correct responses?

If YES, go to the next question.

If NO, repeat the survey testing on lower level (easier) material.

Question: Did the student pass the test?

If YES, discontinue.

If NO, use the following guidelines by finding the description, or descriptions (there may be more than one), that best detail the student's behavior on the maze or cloze test. Then check out the indicated assumed cause(s) by following the specific-level testing recommendations.

Student behavior	Assumed cause	Specific test
Passage was expository	Prior knowledge	SLP 4
No attempt, few correct responses, random errors	A. Student did not understand the cloze/maze test format	Re-explain format and give guided practice. If that doesn't work, try another survey format or begin specific-level procedures
	B. Passage too difficult	Repeat procedure with lower-level (easier) passages
Worked very slowly and scored in the no-pass or marginal range	A. Decoding	SLP 1 and/or chapter 11.
	B. Comprehension strategies	Comprehension specific-level procedure 3 first, then 1 and 4
Errors often syntactically correct but semantically incorrect (e.g., "Yesterday we *ate* to the ball game")	Vocabulary semantics	Go to Chapter 12
Errors often semantically correct but syntactically incorrect (e.g., "Yesterday we *go* to the ball game")	Syntax	Go to Chapter 12
No recognizable error pattern	Unclear	Administer *all* specific-level procedures, beginning with language.

▽ **Question, Paraphrase, and Retell Directions**

1. After the student has finished a cloze or maze exercise, ask him one or more of the following:

   a. "What would have been a good title for this story?"

   b. "What was the main idea of this passage?"

   c. "What did the passage tell you?"

   d. "How can you summarize what you just read?"

3. Questions a and b are somewhat specific and should only be used in conjunction with maze or cloze.

4. Questions c and d are paraphrase/retell prompts. If you are uncertain about how to score these responses read SLP 2: Retell, on pages 203–205. Be aware that even competent adults often have

tremendous difficulty making concise summary statements (Palincsar & Brown, 1984).

Score Interpretation

The difficulty of questions like those above depends on so many things it isn't possible to set meaningful numerical criteria for correct answers. So, in spite of the fact that people do it all the time, scoring is useless.

Qualitative Interpretation

A student should be skilled enough to supply a complete and correct answer to any appropriately developed passage-dependent question. However, you shouldn't interpret failure on questions unless the student failed another procedure (oral fluency, maze/cloze, portfolio).

The one advantage of Retell and Paraphrasing (questions c and d), as related to qualitative interpretation, is in the area of reader awareness. During attempts to answer open questions (rather than those that merely require selection of a choice) readers are more apt to recognize when they are answering incorrectly (Pressley, Ghatala, Woloshyn & Pirie, 1990). Listen for indications of this awareness, or its absence, in the answers students give (Stallman & Pearson, 1990). Asking them how they got their answers or occasionally challenging the answers (see Chapter 8, p. 152) may also provide this sort of insight.

Question: Did the student answer questions correctly?

If NO for a and b, then check prior knowledge with SLP 4 and be sure to use another survey technique.

If NO for c and d, then go to SLP 2.

If YES, then reconsider the possibility that an enabling skill such as prior knowledge is deficient. Go to SLP 4.

Specific-Level Testing

The nine assumed causes for comprehension failure can be lumped into two categories: Comprehension strategies, and enabling skills. Because the enabling skills are covered in some detail in other chapters, this chapter only deals with testing comprehension strategies. That's OK, because these strategies alone provide us with the possibility of multiple explanations for a student's failure to react appropriately to print. However, don't forget that the enabling skills are critical to adequate comprehension. Any indication of a problem within an enabling domain should be checked out with a survey test.

Fortunately, figuring out a comprehension problem is easier than explaining how to do it. In the case of Comprehension SLP 1, a flow chart summarizing the process and explanatory notations are presented.

Comprehension specific-level procedures (SLPs) are used to answer the following questions:

1. Does the student monitor the meaning of the text as he reads?

   SLP 1: Assisted monitoring
   SLP 2: Retell

2. Does the student know about the reading process?

   SLP 3: Awareness of reading

3. Does the student have adequate prior knowledge of a topic to comprehend passages about it?

   SLP 4: Assisted activation of prior knowledge

3. Does the student know how to use what he already knows, along with what he has learned from the text, to make logical assumptions about upcoming material?

   SLP 5: Prediction

4. Does the student know how to use what he already knows about both the topic and text structure to locate targeted information in a passage?

   SLPs 6a and 6b: Assisted search

5. Does the student knows who or what words like *he, they,* or *it* represent?

   SLP 7: Referent knowledge

6. Is the student sufficiently skilled in each of the enabling skill areas to use comprehension strategies?

   All SLPs

Information provided in the interpretation section for each survey-level procedure can be used to select which of these six questions it is most efficient to ask first. The Status sheet in Exhibit 10.1* is particularly helpful. If none of the assumed causes seem any more or less likely, then you will need to test for all of them. To facilitate this, we have arranged them in the sequence that will allow you to use the specific-level interpretation guidelines with maximum efficiency. However, once again, *we strongly recommend that you enter this process through the use of survey-level assessment as illustrated in Exhibit 10.5*.*

A Note on Strategy Assessment Procedures

Questions 1–5 above are all addressed in this chapter (if question 6 comes up, you will be directed to another chapter). These five questions all address strategy use. Strategy use is assessed through direct observation of behavior and interviews with students regarding the procedures they are employing (see Chapter 8, p. 152). Unfortunately, asking a student to tell you what he is doing does not guarantee that he will report accurately, nor does it establish that he will do what he reports. However, it does give you an indication that he knows the components of a procedure and when and why to use it.

The first comprehension strategy category, Active and Reflective Reading, is a combination of each of the other categories. Failure to read actively is indicated whenever there is a breakdown on survey-level measures.

Observe that more than one testing procedure is mentioned for Monitoring, Prior Knowledge, and Clarification. For example, assisted monitoring and story retelling are available for monitoring of meaning. Multiple procedures are available because these comprehension domains are not clearly defined. Our expectation is that, by administering multiple measures, we can better illustrate the student's skill in these domains. We hope this is not a case of collecting a larger sample of the same behavior. It is an attempt to look at each domain from a different perspective. While we advise that you use them all, we also recognize that time constraints may not allow this. Of course, your goal is to continue evaluating until you are satisfied that you have sufficient information to start teaching.

Specific procedures 1, 4, and 6 all involve the use of assisted assessment (see Chapter 5, p. 88). When using these procedures, the evaluator first identifies tasks on which the student is unsuccessful, although apparently adequately prepared. Then the evaluator systematically provides assistance and follows this by retesting. The cycle continues until the student succeeds, allowing the evaluator to map out the zones of support that the student requires (Braun, Rennie & Gordon, 1987; Duran, 1988). Once these have been defined, the goal of instruction is either to teach the student to do without this support, or to provide it for himself.

Comprehension SLP 1: Assisted Monitoring

Assisted monitoring is used to verify that the student monitors the meaning of the text as he reads. The process of SLP 1 is outlined in Exhibit 10.6*. Because of the complexity of this procedure, some steps will also refer to interpretation questions. In order to maintain the flow of the directions, these explanations will all appear in the same place. This means that, on your first pass through, you may need to do some page flipping. (Sorry.)

Directions

Step 1: Collect a Sample. Select a passage that the student reads inaccurately. (You may want to read the survey testing directions in Chapter 11 for information on collecting and scoring reading samples.)

Step 2: Do the Errors Violate Meaning? This is answered by reading the passage the way the student read it and comparing the resulting message to the message of the original text.

Step 3: Is Rate and/or Comprehension Poor? If the errors don't violate meaning, then ask yourself if the student's reading rate and comprehension seem adequate. (Refer to the results of the Survey Comprehension Status Sheet if you've used it.)

See Interpretation Questions 1 and 2

Step 4: Does the Student Self-Correct? Determine if the student self-corrects errors that violate passage meaning.

See Interpretation Question 2

Step 5: Assist the Student's Monitoring. Tell the student "Whenever you make an error, I'm going to tap the table with my pen. When I tap the table, I want you to fix the error." Have the student continue to read the passage. When he makes an error that violates meaning, immediately tap the table with a pen or your finger. Do not wait.

Step 6: Does Assistance Lead to Immediate Error Corrections? Determine if the student immediately self-corrects most meaning-violating errors. If the student does not correct the errors, go on to step 7.

See Interpretation Question 3

Step 7: Test Words in Isolation. Select words the student missed while reading the passage. These should only be words for which the errors violated meaning. Present the words to the student in isolation (on flash cards or paper) and ask the student to read them.

Step 8: Were Words in Isolation Read Correctly?

Interpretation Question 4

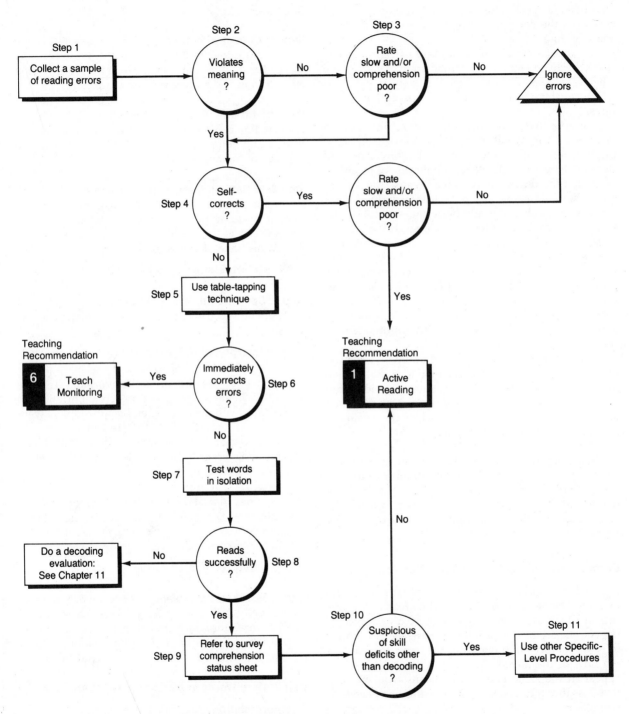

Exhibit 10.6   Flowchart for Comprehension: Specific-Level Procedure 1—Assisted Monitoring

Step 9: Review the Comprehension Status Sheet. If you completed the Survey Comprehension Status Sheet (Exhibit 10.1*), go get it. If you didn't, you need to give it now. Sit down with all the information you have collected and carefully answer the questions on the sheet. Ask yourself (or anyone else who might know) if there is evidence of problems, other than decoding. Mark the problem areas.

Step 10: Were Problems Noted on the Status Sheet? Look at the results obtained from the Comprehension Status Sheet. Give the recommended SLPs for categories marked no or "unsure" on the status sheet. If there aren't any problem categories (other than decoding, which you may have recognized back at step 8), see

Interpretation Question 5

Interpretation Guidelines for Assisted Monitoring

Score and qualitative interpretation guidelines for this procedure are included in the following interpretation questions.

Interpretation Question 1: Does reading rate and comprehension seem OK?

If YES, ignore the errors (they aren't hurting anything).

If NO, go on to step 4.

Interpretation Question 2: Does the student immediately self-correct the errors?

If YES, then assume that he has adequate comprehension strategies for monitoring and clarifying—but does not automatically employ these while reading passages. Go back and reconsider the results you obtained in step 3 to make sure you are confident that the student's rate is slow and/or comprehension is poor. If not, then ignore the errors and consider the student to have passed. If the rate is slow, or comprehension impaired, the student needs to learn to automatically to employ the skills he already possesses. This can be accomplished by using Teaching Recommendation 1 (see p. 213). Select the complementary objective from Comprehension Objectives 1–3 (p. 209) and specify intermediate levels.

If NO, the student does not self-correct, go on to step 5.

Interpretation Question 3: Does the student self-correct when given assistance?

If YES, then it can be assumed that he needs to learn to monitor his own reading (that is, he needs to provide himself with the sort of feedback you were supplying by tapping your pen). Teach this using Comprehension Objectives 4–7 (pp. 209–211) and Teaching Recommendation 6 (p. 216).

If NO, go on to step 7.

Interpretation Question 4: Did the student correctly and quickly (no longer than two seconds per word) read the words in isolation?

If YES, then go on to step 9.

If NO, go to Chapter 11 and conduct a decoding evaluation.

Interpretation Question 5: Is there evidence of any problem other than decoding?

If YES or UNSURE, take one more shot at monitoring by using Comprehension SLP 2: Retell (following). If that doesn't work, you have no choice but to begin systematically checking each area of comprehension strategy. If you don't find anything there, you will next need to check each domain of enabling skill listed in Exhibit 10.1*. (No one said this would be easy!) Obviously, if you can use the indicators of Exhibit 10.1* to narrow this search, it will be well worth your time.

If NO, use Decoding Teaching Recommendation 1: Balanced Instruction (Chapter 11, p. 228), and Comprehension Teaching Recommendation 1: Active Reading (p. 213).

Comprehension SLP 2: Retell

Retell is used to verify that the student monitors the meaning of text. The retell procedure is fairly straightforward. The kid reads a passage and then, upon request, tells you what he read. You score the reaction according to the thoroughness and accuracy of the student's retelling. With this technique, students are permitted to repeat exact words found in the story.

Both the development of a retell scoring procedure and the establishment of criteria are time consuming for the evaluator. Fuchs, Fuchs, and Maxwell (1988), Tindal and Marston (1990) and Lovitt (1984) have all suggested approaches and provide step-by-step descriptions of how to proceed with retell. We prefer the Tindal and Marston procedure because it is the quickest to use. It uses a "scale" for judging the quality of retell (presented in the interpretation section of this SLP).

The way you introduce retell exercises has a great effect on the student's work (Bisanz, Das, Varnhagen & Henderson, 1992). One way to standardize your directions, while clarifying the task to the student, is to go over the criteria with the student before the actual test. This will serve to define retell for the student, just as the Tindal and Marston (1990) criteria have defined it for you.

One drawback of retelling is the difficulty of judging if a student who retells a story with exact words has understood what he has read. Students may need to be taught both to paraphrase and to retell a story. An advantage of the paraphrase and retell formats is that both may also be used as instructional activities to enhance comprehension (Hansen, 1978; Schumaker, Denton & Deshler, 1984; Deshler, 1985).

▽ **Directions**

1. Collect passages of varying difficulty from texts used in the classroom or from published tests. The passages should be about 250 words in length (for primary grades 1 and 2, 100–200 words is adequate).

2. Use written retell if the student has adequate skills; otherwise, set up a recorder to tape student responses.

3. Tell the student that you want him to read a passage and tell you what he has read.

4. Have the student read the passage to himself.

5. Ask the student to tell you what he has read. Record responses.

6. Score responses using Tindal and Marston's (1990) criterion for response quality.

∽ **Interpretation Guidelines for Retell**

Use the following scale to rate the retell:

5—Generalizations are made beyond the text; includes central thesis and major points, supporting details, and relevant supplemental information; exhibits coherence, completeness, and comprehensibility.

4—Includes central thesis, major points, support-ing details, and relevant supplemental information; exhibits coherence, completeness, and comprehensibility.

3—Relates major ideas, includes supporting details and relevant supplemental information; exhibits adequate coherence, completeness, and comprehensibility.

2—Relates a few major ideas, supporting details, and relevant supplemental information; exhibits some coherence, completeness, and comprehensibility.

1—Relates no major ideas, and details only irrelevant supplemental information; low degree of coherence, completeness, and comprehensibility.

Pass: rating of 4 or above.
No-pass: rating of 3, 2 or 1

There really isn't an established standard for the Tindal and Marston scale, although we have found scores 3 and above are easily produced by even primary students when they retell primary passages. You could develop your own (see Chapter 5); it would be tedious, but potentially quite valuable.

Question: Was it possible to score the recall?
If YES, go to the next question.
If NO, (errors cannot be interpreted or incoherent retell), repeat the procedure with progressively easier passages. If none of these produces coherent retell, go to SLP 3 (following).

Question: Did the student score 4 or 5?
If YES, the student does monitor the meaning of text. Explore other assumed causes for failure of the survey procedure, starting with specific procedures 3 and 7 (pp. 203 and 208).
If NO, analyze the retell product for error patterns. Try to recognize these deficits in the retell:
   a. Misses main ideas
   b. Excludes relevant information or includes irrelevant information
   c. Omits references to characters, descriptions, actions, conflicts and/or resolutions
   d. Constructs poor and/or incoherent retell

Question: Did you find a pattern?
If NO, teach Comprehension Objective 7 (p. 210).
If YES, and most errors fall into categories A, B or

C, teach Objectives 7, 8, and 14 using Teaching Recommendations 3, 4, and 6.

Comprehension SLP 3: Awareness of Reading

This procedure is used to investigate the student's awareness of the reading process and how that process is influenced by text difficulty. It is a combined observation and interview procedure drawn directly from the work of Schmitt (1990) and Paris and Jacobs (1984). To use this procedure, you will administer the questionnaire shown in Exhibit 10.7* and a set of questions. Results will be recorded on Exhibit 10.8*.

▽ **Directions**

1. Have the student read material that he has had difficulty understanding (reacting to) in the past. As the student reads, watch for evidence of tactics listed in Exhibit 10.7* and 10.8*. Do not expect to see evidence of each tactic.

2. When you have finished observing, begin to interview the student. Tell the student that you want to ask him some questions regarding reading. Explain that your purpose is to find out what he thinks about reading, *not* how well he reads.

   Remember that different types of passages will elicit different tactics. Therefore, you'll need to make it clear to the student when you are asking about passages read for enjoyment and those read to study. Ask the student to explain how he could go about obtaining the message of a paragraph or the sound of a word.

3. Use the questionaire in Exhibit 10.7*. Some of these items may seem inappropriate to the student, or to the sort of material he is currently reading. In that case skip them. It may also be true that some important topic is omitted from the items in Exhibit 10.7*. In that case you will want to add tactics. Decide which items are missed.

4. Ask the following questions from Paris and Jacobs (1984, pp. 2085–86):

   a. What's the hardest part about reading for you? (complex material, paying attention to the right stuff)

   b. What would help you become a better reader? (help from the teacher, practice)

   c. Is there anything special about the first sentence or two in a story? What do they tell you? (tells you what is important, makes the reading easier)

   d. How about the last sentence; what does it tell you? (what I should have attended to, what is important)

   e. How can you tell which sentences are the most important ones in a story? (where they are in the story, if they tell about the hardest stuff to understand)

   f. If you could only read some sentences in the story because you are in a hurry, which ones would you read? (the ones that tell about important stuff, the first or last ones)

   g. What do you try to tell someone about a story—all the words, just the ending, what the story was about, or something else? (the important stuff, what/who it was about)

   h. The other day I asked a boy to read a story and then tell me what he read. Before he started reading, though, he asked me if I wanted him to remember the story word for word or just the general meaning. Why do you think he asked me that? (because he wanted to know why he was reading the story, so he could decide what to focus on)

   i. Before you start to read a story, do you do anything special? What kinds of plans help you read better? (I try to find out why I'm reading it, I look it over before I start)

   j. If you had to read very fast and could only read some words, which ones would you try to read? (I'd look for clues, like words that are darker)

   k. Do you ever go back and read things over? Why? (yes—because I get confused, because I want to read the stuff the teacher talked about twice, because they are the things I need to attend to)

   l. What do you do if you come to a word you don't understand? (I put another word in its place, then see if the sentence makes sense; I look it up, I ask for help)

Exhibit 10.7   Metacomprehension Strategy Index*

Directions: Think about what kinds of things you can do to help you understand a story better before, during, and after you read it. Read each of the lists of four statements and decide which one of them would help *you* the most. *There are no right answers.* It is just what *you* think would help the most. Circle the letter of the statement you choose.

I. In each set of four, choose the one statement which tells a good thing to do to help you understand a story better *before* you read it.

1. Before I begin reading, it's a good idea to:
   A. See how many pages are in the story.
   B. Look up all of the big words in the dictionary.
   C. <u>Make some guesses about what I think will happen in the story.</u>
   D. Think about what has happened so far in the story.

2. Before I begin reading, it's a good idea to:
   A. <u>Look at the pictures to see what the story is about.</u>
   B. Decide how long it will take me to read the story.
   C. Sound out the words I don't know.
   D. Check to see if the story is making sense.

3. Before I begin reading, it's a good idea to:
   A. Ask someone to read the story to me.
   B. <u>Read the title to see what the story is about.</u>
   C. Check to see if most of the words have long or short vowels in them.
   D. Check to see if the pictures are in order and make sense.

4. Before I begin reading, it's a good idea to:
   A. Check to see that no pages are missing.
   B. Make a list of the words I'm not sure about.
   C. <u>Use the title and pictures to help me make guesses about what will happen in the story.</u>
   D. Read the last sentence so I will know how the story ends.

5. Before I begin reading, it's a good idea to:
   A. <u>Decide on why I am going to read the story.</u>
   B. Use the difficult words to help me make guesses about what will happen in the story.
   C. Reread some parts to see if I can figure out what is happening if things aren't making sense.
   D. Ask for help with the difficult words.

6. Before I begin reading, it's a good idea to:
   A. Retell all of the main points that have happened so far.
   B. <u>Ask myself questions that I would like to have answered in the story.</u>
   C. Think about the meanings of the words which have more than one meaning.
   D. Look through the story to find all of the words with three or more syllables.

7. Before I begin reading, it's a good idea to:
   A. Check to see if I have read this story before.
   B. <u>Use my questions and guesses as a reason for reading the story.</u>
   C. Make sure I can pronounce all of the words before I start.
   D. Think of a better title for the story.

8. Before I begin reading, it's a good idea to:
   A. <u>Think of what I already know about the things I see in the pictures.</u>
   B. See how many pages are in the story.
   C. Choose the best part of the story to read again.
   D. Read the story aloud to someone.

9. Before I begin reading, it's a good idea to:
   A. Practice reading the story aloud.
   B. Retell all of the main points to make sure I can remember the story.
   C. <u>Think of what the pictures in the story might be like.</u>
   D. Decide if I have enough time to read the story.

10. Before I begin reading, it's a good idea to:
    A. Check to see if I am understanding the story so far.
    B. Check to see if the words have more than one meaning.
    C. <u>Think about where the story might be taking place.</u>
    D. List all of the important details.

II. In each set of four, choose the one statement which tells a good thing to do to help you understand a story better *while* you are reading it.

11. While I'm reading, it's a good idea to:
    A. Read the story very slowly so that I will not miss any important parts.
    B. Read the title to see what the story is about.
    C. Check to see if the pictures have anything missing.
    D. <u>Check to see if the story is making sense by seeing if I can tell what's happened so far.</u>

12. While I'm reading, it's a good idea to:
    A. <u>Stop to retell the main points to see if I am understanding what has happened so far.</u>
    B. Read the story quickly so that I can find out what happened.
    C. Read only the beginning and the end of the story to find out what it is about.
    D. Skip the parts that are too difficult for me.

13. While I'm reading, it's a good idea to:
    A. Look all of the big words up in the dictionary.
    B. Put the book away and find another one if things aren't making sense.
    C. <u>Keep thinking about the title and the pictures to help me decide what is going to happen next.</u>
    D. Keep track of how many pages I have left to read.

14. While I'm reading, it's a good idea to:
    A. Keep track of how long it is taking me to read the story.
    B. <u>Check to see if I can answer any of the questions I asked before I started reading.</u>
    C. Read the title to see what the story is going to be about.
    D. Add the missing details to the pictures.

15. While I'm reading, it's a good idea to:
    A. Have someone read the story aloud to me.
    B. Keep track of how many pages I have read.
    C. List the story's main character.
    D. <u>Check to see if my guesses are right or wrong.</u>

16. While I'm reading, it's a good idea to:
    A. Check to see that the characters are real.
    B. <u>Make a lot of guesses about what is going to happen next.</u>
    C. Not look at the pictures because they might confuse me.
    D. Read the story aloud to someone.

17. While I'm reading, it's a good idea to:
    A. <u>Try to answer the questions I asked myself.</u>
    B. Try not to confuse what I already know with what I'm reading about.
    C. Read the story silently.
    D. Check to see if I am saying the new vocabulary words correctly.

18. While I'm reading, it's a good idea to:
    A. <u>Try to see if my guesses are going to be right or wrong.</u>
    B. Reread to be sure I haven't missed any of the words.
    C. Decide on why I am reading the story.
    D. List what happened first, second, third, and so on.

19. While I'm reading, it's a good idea to:
    A. See if I can recognize the new vocabulary words.
    B. Be careful not to skip any parts of the story.
    C. Check to see how many of the words I already know.
    D. <u>Keep thinking of what I already know about the things and ideas in the story to help me decide what is going to happen.</u>

*Underlined responses indicate metacomprehension strategy awareness.
Source: Appendix to "A Questionnaire to Measure Children's Awareness of Strategic Reading Processes," by M. C. Schmitt, *The Reading Teacher*, March 1990, pp. 459-461. Reprinted with permission of Maribeth Cassidy Schmitt and the International Reading Association.

m. What do you do if you don't understand a whole sentence? (pay attention to it, read it over, skip it and come back later, stop and ask for help)

Exhibit 10.8   Status Sheet for Awareness of the Reading Process*

	Adequate	Not Adequate	Unsure
Before reading			
Considers purpose for reading (5, 7)			
Considers title (3)			
Scans illustrations/Figures (2, 8)			
Asks questions (6, 9, 10)			
Makes predictions (1, 4, 9, 10)			
While reading			
Remembers predictions and questions (14, 15, 17, 18)			
Decides if passage makes sense (11)			
Summarizes while reading (12, 19)			
Keeps questioning and predicting (13, 16)			
Seeks clarification (20)			
After reading			
Summarizes (22, 25)			
Reviews questions/predictions (21)			
Fits the story to what is already known (23, 24)			
Items from Paris and Jacobs (1984)			
Reading awareness			
1. What is hard?			
2. What would help?			
3. First sentences?			
4. Last sentences?			
5. What is important?			
Planning			
6. Which would you read?			
7. What would you tell?			
8. Asking before reading?			
9. Planning before reading?			
10. Which would you read?			
Regulation			
11. Do you reread?			
12. Words you don't understand?			
13. Sentences you don't understand?			
14. What do you skip?			
15. What do you read fast?			

*Item numbers from Schmitt (1990) are in parentheses. They are found in Exhibit 10.7.

n. What parts of a story do you skip as you read? (the stuff the teacher won't ask about, the stuff I don't think is important)

o. What things do you read faster than others? (the easy things, the things I know about)

4. If at all possible, tape record the student's responses. At the very least, take good notes on how the student answers.

5. The "correct" answers to each item in Exhibit 10.7* are underlined. Adequate responses to the 15 Paris and Jacobs (1984) questions are more difficult to recognize. General guidelines for adequacy include answers that reflect analysis of the reading task itself, or the application of specific tactics for reading. Some examples are presented in parentheses after each item; these are based on, but not taken directly from, Paris and Jacobs. If you have interviewed the student, use these options as guides to correct responding. The example responses do not reflect any particular grade level, therefore the wording your student uses may be more or less sophisticated than that presented.

6. Combine all of the information you have obtained and mark the status of each item in Exhibit 10.8*.

Qualitative Interpretation

Question: What is the status of each item in Exhibit 10.8*?

If ADEQUATE, then the skill does not need to be taught.

If NOT ADEQUATE, teach the skill. During instruction, utilize tactics the student does know to advance the student's acquisition of knowledge from text, and teach the unknown tactics. Do not emphasize knowing about the tactics—emphasize *using* them. Select Objectives 5, 6, and 9 (pp. 209–210). Use Teaching Recommendations 1, 2, and 6.

If the status is UNSURE, then repeat the observation and questioning by focusing directly on the items in question.

Comprehension SLP 4: Assisted Activation of Prior Knowledge

▽ Directions

This procedure is used to determine if the student lacks sufficient prior knowledge to comprehend a passage.

1. Select four passages from expository texts at the student's expected level. Be sure they cover different topics.

2. Convert two of the passages to cloze or maze format (whichever was used at the survey level).

3. Read each of the four passages carefully and outline their content. You may want to do this by preparing a map of the passage as explained in Teaching Recommendation 3. Recognize topics covered in the passage and any unstated information (prior knowledge) that the reader would need to understand it.

4. Discuss the topics and information you have identified with the student *prior to giving each passage*. (Don't discuss all four then test all four.) Do not "tell" the student about topics. Ask what the student knows and encourage him to remember everything. However, try not to cover the actual material in the target passage. This is important. You are trying to prime the student's recall about the topics. You are *not* trying to teach the content of the passage.

5. Discuss and administer the two cloze/maze tests in standard fashion and score them.

6. Discuss and administer the remaining two passages to get oral-reading fluency rates. Score these in standard fashion.

Score Interpretation

1. Average the scores on the two cloze/maze passages and then average the two oral-reading passages.

2. Compare the scores to those obtained during survey-level testing.

3. If the scores improve into the passing range (see criteria for oral reading on page 195 and cloze/maze on page 196), or if they improve by *at least* 50%, you have confirmed that a lack of prior knowledge is one likely cause of the survey-level failure. (Caution is in order here, as the low survey scores may have been due to the novelty of the survey testing formats. In other words, the improvement you see could simply be the result of practice.)

Qualitative Interpretation

Question: Did the student's work improve into the "pass" range?

If NO, employ Comprehension SLPs 5 and 6. Also consider the possibility that the student lacks a broad base of general information. This is very common among special/remedial readers and results from their limited exposure to information through reading (see Chapter 17). Go to Chapter 12 for information on the assessment of vocabulary, and Chapter 17 for details about general information.

If YES, teach Objective 10 (p. 210) and use Teaching Recommendations 1 and 4.

Comprehension SLP 5: Make Predictions

This procedure is used to investigate how well the student uses what he already knows, along with what he has learned from the text, to make logical assumptions about upcoming material.

Directions ▽

1. Ask the student to begin reading from an expository passage that is appropriate for comprehension instruction (that is, he decodes it and knows what the words mean).

2. At the end of each paragraph, ask the student to predict what will be in the next paragraph. Say "What things do you think the next paragraph will tell us about?" or "What things would you

like to know next?'' Elicit several predictions for each paragraph. Do this for at least four paragraphs.

3. Rate each prediction as correct or incorrect by deciding if the student's reaction follows logically from the text. Consider what the student knows about the topic when making this determination. Criteria for judging predictions are provided later in the description of reciprocal teaching presented in Teaching Recommendation 2.

A prediction need not be true to be correct. This means that if the student's prediction is logical, regardless of what is actually written in the next paragraph, it is correct.

Score Interpretation

There are no established scoring conventions or standards for this test. We believe nearly all (90%) of the predictions should be correct (logical).

Qualitative Interpretation

If the student's accuracy improves after doing a couple of passages, you may want to do a few more. Assume that the initial problem was due to the novelty of the task and interpret the student's final efforts.

Question: Are the student's predictions logical?

If YES, the student is using text and prior knowledge. Check clarification with SLP 7.

If NO, the student cannot make predictions from text. If you believe that the student has adequate prior knowledge, use Objective 11 and Teaching Recommendations 2 and 6. If you used Specific Level Procedure 4, and the student also failed it, consider that the student may be lacking in general knowledge. This means you should go to Chapter 17. However, it does *not* mean you should wait to teach prediction skills. You can begin now by carefully selecting material with which the student is familiar.

Comprehension SLPs 6a and 6b: Assisted Search

These procedures are used to investigate how well the student uses what he already knows about both the topic and text structure to locate targeted information in a passage. They are particularly appropriate for students who are failing to understand topical readings

(like science chapters). SLPs 6a and 6b are designed to examine the student's skill at distinguishing relevant from irrelevant information in the passage. Both procedures attempt to answer the question by telling the student what to look for. Therefore, failure can be attributed to either poor search skills or poor text structure (Guthrie, Britten & Baker, 1991).

A student may have search skills, but still fail to find critical information if the text or the teacher do not adequately signal emphasis.

SLP 6a Directions

1. Select several passages from expository texts that the student is expected to comprehend.

2. Prepare test items for each passage and have the student read a couple of the passages and take the items. If the student passes the items, then repeat with a different topic until you have found an area with which the student has trouble. (If you can't find one, the kid doesn't need this procedure.)

3. Now select passages the student has not read but that cover topics on which the student has previously failed items. Develop pre-reading questions that will serve to focus the student's attention on the topics. These questions should be related to the topics the items sample, but should not exactly duplicate the items. Here is an item for this step.

If this is a question from the test the student will take:
    ''Pre-reading questions should:
        a. cover irrelevant information
        b. exactly match the topic of the test items
        c. complement the topic of the test items
        d. *not* address the topic of the test items''
Then a good question to ask before the student reads would be:
    ''I want you to read this passage to find the answer to this question: 'What sort of pre-reading questions are best?' ''
A bad pre-reading question would be:
    ''I want you to read this passage to find the answer to this question: 'Should pre-reading questions exactly match the topics of test items?' ''

4. Give the pre-reading questions, ask the student to read, and then give and score the test items.

∿ Qualitative Interpretation

Question: Did the student do significantly better on test items after receiving assistance ("significantly better" means he would have passed the test)?

If YES, teach Objective 12 using Teaching Recommendations 2 and 4.

If NO, go to SLP 6b.

▽ SLP 6b Directions

1. Select several passages from expository texts that the student is expected to comprehend.

2. Prepare test items for each passage and have the student read a couple of the passages and take the items. If the student passes the items, repeat with a different topic until you have found an area with which the student has trouble.

3. Now select passages the student has not read, but that cover topics on which the student has previously failed items. Give the student a previously unseen question, and then ask the student to read the passage and underline the words in the passage that answer the question (you may also ask the student to cross out the words that do not answer the question). For example:

"I want you to read passage 3 under SLP 6a. Underline the words that tell you what pre-reading questions should be like."

Given these directions, a student should underline the following parts of Step 3 in SLP 6a:

. . . *questions should be related to the topics the items sample, but should not exactly duplicate the items.*

∿ Interpretation Guidelines for 6b

Question: Does the student underline the correct wording?

If yes, teach Objective 12 (p. 212) using Teaching Recommendations 2 and 4.

If no, assuming you haven't already done so, give SLP 3.

If the student passes SLP 3, use Objectives 13, 14,

and 8, along with Teaching Recommendations 2, 3, 4, and 5.

Comprehension SLP 7: Referent Knowledge

Common referents are words like *he, she, it, they, them,* and *those.* Referents may also include any word that has <u>its</u> meaning designated in a passage. Readers must know what these <u>words</u> mean.

For example, in the final two sentences of the last paragraph two words are underlined. The word *its* refers to, or takes the place of, "any word." *Word* in the last sentence refers to "a word that has its meaning designated in a passage." Here is another example: "Kathy took Claire for a walk and then she read her a story." In this sentence the word *she* refers to Kathy and the word *her* refers to Claire. A student who was ill-suited to determine the correct references for the words *she* and *her* would not understand this sentence correctly. Often when a student loses meaning it is because he has confused referents (Greene, McKoon & Ratcliff, 1992).

Directions ▽

1. Select 250-word passages (for primary grades 1 and 2, 100–200 words is adequate) containing common referents or words that are given designated meaning within the passage. If the student is having problems understanding topic-specific material (a history textbook) use passages covering that content.

2. Have the student read the passage. Then returning to specific referents, point to them and ask "In this sentence to what/whom does the word _____ refer/mean?" Be careful, when you judge how well the student answers these questions, that the student is using referent skills and not logic or personal experience to answer.

3. Collect responses on at least 25 referents. Try to get as much variety as you can in your selection.

Score Interpretation ∿

Accuracy for this task should approach 100%. Any errors, assuming the student decodes the material and understands most of it, are unusual.

~ *Qualitative Interpretation*

Question: Does the student correctly determine the meaning of referents?

If yes, the student's failure to react appropriately to text is not the result of a lack of skill in referent clarification. Try SLPs 1 or 2.

If no, examine errors for patterns. For example, a common <u>pattern</u> involves referents that derive <u>their</u> meaning at a distance from themselves. For example, in the previous sentence *pattern* refers to "error patterns" which was designated in another sentence. The word *their* in that sentence refers to "referents" and was designated in the same sentence. Teach Objective 15 using Teaching Recommendations 2 and 6.

Objectives and Teaching Recommendations

This section begins by listing the objectives referenced in the interpretation sections. These are the objectives which, according to student need, you would put on the IEP and/or lesson plan. The objectives list is then followed by the teaching recommendations mentioned in the interpretation guidelines. The numbering of objectives and teaching recommendations is the same throughout this chapter.

Objectives for Comprehension

Portions of the following goals/objectives have been placed in {braces}. The braced portions require the insertion of wording specific to the student. Therefore, whenever a pair of braces occur, you will need to fill in the information called for at that point. For example, many of the goals use the wording "{passages at expected or intermediate levels}." The expected level is the curriculum level at which students of the same age work. Intermediate levels are those between the expected level and the current level of performance. This wording is used to indicate that the same core goal/objective (the part that isn't between braces) may be combined with a procession of braced wording to establish an instructional sequence. For example, a fifth-grade student currently working at the second curriculum level could have this sequence:

A—Given a series of passages at {the *second* curriculum level}, the student will make predictions about each upcoming passage that reflect a logical extension of the previously read material. CAP 100%

B—Given a series of passages at {the *third* curriculum level}, the student will make predictions about each upcoming passage that reflect a logical extension of the previously read material. CAP 100%

C—Given a series of passages at {the *fourth* curriculum level}, the student will make predictions about each upcoming passage that reflect a logical extension of the previously read material. CAP 100%

D—Given a series of passages at {the *fifth* curriculum level}, the student will make predictions about each upcoming passage that reflect a logical extension of the previously read material. CAP 100%

Comprehension Objectives

1. Given a passage at {expected or intermediate curriculum level}, the student will read it aloud {at specified rate and with specified accuracy}.

2. Given a 250-word cloze passage at {the expected or intermediate curriculum level}, the student will supply correct choices with at least 45% accuracy.

3. Given a 250-word maze passage {at expected curriculum level}, the student will select correct choices with at least 80% accuracy.

4. Given signals, the student will immediately locate and correct errors that violate meaning made in oral reading. The signals may be given after words, phrases, sentences, or paragraphs. CAP: 95%

5. Given passages at {expected or intermediate curriculum levels}, the student will not make, or will spontaneously correct, errors in reading that violate meaning. CAP: no more than 5% uncorrected errors

6. Given passages at {expected or intermediate curriculum levels}, the student will, upon encountering difficult material, employ one or more of the following tactics:

a. reread

b. adjust rate

c. request assistance

d. recognize what information is required. CAP: 90%

7. Given passages at {expected or intermediate curriculum levels}, the student will retell the content. CAP: a rating of 3 or above

8. Given passages at {expected or intermediate curriculum levels,} the student will identify (by underlining, highlighting, or crossing out) material related to one or more of the following specified categories:

a. main idea

b. relevant information

c. irrelevant information

d. characters

e. descriptions

f. actions

g. conflicts

h. resolutions. CAP: 100%

9. Upon request, the student will demonstrate metacognitive awareness of the reading process by supplying and/or explaining the following active reading tactics:

a. predicting and verifying

b. previewing

c. checking purpose

d. analyzing setting

e. self-questioning

f. drawing from background knowledge

g. summarizing

h. applying fix-up tactics. CAP: 100%

10. Given passages at {expected or intermediate level}, the student will maintain passing scores on maze/cloze tests across the following sequence of conditions:

a. comprehensive review of topic with teacher or peer

b. anticipatory discussion of topic prior to reading

c. reminder always to think about topic purpose prior to reading

d. no assistance. CAP: 100%

11. Given a series of passages at {the expected or intermediate levels}, the student will make predictions about each upcoming passage that reflect a logical extension of the previously read material. CAP: 90%

12. Given passages at {the appropriate level}, the student will use his knowledge of the topic and preceding passages to develop his own main-idea pre-reading questions. These questions will cover content that the text author or teacher thinks is critical. CAP: 90%

13. Given passages at {the appropriate level}, the student will locate answers to pre-reading questions. CAP: 100%

14. Given specific topics, the student will identify wording in the passages that is, or is not, related to the topic. CAP: 100%

15. Given passages at {expected or intermediate levels}, the student will supply the correct definitions for referents that are underlined or pointed to by the teacher. CAP: 100%. (These will include referents both near and far from the designated wording in the passage.)

Teaching Recommendations for Comprehension

Comprehension strategies include:

1. Active and reflective reading

2. Adjustment for text difficulty

3. Comprehension monitoring

4. Connection of text to prior knowledge

5. Clarification

The following teaching recommendations have been drawn from a review of literature on comprehension and from classroom teachers. Because the recommendations are presented in a fairly superficial way, many of them are accompanied by references to help you locate additional information. In all cases, because the content being taught is strategic, the information in Chapter 8 on strategy instruction applies to these techniques—particularly the content outlined in Exhibit 8.4.

The following suggestions are broken into two parts. First, there are a set of general suggestions that must be considered regardless of the particular comprehension objectives being taught. These general suggestions are followed by the specific teaching recommendations mentioned in the interpretation sections of the chapter.

General Teaching Recommendations

Promote Awareness of Reading. It is important to teach the student to stop reading and think about applying problem-solving or study skills when his understanding seems inadequate. This application of self-monitoring requires the student to develop an awareness of the reading process (McLain & Victoria, 1991). The content of this awareness was presented in Exhibit 10.7*. It is taught, as are most things, through explanation, demonstration, questioning, and specific feedback. As a teacher, you may easily incorporate the Exhibit 10.8* content into discussion and questioning during your routine reading lessons.

Use of Prior Knowledge. It is important to impress upon the student the idea that he is bringing something to the text, and not just passively receiving its message. This means that the student is continually expected actively to compare what the passage says with what he already knows.

Use of Teacher Questions. Ask questions involving the contrast between the text and information you know the student has learned previously. Ask the student to identify concepts or operations he finds adequately or inadequately described in the text.

Use of Self-Questioning. Self-questioning represents an excellent way to promote active understanding and reading. However, in order for the student to use self-questioning, he must have already developed some comprehension monitoring skills (see Recommendation 6). Monitoring alerts a reader that a task is hard. Tasks are usually difficult because they contain missing (unstated) information, ambiguous cues, or lack distinct criteria for completion (Frederiksen, 1984). Students can learn to directly attack difficult portions

of texts by using their existing knowledge to answer the questions in this table.

Problem	Problem-solving questions students should ask
Missing information	Where did I get lost? What kind of information would help me? Where can I find out more about this?
Ambiguous cues	What do the words I'm dealing with mean? What cause-and-effect relationships have been established? Exactly which pieces of information pertain to which characters or concepts?
Missing criteria	If I understood this, what would I know (be skilled to do)? What are the passage's guidelines (indicators) for understanding? What is a reasonable level of understanding for this kind of passage?

Encourage Prediction. Ask the student to predict upcoming events. Then have the student supply information from the text that supports the prediction. This will be explained in some detail under Reciprocal Teaching (Recommendation 2).

Teach Student to Clarify Vocabulary. Vocabulary evaluation and instruction are covered in Chapters 12 and 17. Remember when you are teaching vocabulary it is important to emphasize multiple meanings and how the meaning of words is altered by context. Give examples of text where context alters meaning. Use examples with familiar words to illustrate your point (Beck, McKeown & McCaslin, 1983). For example, "Having a shallow conversation" does not mean that the speakers are standing in a creek.

Teach Student to State the Unknown.   Encourage the student to recognize points in the text that deserve elaboration. Teach the students to make specific, rather than general, requests for clarification. A student should say "I need to know why the problem in this passage involves the use of tax dollars, not interest payments" rather than "I need to know more about the problem."

Here is a two-step procedure for clarification:

A. First the student is taught to identify the specific topic of concern. This is called the "unknown." The teacher promotes this skill by training the student to ask *himself* "What is unknown in this passage?" and to answer in a full sentence ("I don't know why the problem uses tax dollars and not interest payments").

B. Next the student is taught how to turn the unknown statement into a question. For example, the original ". . . why the problem uses tax dollars and not interest payments" is attached to a stem such as "I need to know." The teacher does this by saying "Now I want you to turn your question into a statement that begins with 'I need to know.'"

The correct response would be "**I need to know** why the problem uses tax dollars and not interest payments."

Teach Search Skills.   Teach the student how to search for needed information. One common search technique involves summarizing a passage and examining the summary for key information. (Teaching the student to summarize preceding and subsequent discussions that can be used as links to the current passage is also a good idea.)

The student must learn to use the structure of the text, including illustrations, titles, and headings, to find information. He must also formulate questions and reread the passage for the purpose of answering the questions. One system for teaching these skills is Multipass (Schumaker, Deshler, Alley, Warner & Denton, 1982). Multipass is described in some detail by Lovitt (1991). Multipass is designed primarily for use with content-area textbooks. Here is an abstract of the Multipass content:

Procedure	Purpose	Method
Survey	Familiarization	Read chapter title, pass introduction, headings and subtitles, illustrations and captions, and summary.
Size-up	Gain	Find textual clues. Turn past information clues into questions. Find answers to questions. Paraphrase answer for yourself.
Sort-out	Self-testing	Recognize when additional past information is needed, think where to look for answers, search for the answer, and search other sections if necessary.

(Schumaker et al., 1982)

Teach Student to Clarify Referent Structures.   Referent, or *anaphoric*, words stand for something. The most common examples are pronouns or pro-verbs such as *she, he, they , it*. Take this passage:

> "Jim and Ken went out to fly their airplane. It was wet, so before they could do that they had to use a towel to dry it."

In the passage each of the referent words are underlined. A student who doesn't match the referent words with either the correct antecedents or with other words not contained in the passage will experience comprehension difficulties. Often students who do not know how to determine the base for a referent will pick the closest word. This tactic, if applied to the words *it* in the sample passage, would work fairly well for the first occurrence but not for the second.

When teaching a student to clarify a referent, the teacher presents a simple six-step tactic:

1. Recognize the unknown word ("it").

2. Picture what is happening in the passage (Jim and Ken need to dry out the airplane).

3. Relate the unknown word to the picture.

4. Select the word that is represented by the unknown ("airplane").

5. Check your answer by substituting the word you have selected for the unknown word and saying the passage out loud ("The *airplane* was wet so they had to use a towel before they could fly the *airplane*").

6. State the relationship ("In this sentence *it* refers to 'airplane' ").

This procedure for clarifying anaphoric referents is explained in some detail by Carnine and colleagues (1990).

Specific Teaching Recommendations

Teaching Recommendation 1: Active and Reflective Reading

This technique is particularly applicable to Comprehension **Objectives** 1, 2, 3, 5, 6, 8, 9, and 10.

Many students seem to think they are meant to be the passive recipients of the author's message, and consequently they do not interact with the passage. Often these students view comprehension strictly as a memory task, and their goal is to try to store the entire passage for recall. Misunderstanding is fostered when the only measures of comprehension they see are post-reading questions. This passive view of comprehension is unfortunate for two reasons: (1) It places unrealistic demands on memory, and (2) it rules out the interaction of the student with the text by elevating the message of the text above the interests and prior knowledge of the student.

Students who are active readers approach passages with an agenda. They do something as they read; for example, they may ask questions and attempt to answer them. In short, active readers employ the comprehension strategies reviewed in this chapter. Students who do not read actively need to be taught to use the comprehension strategies listed in Exhibit 10.1* and referred to in the list of Comprehension Objectives. These objectives are taught using strategic instruction (Reid & Stone, 1991) (see Chapter 8). One such tactic teaches students to recognize that the

source of answers may be in either the text *or* in prior knowledge.

Active and reflective reading, therefore, is not a term that refers to a particular methodology. It is a term that refers to the flexible application of tactics. To promote active and reflective reading, an instructor must teach students two things: (a) how to use particular devices for understanding text, and (b) that it is the use of these devices (that is, tactics), not the act of finishing pages, that constitutes reading. This is a different view of reading than the one portrayed by many teachers and consequently transferred to many students (Rich & Pressley, 1990).

Here is an example of a procedure that promotes active and reflective reading. In a cognitive training study, Raphael and Pearson (1985) taught typical and low-achieving students to determine sources of answers using three mnemonics: (1) *Right There*, (2) *Think and Search*, and (3) *On My Own*. Source (1), Right There, meant that words used to create the question and words used for the answer are "right there" in the same sentence. Mnemonic (2), Think and Search, meant that the answer is in the text, but words used to create the question and those used for an appropriate answer will be found by looking for the answer across sentences and possibly even paragraphs. Source (3), On My Own, meant that the answer is not found in the text—in which case the student should say "I have to find this answer on my own."

Here is an example of Rapheal and Pearson's (1985) training materials:

> "Dennis sat in an old wood rocking chair. He rocked harder and harder. Suddenly he found himself sitting on the floor!"
>
> *Right There*: What kind of chair did Dennis sit in? (old wood rocking chair)
>
> *Think and Search*: What did Dennis do while sitting in the chair? (rocked harder and harder)
>
> *On My Own*: Why did Dennis find himself sitting on the floor? (rocked so hard the chair tipped over) (p. 221)

Teaching Recommendation 2: Reciprocal Teaching

This technique is particularly applicable to Comprehension **Objectives** 1, 2, 3, 6, 7, 8, 9, 11, 12, and 15.

Reciprocal teaching generally refers to the popular trick of having students take on the role of teacher. It is a procedure which, like cooperative learning and peer-mediated instruction, promotes student understanding by encouraging them to reformulate the content.

In reciprocal teaching, the teacher gives an explanation and then asks the student to repeat the explanation as if he were the teacher. The term also has a specific meaning in relation to the topic of reading comprehension.

"Reciprocal teaching of reading comprehension" refers to a particular set of skills and instructional routines developed in part by Day (1980) and packaged for research by Palincsar and Brown (1984). The approach has been picked up by several authors and modified into a general technique (Carnine et al., 1990; Lysynchuk, Pressley & Vye, 1990; Lovitt, 1991; Herrmann,1988). While the practice includes instruction on questioning, clarification, and prediction (Pressley et al., 1990; Sindelar & Stoddard, 1991), its most interesting aspect is aggressive instruction of summarizing. Skill at summarizing what has been read appears to be a fundamental component of both understanding and comprehension monitoring (Gajria & Salvia, 1992; Thistlethwaite, 1991).

The following information about reciprocal teaching has been drawn from the literature just cited. However, we have also modified it as a result of field testing.

In early reciprocal-teaching lessons, the teacher supplies students with these rules for summarizing passages:

1—Find topic sentence:

   1.1 Look at first sentence.

   1.2 If that doesn't work, look at last sentence.

   1.3 If that doesn't work, search the paragraph.

2—If a topic sentence can't be found, invent one:

   2.1 Delete unnecessary information.

   2.2 Delete redundant information.

   2.3 State the "big picture" (principle point of the passage).

   2.4 Say it right (the summary must be stated as a proper sentence).

Once the rules have been presented, the teacher does not repeat this initial explanation but, at the beginning of each session, asks students to supply and explain the rules. After this opening review, the teacher then selects a student to act as instructor. This student (and each other student in turn) then directs the group through the following sequence.

Read. Everyone is given the same materials to read, one paragraph at a time (the paragraphs are cut out and put on separate sheets). The selections, which are read silently, are drawn from expository texts (a history book) and should be challenging to the students. That means they have to have something in them worth comprehending.

Summarize. After the reading, the designated instructor attempts to make a statement summarizing the selection. The teacher compares this summary to the criteria listed here and supplies feedback. In early lessons this feedback often comes by presenting a fully modeled correct summary. Whenever the teacher demonstrates the production of a correct model, the student is asked to repeat the example.

In later lessons the teacher prompts the use of the summary criteria by saying things like "You seem to have included the big picture, and all of the relevant information, but your summary has some redundant information in it. Try again without the redundant information." Prompts such as "This paragraph tells me that . . ." may also be helpful. Praise is given for applying the rules, not for getting the right answer (in fact, there may be many correct summaries).

Here are some guidelines for monitoring the summary statements students make during reciprocal teaching:

A. —Be sure the student:

   • says what he is going to do (summarize)

   • finds or invents a topic sentence

B. —Monitor and adjust:

   • Don't make up your own summary and then compare student's to it. Evaluate the student's summary according to the use of the rules supplied here.

   • If possible, label errors ("That's good, but you have some unnecessary information in it" or

"That's all right so far but it's not a sentence. Try to say it right."

- In early lessons, provide full model corrections that expand/include the student's attempt.

- In later lessons, use prompts or cues (start by saying "This paragraph tells me . . . ," "Another important piece of the paragraph is . . . ," or, "Can you include that in your summary?"

C. Remember the principles of strategy instruction:

- The answer is *not* what the lesson is about. You are teaching the procedure for finding the answer. Talk about, prompt, give feedback, and reinforce the procedure.

- Assure early, active use.

- Make *your* thinking public. Model and demonstrate.

Here are some other activities that may be used to teach summarizing.

a. Select main idea:
Show a complex picture. Then have students pick the part that represents the main action.

b. Select main idea:
Give short stories with one main event and practice picking the foremost words (actions or outcomes).

c. Select main idea:
Introduce passages with redundancy and distractions.

d. Select topic sentence:
Define topic sentence as the author's summary of paragraph.

e. Select topic sentence:
Show that topic sentences can appear anywhere in a paragraph by providing practice selecting them in varying locations.

f. Invent topic sentences:
Explain that not all paragraphs have topic sentences.

g. Invent topic sentences:
Have the student read paragraphs twice, close his eyes and remember/state the essential point of the paragraph. Be sure he states it as a sentence.

Question. After producing an acceptable summary, the instructing student next attempts to convert it summary into a main-idea question. The teacher may facilitate this conversion with prompts such as "Ask a question that begins with the word *what*." In this way, a summary that says "Many Tucson citizens of that day believed the only good wolf was a dead wolf" is converted into a question like "What did many Tucson citizens of that day think about wolves?"

The instructing student then calls on other students to answer the main-idea question. He may also call on students to ask narrower questions about particular events or characters in the passage. In all cases, the teacher encourages students to produce the sort of questions a teacher might put on a test. Students should also be taught to:

a. Change sentences to questions using prompts *who, how, what, when, why,* etc.

b. Change sentences to questions without prompt.

c. Select from three choices the question that matches a paragraph (one distractor will require information not in the paragraph and one will address trivial information).

d. Recognize the main idea (by summarizing) and then ask a question about it.

- Add inflection to existing topic sentence.

- Invent topic sentence and add inflection.

Clarify. In this step the instructing student calls on group members to point out items in the passage that could require clarification. Often these will include text-dependent vocabulary and pronouns. However, clarification may also be requested for more complex or factual references ("In the last passage, to what time period does the phrase 'of that day' refer?"). At the least, students should be prepared to clarify:

a. ambiguous pronominal references

b. unclear protagonist

c. vocabulary from context

d. essential vocabulary (versus words that can be ignored)

e. unfamiliar expressions and metaphors

Predict. Finally, the instructing student calls on several members of the group to predict what might occur in the next passage (they can't look ahead because they are only given one paragraph at a time). These predictions are judged on their logical origin in the passage—not on whether they come true.

After following this sequence, the instructing student then calls on another student and the routine is repeated.

Teaching Recommendation 3: Story Maps and Semantic Webbing

This technique is particularly applicable to Comprehension **Objectives** 1, 2, 3, 7, and 8.

Semantic webs are described in some detail by several authors (Lovitt, 1984; Grossen & Carnine, 1991). (We have put them first in Chapters 1–9 for you to use as study guides.) Semantic webbing is an instructional technique aimed in part at developing knowledge schema (Anderson & Pearson, 1984; Winn, 1991). Cognitive mapping is a device used to organize what is read (Hirumi & Bowers, 1991). "Story maps organize a story visually so specific relationships of selected story elements are highlighted" (Reutzel, 1985, p. 400). A map of a narrative story could contain the following elements: (a) setting, (b) beginning, (c) reaction, (d) attempt, (e) outcome, and (f) ending (Mandler & Johnson, 1977).

While maps are currently extremely popular for summarizing reading and planning composition (McCagg & Dansereau, 1991), you should be aware that there is little research describing exactly who will benefit from their use, or which of the several types available are best (Dunston, 1992).

For additional information refer to Lovitt (1990) and Grossen and Carnine (1992).

Teaching Recommendation 4: Prereading Questioning

This technique is particularly applicable to Comprehension **Objectives** 1, 2, 8, 10, 12, and 13.

Specific questioning is used to develop active and reflective reading and recognition of central and subordinate details in a passage. The student reads specifically to answer a prereading question, so that passage information will be interpreted in terms of that question. This technique is particularly successful if students are taught to develop their own questions. The simplest way to implement the approach is to take all of those end-of-chapter questions authors put in textbooks and give them to the student *before* he starts reading.

Teaching Recommendation 5: Critical Reading

This technique is particularly applicable to Comprehension **Objectives** 1, 2, 3, 9, and 14.

Carnine and colleagues (1990) say that students need to have the skills to:

1. Identify the author's conclusions
2. Determine what evidence is presented
3. Determine the trustworthiness of the author (by judging if he is qualified or biased)
4. Identify faulty arguments (such as tradition, improper generalization, and confusion of correlation with cause (see Appendix A).

Experimental work by Patching, Kameenui, Carnine, Gersten, and Colvin (1983) has demonstrated that instruction in these critical reading skills improves comprehension of low-achieving students. A thorough explanation of the critical reading technique can be found in *Direct Instruction Reading, Second Edition*, by Carnine et al. (1990).

Teaching Recommendation 6: Monitoring Meaning

This technique is particularly applicable to Comprehension **Objectives** 1, 2, 3, 4, 5, 8, 11, 14, and 15.

Comprehension monitoring refers to the student's skill at tracking his understanding of the text. This is accomplished by continual self-inquiry using the question "Do I understand what I'm reading ?" It is essential that a kid realize when he is failing to understand, so that he will begin to use the problem-solving techniques of adjustment and clarification. When they fail to understand what is written, readers who successfully monitor their comprehension will re-read confusing passages, slow their reading rate, refer to reference materials, and even question the text author's skill. Readers who do not monitor their comprehension will either continue to read difficult passages and experience compounded confusion—or give up. Here are some ways to develop comprehension monitoring.

Table tapping is a technique that is a straightforward modification of the specific-level Comprehension Procedure 1: Assisted Monitoring. To employ it, simply follow the directions for assisted monitoring and then systematically move to larger text units. For example, instead of tapping immediately after a meaning violating error, tap when the student reaches the end of the sentence or paragraph in which the error occurred. The direction to the student explicit in the tap is to re-read that unit of text. By requiring the student to re-read the unit (word, sentence, or paragraph) and self-correct the error, you encourage the student to start finding the errors on his own. To put it another way, by extending the text unit you are fading the monitoring assistance you provide. This requires the student to increase his own monitoring.

Other ways to promote monitoring include asking questions prior to reading and emphasizing the need to search the passage for answers. Also, ask passage-dependent vocabulary questions. Allow the student to practice reading with favorite stories, predictable stories, stories chosen by the student, and stories with experiences familiar to the student. Use re-readings (see Chapter 11). Embed nonsense material in the passage (or delete some important material) and reinforce the student for recognizing it. When reading errors do occur, judge their relationships to passage meanings. If the errors jeopardize meaning, talk the student through procedures for using context to correct the error. Several of these tactics are described in the section on blending and word analysis in Chapter 12 (p. 284). Teach the student to make summary statements about sentences, then paragraphs, then whole passages.

Monitoring Reading Comprehension

Once you have selected an objective and an instructional technique, you will need to monitor the instruction to determine if your teaching is effective (see Chapter 5). The best monitoring techniques are those using measures that reflect what you are teaching *and* are sensitive to learning. In the domain of reading comprehension, such measures are difficult to find.

In general we recommend that reading-comprehension instruction be monitored with oral-reading fluency samples. These samples should be collected and charted during each instructional session (Fuchs & Fuchs, 1992). Procedures for using this kind of monitoring are presented in the workbook. Remember, the only way to determine if an instructional approach is effective is to try it, take data, and let the student tell you if it works.

Summary

Because reading comprehension/reaction is complicated and important, this has been a long, complex chapter—in fact, it is probably the most complex chapter in Part 3. And guess what—while the chapter is over, the topic of comprehension isn't. A quick look back at Exhibit 10.1* will remind you that there are still enabling skills, sometimes thought of as the prerequisites of comprehension, to be explained. These enabling skills are presented in the chapters that follow. As for this chapter, it began with an attempt to define comprehension and to explain some of the problems we encounter when trying to evaluate it. From there, Chapter 10 went into considerable detail regarding techniques for measuring comprehension skills, and trouble shooting comprehension problems. The chapter presented survey-level tests, specific-level tests, comprehension objectives, teaching recommendations, and monitoring procedures. Practice exercises are provided in the workbook to allow you to become proficient in the techniques presented here. We strongly recommend you use them.

Chapter 11 / Decoding

The merits of an alphabet are that the symbols are easy to reproduce and interpret, but the cost of this ease is that we have to learn an abstract and conceptually complex code.

—Marilyn Jager Adams (1990)

Focus: Reading and Decoding

There are many ways to teach reading; some are unique, but most are essentially the same. This similarity is the result of the task itself. The task of reading requires students to view print and draw information from it. All reading methods present printed material, and all are expected to teach kids to deal with printed material through a process called *decoding*.

Decoding means breaking the printed code; that is, using the relationship between printed text and sounds to vocalize or understand words. Decoding is based upon the alphabetic principle and grapheme-phoneme correspondence. Decoding may have nothing to do with meaning at all. For example, the word *smek* has no meaning, but you can vocalize it because you can decode it. *Note:* When you are talking to a student don't use the word *decode*, just use *read*.

Adams (1990) undertook an exhaustive examination of the role decoding plays in literacy. This review led to a variety of important conclusions, including the following:

> . . . approaches in which systematic code instruction is included along with the reading of meaningful connected text result in superior reading achievement overall, for both low-readiness and better prepared students. (p. 125)

Adams' efforts support the view that decoding is important for beginning readers. However, for the most part this text focuses on remedial readers. How important is decoding to students who have not benefited from beginning reading instruction?

The importance of code for students with reading problems can be summed up this simply:

- Poor readers make more reading mistakes than good readers.
- These mistakes often include errors in decoding.

- Students should be taught the things they need to know.
- Competent readers know code.
- Problem readers do not know code.

Carnine and colleagues (1990) are such strong believers in code instruction that they state " . . . virtually all the reading failure in the early grades could be avoided if teachers: (1) were given well-constructed code-emphasis instructional materials, and (2) received adequate on-the-job training in how to present reading instruction to groups . . . " (p. 69).

A Closer Look at Code

Some of the confusion about code instruction results from confusion about code curriculum. Decoding includes: concepts of print, phonemic awareness, letter recognition, letter-sound correspondence, knowledge of phonograms (clusters/syllables), knowledge of phonic generalizations, skill at blending, use of contextual cues, automatic word recognition, and reading fluency. These enabling skills do not function in isolation (Teale, 1989), they are compensatory (see Chapter 10, p. 186).

In spite of the complexity of decoding, there is a tendency to think only of code as sounding. This is unfortunate, because it belies the intricacy of decoding and overemphasizes grapheme-phoneme correspondence. In English there are 100–200 possible sound-symbol relationships. However, they are not all equally essential. Therefore, if we teach all 100–200 sound-symbol relationships, we waste our time and the kid's time. It may only take mastery of the 20 to 40 sounds listed in Exhibit 11.1 to begin figuring out new words.

Over-emphasis on low-utility sound-symbol relationships can be doubly dangerous. Because these relationships are not inherently meaningful or strate-

Exhibit 11.1   *Most Common Sounds of Single Letters, Letter Combinations, and Affixes*

I. Single Letters		II. Letter Combinations		III. Affixes	
Continuous Sounds		ai	(maid)	a	(alive)
		ar	(car)	a	(formula)
a	(fat)	au	(haul)	able	(enjoyable)
e	(bet)	aw	(lawn)	ac	(accuse, cardiac)
f	(fill)	ay	(stay)	ad	(address)
i	(sit)	ch	(chip)	age	(package)
l	(let)	ea	(beat)	al	(personal)
m	(mad)	ee	(need)	be	(become)
n	(nut)	er	(fern)	com	(compare)
o	(not)	eu	(feud)	con	(confuse)
r	(rat)	ew	(shrewd)	de	(defeat)
s	(sell)	ey	(honey)	dis	(disappear)
u	(cut)	igh	(high)	ed	(jumped, landed, hummed)
v	(vet)	ing	(sing)	en	(harden)
w	(wet)	ir	(first)	ence	(occurrence)
y	(yes)	kn	(know)	er	(keeper)
z	(zoo)	oa	(load)	es	(misses)
		oi	(boil)	est	(smallest)
		ol	(hold)	ex	(expect)
Stop Sounds		oo	(boot)	ful	(handful)
		or	(short)	ic	(heroic)
b	(boy)	ou	(cloud)	in	(inside)
c	(can)	ow	(own)	ing	(jumping)
d	(did)	oy	(toy)	ion	(action)
g	(got)	ph	(phone)	ish	(selfish)
h	(his)	qu	(quick)	ize	(realize)
j	(jet)	sh	(shop)	ist	(artist)
k	(kiss)	th	(thank)	ive	(detective)
p	(pet)	ue	(cue)	le	(handle)
q	(quit)	ur	(burn)	less	(useless)
t	(top)	wh	(whale)	ly	(sadly)
x	(fox)	wr	(wrap)	ment	(payment)
				ness	(kindness)
				ous	(joyous)
				over	(overtime)
				pre	(preschool)

(continued)

Exhibit 11.1   Most Common Sounds of Single Letters, Letter Combinations, and Affixes (continued)

I. Single Letters	II. Letter Combinations	III. Affixes	
		pro	(protect)
		re	(refill)
		s	(hits)
		ship	(friendship)
		teen	(sixteen)
		un	(unhappy)
		ward	(forward)
		y	(funny)

Source: Reprinted with the permission of Macmillan Publishing Company from *Direct Instruction Reading,* Second Edition by Douglas Carnine, Jerry Silbert, and Edward J. Kameenui. Copyright © 1990 by Macmillan Publishing Company. © 1979 by Merrill Publishing Company.

gic (the sound-symbol relationship is arbitrary) the sound-symbol content is factual (see Chapter 3). When a task is not meaningful, teaching it requires concentrated drill and practice. Drill and practice, particularly if it isn't necessary, is boring.

Sounds are not the only things some people think of when they hear the word decoding. Take a few minutes to review the reading tasks you were taught in school. The odds are that many of you were not simply taught sounds, you were also taught rules. Some of you were taught decoding rules that work on less than 40%, 50%, or 70% of the words students normally decode. For example, "When two vowels go walking the first one does the talking" only works about 45% of the time (Adams, 1990). Maybe the time you spent learning those rules could have been spent more efficiently learning strategies for decoding words through context or vocabulary.

Reading Instruction

Today most students are taught to read with "basal" reading programs. These programs are designed to complement a mode of reading instruction based not on skill instruction, but on the completion of daily lessons (it is not an accident that the basals have as many lessons as there are school days in the year). There is considerable variability in the quality of these programs. Some of them have been developed without consideration of generalization, efficiency, or essential content. For example, Adams (1990) points out that some published programs teach long vowel sounds first. However, most beginning reader words with long vowel sounds in them require the student to know the final/silent e rule (hat/hate). This is a difficult rule to learn. The truth is that almost no one likes basal readers and almost everyone uses them. This curious situation is all the more interesting when we consider that battles over the best way to teach reading seem to go on forever.

It is remarkable to note that, while many authors debate the relative merits of types of reading instruction, there is evidence that very little of it is actually occurring. Even more disturbing is similar evidence that poor readers receive *less* instruction, and poorer quality instruction, than competent readers.

The quality and quantity of instruction provided special and remedial students has been examined by Allington (1983), Haynes and Jenkins (1986), Ysseldyke et al. (1984), Adams (1990), and O'Sullivan, Ysseldyke, Christenson and Thurlow (1990). These authors have noted that the reading instruction typically provided to low-performing students differs from the reading instruction provided to higher performing students. Such problems always seem compounded in the upper grades (Duffy, 1990). Perhaps the most crushing finding is that there is little relationship between student need and total time allocated to reading instruction in both special and general education class settings. Here are some other findings:

There is evidence that poor readers receive poorer quality instruction than competent readers. Further, there is little relationship between student need and total time allocated to reading instruction.

- Problem readers spend more time on letters, sounds, and words in isolation.

- They spend less time reading words in text.

- They spend less time in silent reading.

- Special education students spend more time doing independent and noninteractive worksheets.

- A greater proportion of time is spent on reading tasks in general education classrooms than in special education classrooms.

- The more special reading programs a school has,

the *fewer* minutes the average student in the school spends reading.

Disparities in instructional quality can also be seen in other ways. For example, teachers are more apt to interrupt poor readers and less likely to use semantic cues to correct their errors (Calfee & Drum, 1986). Additionally, in schools with large proportions of at-risk and problem readers, the average student reads nearly 20 minutes less per day than the average student in other schools (Adams, 1990). McGill-Frazen and Allington (1991) noted that, because of the overuse of individual worksheets in Chapter 1 and special education classes, many remedial readers receive as little as 2 minutes of active reading a day.

What has gone wrong with remedial and special reading programs? We see at least three problems.

First, as pull-out programs proliferate, general education teachers lose ownership of reading instruction and decrease emphasis on it in their classes. Anyone observing a general education classroom today is likely to hear a teacher turn to a student and say something like this: "It's time for you to go down the hall to reading." The message to the student, and the one evidently accepted by the teacher, is that reading resides "down the hall."

Second, a peculiar model of "individualized" instruction has evolved in many remedial/special classrooms. In this model, students arrive at the class and collect a folder, shoe box, ice cream bucket, or notebook that is filled with worksheets. They then work on these sheets independently while the teacher circulates through the room giving feedback and/or reinforcement for the completion of the sheets. There is almost no explanation of the purpose of the worksheets, and the emphasis is on task completion—not learning (see Chapter 4).

Finally, the stuff on most of those worksheets is garbage. It is drawn from a very limited view of reading and tends to be selected to conform with the independent seat work mode of instruction—not the demands of literacy (Westby, 1992).

Some Evaluation Concerns

A Note on "Reading Levels"

In a few pages we will address the practice of selecting reading passages for students. But before we do that, we need to make some points about the muddled nature of "readability" levels. In some reading programs the text material is controlled, so that neighboring passages are of somewhat equal difficulty (*Mastery Reading* is an example). But this is not true in all programs, and it is certainly not true of topical textbooks (history, social studies, biology) or the books lined up on a library shelf. It is important to keep this variability in mind, as it limits the degree to which conclusions based on one passage can be generalized to other passages.

Just as it is unsafe to generalize from one passage to another in the same book, it is often dangerous to generalize from one reading series to another. In a study by Beck and McCaslin, cited in Adams (1990), the instructional sequence of eight reading programs was compared. In the first half of first grade the researchers found that one series taught 20 single consonants while another taught only 7. With that much variability introduced before the kid's first winter vacation, imagine what the differences are by the time she reaches third grade.

The concept of grade level is not useful for instructional planning and can even be misleading. In the case of standardized normative measures, grade level is designated according to the way the norming population reacts to the test items. Normative tests establish grade-level scores by giving items to students and calculating the average score of sample populations selected at each grade level. The average score obtained from the fourth-grade sample then becomes "fourth-grade level." On reading tests, the resulting grade equivalence scores may or may not have any relationship to passage difficulty (Jenkins & Pany, 1978). Such scores are so notoriously nonfunctional that the International Reading Association called for an end to their use years ago, as have many other professional organizations.

Passage levels for reading inventories and textbooks are typically set through the use of readability formulas. Often these formulas are based on ratios between the number of words in a sentence and other characteristics like the number of syllables. The formulas—and there are over 1000 of them sampling more than 250 text variables—are under constant examination and modification (Klare, 1984). While it does appear that passages with the same readability score are equivalent in some respect (whatever is summarized by the formula), it is less clear whether these similarities are meaningful or significant. Several

authors have determined that the use of such formulas may even be detrimental to reading instruction. For example, Sabers (1992) notes that some of the original standards for grade level were determined by averaging scores derived from texts available *in the 1940s*. This yielded average levels of sentence length and word/syllable ratios for texts in the 1940s. Unfortunately, reading text publishers adopted these levels as ceilings and insisted that subsequent books not exceed those averages. This had the effect of removing more difficult texts from the market and, as a result, effectively "dumbed down" (Bowen, 1984) the entire body of classroom reading texts.

Taken together, attempts at defining levels of reading passages have not been particularly functional. So where does this leave the evaluator? Our best advice is that survey-level reading samples be taken from multiple passages drawn from the text series, or other books, that students without decoding problems are expected to read.

Testing to Select Texts Because of the basal influence, it is not uncommon for teachers to believe that the key to teaching decoding lies in the selection of the right book. In reading jargon this is called the search for the "instructional level." These teachers will ask things like "What book should Emily be in?" instead of "What skill does Emily need to be taught?" Consequently, there are many techniques for finding the "best" book for each student. The assumption behind these techniques is that there *is* a best book for each student. That's putting too much responsibility on book publishers, and it is especially futile in the upper grades, where texts are designed for purposes other than reading instruction (Durkin, 1990).

Remedial/special teachers should not test for the purpose of placing the student into a book or series of books. They should test for the purpose of placing the student within the sequence of decoding skills—the curriculum. Then they look for a book (or books) that include opportunities for instruction and practice on the skills the kid needs. A competent teacher/evaluator compares both the student *and* the materials to the curriculum (see Chapter 5).

Testing "Pre-Reading" Skills Many tests are available to measure things that aren't really reading but are supposed to be prerequisites for decoding. Auditory and visual discrimination are two popular exam-

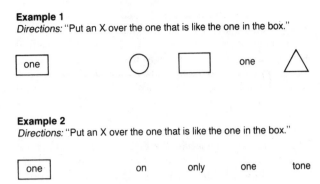

Example 1
Directions: "Put an X over the one that is like the one in the box."

Example 2
Directions: "Put an X over the one that is like the one in the box."

Exhibit 11.2   A nonreading item and a reading item.

ples of these so-called pre-reading skills. There is no question that discrimination is necessary for decoding. But there are questions about our success at teaching discrimination and about the types of discriminations that are relevant to decoding. When students are asked to discriminate between the sounds of letters, some people say they are doing a pre-reading task. We think they are decoding. When students are asked to discriminate between animal sounds, some people will say they are doing a pre-reading task. We think they are discriminating between animal sounds. Tests that sample geometric shapes or animal noises are dealing with content that is too far removed from the decoding curriculum to have instructional utility (see Chapter 3, p. 41).

A typical visual-discrimination test supplies one letter, word, or shape, and then asks the student to recognize it somewhere else (see examples 1 and 2 in Exhibit 11.2). Each format tests something that is in part visual, and each requires the kid to make a discrimination. However, in all tests of this kind, it is important to recall that both the required response and the content (what is being discriminated) will affect the student's performance. Example 1 is easier than example 2 because a student may be more successful at discriminating words from nonwords than words from words.

If changes in the content can influence test behavior, then the conclusions drawn from the test should be applied to the content and not just to the kid. In other words, *don't make general statements about someone having good or bad visual discrimination. Instead make statements about what she does or doesn't know how to discriminate.* For example, "Rebecca doesn't know how to tell a's from o's when they are in the middle of words." This kind of statement won't encourage anyone to try to teach visual discrimination (which is outside of the curriculum), but might encourage someone to teach Rebecca what the critical differences are between a's and o's.

Work by Ball and Blachman (1991), Teale (1989), Ehri and Wilce (1985), Juel (1985), Yopp (1988) and Pany (1987) suggests that there is an auditory reading skill that is teachable (and therefore should be evaluated). This skill is linked to decoding success and can be taught as a part of decoding instruction (Byrne & Fielding-Barnes, 1988; Griffith & Olson, 1992). The skill is called *phonemic awareness* (or *segmentation*), and it will be covered later in Decoding SLP 1.

One final caution about the popular use of perceptual processing tests to examine pre-reading skills: If nonreaders do poorly on discrimination tests, it may seem that their lack of discrimination skills has resulted in poor decoding. However, the opposite could also be true; that is, their poor decoding could result in the poor discrimination test scores. Many of the perceptual discrimination, coding, and sequence skills presented as prerequisites for decoding are actually taught during decoding instruction and should be part of the decoding curriculum. Therefore, students fail tests on these skills because they don't know how to decode—they don't fail to decode because they don't discriminate or sequence.

Testing Decoding Rate   The relationship between decoding and comprehension was discussed in Chapter 10 (p. 188). Decoding enables comprehension. However, comprehension also enables decoding. It really is a mistake to try to impose a sequence on this interaction. It is also a mistake to ignore decoding rate because of a commitment to comprehension.

When nonreaders attack an unknown word, they prefer to use letter cues. This may be because other cues, such as word meaning and syntax, can only be accessed after some facility at decoding enables this access. (It may also be that they are so bad at those other skills that they must use letters.) Students must have knowledge of letter/cluster sounds and how to blend them to decode unfamiliar material. A comprehensive reading evaluation has to include assessment of decoding rate, because this skill is so important that the lack of it accounts for a large portion of nonreaders (Anderson et al., 1985). We do not mean by this that students who comprehend passages should be tested on *all* decoding skills. However, the literature supports the position that students need to decode rapidly in addition to knowing how to comprehend (Allington, 1983; Adams, 1990; Carver, 1992). This means that decoding fluency should be evaluated (Hasbrouck & Tindal, 1992).

Without rapid, accurate decoding, students will not use reading as an efficient tool for acquiring large amounts of information (imagine trying to decode this book at a rate of 50 words per minute). Since the ultimate goal of reading is to construct meaning from text, students who decode slowly, even if they understand what they decode, will learn less because they take in fewer ideas per minute than students who decode fluently. Thus evaluators need to check rate of decoding even when students pass all measures of comprehension.

Testing with Isolation, Time, and Nonsense Words

At the specific level, evaluators will sometimes test sounds in isolation, not in a word. Whenever testing a skill in isolation, remember that you are asking the student to do something successful readers seldom do—decode individual letters. Testing decoding subskills in isolation is a classic example of how evaluation procedures may differ from teaching procedures (although these differences should never be in content). Sounds are best taught within words, but if they are tested within words, the other letter sounds may obscure or affect the way the student pronounces the target letter. This can distort your conclusions. (Similarly, passage decoding tests are timed to test for skill mastery; however, teaching with timed decoding drills is not always a good idea.)

Timing and isolation are not the only testing procedures that are different from teaching procedures. Another technique is to test with nonsense words. Nonsense words (nok, noke, nook) are used to sample the student's skill at sounding and blending. Often, poor readers need to be tested on short words, not long ones. However, these same readers may already know most short words as sight words (no, nose, noon). Therefore, to test their knowledge of sounds, you must either risk confusing the results with the complexity of longer words or with the novelty of nonsense words.

If an evaluator is forced to use nonsense words, then the risk of obtaining a bad sample because of novelty can be diminished by taking steps to inform the student that, while the words aren't real, she should decode them as if they are. If the student reads the nonsense words, one can be sure she is doing so based on her skill at sounding and blending. Although nonsense words make sense for testing pure grapheme/phoneme decoding, they make no sense for teaching reading.

Error Analysis

Error analysis allows an evaluator to gain insight into the thought processes of the student. It is very popular among reading evaluators, and is the backbone of most of the so-called informal reading inventories on the market. It does have a couple of problems, however.

One problem with categorizing errors is that the evaluator needs some sort of error classification system. Such systems seldom enjoy the empirical support their popularity indicates (Allington, 1984). Therefore the same error might be categorized several different ways. This variability among evaluators confuses judgments about the utility of error analysis. (Whole Language Reading advocates don't even call the process error analysis. They prefer the term *miscue*, as they think it more accurately reflects the student's correct application of her own thought process—whereas *error* implies that the student has done something wrong. Therefore one might conclude that, from a whole language perspective, "To error is human—but to miscue is divine").

A second factor influencing the quality of error analysis also relates to its dependence on the thinking of individual evaluators. This is the problem of interrater agreement. Philosophical orientations aside, two different evaluators may disagree about what a student has done and, as a result, categorize the same error differently. For this reason we recommend that you practice categorizing errors and receive feedback on your efforts.

A final problem with error analysis is that the errors a person makes depend in large part on the questions they are asked. All of the error-analysis procedures discussed in this chapter depend on the availability of an appropriate error sample. This is critical. The types of errors a student makes are, in part, a function of the passage the student is reading, and the directions you give when you ask her to read. If the passage is too hard, the student will respond by making errors that reflect as much desperation and anxiety as skill. If the passage is too easy, the errors will often be of little consequence, as they merely reflect attempts at efficiency. We recommend that error samples be drawn from passages the student reads with 80–85% accuracy.

Evaluation Procedures

Survey-Level Testing

Survey-level testing involves oral decoding of passages from books used at the student's expected level (the level at which the student would decode if she had no decoding problem). As pointed out earlier, it's better to use multiple passages from texts the student will actually need to read than it is to trust the "levels" assigned to passages by publishers. Published tests with passages arranged according to levels of difficulty may also be used. The advantages of these tests (usually called reading inventories) are that they cover many levels quickly and they are well-organized. The disadvantage is that these tests may not require the kids to decode the kind of material they typically decode in school.

▽ Directions

1. Collect at least three passages that the student would be expected to read if she had no problems in reading. Get them from texts used in class or from published tests. Have copies for yourself and for the student. Each passage should be about 250 words long.

2. Set up a tape recorder.

3. Get a stopwatch.

4. You will need something to write with to code or score student responses. A calculator may also be useful for determining percentage scores.

5. Administer passages at the student's expected level. (Once again, this is the level at which any other student of this kid's age is expected to decode. Don't decide to use a simpler passage because you think the student is a problem learner.) You may adjust the wording of these directions according to the age of the student and the type of passage.

Say to the student: "I want you to read part of this story out loud. Read it as quickly and carefully as you can. If you come to a word you do not know, skip it. Please begin."

Time the student for 1 minute and make a slash (/) after the last word decoded in the 1-minute time limit. As the student reads, mark all errors on your copy of the passage. It is not necessary to note different types of errors right now.

6. To establish decoding rate, count the number of words decoded correctly and the number of word errors during the first minute (up to your slash mark). Omissions are not errors. To obtain the student's passage accuracy, divide the words correct by the total number of words decoded.

Note: Any time a student clearly is unable to progress through the passage, and you perceive that the attempt is disagreeable for the student (she has tipped over in her chair and started to weep), base an estimated score on the initial effort, then discontinue and go to an easier passage.

Score Interpretation

Compare the student's scores to the criteria for acceptable accuracy and fluency for oral passage reading that are shown in the passage reading summary form in Exhibit 11.3* (or to a criterion you establish using procedures outlined in Chapter 6). The criteria in Exhibit 11.3* are behavioral expectations based on a review of research into functional skill levels (Howell et al., 1985). They are not norms. However, they are consistent with the expectations established by studies that report rates for successful students. Exhibit 9.4 presented the results of a local norming study conducted in Oregon. Note that students at the +1.5 level are scoring within the range of criteria listed in Exhibit 11.3*.

Qualitative Interpretation

Register if the student is either accurate and fast, accurate and slow, or inaccurate. Respond to the following questions according to the student's performance and the criteria for the passage.

Question: Is the student's accuracy (percentage correct) and fluency (rate) on oral decoding at or above the criterion for grade level?

Exhibit 11.3* Passage Summary Sheet with Criteria for Acceptable Performance

Directions: For each passage used, record the number of corrects and errors per minute. Also record the accuracy. For each passage, check the rate and accuracy status (pass, marginal no-pass, or no-pass) for each curriculum level.

Curr. Level	Form	Expected Rate Correct	Error	Obtained Rate Correct	Error	Pass	M. No Pass	No Pass	Exp. Acc.	Obt. Acc.	Pass	M. No Pass	No Pass
8		140	0-7						100-95%				
7		140	0-7						100-95%				
6		140	0-7						100-95%				
5		140	0-7						100-95%				
4		140	0-7						100-95%				
3		140	0-7						100-95%				
2		Late 120 Early 80	0-5						100-95%				
1		Late 50 Early 30	0-3						100-95%				

Expected Level (Current Grade Placement) _____

Curriculum Level (Highest level at which mastery criterion is met) _____

Levels above (+) or below (−) Expectation _____

Rate Discrepancy at Instructional Level
Obtained Rate _____ ÷ Expected Rate _____ = Rate Discrepancy _____

Accuracy Discrepancy at Instructional Level
Obtained Accuracy _____ % ÷ Expected Accuracy _____ = Accuracy Discrepancy _____

Source: From K. W. Howell, S. H. Zucker & M. K. Morehead (1982) *Multilevel Academic Skills Inventory.* H & Z Publications, 6544 E. Meadowlark, Paradise Valley, AZ 85253. Reprinted with permission.

If YES, the student has passed decoding: discontinue.

If NO, repeat steps 1–6 with sequentially easier passages until you have found a level at which the student meets the criteria in Exhibit 11.3*. (If the student is accurate and scores within 15% of the fluency criterion, consider readministering the test with another passage at the original level. Some students have never been asked to decode a passage at rate before.)

When a level of decoding success has been recognized, use the information to fill out the discrepancy information on the bottom of Exhibit 11.3*.

Question: Did the student decode some words?
    If YES, go to the next question.
    If NO, test awareness of print and sounds (Decoding SLP 1).

Question: Does the student decode accurately but slowly?

If YES, go to Decoding SLP 2.
If NO, go to Decoding SLP 3.

Specific-Level Testing

This section describes seven procedures used to verify (test) the most functional assumed causes for decoding failure. Each procedure will begin with a question and then illustrate how that question might be answered. Here are the questions:

1. Is the student aware of the basic concepts of print and sound?

   SLP 1: Awareness of Print and Sounds

2. Is the student's fluency constrained by slow decoding, poor understanding of the passage or lack of experience in reading quickly?

   SLP 2: Passage Rereading

3. Do the student's errors occur because she does not monitor her decoding or always make her *best effort* (therefore failing to consistently employ the decoding skills she has mastered)?

   SLP 3a, 3b, and 3c: Assisted Self-Monitoring

4. Are you sure that the student is making important errors?

   SLP 4: Elicit Error Sample

5. Are error patterns so predictable that they indicate what sort of instruction the student should receive?

   SLP 5a, 5b, and 5c

6. Is instruction emphasizing phonics justified?

   SLP 6: Consider the Big Picture

7. Which phonetic content should be taught?

   SLP 7: Evaluate Phonics

As the description of decoding specific-level testing continues, be aware that this discussion is more complex than its application. There are two reasons for this. First, we are supplying explanations and rationale. Second, we are trying to make the thought processes of a skilled evaluator visible. Some of these steps that take paragraphs to describe only take seconds to accomplish.

Exhibit 11.4 illustrates the process for deciding what to teach in decoding. It's a flow chart and—once again—we recognize that these things will really nauseate some readers. If you are one of those readers, take scissors and cut Exhibit 11.4 out of the book (this way you won't have to look at it, and you won't be able to resell the text!).

We have transformed the assumed causes for failure at the survey level into the questions in the flow chart. Each decoding procedure is used to answer a question. For example, you will use Decoding SLP 2 when you want to answer this question: "If oral decoding is accurate but slow, will practice improve rate?"

Decoding SLP 1: Awareness of Print and Sounds

This material, which we have called "awareness of print and sound," is typically described under the headings of phonological and orthographic awareness (Adams, 1990; Peterson & Haines, 1992; Schmitt, 1990; Yopp, 1992a, 1992b). A list of this content can be found in Exhibit 11.5*. While the list in Exhibit 11.5* gives the appearance of many isolated skills, we doubt that is the case. Therefore, we want to remind you than many enabling skills, even if discrete, are most effectively acquired in tandem with more complex tasks. We think the evidence is clear that preliminary print knowledge and enabling phonological skills interact with, and are causally or reciprocally linked to, beginning reading. So we want to encourage you to test and teach these processes. We do not, however, want to encourage instructional interventions in which students are drilled on tracking tasks, phoneme counting tasks, and sound discrimination tasks in isolation. We do want to encourage an instructional focus accompanied by some hands-on teaching.

The following is a very brief description of how to assess a student on both enabling phonological knowledge and preliminary print knowledge. You will want to attend closely to these evaluation techniques, as the same procedures are also used for instruction.

Evaluation techniques   The assumption that a student is missing awareness of the basic reading processes will most often be made for young readers. As with any assessment, and especially with the assessment of young children, the evaluator needs to be

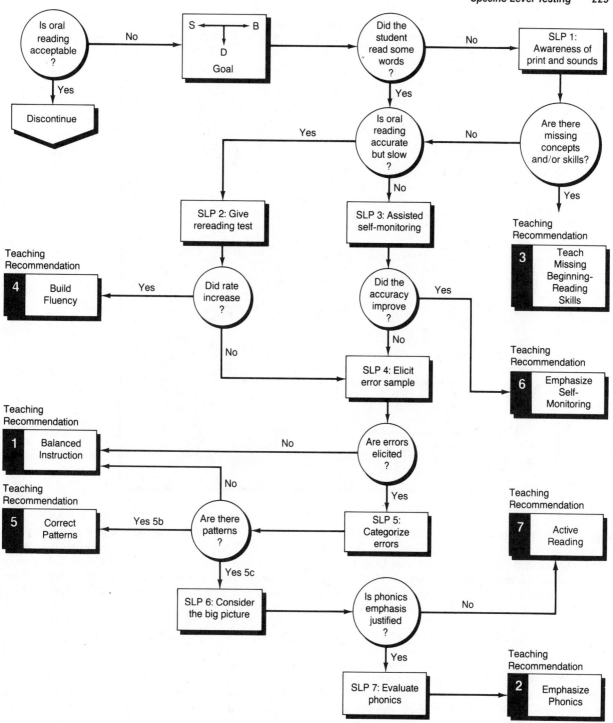

Exhibit 11.4   Deciding what to teach in decoding.

Exhibit 11.5*   *Awareness of Print and Sound*

Directions:

1. Test the student.
2. Whenever an error occurs, write down the exact content and conditions of the test.
3. Start with production. If the student does not produce answers, move to identification.
4. Record accuracy.

	Record Accuracy		
Print knowledge	Identification	Production	Note Conditions/ Content of Test
Page conventions	————	————	
left to right	————	————	
top to bottom	————	————	
Book conventions	————	————	
page by page	————	————	
front to back	————	————	
right side up	————	————	
Book length	————	————	
Word length	————	————	
Word boundaries	————	————	
Sentence boundaries	————	————	
Lower-case letter names	————	————	
Upper-case letter names	————	————	
Environmental print and logos	————		
Phonology with spoken language			
Distinguish word in speech streams	————	————	
Delete words	————	————	
Blend words	————	————	
Segment words	————	————	
Rhyme	————	————	
Blend syllables	————	————	
Segment syllables	————	————	
Delete onset/rime or phoneme	————	————	
Discriminate same/different phonemes	————	————	
Segment and blend phonemes	————	————	

mindful of the challenge of obtaining a reliable and valid sample of the students' knowledge and skills. The procedures we describe here can be integrated into routines for group play or instruction if the evaluator has reason to think that such contexts are more likely to support a young child in displaying what she knows.

If the student is not observed spontaneously to produce knowledge of the targeted skills, you will need to probe her understandings. This will often be accomplished by turning the assessment into an "identify" (select-response) task.

For each task, present ten or more opportunities. If the student makes an error, provide assistance by modeling the correct response before presenting the next item. The purpose of this assessment is not simply to determine if the student has the skill. It is also to determine how much assistance/instruction the student is going to need to use the skill when reading. Preliminary print and sound knowledge can be observed in classroom contexts as well as directly assessed (Cunningham & Stanovich, 1990). Therefore, assessment of preliminary print can be incorporated into story-reading activities, especially a rereading of a familiar story. In some cases, with students who have almost no reading skills, you may need to make use of pseudo-reading ("pretend" reading). In these cases, you sit with the student and read with her as you would with a toddler, carefully providing those segments of the task the student cannot supply. In this way you will move through the material as the child "reads," even if the only contribution she makes is to turn the pages.

Each of the areas of content in Exhibit 11.5* are addressed in the following. As you check each area, note the status of the student's skills. Be sure to include comments regarding the exact content (sound or print convention) of any errors.

Question: Is the student aware of the basic concepts of print?

▽ **Directions**

Book and Page Conventions   Observe to see if the student in "pretend" reading or in "reading with you" follows book and page conventions, especially when pretend-reading a familiar or memorized book.

Does the student consistently hold the book right-side up? start at front and go to the back? go page by page? start at the top of the page and go to the bottom? scan from left to right? When a page is skipped in a familiar story to arrive at a favorite passage or illustration, the skipping is not an error. It actually documents considerable awareness of text.

Playfulness by the evaluator may be useful (hold the book upside down, start at the back page, read the last sentence on a page first) especially if you pause, look confused, and (while holding the text sideways) ask "Now why can't I read this?"

Book Length   Show the student two books and ask which will take longer to read. (Try to trick the student into accepting a 90-second story time when she is accustomed to 15 minutes. See if she notices.)

Word Boundaries and Length   Ask the student to "finger-paint" as you read each word (Ehri & Sweet, 1991). Model with a memorized or familiar story.

Sentence Boundaries   Ask the student to show you the beginning of a sentence and the end. If necessary, prompt with information that "a sentence begins with a capital and ends with period," and so on. You may use a story the student has memorized or one of the student's own stories that you have transcribed.

Letter Names   Assess letter names in the context of story reading or by using letter cards. Ask the student to name all 52 (upper and lower) in an unordered presentation. This presentation can occur over several assessment/instructional sessions if necessary.

Environmental Print and Logos   When a child starts chanting "Cheeseburger, cheeseburger" four blocks from McDonald's, and all you can see is a tiny view of golden arches through a break in the billboards, you know the student has started processing symbols. Recognition of Pepsi logos, stop signs, and seat-belt warning lights are all indicators of symbolic learning. The presence of this knowledge should be noted, but if it is missing it does not need to be taught.

Question: Is the student aware of basic concepts of phonology?

Phonology can also be assessed in the context of group play or instructional activities. All of the phonological procedures are used with spoken language and are *not* paired to print symbols. If you have a speech defect or a particularly strong regional accent, get someone else to carry out these tests for you. Summarize the results, in terms of percent right and wrong, on Exhibit 11.5*.

Distinguish Word from Other Words in Spoken Language   Read from a familiar book, say a familiar rhyme, repeat the name of a classroom object or use the student's name as a word-of-the-day. For example, if the word today is *jump*, ask the kid to "Raise a finger each time I say *jump*. Listen." Pause. "Jump, frog, jump."

Delete Words from Sentence   When using this technique, say *"Brown bear, brown bear, what do you see?"* without the word *see*. The student is expected to respond by providing the missing word. Use sentences with which the student is familiar (*Brown Bear* is by Martin & Carle, 1983).

Blend Words   Treat this task like a guessing game. Using rainbow, say "Today's word is *rain* [pause] *bow*. What is our word today?" or "I am thinking of a word. Listen. *Help. Ful.* What word?" Use a variety of words, including compound words and other multisyllable words. Provide unprompted individual turns for ten or more words for each student. Continue to check during instruction until you are confident the student can blend syllables into words.

Segment Words   In this procedure, you want students to indicate the number of syllables in a word. We have students clap as they say words to indicate each syllable. Some practitioners use tapping, moving small blocks forward, or raising fingers as indicators for the syllable count. If your student has trouble clapping, you could use an alternate means for the student to show the syllable count. Some research suggests the use of compound words for initial assessment (rainbow: "rain-*clap*, bow-*clap*. Football: "foot-*clap*, ball-*clap*"). Other work indicates that using students' names is a good way to model how to play the game. For example, "Listen—I am going to clap for the parts of my name: 'Ma-'*clap*, 'duh'-*clap*, 'ka'-*clap*. Now listen while I clap for your name: 'Ken'-*clap*, 'neth'-*clap*. Let's do your name together: 'Shel'-*clap*, 'ly'-*clap*." After the student learns the game, provide unprompted individual turns. Do not exaggerate syllable boundaries in the unprompted individual turns. Include one-, two-, and three-syllable words. Assess the skill over ten or more words and continue to check until you are confident the student has the idea of segmenting words.

Rhyme   Ask the student to indicate if words rhyme. Model with two or more pairs of words. Include at least one pair of words that do not rhyme:

> "Listen, these rhyme: mat-bat
> car-far
> phone-cone
> These do not rhyme: fall-car
> boy-big.
> Your turn:"

Present the student with at least ten pairs, half of which do not rhyme. Note how many the student correctly identifies.

Blend Syllables   Syllables have a beginning sound called the *onset* and an ending sound called a *rime* (Treiman, 1985). In this assessment, you want to see if a student can put the two together. The assessment for this skill parallels the procedure for blending words.

> "Listen—I am going to say parts of a word. Then I will put the word together. Mmm-at, 'mat.'
> Listen again: h-orse, 'horse.' Here is another one:

b-ig, 'big.' Your turn. I say the parts, you put them together."

Present ten or more and note accuracy.

Segment Syllables   Segmenting syllables is analogous to segmenting words. In syllable segmentation, you want to see if the student can separate the initial part of a syllable, the onset, from the final part of a syllable, the rime.

Model a "game" where you start with a syllable and then segment it. Then present the student with a syllable.

> "Listen—I can make two parts. 'Rat,' Rrr-at;
> 'Sam,' Sss-am, 'far,' fff-ar; 'chair,' ch-air. I will
> say one part, you make two parts."
> Teacher—"hat" Student—"hhh-at"
> Teacher—"lake" Student—"lll-ake"

Record accuracy and note any error patterns.

Delete Onset/Rime or Phoneme   In this technique, you say a word and then designate a portion (onset, rime, or phoneme) that you would like omitted. For example, the teacher says, "Say *Sam* without *am*" and the student replies "sss." When doing this, be sure to ask for deletions from different portions of the word, and to ask that a range of units be deleted. Note accuracy and any patterns to errors.

Distinguishes Phoneme from Phoneme   Using colored blocks as indicators for same and different, model the following procedures. Place two blocks of one color and two blocks of another color in front of you. Say "Mmm, mmm," then move two blocks of the same color forward and say "'mmm' and 'mmm' are the same." Present several more two-phoneme combinations, some of which are the same and some of which are different. (When you present two that are different, move forward two different colors.) Next, ask the student to move blocks forward to indicate same or different when you say two sounds. After the student is successful with two sounds, increase the difficulty to combinations with one sound that is different (mam) and then three that are different (bat). Record accuracy.

Segmenting Phonemes and Blending Phonemes
Use the procedure you employed to assess syllable blending and syllable segmentation. Break the stimu-

lus item into phonemes rather than the onset and rime you used for the syllable task (hat = *h, a, t*).

∿ Score Interpretation

There are no established scoring conventions or standards for this procedure. Yopp (1992a) has noted that younger students generally are less than 70% accurate at many of the phoneme tasks. However, we have found that students who can read successfully are almost always 100% accurate at these very basic skills. Therefore, we would treat any errors made by a school-age child with concern. (Remember that the only reason you got to this content was that the student has failed to read simple words.)

∿ Qualitative Interpretation

Review the results recorded on Exhibit 11.5*. Pay particular attention to the comments. Then answer the question.

Question: Are there missing concepts and/or skills?

If NO, return to the survey-level passages, select the easiest one you can find, and try again. However, this time employ SLP 3a in conjunction with the passage decoding. This is done to try to get a decoding sample from a passage. If it fails, then move to words in isolation and ask the student to decode them. A student at this very low level may simply need to be placed in beginning decoding instruction using Intensified Balanced Instruction (Teaching Recommendation 1).

If YES, then note those concepts or skills on which the student appears to need instruction and teach them, using the objectives and techniques outlined in Teaching Recommendation 3.

Decoding SLP 2: Passage Rereading

Is the student's fluency constrained by slow decoding, poor understanding of the passage and/or lack of experience in reading quickly? Given the fact that the student is accurate but slow, three questions, reflecting three assumed causes, need to be answered:

1. Is the fluency problem the result of a previous neglect of fluency instruction?
2. Is rate impeded by uncertainty about the context?
3. Is rate impeded by decoding skills other than oral decoding fluency?

Question 3 will be dealt with in Decoding Procedure 4. Questions 1 and 2 can both be addressed through SLP 2, the rereading procedure.

Rereading provides practice and (because she is accurate) allows the student to learn the context during the first reading and use it in the second. The purpose of this test is to determine if the student's oral decoding rate (words correct per minute) increases when she has an opportunity to practice decoding the material.

Directions

1. Select a new passage from the highest level at which the student failed to meet the rate criterion but was +90% accurate.
2. Say to the student "I want you to read this story aloud. Begin."
3. Note where the student is after one minute (/), but don't stop her. Allow her to keep reading until she has doubled the amount decoded in the first minute. When she finishes decoding the additional material, point to the beginning of the passage and say "Now I want you to read it aloud again as quickly and carefully as you can. Are you ready? [pause] Begin."
4. Again, time the student for one minute. Stop the student after the minute is up.
5. Count the number of words correct to obtain rate on corrects-per-minute on both readings. Do the same for errors.
6. Record the correct words per minute and error words per minute.

Interpretation Guidelines

Compare the student's rate during the initial reading and her rate during the timed rereading. Compute the percentage increase by dividing the initial rate by the rereading rate and subtracting the result from 100. For example, if the original rate was 60 and the rereading rate was 80 the improvement was $60 \div 80 = 100 - 75 = 25\%$.

Pass Student's decoding rate is 35% or more than it was on the first decoding.

The student's slow initial rate can most likely be attributed to a lack of fluency instruction and/or failure to derive context cues from passages during decoding. It could also be the result of a lack of familiarity with fluency testing. In either case the student needs fluency building.

Objective. "Given passages the student reads with 90% accuracy or better, the student will decode the passage on the first try at {the rate specified for her curriculum level in Exhibit 11.3*}."

Use Teaching Recommendation 4: Build Fluency.

No-pass   Student's re-reading rate is less than 35% faster.

The student's slow rate may be the result of accurate but nonfluent decoding skills. The student may even be making errors and self-correcting them subvocally (so you aren't aware of it).

Go to Decoding SLP 4.

Decoding SLPs 3a and 3b: Assisted Self-Monitoring

These procedures are designed to test the possibility that the student makes errors because she is consistently failing to employ the decoding skills she has mastered. The assumption here is that a student may have the skills required to decode a passage, but does not use them. In some cases this could be because the student is not monitoring her own reading. There is, however, another, related explanation.

This will not sound overly theoretical, but it is our experience that students sometimes fail to decode accurately because they don't think anyone cares if they do. The research cited earlier tells us that in many classrooms reading is unmonitored and unmotivating. Additionally, reading assignments sometimes seem to emphasize the completion of pages over the quality of reading. Under such conditions, it is not difficult to imagine that even the most conscientious of students might occasionally decide to blow off a page or two, a book, or a testing session. Their errors in such circumstances would fall into the "know/display" category (see Chapter 7) and it would be a mistake to spend much time analyzing them.

Decoding SLP 3a answers this question:

"Will knowing the purpose for reading increase accuracy?"

We call 3a the "pep talk" test.

Decoding SLP 3b is designed to answer a slightly different question:

"Are the student's errors the result of insufficient, or inefficient self-monitoring?"

This is what was checked in Comprehension Specific-Level 1. You need to administer *both* 3a and 3b to all students who decode without accuracy.

Directions

Decoding SLP 3a: The Pep-Talk Test

1. You may need to do this several times, as you must assume that the student has *learned* to decode without attention to accuracy.

2. Tell the student that you are interested in finding out how long it takes her to read the passage *correctly*. Tell her it is important that she do her best work.

3. Emphasize the importance of reading accurately and your own need to get good information about her decoding skills. If you know that the student has experience with some form of reinforcement program, then you may want to offer a reward for her best efforts.

4. *Don't* help the student with word or letter cues. The idea is to get the student to try, not to help her.

Score Interpretation

Pass   Fifty percent or better improvement in accuracy.

You are looking for a significant improvement between the original decoding accuracy obtained at the survey level and the accuracy obtained after the pep talk. In some cases this may mean a score as high as Exhibit 11.3* criteria. However, an increase of 50% is sufficient to consider this test a pass.

Qualitative Interpretation

No-pass   Go on to Decoding SLP 4.

Pass   If the student improved to acceptable levels after you emphasized accuracy, she needs to learn to provide this emphasis on her own. This is done by using Teaching Recommendation 6. Administer Decoding SLP 3b and follow the interpretation guidelines supplied there.

▽ **Directions**

Decoding SLP 3b: Assisted Monitoring

Note: This is the same as Comprehension SLP 1. Therefore, these directions are considerably reduced. However, the interpretation guidelines are somewhat different.

1. Select a passage that the student reads without accuracy.

2. Note if the errors violate meaning.

3. Note if the student self-corrects errors that violate passage meaning.

4. Tell the student, "Whenever you make an error I'm going to tap the table with my pen. When I tap the table, I want you to fix the error." Have the student continue to decode the passage. When she makes an error that violates meaning, immediately tap the table with a pen or your finger. Do not wait.

5. Note whether the student immediately corrects errors after you tap.

～ **Interpretation guidelines Decoding SLP 3b**

If the student corrects errors when you provide monitoring assistance, you can assume that she has adequate clarifying strategies, but does not automatically employ them while passage reading. Go back and reconsider step 2 in the procedure to make sure you are confident that the errors are important. If the errors don't violate meaning, ignore them. If they are important, the student needs to learn to employ monitoring automatically (that is, she needs to provide herself with the sort of feedback you were supplying with your tapping pen). Teach this using Teaching Recommendation 6.

If the student does not correct errors go to SLP 4.

Decoding SLP 4: Elicit Error Sample

▽ **Directions for Collecting the Error Sample**

1. Select a 250-word passage on which you estimate that the student will be about 80–85% accurate. Use the results from the survey oral-reading test to help make your selection. You will need about 25 errors for students in grade 1; at grades 2 and above, at least 50 errors are recommended.

2. Disregard the student's decoding rate for this measure.

3. Point to the passage and say "I want you to read these words aloud. Take your time and read them as carefully as you can. Try all the words. Begin."

4. If the student is not near 80–85% accuracy, discontinue and select another passage.

5. Continue moving up or down in passage difficulty until you find a passage on which the student is about 80–85% accurate.

6. Using the passage you found in step 5, record the student's errors on your copy of the passage. You are marking these errors now so that you can categorize them later. Your efforts at categorization will involve the use of Exhibits 11.6*, 11.7* and 11.8* so take a look at them and be sure you can mark errors in a way that will let you fill them out. Exhibit 11.9 illustrates this system of error recording. Here is some other advice:
   • Use a tape recorder to confirm your scoring.
   • When the student makes a mistake, write what she said directly above the words as they appear in the passage.
   • Circle omitted words.
   • Indicate insertions and write in the insertion.
   • Mark hesitations with an *H*.
   • Underline repeated words, phrases, or portions of words each time they are repeated.
   • Write *C* next to any errors the student self-corrects. Because they reflect the student's awareness of her own reading, and because they are something you should promote, it is important to register all self-corrections.

7. Be sure to jot down whether the student reads with appropriate intonation, attends to punctuation, or makes any relevant comments about her decoding.

Exhibit 11.6*   Error Pattern Checklist: Specific-Level Procedure 5b

Compare each error in the passage to the checklist (ignore errors on proper names). Make a mark next to the category in which the error seems to fit. Identify the strategic categories in which most errors occur and begin additional testing in those areas. Continue to monitor changes in error patterns.

Error Categories	No. Errors

Mispronunciations

Errors are substitutions of real words

Errors are not real words

Errors are phonetically similar to stimulus word

Insertions

Insertions are contextually appropriate

Insertions are contextually inappropriate

Omissions

Omission affects passage meaning

Omission does not affect meaning

Hesitation
Repetition

Repeats a portion of target word

Repeats preceding word

Repeats preceding words or phrases

Does not attend to punctuation

Does not pause at punctuation

Pauses at end of line

Self-corrects

Directions for Using the Error Pattern Checklist: Use the Error Pattern Checklist to categorize all decoding errors made on the passage. Ask yourself what the most probable reading strategy explanation is for each error. Check it off by marking the appropriate category. If more than two errors were made on a word, categorize only the first two.

Question	Recommendation
1. Are there clear patterns of errors?	If yes, correct the erroneous pattern by targeting it as an instructional objective.

Source: From K. W. Howell, S. H. Zucker & M. K. Morehead (1982) *Multilevel Academic Skills Inventory.* H & Z Publications, 6544 E. Meadowlark, Paradise Valley, AZ 85253. Reprinted with permission.

Exhibit 11.7*   Decoding Content Checklist: Specific-Level Procedure 5c

Compare the words in the passage to the student's errors and categorize errors by content area and content subskill. Make a mark next to the subskill indicated by each error. Do not record more than two errors per word. Identify the content areas in which the most errors occurred and begin additional testing in those areas. Continue to monitor changes in error patterns.

Content Categories	No. Errors

Words: errors involving whole words

Polysyllabic Words

Contractions

Compound Words

Sight Words

Silent Letters

Units: errors involving combined letter units

Endings (Suffixes)

Clusters

R-controlled Vowels

Vowel Teams

Consonant Digraphs

Consonant Teams

CVC Words

Conversions: errors involving sound modification

Double Consonant Words

Vowel + e Conversions

Sounds: errors involving individual letters and sounds

Vowels

Consonants

Sequence

Sounds

Symbols

Directions for Using the Decoding Content Checklist: Use the Content Checklist to categorize all errors made on the passage. Ask yourself what the most probable content explanation is for each error. Decide what content category the error is from and check it off by marking the appropriate category. If more than two errors were made on a word, categorize only the first two.

Question	Recommendation
1. Are there identifiable problems of content?	If yes, conduct specific-level testing of decoding skills reflected in the errors.

Source: From K. W. Howell, S. H. Zucker & M. K. Morehead (1982) *Multilevel Academic Skills Inventory.* H & Z Publications, 6544 E. Meadowlark, Paradise Valley, AZ 85253. Reprinted with permission.

～ Interpretation Guidelines

Question: When you moved to harder passages, did the student make more errors (as opposed to simply decoding slower and slower)?

If YES, go to Decoding SLPs 5a–c.

If NO, employ Teaching Recommendation 1: Intensified Balanced Reading Instruction.

Decoding SLPs 5a, 5b, and 5c: Error Analysis

The decoding sample collected in SLP 4 is used for these analyses. Employ all three of the procedures (5a, 5b, and 5c) with each student. Interpretation for all procedures will occur at the same time. It is permissible, and even a good idea, to categorize a single error as many ways as logic will permit.

Decoding SLP 5a: Meaning Violating Errors

Decoding SLP 5a: Meaning Violating Errors is

Exhibit 11.8* Error Category Checklist for Meaning Violations: SLP 5a

Directions: Tally *each* error under the appropriate category. An error violates meaning if it has the *potential* to impair the student's understanding of the author's message. Do *not* tally mispronunciations of proper nouns as meaning violations.

	Category 1 Violates Meaning	Category 2 Does Not Violate Meaning	Category 3 Cannot Classify	Errors Self-Corrected
% of total errors this category	_____	_____	_____	
% or errors this category self-corrected	_____	_____	_____	

designed to answer the question "Do errors in decoding seem likely to impair the student's understanding of the text?" Errors that reflect inattention to context are likely to interfere with meaning. They can be differentiated from those that are consistent with context (not likely to interfere with meaning).

▽ **Directions**

1. Make sure you are familiar with the passage. Reread it if necessary.

2. Use the meaning violation tally sheet in Exhibit 11.8*. Tally all errors, even if they are self-corrected. Note which errors are self-corrected; if an error is self-corrected, circle the tally mark. Tally repeated errors each time they occur. Tally errors under the following categories:
   • Category 1: The error response has the potential to impair understanding of the author's message; that is, the error does not make semantic or syntactic sense in the context of the passage. (Judge errors in terms of the story as written, not the story as the student may have

misread or modified it.) Don't tally mispronunciations of proper nouns as meaning violations. If, however, the student substitutes proper nouns for each other, these should be counted.
   • Category 2: The error response does not violate the message of the author; that is, it is appropriate or does not significantly disrupt the context of the story.
   • Category 3: Any error you are not certain how to classify; include in this type all errors involving the mispronunciation of proper names.

3. Divide the number of errors in each category by the total errors tallied to get a percent for that category. Also record what percent of each error type the student self-corrects.

4. Compute the number of errors in each category and summarize the results by percentage (50% category 1, 40% category 2, 10% category 3).

Decoding SLP 5b: Error Patterns

Decoding SLP 5b: Error Patterns addresses the question "Do errors in decoding seem to fall into

Exhibit 11.9 Scoring a reading passage.

yuca   pant   spinny   winter c
The yueca is a desert plant. It has long, spiny leaves. Once a year, it bears beautiful white flowers.
These   loom   This   sed   yuca
The flowers bloom only at night or on a very dark day. The flowers produce seeds for more yueca plants.
yuca   the   parking yuca mother yuca mother   girls
The yueca could not produce seeds without its partner, the yueca moth. The yueca moth has only one goal
                    pace C   egg   yuca   all   mother
in life. Its goal is to find a safe place to lay its eggs. The yueca plant and the yucca moth became partners

because each one had something the other needed.

Source: From K. W. Howell, S. H. Zucker & M. K. Morehead (1982) *Multilevel Academic Skills Inventory.* H & Z Publications, 6544 E. Meadowlark, Paradise Valley, AZ 85253. Reprinted with permission.

certain types or patterns, i.e., insertions, substitutions, omissions?'' Reading strategies are learned. Often these strategies are the result of our attempts to shortcut the decoding task or to avoid difficult material. Sometimes they work and sometimes they don't. For example, one student may get in the habit of avoiding errors by simply omitting troublesome words, while another may substitute known words, and a third may mispronounce. As all students practice decoding, they practice using these strategies and develop what might best be described as ''error patterns.'' These error patterns are actually poor decoding habits, which must be countered with direct intervention, as will be described in Teaching Recommendation 5: Correct Error Patterns. However, before this can be done the specific error pattern must be recognized. To do this we will recognize patterns of errors (substitution, insertion, omission) that may or may not relate to the categories of errors (violate meaning, do not violate meaning) we have already discussed.

Directions

1. Use the information you obtained by following the seven steps of Procedure 4.

2. Categorize and tally the errors according to pattern type (hesitation, mispronunciation, insertion) by using the error pattern tally form in Exhibit 11.6*.

Decoding SLP 5c: Decoding Content

The Decoding SLP 5c: Decoding Content test is used to answer the question ''Do errors seem to occur whenever certain code content is present in the word?'' If a student does not seem accurate at passage decoding or if she is accurate but slow, she may be having trouble using phonics. Students who are slow but accurate or who omit or substitute words are often compensating for weak phonics skills by slowing down or avoiding difficult words. Obviously students who are very inaccurate or very slow are having trouble with phonics. Consistent phonics and word recognition errors indicate specific code skills that the student is not adequately employing. Once recognized, these skills can be taught using Teaching Recommendation 2: Emphasize Phonics.

Directions

1. Use the information you obtained by following procedure 4, Directions for Collecting Error Sample.

2. Note the phonetic content associated with each error. Use a form like the one in Exhibit 11.7* to tally the errors.

3. Identify those phonetic units or strategies that seem to account for a large proportion of errors.

Score Interpretation

There are no established scoring conventions or standards for these procedures. The information of most value is obtained by comparing the frequency of errors in the many different categories presented in SLPs 5a–5c. However, because opportunities for errors vary, and the skills are compensatory, criteria cannot be established.

Qualitative Interpretation

You got this far because the student started out as an inaccurate or slow reader at the expected curriculum level. Performance did not improve after assisted self-monitoring or rereading. After eliciting an error sample in procedure 4 you next used Decoding SLPs 5a–5c to see if you could find patterns in the errors the student is making.

You have now collected considerable information about the student's decoding. The next challenge is figuring out what it all means. We'll try to facilitate the process by framing key decision-making factors as questions. Because we can only write one thing at a time, and you can only read one thing at a time, the questions will appear in a series. But they are not sequential. In practice, an expert evaluator asks all of these questions all of the time—not each question one at a time. It's like a crossword puzzle. The solution to one item affects the solution to the others. But the puzzle is not finished until all questions have been asked and all the blanks filled in. It is possible, therefore, for a student to have error patterns *and* phonic mistakes. *Don't assume that a YES on 5b is the same as a NO on 5c.*

Question: Are certain patterns of errors, or phonetic skill weaknesses, illustrated by SLPs 5b and/or 5c?

If NO, there is nothing arguing for, or against, a

particular instructional emphasis. The kid needs intensified balanced decoding instruction. Put her in Teaching Recommendation 1 and monitor her decoding closely using an **Objective** like this: "Given passages at the {expected or an intermediate} level, the student will decode them at {specify the rate} while maintaining 95–100% accuracy."

Question: Are there error patterns illustrated by SLP 5b?

If YES, the student needs to learn to correct these inefficient decoding habits. You'll accomplish that by using Teaching Recommendation 5 and this **Objective:** "Given passages at the {expected or an intermediate} level, the student will decode the passage fluently while making no more than 5% {specify pattern} errors."

Question: Are there phonic errors illustrated by Procedure 5c?

If YES, go to Decoding SLP 6.

Decoding SLP 6: Consider the Big Picture

It's time for a little reflection; stop to think about where you are. You and the student are now well down the flow chart in Exhibit 11.4*. There is only one decision left to make, but it is a big one—and there is not a set criterion to help you make it.

What you have is a kid who doesn't decode at her expected level. Additionally, practice doesn't help, and pep talks don't help. This reader makes errors. There may or may not be SLP 5b patterns to these errors, but there *are* phonic patterns (illustrated by Decoding SLP 5c). The question is, do you teach her phonics?

On the face of it the answer seems to be a fairly easy YES. However, there are some considerations. For example: What if this "kid" is 23 years old? What if she self-corrects most of the errors that violate meaning? What if she seems to decode too quickly? What if she comprehends everything you give her? What if the phonics errors she makes are relatively trivial? Finally, what if you are sure high quality phonics instruction has been tried on a consistent basis for a long time?

Two of these questions deserve some explanation. First, the issue of age. The main reason to avoid putting older students into phonics is that, because phonics are taught in the early grades, the decision to put older students into phonics has the effect of sending the student backwards in the curriculum. This risk must be weighed against the very real need for students to learn phonics because it is a basic skill. If there is a way out of this, it is to place the student into age-appropriate code instruction. We like the *Corrective Reading Program* published by SRA.

The last question is important, given our previous observations on the quality of reading instruction that is occurring in some classes. You cannot assume that a student has received phonic instruction simply because workbook pages with code emphasis items were placed on the desk before her. (For an idea of what we think quality instruction looks like, review Chapter 8 and attend to the teaching recommendations at the end of Chapter 11). Obviously, if effective code instruction has not been used, it should be tried. Every year thousands of previously illiterate adults are taught to read, and most of them are taught phonics. These variables—age, instructional history, comprehension, self-monitoring, decoding fluency, and phonic content—are all important.

Directions
Gather everything you have on the student (tape recordings, tally sheets, notes) and ask yourself this question: "Should I emphasize phonics?"

Score Interpretation
There are no established scoring conventions or standards for this procedure.

Qualitative Interpretation
Most students learn phonics, either through direct or indirect means, before the end of the second grade. Most students achieve mastery and automaticity with phonics by the end of the third grade. Phonics skills *are* important. However, because they are from the early elementary curriculum, emphasizing them with older students can be a mistake. As you recall, one of the rules for thinking presented in Chapter 7 was "Stay close to the main task." Phonics is one of the main tasks in the first grade. It is a long way from being one of the main tasks in the eighth grade. Therefore, electing to emphasize phonics in assessment and instruction with an eighth-grade student could violate the rule. (The key term here is *emphasize*. When phonics is emphasized in the early grades it isn't the only thing that is taught. If it is not emphasized with older students, it still is taught;

Exhibit 11.10   Is Phonics Indicated?

Student A: This is a tenth-grade student who was taught to read in a code emphasis reader. Her comprehension is good and her reading errors tend not to violate the meaning of the passage.

Student B: This is a first-grade student who has been taught to read through a discovery learning emphasis. Her comprehension is very bad and her reading errors violate the meaning of the passage.

Student C: This is a tenth-grade student who was taught to read in a code emphasis reader. Her comprehension is poor and her reading errors tend to violate the meaning of the passage.

Student D: This is a first-grade student who was taught to read in a code emphasis reader. Her comprehension is good and her reading errors tend not to violate the meaning of the passage.

however, it is taught along with other decoding strategies such as context analysis and summarizing. The decision should never be to ignore phonics, or to focus exclusively on it.)

How do you decide if phonics should be emphasized? First of all, you need to turn to the results obtained through Decoding SLP 5a. These will give you information about the degree to which the student's errors violate meaning. Next, look at Exhibit 11.10. It describes both a kid who clearly needs phonic emphasis (student B) and one who does not (student A). The closer your student is to student B, the more justified a code emphasis approach seems. In the case of students C and D, the need for phonics is much harder to determine. That is because, in devising these examples, we have counterbalanced every other variable (kid D is in a lower grade than kid C, but her errors don't violate meaning as much). We asked a group of teachers which of these students they thought should have a phonics emphasis, and how confident they were that their decision was correct. Sure enough, most of them thought B needed phonics and A did not. Additionally, the confidence went way down for students C and D. What this means, in evaluative terms, is that subtle decisions must be monitored closely—no matter which way.

Question: Is a phonics emphasis justified?

If YES, go to Decoding SLP 7.

If NO, employ Teaching Recommendation 7 and use this **Objective:** "Given passages at the {expected or intermediate} level, the student will decode the passages with 95% accuracy at {the specified rate}."

Decoding SLP 7: Evaluate Phonics

You have already decided to emphasize phonics with this student. The question now is, which phonetic content? To answer this, you need to treat the information obtained through SLPs 4 and 5 as survey-level test results. Starting with the tallied product obtained in Exhibit 11.7,* select objectives and/or conduct additional assessment to determine which phonetic content seems to be most problematic. This requires some explanation.

Testing Letter Sounds

There are many hierarchies of decoding content. Most of them are essentially the same and move in a progression from single-letter sounds (vowels and consonants) to sounds associated with clusters of letters (blends and digraphs), to words (contractions and compounds). The letter and cluster sounds can be tested in words or in isolation. For example, if you are interested in finding out about the student's use of the *a* sounds, you can test by giving a flashcard with only that letter on it and asking "What sounds does this letter make?" You may also test by giving a word with the letter in it: "Read this word: *abate*." In this case, you would score only the use of *a*. If you present the letter in isolation, keep in mind that the letter can make more than one sound. You might say "This letter makes two sounds, long and short. Give me the two sounds this letter makes."

If you are interested in the student's skill at converting *a*'s from the long to short sound, you might give a probe such as the vowel conversion probe shown in Exhibit 11.11. Once again, you would score only the student's response to the targeted vowel; the *t*'s and *p*'s are carriers that increase the validity of the sample, in spite of the fact that real words are not used. (Some evaluators test conversions through the use of diacritical markings. Unless these markings are used in the student's decoding program, such a test will not be useful because it requires knowledge not normally used in decoding.

Exhibit 11.11   A Vowel Conversion Probe

					tip	tipe	tap	tappe
tip	tupp	tep	topp	tope	tupe	tape	tepe	tipe
tap	tipe	tupe	tepe	top	tope	tupe	tape	tepe
tep	tape	tippe	tuppe	teppe	topp	tope	tupe	tape
tip	tepe	tappe	tipp	tupp	tepp	toppe	tope	tupe
top	tipe	teppe	tapp	tip	tup	tepe	tope	tope
tup	tope	tippe	tepp	tap	tipe	tupe	tep	top
tape	tupe	toppe	tipp	tep	tape	tippe	tupe	tepe
tappe	tap	tuppe	topp	tip	tepe	tappe	tipp	tup
toppe	teppe	tapp	tupp	top	tipe	teppe	tapp	tip
tap	tippe	tuppe	tappe	tupe	tope	tip	tepe	tap

Source: From K. W. Howell, S. H. Zucker & M. K. Morehead (1982) *Multilevel Academic Skills Inventory.* H & Z Publications, 6544 E. Meadowlark, Paradise Valley, AZ 85253. Reprinted with permission.

While decoding this text, for example, you are not depending on diacritical cues).

Formats   Sounds can be tested with probe sheets or flashcards. Probe sheets, like the one in Exhibit 11.11, can be used for testing mastery and accuracy, whereas flashcards are only useful for accuracy. The student must give an oral response to the probe if you wish to grade it, and because the oral response is gone in an instant, you must either tape the behavior or score it as the student reads. Simultaneous scoring can be simplified by having your own copy of the probe in a clear plastic binder; then you can use a transparency pen to write what the student said over each sound missed. After transferring findings you can wipe the plastic clean. Incidentally, remember to sit behind the kid so that she isn't distracted by your scoring.

The main limitation of flashcards is that they are not practical for timing, because you control the student's decoding rate with the rate at which you flash the cards. The amount of time it should take a student to decode a word on a flashcard is not well-established and is difficult to test. The task is quite different from decoding a line of print; it is probably more analogous to reading highway signs on a curved mountain road at night. Some commonly used measures allow students as long as 5 seconds, but a proficient reader (which is what you want the kid to be) can decode a

single word of nearly any length in about a half-second. As a rule, single units (letters and syllables) should be decoded with 100% accuracy at a rate of 60 per minute, while words in isolation should be decoded with 100% accuracy at 80 per minute.

Testing Words

Word Errors   Students will often substitute whole words or parts of words. This is sometimes called *word calling,* and is typical of older readers. These errors may include whole-word substitutions (is-at, in-to) or partial substitutions (the-them, display-discuss). Characteristically, when a partial word error is noted, the first or last few letters of the substituted word will be correct.

To gain insight into the skill deficits promoting this error pattern, take the words missed and present them in isolation (on flash cards). If the student doesn't decode the phonetically regular portions of them accurately and quickly in isolation, she is having sound or blending problems. Test and teach those skills.

If the student reads the previously missed words correctly, ask yourself if these are ''sight'' words. Should that be the case, move to the use of nonsense words. If the student makes errors on nonsense words, test and teach phonics. If phonics does not seem to be a problem, recheck to see if she is making errors that affect her comprehension (Decoding SLP 5a). If the errors do affect comprehension, have the student decode the passage while you provide assisted self-monitoring (Comprehension SLP 1). If her accuracy improves, she needs to learn to monitor for meaning while decoding quickly. Use Decoding Teaching Recommendations 6 and 4. If the errors don't affect her comprehension, you have found a pattern unique to oral decoding. In other words, there would be no problem were there not an oral decoding test, so forget the errors.

Blending and Word (Sound) Analogy   When using phonics to decode a word, a student first segments it into units, recalls the grapheme-phoneme relationship for each unit, and then combines the sounds to say the word. These segmenting and combining activities are called *blending*. Blending is viewed as a separate task from sounding; however, blending is of primary importance to decoding (Williams, 1984; Yopp, 1992b). Some of the formats for testing blending were described in depth in Decoding SLP 1: Awareness of Print and Sound. (You probably didn't read that section because it was targeted at students who are beginning readers. Guess what! The decision to emphasize phonics was a decision to treat this student as a beginning reader. So go back to Decoding SLP 1 and read it for background value.)

A student who knows the *at* in *pat* can use that information in analogous words such as *fat, rat, mat,* or *bat*. A student who knows *icker* in *sticker* can use that information to decode *flicker* or *bicker*.

The technique of word-analogy testing can be used to evaluate and teach decoding. This is particularly effective when the teacher utilized morphemes as the clusters targeted for the analogy exercises. That is because morphology (Chapter 12, p. 257) introduces meaning into the decoding task (Carnine, et al., 1990). Many of the affixes in Exhibit 11.1 are morphographs.

Decoding by word analogy requires the blending steps of unit recognition, word segmenting, sound recall, and combining. Proficient readers use the analogy strategy automatically. Explicit instruction that prepares students to use word analogy strategies appears in a number of reading materials. It is sometimes called rhyming. We will describe three assessment procedures that will let you analyze blending with word analogy strategies.

Blending Procedure 1:   To see if a student blends two units, show a letter (or cluster) and supply the sounds of the units before asking for the sound of both together. Example:

Teacher	Student
"This is 'b'."	Pronounces the sound "b"
"This is 'igh'."	Pronounces the sound "igh"
"What is 'b' [pause] 'igh'?"	Pronounces the sound "bigh"

Because the sounds are supplied, this test is evaluating the blending of the "b" to "igh." Sounding of "b" and "igh" isn't being tested.

A blending test can be assembled by making up flashcards for each code unit in Exhibit 11.1 and putting them in order, either by numbering them or affixing them to metal rings. You can make up a record form that corresponds to the order of the cards. By using the record form, you can flip through various code combinations and mark the student's performance on each.

Another technique is the use of rhyming word teams. For example:

> "This word is br/eam."
> [Pronounce the word.]
> "What word would this be?" *Bleam*.

The sound that is supplied ("eam") is not being tested. Instead, the production of the "bl" sound and the blending of "bl" to "eam" are being tested. Remember to change the position of the sounds, because some students may be skilled enough to blend a letter in the initial position but not in the medial or final positions. For example, to test "b" in the initial place:

> "This word would this be?" *Bap*.
> [Pronounce the word.]
> "What word is this? *B/ap*."

To test "b" in the final place:

> "This word is ta/p."
> [Pronounce the word.]
> "What word would this be?" *Tab*.

Blending Procedure 2: Another Decoding Procedure, the Glass Analysis System (Glass, 1971), is ideal for testing both production and identification of blending as well as cluster sounds. It is also an excellent spelling test. In the Glass system, the whole word is shown and the student is given the sound of the word. Next, the student is asked to indicate which letter makes each sound in the word and then what sound the letter makes. The system requires students to find letters and clusters within the word. This task (identification of the code units) is a necessary part of blending. Remember that blending is not just putting the sounds together. First, the kid must recognize code units within the word. Here is how the Glass system might be used to test segmenting, sounding, and combining subskills:

	Teacher	Student
Step 1.	"This word is *bring*." [Show and pronounce the word.] "Say it."	"Bring"
Step 2a.	"In the word *bring*, which letters make the sound 'br'?"	"B-R"
Step 2b.	In the word *bring*, what letters make the sound 'ing'?"	"I-N-G"
Step 3a.	"In the word *bring*, what sound do the letters 'B-R' make?"	"brrr"
Step 3b.	"In the word *bring*, what sound do the letters 'I-N-G' make?"	"ing"
Step 4.	"Say the word."	"Bring"

You can easily modify the Glass (1971) procedure to incorporate the content already discussed. Now that you know the kid knows the sounds of "br," "ing," and "bring," new words can confidently be built using them. For example:

brick sing bride
or
fling broke swing

Blending Procedure 3: The Glass questions can also be used to obtain insight into the student's skill at combining. Let's say the student failed at working with rhyming words. You could go through the Glass (1971) technique with the words and then combine them, as shown in the following.

Word A	Stimulus	Response
Step 1.	(Show the word *drain*.) "This word is *drain*. What word is it?"	"Drain"
Step 2.	"In the word *drain*, what letters make the sound 'ain'?"	"A-I-N"
Step 3.	"In the word *drain*, what sound do the letters 'A-I-N' make?"	"ain"
Step 4.	"Say the word *drain*."	"Drain"
Step 5.	(Show the word *train*.) "Now say this word."	"Train"

Word B	Stimulus	Response
Step 1.	(Show the word *trade*.) "This word is *trade*. What word is it?"	"Trade"
Step 2.	"In the word *trade*, what letters make the sound 'tr'?"	"T-R"
Step 3.	In the word *trade*, what sound do the letters 'T-R' make?"	"tr"
Step 4.	"Say the word *trade*."	"Trade"
Step 5.	(Show the word *drade*.) "Now say this word."	"Drade"

Sight Words Evaluating sight words is somewhat like evaluating letter sounds. That is because the basic strategy involved in learning them is the recall of grapheme-phoneme correspondence. Just as "e" says *eh*, "boy" says *boy*. There is, however, one big difference between "e" and "boy." The difference is that *boy* has meaning. Letters, unless they are morphographs, have no meaning. Therefore, the domain of letter decoding is consolidated (see Chapter 3, p. 52) only by the rules of sounding. Those rules tend to be arbitrary, and as a result the domain is not easily approached through conceptual instruction. However, the domain of words/morphographs is consolidated by meaning and may even be taught, in part, through a generative approach (Westby, 1992).

Sight words become sight words because they are either frequently used or phonetically irregular. Therefore, some are regular (*man*), while others are irregular (*was*). Before you get too interested in classifying words as regular or irregular, remember that as students acquire more knowledge of coding rules more words become regular to them. If a student does not know the final–e rule, then *mane* and *cane* are irregular (Carnine et al., 1990). The way you test sight words is to show them to the student (ideally within sentences or phrases) and ask her to decode them. If she gives an immediate response (1 half-second for the targeted sight word), then she either knows it as a sight word or has decoded it successfully.

Theoretically, no sight word requires more energy to learn than any other, just as the sound "b" is not harder to learn than the sound "n." However, ease of learning has nothing to do with ease of usage. Some sight words are more commonly confused than others. This is particularly true of those that begin with *th* (that, those, these, them, this, thought, throw, threw). Therefore, when testing sight words at the automatic level, you will want to select a passage with a lot of these items.

High-frequency word lists, like the one in Exhibit 11.12, are available in most reading texts. The exhibit list was developed by Eeds (1985), who distinguishes between high-frequency words found in basal texts (in which words are selected for their conformity to skill sequences) and high-frequency words found in children's literature. Most other compilers of word frequency lists have used basals to establish their samples. Eeds advocates teaching a core of words found in literature, rather than basals. She argues that a goal of reading instruction is reading from all texts. As it turns out, Eeds' list contains most of the words on Adams' 1990 list of the highest-frequency words in texts.

Sight words can be tested in context, in phrases, and in isolation. Because some readers substitute one sight word for another, it is a good idea to repeat each word on the probe sheet several times. This repetition makes the student use the word more than once, which increases the validity of the test by decreasing the likelihood of lucky guesses. As a rule, only use from 10 to 20 different sight words on any probe sheet. CAPs for sight words are slightly higher than for sounds but lower than for passage decoding. A reasonable criterion is 80 correct with 0–2 errors per minute.

Testing Attention to Code   A commonly stated assumed cause for decoding errors is inattention to portions of words. This is the cause most often assumed when students make whole-word substitutions of words sharing initial sounds (the-their, who-what, is-if), or when they omit endings (-ed, -ing, -ion, -s). There is a simple procedure to find out if these errors are the result of either a failure to attend to the whole word or lack of decoding skill. (Remember, if the errors aren't affecting meaning you don't need to worry about them.)

Select two passages of equal difficulty and underline the characteristically omitted or substituted portions of one passage in red. Time the student's reading of both passages and note accuracy and rate. If, when these words are underlined, the accuracy improves considerably but rate maintains, then the student knows how to decode the endings but isn't doing so. To remedy this problem, place greater emphasis on accuracy and comprehension monitoring (Teaching Recommendation 6). If accuracy does not improve, or if it improves but rate decreases significantly (more than 20%), teach the words or units themselves.

Teaching Recommendations

A Note on Monitoring Decoding

Once you have selected an objective, you will also need to monitor the effect of teaching to determine if your teaching is effective (see Chapter 5). Most of the monitoring procedures we discuss are presented in the workbook. However, the best monitoring techniques are those that use measures that reflect what you are teaching and are also sensitive to learning. In the domain of decoding, this is fairly easy.

Exhibit 11.12   Wordlist Based on Frequency in 400 Storybooks for Beginning Readers

the	1334	good	90	think	47	next	28
and	985	this	90	new	46	only	28
a	831	don't	89	know	46	* am	27
I	757	little	89	help	46	began	27
to	746	if	87	grand	46	head	27
said	688	just	87	boy	46	keep	27
you	638	* baby	86	take	45	* teacher	27
he	488	way	85	eat	44	* sure	27
it	345	there	83	* body	43	* says	27
in	311	every	83	school	43	* ride	27
was	294	went	82	house	42	* pet	27
she	250	father	80	morning	42	* hurry	26
for	235	had	79	* yes	41	hand	26
that	232	see	79	after	41	hard	26
is	230	dog	78	never	41	* push	26
his	226	home	77	or	40	our	26
but	224	down	76	* self	40	their	26
they	218	got	73	try	40	* watch	26
my	214	would	73	has	38	* because	25
of	204	time	71	* always	38	door	25
on	192	* love	70	over	38	us	25
me	187	walk	70	again	37	* should	25
all	179	came	69	side	37	*room	25
be	176	were	68	* thank	37	* pull	25
go	171	ask	67	why	37	* great	24
can	162	back	67	who	36	gave	24
with	158	now	66	saw	36	* does	24
one	157	friend	65	* mom	35	* car	24
her	156	cry	64	* kid	35	* ball	24
what	152	oh	64	give	35	* sat	24
we	151	Mr.	63	around	34	* stay	24
him	144	* bed	63	by	34	* each	23
no	143	an	62	Mrs.	34	* ever	23
so	141	very	62	off	33	* until	23
out	140	where	60	* sister	33	* shout	23
up	137	play	59	find	32	* mama	22
are	133	let	59	* fun	32	* use	22

(continued)

Exhibit 11.12   Wordlist Based on Frequency in 400 Storybooks for Beginning Readers (continued)

will	127	long	58	more	32	turn	22
look	126	here	58	while	32	thought	22
some	123	how	57	tell	32	* papa	22
day	123	make	57	* sleep	32	* lot	21
at	122	big	56	made	31	* blue	21
have	121	from	55	first	31	* bath	21
your	121	put	55	say	31	* mean	21
mother	119	* read	55	took	31	* sit	21
come	118	them	55	* dad	30	* together	21
not	115	as	54	found	30	* best	20
like	112	* Miss	53	* lady	30	* brother	20
then	108	any	52	soon	30	* feel	20
get	103	right	52	ran	30	* floor	20
when	101	* nice	50	* dear	29	wait	20
thing	100	other	50	man	29	* tomorrow	20
do	99	well	48	* better	29	* surprise	20
too	91	old	48	* through	29	* shop	20
want	91	* night	48	stop	29	run	20
did	91	may	48	still	29	* own	20
could	90	about	47	* fast	28		

*Indicates words *not* on Durr list.
Source: "Bookwords: Using a Beginning Word List of High Frequency Words from Children's Literature K–3." by M. A. Eeds, January 1985, *The Reading Teacher*, 38, p. 420. Reprinted with permission of Maryann Eeds and the International Reading Association.

While you can monitor a student's acquisition of a specific decoding subskill (converting vowels to the long sound when a silent *e* is present) we also recommend that, whenever teaching reading, passage reading be monitored with timed reading samples. These samples should be collected and charted during each instructional session. Procedures for using this kind of monitoring are also presented in the Student Workbook.

Remember, the only way to determine if an instructional approach is effective is to try it, take data, and let the student tell you if it works.

Seven kinds of reading intervention are represented in Exhibit 11.4: (1) intensify balanced instruction, (2) emphasize phonics, (3) teach beginning skills, (4) build fluency, (5) correct error patterns, (6) emphasize self-monitoring, and (7) emphasize higher level strategies.

Teaching Recommendation 1: Use Intensified Balanced Instruction

This recommendation is usually indicated when a student is progressing slowly through an initial, largely code-dominated, reading curriculum. The student will be decoding below an expected level. While progress is not adequate, the pattern of errors does not seem to indicate the need to take a radically biased (all-code or all-language-based) approach. Instead, an intensive, balanced approach is recommended, including direct instruction on phoneme-grapheme correspondence made meaningful through the periodic use of language-based exercises such as student-generated stories, teacher-student shared decoding, and teacher readings from more sophisticated texts (Cognition and Technology Group, 1991). While both code strategies and context strategies are taught in an intensified balanced approach, in the early grades the correct "balance" must favor phonics.

While the relative merits of code and language emphasis continue to generate debate, there is one thing we know. Students need to read, and they need to read a lot! Therefore, no matter what your orientation to the content of decoding might be, you need to do everything you can to increase reading activity.

Teach Code—"Sounding it Out"

There is an endless list of programs that were developed to teach beginning reading, so it hardly makes sense for a teacher to generate more. However, not all published programs, even those that sell well, are necessarily good. You need to select instructional materials carefully. In addition to using a published program, there are other things a teacher should do. With students who are just beginning to learn to read, teach sound/symbol relationships directly. This is done by showing the letter, modeling the sound, and prompting the student to produce the sound (Simmons & Kameenui, 1989). In addition, as Adams (1990) reminds us, "the single most important activity for building the knowledge and skills eventually required for reading appears to be reading aloud to children regularly and interactively" (p. 124).

When a student has developed some skills, it is necessary to skip through the reading sequence in order to bypass what is already known. Focus on specific grapheme or phoneme problems by teaching what the student needs to know to correct them. Highlight the content, refer to it frequently, and reinforce the student for improvement.

Time spent in listening to reading, and reading for enjoyment, out of texts at the student's skill level must be augmented by periods, even if short, of intense work on skill acquisition. During these sessions insist on accuracy in decoding by taking steps to minimize errors or by insisting that the student correct errors made during monitored reading (Spaai, Ellermann & Reitsma, 1991). If necessary, separate the words by pointing to each one and not allowing the student to go on until you move your finger in response to the correct decoding of the word. Remind the student that after sounding out a word in a story she should remember it, so it isn't necessary to sound it out again.

At first you may want to carefully reduce overuse of context clues in order to increase reliance on code. If that is the case, do not attack or criticize the use of context, but select passages that deal with novel content and are not redundant. This way, fewer context clues will be available. Encourage the student to attempt unknown words by applying her knowledge of code content. Employ an explicit approach to code in which essential sound-symbol relationships are directly taught. Avoid teaching all the sounds in the world. Have the student master a core of high-utility sound-symbol relationships along with strategies for using them in new words (Simmons & Kameenui, 1989). High-utility sound-symbols are those that appear frequently in text and are regular. Do not teach the student decoding terminology (digraph, blend, CVC), but *do* teach her sequential, code-based generalizations for word attack. Don't forget blending. Use drill and practice to achieve fluency in code content.

Teach Context Strategies—"Making Sense"

To balance code instruction, you will also need to focus on the student's skill at using context (titles, vocabulary, story line) to predict upcoming events and words in the story. These activities are often influenced by the size of the instructional group (Morrow & Smith, 1990). Require the student to explain how she can confirm a prediction and how to provide evidence from the passage to support both predictions and confirmations. Minimize the use of post-reading/summary questions. Encourage the student to "look ahead" and "look back" for context clues. Have the student close her eyes and try to visualize what occurred in a given sentence or paragraph. Encourage her to paraphrase or repeat what was just read and to ask "Does that make sense?" See Teaching Recommendations 6 and 7 for more information about context strategies.

Teaching Recommendation 2: Emphasize Code Content

This is for the student who does not seem to have adequately mastered basic grapheme-phoneme correspondence. This may mean the student is inaccurate at these skills or that she has not become fluent enough at them to use them automatically when decoding.

For this student, decoding instruction should be targeted directly on content areas indicated by high-frequency errors. Before beginning instruction you may wish to test several code objectives to be sure of the exact content or level of proficiency on which the student needs instruction. If you do, begin with the more advanced decoding skills and work backwards to identify weak or missing subskills. As a rule, letter sounds are best taught within words and words within phrases. Extensive drill on words or phonemic units in isolation is generally not recommended, though those procedures are justified if you have tried other methods and failed.

Teaching code in context does not preclude explicit skill instruction. Explicit (supplantive) code instruction (synthetic phonics) appears to be superior to implicit (generative) phonics (Johnson & Baumann, 1984). Analytic-implicit phonics approaches, those in which students ''see'' how words are similar in order to infer code, often require that a kid know how to decode the words in the practice exercise from which the phonics rules are to be inferred. If she knows how to do that, she doesn't need the instruction in the first place!

While good readers make a large number of appropriate analytic code inferences, poor readers do not. Explicit code instruction is efficient and is supported by current research. In an explicit code lesson, students are taught a sound and asked to decode words that have the sound. Here is an example of explicit instruction:

TEACHER: "The sound of this letter *s* is 'sss'."
"What sound will you say when you see this letter?" [Hold up *s*.]

STUDENTS: "sss."

TEACHER: "These new words will be in our story. Let's read them together. Remember to say 'sss' when you sound out a word with this new letter."

[Word List on Board]
Sam   sis   mist   sun

A caution: When explicitly teaching very specific content (such as vowel teams or word lists), be aware that you are asking the student to perform an essentially meaningless task. The promise that working on these subskills will eventually enable her to make sense of printed matter is far-removed and hollow for most special/remedial students. Therefore, be careful to supply meaning while maintaining the focus on target skills. The following recommendations may help

students who need direct instruction on particular skills:

- Be sure of the content you are teaching. Don't isolate (decontextualize) material the student has already learned.

- Be sure the student knows what she is trying to learn (this does not mean you should use teaching terminology like *digraphs* or *vowels*).

- Use the blending/analogy procedures described in Decoding SLP 7 as instructional techniques.

- Provide short, high-intensity practice sessions that require high rates of student response. Avoid long sessions that will bore the student.

- Maintain a quick pace by moving to a new objective as soon as a skill has been learned.

- Reinforce the kid frequently but keep statements of praise or distribution of rewards brief. Tie rewards directly to acquisition of the content ("Good work! You learned the word" not "Great work! You're really being good").

- Mix specific lessons with whole reading experiences such as being read to by the teacher.

- If at all possible, teach students with similar skill deficits in groups to derive the motivational advantage of peers and to promote vicarious learning. However, be aware that the membership of such groups should change quickly. If it doesn't, the grouping isn't working.

- Modify the presentation frequently, but never at the expense of focus on the content.

- Monitor progress and expect rapid improvement. If the student does not acquire the skills in a matter of weeks, you may wish to consider an intensified balanced approach that emphasizes both code and context.

Teaching Recommendation 3: Awareness of Print and Sound

Objectives: Enabling Phonology

Segment Phonemes   When presented with ten spoken words of three phonemes each (man, hit, sit, ram, job, etc.) the student will say the phonemic sounds in sequence with 80% accuracy on five of five trials (student says, "mm-aa-nn" when teacher says *man*).

Blend Phonemes   When presented with ten spoken words segmented into phonemes (ss-ii-t, mm-o-mm, b-aa-t, p-o-p, etc.) the student will blend the sounds to make a word with 80% accuracy for five of five trials (student says *sit* when teacher says "ss-ii-t").

Discriminate Same and Different Phonemes   When presented with ten spoken words of two and three phonemes, the student will indicate which sounds are the same and which sounds are different, using colored blocks as indicators, with 80% accuracy on five of five trials (teacher says *pet* and student pushes forward three different-colored blocks; teachers says *Mom* and student pushes forward two blocks of same color and one of different, "m" = red, "o" = white, "m" = red).

Segment Syllables   When presented with ten spoken (one-syllable) words, the student will segment initial sound (onset) from remaining sound (rime) with 80% accuracy on five of five trials (teacher says *lake* and student says "l-ake"; teacher says *pat* and student says "p-at," etc.).

Blend Syllables   When presented with ten spoken, segmented, one-syllable words, the student will blend the parts into a whole with 80% accuracy on five of five trials (teacher says, "p-in," student says *pin*; teacher says "r-am," student says *ram*; teacher says "t-ake," student says *take*, etc.).

Rhyme   When presented with ten pairs of spoken, one-syllable words, the student will identify whether the pair of words rhyme or do not rhyme with 80% accuracy, on five of five trials (teacher says *pat-hat*, student says yes; teacher says *top-boy*, student says no, etc.).

Segment Words into Syllables   When presented with words of one to three syllables, the student will indicate the number of syllables heard by clapping for each syllable with 80% accuracy for five of five trials (teacher says *football*, student claps twice; teacher says *rainbow*, student claps twice; teacher says *dog*, student claps once, etc.).

Blend Words   When presented with ten spoken words, of one to three syllables, segmented into sylla-

bles, the student will say the word with 80% accuracy on five of five trials (teacher says "help"-"ful," student says *helpful*; teacher says "foot"-"ball," student says *football*; teacher says "Nin"-"ten"-"do," student says *Nintendo*, etc.).

Distinguish Word from Other Words in Spoken Language   When presented with ten target words in ten separate sentences, the student will indicate when she hears the target word with 80% accuracy on five of five trials (target word is *bark*; teacher says "I heard the dog bark and bark." Student indicates hearing *bark* two times).

Objectives for Print Knowledge

Letter Names   Given all 52 letters (upper and lower case, randomly ordered in a typical print style), the student will name each with 100% accuracy, on five of five trials.

Sentence Boundaries   When shown pre-primer or primer text with conventional sentence/paragraph format, the student will identify sentence boundaries with 100% accuracy for ten or more sentences on five of five trials.

Word Length   When shown five one-syllable words and five three-syllable words, the student will identify short words and long words with 100% accuracy on five of five trials.

Word Boundaries   Given sentences in pre-primer or primer text in conventional sentence/paragraph format, the student will identify word boundaries (space between words) with 100% accuracy.

Book Length   When shown five very short books and five long books (that have been previously read to the student), the student will indicate with 100% accuracy which books are short and which books are long.

Page Conventions and Book Conventions   Given a familiar memorized book, the student will pretend-read

- holding the book upright
- from front to back

- page by page
- left to right per column
- top to bottom per column

with 100% accuracy, five of five trials.

Logos/Signs   Student will spontaneously recognize familiar logos or signs in the environment with 100% accuracy (fast-food restaurants, grocery stores, favorite foods, restrooms); or, given 20 Polaroid pictures of familiar logos or signs in the environment, the student will name places and items the pictures represent with 100% accuracy.

These objectives may need to be modified depending on the prior knowledge of the student. Because these skills are so basic, it can be assumed that the student will need considerable teacher assistance (Mason, Herman & Au, 1990). Therefore, the sequence of instruction is often more one of assistance (conditions) than content (see Chapter 17, p. 416). Review the techniques you used to recognize the missing skills and then include them within the condition portion of the objectives where called upon by the {braces}. For example, the content specified in "sentence boundaries" would change depending on the results noted on the status sheet. The condition "during pseudo-reading exercises" is drawn from notes taken during the testing:

> "{During pseudo-reading exercises with the teacher} the student will identify (point to) {sentence boundaries} with {100% accuracy}."

By recombining targeted content and relevant levels of assistance, you will produce objective lists that reflect the student's instructional needs.

See the note on criteria under the Score Interpretation guidelines (p. 233). If the student is below first-grade level, insert 70% into the braces; if the student is above first-grade level, use 100%. You may prefer to sample some successful students at each grade level to verify these criteria, as different approaches to beginning reading instruction will likely result in different proficiency patterns. Sampling can also establish expectations for intermediate dates through first grade.

The procedures for teaching awareness of print and sound are the same as the procedures we recommended for evaluating that awareness. Rather than repeat them here, we simply refer you back to those techniques you used to decide if a particular phonological or print skill required instruction. However, we will give you some advise about teaching for awareness of print and sound.

Phonetic segmentation is an essential skill more basic than recalling sound-letter or sound-cluster correspondence (Ball & Blachman, 1991; Daneman & Stainton, 1991). With phonetic segmentation, students determine the presence, boundaries, and number of sounds (phonemes) in a word (Griffith & Olson, 1992; Hoogeveen, Birkhoff, Smeets, Lancioni & Boelens, 1989). Phonemic segmentation is not syllabication. In a syllabication task, students would tell how many syllables there are in a word. In a phonemic segmentation task, they would isolate the phonemes "m-a-n" in order to demonstrate that they can conceptualize and manipulate phonemes. In the word *man* there is one syllable but three distinct phonemes.

You may have noticed that we included logos and signs on our content list for preliminary print knowledge. We actually wrote a procedure for assessing it but decided not to include it in the text for the following reason: While there is a highly positive correlation between kids who notice that signs and logos carry messages and kids who learn to read, we do not think the evidence is as clear that taking instructional time to teach signs will lead to learning to read sooner (in fact we suspect the converse—that learning to read will help the student with logos). Teachers can teach that print carries meaning in a variety of ways without making up flashcards to advertise McDonald's.

Mixed results have been reported on the benefits of teaching at the phoneme level (Adams, 1990; Haskell, Foorman & Swank, 1992). Consequently, we include the content of phoneme blending and segmentation with caution and encourage the reader to follow the research. Current research does tell us that good readers have advanced phoneme skills.

As authors, we are concerned that by including the suggestion that some students be taught "preliminary print knowledge" and "enabling phonemic knowledge" we may promote inappropriate instruction. So here is what we don't want to see: a child in a room with no books where she is required to master choosing same and different letter sounds before anyone will read a story to her. Here is what we *do* want: hours of interactive reading and writing activities infused with explanations, questions, and activities designed to focus the student on preliminary print and phonological skills. These skills are best taught explicitly, but within the context of reading, listening, and conversational routines.

Many of the techniques for teaching beginning-reading skills can take the form of games, including the learning of nursery rhymes and songs (Thompson & Majsterek, 1992). Once the student has learned a song, you can sing it together and then omit words for the student to fill in. One teacher we know uses the methods we recommended for assessing phonological knowledge to teach it. He does this across the school day on the way to recess, in the lunchroom, waiting for the bus, at the drinking fountain, as well as in the classroom. Often these teaching activities come in the form of word games. For example, you can introduce a procedure as an integrated activity in a daily routine ("I have some secret words. Can you guess what they are? Listen: 't-ake?' ") (O'Connor, 1992).

Teaching Recommendation 4: Build Fluency Rate

Students who are accurate but slow may know a particular reading strategy but not employ it efficiently because it has not been learned to fluency (Carver, 1992). Lessons designed to build fluency typically use rapid-paced drill and practice with material on which the student is at least 90% accurate. During these lessons, the student is reinforced for rapid responding and daily improvement in fluency. Errors are typically viewed as rate-induced and are ignored to the extent that error correction procedures are not used. (Feedback may be given after the student reads the passage.)

One popular technique for building oral-decoding rate, suggested by Carnine and colleagues (1990), is summarized here:

1. Select a passage on which the student is accurate.

2. Instruct the student to read for one minute as quickly and as accurately as possible and then note the student's rate (60 words per minute).

3. Set a target rate for the passage that is 20% to 40% above the initial rate of the student (60 wpm × .40 = 24 and 24 + 60 = 84 wpm).

4. Mark the target in the student's book and have

her reread the selection, just as before (step 2), as many times as necessary to reach the target.

5. Continue this procedure on various selections until the student's average rate reaches the criterion for her grade level (and accuracy is maintained).

It is important to remember that you are building fluency, not having a race, when you conduct rate-building lessons. If you look up fluency in the dictionary you'll find that it mentions *effortless* and *laid back* as well as speedy. The fact is the rate criteria in Exhibit 11.3* were not all that high, and a student can easily reach them without sacrificing the smooth, flowing patterns that we associate with competent performance. Try to promote ease of reading at the same time you are promoting speed.

In addition to the suggestions above, Carver (1992) recommends the following:

> Don't worry about the student "talking to herself" (reading subvocally).
>
> Have the student read every word.
>
> When the student slows down, assume it is because the vocabulary or concepts are unfamiliar.
>
> Don't encourage the student to skip unimportant words.
>
> Have the student read relatively easy material often to practice and maintain rate.

Teaching Recommendation 5: Correct Error Patterns

Error patterns are learned. In fact different forms of reading instruction, by emphasizing code or meaning, frequently lead to different error patterns (Johnson & Baumann, 1984).

When working with a student who clearly illustrates a pattern of decoding errors, consider immediately implementing a program for that pattern. Students whose performance shows evidence of consistent error patterns are typically beyond initial decoding instruction, but have learned some erroneous strategies for decoding passages. These students are not *tabula rasa* (blank slates). They are employing, often automatically, strategies they have practiced for years. Sometimes corrective readers have a habit of making certain errors that they are actually skilled enough to avoid. Often these error patterns can be recognized and attacked directly.

Most students take a balanced approach to reading (code and context), but some may rely too heavily on only one kind of information as they read. There are two reasons why problem readers become over-dependent on one kind of information: (1) their skills with one kind are so weak that they must compensate, or (2) past instruction so heavily emphasized one kind of information that the student automatically employs only those strategies. Because either explanation can account for the same error patterns, it is important to gather information to determine which reason best explains a student's difficulty. Ideally, you should collect data continually during a period of instruction to make this determination.

There are two approaches to correcting error patterns: (1) break bad decoding habits, or (2) correct over-reliance on one pattern.

Direct Intervention on Bad Reading Habits

This technique isn't highly theoretical—just a straight-forward set of steps.

1. Identify the error pattern.

2. Count the occurrence of the error pattern per 100 words and chart it.

3. Be sure the student knows how to recognize and count the same error pattern (listening to a tape of her decoding is useful here).

4. Provide feedback on the occurrence of the error pattern.

5. Reinforce the student for decreasing the number of errors or increasing self-corrections.

6. If the student does not begin to decrease the error pattern in a few days, have her work on one of the following instructional exercises. Some of these exercises are taken from Lovitt's *Tactics for Teaching* (1984).
   - Have the student listen to tapes of herself decoding while you mark (or correct) errors that affect meaning.
   - When errors violate meaning, show the student how the words before and after the error can be used to help figure it out.
   - As the student listens to her taped decoding,

show how errors do not convey the message of the text. Point out how errors are syntactically wrong, redundant, superfluous, or misleading.
- Ask the student to explain how each error might hurt understanding of the text.
- Read in unison with the student or have her check the decoding of other students.
- Make up sentences for the student to read in which all words are very easy except for words typically missed.
- Put problematic words in short phrases on flashcards and drill the student.
- If the student is decoding at an appropriate level and comprehension seems adequate, tell her that it isn't necessary to read each word perfectly. Tell her simply to attempt the word and then use context to see if the attempt was correct.
- Accentuate punctuation marks by coloring them, or over-correct by having the student pause a set time (a count of 5) every time there is any punctuation mark.

Correct Over-Reliance on One Type of Information

When direct instruction on bad decoding habits does not seem to work, it may be that the student is actually over-reliant on either code information or context information. In these cases, corrective instruction should follow this sequence:

1. Identify an error.

2. Recognize the kind of information (code or context) on which the student is relying. To do this, answer the following questions about the types of errors made by the student during oral decoding:
   - Are errors that do not make sense real words?
   - Do errors on portions of words sound or look dissimilar to the stimulus word?
   - Do inserted words make sense in the sentence?
   - Is the student unwilling to attempt words or to guess?
   - Does the student omit words containing graphemes read correctly in other words?
   - Does the student omit function words (of, the, it, a)?
   - Does the student hesitate on short, familiar words as well as on longer ones?

- Does the student repeat several of the words preceding a difficult word?
- Does the student repeat only words and not portions of words?
- Does the student correct only errors that affect passage meaning?

Yes answers indicate errors that result from reliance on context information; no answers indicate errors that result from reliance on code information. If the yes and no answers are about evenly distributed, assume the student is not over-reliant and use an intensified-balanced approach of code and context (see Teaching Recommendation 1). If over-reliance is evident, first decide which specific skills need to be addressed and then employ the following recommendations:

1. Tell the student that she has made an error.
2. Show how the erroneous strategy led to the error.
3. Show how the appropriate use of the other (nondominant) kind of information would have led to correct decoding.
4. Test the student's skill at using this other kind of information.
5. Provide practice to make the use of the appropriate information automatic.
6. Throughout the process, analyze the text to determine if there are adequate opportunities to use appropriate information. Some text may contain only one or two opportunities every 200 to 300 words. To practice, more opportunities will be needed.

Teaching Recommendation 6: Teach Self-Monitoring

Various authors have noted that successful students routinely self-correct from 30% to 50% of meaning-violating errors (Clay, 1985). We have noted that, when given a pep talk like the one described in Decoding SLP 3a, most kids will self-correct *at least* 50% of meaning-violating errors. When given SLP 3b (the table-tapping test), successful readers will correct almost every error. Therefore, if your student is not attending to errors, she is reading very differently than a successful reader would read. Go to Chapter 10 and employ Teaching Recommendation 6: Self-Monitoring.

Teaching Recommendation 7: Teach Active and Reflective Reading

See Teaching Recommendation 1 for Active Reading in Chapter 10, p. 215.

Summary

Reading is an interactive process, and there is some validity to concerns that subdividing such a process distorts it. However, our inability to write about everything at the same time, and the considerable body of evidence demonstrating that decoding is important, have led us to separate the discussions in Chapters 10 and 11. *That doesn't mean that they should be separate within instruction.*

This chapter has reviewed issues relative to decoding as a curriculum domain and presented tactics for evaluating and teaching knowledge in that domain. You will need to consider all the guidelines within this chapter and those in Chapter 10 in order for these tactics to be useful. You will also need to do the exercises in the workbook in order to become familiar with the multiple processes and decision points outlined in the reading chapters.

Chapter 12 / Language

One of the lessons of history is that nothing is often a good thing to do and always a clever thing to say.

—Ariel and Will Durant

Focus: Language

This chapter provides an introduction to oral-language evaluation. As was pointed out in Chapter 3, language is the exclusive tool for obtaining knowledge, for communication, and for thought. Additionally, as cognitive processes become both more complex and more abstract, language plays an increasingly important role in the way we learn. Consequently, children with language problems are often unable to fully benefit from school programs. Such children have difficulty gaining information from both verbal and printed messages. They may also have problems demonstrating what they know, and in expressing the need for help.

There are a number of theoretical bases from which to assess language, but this chapter includes neither an in-depth discussion nor a resolution of these theoretical bases. Nor does it focus on the evaluation of the various processes theorists believe children use to understand and produce language. Instead, this chapter describes assessment procedures that will enable you to decide what to teach mildly disabled/remedial students with functional language problems, and what you should teach students with limited English proficiency (LEP).

The Content of Language

The four general areas of language are:

- Syntax and morphology
- Semantics
- Pragmatics—communication
- Phonology, voice, and fluency

This chapter is limited to a discussion of syntax, semantics, and pragmatics. Because of space limitations we will not cover phonology.

As in other fields, the first step in language assessment is to decide what to evaluate. The major components of syntax, semantics, and pragmatics are presented in Exhibit 12.1. The Exhibit is a compilation of elements most frequently noted as essential by language specialists. Throughout this chapter, Exhibit 12.1* will serve as the primary reference in this chapter—so let's take a look at it now. Exhibit 12.1 shows things that students must have the skills to do—but they are not necessarily things that students need to know about. This means that while competent speakers may not have the skills to state the syntactical rules that govern word order, they use the rules correctly.

The content included in Exhibit 12.1 is most likely appropriate for school-age children who have moderate language problems. It would need to be extended downward to accommodate children with severe language problems. The sequence of the content is appropriate for children with typical language development, as well as for children with language delays. (Children with typical language development would include those who are acquiring English as a second language.) Most children with language delays follow the common sequence of language development followed by other students; they just do it more slowly (Hallahan & Kauffman, 1986; Wiig & Semel, 1984). Since it often is not known whether a specific set of language skills must be learned in a particular sequence, the educational differences between children with language delays and children with more complex language disorders may not be significant.

The content of Exhibit 12.1 is not necessarily arranged in prerequisite order. So don't assume that because a child passes a higher-level skill he has mastered all lower-level skills. In general, however, skills with higher numbers are more complex than skills with lower numbers.

Exhibit 12.1 includes both receptive and expressive

Exhibit 12.1   Content Analysis of Language Domains

I Syntax/Morphology	II Semantics/Vocabulary	III Pragmatics
A. Syntax/Morphology	A. Basic Vocabulary	A. One-Way Communication
1. Noun Phrase/Verb Phrase	1. Body Parts	1. Expresses Wants
2. Regular Plurals	2. Clothing	2. Expresses Opinions
3. Subject Pronouns	3. Classroom Objects	3. Expresses Feelings
4. Prepositional Phrases	4. Action Verbs	4. Expresses Values
5. Adjectives	5. Verb Tasks	5. Follows Directions
6. Interrogative Reversals	6. Animals and Insects	6. Ask Questions
7. Object Pronouns	7. Outdoor Words	7. Narrates Event
8. Negatives	8. Family Members	8. States Main Idea
9. Verb *be* Auxiliary	9. Home Objects	9. Sequences Events
10. Verb *be* Copula	10. Meals	10. Subordinates Details
11. Infinitives	11. Food and Drink	11. Summarizes
12. Determiners	12. Colors	12. Describes
13. Conjunction *and*	13. Adverbs	13. Compares and Contrasts
14. Possessives	14. Occupations	14. Gives Instructions
15. Noun/Verb Agreement	15. Community	15. Explains
16. Comparatives	16. Grooming Objects	B. Two-Way Communication
17. *Wh-* Questions	17. Vehicles	1. Considers the Listener
18. Past Tense	18. Money	2. Formulates Messages
19. Future Aspect	19. Gender	3. Participates in Discussions
20. Irregular Plurals	20. School	4. Uses Persuasion
21. Forms of *do*	21. Playthings	5. Resolves Differences
22. Auxiliaries	22. Containers	6. Identifies Speaker's Biases
23. Derivational Endings	23. Days of the Week	7. Identifies Speaker's Assumptions
24. Reflexive Pronouns	24. Months	8. Formulates Conclusions
25. Qualifiers	25. Emotions	C. Nonverbal Communication
26. Conjunctions *and, but, or*	26. Numbers	1. Gestures
27. Conjunctions	27. Celebrations and Holidays	2. Proximity
28. Indirect and Direct Objects	28. Spatial Concepts	3. Position
29. Adverbs	29. Quantitative Concepts	4. Expression
30. Infinitives with Subject	30. Temporal Concepts	5. Eye Contact
31. Participles	31. Shapes	D. Executive Function
32. Gerunds	32. Greetings and Polite Terms	1. Develops Intent
33. Passive Voice	33. Opposites	2. Plans
34. Complex Verb Forms	34. Materials	3. Monitors
35. Relative Adverb Clauses	35. Music	4. Identifies Problems
36. Relative Pronoun Clauses	36. Tools	5. Analyses Problems
37. Complex Conjunctions	37. Categories	6. Recognizes Needed Assistance
	38. Verbs of the Senses	7. Recognizes Solutions
	B. Topical Vocabulary	8. Seeks Help
	1. Reading Material Vocabulary	9. Adjusts Message
	2. Content Area Vocabulary	10. Uses Alternative Messages
	3. Idioms/Figurative Language	11. Incorporates New Language Skills
	4. Multiple Meaning of Words	12. Attributes Events
	5. Influence of Context on Meaning	13. Reflects
		14. Speculates
		15. Regulates
		16. Repairs Communications

tasks. *Receptive tasks* are those in which students identify or select answers. *Expressive tasks* are those in which students produce a verbal or written response.

The criteria for acceptable performance (CAP) is not listed within the table because information relating to the CAP for language skills is not available. However, there is a standard for language use that has been established by general consent and is universally recognized. That standard is conventional adult speech. Adult speakers of Standard English virtually never say such things as "I goed there," "Her and him are coming," "The boys is playing," "She gots a big dog," or "I out the window saw them." Therefore, the criteria for all skills approaches 100% accuracy. This means that even a few errors indicate a need for specific-level assessment.

The content of language, particularly that of syntax, tends to unnerve some evaluators. Evoy (1992) has suggested a logical analogy that may clear up some of the complexity represented in Exhibit 12.1. According to Evoy, sweeping variations of speech and language are like the assortment of colors we see painted around us. These distinct shades, hues, and tones are the result of mixing only three primary pigments—just as the messages we send through language result from a blend of semantics, syntax, and pragmatics.

Syntax and Morphology

Syntax is the rule system that governs word order in sentences. While there are many acceptable arrangements of words in English sentences, some arrangements are not acceptable. For example, we could say "The ball is bouncing," "Bouncing is the ball," "Ball bouncing." However, we would not say "Ball the is bouncing." English rules of syntax do not permit this arrangement of nouns and verbs (the reference for combining noun phrases and verb phrases is shown in Exhibit 12.1,* column I, number 1).

Morphology is a subset of syntax that depends on a particular type of semantic knowledge. Basic units of meaning within English words are called *morphemes* (see Chapter 14, p. 311), and they will be discussed in greater depth under the heading of semantics/vocabulary. However, there is a the rule system that governs how to combine morphemes to make words; it is called *morphology* and it is part of syntax. "Free" morphemes stand alone; they are often referred to as *root words*. Examples of free morphemes are *talk, group,* and *tie*. There are also "bound" morphemes, which

cannot stand alone. These are the affixes we add to the beginning or ending of words to modify the meaning. Examples of bound morphemes are -s, -er, -ed, -ing, -un, -al, and -sur. When the morpheme *talk* is changed to mean *a person who talks*, the morpheme *-er* is added to make the word *talker*. When we want to show the past tense of talk we add the morpheme *-ed*. *Talk* is a free morpheme; *-er* and *-ed* are bound morphemes. Syntax guides how morphemes may be combined to form words and to alter meaning.

Teachers must have knowledge of the syntactic structure of the English language to determine what a child knows how to use and what he has not yet mastered. On first observation, it may appear that there are an infinite variety of types of sentences one can produce using English syntactic structures. While there is an infinite variety of ideas to express, actually there is a finite number of structures speakers use to produce sentences. These structures are combined to produce basic sentences at lower levels of language functioning. At higher levels of language functioning, speakers expand basic sentence patterns to produce more complex sentences using syntax to modify, coordinate, substitute, and subordinate. The basic sentence "The girl ran" has been expanded in Exhibit 12.2 to illustrate the use of additional syntactic structures. "The girl ran" is correct. But if a student only communicated using such simple structures we would be concerned about his sophistication with language.

The syntactic structures listed in Exhibit 12.1 are described in Exhibit 12.3. Few of us have committed those structures to memory, so Exhibit 12.3 can be a helpful reference.

The syntactic structures listed in Exhibits 12.1* and 12.3 can be combined with behavior and conditions to form tables of specifications. For example, the behaviors listed in the table of specifications for syntactic structures (Exhibit 12.4*) are: (a) imitates sentences, (b) produces sentences with prompts or in controlled settings, and (c) produces spontaneous sentences. When the content and behavior are combined, they form tasks. When *pronoun* is the content and *imitates* is the behavior, the task requires the kid to "imitate sentences that include pronouns.'" (There is evidence to support the idea that a child's skill at imitation is closely related to his current level of linguistic competence and to his comprehension of utterances. Modeling with imitation is a valuable language training procedure for children with language problems [James, 1990]).

Exhibit 12.2   The Expansion of a Sentence Using Additional Syntactic Structures (Prepared by John Freeman)

Sentence	Additional Syntactic Structure
The girl ran.	
The sanguine girl ran.	Adjective
The sanguine girl ran quickly.	Adverb
The sanguine girl ran up the hill quickly.	Prepositional phrase
The sanguine girl, who wore the wild shoes, ran up the hill quickly.	Relative pronoun clause
The sanguine girl, who wore the wild shoes, ran up the hill quickly, but another runner won the race.	Conjunction coordinating two independent clauses
The sanguine girl, who wore the wild shoes, ran up the hill quickly, but another runner won the race because she was in better shape.	Relative adverb clause

Not only are the rules of syntax and morphology consistent within a language, but the chronology or sequence in which typical learners acquire these rules is predictable. For a detailed discussion of syntax and morphology, we encourage you to read Wiig, Freedman, and Secord (1992) and James (1990).

Semantics

Semantics is the study of meaning within a language. It includes:

- Meaning of morphographs
- Meaning of single words and word combinations
- Multiple meaning of simple words
- Figurative language
- Influence of content and structure on meaning

Semantic skill is more than definitions. It is also knowledge and application of the constraints meaning imposes on the ways words are combined. English syntax permits "The book reads the child." However, *semantic* rules (meaning rules) preclude that word combination. Books do not read, so the ways the word *book* may be used in a sentence are constrained by semantics.

A list of vocabulary categories was suggested in Exhibit 12.1. This listing is representative of words commonly used by children in the early stages of language development. In addition to basic vocabulary, there are words that have immediate utility for the child, as well as content (specific vocabulary) that is necessary for learning about particular topics. These words fall into the second subdomain of vocabulary: "Advanced." The need to acquire vocabulary in particular content areas is discussed in Chapter 17 as part of task-related knowledge.

Semantics takes into account meaning, underlying concepts, and the relationship of words and sentences to contexts and ideas. *Vocabulary,* the meanings of individual words, is a component of semantics. Vocabulary and semantic content are unlike the content for syntactic structures. Whereas there is a finite number of syntactic structures commonly used in English, the individual words and the contexts in which they are used are limitless. One can continue learning and using new vocabulary and developing new meanings for previously learned words throughout life. A person's knowledge of words is so important that it has been suggested that "working memory capacity" (see Chapter 2) is really nothing more than word knowledge (Engle, Nations & Cantor, 1990).

Pragmatics

Children and adults use language for a reason—to communicate. Language is used to affect the behavior and attitudes of others and to regulate activities and attention. These functions are referred to as *pragmatics.* The goal of pragmatics instruction is to increase the child's repertoire of communication strategies for use in critical communication situations.

A critical aspect of pragmatics is code or style

Exhibit 12.3 Explanations of Syntactic Structures (Prepared by John Freeman)

Syntactic Structures	Purpose/Function	Example(s)	Sample Error(s)
1. Noun/Noun phrase	Identifies person, place, thing, or idea to act or be acted upon.	Girl, the girl, the wonderful girl, the girl with the wild shoes . . .	Errors for the noun/noun phrase, verb/verb phrase generally occur through omission or a consistent lack of production.
Verb/Verb phrase	Describes the action or state of being for the noun phrase.	runs, runs fast, runs with abandon, lightly runs over the hill . . .	
2. Regular plurals	An added -s to nouns. Indicates more than one	Boys, girls, etc.	Many girl, Three boy
3. Subject pronouns	Substitutes for nouns which act as subjects or predicate nouns.	I, you, he, she, it, we, you, they play.	It hit he. The car ran over he.
4. Prepositional phrases	Consist of a preposition and a noun or pronoun object. Act as adjectives or adverbs.	The boy went *around the bush.* The girl *in the new car.*	Girl go town. Boy sit chair.
5. Adjectives	Modify nouns. Can be single words or phrases.	The *quiet* cat, The dog is *silent.*, the horse *with the spots*	The dog silent, cat quiet
6. Interrogative reversal form for questions	The subject of the question, comes between the helping verb and the main verb	Could I do that?	I could do that?
7. Object pronouns	Receive the action of the verb or follow prepositions as objects.	She saw *him* with *her.*	Him walked there. It's me.
8. Negatives	Serve to negate an action or description	*not* green, could*n't*, *never* would, *nobody*, *hardly*	Double negatives: don't never, hardly nobody, no-one doesn't
9. Verb *to be* as a helping verb	am, is, are, was, were, be, been	has been seen, is looking, was peering	She looking, Boy peering
10. Verb *to be* as a linking verb	Links a predicate noun or predicate adjective to its subject.	The girl is a *genius.* The boy was *smart*	That girl big. This boy large.
11. Infinitives	*to* plus the present tense of a verb.	The boy wants *to study.* The girl likes *to learn.*	The girl wantsa learn. The boy likesoo study.
12. Determiners	Precede nouns.	a, an, the, that, this, these, those. *This* type, *Those* types	This kinds, Those kind
13. Coordinating conjunctions	Join or connect words and/or phrases	and, but, or, nor, for, yet	The girl boy run jump.
14. Possessive nouns and pronouns	Establish possession or ownership	Singular possessive nouns add an 's, plurals add an s'. Possessive pronouns-my, your, his, our, his, her, etc.	The *girls* shoes, The *boy* eyes
15. Noun/Verb agreement	A singular subject (noun) agrees with a verb which ends in s in the present tense.	The girl *considers.* The boy *jumps.*	There *goes* the *boys.* The *girl run* to the store. There*'s* is two of them.
16. Comparatives and superlatives	Adjectives which imply comparisons add 'er or 'est.	large, larger, largest good, better, best	She's the smartest of the two. He's more smarter.
17. Questions beginning with an interrogative pronoun.	Wh- pronouns used to set up a question	Who, what, when, where, why, which, etc.	Subject does not use the *wh*-structure to begin questions.
18. Past tense of the verb	Regular verbs add -ed to form the past tense. Irregular verbs take their own forms in the past tense.	jump*ed*, look*ed*, jerk*ed* see/*saw*, eat/*ate*, think/*thought*	Yesterday, the girl look. The boy thinked she eated it.
19. Future aspect	Helping verbs that indicate an action in the future.	may, can, going to, will, should	It happen tomorrow. She do it later.
20. Irregular plurals	Nouns which take their own forms for the plural	Man/*men,* deer/*deer,* mouse/*mice*	mans, deers, mouses
21. Forms of *do*	*Do* is an irregular verb which is often misused.	I/we/you/they *do,* he/she/it *does.* Past tense-*did.* have/has/had *done*	She *done* it. He has *did* it.
22. Auxiliaries (Helping verbs)	Add tense or intention to the action verb	has, have, had, would, should, could, might, must, ought, will, shall	Omission: She _____ do it if she could.
23. Derivational endings which change verbs to nouns	-or, -er, -ist, -ian when added to verbs indicate that the action is carried out by a noun	creat-or, operat-er, pian-ist, compan-ion	Omission
24. Reflexive pronouns	Reflect back to and intensify a noun in the sentence	myself, yourself, him-her-it-self, ourselves, yourselves, themselves	We did it *ourself.* The girls took care of *theirselves.* The boys watched *themself.*

(continued)

Exhibit 12.3 Explanations of Syntactic Structures (Prepared by John Freeman) (continued)

Syntactic Structures	Purpose/Function	Example(s)	Sample Error(s)
25. Qualifiers	Added to verbs to indicate to what extent or under which conditions the action is carried out.	very, much, more, most, less, least, too, so, quite, almost, just, little, somewhat, anyway	Omission. Overuse: So . . . So . . . So, anyway.
26. Coordinating conjunctions	Join clauses or simple sentences.	and, but, or, nor, for, yet	Omission: Production of short, choppy sentences. Overuse: Production of run-on sentences.
27. Conjunctions commonly used to coordinate clauses	Relate two clauses or simple sentences.	after, before, because, if, since, so	Omission: Short, choppy sentences. Overuse: cuz . . . cuz . . . etc.
28. Indirect and direct objects	Receive the action of the verb (Direct object-DO). Receive the DO (Indirect object-IO).	She hit the *ball* (DO). He gave the *girl* (IO) the cake.	Ommission
29. Adverbs	Modify verbs, adjectives, and other adverbs.	*Sometimes* he wins. She felt *really* good. I do *much* less.	She felt *real* good. I want to go, *to.*
30. Infinitives with subjects	Add a noun or pronoun to an infinitive=an infinitive phrase.	The boy wants *her to play.*	The girl wants him play.
31. Participles	Formed by adding -ed or -ing to verbs. Precede nouns and serve as adjectives.	She felt better after *running* laps.	Omission
32. Gerunds	Nouns formed by adding -ing to verbs.	*Running* is fun.	Omission
33. Passive voice	Occurs when the subject/noun is acted upon by the verb.	The boy was seen in her company.	Omission. Overuse: Use of the passive voice is often discouraged in written communication.
34. Complex verb forms-multiple auxiliaries	Usually indicate tense and intention.	He *would have been teased* if he had gone.	Omission
35. Relative adverb clauses	Clauses usually preceded by where, why or when, which modify the verb in the sentence.	The boy ran *when he was chased.*	Omission
36. Relative pronoun clauses	Clauses usually preceded by which, that or who, which act as adjectives in the sentence.	The boy, *who was chased,* ran away.	Omission or agreement problems- The boy *that*
37. Complex or subordinating conjunctions	Used to set up a complex relationship between clauses in a sentence.	*While* the girl lifted weights, the boy skied. When, as if, where, until, before, after, etc.	A clause beginning with a complex conjunction requires an independent clause to complete its action (i.e. make it a complete sentence). Errors often occur when the action in the complex sentence is left incomplete. *While the girl was lifting weights . . .*

switching. Competent language users adjust their presentations according to the characteristics of the person to whom they are speaking (James, 1990). To put it simply, most people speak differently in church on Sunday morning than they do at a bar on Saturday night. Those who don't—no matter to which place they fail to adjust—are apt to be considered inappropriate. However, style switching routinely occurs across less extreme boundaries. For example, in a social gathering some individual's tone and word choice may be modified considerably by the simple presence of a wedding ring.

Most discussions of pragmatics also address skills linked to understanding and applying shifts between the roles of speaker and listener. These skills have verbal and nonverbal components. Some nonverbal components are physical proximity, gestures, and eye contact (Banbury & Hebert, 1992). Verbal components include turn taking, responding, and voice control. (Good speakers use their voices to influence outcomes and good listeners interpret the intent not only of words but also of intonation and volume.) In Exhibit 12.1, column 3, notice that skills associated with the role of listening and being responsive to others are summarized under part B, "two-way communication."

Exhibit 12.4*   *A Table of Specifications for Language Syntactic Structures*

Student's Name _____

Evaluator's Name _____

Date _____

	By Imitation	Produces With Prompts or in Controlled Situations	Spontaneous
1. Noun phrase/verb phrase			
2. Regular plurals			
3. Subject pronouns			
4. Prepositional phrases			
5. Adjectives			
6. Interrogative reversals			
7. Object pronouns			
8. Negatives			
9. Verb *be* auxiliary			
10. Verb *be* copula			
11. Infinitives			
12. Determiners			
13. Conjunction *and*			
14. Possessives			
15. Noun/verb agreement			
16. Comparatives			
17. *Wh-* questions			
18. Past tense			
19. Future aspect			
20. Irregular plurals			
21. Forms of *do*			
22. Auxiliaries			
23. Derivational endings			
24. Reflexive pronouns			
25. Qualifiers			
26. Conjunctions *and, but, or*			
27. Conjunctions			
28. Indirect and direct objects			
29. Adverbs			
30. Infinitives with subject			
31. Participles			
32. Gerunds			
33. Passive voice			
34. Complex verb forms			
35. Relative adverb clauses			
36. Relative pronoun clauses			
37. Complex conjunctions			

While pragmatics are typically thought of as the functions of language between two or more people, pragmatics can also be conceptualized in an "executive-control" (see Chapter 2) framework of inner language or thinking. The executive function of language serves to cue or prompt action, to coordinate information, to question, to control, to problem solve, and to mediate both thought and action.

The Social Context of Language

The use of language occurs in the context of four variables (Wells, 1973; Wiig & Semel, 1984):

- Characteristics of participant's sex, age, status
- Setting/situation for exchange (time and place)
- Topic of communication
- Goal, task, or intent of speaker(s)

Language has a social framework that teachers must understand if they are going to adapt instruction for individual learners (Gruenewald & Pollack, 1990). In a social framework, the function of language is to initiate and sustain interaction. A kid's language development depends, in part, on his involvement with this linguistic environment. Therefore, a person's language is shaped by the extent to which the people around him are willing to communicate with him, to respond to what he says, to encourage him by their understanding, and to allow him to learn to modify and expand his language. Family members, other adults, TV, and peers all play an important role in the child's social linguistic environment, as do teachers, books, and computers.

Social Rules

The child's understanding of sociolinguistic rules is another important aspect of language. Students who do not know the social rules of language usage may appear rude or insubordinate (Iglesias, 1985; Saville-Troike, 1976). This applies to all elements of language, not just to verbal usage. For example, when the teacher says "Would you like to do your spelling now?" the child who understands the sociolinguistic rules (but does not want to do the assignment) could say "Can I do it later?" or just sharpen his pencil with great enthusiasm. A child who does not understand sociolinguistic rules might just say *no* and be considered unresponsive or rude. Some children may not participate (people surmise they are shy) when the social conditions they're accustomed to are missing (Philips, 1970).

Second-Language Learners

Bilingual conflicts were once cited as a cause of childhood language impairments. However it is now recognized that this need not be the case. Typical youngsters seem to benefit from rich multilingual

Students whose first language is not English should not be considered disabled, although they may be "handicapped" by a nonsupportive classroom environment.

environments and do not suffer from opportunities to experience more than one language, as long as these various languages are appropriately presented. When children from multilingual environments have communication disorders, another factor is probably operating.

Today in the United States there is a rapidly growing number of school-age children who are not proficient in English. They have a primary home language other than English or a dialect that is significantly different from the language used in classroom settings. In California, for example, there has been a 52% increase of language-minority students in the last five years! Language minorities represent 31% of the K–12 students in that state (California Department of Education, 1991). While these kids are not disabled, their language differences place them at risk for school failure. Of the students who have a dialect or a primary home language other than English, 75% (or 2.5 million) may have language differences great enough to interfere with their school performance (National Coalition of Advocates for Students, 1985). This diversity could be parlayed into a rich foundation on which to base instruction. Unfortunately, it is estimated that in two-thirds of classrooms, instruction is not differentiated to accommodate linguistic differences (U.S. Department of Education, 1984). Approximately 25% of the classrooms in America serve students with limited English proficiency (LEP) and this percentage is growing. But consider this: In 1985 less than 4% of the teachers in the United States indicated that they had any training that would prepare them to differentiate instruction for LEP students (National Coalition of Advocates for Students, 1985). In California, as of 1990, there were available positions for 22,365 bilingual/cross-culture teachers and 14,332 LEP teachers. However, only 358 teachers were credentialed in bilingual education from 1988 to 1989 in California (California Department of Education, 1991). This shortage highlights a long overdue need to reassess the role and qualifications of all school professionals (Valdez, 1986).

An LEP child may use nonstandard English codes that are considered inappropriate in social communications outside his linguistic community. The child's nonstandard language code could include syntax, vocabulary, pragmatics, or even phonology different from that of standard English. It is important to recognize that these codes, while different, are *legitimate*. They are not deficient. Still, the child with competence in the code used in his own environment may also need instruction and practice in Standard English as an alternate language code (Harris, 1991).

Note: We recognize that by juxtaposing a discussion of LEP students with a discussion of language-disabled students, we risk incurring the disapproval of professionals in the fields of bilingual instruction and ESL, proponents of nonstandard English, and special educators. However, it is important to recognize that these constituencies do not demand unique evaluative techniques. Our experience indicates that: (a) students who are not competent in social or academic communication are functionally disabled, and (b) that the techniques required to correct a lack of competency do not vary by constituency (LEP, ESL, bilingual, remedial

or special). While the source of difficulty for LEP students and special/remedial students may not be the same, evaluation of language is.

When a student arrives in a classroom that uses unfamiliar language configurations, he must acquire the new language to succeed. Sometimes this is easy and sometimes it isn't. The difficulty of accommodating an unfamiliar language framework is determined, to some extent, by the interference points between the student's existing language and that of the class. *Interference points* occur when a student's prior knowledge inhibits understanding—just as your own understanding of this text would be inhibited if we suddenly began to use the word *alumno* instead of *student*. Some languages interfere with English more than others.

In order to elaborate on the concept of interference, here are some examples specific to Spanish-speaking students. In Spanish syntax, nouns precede modifiers; this means that a student saying "The broken chair is in the kitchen" in Spanish says *"La cilla quebrada esta en la cocina."* If the student carries this syntactic structure into English, he will say "The chair broken is in the kitchen." Here's another. A friend of ours who teaches special education in Tucson reported that one of her regular education colleagues was very concerned that a first grader in her class had become inexplicably fixated on the letter "L." This student was writing "L" over and over in his work. Our friend looked at the work and realized that, because in Spanish the "Y" sound is spelled "ll," this student was spelling words like "yoyo" *llollo*.

Such confusion is common and often very hard for teachers to deal with. In addition, this confusion isn't limited to the public schools, as the makers of Nova cars can testify. Novas never sold well in Mexico because the word means "no go" in Spanish. (The owners of Osco Drug Stores have had a similar problem, and if you don't get this joke you have just experienced language interference.)

One final point about interference: Because language is the proprietor of culture, merely translating messages without an awareness of their cultural meaning is not sufficient. For example, in the United States many students grow up in a composite linguistic environment of Spanish and English. Often these kids learn to put the Spanish gender-related "ea" on the end of English words. Therefore "line" becomes *linea*. This means that when a teacher wants the class to line up he should say *"Ponganse en linea."* However, college-educated teachers are apt to use the formal Spanish translation of "line," which is *fila* and say *"Ponganse en fila."* There are two problems with this. First, some students simply don't know the word *fila*. Second, those who do know it may be more familiar with its slang meaning, which is "blade" or "knife."

So, what does this all mean? One thing it means is that people who speak other languages should not be considered disabled (although they may be "handicapped" by a nonsupportive classroom environment). It also means that students need to be taught the relevant language of schools in order for them to get along there. Directly teaching children about classroom interaction styles will improve classroom learning (Kawakami & Hupei Au, 1986).

Note: We want to state clearly that we do not advocate a "learning styles" approach to LEP students (see Chapter 2, p. 18). We do not agree with statements like this one: "When teaching LEP students it is important to provide more wait-time after asking questions." The idea of increased wait-time for students experiencing difficulty in a content area is excellent. However, the decision to increase wait-time should be based on the student's individual and task-explicit skills, not on the fact that the student is bilingual or has limited English proficiency.

The teacher's perception of a student's primary language and culture influences second-language acquisition (Cummins, 1986). In assessing the language environment of second-language learners, you may need to note the status of their language in the school society. If a student's language is not held in regard by the general population, his peers, or yourself, his communication within the classroom may be damaged. This is paradoxical, in that it means if a teacher wants a student to learn English, the best way to do it is to honor the language the student already possesses. It is possible to enhance the status of all languages and cultures within the classroom by demonstrating the acceptance of diversity.

General Beliefs, Assumptions, and Misunderstandings About Language

Some children do not learn language as quickly as their peers. Consequently, instruction that is appropriate for their peers may be inappropriate for them.

These students must be taught language skills directly and systematically if they are to benefit from educational programming. However, certain beliefs appear to encourage educators to disregard language problems and neglect language instruction.

The Child Is Just Quiet and Shy

The belief that the child is just shy and will come around in time may have damaging consequences if in fact he does need instruction and that instruction is not provided. Children who have language problems but who are not behavior problems and who smile when we talk to them are frequently not identified as needing special help. Therefore they are not provided with appropriate language instruction. Shyness refers to a student's temperament—not to his skill in communication. When a shy child decides to say something, he should be just as skilled as any other student.

It's OK as Long as I Know What He Means

Sometimes teachers respond to the message the child sends and ignore the way in which he sends it. For example, the child may ask "Her coming, too?" and the teacher may respond *yes*.

Although it is always appropriate to respond to the message, if a child has a language problem it is also important to notice the way he uses language. Sometimes teachers get used to hearing certain sentence patterns. As a result, their sensitivity to a child's language errors diminishes over time. In addition, teachers are often unaware of the degree to which they fill in the gaps for the child. For example, one teacher we know was so convinced that all children in his junior-high special class had adequate language that he recorded a conversation between himself and one of his better students just to prove it to us. When he played back the tape, the conversation went like this:

TEACHER: What is your favorite sport? [pause] Basketball?

STUDENT: Yes, basketball.

TEACHER: How long have you been playing basketball? [pause] Three or four years, hasn't it been?

STUDENT: Yes.

TEACHER: Are you glad we're going to be dismissed early today?

STUDENT: Yes.

TEACHER: Do you know why we'll be dismissed early today?

STUDENT: Mud.

TEACHER: Yes, the rain is so bad that the buses need to get children home before the roads become too muddy.

The teacher had not been aware of the extent to which he had been supplying both the questions and the answers until he listened to the tape.

He'll Grow Out of It

Another common misconception concerning language is that children's language problems are the byproduct of immaturity. Some educators and pediatricians have been known to say "Don't worry, he'll grow out of it" to parents of a 5-year-old who still isn't talking. This may not be true. While some children do outgrow language problems, most don't.

Language tends to be discussed in developmental terms, because almost all of it emerges when students are very young. Unfortunately, numerous educators confuse the term *develop* with the term *mature*. While it is common to provide "developmental expectations" for language acquisition (we'll do that in a minute) it is a mistake to assume that these milestones are only achieved through the passage of time. In most cases the milestones, like the ones in Exhibit 12.5, contain normative data collected from a representative cross section of society. A student who for some reason misses out on a critical language lesson (even because of something as innocuous as an earache) may not acquire a particular language skill by the normal age. This deficit is not the result of the aging process; it is the result of something that did, or didn't, happen while the student aged.

Developmental norms are not dictated exclusively by the age of students. These norms reflect environments as well. What is "normal" at a particular age in one environment may not be normal in another. Therefore, it is a mistake to assume that a student who has not achieved a particular developmental skill is somehow immature and in need of limited challenge. The opposite assumption may be true.

A corollary to the "grow out of it" misconception is that, as children are exposed to language models every day in school, they will spontaneously learn to understand and use language. A study of the vocabulary and language structure of normal language learners and linguistically different children indicated that language deficiencies were maintained throughout the elementary school years (Serapiglia, 1978). Everyday exposure to standard language is not sufficient in itself to enable linguistically different students to learn and use language. They need instruction.

Language Isn't Taught in School

Most children learn language without supplantive instruction at home or at school. Language is usually learned so naturally that we seldom think about it as a remarkable feat. Language development norms, like the ones in Exhibit 12.5, indicate that children in typical environments master basic language structures between 3 and 5 years of age. Three-year-olds speak in three- to four-word sentences and use speech that is 75% to 90% intelligible. Four-year-olds use more complex sentences and can give an accurate, connected account of some recent experience. Ninety percent of 4-year-old speech is intelligible. By the time children with normal language development are 5 years old, they use fully developed complex sentences of about seven to eight words and can carry on meaningful conversations with adults and children. Templin (1957) has stated that children learn to use an estimated vocabulary of about 13,000 words by age 6, 21,000 words by age 7, and 28,300 words by age 8. They also pick up another 5000 per year while in school (Nagy & Scott, 1990).

It is generally taken for granted that once children reach elementary school, and especially the upper elementary grades, they will have become proficient in language. Therefore, they are expected to understand and interpret complex information, instructions, and explanations presented in oral and written form. Furthermore, the language of instruction is not only complex, but it is also an academic language that may differ significantly from the language of social communication. This is especially true of the interactive pragmatics components.

So language usually isn't taught in school. As a result some teachers don't think it is their job to deal with it. Unfortunately this attitude cannot be justified,

Exhibit 12.5   Developmental Milestones

By age	Syntax	Morphology	Other
4	Pronouns—present and past tenses used consistently. Verbs—present and past tenses used consistently. Conditionality (You eat your dinner, you have banana.) and causality (Don't sit on 'at radiator—very hot.) Expressed by *why, because,* and *if* are implicit in children's language. Complex sentences—appear frequently. Average number of words per communication unit in oral language, approximately 6.8.	Plural—Uses -s and -z, but not consistently. Tenses—Uses progressive (-ing); simple past (-t and -d) not consistent. Progressives—*My/mine* emerging; uses nouns and with final -s; *his, her.* Comparatives—not used.	Adjectives—Adjectives (simple) used. Adverbs—Adverbs of location (there, here) used. Pronouns—*I* and *me* inconsistent; *it.* Conjunctions—*And* used consistently to coordinate; *because* emerging; *if* and *so,* not used. Negation—*Not, no, can't,* and *don't* used. Questions—Upward intonation at end of sentences; *what, what do* used. Prepositions—*In, on, with, of, for, to, up,* and *at, beside, under, behind,* used.
5		Plurals—Uses -s and -z more consistently; -es, -ez, not consistent. Tenses—Simple past, future tense, and present progressive more consistent; *have* and *have not,* not used.	Adjectives—Errors in agreement between adjective and noun. Adverbs—Adverbs of time and manner in addition to location. Pronouns—Consistently used; reflexive pronoun emerging. Conjunctions—*Because* used more consistently; *if* and *so* emerging. Questions—Why questions inconsistent; inversion of subject and auxiliary. Prepositions—*After, before, until, down, through, between, around, over, under,* and *near,* used.
6		Plurals—Uses -es and -ez more consistently; irregular form emerges. Possessives—Uses correctly with greater consistency. Comparatives—Regular.	By Age 6–7 Conjunctions—*But, after, before* (temporal), *if,* and *so* more consistently used; *because* and *therefore* used as *then* with no causal relationship. Pronouns—Reflexive pronoun used. Prepositions—Correctly used. Questions—*How* emerging.

(continued)

Exhibit 12.5   Developmental Milestones (continued)

By age	Syntax	Morphology	Other
7	Complex sentences—Further progress, especially those with adjectival clauses. Conditional dependent clauses, such as those beginning with *if*. Average number of words per communication unit in oral language—about 7.5 with a variation between 6.6 and 8.1.	By ages 7 and 8: Plurals—Improves use of irregular form. Tenses—*Have* and *had* developed. Comparatives—Uses irregular correctly.	
8	Relative pronouns—As objects in subordinate adjectival clauses (I have a cat that I feed every day.) Subordinate clauses—Frequent use of clauses beginning with *when, if,* and *because.* Gerund phrase—Object of verb appears (I like washing myself.). Average number of words per communication unit in oral language—about 7.6.		
10	Connectors—*meanwhile, unless, even if,* used to related particular concepts to general ideas. About 50% of children begin to use subordinating connectors correctly. Present participle active appears (*Sitting* up in bed, I looked around.). Perfect participle appears—(*Having* read *Tom Sawyer,* I returned it to the library.). Gerund as object of preposition appears—(By seeing *the movie,* I didn't have to read the book.). Average number of words per oral communication unit will be 9 with a variation from 7.5 to 9.3.		
12	Complex sentences—Subordinate clauses introduced by connectives *like, provided that, nevertheless, in spite of,* and *unless,* to form hypotheses and envision their consequences. Auxiliary verbs—*might, could,* and *should* appear more frequently.		

(continued)

Exhibit 12.5   Developmental Milestones (continued)

By age	Syntax	Morphology	Other
	Past, past perfect, and present perfect tenses—have difficulties in distinguishing and using these forms of the verb. Almost none of the children use the expanded forms of the past perfect or future perfect. Conditionality—The stage of thinking *if this, then* (probably), which is emerging, usually appears to be temporal things rather than nontemporal ideas and relations—(If the cost of higher education escalates, *then* (probably) enrollment will falter.). Average number of words per spoken communication unit—about 9.5 with a variation from 8 to 10.5. The average number per written unit was 9, with a range from 6.2 to 10.2, depending on the child's verbal proficiency.		

Source: Language Interaction in Curriculum and Instruction, 2nd Edition, by L. J. Gruenewald and S. A. Pollack. Copyright © 1990 by Pro Ed. Reprinted by permission.

especially when there are special/remedial students in the class. Estimates of the prevalence of speech and language disabilities vary. A 1984 report of school-age children receiving special education and related services under PL 94-142 and PL 89-313 indicated that, of the general school population, about 2.5% were categorized as speech or language disabled (American Speech-Language Hearing Association, 1986). However, determining the exact extent of the problem is complicated due to definitional problems and the fact that language problems often occur in the presence of other handicapping conditions (Hallahan & Kauffman, 1986). A large proportion of children with language problems (not speech problems) can be found within the traditional handicapping categories. These children are not included in the 1986 2.5% prevalence figure.

Here are some estimated percentages of children ages 4 to 17 with oral language disabilities in each special education category (Marge, 1972):

- 100% of the profoundly mentally retarded
- 100% of the severely and moderately mentally retarded
- 80% of the mildly mentally retarded
- 100% of the congenitally deaf and hard of hearing
- 10% of the behaviorally disordered
- 50% of the specific learning disabled
- 95% of the speech disabled (not included in other categories)

OK, But It's the Speech/Language Clinician's Job

Yes and no. It is true that speech/language teachers have been trained to assess and teach language. It's also true that in many school districts speech/language teachers carry a heavy caseload. Often their teacher-to-pupil ratio can be as high as 1 to 45. We know of situations where it is 1 to 95. In some cases, there is no language teacher. This scarcity of service is professionally unacceptable and often illegal. However, while we are all waiting for society to adopt more constructive patterns of school funding/staffing, someone has to teach. Given the numbers, it is unrealistic to expect language teachers to provide all language instruction.

A speech/language teacher may be able to work with a child for only 20 or 30 minutes twice a week. Yet children who need language instruction need lots of it. Besides, language instruction seems to be more successful when it is integrated into the daily school program. This requires the involvement and participation of regular and special teachers.

Causes of Inadequate Language Development

Various environmental, sensory, and psychological factors have been found to be related to inadequate language development. Some of these are: insufficient stimulation, improper training, impaired hearing, excessive parental or social pressure, inadequate speech mechanisms, lack of good speech models, parental over-protection, and emotional trauma. However, in most cases there is no apparent reason for language deficits.

The cause of a problem is often of little importance to its solution. (We know we've said this before, but really, if educators would spend as much time looking for *solutions* as they do looking for causes, more students would be helped). However, some causative factors such as impaired hearing, inadequate speech mechanisms, and inadequate socio-linguistic environments need to be considered before or during the assessment process. These factors need to be considered because they are related to teaching. This is especially true of hearing (Berry, 1992).

Some indications of a hearing impairment are trouble with consonant sounds (which are softer than vowel sounds), voice production problems such as unusual pitch or quality of voice, unusual rhythms, persistent articulation errors, and trouble remembering and understanding long sentences. A child may also have different hearing efficiency at different times. When a speech or language problem is suspected, be sure that a complete audiological evaluation is part of the assessment. New techniques make hearing evaluations of even young children feasible and reliable.

Evaluation of Language

Language Samples

The following section will provide an extensive explanation of the language sampling procedure. This explanation will be followed by a more functional set of directions and interpretation guidelines.

Many teachers, psychologists, and speech/language clinicians believe that language assessment should be conducted with norm-referenced tests under conditions in which the stimulus, time, and circumstances are held constant. Muma (1973, 1978) has addressed the issue of fixed-format language assessment and has concluded that regulated conditions are actually contrary to what we know about language behavior. Many tests place too great a constraint on the student's responses, making them less representative (Gerber & Bryen, 1981). For these reasons we recommend the language-sampling procedure.

Collecting the Language Sample

The language-sampling procedure involves obtaining an example of the student's language behavior and then transcribing and analyzing it. The more skilled you are in collecting a good language sample, the more information you will derive and the less assessment you will need to do at the specific level.

The language sample should be representative of the child's language performance. When collecting a language sample, you must be extremely aware of the "know/display" dichotomy (see Exhibit 7.5). To be completely representative, the sample would have to include a large number of sentences collected in a large number of situations. As with any testing procedure, reliability (and hopefully validity) will tend to increase with the number of items included. The number of utterances people recommend for use during language sampling varies (Herbert, 1979; Wiig and Semel, 1984). We recommend collecting at least 50 utterances.

Collect the language sample in at least three typical language situations. A good way to do this is to simply "cruise" by the target student and write down whatever he happens to be saying at the time. It is often useful to allow the target student to work or play in an activity area and record his language as he interacts with other children or adults. In this case, it is necessary to have a tape recorder with automatic volume control that can pick up the child's voice as he moves around. It may also be appropriate to evaluate the child's language as he interacts with a parent or other adults.

If you cannot collect a spontaneous sample, you will have to prompt a discussion and, because various factors affect language production, the evaluator must create an environment that will encourage the child's performance and elicit the best possible sample. This can be done by preparing and selecting the settings carefully (see Chapter 6).

When collecting a language sample, you must be willing to subordinate your interests to those of the child and to follow what the child says. This means responding to the child with vocabulary and grammatical forms he understands; however, you should not be instructive or corrective. Let your face and voice show the child that it is safe and that you are interested in what he says.

Have objects, devices, toys, and photographs immediately available. Some children may require these tangible objects. You can present the stimulus materials one at a time as appropriate, but do not try to elicit responses by asking questions about the objects. Rather, simply use them to promote conversation. While trying to hold this kind of discussion it is often a good idea to sit on the same level as the student. It is also a good idea to have a list of topics that may be of interest. These can include familiar events, school and community activities, visits the student may have made, what he likes to do after school, whom he plays with, what shows he watches on TV, current events, and brothers and sisters. With young children, one topic that has a high probability of success is the child's dog, other pets, or just animals in general. Pictures, photographs, films, and TV may also be used to stimulate discussion by asking the child to relate an episode or explain how or why something happened.

The question-answer format, which is easy to fall back on when things get uncomfortably quiet, should be avoided if possible. If you do use questions, be sure they are likely to elicit a whole sentence rather than a short phrase or a one-word answer. Direct questions such as "What is the boy doing?" elicit single-word responses such as "running." A language sample composed of "yes," "Tuesday," "blue," "maybe," and "Ralph" would be hard to analyze. Open-ended questions like "What happened at recess, and how did the fight get started?" may elicit more complex responses.

If the child produces a high percentage of phrases or partial sentences, you may need to prompt with leads such as "Tell me more about it."

Be sure to provide an opportunity for the child to use the various structures that were listed in Exhibit 12.1. Have him discuss something a group did, or something that either happened in the past or will happen in the future, in order to elicit plurals and past and future tense.

Puppets, if you are accomplished in their use, can provide versatility in the display of language by a young child. (The use of puppets with teenagers sometimes elicits more versatility than most of us prefer!) You may direct the child to ask the puppet something so as to elicit interrogative reversals and wh-questions. Having the student tell the puppet to do something will elicit prepositions, and telling the puppet not to do something will elicit negatives.

Some children will be unresponsive. It may help to have another child present on these occasions. It may also be useful to provide a game to promote communication between the youngsters. Record both children and transcribe the language sample for the target student only.

The social situation is one of the most powerful determinants of verbal behavior (Labov, 1969). This point is often illustrated with the example of two interviews with a young black boy. The first interview was conducted by a friendly white interviewer who put an object on the table in front of the boy and said "Tell me everything you can about this." The child's responses were defensive and monosyllabic. The second interview was conducted by a black man who was familiar with the child's neighborhood. The interviewer brought along potato chips and the child's best friend. The three of them sat on the floor and discussed what are normally considered taboo topics. The child's language was strikingly different, as this previously "nonverbal" child became quite outspoken.

Make tally marks to indicate the approximate number of sentences a child has uttered during your conversation so that you know when you have reached the 50-sentence minimum. (That is the minimum for any individual sample. It is a good idea to collect multiple samples across multiple contexts.) After you have taken the language sample, next try to decide if what the child produced was comparable to the language he usually produces. If you do not know the child well, ask someone who does to make the comparison. If you judge that the language is not typical, then add to the sample.

Transcribing the Language Sample

Tape record the language sample. You may also try to write down the child's utterances at the time of the sample, but this can cause problems. First, writing down a child's responses in front of him may inhibit his language performance. Second, you may not write fast enough or remember what the child actually says, and it is essential in this procedure to record exact utterances. Novice language evaluators tend to change what the child actually says to correspond more closely to conventional English. It is also extremely difficult for adults to copy unconventional phrasing. The student may say "She running" and the evaluator will write "she's running." Therefore, compare the sentences written during the time the language sample was taken with the sentences on the tape to eliminate this type of error. Never let an uninformed person transcribe the tape of a language sample. (While conducting research, Dr. Theresa Serapiglia once recorded the language of a number of students and her unwary typist systematically corrected all the students' errors.)

Transcribing the language sample is a critical part of the assessment process and must be done with precision. After the sample is collected, it should be transcribed and analyzed immediately by the person who took it. This allows that person to analyze the sample before forgetting valuable information about inflection and voice. Because each transcribed sentence must ultimately be judged within the context of the stimulus materials and conversational circumstances in which it was collected, this context must also be recorded. For example, with the utterance "He is running up the hill," it is only possible to evaluate the use of the pronoun *he* if the evaluator knows the runner was a male. Moreover, the use of the verb phrase *is running* and preposition *up* can only be evaluated by comparison to the stimulus or event being related.

Obviously, a sentence does not need to be correct to be included in the transcription. Sentences may contain incorrect grammar, vocabulary, and/or word order. Only different utterances are counted; repetitions of utterances are not counted. If the child repeats the same sentence several times, use only the first of the series. If the sentence is so garbled that it is unintelligible, it should not be included in the sample.

None of us speaks in sentences all the time. However, although we do not always expect children to speak in full sentences, single-word utterances are not to be included for analysis. The number of partial sentences and one-word responses should be tallied and recorded. The number of repetitive utterances and the number of unintelligible utterances should also be noted, as well as the number of hesitations.

Decisions need to be made during the transcription process. One decision to be made is where each sentence stops and the next one begins. The most useful indication of the beginnings and endings of sentences is the child's intonational patterns and pauses. Some children use "and" frequently to begin sentences. You should recognize that the *and* in these cases is not joining thoughts to form compound sentences, but is used as a filler at the beginning of a sentence. Other conjunctions such as *because* may be overused by children to start sentences. As is the case of *and*, you should not consider these words to be conjunctions joining two sentences.

A child may produce a long, rambling sentence by stringing together several noun phrases such as "There is a boy and a truck and a dog and a ball and a tree and a flower and a cloud and the sun." In sentences like this, count only two repeated elements (you would count "boy *and* a", and "dog *and* a" but not the other occurrences of *and a*).

Analyzing and Interpreting the Language Sample

Once the sample has been transcribed, you are ready to begin analysis. Because of the complexity of language, it is best to handle each of its domains separately. We'll explain each one before providing the Interpretation Guideline.

Syntax   The first step in your analysis of the sample is to identify those utterances with syntactic errors or omissions. Read over each, and then determine if the utterance sounds like something that an adult speaker with conventional usage would say. It may help to rewrite the sentence in conventional form, using information you remember about the context of the sentence. For example, if the child's utterance was "I gots three pencils" you might determine that the conventional form would have been "I have three pencils."

Next, you need to identify the type of error(s) evident in the sample. If you know the content, you can do this from memory, but it is easier to tally the errors.

Exhibit 12.6   Language Transcription Examples

What Was Said	What Should Have Been Said	Syntax Error Type (keyed to Table 12.1)
1. After wash her hair what did her do?	What did she do after she washed her hair?	3 and 18
2. I could do that Connie? [intonation indicates question]	Could I do that, Connie?	6
3. I ran.	This morning before school I went out running.	Not complex

Use Exhibit 12.1 or, better yet, the Spontaneous column of Exhibit 12.4* (this will save time if you eventually get to Language SLP 5).

Remember that a sentence may be correct but lack desired syntactic sophistication. Because of this, you must also search the language sample for evidence of *each* syntactical structure. If you find that the student has not produced a structure, mark it for later specific-level testing. This exercise must be carried out to see if the student simply failed to display the missing structure, or if he doesn't know how to use it.

Look at the example in Exhibit 12.6. The first utterance has an error in subject/pronoun, and an error in past tense. Sentence two contains an interrogative reversal error that was identified with the aid of a comment about the student's intonational pattern. Sentence three has no syntactic errors, but is simple. The numbers after each utterance refer to the structures in Exhibit 12.1.

Syntactic Interference   After you've identified errors, decide if they are related to interference points between other languages or dialects and English. This will require you to become familiar with the other language. We will briefly supply this information for Spanish and Black English, as they represent the larg-est language minorities in the United States. Canadians will be interested in defining the intersections of English and French.

The syntactic interference points between Spanish and English are as follows:

1. The -s ending is often omitted in plural possessives, and third-person singular verbs. Also, past-tense endings may appear to be absent. ("They *play* there yesterday.")
2. Spanish employs added words rather than suffixes to show comparatives. ("Her shirt is *more* pretty.")
3. Negative commands may be expressed by *no* instead of *don't*. ("*No* go there.")
4. Articles (the, a, an) may be absent. ("She is teacher.")
5. Spanish employs *to have* in many instances where, in English, *to be* would be used. ("I *have* hunger" or "She *has* 6 years.")
6. *Do* may be absent from questions. ("You like ice cream?")

Syntactic features of Black English (Hopper & Naremore, 1978) that differ from Standard English follow.

1. The expression of possession is different. ("Joe book.")
2. Negation is expressed by a double negative or *ain't*. ("I *haven't/ain't* got no car.")
3. Subject-verb agreement differs. ("We *is* here.")
4. The -s ending is omitted from third-person singular verbs. ("She laugh.")
5. The word *is* is not necessary in present tense. ("She here.")
6. *If* constructions are changed. ("I find out *do she want* to stay.")
7. Past-tense *ed* may be omitted. ("She walk.")
8. Future tense of verbs may be expressed differently. ("She *gon* [going to] go.")
9. *Be* expresses habitual action. ("She *be* sick.")

While this chapter does not deal extensively with articulation problems, they are so alarming to teachers that we'll briefly mention dialect and culturally different speech codes. The major differences between Standard English and (nonstandard) Black English and the major interference points for Spanish speakers learning English have been summarized by Hopper and Naremore (1978). Phonological interference points between Spanish and English are:

1. Initial and final voiceless plosives are not aspirated in Spanish. *Coat* may sound like *goat*; *pig* may sound like *pick*.

2. Spanish has neither voiced nor voiceless "th," so the child may substitute "d" for voiced "th," giving *dis* instead of *this*; "s" may substitute for voiceless "th," giving *sing* instead of *thing*.

3. Spanish makes no distinction between "b" and "v."

4. Spanish has the "s" sound but not the "z," "zh" (as in *treasure*), "sh" (as in *shop*), and "j" (as in *jump*).

5. "r" and "l" may be substituted for one another.

6. The vowel sounds in the English words *pig*, *fat*, and *sun* are not used in Spanish. (*Pig* may become *peeg*, *fat* may become *fet*, rhyming with *set*, and *sun* may sound as though rhymed with *John*.)

Phonological interference points between Black English and Standard English are as follows:

1. "r" and "l" may be omitted before consonants in the last sound in a word (*short* becomes *shot*).

2. Consonant clusters at the end of words will be shorter.

3. Final consonants will be weaker.

Semantics/Vocabulary   It is difficult to make good survey decisions about a child's functional level in vocabulary by analyzing a language sample alone. Sometimes it is obvious in the sample that a child's vocabulary skills are deficient because of his limited word choice or the use of such fillers as "that," "you know the stuff," or "thing." Other times you come away just feeling unsure. In either case, specific-level assessment will be needed.

Pragmatics   The language sample may also be used to determine the child's skills in communication, though an interview of teachers or family will help. While performance standards for communication are not precise, the child's peer group can be used as a comparison standard. Using the pragmatic content in Exhibit 12.1, try scanning the language sample or inquiring during the interview for evidence of successful use of each function. Here is an excerpt from a child's language sample (remember that the punctuation you see here was supplied by the evaluator during transcription of an oral sample):

> "I seen them on television. And this other guy got robbed and the other guy got mad. And he, and he, well there was a bad guy. The car was all torn up. The lady said. 'Give me the money.' They bombed the vices. They cops, do you know?"

In this sample the child does not appear to be telling events in sequence or using subordination as an aid in organizing his material. Since he has not used subordination to decide what to feature and what to suppress, his story lacks order. You would record this information under the pragmatic column in Exhibit 12.4 as no-pass (NP) for Sequence Events (part A, item 9) and Subordinate Details (part A, item 10). This indicates that specific-level testing may be needed in those areas.

The executive function of pragmatics, because it is covert, presents measurement problems. Refer to Chapter 16 for information about the assessment of "Type 2" prerequisites.

Mean Length of Utterance

A traditional method for assessing children's language development is to determine the average length of their utterances. After the language sample has been transcribed onto the transcription sheet, the evaluator can then determine the mean length of the child's utterances (MLU). Exhibit 12.7 shows an example of calculating the MLU. Count the number of words and divide by the total number of sentences. If the child repeats, count each word only once, as in the utterance, "I . . . I am going to see the dolphins" or "That . . . that dolphin has a ball." In this example you would count the words *I* and *that* only once. If the child corrects his sentence, as in sentence 2 in Exhibit 12.7, count the corrections and not the words the corrections replace. Do not count filler expressions such as "you know" or "ah, ah" as in sentence 4. Count contractions as two words. Do not count more than

Exhibit 12.7   Calculating the Mean Length of Utterance

Sentence	Repetitions and Fillers Not Counted	Number of Words per Sentence
1. That . . . that dolphin has a ball.	that	5
2. And, uh, the dolphin the fat dolphin has a big nose.	and, uh, the dolphin	7
3. And, uh, it's the ball I liked.*	and, uh	6
4. Pretty soon he swam uh uh away under the water.	uh, uh	8
5. And, uh, we bought drinks and sandwiches and chips and salad.	and, uh, and, and	7
	Total Words	33
	MLU	6.6

*Count "It's" as "it is."

two *and*s plus the words that *and* connects (as indicated by sentence 5 in Exhibit 12.7). Do not count stereotypic starters such as those in sentences 2, 3, and 5 ("and uh").

Developmental norms indicate that the approximate mean number of words per utterance is from 2 to 3.5 words for 2- to 3-year-olds, 4 to 6 words for 4- to 5-year olds, 6 to 7 words for 6-year-olds, and 7 to 8 words for 7- to 8-year-olds (Gruenewald & Pollak, 1990; Templin, 1957). In cases in which the child's mean length of utterance is low compared to developmental norms and there are no errors in syntactic structures, one appropriate language goal would be to increase the child's mean length of utterance to the norm (although a locally established behavioral criterion would better serve your needs [see Chapter 6, p. 95]).

When analyzing the language samples of children who are functioning at higher levels in language, both the mean number of words per sentence and the number of different kinds of structures included in the sentences should be considered simultaneously. A low number of words uttered per sentence is a signal that the student is probably not incorporating various syntactic structures into his sentences and is not producing complex, expanded sentences. However, some caution is needed here.

Listeners are inclined to credit speakers who have a high mean length of utterance with advanced language performance, when in actuality the primary characteristic of their language is verbosity. Verbose speakers use stylistic devices to modify, qualify, repeat, and pad the main argument. Listeners often credit speakers like this with saying something intelligent (Labov, 1969). But, have you ever felt overwhelmed and impressed with a person's speech, only to wonder later what he really said? (Of course we notice this phenomenon most frequently in election years.)

Evaluation Procedures

Survey-Level Testing

Directions for Collecting the Language Sample

The language sample is taken to find out if the child has a language problem, and to obtain guidance for additional testing:

1. Decide on settings for conversation and assemble any stimulus materials you may need. Select these settings with the goal of eliciting a large number of natural responses. Plan to draw samples from at least three settings.

2. If you plan to include other students and if you plan to sample across several settings—more

than one class, recess, lunch, at-home, or on the bus—then schedule appointments ahead of time.

3. Set up a tape recorder.

4. Elicit at least a 50-utterance sample.

   a. One-word utterances or short phrases are not counted as part of the 50-utterance minimum, but they are included in the transcription.

   b. Sentences with incorrect grammar are counted as part of the 50-utterance minimum ("Her gonna cry?" or "Why Lee Lee barking?").

   c. Structure the conversation to elicit plurals, past and future tense, vocabulary, and so on. Use Exhibit 12.1 to guide you.

5. Use props (pictures, comics, games, toys) and even other students to create a context for conversation. Avoid asking questions.

6. Transcribe the sample.

∾ *Interpretation guidelines*

It is important to remember that language is a complex process. Rarely does any student need instruction in only semantics, syntax/morphology, or pragmatics. Therefore, it is a good idea to carry out all of the following directions on the basis of the survey-level sample and to use each Language SLP indicated:

1. Determine if the student produces complete sentences 50% of the time. If not, you will need to go directly to specific-level testing in all areas.

2. Analyze and tally errors using tally sheets or tables of specifications based on Exhibit 12.1. Summarize errors across syntax, semantics, and pragmatics.

   a. Determine sentence boundaries.

   b. Analyze each sentence in the context of the conversation.

   c. Do not analyze unintelligible responses; just total them.

   d. Count only the first utterance of a repetition. Analyze and record only two repeated elements in a sentence where there are strings of the same element.

   e. Tally the number of partial and one-word responses, repetitions, hesitations, disfluencies, and unintelligible responses.

3. Note any areas where errors or omissions occur.

4. The CAP is either acceptable adult speech, the usage of an exemplar in the same setting, or the norms in Exhibit 12.5. When the target of instruction is accuracy, the CAP should be set very high—usually near 100%. When an objective calls for increases in frequency or fluency, standards should be set by collecting ecological data (see Chapter 16, p. 387).

Question: Is the student's language competence at acceptable levels?

If YES, then cease evaluation, check referral, or repeat the survey-level procedure in another setting. You may still be interested in Teaching Recommendations 1, 2, and 7.

If NO, then compare the student's behavior to the standard and derive a discrepancy. This discrepancy can then be converted into an instructional goal. For example, if the standard for noun/verb agreement is 100% but the student only demonstrates agreement 80% of the time, the goal would be to improve agreement by 20% (or a factor of 1.25).

Once the goal has been specified move to the next question.

Question: Does the classroom setting appear to inhibit communication?

If YES (or if you are unsure), then observe the classroom (Language SLP 1).

If NO, then check the next question.

Question: Does the student seem to produce utterances of adequate sophistication?

If YES, then, check the next question.

If NO, then test mean length of utterance (Language SLP 4).

Question: Are there consistent error patterns in one or more domains—syntax/morphology, semantics, or pragmatics?

If YES (or UNSURE), then test error patterns (Language SLPs 2, 5, and 6). If NO, then ask *both* of the following questions.

Question: Are there errors in fluency, phonology, and/or voice?

If YES, then refer student to a specialist for further evaluation.

If NO, then check the next question.

Question: Does the student fail to communicate in spite of adequate prerequisite skill?

If YES, then test executive pragmatic/communication strategies (Language SLP 2).

If NO, then repeat analysis by returning to the first of these questions.

Specific-Level Testing

Specific-level testing is used to answer the following questions:

1. Does the setting inhibit the student's verbal communication?

   Language SLP 1: Setting Observation

2. Are there patterns of pragmatic errors?

   Language SLP 2: Executive Function of Pragmatics

3. Is the student competent in communication?

   Language SLP 3: Communication Checklist

4. Are the student's utterances adequately complex?

   Language SLP 4: Mean Length of Utterance

5. Are there patterns of syntactical errors and omissions?

   Language SLP 5: Syntax/Morphology Probe

6. Are there patterns of errors or omissions in the student's vocabulary usage?

   Language SLP 6: Probe for Word Meaning

7. Can the student use context to determine the meaning of words?

   Language SLP 7: Determining Word Meaning

Language SLP 1: Setting Observation

This SLP involves observing and analyzing communicative transactions within the classroom. For a review of general-observation procedures see Chapter 6, Chapter 16, and Chapter 17. You may also want to take a look at the TIES classroom descriptors in

Appendix B. The most relevant TIES components and subcategories are: Component 1 (clarity of directions, checking for student understanding); Component 2 (class climate); Component 3; Component 5; and Component 12.

The checklist in Exhibit 12.8*, which is based in part on work by Rueda, Goldenberg, and Gallimore (1993, in press) can be used to organize your observations. The exhibit asks about teacher actions that have an impact on the flow of communication within the room. However, remember that you are not actually attempting to examine the communicative properties of the class—only the opportunities for this particular student. Often the language opportunities of some students are limited because of their academic skills or social skills.

Directions

1. If the classroom in question is your own, attempt a self-evaluation. Also, arrange to have someone else come in and observe.

2. Review the content of Exhibit 12.8* and related *TIES* descriptors to clarify the focus of the observation.

3. Observe over several intervals and sample various times of the day.

4. Answer the questions.

Interpretation Guidelines

This is a highly subjective exercise but it deals with an extremely important factor in language competence. As you know from personal experience, your own use of language and communication, as well as your acquisition of new vocabulary, depends on the setting in which you find yourself. If your class, or the class you have observed, does not seem to provide this particular student with opportunities to learn language, you should employ the suggestions found under Teaching Recommendation 2. The following objective can be used to define the expected impact of following that recommendation.

Objective

The student will demonstrate language usage at {a level comparable to that of other students in the setting} by increasing the frequency of {specify target utterances and/or responses}.''

Exhibit 12.8*   Setting Observation

Opportunity to Learn Language	Yes	No
1. Is the presentation understandable—semantics and syntactic structure at correct level?	_____	_____
2. Is the presentation meaningful—linked to prior knowledge or interest of student?	_____	_____
3. Is there visual support for verbal input—pictures, graphs, role playing, objects, gestures, etc.?	_____	_____
4. Is the student given frequent opportunities to respond?	_____	_____
5. Is there monitoring for understanding?	_____	_____
6. Are corrections linked to critical attributes of skill and to meaningfulness?	_____	_____
7. Are there multiple models (peers and teachers) available?	_____	_____
8. Is the classroom structured to increase frequency of communications?	_____	_____
9. Do peers and teacher have strategies for engaging a shy student who would remain silent if given a choice?	_____	_____
10. Are peers and teacher comfortable communicating with all students or do they look away or move away when some students initiate contact?	_____	_____
11. If student is acquiring English as a second language, is the primary language and culture of the student valued?	_____	_____
12. Is there collaboration with other classes, activities, and the home to insure focus, quality, and frequency of opportunity?	_____	_____
13. Is the teacher responsive to student contributions?	_____	_____
14. Do class discussions typically revolve around a theme?	_____	_____
15. Do TIES descriptors relate to this class's:		
Clarity of directions?	_____	_____
Checking understanding?	_____	_____
Class climate?	_____	_____
Teacher expectation?	_____	_____
Motivational strategies?	_____	_____
Student understanding?	_____	_____

Language SLP 2: Executive Function of Pragmatics

This assessment can be conducted over a period of time using either simulated or real events. Follow a procedure similar to the one used for obtaining the survey sample, except with this procedure you must structure opportunities for the student to display pragmatic skills. For example, if you want to sample "seeks help" (Exhibit 12.1, Pragmatics, section D, number 8), you would need to create a situation where the student faces a problem. This situation could be either a game or a lesson in a cooperative group.

Some of the content in Exhibit 12.1 is hard to observe and, even if you can initiate it, may not be displayed spontaneously. If that is the case, it may be better to treat the assessment as an interview. When interviewing a parent or teacher, be sure to ask about each item of content. One of us once asked a teacher if his 10-year-old student had any communication problems. The teacher said no. However, when asked about each item, the teacher indicated the student could actually pass only items 1 and 6 on the Pragmatics list in Exhibit 12.1.

Exhibit 12.9*   Table of Specifications for the Executive Function of Pragmatics

Directions: Beginning with the column on the right, judge the quality of usage for each example of content. If use is inadequate, move to the condition(s) found to the left. Criteria will need to be established according to context. Items marked "no pass" become objectives.

Content and Behavior	Conditions			
	Identify Correct Example	Produce After Model	Produce After Prompt	Produce Spontaneously
Plan ways to accomplish intent?				
Monitor to see if intent is being met?				
Recognize when a problem occurs?				
Analyze problem for solution?				
Recognize when assistance is needed?				
Recognize resources for solution?				
Seek appropriate help?				
Adjust responses as result of analysis?				
Recognize when intent is met?				
Verify intent is met through alternative message?				
Actively plan to incorporate new language skills into old?				

▽ **Directions**

1. Based on part D of Exhibit 12.1, create a table of specifications by imposing a sequence of production on the list of pragmatics content. This is illustrated by the example found in Exhibit 12.9.*

2. Conduct an interview or arrange situations that permit you to observe the skills. If skills are not spontaneously displayed, work to the left of the production sequence at the top of the table of specifications.

3. When prompting, include situations in which the student must decide when to use the skill as well as situations in which he uses the skill in response to a direction.

4. Record student responses during the situation.

∿ **Interpretation Guidelines**

Judge if the responses reflect adequate executive functioning for the student's communication settings. This may require you to observe other students, including exemplars, in order to establish an expectation.

○ **Objective**

Given a {specified level of assistance (prompts, cues, or models) up to spontaneous use}, the student will decrease {targeted pragmatic errors}, and/or increase {correct use of targeted pragmatic skills} to the level of other students in {the specified setting}.

Use Teaching Recommendations 5 and 6 to teach missing skills.

Language SLP 3: Communication Checklist

Directions   ▽

1. Develop a checklist based on your observations of communication demands, or use the one shown in Exhibit 12.10.*

2. Conduct an observation or interview and record the status of each item. This table is best filled out by a group of individuals who are familiar with the student.

3. Follow the directions and summarize and analyze the information.

Interpretation Guidelines   ∿

Disregard items marked YES. List items marked NO as instructional objectives. Continue to test items marked UNSURE.

Objective   ○

Given {a specified communication task} the student will correctly employ the {strategies marked NO in Exhibit 12.10*} at a level consistent with that of his classroom peers.

Exhibit 12.10* *Table of Specifications for Communication Skills*

Directions: Beginning with the column on the right, judge the quality of usage for each example of content. If use is inadequate, move to the condition(s) found to the left. Criteria will need to be established according to context. Mark items YES, NO, or UNSURE.

Content and Behavior	Identify Correct Example	Produce After Model	Produce After Prompt	Produce in Familiar Content	Produce with Strangers
A. One-way communication					
1. Expresses wants					
2. Expresses opinions					
3. Expresses feelings					
4. Expresses values					
5. Follows directions					
6. Asks questions					
7. Narrates event					
8. States main idea					
9. Sequences events					
10. Subordinates details					
11. Summarizes					
12. Describes					
13. Compares and contrasts					
14. Gives instructions					
15. Explains					
B. Two-way communication					
1. Considers the listener					
2. Formulates messages					
3. Participates in discussions					
4. Uses persuasion					
5. Resolves differences					
6. Identifies speaker's biases					
7. Identifies speaker's assumptions					
8. Formulates conclusions					
C. Nonverbal communication					
1. Uses gestures					
2. Uses proximity					
3. Uses position					
4. Uses expression					
5. Uses eye contact					

Use Teaching Recommendations 1, 6, and 7 for those skills missed on the checklist.

A Note on SLPs for Syntax

The language-sampling process is rarely sufficient for selecting syntax objectives. Because of the limited sample the process yields, a child seldom has the opportunity to produce all possible syntactic forms. Specific-level assessment should be conducted to systematically assess those syntactic structures that were *not* produced in the language sample. Specific-level work should also be carried out for those structures about which you have conflicting or insufficient information.

A typical specific-level test in this content domain is usually nothing more that a direct statement or question designed to prompt the use of a particular structure. Caution is necessary because kids will often respond in ways that are unexpected, but not necessarily incorrect. For example, "Tell me what you did yesterday'' is a request designed to elicit a response that includes a verb in the past tense (e.g. ''played''). If the child responds by saying ''Boyd and me like to play ball,'' the response is not incorrect. It is simply not the target response.

To determine if the child can imitate an utterance, model a sentence and then ask him to repeat it. If he is speaking in phrases, ask him to expand his response (see Teaching Recommendation 7 for an explanation of expansion) to determine if he has the skills to speak with more complex utterances. You can ask him to ''Say the whole thing'' or ''Tell me some more.''

Language SLP 4: Mean Length of Utterance

▽ **Directions**

Use the language sample and Exhibit 12.7 to follow these steps:

1. Count the number of words in each utterance (sentence).
   a. Do not count repetitions and fillers.
   b. Count contractions as two words.
   c. Count self-correction, but not the words that corrections replace.
2. Count the number of words.
3. Divide the number of words by the number of sentences.

〜 **Interpretation Guidelines**

Compare the result of step 3 to standards for average number of words per unit (mean length of utterance) in Exhibit 12.5.

◯ **Objective**

Given a {specified level of assistance (prompts, cues or models) up to spontaneous use} student will express himself with an average MLU of {specify level}.''

Build fluency and sophistication by using Teaching Recommendation 7, as well as 2.

Language SLP 5: Syntax/Morphology Probe

▽ **Directions**

1. Review the summary of syntax errors in Exhibit 12.4*. Recognize both structures the student used

incorrectly and those the student failed to use at all.

2. For each structure recognized in step 1 you will need to develop a probe. Use the Purpose/Function column of Exhibit 12.3 as a guide. That column can be used to generate either open-ended questions or prompts. For example, here is how you can try to probe the student's knowledge of ''possessive nouns and pronouns'' (item 14). Pick objects owned by individuals and objects owned by groups. Then ask the student to tell you who owns them (''Who does Ms. Kelly coach?'' Answer: ''The girls' team''). Elicit about ten responses for each structure of concern.

If the student does not produce responses, then move to an imitation format. For an ''imitate'' response say to the student ''Say this, 'That is *his* fish.' '' Again, provide about ten items for each form.

3. Record the accuracy of response on Exhibit 12.4*.

〜 **Interpretation Guidelines**

Analyze, tally, and summarize the responses to identify structures omitted or used incorrectly. Then use an objective like the following:

◯ **Objective**

Given a {specified level of assistance (prompts, cues or models) up to spontaneous use} the student will decrease errors and increase correct usage of {structures specified in Exhibit 12.4*} at a level {equivalent to peers or specified in Exhibit 12.5}.

Teach structures using Teaching Recommendations 3 and 6.

A Note on SLPs for Vocabulary

When you test semantics/vocabulary you are testing two things:

1. Knowledge of word and morphograph meaning (i.e. vocabulary)
2. Skills at finding out what words mean.

If a student doesn't know what a word means, then you should obviously teach it. However, instruction on one set of words won't necessarily generalize to other words. Vocabulary is best learned in a natural reading and speaking environment; often it turns out that special and remedial students have the skills to

Exhibit 12.11   Formats for Vocabulary Sampling

Format A
Target word: *drill*
Synonyms: A. practice   B. tool
Directions: "Match the synonym to the correct sentence."
1. Hand me the *drill.*
2. We need *drill* on our skills.
Answer(s): Sentence 1—synonym B.   Sentence 2—synonym A.

Format B
Target word: *drill*
Directions: "Select the words which make sentence 2 most like sentence 1."
Sentence 1. We need *drill* on our skills.
Sentence 2. If we want to get better at our skills, we should
    . . . study them.
    . . . put a hole in them.
    . . . do them a lot.

Format C
Target word: *drill*
Directions: "Write a synonym for the target word which can be used in each of the following sentences."
Sentence 1. Hand me the *drill.*
Sentence 2. We need *drill* on our skills.
Synonym 1: _____
Synonym 2: _____

Format D
Target word: *drill*
Directions: "Read this sentence—"We need *drill* on our skills." In this sentence, does the *drill* mean to:
a. make a hole in something?
b. work on something over and over again?

derive word meanings from context without direct and explicit vocabulary instruction (Elley, 1989). However, they are deprived of the opportunity to learn in this fashion by their limited reading and social skills. In addition, because of study skill and reading problems, these students often accumulate great deficits in general knowledge as they advance through school (see Chapter 17). Without adequate prior knowledge they cannot acquire new vocabulary because they don't have the knowledge necessary to learn new words (Graves, 1986; Nagy & Scott, 1990). Therefore, explicit instruction is needed.

Exhibit 12.1 presented two subdomains of semantics/vocabulary. The "basic" subdomain is composed of categories of concepts and things that typical students are familiar with *before* they come to school.

However, it is likely that a remedial/special student will be missing some of this information. Therefore, this domain of basic knowledge should be checked. As it turns out, this is the sort of content that is featured in published concept inventories, adaptive behavior scales, and developmental checklists. It is easiest to pick one or two of these existing devices by using the content in Exhibit 12.1 as your selection criterion.

Next, the student should be tested regarding knowledge of the vocabulary he needs to comprehend both topical instruction and/or reading material. This is called "topical" vocabulary (see Chapter 17). It is recognized by reviewing the material the student needs to know and selecting words important to understanding of the topic.

Exhibit 12.11 illustrates four different formats we

Exhibit 12.12   Vocabulary Specifications

Content and Conditions Under Which the Behavior Will Occur	Behavior (What the student will do) →	
	Identify correct synonym or definition	Produce (supply) the correct synonym or definition
Words in Context	Format 3	Format 1
Words in Isolation	Format 4	Format 2

might use to test a student's knowledge of vocabulary. These tests may be used by having the student read them, or by reading them to the student. Formats A through C are identification items, whereas D is a production item. Note that each format attempts to get at the word's context-dependent meaning—not its dictionary definition. Making up items like those in Exhibit 12.11 can be time-consuming; however, published vocabulary tests would never be adequately aligned with a particular student's needs to test topical vocabulary sufficiently.

Exhibit 12.12 may help you organize your testing of vocabulary. Notice that there are four levels of complexity represented by the different formats. When testing word meaning, elementary students (and possibly older special-needs students) prefer to define words by describing either how the word is commonly used or by referring to concrete examples. Older (secondary) students tend to define words with synonyms and to use abstract examples such as classifications (Farr, 1969). Synonym items may not be natural to younger students.

Format 1: Produces Word Meaning in Context.

This skill is checked by underlining important words in the passage and then asking the student to read the passage. When the student comes to an underlined word, have him stop and define it or use it in a sentence (other than the one in the story). If the definition or sentence is in keeping with the context, the word is correctly defined. Note that this format, because it relies on reading skill, shouldn't be used with nonreaders.

Format 2: Produces Words in Isolation.

Take the underlined words from test 1 and present them in isolation (by dictation and/or flashcards). The student is asked to supply a definition or synonym or to use the target word in a sentence. In this case, any acceptable definition is counted as correct.

Format 3: Match the Word to Correct Context.

This type of test was illustrated in Exhibit 12.11. Have the student read the passage until he reaches an underlined word. Then supply two definitions, both of which match the word but only one of which matches the context, and ask him to select the better one. He will be right if the definition (or synonym) selected makes sense in the context of the passage. Once again, this is a format that should not be used with nonreaders.

Format 4: Match Words in Isolation to Their Definitions.

In this test, the student is shown or read the underlined word and then given age-appropriate definitions. If the student matches the word to a correct definition (regardless of context), it is correct.

Language SLP 6: Probe for Word Meaning

Directions

1. Select or develop a test to sample categories of words that the student does not seem to know. Construct these tests using one of the four formats presented in Exhibit 12.11. The words may be drawn from materials used in the classroom,

vocabulary used for instruction, or vocabulary used for social interaction. Reference the words to the categories presented in Exhibit 12.1*. At *least* a 25-word sample is recommended.

2. Administer the tests. Say to the student "What is a _____?" for a production response. Say "Point to the _____," for an identification response. If you must give multiple tests, follow the sequence (1 through 4) in Exhibit 12.12. If the student passes a test, discontinue testing.

3. Score responses.

Interpretation: Format 1

Pass. The student knows the words. Vocabulary is not a problem.

No-pass. Go to Format 2.

Interpretation: Format 2

Pass. The student knows word meanings but doesn't adjust them to fit context (as required in Format 1), so that's what needs to be taught. This is often referred to as "multiple-meaning" instruction.

Objective

The student will use context to develop definitions to {specified words} with 95% accuracy.

Teaching Recommendation: Use Teaching Recommendations 1, 4, and 7.

No-pass. See Format 3.

Interpretation: Format 3

Pass. The student can identify correct definitions by using context clues but isn't sufficiently skilled to supply these definitions.

Objective

The student will supply context-specific definitions to {specified words} with 95% accuracy.

Teaching Recommendation: Use the Teaching Recommendation given for Format 2, but begin instruction by building from the student's existing identification skills. This would include instruction that

gradually fades out choices and requires him to provide the definitions.

No-pass. Go on to Format 4.

Interpretation: Format 4

Pass. The student has some knowledge of word meanings, but only at the identification level (not production). Previous testing has already indicated that context does not improve his performance. You probably should go to Language SLP 7.

Teaching recommendations: The student needs to be moved from identification in isolation to production within context. Begin by teaching production of correct definitions. See Teaching Recommendation 4, and related information in Chapter 10 and Chapter 17.

No-pass. Give Language SLP 7.

Language SLP 7: Determining Word Meaning

This test is used to see if the student can employ context to determine the meaning of words. Because this skill is critical to reading comprehension, you might want to take a look at the way vocabulary is handled in Chapter 10, especially through Comprehension SLPs 6 and 7.

Directions

1. Devise a pretest, or use information from other procedures, to recognize a body of words (at least 20) that the student cannot define or use in sentences. These should be words the student is expected to know.

2. Locate, or produce, passages containing the targeted words. Underline these words.

3. Ask the student to read or listen to the passages and then define the words.

4. Ask the student how he attempts to figure out what the underlined words mean.

Interpretation Guidelines

If the student can define previously unknown words once they are placed in context there isn't a problem.

Use Language SLP 6 to recognize unknown words and teach them.

If the student cannot define the words, check (through an interview) to see if the student is aware of the following strategies for context analysis:

1. Comparing the word to the message that preceded it.
2. Comparing the word to the message that followed it.
3. Inserting a word that is known, and makes sense, in the place of the unknown word (assuming that the unknown word and the known word mean the same thing).
4. Using gender, tense, and number clues to include or rule out possible meanings.
5. Using syntax clues to test the appropriateness of possible synonyms.
6. Using reference materials such as glossaries or dictionaries.
7. Asking someone what the word means.

Objective

Given words which he does not know, the student will use {specified strategies 1–7, or their enabling skills} to determine and then supply {in a specified way} the words' meanings. Word meanings will be determined with 100% accuracy.

Teaching Recommendation: Use Teaching Recommendations 1 and 4.

Teaching Recommendations

The following instructional recommendations will be briefly explained:

1. Use a direct approach to teach syntax/ morphology, semantics, and pragmatics.
2. Modify settings to increase opportunities for communication.
3. Teach syntax and morphology.
4. Teach semantics.
5. Teach pragmatics.
6. Focus instruction on error patterns within syntax, semantics, and pragmatics.

7. Use expansion.

Because these Teaching Recommendations will be covered in a very cursory manner, you may need to consult the references provided to understand them. A good basic resource for teachers working with language is: Gruenewald, L.J. & Pollak, S.A. (1990). *Language Interaction in Curriculum and Instruction* (2nd ed.). Austin, TX: Pro. Ed.

Teaching Recommendation 1: Use a Direct Approach

Direct teaching is rich with teacher-controlled models and meaningful opportunities for students to use "new" skills. *Direct* does not imply *meaningless* drill or absence of context. What it does mean is focused hands-on, supplantive instruction, for optimal use of learning time. In a direct, hands-on intervention, you tell the student what you want him to do, show him how to do it, and provide opportunities for practice. However, there is no reason that this focus must exclude those holistic-thematic aspects of language instruction that have been found to be effective (Wiig et al., 1992).

Supplantive instruction (see Chapter 4) is most appropriate when the current context of communication, or the student's enabling skills, do not afford sufficient opportunities for generative instruction and practice in language (Tharp & Gallimore, 1989). When this is the case, you must introduce the target skill and the necessary prompts to generate instructional opportunities. This is mandatory, because the student must become an active, not passive, receiver of language instruction. Therefore, the most important thing for you to do is to recognize a series of unambiguous models, prompts, and cues that will illustrate and activate the targeted skills.

It is important to try to determine if the child can produce the targeted skills with or without the use of cues and prompts. This is usually established through assisted assessment (see Chapter 5). The child's progress can be assessed on a continual basis by evaluating his reliance on prompts and recording the progression from dependence on explicit assistance to more subtle prompts, and finally to spontaneous and accurate production. The child's reliance on explicit prompts over a long period may indicate that the level of difficulty of the target is too high.

Teaching Recommendation 2: Modify Settings to Increase Opportunities for Communication

This particular recommendation should probably be applied to every student with language or communication difficulties. Classrooms are not always the best place to learn language. As Tharp and Gallimore (1989) have noted, many classrooms are characterized by teacher-dominated discourse and a lack of attention to student attempts at language usage. In addition, because many of the students with communication difficulties also have problems in the area of reading, they often miss out on the language models provided by higher-level reading lessons (see Chapter 17) (Allington, 1990).

Use the results obtained by completing the observation form in Exhibit 12.8* to recognize needed classroom modifications. Students are most apt to develop language competence in warm and supportive classrooms where there are high expectations for communication from all members of the group. In settings that support all students, there is both encouragement to communicate and direct instruction (Westby & Rause, 1985). Such a setting can be developed by producing the conditions listed on the setting observation in Exhibit 12.8*.

In the case of second-language learners, particular care must be provided to be sure that:

1. respect for the student's primary language is maintained by conveying the message that, while English is being added, his primary language is not being removed

2. the student receives instruction and is not simply bombarded with corrections

3. teaching for generalization is always primary (the goal of the instruction must reach beyond the classroom)

4. opportunities are provided for the student to make use of his own knowledge, so that language development depends as much on the student's everyday experiences as it does on the "academic" experiences of the classroom.

Schloss & Sedlak (1982) provide guidelines for working with language that can be applied to second-language learners in the classroom.

Teaching Recommendation 3: Teach Syntax and Morphology

Teaching sentence structure and word formation requires knowledge of the content and allocation of instructional time. Interventions may vary from low-context to high-context and may require identification (receptive) responses or production (expressive) responses. Wiig and Semel (1984) point out that there are some general principles for selecting instructional formats and for designing instruction for syntax:

1. Unfamiliar word- and sentence-formation rules should be introduced and sequenced according to normal developmental sequences (refer to Exhibit 12.5) or established orders of difficulty.

2. The words featured in example phrases, clauses, and sentences should be highly familiar. One way to assure that this is the case is to select words from vocabulary lists at or below (by as much as 3 years) the child's current age or grade level.

3. Sentence length should be kept to an absolute minimum. This may be achieved by limiting sentence length to 5–10 words, while phrase or clause length should be limited to 2–4 words. Minimum sentence length will depend upon the complexity of the structure being taught.

4. Pictorial or printed representations of words, phrases, or clauses should be given for all spoken sentences. Pictures of the source for words, particularly referents and function words, may also be used.

5. Unfamiliar word- or sentence-formation rules should be introduced in at least ten illustrative examples. These rule examples should feature different words.

6. Knowledge of word- or sentence-formation rules should be established first through recognition and then through production tasks.

7. The knowledge and control of word- and sentence-formation rules should be established first with highly familiar word concepts. It should then be extended to less familiar concepts.

8. The knowledge and use of word and sentence formation rules should be tested in at least ten examples that feature vocabulary not previously used.

Teaching Recommendation 4: Teach Semantics

Even students who succeed in school require repeated exposures before learning new words. Unfortunately, few teachers or reading programs provide adequate vocabulary instruction (Anderson, Osborn & Tierney, 1984). The traditional word list and dictionary approach to vocabulary instruction cannot begin to provide kids with the rich knowledge of vocabulary they need (Jenkins & Dixon, 1983). Effective explicit vocabulary instruction requires careful planning, a focus on context, and structured opportunities for practice (Beck, Perfetti & McKeown, 1982; Graves, 1986). The vocabulary lesson formats we will discuss here include questions, examples, synonyms, morphemes, definitions, and semantic features. For additional information on these formats, review Carnine et al. (1990); Gruenewald & Pollak (1990); and Johnson (1983).

Questions

A sequence for questioning will be presented in Chapter 16 (p. 382) that can be readily adapted to instruction. The sequence involves beginning with an "open question" and then, depending on the student's response, moving to "multiple choice," "restricted alternative," and "full model" questions (Stowitschek, Stowitschek, Hendrickson & Day, 1984). Here is an example of the sequence applied to vocabulary instruction:

> *Open Question*
> "What does *alacrity* mean?"

If the student correctly defines the word, go to the next one. If the student incorrectly defines the word, follow up with a multiple-choice question:

> *Multiple Choice*
> "Does *alacrity* mean:
> cute?
> travel?
> eagerness?
> anxiety?"

If the student correctly identifies the answer (eagerness) go back and ask the open question again. If the student answers the open question this time, go to the next word. If the student does not get the multiple-choice question correct, notice what word he did select

and go to a "restricted alternative" question. For this example we'll assume the student selected *anxiety*:

> *Restricted Alternative*
> "*Alacrity* does not mean "anxiety," so what does it mean?"

If the student correctly identifies the answer (eagerness), go back and ask the open question again. If the student answers the open question this time, go to the next word. If the student does not get the restricted-alternative question correct, then go to a "full model" question:

> *Full Model*
> "*Alacrity* means "eagerness." What does *alacrity* mean?"

If the student gets it right this time, go to the next word—but within a few items go back to *alacrity* and try the open question again. If the student gets it wrong this time, repeat the model.

Examples. Teach new words by example when the student does not have a synonym for the word, does not know the morpheme, or lacks the vocabulary to acquire a definition. Concepts are frequently best defined by examples and nonexamples that focus on critical attributes (see Chapter 3). Here is an illustration: Teach the definition of *opprobrious* by showing the student that the word matches photos of Hitler, Saddam Hussein, and Hannibal-The-Cannibal; but not Mother Teresa, Albert Schweitzer, or Lassie.

Synonyms. If a student already knows the meaning of a synonym, introduce a new word by linking it to the old. For example:

TEACHER: "*Sclerosis* [new word] means "hardening" [known word]. What is another word for *hardening*?"

STUDENT: "Sclerosis."

TEACHER: "Yes, *sclerosis* means hardening. We sometimes say "hardening of the arteries." What's another way to say "hardening of the arteries"?

To ensure the student knows that the new word is not exclusively linked to the words used in the example, be sure to change the example. In the case of *sclerosis*, to ensure that it's not linked to arteries alone, you might practice a sentence in which you meant hardening of plant cell walls.

TEACHER: "Plants become woody when hardening of the cell walls occurs. Use your new word in this sentence. Plants become woody when _____ of the cell walls occurs."

STUDENT: "Plants become woody when *sclerosis* of the cell walls occurs."

Morphemes. Morphemes were discussed in Chapters 10, 11, and 14 (see Chapter 14, p. 311). Opportunities for generalization occur when the learner sees that something can be used many ways. When units of meaning are taught and then the student is given opportunities to use that information to define new words, it is likely that he will learn more words. For example:

> Teach the student that "re" means "do again." Next teach that *unite* means "join." Then ask "What does reunite mean?" The answer: "Join again."

"Morphological word families" may also be of use when teaching semantics (Nagy, Anderson, Schommer, Scott & Stallman, 1989). These are words that share semantic features (decide, decision, decided) not a simple overlapping of letters (decide, decimal, deciduous).

Definitions. When you're teaching definitions, do not ask students to go to the dictionary and look something up. Teach the meaning of the word by defining it as you did when teaching morphemes. Check the learning by asking questions that verify that the student has a deep understanding of the word's meaning and recognizes critical components of the definition. An example from Carnine et al. (1990, p. 282) illustrates this kind of definition teaching:

TEACHER: "*Respite* means "short rest." John worked hard all day. Then he went home and slept for ten hours. Did he take a respite? Ann worked hard all morning. At twelve she stopped and ate a quick lunch and then went back to work. Did she take a respite? How do you know?"

Semantic Features. This format for enriching the meaning of new words is often effective. First, stu-

dents are engaged in a discussion. Old words are linked to new ones by use of defined words, and classification is used to clarify and expand student's word knowledge. Exhibit 12.13 illustrates a semantic-features list. Semantic features can be used to augment more traditional vocabulary instruction such as examples, synonyms, morphemes, and definitions. However, do not expect students to discover the meaning of new words through semantic feature analysis. New word meanings must be taught.

Nagy (1988) has identified three properties of effective vocabulary instruction. Noting the failures of traditional "definition" and "contextual" approaches, he recommended that vocabulary instruction include these three properties:

1. **Integration:** The new word is related to the student's prior knowledge. Relationships, rather than facts, are stressed during the presentation of new words.

2. **Repetition:** Students are taught to be automatic in word usage.

3. **Meaningful use:** The focus of instruction is on the student using the word, not on the student defining it. This includes work with analogies and inference.

Teaching Recommendation 5: Teach Pragmatics

The following comments assume that you have limited the number of particular skills listed in Exhibit 12.10* and identified objectives. Instruction in pragmatics requires integration of skills in syntax and semantics as well as application of knowledge of specific language functions. Another way of describing pragmatics is to link it to codes, or styles (James, 1990): one code is used when seeking help from a friend; another code is used when seeking help from a stranger.

Role playing is a good format for teaching pragmatics. Students can practice a variety of roles as they learn critical information linked to a variety of communication purposes. These lessons should include information about: (a) the purpose of the skill, (b) a variety of example situations in which the student needs the skill, and, (c) critical components of the skill. During initial acquisition, lesson formats should include models, demonstrations, and guided practice. This practice should include verbal rehearsal of what

Exhibit 12.13   Semantic Features—Vehicles

	Concept: Vehicles Features							
Words	Carries Things	Land	Air	Sea	Windows	Wheels	Wings	Fuel
Tricycle	+	+	–	–	–	+	–	–
Bicycle	+	+	–	–	–	+	–	–
Automobile	+	+	–	–	+	+	–	+
Truck	+	+	–	–	+	+	–	+
Bus	+	+	–	–	+	+	–	+
Train	+	+	–	–	+	+	–	+
Tanker	+	–	–	+	?	–	–	+
Airplane	+	+	+	–	+	+	+	+
Helicopter	+	+	+	–	+	+/–	–	+
Space shuttle	+	+	+	–	?	+	+	+
Wagon	+	+	–	–	–	+	–	–
Rickshaw	+	+	–	–	–	+	–	–

Key: +   Applies to concepts
　　 –   Does not apply to concepts
　　 ?   May apply to concepts
　　 +/– Sometimes applies to concepts
Source: Adapted from D. D. Johnson, ''Three Sound Strategies for Vocabulary Development.'' *Ginn Occasional Papers: Writings in Reading and Language Arts.* Columbus, OH: Ginn & Co., 1983.

the student will think as well as rehearsal of what he will say and do. Next, there is guided practice across settings. Finally, there is independent practice. Since all pragmatics require that the communicator recognize what skill is needed, and under what conditions, practice across settings is essential.

Teaching Recommendation 6: Focus Instruction on Error Patterns

Whenever a student is making consistent errors, regardless of the content, a direct correction procedure may be required. It has been said if an error occurs in the first 30 attempts during new learning *and is corrected,* only a few corrections will be required. However, if an error goes uncorrected and is practiced (learned), it could take thousands of corrections to eradicate the error and instill a correct alternative. This is especially true if opportunities to make the response occur in unstructured situations. If there is any content

area that matches that description, it is interpersonal communication. This is why early and extensive use of guided practice is so important.

Error correction needs to be immediate and frequent. Opportunities to make the specific errors of concern need to be built into instruction. Corrections should be based on the cause of the error. The following causes of errors are the most likely:

1. Failure to see how things are different. This is called a ''discrimination error.''

2. Failure to see how things are the same—a ''generalization error.''

3. Missing information.

Discrimination errors occur when students carry old rules into new situations. For example, a student has learned that you add *s* to make English words plural, but does not know words for which the rule does not apply (deer, goose, man). The solution here is to teach the needed discrimination. For example:

TEACHER: "We say two boys, four hats, ten pencils—but we say six sheep. We say one sheep, two sheep, three sheep—but we say one boy, two boys, three boys."

A generalization error occurs when the student fails to see how two things are the same. A correction for this kind of error would include information of the critical ways things are similar. A student who can ask for help in one classroom and not in another needs to be taught that ways of seeking assistance are frequently the same across situations.

When a student makes errors because he just doesn't know something (e.g. how to ask for directions) simply supply the information.

Teaching Recommendation 7: Expansion

To increase both the number and the richness of ideas and structures a student uses, the child has to incorporate new material into his current speech. In terms of syntax, structures such as adjectives, adverbs, prepositional phrases, and coordinating elements are targets to be included in existing utterances. Structures such as complex verb forms and clauses are added to already complex utterances to increase the number of words per utterance. The long-range goal of expansion is to increase the mean length of the child's utterances by including various language structures; the short-range objective is that the child produce sentences using specific structures. An example of an objective at a lower level is "The child will produce sentences using prepositional phrases." The format of higher-level objectives stays the same ("The student will produce sentences using the relative adverb clauses").

In order to increase the richness and conceptual sophistication of the student's speech it is often good practice to focus on the purpose, intent, and audience of communication (see Chapters 3 and 13). Palincsar and David (1992), for example, have found that successful students listen very differently to classroom dialogue than those who are not so successful. Unsuccessful students explain their approach to listening this way: "I stay still," "I do nothing," and even "I don't know this. I'm only 7 years old!" Such passive listening strategies were changed dramatically, along with scores on listening-comprehension measures, through dialogues in which teachers provided guided practice, extensive teacher modeling, and the systematic expansion of student efforts. These are principle elements of the reading comprehension technique called reciprocal teaching (see Chapter 10, p. 213).

The process of expansion is simple. It is used by taking the student's incorrect, or simple, utterance and changing it into one that is closer to the student's language goal. For example, if a student with a syntax goal were to say "Ask do he want a Pepsi," the correct expansion would be "Ask if he wants a Pepsi." If a student with a semantic or advanced syntax goal were to say "Look at the bird," a good expansion might be "Look at the bird as it flies slowly across the sky." Similarly, a pragmatic objective for listening might start with a student saying "I stay still," and expand this kernel into "I stay still so I can think about what I hear."

There are a couple of rules to remember when using expansion:

1. Expand the utterance into what the *student* should have said. This means "I go bathroom?" should not be expanded into "May you go to the bathroom?" but into "May I go to the bathroom?"

2. Accompany the expansion with a standard cue, such as a hand on the student's shoulder, to signal that a brief language lesson is about to occur.

3. Do not expand every utterance—the kid will quickly get sick of it.

4. Always respond to the message the student is trying to convey. If you become too interested in how everything is said, and ignore the conversation, the student will stop talking to you. In other words, building from the example above, say "May I go to the bathroom? Yes, you may." (You don't want to fix the kid's syntax but leave him with a stressed bladder.)

5. Use expansion in many different situations and times. Try to fit it into the normal course of the day, and not just into language lessons.

Summary

This chapter defined oral language and explored some beliefs, assumptions, and misunderstandings about language acquisition. It also discussed in detail what to consider when conducting an evaluation of language. We have linked these considerations to explicit procedures for conducting survey- and specific-level tests. The specific-level procedures described match the most probable causes for language difficulties. Guidelines for interpreting test results were also linked to instruction recommendations.

Chapter 13 / Written Expression

How can I know what I think till I see what I say?"

—E.M. Forster

Reading is not a duty, and has consequently no business to be made disagreeable.

—Augustine Birrell

Many times in this text we have pointed out that the measurement and analysis of literacy hinges on two things: the student's knowledge, and how the student displays that knowledge. While obviously associated, these two are not entirely linked. Some people who know things can't seem to display them, and some people who know very little present what they know with considerable skill. The know/display association, which is particularly important in written communication, was recognized by Smith (1982) when he drew a distinction between the "writer as author" and the "writer as secretary." This chapter deals with the writer as author. Chapter 14 deals with the writer as secretary.

Authorities suggest there are three aspects of the author role in communication: (1) purpose, (2) process, and (3) product (Scardamalia & Bereiter, 1986; Isaacson, 1985). This discussion of written communication will focus on these three aspects as they relate to the concepts of literacy outlined in both Chapters 3 and 12. It may have been a long time since you read Chapter 3, so some of the early discussion in this chapter will serve as a review.

Components of Written Communication

Purpose

While some specialists make a distinction between them we will be using the terms *purpose* and *intent* as if they are synonymous. Purpose in written language is analogous to pragmatics in oral language. Several guides have been suggested by authors attempting to establish frameworks for defining purpose (Britton,

1978; Wiig & Semel, 1984). These guides generally take the form of lists based on categories of genre (kinds of writing, message type or intent) (see Exhibit 3.3).

There are two ways to look at the assessment of purpose. First, as a reader you must know the writer's intent in order to judge whether a written communication is acceptable. If you don't know what the writer intended, then you can't discern whether the writer followed the conventional form (if the writer intends to ask for a job, she needs to follow the form of business-letter writing). The other view of purpose places the responsibility more directly on the author by presupposing that, if you can't tell the intent, the writer hasn't done a very good job of expressing it. We prefer the second approach. This preference stems from the same view of communication that holds there is no greater linguistic value in complex sentences than in simple ones (see Chapter 12). The message is the most important aspect of communication. If we understand the purpose, we won't reject the message because it fails to conform to a particular style. If we don't understand the purpose, then we aren't impressed by the style.

Process

The process of writing has four stages (Isaacson, 1985): planning, reviewing, revising, and transcribing. These are shown in Exhibit 13.1. Transcription is discussed in Chapter 14, as it is secretarial.

Planning includes a pre-writing stage in which the writer formulates a purpose for writing, decides what to write, selects a style that is likely to accomplish the purpose, and then organizes the message. Planning also occurs during writing and includes both the plan-

Exhibit 13.1   Process in Writing

Planning	Transcribing	Reviewing	Revising

Prewriting
   Formulate purpose
   Match style to
   purpose
   Organize message
	Modes
	   Dictation
	   Typing
	   Computer keyboard
	   Pen or pencil
		Monitor
		   Match of message to
		   purpose
		   Accuracy of
		   mechanics
			Modify to meet purpose
			   Style
			   Content
			   Word selection
			   Sentence complexity
			   Organization

During writing
   Develop message
   Manipulate mechanics
	Mechanics
	   Handwriting, typing,
	   etc.
	   Spelling
	   Capitalization
	   Grammar
	   Form—Margins,
	   heading, etc.
			Correct errors in
			   mechanics
			   Handwriting, typing,
			   etc.
			   Spelling
			   Capitalization
			   Grammar
			   Form—Margins,
			   heading, etc.

ning for development of a message, as well as the planning for manipulation of mechanics. The focus of planning should be to accomplish the purpose of the communication. As writers of this text, we planned our content and how to present it to you. We also planned our format. Certain planning occurs before writing; other planning takes place during writing. On large projects like this text, allocation of time also requires planning. Some of the plans we developed for this book actually made it all the way through the process. Others, like the musical version of Chapter 6, had to be dropped.

Reviewing appears to interact with planning. Good writers frequently look back over their work to check on how things are going, just as good readers look back on what they have read to check understanding. As writers review their work, they invariably revise it. This means the stages in Exhibit 13.1 are not really sequential (or even separate).

Revision may include changes in style, content, word selection, and sentence complexity, to assure that the message is either as clear or vague as the writer intends (Raymond, 1989). Sometimes, most obviously in poetry, ambiguity is the goal. The final stages of the revision process tend to focus only on the secretarial aspects of the work and include corrections in spelling, punctuation, grammar, and appearance. (Good writers are aware that the physical organization of a written message influences how it is received and whether it is understood. That is why students with laser printers tend to get the best grades.)

Product

Products are the result of purpose and process. These products are what evaluators analyze to determine how well a student has mastered writing. Isaacson (1985) has identified five writing products: fluency, syntactic maturity, vocabulary, content, and writing conventions (which include mechanics). Each can be directly observed. Isaacson's descriptions of these components are summarized in Exhibit 13.2. Because both ease of evaluator acquisition and use are factors that should be weighed along with reliability and validity, we have added an efficiency rating to Isaacson's original summary. Some of the procedures Isaacson suggests are easy for an evaluator to use and others are not.

Strategies

Writing strategies are embedded in purpose, process, and product. They include (a) procedures for deciding

Effective writing skills, along with competence in reading, are expressions of literacy. The failure to acquire reading and writing as functional extensions of language accounts for the greatest number of referrals to special and remedial education.

what to do, and (b) procedures for doing it. As in reading, math, and oral language, there are both general strategies and task-specific strategies. A general strategy is characterized by a question such as "What should I be doing?" A task-specific strategy is characterized by the question "How do I start a letter of apology to the Principal?"

The Flow of Composition   As we've already pointed out, the various components of the writing process do not take place in a fixed progression. One does not finish planning, then transcribe, then review/revise, and finally hand the product in for publication. Writers do all of these things at the same time. However, there is an interactive element of composition that is important if we are to understand the process. It is a "temporal-experiential-interaction" (we love making up these terms) and it occurs as the writer's personal history is converted into the messages she is generat-

ing for the future. As illustrated in a chapter by Scardamalia and Bereiter (1986), during composition the author does two things: she looks back upon her own experience, and she looks forward to predict what sort of presentation will have the desired effect on her reader (Beaugrande, 1984). The writer, therefore, is attempting to govern the experience of the reader from a position between reflection and prediction. This is a very sophisticated undertaking.

Problems in Written Communication

Effective writing skills, along with competence in reading, are expressions of literacy. The failure to acquire reading and writing as functional extensions of language accounts for the greatest number of referrals to special and remedial education (Hallahan & Kauffman, 1986).

Exhibit 13.2   *Components of Written Communication Products*

Component	Evidence	Direct Measures	Training Time Low	Training Time Medium	Training Time High	Scoring Time Low	Scoring Time Medium	Scoring Time High
Fluency	Production of simple sentences and elaboration into compositions of gradually increasing length	Total number of words	X			X		
		Ratio of correct word sequences	X				X	
Syntactic maturity	Production of sentences of increasing complexity	Total number of sentences by type: fragment, simple, compound		X			X	
		Total number of T-units per sentence			X		X	
		Length of T-units per sentence			X		X	
Vocabulary or semantic maturity	Fewer repetitions of favored words and use of more sophisticated words	Total number of unusual words (teacher's best guess about unusual)	X				X	
		Proportion of mature words (from a word frequency list)	X				X	
		Proportion of unrepeated words	X					X
Content	Attention to organization of thought, originality, and style	Text cohesion			X			X
		Holistic rating		X			X	
		Analytic rating			X			X
Conventions	Mechanical aspects of writing such as margins, grammar, spelling, and punctuation	Proportion of errors in each category		X			X	

Source: From Isaacson (1984, 1985).

No one argues the importance of writing instruction. However, exactly what to teach and how to teach it are hotly debated (Du Charme, Earl & Poplin, 1989; Englert, 1992; Isaacson, 1989a, 1989b, 1992).

Before we get into how writing should be taught, the question of whether it should be taught at all should probably be considered. Numerous researchers have noted that most students spend little time in writing activities (Applebee, 1981; Petty & Finn, 1981; Bridge & Hiebert, 1985; Isaacson, 1990). Some studies have found that, beyond the primary grades, the average student in the United States spends only about 15 minutes a week in writing instruction. These authors also report that most of the scant time spent in writing is spent copying verbatim from workbooks or teacher-prepared worksheets. Students seldom compose written messages and almost never write for an audience other than the teacher.

This means we are in something of a bind with Chapters 13 and 14. It takes several pages (which you will have to pay for) to do a good job explaining written communication. In some ways it is hard to justify spending about 15% of the content discussion in this text on something teachers only teach about 2% of the time. However, writing is one of the "3 Rs," and failure at it can be disabling to communication and stigmatizing to students. Also, with the advent of word-processor access, much of the traditional focus on writing mechanics is becoming obsoleat (for example, do you want to know how to spell *obsolete*? Press shift F4).

Debate on How to Teach

Today, in conjunction with an interest in literacy and generative instruction (Englert, 1992), tremendous emphasis is being placed on the writing process within the professional literature on education (even though it is hard to find this emphasis reflected in common classroom practice). Proponents of the writing process appear to be reacting to what they see as an historic over-emphasis on the secretarial skills (Huot, 1990). These advocates worry that, by accentuating enabling secretarial skills, teachers neglect the more complex tasks that are linked to print communication (planning, reviewing, revising). They also believe that an emphasis on enabling skills fails to produce good writers (Du Charme, Earl & Poplin, 1989). While we agree that writing should be an integrated activity, we think that to reduce the discussion of written communication to an argument on whether the writing process is any more important than the mastery of mechanics misses the point. Sometimes it takes more than one set of skills to get something done.

Writing and Reading

It is popularly believed that gains in reading competence influence gains in writing competence and that competence in writing influences reading (Assink, Kattenberg & Wortmann, 1992). The nature of the writing-reading relationship is still being explored. Tierney and Leys (1984) have pointed out that the magnitude of the relationship seems to vary with the age of the writer and the kind of test employed to measure the interaction. However it is safe to say that, while there are good readers who are not good writers, there are probably no good writers who are not also good readers. Among other explanations, this is because good writing includes reading your own text for planning and review, and often reading the text of others as an informational source.

Eckhoff (1983), Geva & Tierney (1984), and Bereiter and Scardamalia (1984) have all observed that what a person reads influences her writing style. This is a big problem for teachers and students because, as Armbruster (1984b) has pointed out, school texts are often poorly organized, obscurely written, and insensitive to their audience. She has however suggested a possible advantage to these inferior communication models. Armbruster recommended teaching students to rewrite poor texts. She believes that analysis and revision of a poorly written text provides kids with practice in critical reading *and* critical writing. Maybe by teaching kids to become critics and editors we will teach them strategies to improve both their reading comprehension and their own writing skills.

Collecting a Writing Sample

There are a number of ways to obtain samples of written work (Tindal & Parker, 1991). One is to collect existing samples from class assignments. If these samples are not readily available, you can provide the student with a "story starter." This writing prompt can be a picture(s), a description of an age-appropriate situation, or a question. Since a student's prior knowledge and current interest in the topic are critical, it is important to consider starters that are flexible. The disadvantage of using samples from a structured assignment is that the purpose is not generated by the kid. Pictures also have problems, as many students will simply describe what they see in them (therefore making originality and plot hard to judge). If you are going to use a picture prompt, try asking the student to write about "What you think will happen next."

Prompts should be as free from cultural bias as possible. Consider the three prompts in Exhibit 13.3. In prompt A, it does not matter where a student has lunch or what they have for lunch. In prompt B, however, if they do not live with both a mom and a dad

Exhibit 13.3   Three Story Starters

Prompt A	Prompt B	Prompt C
"What is the best thing and the worst thing about lunch?" (Hutchinson, 1987)	"Families are special people. I'd like to learn who is special in your life. Who are the members of your family? Do you have brothers and sisters? What do you like to do with your mom or dad? What do you like about your family times together?	A flying saucer that you suspect is filled with Martians lands near the fire hydrant in front of your house. Describe the scene and write about what happens.

and have brothers and sisters, they may have trouble with this "story starter." Even if the student were a good writer, the topic could be culturally and conceptually difficult to address. A second problem with prompt B is that it is lengthy. If a student has difficulty listening or difficulty remembering more than a few sentences, she may miss part of the prompt. Prompt C is fairly typical of the sort of story starters found in many published classroom programs. Its heavy dependence on imagination, while instructionally attractive, may not be good for evaluation. Many students would find it much easier to write about how they spent their weekend than how they would handle a visit from spacemen (Graham & Harris, 1988).

Heward, Heron, Gardner and Prayzer (1991) provide a list of writing topics and story starters including: "We searched for hours and hours and couldn't find. . . . "; "If I were. . . . "; and "What could you do with a deflated basketball?"

A Note on Standards

Perhaps the greatest problem associated with samples of written communication is deciding how to rate them. One reason this is such a tremendous problem is that standards for comparison often do not exist. In a minute when we get to the evaluation procedures we'll recommend a standard suggested by Tindal and Hasbrouck (1991). However, because the approach to writing instruction varies so much from school to school, many teachers like to have a local standard.

The Tindal and Hasbrouck scale is shown in Exhibit 13.4*. It is useful for determining the initial quality of a sample, setting long-term goals, and for

recognizing problems in three areas: story/idea, organization/cohesion, and conventions/mechanics. We recommend that you use the scale as an absolute standard and do not attempt to norm it. In other words, you would assume that any student should get a 5 in each area regardless of the typical rankings in your class/school (allowing some consideration for grade-level and genre, particularly in the domain of conventions/mechanics). As students get older they are expected to maintain the 5 rating as their work moves to different genres such as letters, job applications, and essay test writing.

If you think you need a locally derived standard, and it is probably a good idea, here is one approach. It isn't particularly easy to carry out, but once it is done it should not need to be repeated for some time. The approach is used to identify exemplar writing along with clusters of less expert products that can be used to anchor the ratings of writing samples.

This needs to be done for each grade level at the school. It will also need to be done for each school in a district, as you can expect considerable variation between schools:

1. Give all students a pre-writing prompt (called a story starter), 2 minutes to plan, and 3 minutes to write.

2. For each student, record:
   - total words written (even if they have errors)
   - total words spelled correctly
   - total words spelled incorrectly
   - total words in correct sequence

3. Summarize the scores obtained in step 2 by grade (it is a good idea to have beginning-,

Exhibit 13.4*   Analytic Scales for Dimensions of Writing Using a Five-Point Anchors of Quality

Story-Idea	Organiz.-Cohesion	Conven. Mechanics
5	**5**	**5**
—includes characters —delineates a plot —contains original ideas —contains some detail —word choice —contains descriptors (adverbs and adjectives) and colorful, infrequently used, and/or some long words	—overall story is organized into a beginning, a middle, and an end —events are linked and cohesive —sentences are linked, often containing some transitions to help with organization (finally, then, next, etc.)	—sentence structure generally is accurate —spelling does not hinder readability —sometimes contain dialogue —handwriting is legible —punctuation does not effect readability too much —word usage generally is correct (s.v.o./homophone/s-v agreement)
4	**4**	**4**
—includes characters, but they are not original, often coming from movies —delineates a plot, although it is not as clear as 5 —contains some original ideas but is fairly predictable —contains some detail —includes descriptors (adverbs and adjectives) —word choice: contains some descriptors (adverbs and adjectives) and some colorful, infrequently used, and/or long words	—story has somewhat of a beginning, middle, and an end —events appear somewhat random, but some organization exists —sample may contain some transitions to help with organization: finally, then, next etc.) —story often contains too many events, disrupting cohesion	—sentence structure generally is accurate but not as good as 5 —spelling does not hinder readability too much —sometimes contains dialogue —handwriting is legible —punctuation does not affect readability too much —word usage generally is correct (s.v.o./homophone/s-v agreement)
3	**3**	**3**
—characters are predictable and undeveloped —plot is somewhat haphazard —may or may not contain original ideas —lacks detail —word choice is somewhat predictable only sometimes contains descriptors (adverbs and adjectives)	—somewhat of a plot exists but story may still lack a beginning, middle or an end —events are somewhat random —often lacks transitions —sometimes lack referents	—sentence structure has a few problems —spelling is somewhat of a problem —may use dialogue but does not punctuate it correctly —handwriting is legible —punctuation is fair —problems sometimes occur with word usage (s.v.o/homophone/s-v agreement)
2	**2**	**2**
—includes few if any characters —plot is not developed or apparent —contains virtually no original ideas —detail is significantly absent —events are very predictable —word choice is predictable, lacking descriptors (adverbs and adjectives)	—plot lacks organization into a beginning, middle and an end —events are random, lacking in cohesion —lacks transitions —often lacks referents	—sentence structure makes story difficult to read —spelling makes it difficult to read —may use dialogue but does not punctuate it correctly —handwriting is not very legible —punctuation is inconsistent and problematic —word usage is problematic (s.v.o/homophone/s-v agreement)
1	**1**	**1**
—includes few if any characters —plot is non-existent —contains no original ideas —detail is significantly absent —events are few and predictable —lacks descriptors (adverbs and adjectives)	—plot is virtually nonexistent —events are few and random —lacks transitions —lacks referents	—sentence structure is problematic —spelling makes it extremely difficult to read —handwriting is illegible, making it extremely difficult to decode —punctuation is virtually nonexistent —word usage is problematic (s.v.o/homophone/s-v agreement)

From "Analyzing Student Writing to Develop Instructional Strategies," by G. Tindal and J. Hasbrouck, 1991, *Learning Disabilities Research & Practice*, 6, (4), p. 239. Reprinted by permission.

middle-, and end-of-the-year norms for grades 1–3). Find the medians and divide by 1.5 and 2.0 discrepancy-cutting scores (see Appendix A) for each grade, as illustrated back in Exhibit 9.4. Put that information in a notebook.

4. Next, have at least three teachers sort the products at each grade level into five groups on the basis of their overall impression of quality as follows:

a. Divide number of students at each grade level by 5 (45 kids ÷ 5 = 9).

b. Use a "holistic" standard for sorting the samples. This means judging the quality of the overall product. Therefore the raters must try to balance consideration of *both* the quality of the message and the mechanics of the presentation.

c. Teachers first identify the best nine papers

and the worst nine. The best are ranked 5, and the worst ranked 1.

d. From the remaining papers, the teachers select the 9 that are next to best (these will be called 4) and the 9 that are next to the bottom (called 2).

5. For each grade select several papers at each level (1–5) and put them in the notebook with the scores you developed for step 3. These will be used to illustrate each rank so that in the future teachers can use the notebook to rate students. The notebook will, therefore, have dividers separating the samples by grade level and samples representing each rank for each grade. This will make the folder a static standard, which means, for example, that when future papers are rated, 20% of them need *not* be ranked 1.

Evaluation Procedures

The process of evaluation for written communication is outlined in Exhibit 13.5. It begins with survey-level testing.

Survey-Level Testing

▽ **Directions for Collecting and Scoring Written Language Samples**

1. Collect at least two samples. One should be collected without time for review/revision, and the other should allow time for review/revision.

2. If existing samples are not available, then provide a verbal or pictorial prompt. For the "no revision" sample tell the student that she will have 2 minutes to think about the prompt and 3 minutes to write (these times may be varied but should match those used to establish standards). For the "revison" sample, allow the student to take whatever time she wishes to improve a previous 3-minute work.

3. Score each product using the Tindal and Hasbrouck (1991) rating form in Exhibit 13.4*, or local rating standards you have established. When using the Tindal and Hasbrouck rating,

select the number that most closely describes the student's work. Each indicator for a particular rank need not apply.

Score interpretation

1. All students receiving a rank of 1 or 2 on the local standard, or a rank below 4 from Exhibit 13.4*, should be given another story starter the next day to confirm their low rank.

2. All students still ranked 1 or 2 by local standards, or below 4 on Exhibit 13.4*, are considered to have inadequate skills; they need additional testing.

3. Students scoring 1.5 below the median on total words, words spelled correctly, letters in correct sequence, and/or writing letters should also be referred for additional testing *regardless* of their ranking.

4. Students currently viewed as at-risk who score *above* the 1.5 cut, or who have ranks of 3 or above, should be reevaluated to determine if special services are no longer needed.

Qualitative Interpretation

Question: Did the student obtain an acceptable rank?
If YES, you can discontinue.
If NO, and the problem seems to be strictly mechanical, go directly to Chapter 14. If it isn't mechanical, you will employ both SLP 1 and SLP 2.
Before starting specific-level testing, you need to set a goal. If the standard is a ranking of 4, for example, and the student's work has been ranked 2, then the discrepancy is 2. This would produce an **Objective** like this: "The student will write a {insert a description of the type of writing you will request} passage which ranks 4 on the Tindal and Hasbrouck (1991) scale."

Specific-Level Testing

Written Expression SLP 1: Interview/Observation

Most behaviors for written communication purposes and processes are cognitive. While you cannot directly observe these behaviors, they may become apparent through interviews with the student.

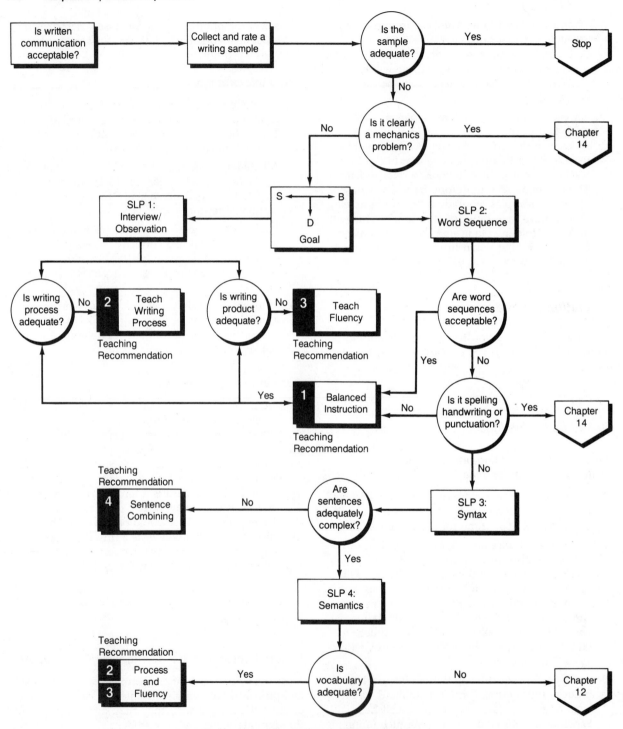

Exhibit 13.5*   Evaluating written expression.

Exhibit 13.6* **Status Sheet for SLP 1: Interview/Observation of Writing Process and Product**

The Writing Process			
Planning	yes	no	unsure
Did the writer define a purpose or establish an intent before beginning to write?			
Did the writer develop a list of content items appropriate to purpose or intent?			
Did the writer formulate a <u>model, map</u> or outline (plan) to structure content appropriate to purpose or intent?			
Did the writer use the plan as a basis for writing the first draft?			
Reviewing	yes	no	unsure
During the writing of the draft(s) does the writer go back and read what was written to check on development and structure?			
Revision	yes	no	unsure
Is there evidence in the drafts to indicate that the writer made changes to accomplish purpose/obtain intent?			
Product			
Structure	yes	no	unsure
Does the thesis sentence focus the reader on the writer's intent or purpose?			
Does the final sentence provide an appropriate ending/conclusion?			
Are the subtopics and/or events arranged in a recognizable order?			
Cohesion	yes	no	unsure
Do all the sentences relate to the writer's intent or purpose?			
Is there an apparent order in the presentation of the sentences?			
Does the writer make use of transitional words and devices?			

Exhibit 13.7 **Examples of Scoring Using Correct Word-Sequence Count**

Sample Scored Sentence
^ Jack ^ and ^ Paula ^ and ^ Mary ˅ last ^ week ^ to ^ shell ˅ peacans ˅

Key — Carets above words indicate correct counts.
Carets below words indicate incorrect counts.

1. A correct caret is placed before "Jack" to indicate a correct starting word.

2. An incorrect caret is placed before "last" to indicate that "Mary last" is not a correct sequence in this sentence. A word like *met* was probably omitted and would have been correct.

3. An incorrect caret is placed before and after "peacans" because it is misspelled. It cannot be counted as a correct sequence after "shell" nor can it be counted as a correct ending word, which the last caret would indicate, because it is misspelled.

Score: 73% correct, 29% error.

▽ **Directions**

Observe the student during the process of writing. You may need to do this more than once. Ask the student to explain what she is doing, and how she decided on the actions she is taking. Through observations of the student, and questions, rate the student on each item in the status sheet found in Exhibit 13.6*.

〜 **Interpretation Guidelines**

Question: Are there indicators that the student uses the *process* of writing effectively?

If YES, then consider the items marked adequate to be passed. Use Teaching Recommendation 1.

If NO, the **objectives** become the skills or strategies marked "not adequate" or "not observed." Use Teaching Recommendation 2.

Question: Are there indicators that the student has produced an adequate *product*?

If YES, then use Teaching Recommendation 1.
If NO, then use Teaching Recommendation 3.

Written Expression SLP 2: Word Sequence Test

This procedure focuses on correct sequences of written products (Parker, Tindal & Hasbrouck, 1991; Videen, Deno & Marston, 1982). It may be applied to letters, words, phrases, sentences, or even paragraphs. Implicit in this system is the notion that a correct sequence of words or phrases reflects not only fluency but syntactical maturity. Exhibit 13.7 illustrates the procedure applied to words. While correct sequence scoring does not sample all the components of writing, it takes very little time and correlates with a number of more time-consuming techniques.

▽ Directions

1. Obtain samples of the student's writing. Either use the samples from the survey level, or obtain others. If there seems to be variability in the student's production, look at more than two samples.

2. To score the samples, give one point for (a) each word that is in correct sequence, and (b) for appropriate ending. Correct sequence means the word conforms to both semantic and syntactic constraints (that is, it makes sense, in that place, in that sentence). This is illustrated in Exhibit 13.7. A practice scoring exercise can be found in the workbook.

3. Summarize data.

4. Compare to established standards. To determine standards for this task, you could compare your students' scores to scores of students whom classroom teachers judge to be competent writers. However, we have observed that since inaccuracy in word sequence is not acceptable to most recipients of written messages, an absolute standard of 100% is advisable for revised samples.

≈ Interpretation Guidelines

Question: Are word sequences correct?

If YES, use Teaching Recommendation 1, and this

Objective:

"In response to writing prompts the student will produce passing levels of word sequences. CAP: {as specified in the section on survey level testing}."

If NO, does the problem appear to be in spelling, handwriting or punctuation?

If YES, go to any to Chapter 14.

If NO, then go to SLP 3 for syntax.

Written expression SLP 3: Syntactic Maturity

One way to judge syntactic maturity is to use T-units. A T-unit is a minimal-terminal unit such as a main clause plus attached subordinate clauses. In our experience, whereas numerous authors talk about the use

of T-units (Loban, 1963; Hunt, 1965; Polloway & Smith; 1982), almost no one actually uses them. In case you decide to be one of those who do, Exhibit 13.8 illustrates how to calculate the mean T-unit to summarize sentence complexity.

We prefer the simpler approach advocated by Isaacson (1990), as adapted from Powers and Wilgus (1983) and shown in Exhibit 13.9.*

▽ Directions

1. Collect samples of the student's written communication or analyze the sample obtained in the survey-level procedure.

2. Using the guidelines presented in Exhibit 13.9*, determine the number of sentences at each level, and the percent of total sentences at each level.

Score Interpretation

There are no established standards for this procedure. However, standards could easily be established from the school-wide writing samples used in the initial ratings. Obviously it is assumed that, as students advance in grade, a larger proportion of their sentences should be at levels 2 and 3.

Qualitative Interpretation

Question: Does the student's syntax seem adequately mature?

If YES, use SLP 4.

If NO, teach specific-level skills for expanding and increasing sentence complexity using Teaching Recommendation 4. Also consult Chapter 12.

Objective

"The student will, within writing samples and revised work, develop sentences reflecting syntactic maturity. CAP: {specified T-unit and/or Exhibit 13.9 rankings}."

Written Expression SLP 4: Semantic Maturity

SLP 4 is similar to the semantic test in Chapter 12. It is summarized in Exhibit 13.10. A limitation of this approach is that counting words and comparing them to a word-frequency list is time consuming. Therefore, not many teachers use this one either. Instead, they tend to simply judge whether word choice is adequate. Judgment is fine with us as long as it is double-checked with another teacher. The following, more

Exhibit 13.8   Calculating Mean T-Unit and Rating Sentence Complexity

Directions	An Example

Directions

1. Count the total number of words in the sample.
2. Count the total number of T-units in the sample.
3. Divide the total number of words by the total number of T-units. The quotient will be the mean length of T-unit.
4. Rate each sentence as a fragment, simple, compound, compound run-on (more than 2 independent clauses), or complex sentence.
5. Summarize T-units and sentence types. Compare to a standard and decide if and where improvement is needed. (Fragments and run-on sentences would be intervention targets.

Practice Example
Score this Passage:
Howard rides his bicycle and Thad rides in a seat on the back. They wear hats to shade their eyes. They go to the park and they go down the big slide.

Key
Howard rides his bicycle / and Thad rides in a seat on the back. / They wear hats to shade their eyes. / They go to the park / and they go down the big slide. /

Number of words   32
Number of T-units   5
32 (words) ÷ 5 (T-units) = 6.4 (mean length of T-unit)

An Example

Definition
T-unit = One group of words that will stand alone with all subordinate clauses.

Practice

Sentence	T-units	Type of Sentence
Thad likes to run.	1	Simple sentence
While Thad likes to run, he also likes to swim.	1	Complex sentence: one independent and one dependent clause
Thad likes to run and he also likes to swim.	2	Compound sentence: 2 independent clauses
When Thad collects shells	0	Sentence fragment
Thad collects shells and he builds sand castles and he splashes Christopher and he also read to Tonya.	4	Compound run-on sentence

exacting, techniques should be used with students who both teachers agree have problems.

▽ **Directions**

1. Obtain samples of written work or analyze samples from the survey-level writing exercise.

2. Obtain a graded list of frequently used words (for example, from Barrett, Huisingh, Jorgensen & Zachman, 1983).

3. Use the procedure described by Isaacson (1985) and presented in Exhibit 13.10.

4. Summarize the student's performance and compare it to locally developed standards.

Score Interpretation

Once again there are no established standards for this procedure. (This may not be bad. To attempt to develop anything but a local standard would probably be a mistake, because it would contradict the assumptions about local patterns in literacy held by most experts).

Qualitative Interpretation

One indication of the semantic quality of a student's writing is its similarity to the semantic usage the student produces when talking. The levels should at least be equivalent. Another indicator, if you developed school writing samples, is the similarity of the student's usage to exemplars in his class.

Exhibit 13.9*   A Modification of Isaacson's Syntax Scale

Syntax

Count the number of sentences in the writing that are representative of each syntactic level. Record the number of sentences for each level in the rectangle provided. Divide the number in each rectangle by the total number of sentences and record the percentage on the line provided.

Level 1
Repetitive use of simple (kernel) sentences. For example:

    I like hamburgers.
    I saw a dog.
    The dog ate a burger.
    He was sick.

Level 1

_____ %

Level 2
First expansions-kernel sentences + various phrases. For example:

    The dog ran away *from McDonald's.* (prepositional phrase)
    Putting its tail between its legs, the dog ran around the corner. (participial phrase)
    The dogs wants *to hide under the porch.* (infinitive phrase)
    Lying in the cool darkness is the cure for the dog's illness. (gerund phrase)

The writer may also use simple compound sentences. For example:

    The hamburger was bad, but the dog liked the fish.
    The dog felt better, and he chased the squirrel.

Level 2

_____ %

Level 3
Transformations that combine kernel sentences with relative and subordinate clauses. For example:

    The fish *which was freshly caught* smelled like the sea. (relative clause)
    While the dog slept under the porch, the moon rose. (subordinate clause)

Level 3

_____ %

Question: Is the student's vocabulary skill adequate?
    If YES, use Teaching Recommendations 1 and 3.
    If NO, teach vocabulary. Refer to recommendations in Chapter 12.

Objective
"The student will, within writing samples and revised work, produce writings reflecting adequate levels of vocabulary use. CAP: {specified levels from word lists and/or ratings from Exhibit 13.10}."

Teaching Recommendations

Teaching Recommendation 1: Balanced Instruction

Many classrooms do not provide time for instruction in writing (other than copying tasks). This isn't good, because students need time for writing (Graham and Harris, 1988; Heward, Heron, Gardner & Prayzer, 1991). This instructional time needs to provide for

Exhibit 13.10*   *Semantic Maturity/Vocabulary*

Count the number of words = w

Count the number of words longer than seven letters = 7 +

Calculate the proportion of large words using the formula:

$$\frac{7+}{w} = \text{proportion/percentage of large words}$$

Count the number of words not found on a list of common, frequently used words = cf

Calculate the proportion of "uncommon" words using the formula:

$$\frac{cf}{w} = \text{proportion/percentage of "uncommon" words}$$

Calculate the number of repeated words = u

Calculate the proportion of unrepeated words using the formula:

$$\frac{u}{w} = \text{proportion/percentage of unrepeated words}$$

both explicit instruction in the writing process (strategies for being an author) as well as explicit instruction in the mechanics of writing (skills for being a secretary). Without an adequate allocation of instructional time, there is little likelihood that a student's writing will improve. If you don't know how much time the student has to write, find out by observing both the student and the classroom time schedule.

In planning what to teach, priorities need to be set based on the student's current learnings and the concepts, strategies, rules, and facts needed to gain additional writing skills and to increase fluency. It is critical in a process as complex as writing to achieve a balance between enabling skills like handwriting, spelling, punctuation, sentence and paragraph conventions, and the broader purposes of skilled communication. One way to assure this balance is to integrate reading and writing activities by stressing the fact that books are models of authorship.

The role of teacher and the role of student change as the student becomes increasingly more competent in deploying both secretary and author skills (Isaacson, 1989a). In initial stages of acquisition, the teacher explicitly explains how to plan, review, revise, and transcribe (Graham, MacArthur, Schwartz & Page-

Voth, 1992). The following strategy from Englert and colleagues (1991) illustrates the *planning* questions a teacher has students repeat during initial stages of instruction:

What is my topic?

Who am I writing for?

Why am I writing this?

How can I group my ideas?

How will I organize my ideas?

Whenever teaching this sort of strategy, the teacher shows and labels the correct performance. In later stages of acquisition, the teacher enlists the student as a collaborator—one who helps with the steps. The instruction is highly interactive as the teacher asks questions about the task and the student responds, having heard the teacher's thinking out loud and having seen the teacher carry out the steps. If the student's poor handwriting or spelling interfere with strategy acquisition, the teacher, or a cooperative work group, can take dictation. You may also encourage the use of invented spelling or, where available, have the student use a computer. (We recommend using a keyboard only when it is truly an aid. Often the keyboard becomes nothing more than a temporary novelty in classrooms and, because the student is not taught to use it with proficiency, its introduction actually reduces the student's productivity.) When teaching writing, you may select topics that are familiar to the student to increase the opportunity for her to focus on the steps in the strategy rather than new topical information.

Because planning is a hard concept for younger students, you may wish to use a strategy introduced to us by a first-grader. Prior to writing, this student would draw a picture about the topic of his story starters and then, during composition, look at the picture and describe what he had drawn.

In balanced instruction, lessons are designed to provide the student with instruction in a variety of writing forms. Even though there is a growing bias to use only student-initiated forms of communication, we agree with Isaacson (1992) and with Graham and Harris (1988) that students need instruction in forms that they may not spontaneously generate but are likely to be required to use in school and in life (note taking, job applications, test responses). Student-initiated forms can be employed to build fluency and to increase interest, but should not be the only genre for students who need instruction.

As the student becomes more accurate in employing a writing process, the teacher can introduce strategies that are specific to different writing genres. Examples of these different kinds of written communication are presented by the teacher as each new genre is taught. Examples and nonexamples are shown to illustrate communication forms such as information, persuasion, argument, and entertainment. Isaacson (1989b) suggests that instruction in the secretary skills of writing be separate from those of the author role when the student's secretary skills hinder fluent writing.

For a well-developed and thorough explanation of effective writing instruction, we highly recommend a chapter on the topic by Heward et al. (1991).

Teaching Recommendation 2: Teach the Writing Process

An example **objective** for a student who needs this intervention would be: "In response to writing cues the student will compose {define the type of composition}. In order to be acceptable, a composition must conform to {insert appropriate indicators found in either Exhibit 13.4* or 13.6*}."

We have described a general approach for teaching the writing process in the context of a balanced instructional approach. Balanced instruction targets both mechanics and process (never delay teaching about the writing process while waiting for the student to become skilled in mechanics). However, if a student has already mastered the mechanics of writing, the focus of instruction will be on the processes of planning, reviewing, revising, and transcribing.

As with any other strategy, writing is best taught through explicit explanation and demonstration by the teacher (Gambrell & Chasen, 1991). In our experience we find that teachers often explain and show models of completed work, but they don't demonstrate the actual use of procedures—especially planning procedures. Today the use of maps and diagrams (like those presented in Parts 1 and 2 of the text) has replaced the more traditional approach of planning by outline. This is because the maps seem more accurately to represent the interactive nature of information processing (see Chapter 2) (Winn, 1991). However, it should be noted that there is little information on the effectiveness of different map types, or on their appropriateness for students with different skill levels (Dunston, 1992).

A variety of strategies for text production have been described in recent literature. Good sources for these strategies include Lovitt (1991) and Welch (1992). Also remember that students may benefit from constructing their own strategies (Pressley, Harris & Mark, 1992). We first encountered the strategy of drawing a picture before writing, as described in the section on balanced instruction, when a student thought it up during an evaluation. Be sure to:

- Teach strategies for planning, reviewing, revising, and transcribing;
- Teach goal-setting and self-monitoring (Graham et al., 1992);
- Teach peer collaboration strategies to enable student to interact with an audience to gain feedback on effects of communication.

Revision is a major part of the writing process (Raymond, 1989). However, students seldom, if ever, see revision take place. (This text has been reviewed and revised many times but the endless cross-outs, margin notes, and giant red Xs don't appear in the final version.) Students need to see the effort and revision that goes into the writing process. They also need to understand that composition and revision often occur at the same time. They can only learn this through public demonstration. This is most effectively provided by teachers who are willing to display public composition and revision. Have the students suggest a topic and then write about the topic on an overhead projector so they can see your effort and revision (don't prepare for this, do it the way *they* have to). Talk your way through the writing in order to demonstrate strategy use for the student.

Teaching Recommendation 3: Teach Fluency

Fluency in writing means producing more ideas and expressing them well in a shorter period of time. This is an aspect of writing for which there seems to be little empirical work specific to instruction. The following ideas are ones we share, more because they make sense than because of any compelling evidence that they are the most useful or efficacious.

Have students:

- increase the quantity of writing and reading

- write and read a variety of genre

- write for and interact with an audience

- rewrite in response to advice from peers

- assist peers in checking work for specific attributes

- assist peers in planning, reviewing, and revising for a variety of purposes

- self-monitor increases in fluency and quality for specific components/tasks that are less fluent than others

- rewrite the same topic for different audiences or purposes

Teaching Recommendation 4: Sentence Combining

Sentence-combining instruction consists of explicit instruction in taking short sentences and making them into big sentences. Theory suggests a link between the development of complex syntax in oral language and its use in writing (Lawlor, 1983; Reyes, 1990). To decide what to teach, review literature on syntax changes in oral-language development (see Chapter 12, p. 257), look at written syntax of capable peers, or use the guidelines in Exhibit 13.9.

During sentence combining, the teacher models how to combine ideas by using conjunctions such as *and* and *but*. Short sentences with parallel ideas can be taken from the student's work to illustrate the strategy of making them into bigger sentences. For example, the sentences "Thad likes to play Nintendo" and "Hannibal likes to swim" can be converted into "Thad likes to play Nintendo but Hannibal likes to swim."

In addition to combining short parallel constructions, students can be taught to combine structures that are not parallel. Students can also be taught how to manipulate single sentences. For example, the declarative sentence "Claire ran upstairs after she heard the airplane," can be inverted to "After she heard the airplane, Claire ran upstairs." Teacher-modeled instruction followed by prompted and unprompted practice will provide students with opportunities to learn how to manipulate sentence structure so as to gain more control over the way they communicate their ideas (Englemann & Carnine, 1982).

Summary

Chapter 13 defined written communication as a complex system that includes purpose, process, and product. We discussed evaluation issues in writing and addressed concerns regarding the absence of writing instruction in schools. We then outlined procedures for analyzing written communication.

Frequent references were made within this chapter to Chapters 14 (written mechanics) and 12 (language).

Chapter 14 / Written Mechanics

This morning I took out a comma and this afternoon I put it back again.

—Oscar Wilde

It's an impoverished mind indeed that can only think of one way to spell a word.

—Andrew Johnson

That's fine phonetically, but you're missing just a little bit."

—Dan Quayle, to Trenton, New Jersey, sixth-grader William Figueroa, after the youngster correctly spelled the word *potato,* which Quayle thought was spelled "potatoe." *Newsweek*

This chapter is about the enabling skills that allow people to display messages in writing. Don't even start reading it if you haven't read Chapter 13. Any discussion of transcription must assume there is a message to transcribe—and Chapter 13 is about messages.

Transcription is the process of putting a message into print. Some people dictate messages into tape recorders for others to put in print. Some people write with pencil and paper or use a keyboard to transfer messages to a written form. There are even computers that translate voice messages into print. No matter what the medium, transcribing requires the simultaneous integration of a number of "secretarial" skills (Flower & Hayes, 1990; Isaacson, 1989a). These skills include the mechanics and conventions of writing.

In Exhibit 13.1, handwriting, spelling, capitalization, and punctuation are listed under Mechanics. These skills are also listed by Tindal and Hasbrouck (1991) as Conventions and Mechanics in Exhibit 13.4*. In general these skills are thought to enable the display of messages developed through the processes explained in Chapter 13. However, in spite of their secondary role in written communication, many teachers find spelling and handwriting to be the most immediately alarming aspects of written communication. As a result, they are the source of many requests for remedial writing instruction (Isaacson, 1992).

The role of written mechanics in the modern classroom is somewhat dubious (note that many of the references in this chapter are old) because existing computer software can already replace handwriting and spelling with keyboard skills. However, until all students have the same access to computers that they now have to pencils (and remarkably, in spite of what one might conclude from reading journals and school district PR, only a small proportion of them do), handwriting and spelling will remain major components of transcribing.

Your authors (incidentally, one of us is a poor speller—it's his vowels—and uses a rather primitive style of printing) consider mechanics to be less important than the process of written language explained in Chapter 13. So why include a chapter about it? "Because it's there." Spelling and handwriting are taught in schools all over this country. One day a week, most elementary- and middle-school students have to write and take spelling tests. Spelling and writing are part of the curriculum. Teachers and students seem to be stuck with them, for better or worse. Actually, even if spelling and handwriting were not in the curriculum, we'd probably address them anyway in Chapter 17 (task-related behavior). That is because they account for bias in grading, which is an added hurdle that few special/remedial students need (Holbrook, 1990).

Handwriting

It is safe to say that most teachers teach both spelling and handwriting the way it was taught to them. It is also safe to say that, in spite of the fact that almost

Spelling and handwriting errors contribute to bias in grading, an obstacle special and remedial students cannot afford.

tion. Additionally, few teachers give task-specific corrections and feedback regarding letter formation (Scardamalia & Bereiter, 1986).

It is good to remember that handwriting can have an effect on a student's formulation of messages as well as his spelling performance. Students who have not mastered the skill of handwriting are often unable to concentrate on the processes of composition and transcription. This means that these skills should be taught to automaticity.

A Note on Style

Even today most students are taught manuscript and then switched to cursive writing; however there is some controversy about whether both should be taught. One argument against cursive is based on studies that show that the farther handwritten forms depart from the vertical, the less legible they become (Hildreth, 1964). The joining of letters, the increasing of their slant and elongation, as well as the addition of loops, all serve to decrease the legibility of cursive writing. There is also wide variation among individuals' writing in cursive, while manuscript writing tends to vary less among people. This makes manuscript more standard and less open to interpretation, thus facilitating communication. Also, contrary to popular belief, there do not appear to be any significant differences in writing rates between the two styles when experience and practice are comparable for those people tested (many of the studies suggesting that cursive is faster contrast the rates of older students with those of first- and second-graders). Instead, handwriting rates are thought to be more closely related to the quality of instruction, the duration of practice, and the individual skills of the writer than they are to writing style.

In this domain, which is so dominated by custom, some teachers and parents are quite inflexible in their expectation that all students write in a preferred style. They may even refuse to accept manuscript writing from older students. In such cases it can make more sense to arrange for a change in teachers (parents are harder to change), than to have the student spend valuable time on a subjective concern about style.

The one thing that is clear is that success in cursive writing is not contingent upon prior instruction in manuscript (Lovitt, 1973; Staats, Brewer & Gross, 1970). This means that manuscript is *not* a prerequisite

every primary classroom has a representation of the alphabet posted above the chalk board, *no one* in the school has penmanship that looks like that model. About 40 years ago it was noted that "No subject in the curriculum is as neglected or as poorly taught . . . as handwriting. And in no other subject are the results of instruction less impressive" (Cole, 1956, p. 97). The same statement applies today. Handwriting instruction is still limited largely to copying exercises that students complete in the absence of explanation or demonstrato cursive. Therefore, if a student is having difficulty learning to write, then teachers should pick a style early on and adhere to the selection. Someone who has had trouble learning to write, and has made some progress in a particular style, should *never* be asked to switch.

Spelling

There isn't any syndrome or set of characteristics that typifies bad spellers. Hardly anyone ever says a kid is suffering from "dyspellia," because the only characteristic that seems to separate spellers from nonspellers is the number of words they spell correctly (that is one reason spelling is excluded from the domains which can be used by themselves to justify eligibility for learning disabilities).

As an oversimplification, spelling can be viewed as the flip side of phonetic decoding. When you ask a student to decode, you show him letters and ask for sounds. When you ask a student to spell, you give him sounds and ask for letters. (Therefore the predictability of the sound-letter correspondence in words is an important concern.) To be a good speller, a student must determine how the word is pronounced, if it is spelled as it is sounded, and how it is spelled if it isn't spelled as it is pronounced (Spache, 1940).

There are prerequisites to good spelling. One of the most important prerequisites is the skill to selectively attend to and perceive letter, cluster, and word sounds (Assink et al., 1992). If a kid thinks the word *dropped* is pronounced "drop" because he doesn't attend to the endings of spoken words, he will probably write d-r-o-p in those instances where d-r-o-p-p-e-d would be correct. (As an evaluator, whenever you come across a misspelled word in the student's written work, ask him what word he was trying to write. If he mispronounces the word, you may have speech, or regional-accent, interference.)

The clearest prerequisite to spelling is skill at recalling the letters (either single letters or clusters) that make sounds. This phonetic skill is so similar to what is expected while reading, that reading and spelling instruction can be used nicely to reinforce each other (Cataldo & Ellis, 1988). Also, spelling skills can be tested by simply selecting a decoding sequence and asking "What letter(s) makes this sound?" In addition, some phonetic generalizations occur reliably enough

that students may be able to use them to attack unfamiliar words. These generalizations are outlined in Exhibit 14.1. Of course, these generalizations cannot be used at the automatic or even mastery levels, but they may help a student reach accuracy.

Phonetic spelling is like blending, in that it requires the student to break the word down, translate it into code, and reassemble it. During the analysis ("breaking") step it is best to attend to clusters within the word as opposed to its individual letters. That is because, when we are dealing with clusters, the amount of material that must be processed is reduced (see Chapter 2). Also, the clusters are more phonically regular than words (while the "i", "n," and "g" sounds may vary from word to word, "ing" is always sounded the same way). In the word *string*, therefore, a student is better off focusing on the clusters "str" and "ing" (see Chapter 11, p. 240).

Many of the skills important to spelling seem related to phonemic segmentation (see Chapter 11, p. 232). Research in phonemic segmentation indicates that it is a skill linked to both reading and spelling and that it can be taught (Liberman & Shankweiler, 1985; Pany, 1987; Read & Ruyter, 1985; Williams, 1984; Yopp, 1988). Research has not yet confirmed whether phonemic segmentation is truly a prerequisite for spelling, an enabling skill, or part of spelling itself (Yopp, 1992b). However, a complete spelling evaluation of young children and poor spellers needs to include tests of phonemic segmentation like those explained in Chapter 11 under SLP 1.

Morphographs

There is a content domain within language that permits writers to increase geometrically the number of letters they can spell. This domain is really a way of subdividing spelling by organizing the content into units of meaning—morphographs—rather than letters. Morphographs (see Chapter 12, p. 257) are the building blocks of all words. Some morphographs are words, some are affixes (the parts you use at beginnings and endings of words), and some are bases (the parts you use with affixes to form words) (Dixon, Englemann & Olen, 1981; Wiig & Semel, 1984). In Exhibit 14.2 we list morphographs that can be easily combined to form a number of words. Once the spelling of a morphograph has been learned, one can apply phonics rules to combine it with others to spell new

Exhibit 14.1   Phonics Generalizations Applied to Spelling

1. Double the letters *f, l, s,* or *z* in most one-syllable words when preceded by a short vowel. Examples are *cliff, sniff, bluff, whiff, cuff, puff, fell, tell, swell, ball, spill, fill, spell, brass, press, cross, miss, fuss, pass, buzz, fizz, jazz.* Exceptions are *bus* and *gas.*

2. The silent *e* at the end of a word makes a short vowel long. Examples are *pin* and *pine, dim* and *dime, hat* and *hate, mat* and *mate, rat* and *rate, cub* and *cube, plan* and *plane, cap* and *cape, at* and *ate, mad* and *made, mop* and *mope, kit* and *kite, rod* and *rode, hid* and *hide, rip* and *ripe, fad* and *fade, cut* and *cute, tub* and *tube, can* and *cane, hop* and *hope, not* and *note,* and *fin* and *fine.*

3. When you hear *k* after a *short vowel,* spell it *ck;* when you hear *k* after a *long* vowel or consonant, spell it *k.* Examples are *neck, dusk, flank, track, hunk, slack, stuck, deck, rink, milk, check, tuck, task, fleck, lack, coke, make, rock, knock,* and *stink.* Use *c* at the end of polysyllabic words when you hear *ik.* Examples are *attic, plastic, metric, cosmic, classic, Atlantic, optic, frantic.*

4. When you hear *j* after a short vowel, you usually spell it *dge.* After a long vowel or consonant you use *ge.* Examples are *age, gadget, lodge, huge, strange, cage, nudge, stage, page, bridge, change, hinge, edge.*

5. When you hear *ch* after a short vowel, use *tch.* When you hear *ch* after a long vowel or consonant, use *ch. Ch* is always at the beginning of a word. Examples are *chop, bench, batch, pinch, church, witch, blotch, pitch, porch, crutch, lunch, sketch, fetch, patch.* Exceptions are *rich, which, much, such, sandwich.*

6. When you have a one-syllable word with a consonant at the end of a word that is preceded by a *short* vowel and the suffix begins with one vowel, double the consonant. If any one of these conditions is not met, don't double. Examples are *ship* and *shipper, ship* and *shipping, hot* and *hottest, slop* and *sloppy, mad* and *madder, rob* and *robber, star* and *starry, fat* and *fatter, fog* and *foggy, wit* and *witness, grin* and *grinning, mad* and *madly, cold* and *colder, farm* and *farming, dust* and *dusty, rant* and *ranted, boat* and *boating, weed* and *weeding, blot* and *blotter, grim* and *grimmest, rest* and *restless, flat* and *flatly, slim* and *slimmer, feed* and *feeding,* and *win* and *winning.*

7. A word ending in a silent *e* drops the *e* before adding a suffix beginning with a vowel, but does not change before an ending beginning with a consonant. Examples are *hope* and *hoping, dive* and *diving, write* and *writing, tune* and *tuneful, shine* and *shiny, time* and *timer, hope* and *hopeless, take* and *taking, sore* and *soreness, flame* and *flaming, fame* and *famous, care* and *caring, hide* and *hiding, hope* and *hoped, lone* and *lonely, use* and *useful, sure* and *surely, close* and *closely, make* and *making, life* and *lifeless, like* and *likeness, shade* and *shady, noise* and *noiseless,* and *tire* and *tiresome.*

8. Double the consonant when adding a suffix after a short vowel. Examples are *capped, caper, capping, moping, mopping, mapped, filling, filed, filing, filled, taping, tapping, taped, tapped, tapper, hopped, hoped, hopping, hoping.*

9. In words ending in *y* preceded by a consonant, the *y* changes to *i* before any ending except *-ing* or *-ist.* In words ending in *y* preceded by a vowel, keep the *y.* Examples are *cry* and *crying, rely* and *reliance, pray* and *prayer, worry* and *worrying, joy* and *joyful, enjoy* and *enjoyment, say* and *saying, sleepy* and *sleepiness, glory* and *glorious, delay* and *delayed, merry* and *merriest, study* and *studying, lonely* and *loneliness, pay* and *payable, carry* and *carried, stray* and *strayed, fly* and *flier, supply* and *supplied, healthy* and *healthier, spy* and *spying, funny* and *funniest, tiny* and *tiniest, injury* and *injurious.*

10. When adding *ble, dle, fle* to a word, consider the initial vowel sound. A long vowel or consonant simply needs *ble, dle, fle.* A short vowel continues to need all the help it can get. Examples are *buckle, freckle, puddle, ruffle, stable, rifle, stifle, staple.*

11. While most nouns form the plural by adding *s* to the singular, nouns ending in *s, x, sh,* and *ch* form the plural by adding *es.* A noun ending in *y* preceded by a consonant forms the plural by changing the *y* to *i* and adding *es.* Examples are *cats, dogs, kisses, boxes, fishes, churches,* and *candies.*

12. An apostrophe is used to show the omission of a letter or letters in a contraction. The possessive of a singular noun is formed by adding an apostrophe and *s.* The possessive of a plural noun ending in *s* is formed by adding an apostrophe. Examples are *cannot* and *can't, will not* and *won't, I had* and *I'd, I will* and *I'll, had not* and *hadn't, Jim's car, the dog's bone, the groups' scores.*

Exhibit 14.2 Example of Morphographs in English

Affixes	Nonword Bases	Words
be-	tain	born
de-	astro	gain
dis-	cant	listen
-ed	stance	talk
-ing	ject	tear
re-	gress	time
un-	lief	grade
-s	ceed	act
-ship	spect	grace
pro-	quire	
-ion	vise	
-ive	semble	
-or	sist	
in-		
ad-		

words. Take a few seconds to see how many new words you can make by combining the morphographs in Exhibit 14.2 with words. Dixon and colleagues (1981) suggest that if teachers teach a few phonics rules with high-utility morphographs, even very poor spellers will become successful.

Evaluation Procedures

The process of evaluation for mechanics is illustrated in Exhibit 14.3.

Survey-Level Testing

Directions
Follow the survey-level directions for collecting a writing sample given in Chapter 13. The interpretation guidelines in that chapter will lead you here if necessary (if they don't, you shouldn't be here).

As in written communications one of the biggest

problems in written mechanics is the absence of standards for comparison. Therefore, before you can go too far, you may need to follow the process for developing a holistic scale as explained on pages 297–99 of Chapter 13. If you don't want to do that, then employ the scale presented in Exhibit 13.4*. You may also want to consult the rate norms that were supplied for written communication in Exhibit 9.4, but remember that these are local norms and not performance criteria.

Interpretation
Using the indicators in the mechanic/convention column of Exhibit 13.4*, answer these questions.

Question #1: Is the writing sample adequate?
 If YES, discontinue.
 If NO, ask question 2.

Question #2: Does the student have a problem with the use of mechanics and conventions?
 If NO, discontinue or return to Chapter 13.
 If YES, the first thing you need to do is compare the student's current rating on the scale in Exhibit 13.4* to your expectation, in order to state a long-term goal for written mechanics. Then, in order to have an adequate sample for analysis, employ SLP 1.

Specific-Level Testing

Mechanics SLP 1: Writing Fluency

If you do not have an adequate sample of writing, you will need to collect one now. If you do have an adequate sample, you still need to score it in order to engage in decision making.

Directions

1. Look at Exhibit 14.4*. It presents four different writing conditions. Whenever you collect a sample, it is best to collect at least three different ones under the condition you chose. (Be sure to note the condition on the sample so that you can tell the difference between words copied and those written from dictation.) When scores are called for, mark each sample as explained in the

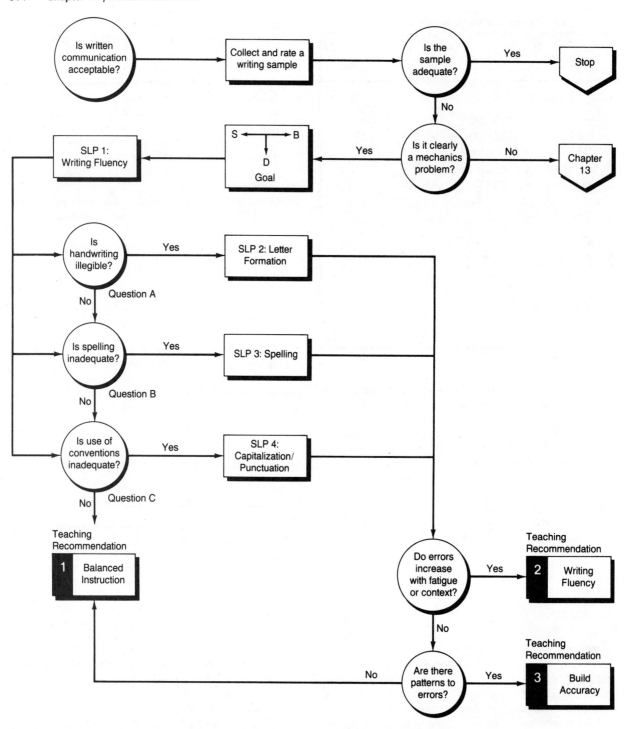

Exhibit 14.3   Decision making for written mechanics.

Exhibit 14.4* Writing Sample Summary

Error Category		Type of Condition			
		Copy Total Letters _____ Rate _____	Dictation Total Letters _____ Rate _____	Story Starter Total Letters _____ Rate _____	Assignment Total Letters _____ Rate _____
Letters **formed** incorrectly	Number				
	%				
Letters **spelled** incorrectly	Number				
	%				
Words **capitalized** incorrectly	Number				
	%				
Words **punctuated** incorrectly	Number				
	%				
Total errors **Total accuracy**					

following and use the *median* scores of the three samples for decision making.

While it is best to start analysis with samples taken from writing in assignments, sometimes these samples cannot be analyzed (because they are so limited). If that is the case, move left to the next column in Exhibit 14.4* to get samples of writing from story starters, dictation, or copying. If the student is having spelling troubles, be sure to include a sample from dictation (poor spellers often avoid words with which they know they have trouble). Have the student use the writing style (cursive or manuscript) being taught.

Try to collect samples of at least 100 *letters* (for spelling and letter formation), or *words* (for capitalization and punctuation). A format for scoring running text was introduced in Chapter 13 and illustrated in Exhibit 13.7. There are practice items in the workbook to clarify that process. Note that in written mechanics, spelling and letter formation are usually scored *by letter* whereas capitalization and punctuation are usually scored *by word*. To illustrate this, the same sentence has been scored for spelling, capitalization, and punctuation in Exhibit 14.5.

2. We will worry about scoring legibility in a minute. For now, record spelling, capitalization, and punctuation results from each sample on the summary sheet shown in Exhibit 14.4*. Do this by first totaling the number of errors in each category (spelling, punctuation, capitalization). Next, divide the totals by the number of *letters* (for spelling) and *words* (for capitalization and punctuation) in the entire sample. This computation will give you a percent that summarizes the ratio of errors per letter or word for each sample. Summarize this information on the writing sample summary in Exhibit 14.4*.

3. If the student's writing seems to get worse as he writes, you may want to repeat step 2 at intervals

CORRECT SENTENCE

The squirrel, or one of its band, ate Norvic's cinnamon bun.

INCORRECT SENTENCE

the squrrul or one of it's band atte novics cinamon bun

Spelling

the squrrul or one of it's band atte novics cinamon bun   4| *Correct*
6 *Errors*

Capitalization

the squrrul or one of it's band atte novics cinamon bun   0 *Correct*
2 *Errors*

Punctuation

the squrrul or one of it's band atte novics cinamon bun   0 *Correct*
4 *Errors*

Exhibit 14.5   Scoring a writing sample.

of 100 words to see if he has an obvious "fatigue point" beyond which accuracy falls off sharply.

Interpretation Guidelines

Question A: Using the grade-by-grade ranked writing samples you developed for Chapter 13, or your own judgment, ask "Is the handwriting illegible?"

If YES, then use SLP 2.

If NO, then use Teaching Recommendation 1, and also check question B.

Question B: Is spelling inaccurate?

If YES, then use SLP 3.

If NO, then use Teaching Recommendation 1, and also check question C.

Question C: Is the student's use of punctuation and capitalization inadequate?

If YES, then use SLP 4.

If NO, then use Teaching Recommendation 1.

Mechanics SLP 2: Letter Formation

Letter formation is important to teachers, as it accounts for most of what we think of as "legibility." Exhibit 14.6* lists ten types of formation errors. In Exhibit 14.7, a phrase has been scored for formation by drawing arrows to each error. The number for each error,

by type listed in Exhibit 14.6*, is noted with the arrow pointing to it in Exhibit 14.7.

Directions
Score a writing sample as shown in Exhibit 14.7.

Interpretation
Question: Do more errors occur at the end of longer writing samples and/or in the context of other tasks?

If YES, then fatigue or lack of automaticity is confirmed as a problem. Teach for fluency, using Teaching Recommendation 2.

If NO, then ask the next question.

Question: Does the student make important errors in letter formation?

If YES, note the kind(s) of errors the student makes and use Teaching Recommendation 3 to build accuracy.

If NO, return to SLP 1 and reexamine the evidence that led you to letter formation. This may mean questioning the relevance of the criteria you used in SLP 1.

Mechanic SLP 3: Spelling Accuracy

Misspellings fall roughly into two categories: phonetic and nonphonetic misspellings. Phonetic misspellings can be read as the stimulus word ("ordr" for "order"). Nonphonetic misspellings can't be recognized ("atus" for "order"). The type of misspellings a student makes is critical. The phonetic speller is actively using phonetic clues (although they are sometimes the wrong ones), while the nonphonetic speller does not seem to be using letter sounds. In any case, we are going to take the stance that remedial spelling instruction needs to present students with a code-based strategy. The one we recommend is illustrated in Exhibit 14.8. This strategy is recommended because we believe that spelling should not be taught by presenting lists of words (unless these are words derived from a set of technical vocabulary the student must master in order to do well in a specialized content area, like personal information for filling out job applications (see Chapter 17, p. 411). Students, especially those who have encountered difficulty, need to learn procedures they can apply to decode and spell words they have not specifically studied.

The phonetic spelling strategy in Exhibit 14.8 is presented as a series of objectives. During assessment you will ask the student to demonstrate competence on these objectives in the sequence presented in the

Student _____   Grade _____   Evaluator _____   Date _____

Task _____

TIMED/UNTIMED   COPY(NEAR/FAR)/MEMORY   TOTAL NO. OF LETTERS _____

1. ALIGNMENT	2. RELATIVE SIZE	3. RELATIVE SPACING	4. PROPORTION OF PARTS	5. INCONSISTENT STYLE	6. INCONSISTENT MODE	7. INCONSISTENT SLANT	8. CLOSED LOOPS	9. STRAIGHT & CURVED LINES
YaK ↓ K	cat ↑↑ Ca	ca t ↔ ↔	bird ↑ ↑ r d	bir d cursive	birD ↑ cap	cax / / \	cut ↑ a	cat ↑ ↑

Exhibit 14.6   Handwriting errors.

exhibit. The words to use will be words the student has previously misspelled. If the student fails an objective, it should be listed on his instructional program.

▽ **Directions**

1. Recognize spelling errors within the student's classroom portfolio or construct and administer a spelling test that will permit you to collect at least 75 errors (there may be more than one error per word). Be sure that the test provides an opportunity for each type of spelling error. Use the error types identified by Spache (1940) that are shown in Exhibit 14.9.

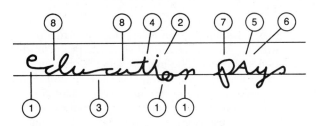

Exhibit 14.7   Letter formation errors.

2. Score the sample and categorize the errors using a format like the one illustrated in Exhibit 14.10.

3. Identify error patterns.

4. If patterns are not apparent, then use the informal phonetic spelling inventory outlined in Exhibit 14.8. The steps in that Exhibit should be applied to words the student has previously misspelled.

Interpretation Guidelines

Question: Do more errors occur at the end of longer writing samples and/or in the context of other tasks?

If YES, then fatigue and/or lack of automaticity is confirmed as a problem. Teach for fluency using Teaching Recommendation 2.

If NO, then ask the next question.

Question: Do there seem to be identifiable spelling error patterns?

If NO, then go to Teaching Recommendation 1. You may also need to teach proofreading and text-revision skills (see Chapter 17) using Teaching Recommendation 2 in Chapter 13. When using either teaching pro-

Exhibit 14.8   Informal Phonetic Spelling Inventory

1. *Word reproduction:* Given words dictated one at a time by the examiner, the student will correctly repeat each word with _____ % accuracy taking no more than _____ seconds per word.

2. *Syllable isolation:* Given words dictated one at a time by the examiner, the student will correctly say each word with an obvious pause between syllables (clusters). This will be done with _____ % accuracy taking no more than _____ seconds per word.

3. *Sound isolation:* Given syllables (clusters) dictated one at a time by the examiner, the student will correctly say each sound (phoneme) in a syllable with an obvious pause between sounds. This will be done with _____ % accuracy taking no more than _____ seconds per syllable.

4. *Sound-symbol correspondence:* Given sounds (phonemes) dictated one at a time by the examiner, the student will correctly write the letters (graphemes) that make each sound. This will be done with _____ % accuracy taking no more than _____ seconds per sound.

5. *Operational knowledge:* Given the directions to do so, the student will correctly say and describe all of the steps necessary to phonetically spell unknown words. This will be done with _____ % accuracy taking no more than _____ seconds.

Exhibit 14.9   Common Spelling Errors

1. Omission of a silent letter (e.g., *wether* for *weather*, *reman* for *remain*, *fin* for *fine*)

2. Omission of a sounded letter (e.g., *requst* for *request*, *plasure* for *pleasure*, *personl* for *personal*, *juge* for *judge*)

3. Omission of a doubled letter (e.g., *suden* for *sudden*, *adress* for *address*, *sed* for *seed*)

4. Doubling (e.g., *untill* for *until*, *frriend* for *friend*, *deegree* for *degree*)

5. Addition of a single letter (e.g., *darck* for *dark*, *nineth* for *ninth*, *refere* for *refer*)

6. Transposition or partial reversal (e.g., *was* for *saw*, *nickle* for *nickel*, *bron* for *born*)

7. Phonetic substitution for a vowel (e.g., *prisin* for *prison*, *injoy* for *enjoy*)

8. Phonetic substitution for a consonant (e.g., *prixon* for *prison*, *cecond* for *second*, *vakation* for *vacation*)

9. Phonetic substitution for a syllable (e.g., *purchest* for *purchased*, *financhel* for *financial*, *naborhood* for *neighborhood*, *stopt* for *stopped*)

10. Phonetic substitution for a word (e.g., *weary* for *very*, *colonial* for *colonel*)

11. Nonphonetic substitution for a vowel (e.g. *rad* for *red*, *reword* for *reward*)

12. Nonphonetic substitution for a consonant (e.g., *watching* for *washing*, *inportance* for *importance*)

Source: G. D. Spache. (1940). "Characteristic errors of good and poor spellers." *Journal of Educational Research, 34*, 182–189. Reprinted with permission.

cedure, emphasize strategies for problem recognition and self-monitoring.

If YES, then provide error-correction instruction that targets the student's patterns, using Teaching Recommendation 3 in this chapter.

Note: If the student has problems spelling in the context of another task, then, in addition to Teaching Recommendation 3, you need to teach for fluency using Teaching Recommendation 1.

Mechanics SLP 4: Capitalization and Punctuation

▽ **Directions**

1. Collect a writing sample that contains at least 75 errors (this means students who are fairly accurate will have to write more than those who are

not). Be sure that the sample provides an opportunity for each type of punctuation/capitalization error. Use the error types shown in Exhibit 14.11*.

2. Score the sample and categorize the errors by inserting an arrow and labeling the problem (this will look something like the letter formation example in Exhibit 14.7). *Don't bother with skills the student isn't expected to know yet* (that is, don't score a first-grade student downward for failure to use commas before conjunctions joining an independent clause).

Exhibit 14.10 Categorization of Spelling Errors

Stimulus	Response	Error Type from Exhibit 14.9 (listed as it occurred)
1. keeper	kepr	3, 2
2. stories	strz	2, 9
3. team	tem	1
4. teach	tesh	1, 12
5. cowboy	kboy	8, 2
6. why	y	2, 1
7. funny	funy	3
8. that's	thats	apostrophe
9. kite	kit	1
10. sorry	sry	2, 3
11. line	lin	1
12. air	ar	1
13. became	becm	2, 1
14. mile	mil	1
15. bigger	bigr	3, 2
16. birds	brdz	2, 8
17. animal	aminl	6, 2
18. I'll	Il	apostrophe, 3
19. tribe	trb	2, 1
20. truck	truk	2
21. eight	at	7, 1
22. won	on	2
23. merry	mry	2, 3
24. helper	helpr	2
25. fair	fr	2, 1
26. send	sen	2

3. Summarize the errors by category and identify patterns of concern.

Interpretation Guidelines

Question: Do more errors occur at the end of longer writing samples?

If YES, then fatigue and/or lack of automaticity is confirmed as a problem. Teach for fluency using Teaching Recommendation 2.

If NO, then ask the next question.

Question: Do there seem to be identifiable error patterns?

If YES, then teach the recognized skills using Teaching Recommendation 3.

If NO, then use Teaching Recommendation 1 with an emphasis on proofreading.

Teaching Recommendations

In this chapter we will not discuss instructional recommendations in any detail. The emphasis in earlier chapters, and the relationship of this chapter to Chapter 13, serve as a model for organizing interventions.

Teaching Recommendation 1: Balanced Instruction

Teaching Recommendation 1 in Chapter 13 covered balanced instruction for writing. Those recommendations should be followed for this student with one important addition—an emphasis on proofreading strategies for self-monitoring and correcting work (Okyere & Heron, 1991). Several explicit strategies for proofreading have been recommended, including those discussed by Gleason, Colvin and Archer (1991) (see Chapter 17, p. 404). An emphasis on self-monitoring is typically provided by using, and then gradually withdrawing, varying levels of assistance (prompts and cues) (Borkowski, Estrada, Milstead & Hale, 1989; Daiute & Kruidenier, 1985; Flower & Hayes, 1990).

When teaching handwriting or spelling use the following **Objective:** "Given writing tasks requiring the student to write {in assignments, from story starters, from dictation, or from copy} the student will make no more than {_____ spelling/writing} errors per symbol, while maintaining a rate of {_____} symbols per minute."

The criteria you will place within the braces of the objective should come from the same standards you used to determine that the student has a written communication problem (the first question in Exhibit 14.3), or the criteria that led you to answer NO to question A, B, or C.

Because writing is an active, constructive process,

Exhibit 14.11*   Mechanics Error Summary

	Error Tally	% Errors per 100 Words		Error Tally	% Errors per 100 Words
Capitalization			**Apostrophe**		
First name in sentence	____	____	Contractions	____	____
Name of person	____	____	Possessions	____	____
Title	____	____	**Semicolon**		
Days of week	____	____	Separation of series	____	____
Month	____	____	Other	____	____
Street names	____	____	**Colon**		
Towns, cities, states, countries	____	____	Salutation of letter	____	____
Personal pronoun "I"	____	____	Expression of time	____	____
Buildings, companies, products	____	____	Appositives	____	____
Geographical names	____	____	Other	____	____
Family relationships used for name	____	____	**Hyphen**		
First word of quotation	____	____	Compound word or phrase	____	____
Other	____	____	Prefix when base is capitalized	____	____
Punctuation			Other	____	____
Period			**Quotation marks**		
End of sentence	____	____	Direct quotations	____	____
Initials and abbreviations	____	____	Single within direct	____	____
Question mark			Block quotations (no marks)	____	____
End of sentence	____	____	Dialogue	____	____
Exclamation point			Titles	____	____
Exclamatory sentence	____	____	Words used as words	____	____
Emphasis	____	____	Foreign words	____	____
Comma			Special use words	____	____
Items in a series	____	____	**Parentheses**		
Month, year	____	____	Interruptions	____	____
City, state	____	____	Technical information within text	____	____
Day, month	____	____	**Underline**		
Direct address	____	____	Titles	____	____
After year in sentence	____	____	Stress	____	____
After state or country in sentence	____	____	**Ellipses**		
After introductory word in sentence	____	____	Omissions	____	____
Before conjunction joining independent clause	____	____	**Dash**		
Surround appositive	____	____	Interruptions	____	____
Set off dependent clause	____	____			
Set off adverbial clause	____	____			
After greeting and closing in letters	____	____			

student involvement is paramount. This involvement is characterized by reflection and self-monitoring. Even something as mechanical as handwriting can be improved with self-monitoring. Students who monitor their work will review what they need to do, check what they have done, and judge the adequacy of their responses.

Begin by making it clear to the student that quality of production is more important than simply finishing assignments. Next create a "strategic environment" (see Chapter 8, p. 158) in the class by holding students accountable for locating and correcting their own errors. Finally, present specific proofreading strategies such as COPS.

The COPS strategy, and a number of other writing strategies, were developed at the Kansas Institute on Learning Disabilities. *COPS* stands for "capitalization, organization, punctuation, and spelling." The use of this procedure is explained, along with a number of others, by Lovitt (1991). Each of these strategies uses the device of a "name" (COPS) to focus the student on the essential monitoring actions. The student is then taught to employ the actions through explanation, demonstration, and the gradual removal of self-talk. These techniques were all explained back in Chapter 8.

Teaching Recommendation 2: Writing Fluency

Review the instructional recommendations in Chapter 13. Remember that students need frequent, meaningful opportunities to write (and that they seldom get this in schools). They also need explicit instruction in the purpose, process, and product development of written communication. Even after they have mastered individual components, they will probably need instruction in how to integrate these complex skills. This integration is best assured through explanation, accompanied by the demonstration of good writing by the teacher, and followed by a great deal of writing. Without this integration, and considerable practice, the student will not learn to use writing automatically (Ivarie, 1986). See Chapter 13, Teaching Recommendations 1 and 3, for additional guidance.

The first fluency objective will be to reduce the error-per-symbol ratio for later passages to the level found in earlier passages. For example, assuming that the student currently misspells 12 out of every 100 *letters* within the first 100 *words* of a sample, 16 for the next 100 *words*, but 30 for the next 100 *words*. That student's **Objective** could read: "Given a story starter, the student will spell no more than {16% of the *letters*} incorrectly from any lot drawn more than {200 *words* into a sample}."

The second fluency objective should target specific conditions for writing. Here is an example: "When writing {during classwork} the student will maintain a rate of 90 correct letters per minute with 97% accuracy."

Teaching Recommendation 3: Build Accuracy

Accuracy is developed by carefully demonstrating strategies for correct performance, and by extensive guided practice. In the case of students who have practiced incorrect usage, the teacher may need to employ highly targeted lessons and correction procedures. The overall format of this process is simple. Return to the exhibits that contain error pattern information (14.4*, 14.6*, 14.9 and 14.11*) and select the most problematic types of errors. Then sit down with

the student and show him exactly what he is doing wrong—as well as exactly what he should be doing. Next, have the student explain it back to you. When the student can explain the correct usage, begin to have the student practice. Use lead questions (Stowitschek, et al., 1984) and prompts to maintain accurate performance. Then gradually withdraw the prompts while emphasizing the need for accuracy.

Write **Objectives** like the ones following. Specify the error type and use criteria as established in the survey-level procedure. If you haven't established criteria, we recommend 90% for grades 3 and above, and 80% for grades 1 and 2. Here are some sample objectives:

Handwriting Objective: "Given an {assignment, story starter, dictated prompt, copy exercise}, the student will make no more than {____%} {specify error type} errors per 100 letters."

Spelling Objective (for failure to use generalizations in Exhibit 14.1): "When spelling phonetically regular words, or portions of words, the student will use the {_____} generalization to write or say the correct spelling. CAP: 100% accuracy."

Spelling Objective (for failure to use the morphographs in Exhibit 14.2): "When spelling phonetically regular words, or portions of words, containing {specified morphographs}, the student will write or say the spelling of the morphograph. CAP: 100%."

Summary

Chapters 13 and 14 are separated for convenience. In practice the process of writing should be evaluated and taught along with the conventions and mechanics of transcribing. This chapter has focused on the secretarial skills required to transcribe written messages. We have described techniques for evaluating these skills and provided appropriate teaching recommendations.

Chapter 15 / Mathematics

I'm distressed by a society which depends so completely on mathematics and science and yet seems so indifferent to the innumeracy and scientific illiteracy of so many of its citizens; with a military that spends more than one quarter of a trillion dollars each year on ever smarter weapons for ever more poorly educated soldiers; and with the media, which invariably become obsessed with this hostage on an airliner, or that baby who has fallen into a well, and seem insufficiently passionate when it comes to addressing problems such as urban crime, environmental deterioration, or poverty.

. . . The discrepancies between our pretensions and reality are usually quite extensive, and since number and chance are among our ultimate reality principles, those who possess a keen grasp of these notions may see these discrepancies and incongruities with greater clarity and thus more easily become subject to feelings of absurdity. I think there is something divine in these feelings of absurdity, and they should be cherished, not avoided.

—J.A. Paulos (pp. 134–35)*

Mathematics is a language used to describe relationships between and among various objects, events, and times. Those fluent in the language interact appropriately with a system of symbols—just as you are interacting with alphabetic symbols, words, and punctuation marks as you read this text. This system of symbols works according to certain rules, just as words are assembled into sentences according to the rules of syntax. In mathematics, the ideas (the messages conveyed) have meaning and can be recognized in other forms—but the symbols are essentially arbitrary. By *arbitrary,* we mean that they are made up and agreed upon. As long as everyone agrees that "+" is a plus sign, it is. If, tomorrow, everyone decides that "−" is plus and "+" is take away, we would still be able to explain all the ideas we can explain today.

Evaluation in math centers on two broad content domains: the students' knowledge of the relationships of number and chance (the ideas) expressed through math; and the students' knowledge of the language used to communicate these relationships. The value of the language resides in the need to understand and to communicate. Therefore, it is an important aspect of literacy—or, in this case, *numeracy.*

Many students think that math is something one learns about, but do not understand that it is a tool for learning about other things. It is important to remember that, without a message, a language becomes nothing more than technique (that is the point of the quote we selected for the beginning of this chapter). Therefore, as teachers, we must somehow assure that students get *both* something to talk about and some way to say it.

Mathematics in Schools

It is difficult to say exactly which domain of mathematics gets the least instructional attention. However, it is fairly common to hear that the conceptual side of math is shortchanged within schools. As Paulos (1988) points out, "A discussion of informal logic is as common in elementary mathematics courses as a discussion of Icelandic sages" (p. 74).

Mathematics is very different from curricular areas such as reading, language, and written communication. One of the biggest differences is that skill in math is not reflected in global tasks like oral reading, lan-

Students who are literate in numeracy are competent in both knowledge of number relationships and in the language used to communicate those relationships. They understand that math is a tool for learning about other principles.

guage samples, or story starters. This means that a student may know a great deal about some aspect of math but completely bomb a test that doesn't cover that material. Therefore, it is necessary for an evaluator to know exactly what a student has been taught, and what she is expected to know, in order to conduct a functional math evaluation. In math, as in other areas, your own knowledge of the curriculum will have a major impact on how you evaluate and teach (Livingston & Borko, 1990).

In spite of heroic efforts at defining the curriculum of mathematics (Cawley, Baker-Kroczynski & Urban, 1992) and integrating it into a more holistic/thematic view of learning (Cawley & Parmar, 1992), most teachers teach mathematics out of basal textbooks. These basals vary dramatically in the sequence of skills they present, and the depth at which they cover these skills. For example, all programs teach two-place addition without regrouping prior to two-place addition with regrouping. However, in one version of the Harper & Row basal series, the shift from first to second of these skills is taught for nine days, whereas the *Heath Mathematics* series allocates 23 days for the same skill transition.

Howell, Zucker, and Morehead (1985), in preparation of a computation test, placed the sequence of skills from the five top-selling elementary math programs on a computer. We then asked the computer to supply skills introduced by four of the five programs at each grade level. The computer almost blew up. While there was some agreement between the basals at the first-grade level, there was essentially no agreement above that level. We found one program that introduced decimals in the second grade and another that didn't mention them until the seventh grade. Imagine what must happen to students as they move from school to school when this sort of misalignment exists (incidentally, census figures indicate that around 80% of students in the United States will graduate from a different school district than the one they originally enter).

However, math basals aren't the only problem facing evaluators. Math tests approach the math curriculum in the same motley fashion as basals (Brown & Bryant, 1984; Shriner & Salvia, 1988). In some ways the tests are even worse than the texts, because they present an image of consensus about math curriculum when no such consensus exists (Freeman et al., 1983). The basic problem is this: *given the variability in sequencing among tests and programs—the grade level statements from all math tests are useless.* Don't even think about taking a student who scores at the third-grade level and simply putting that kid in a third-grade text. The odds that such a decision will be advantageous are less than the odds of this book's being made into a movie. Consequently you should never state math objectives in terms of growth on published math tests ("Student will improve by 7 months on the {Brigance, WRAT-R, Woodcock, etc.}''), as the test items are unlikely to be aligned with your sequence of instruction.

While the sequences of skills in texts and tests are not to be trusted, some tests do collect adequate and useful samples of math behavior. This is particularly true in the domains of computation. Therefore, the tests may be used to track knowledge of particular skills. However, in order to make these tests useful for assessment in special/remedial education, it is necessary to cross-reference the items they present to a sequence of skills, and then to cross-reference the instructional programs you will use to the same sequence. Some tests and programs make cross-referencing easier than others by presenting clear content specifications. This cross-referencing may seem like a hassle, but it is absolutely necessary in order to interpret the results of testing in mathematics. Besides, as long as no one changes programs on you, it only has to be done once.

Recently there's been a major move toward "authentic" assessment in the area of mathematics. This movement is typified by work on portfolio and open-ended performance measures completed in California (Stenmark, 1989; California Mathematics Assessment Advisory Committee, 1990) and is promoted in large part by the almost universal dissatisfaction math educators experience when it comes to the use of math tests. While these procedures are still evolving, some of their implications for functional evaluation are clear. The main one is that math *isn't* simply about the language of numbers. Therefore, assessment procedures that only ask students to look at and write numbers are too narrow to reflect current views of mathematics instruction. This is one reason we recommend that student interviews accompany all testing at the specific level.

Mathematics Curriculum

Computation and Operations

Computation means working problems. Individuals who have obtained functional literacy can compute using the addition, subtraction, multiplication, division, and decimal-ratio-percent operations. For a student to compute, she must: (a) accurately and quickly substitute the various symbols for the quantities being computed, (b) arrange the symbols according to the rules for their use, and (c) know the correct messages to convey. These three actions correspond to the domains (facts, strategies, concepts) illustrated in Exhibit 15.1. The three domains should be taught together, although teachers may emphasize one over another depending on a student's needs.

The failure to integrate facts, strategies and concepts can best be seen through the process of error

Exhibit 15.1 Computation Domains

Facts	Strategies	Concepts
Has mastery of basic tools (e.g., addition, subtraction, multiplication, division)	Knows how to use basic skills (e.g., step-by-step procedures and algorithms)	Knows why the skills are used (e.g., understands quantitative or qualitative relationships)

Source: Adapted from J. Silbert, D. Carnine, and M. Stein, *Direct Instruction Mathematics.* Columbus, OH: Merrill Publishing, 1981.

analysis. For example, a student who produces the answer "17 + 8 = 16'" has failed to carry out a strategy correctly (she has accurately used factual knowledge to add the numbers 1, 7, and 8 together but failed to adjust for their relative positions). She has also violated the concept of addition by producing an answer that is smaller than the numbers with which she started. Here is a quick review of concepts, strategies, and facts.

Concepts

Concepts can be understood and recognized in terms of concept analysis. As you recall, concept analysis is a process through which the defining characteristics of an idea are identified (see Chapter 4, pp. 62-63). These characteristics are called attributes. Exhibit 15.2 lists concepts associated with different computational and problem-solving operations discussed in this chapter. This list of concepts is based on information presented in the book *One Step At a Time* by Bitter, Engelhardt, and Wiebe (1977), an analysis of math concepts by Howell and others (1985), material in *Direct Instruction Mathematics* by Silbert, Carnine and Stein (1990), and information in *Critical Thinking: A Functional Approach* by Zechmeister and Johnson (1992). Exhibit 15.2 also gives examples of problems related to these concepts. Most of the concepts are basic to the successful computation of addition, subtraction, multiplication, division, and fraction problems (Fuson, 1992). However, every concept is not necessary for every computation. The "common denominator," for example, isn't necessary for multiplication.

Exhibit 15.2   Basic Concepts and Example Problems

Concept	Example Problem	Solution
40. Cause-and-effect	Why are people who drink cold beverages more likely to drown in a pool?	They are more likely to go swimming because they are hot.
39. Correlation	If you observe a group of people during the winter and find that they drink a lot of cold beverages, do you think they are more or less likely to drown in a pool?	Likelihood same as average person
38. Representativeness	"How can you explain why I flipped a coin and got 'heads' 3 times in a row?"	What is true of large samples of items may not always be apparent when examining a few items.
37. Probability	"What is the probability of getting 'heads' when I flip this coin?"	50–50
36. Chance and coincidence	"How likely are two people in a room to have the same birthday?"	"It depends on how many people there are and how they were selected to be in the room."
35. Estimation	Would the answer to $710 + 50$ be closer to 700, 800, or 900?	800
34. Algorithms for checking problems	$9\overline{)252}$ with $\frac{28}{}$, $\frac{18}{72}$, $\frac{72}{0}$ "Show me how you would check this answer."	$\begin{array}{r} 28 \\ \times\ 9 \\ \hline 252 \end{array}$
33. Algorithms (procedures)	1. $\begin{array}{r} 44 \\ \times 22 \end{array}$ 2. $\frac{3}{8} \div \frac{5}{8} =$	1. $\begin{array}{r} 44 \\ \times 22 \\ \hline 88 \\ 88 \\ \hline 968 \end{array}$ 2. $\frac{3}{8} \div \frac{5}{8} = \frac{3}{8} \times \frac{8}{5}$ $\frac{24}{40} = \frac{12}{20} = \frac{6}{10} = \frac{3}{5}$
32. Set up equation This is a 1-step problem. (In a 2- or more step problem a critical concept would involve which step to complete first as well as how to set up each step.)	There are 5 children in the math group. Today 4 are absent. How many are present? a. $5 - 4 = \square$ b. $4 - 5 = \square$ c. $\begin{array}{r} 5 \\ +4 \\ \hline \square \end{array}$ d. $\begin{array}{r} 4 \\ -5 \\ \hline \square \end{array}$	There are 5 children in the math group. Today 4 are absent. How many are present? (a.) correct b. set up incorrectly c. incorrect operation d. set up incorrectly
31. Select operation	Thad has 7 miles to walk to get home. He walks 4 days a week. How many miles does he walk in 4 days? a. $7 - 4 = \square$ b. $7 + 4 = \square$ c. $4\overline{)4}^{\square}$ d. $4 \times 7 = \square$	Thad has 7 miles to walk to get home. He walks 4 days a week. How many miles does he walk in 4 days? a. wrong operation b. wrong operation c. wrong operation (d.) correct

(continued)

Exhibit 15.2   Basic Concepts and Example Problems (continued)

Concept	Example Problem	Solution
30. Irrelevant information	Chris catches 14 lobsters and releases 3 because they are too small. Kathy catches 9 and keeps them all. Jack notices that 5 are "in berries" (carrying eggs). How many lobsters do they have?	
	a. 14 11 − 3 + 9	(a.) correct
	b. 14 5 − 9 +3	b. set up incorrectly
	c. 14 17 + 3 + 9	c. wrong operation

	d. 14 11
	     − 3 9
	           + 5
		d. irrelevant information

29. Missing information	Howard and Tom play racquetball 3 days a week. Howard wins 2 of every 3 games they play. Howard is 5'11" tall and Tom is 6'. Tom weighs 150 pounds. How much does Howard weight?	Can't tell. There is not enough information.
28. Decimals	$1.7 \underline{\hspace{1cm}} 1.8$ $\frac{1}{4} = .\underline{\hspace{1cm}}?$	$1.7 \underline{<} 1.8$ $\frac{1}{4} = \underline{.25}$
27. Inverse of fractions	$\frac{3}{8} \div \frac{5}{8} = \frac{3}{8} \times \underline{\hspace{1cm}}$	$\frac{3}{8} \div \frac{5}{8} = \frac{3}{8} \times \underline{\frac{8}{5}}$
26. Mixed numbers	$\frac{5}{8} + \frac{1}{2} = \underline{\hspace{1cm}}$	$\frac{5}{8} + \frac{1}{2} = \underline{1\frac{1}{8}}$
25. Equivalent fractions	$\frac{1}{2} = \frac{?}{4}$ $\frac{2}{4} = \frac{?}{8}$	$\frac{1}{2} = \frac{2}{4}$ $\frac{2}{4} = \frac{4}{8}$
24. Fraction equal to "one"	$1 = \frac{?}{2} = \frac{?}{3} = \frac{?}{4}$	$1 = \frac{2}{2} = \frac{3}{3} = \frac{4}{4}$
23. Common denominator	$\frac{1}{2} + \frac{1}{4} = \underline{\hspace{1cm}}$	$\frac{1}{2} + \frac{1}{4} = \underline{\frac{3}{4}}$
22. Unity	$1 \times 4 = ?$ $4 \div 1 = ?$	$1 \times 4 = \underline{4}$ $4 \div 1 = \underline{4}$
21. Remainders	$17 \div 4 = 4r\ \underline{?}$	$17 \div 4 = 4r\ \underline{1}$
20. Distributive property	$10 \times 6 = 60$ $(2 \times 5) + (10 \times 5) = ?$	$10 \times 6 = 60$ $(2 \times 5) + (10 \times 5) = \underline{60}$
19. Multiplication/Division by 1 and 0	$\begin{array}{ccc} 8 & 8 & \frac{8}{1} = \\ \times 1 & \times 0 & \end{array}$	$\begin{array}{ccc} 8 & 8 & \frac{8}{1} = 8 \\ \times 1 & \times 0 & \\ \hline 8 & 0 & \end{array}$

(continued)

Exhibit 15.2   Basic Concepts and Example Problems (continued)

Concept	Example Problem	Solution
18. Associative property	$2 + 2 + 2 = \underline{?}$ a. $4 + 2$ c. $8 + 2$ b. $1 + 2$ d. $2 + 2$	$2 + 2 + 2 = \underline{a}$ a. $4 + 2$ c. $8 + 2$ b. $1 + 2$ d. $2 + 2$

17. Set separation	xxx − xx = <u>?</u>
	a. x x b. xx
	    x xx
	  x x xx
	c. x d.
	   x x
	  x
	  x
		xxx − xx = <u>d.</u>
		a. x x b. xx
		    x xx
		  x x xx
		c. x d.
		   x x
		  x
		  x

16. Union of sets	xxx + xx = <u>?</u>
	a. x x b. xx
	    x xx
	  x x xx
	c. x d.
	   x x
	  x
	  x
		xxx + xx = <u>a.</u>
		a. x x b. xx
		    x xx
		  x x xx
		c. x d.
		   x x
		  x
		  x

15. Sets	Circle the set of Δ's x Δ Δ x x Δ x x	x (Δ Δ) x x (Δ) x x
14. Equality	__ + __ = 8. __ − __ = 8. __ × __ = 8. __ ÷ __ = 8.	<u>5</u> + <u>3</u> = 8. <u>24</u> − <u>16</u> = 8. <u>2</u> × <u>4</u> = 8. <u>16</u> ÷ <u>2</u> = 8.
13. Expanded notation	763 is equal to __ hundreds __ tens __ ones	<u>7</u> hundreds <u>6</u> tens <u>3</u> ones
12. Zero as a place holder	"Write this number" <u>7</u> hundreds <u>0</u> tens <u>3</u> ones	<u>703</u>
11. Place Value	$\begin{array}{r} 27 \\ +11 \\ \hline \end{array} = \begin{array}{r} 20 \\ + \ ? \\ \hline 30 + \end{array} \begin{array}{r} ? \\ + 1 \\ \hline 8 = ? \end{array}$	$\begin{array}{r} 27 \\ +11 \\ \hline \end{array} = \begin{array}{r} 20 \\ +10 \\ \hline 30 + \end{array} \begin{array}{r} 7 \\ + 1 \\ \hline 8 = 38 \end{array}$
10. Regrouping	7 tens and 8 ones can be written as _ tens and 18 ones	<u>6</u> tens and 18 ones
9. Addition, subtraction, multiplication, division	$\begin{array}{r} 2 \\ +2 \\ \hline \end{array}$ $\begin{array}{r} 2 \\ -2 \\ \hline \end{array}$ $\begin{array}{r} 2 \\ \times 2 \\ \hline \end{array}$ $2 \div 2 =$	$\begin{array}{r} 2 \\ +2 \\ \hline 4 \end{array}$ $\begin{array}{r} 2 \\ -2 \\ \hline 0 \end{array}$ $\begin{array}{r} 2 \\ \times 2 \\ \hline 4 \end{array}$ $2 \div 2 = 1$
8. Multidigit numbers	"Read these numbers" 14 87 172	"Fourteen, eighty-seven, one hundred seventy-two"

(continued)

Exhibit 15.2 Basic Concepts and Example Problems (continued)

Concept	Example Problem	Solution
7. Mathematical symbols, terminology, and notation	$+, -, \times, \div, =, <, >$	$+$ = add, $-$ = subtract, $\times$ = multiply, $\div$ = divide, $=$ = equals, $<$ = less than, $>$ = greater than
6. One to many correspondence	"Draw lines from each □ to three 0's"	
5. One-to-one correspondence	"Draw a line from each □ to one 0"	
4. Numeral values	"Circle 7 x's"	
3. Groups of 1's, 10's, 100's, 1,000's	"Write this number" 9 thousand 7 hundred 6 tens 3 ones	9000 700 60 3
2. Cardinal numbers (especially "0")	"Count the x's" x x x x x	"1, 2, 3, 4, 5,"
1. Number order	"Place these numbers in sequence" 12 7 18	7, 12,18

Source: Adapted from G. G. Bitter, J. M. Englehart, and J. Wiebe, *One Step at a Time,* St. Paul: EMC Corp., 1977; and K. W. Howell, S. H. Zucker, and M. K. Morehead, *Multilevel Academic Survey Test.* San Antonio, TX: The Psychological Corp. 1985.

Strategies

A friend of ours once observed in several primary classrooms. In one of these classrooms students had been taught strategies for efficiently working with numbers. One strategy was "counting-on" from any number. (An example of counting-on *forward* would be, "Let's start with 6 and count to 10. Six . . . 7 . . . 8 . . . " The same exercise in reverse: "Ten . . . 9 . . . 8

. . . 7 . . . 6." Another strategy taught in the room was "counting-by." This traditionally covers counting by 2's, 5's, 10's, and 100's. When introduced to addition and subtraction, students trained in these strategies will know how to use their counting-on strategy to determine answers. When they are introduced to multiplication, they can use their "count-by a number" strategy to determine answers. Both count-on and count-by are very simple strategies that can be generalized to a range of problems (Silbert et al., 1990).

In another classroom, our friend observed students that were not as fortunate as those who had been taught efficient strategies. These students had been left to generate their own counting strategies. For example, one 8-year-old was observed counting her fingers to solve an addition problem. On one problem, however, she ran out of fingers. At first she appeared to give up, but then she got out scissors, plain paper, and tape. As our friend watched, the student then proceeded to fashion several tubes that she taped to one hand. No, she had not given up on her math problem. Yes, she had made more fingers! While her solution was entertaining, it was also very inefficient, as she spent a good portion of her math period constructing extra fingers, which would have been unnecessary if her teacher had taught her the count-on strategy.

Facts

In math, facts are simple numerical statements that must be used correctly in order for calculations to occur properly. For example, 2 + 2 had better equal 4 whenever a student is computing. In some ways "facts" are like "irregular sight words" in reading (see Chapter 11, p. 243), in that the regularity of those words depends on the skills of the reader. 2 + 2 = 4 may be a fact for both an eighth-grader and a first-grader, but the fact that 6 × 8 = 48 usually would not be a fact for a first-grader.

Application

Many teachers allocate time for instruction in computation and operations but do not include adequate time for instruction in problem solving and application (Carpenter, Matthews, Lindquist & Silver, 1984; Algozzine, O'Shea, Crews & Stoddard, 1987). To some extent the practice of emphasizing the factual and strategic content of computation over the more utilitarian content of application and problem solving may actually increase the time it takes students to acquire computation skills and decrease the likelihood that they will maintain proficiency. When computation and operations are taught separately, it is difficult to make them meaningful (Baroody & Hume, 1991). Meaningless material requires more practice if it is to be retained and is more likely to be forgotten than material that is useful in daily tasks.

Application is the utilization of math. Application as a content domain is familiar to us as the "stuff" we erroneously want to get to after students master computation. Application includes measurements of time, temperature, money, length, surface, volume, and weight. Subdomains within each of these areas include (a) tool use (how do you use a meter stick?), (b) content knowledge (how many centimeters in a meter?), and (c) vocabulary knowledge (what is the definition of length?) (Howell et al., 1982).

Exhibit 15.3 illustrates what we mean by content knowledge, tool use, and vocabulary knowledge. This example contains content lists for the measurement of time and surface. The lists in Exhibit 15.3 are not exhaustive. Other content could be included, or the same content could be arranged or calibrated differently. However, do not assume that all content covered in all texts or represented on all math tests is worth instructional time. Math curricula are often saturated with marginal content—the first example that comes to mind is the topic of roman numerals. This sort of curricular residue should not be allowed to compete with things the student genuinely needs to know and use. (Dr. Morehead has suggested that, if you really want to test and teach roman numerals, you can send her $500 and she will answer all of your questions about them.)

Problem Solving

Problem solving requires the functional combination of computation knowledge and application knowledge. It has two steps: step 1 involves deciding what to do (selecting correct operations, selecting relevant information, ignoring irrelevant information, noting missing information, and estimating correct answers); step 2 involves carrying it out (setting up equations and judging which numbers go with which operation, working equations using procedures that result in correct answers, and checking results).

Exhibit 15.3   Application Example of Subdomains

Domains	Subdomains		
	Vocabulary Knowledge	Tool Use	Content Knowledge
Time	*Tools*—definition of function	*Uses*	*Units*
	Clocks	Calendar	60 seconds = minute
	Watches	Digital clock–watch	60 minutes = hour
	Calendars	Telling time	24 hours = day
	Units—definitions	Setting alarm	___ days = month
	Seconds	Stop watch	12 months = year
	Minutes	Analog clock–watch	10 years = decade
	Hours	Telling time	10 decades = century
	Months	Setting alarm	100 years = century
	Years	Stop watch	
	Decade		*Concepts*
	Century		Early
	Morning		Late
	Night		Duration
	Fall/Autumn		
	Winter		
	Spring		
	Summer		
Surface Measurement	*Terms*	*Kinds of Tools*	*Units*
	Area	Ruler	Metric
	Perimeter	Yardstick	10 mm = 1 cm
	Circumference	Meterstick	100 cm = 1 meter
	Radius	Tapemeasure	1000 m = 1 km
	Angle	T-Square	
	Line		Customary
	Base		12 inches = foot
	Height		3 feet = yard
	Shapes		5280 feet = mile
	Square		640 sq. feet = acre
	Rectangle		*Algorithms*
	Triangle		Perimeter of a rectangle = (2) length + (2) width
	Circle		Perimeter of a triangle = Σ of sides
	Polygon		Perimeter (circumference) of a circle = $2\pi r$
			Area of a rectangle = length $\cdot$ width
			Area of a triangle = 1/2 base $\times$ height
			Area of a circle = πr^2

Exhibit 15.4   Self-Talk in Problem Solving

Problem-Solving Step	Self-Talk
Select correct operation(s)	"Will I add or subtract to solve the problem? I will add how many Thad and Paula read and subtract that from 38."
Select relevant information	"What information do I need to solve the problem? How many pages were read and how many pages were there altogether? Is everything I need to know there? Yes. Is there information I do not need? Yes, Christopher is 2½."
Estimate correct answer	"About how large a number could I get and not exceed 38?"
Set up equation and carry out	"First I'll find the sum of 26 + 7 = _____ and then I'll subtract that sum from 38. 26 + 7 = 33. 38 − 33 = 5."
Check results after problem solution	I have trouble with adding 7's so I'll check as I go. "I'll add my solution to the sum of 26 + 7 and see if it equals 38. 33 + 5 = 38."

Exhibit 15.4 illustrates what a student might say to herself as she goes through each problem-solving step. These steps are linked to math, but their relationship to general problem-solving strategies (see Chapter 5) should be apparent. Problem solving is another neglected and misunderstood topic in the math curriculum (Cummins, 1991; Englemann, Carnine & Steely, 1992; Schoenfeld, 1989). This is puzzling, as most math teachers are as interested in the conceptual material of numbers as reading teachers are in recreational reading. (It may be that little or no emphasis is placed on problem solving because so many teachers confuse "problem solving" with working word ("story") problems (Howell & Barnhart, 1992). This is a dangerous confusion, because story problems are often just a prose form of computation. When this confusion occurs, "problem solving" may be approached as simply a matter of putting computation into words.

Sampling Math Behaviors

Math tests have all the problems of other published tests (see Chapter 6): their norms are irrelevant to teaching; their formats and problems don't resemble class assignments; they don't adequately sample the student's behavior; and they don't make it clear why errors are made. To evaluate math, we need instruments that sample computation, applications, and problem solving. These instruments also need to be sensitive to all of a student's factual, procedural, and conceptual understandings. While many instruments sample the factual aspects of computation, few sample applications and problem solving adequately; fewer still are designed to examine concept knowledge and strategy use.

To see if a student uses estimation or monitors her own answers, the evaluator will need to use techniques that elicit more than numerical answers. Interviews and other less customary procedures need to be employed. For example, the two test formats in Exhibit 15.5 are meant to sample a student's mastery of the algorithm for addition of a two-digit addend to a one-digit addend with regrouping. In format A, all the problems require regrouping. In format B, some of the problems do not require regrouping. Format B is the better test.

In format B the problems that do not require regrouping are nonexamples (noninstances) of regrouping. The systematic and judicious use of noninstances forces the student to do more than compute. To pass this test she must utilize conceptual knowledge to discriminate when regrouping is and isn't required. The directions for this test could simply ask the student to "point to the items requiring regrouping" and involve no item solution at all. (The test also includes a diagonal grid for error analysis originally developed by Hofmeister [1975]. Of course the lines do not appear on the student's copy.)

To sample problem-solving skills such as selecting the correct operation, selecting relevant information, or setting up equations, one may choose not to have the student actually work the problem but to select how she would work the problem. Examples of stimulus formats that accomplish this are illustrated for concepts 29–32 in Exhibit 15.2.

Exhibit 15.5   Examples of Stimulus Formats

Format A

Name _____ Date _____ Grade _____ Count: correct _____ errors _____ Time: 1 min.

Addition – Double Digit with Carrying

48	25	15	78	16	77	17	18	14	26
+38	+78	+29	+13	+49	+15	+54	+49	+37	+19

29	16	17	13	15	17	19	76	17	18
+18	+18	+14	+28	+39	+43	+55	+17	+79	+19

23	36	48	53	64	18	68	15	39	42
+18	+15	+14	+18	+17	+69	+19	+17	+19	+19

16	19	17	19	19	69	17	18	14	15
+18	+18	+18	+19	+18	+16	+68	+23	+36	+48

Format B

Practice Items

45	28	94	76
+ 7	+ 6	+ 8	+ 4
52	34	102	80

28	53	16	94	87	63	60	32	42	51	Digit count
+ 4	+ 9	+ 8	+ 8	+ 7	+ 9	+ 8	+ 9	+ 2	+ 9	
32	62	24	102	94	72	68	41	44	60	1s (21)
31	58	13	26	74	69	83	49	22	93	
+ 5	+ 2	+ 7	+ 4	+ 7	+ 9	+ 7	+ 0	+ 8	+ 3	
36	60	20	30	81	78	90	49	30	96	Non-instance (41)
39	62	78	43	56	24	18	73	83	92	
+ 9	+ 4	+ 3	+ 8	+ 5	+ 9	+ 8	+ 8	+ 5	+ 9	
48	66	81	51	61	33	26	81	88	101	2s (62)
28	49	93	98	15	85	34	45	63	71	
+ 1	+ 6	+ 6	+ 5	+ 7	+ 9	+ 6	+ 5	+ 9	+ 4	
29	55	99	103	22	94	40	50	72	75	Non-instance (83)
31	97	19	70	48	65	95	84	36	83	
+ 9	+ 2	+ 5	+ 9	+ 8	+ 8	+ 6	+ 8	+ 6	+ 8	
40	99	24	79	56	73	101	92	42	91	3s (104)
1s	Non-instance	9s	Non-instance	8s	3s 5s	6s 5s	4s	Number added to itself		

Source: From K. W. Howell, S. H. Zucker & M. K. Morehead (1982) *Multilevel Academic Skills Inventory.* H & Z Publications, 6544 E. Meadowlark, Paradise Valley, AZ 85253. Reprinted with permission.

Interviewing

Some of the best procedures for evaluating math don't rely on tests at all. Interviews and assisted assessment can be considerably more useful than tests for gaining insight into conceptual and strategic knowledge (Stenmark, 1989; Madden, 1991). The easiest interview format is simply to ask the student to "be the teacher" and to show you how to work problems. This forces the student to make her thought processes, like those illustrated in Exhibit 15.4, observable.

If an open-ended request ("Be the teacher") is not sufficient, then a more structured interview should be given. Exhibit 15.6* provides a set of questions for conducting this kind of interview. The questions in Exhibit 15.6* are from *Assessment Alternatives in Mathematics* (California Mathematics Assessment Advisory Committee, 1990).

Error Analysis and Task Analysis

Task Analysis

A math problem is a task. Like any other, it places certain requirements on the student. In other words, the nature of the task itself requires the worker to do certain specific things. For example, adding fractions with *unlike* denominators ($1/16 + 1/4 = $ ____) requires skill at adding fractions with *like* denominators ($1/16 + 4/16 = $ ____). Therefore, if a kid fails, one way to find explanations for her failure is to task-analyze the problem. The subtasks that result from the analysis will be the same for all students who work the problem. Everyone who computes the solution to "$1/6 + 1/4 = $ ____" must do the things listed in Exhibit 15.7.

If a student does not solve $1/6 + 1/4$ correctly, any of the five subtasks in Exhibit 15.7, or their subtasks, could be used to explain the failure. In Appendix C.2, computation objectives for major operations have been task-analyzed. Each objective has an identifying number and letter designation. Listed with each objective are three other vital pieces of information: a list of prerequisite computation skills needed to work the objective; a reference to information about how to teach it if it is pivotal; and the grade level at which it is typically taught. You might want to take a look at Appendix C now because you'll be referring to it frequently.

An alternative explanation for any error is that, while the student knows the necessary prerequisites,

she does not have a strategy for combining them. As explained earlier, strategy problems can often be identified through error analysis.

Error Analysis

Basic computation (like spelling) is not an area where creative responses are highly prized. Because computation responses are controlled by the problem, errors often occur by types. These types correspond to the requirements of the problem. Some researchers have studied computational error patterns and proposed categories for them. The categories that are most frequently used are those originally identified by Roberts (1968). They are:

1. Wrong operation
2. Obvious computational error
3. Defective algorithm
4. Random response

Enright (1983) expanded these basic categories to seven error clusters:

1. Regrouping errors
2. Process substitution errors
3. Omission errors
4. Directional errors
5. Placement errors
6. Attention to sign errors
7. Guessing errors

Exhibit 15.8 shows examples of Enright's computation process errors.

Ashlock (1982) has advised teachers using error analysis to (a) be accepting of the student, (b) collect data, (c) be thorough, and (d) look for patterns. (Looking for patterns is obviously the main thing we need to do, but the other three suggestions will have an effect on what we find.)

Follow these steps when analyzing errors:

1. Collect an adequate behavior sample by having the student work several problems of each type in which you are interested.
2. Encourage the student to work and talk aloud about what she is doing, but do nothing to influence her responses.

Exhibit 15.6* **Asking Questions**

Asking the right question is an art to be cultivated by all educators. Low-level quizzes that ask for recall or simple computation are a dime a dozen, but a good high-level open-ended question that gives students a chance to think is a treasure!

These questions might be used as teaching or "leading" questions as well as for assessment purposes. Both questions and responses may be oral, written, or demonstrated by actions taken. The questions and their responses will contribute to a climate of thoughtful reflectiveness.

Some suggestions about assessment questioning:

- Prepare a list of possible questions ahead of time, but, unless the assessment is very formal, be flexible. You may learn more by asking additional or different questions.

- Use plenty of wait time; allow students to give thoughtful answers.

- For formal assessment, leading questions and feedback are not generally used, although some assessment techniques include teaching during the examination.

- Make a written record of your observations. A checklist may or may not be appropriate.

This is a starter list. You will want to build a collection of your own good questions.

Problem Comprehension
Can students understand, define, formulate, or explain the problem or task? Can they cope with poorly defined problems?

- What is this problem about? What can you tell me about it?
- How would you interpret that?
- Would you please explain that in your own words?
- What do you know about this part?
- Do you need to define or set limits for the problem?
- Is there something that can be eliminated or that is missing?
- What assumptions do you have to make?

Approaches and Strategies
Do students have an organized approach to the problem or task? How do they record? Do they use tools (manipulatives, diagrams, graphs, calculators, computers, etc.) appropriately?

- Where could you find the needed information?
- What have you tried? What steps did you take?
- What did not work?
- How did you organize the information? Do you have a record?
- Did you have a system? a strategy? a design?
- Have you tried (tables, trees, lists, diagrams . . .)?
- Would it help to draw a diagram or make a sketch?
- How would it look if you used these materials?
- How would you research that?

Relationships
Do students see relationships and recognize the central idea? Do they relate the problem to similar problems previously done?

- What is the relationship of this to that?
- What is the same? What is different?
- Is there a pattern?
- Let's see if we can break it down. What would the parts be?
- What if you moved this part?
- Can you write another problem related to this one?

Flexibility
Can students vary the approach if one is not working? Do they persist? Do they try something else?

- Have you tried making a guess?
- Would another recording method work as well or better?
- What else have you tried?
- Give me another related problem. Is there an easier problem?
- Is there another way to (draw, explain, say, . . .) that?

Communication
Can students describe or depict the strategies they are using? Do they articulate their thought processes? Can they display or demonstrate the problem situation?

- Would you please reword that in simpler terms?
- Could you explain what you think you know right now?
- How would you explain this process to a younger child?
- Could you write an explanation for next year's students (or some other audience) of how to do this?
- Which words were most important? Why?

Curiosity and Hypotheses
Is there evidence of conjecturing, thinking ahead, checking back?

- Can you predict what will happen?
- What was your estimate or prediction?
- How do you feel about your answer?
- What do you think comes next?
- What else would you like to know?

Equality and Equity
Do all students participate to the same degree? Is the quality of participation opportunities the same?

- Did you work together? In what way?
- Have you discussed this with your group? with others?
- Where would you go for help?
- How could you help another student without telling the answer?
- Did everybody get a fair chance to talk?

Solutions
Do students reach a result? Do they consider other possibilities?

- Is that the only possible answer?
- How would you check the steps you have taken, or your answer?
- Other than retracing your steps, how can you determine if your answers are appropriate?
- Is there anything you have overlooked?
- Is the solution reasonable, considering the context?
- How did you know you were done?

(continued)

Exhibit 15.6*   Asking Questions (continued)

Examining Results *Can students generalize, prove their answers? Do* *they connect the ideas to other similar problems or* *to the real world?*	• What made you think that was what you should do? • Is there a real-life situation where this could be used? • Where else would this strategy be useful? • What other problem does this seem to lead to? • Is there a general rule? • How were you sure your answer was right? • How would your method work with other problems? • What questions does this raise for you?
Mathematical Learning *Did students use or learn some mathematics from* *the activity? Are there indications of a* *comprehensive curriculum?*	• What were the mathematical ideas in this problem? • What was one thing you learned (or 2 or more)? • What are the variables in this problem? What stays constant? • How many kinds of mathematics were used in this investigation? • What is different about the mathematics in these two situations? • Where would this problem fit on our mathematics chart?
Self-Assessment *Do students evaluate their own processing,* *actions, and progress?*	• What do you need to do next? • What are your strengths and weaknesses? • What have you accomplished? • Was your own group participation appropriate and helpful? • What kind of problems are still difficult for you?

From: *Assessment Alternatives in Mathematics*, by J. K. Stenmark. Copyright © 1989 by EQUALS, Lawrence Hall of Science, University of California, Berkeley. Reprinted by permission.

3. Record all responses the student makes, including comments.

4. Look for patterns in the responses.

Exhibit 15.7   A Task Analysis of 1/6 + 1/4

Add fractions with unlike denominators.
1/6 + 1/4 = 5/12

5. Add fractions with like denominators.
   2/12 + 3/12 = 5/12

4. Convert unlike-denominator fractions to like-denominator fractions.
   1/6 + 1/4 = 2/12 + 3/12

3. Multiply fractions by a fraction equal to 1, using the factor that produces a denominator equal to the Lowest Common Denominator.
   1/6 × 2/2 = 2/12   and   1/4 × 3/3 = 3/12

2. Find factors of the Lowest Common Denominator.

1. Find the Lowest Common Denominator.
   6, 12, 18, 24, 30
   4, 8, 12, 16, 20, 24

5. Look for exceptions to any apparent pattern.

6. List the patterns you have identified as assumed causes for the student's computational difficulties.

7. Interview the student. Ask her to tell you how she worked the problem to confirm suspected patterns.

A task-analysis of basic computation is presented in the workbook. This analysis provides a cross-referenced mechanism for recognizing the prior knowledge assumed to be required for a student to learn a particular computation skill.

Standards

Tables of specifications for computation are provided in the workbook. In these tables each criterion for acceptable performance (CAP) is written in the squares. In some cases, CAP is listed as "undetermined." This is because those intersections cover tasks that are too variable, in either content or format, to allow a single statement of CAP. Therefore, before testing those squares, you will need to make or select materials and obtain CAP.

The CAPs listed in the workbook and Appendix C-1 are reasonable for all students; however, they are approximate. The criteria come from a variety of sources including the authors' judgment and experience. Standards for mastery were obtained by testing successful elementary students, junior-high

Exhibit 15.8   Computation Process Errors

Computation Error	Correct Answer	Student Response	Analysis
General Errors *Fact Error*—student makes errors on specific facts or fails to respond correctly to all or most facts within a particular operation.	8 +7 *15*	8 +7 *16*	
Sign error—student fails to use sign in selecting operation. Adds instead of subtracting, multiplies instead of adding, etc. This error type may be difficult to observe when entire page requires use of one operation.	3 −2 *1*	3 −2 *5*	Added when subtraction was called for.
Placement error—student writes digits in incorrect sequence or fails to align parts of problem correctly for required computation.	13 + 6 *19*	13 + 6 *91*	Added correctly but reversed digits in answer.
	6.021 *6.021* +51.30 = *51.30* *57.321*	6.021 +51.30 *111.051*	Failed to align decimals properly prior to computation.
	22 ×86 *132* *176* *1892*	22 ×86 *132* *176* *308*	Failed to align partial products correctly.
Faulty Algorithms *Wrong steps*—student used steps which do not appear to be correct for any problem solution.	22 +53 *75*	22 +53 *12*	Added all digits together.
	64 + 2 *66*	64 + 2 *6 + 4 + 2 = 12* *12*	Treated 64 as an addition problem and added sum of 6 + 4 to 2.
Missing steps—student fails to use necessary steps to complete problem. Regrouping errors are a frequent missing step error type.	18 +96 *114*	18 +96 *1014*	Added ones and tens and failed to regroup.

(continued)

Exhibit 15.8   Computation Process Errors (continued)

Computation Error	Correct Answer	Student Response	Analysis
	$\begin{array}{r} 8942 \\ -5961 \\ \hline 2981 \end{array}$	$\begin{array}{r} ^{8}8942 \\ -5961 \\ \hline 3181 \end{array}$	Borrowed in tens column but failed to borrow in hundreds and subtracted 8 from 9.
	$\begin{array}{r} 40 \\ \times 31 \\ \hline 40 \\ 120 \\ \hline 360 \end{array}$	$\begin{array}{r} 40 \\ \times 31 \\ \hline 0 \\ 12 \\ \hline 120 \end{array}$	Multiplied ones digit by ones digit and tens digit by tens digit and summed.
	$\frac{3}{13} + \frac{1}{3} = \frac{9}{39} + \frac{13}{39} = \frac{22}{39}$	$\frac{3}{13} + \frac{1}{3} = \frac{3}{39} + \frac{1}{39} = \frac{4}{39}$	Found common denominator but retained numerator. Failed to use steps to change numerator.
	$\begin{array}{r} 20 \text{ r } 49 \\ 58\overline{)1209} \\ 116 \\ \hline 49 \end{array}$	$\begin{array}{r} 2 \text{ r } 49 \\ 58\overline{)1209} \\ 116 \\ \hline 49 \end{array}$	Derived an answer before operation was complete, failed to calculate $49 - 58 = 0$ r 49
Wrong algorithm for given operation—student may use steps which are suitable for a different operation.	$\begin{array}{r} 24 \\ \times\ 3 \\ \hline 72 \end{array}$	$\begin{array}{r} ^{1}24 \\ \times\ 3 \\ \hline 32 \end{array}$	Multiplied in ones column and carried but failed to multiply in tens column and simply added carried number to tens. Procedure used in tens column would have been correct for an addition problem.
	$\begin{array}{r} 43 \\ +\ 5 \\ \hline 48 \end{array}$	$\begin{array}{r} 43 \quad 5 + 3 = 8 \\ +\ 5 \quad 5 + 4 = 9 \\ \hline 98 \end{array}$	Added ones and then added ones and tens. Order of these steps would be appropriate for multiplication.
	$\frac{1}{8} + \frac{3}{8} = \frac{4}{8}$	$\frac{1}{8} + \frac{3}{8} = \frac{4}{16}$	Added both numerator and denominator.

From K. W. Howell, S. H. Zucker, and M. K. Morehead (1982), *Multilevel Academic Skills Inventory.* H & Z Publications, 6544 E. Meadowlark, Paradise Valley, AZ 85253. Reprinted with permission.

students, and adults. There is not a terrific relationship between the CAP and grade level; a fourth-grader who has mastered addition isn't any slower than a high-school student who has also mastered it. Our criteria seem to be consistently higher than those recommended by White and Haring (1982). Obviously the criteria apply only if the student has received instruction in the content (first-graders don't learn fractions, so the fraction CAPs don't apply to them). The computation rate criteria do not apply to students until they can write digits at a rate of 100 correct per minute. If the student cannot write digits at this rate (most first- and second-graders cannot), a formula can be used to set intermediate aims. This will be explained in Computation SLP 1.

Criteria for the domains of application and problem solving are generally set at 100% accuracy (specifying an objective that calls for a student to "make change" at anything less than that seems a bit indifferent). If that appears unreasonable, or if you desire fluency criteria for application and problem solving, you can base application criteria on the "automatic" (See Chapter 2, p. 26) use of computation. Following this reasoning you specify a task—"Determine how many minutes remain until recess" for example—and expect that the solution be obtained at the rate and accuracy levels specified for subtraction in the workbook.

Evaluation Procedures

Note: Materials for use in evaluation of mathematics can be found in the student workbook that accompanies this text. We will refer directly to these materials by giving the number of the test, but will also provide a brief description of each in case you prefer to develop your own. One principle advantage of the materials we are providing is that they have been cross-referenced to the objectives supplied in Appendix C.1, C.2 and C.3.

Survey-Level Testing

Survey-level materials are used to answer questions (listed later) about the student's general status in math. The student's classwork is probably the best source of information to answer these questions. Other sources are tests that sample a range of math tasks. However, if any survey material (test or class assignment) is too difficult, then the resulting behavior sample will be composed mostly of random responses or desperate guesses. Where one disadvantage of many normed tests is that they lack content validity, one advantage is that they usually have a range of items. You need this range if you have no idea where a student is currently functioning. Some math texts have chapter reviews in their appendices, and these can be used to assemble a comprehensive survey-level test. Be sure to add problems that sample strategy behavior if the test you select doesn't include them.

Here is some more advice:

1. Select stimulus materials that sample a broad range of computation, applications, and problem-solving objectives, focusing only on objectives typically taught at or near the student's expected grade level. For example, if the student is only in the second grade, simply cross out problems in multiplication and division.

2. Have scrap paper and extra pencils available for the student and a stopwatch for yourself.

3. Plan to collect the survey-level information first and the specific-level samples after you analyze survey-level responses. Because math tests frequently use written responses, it may be possible for you to have the student work the survey tests in another class, or during separate sessions over a period of days.

4. Use Exhibit 15.9 to guide you through computation and 15.13 to guide you through application.

5. Keep records and copies of everything. Record summaries of the various procedures on the math summary sheet you will find in Exhibit 15.10.*

6. Remember to refer to the rules for developing assumed causes, and the 15 evaluation actions presented in Chapter 8, whenever you are interpreting the results of the various procedures. The interpretation guidelines all assume that the rules and actions have been followed.

Survey-Level Computation

The process for decision making in computation is outlined in Exhibit 15.9. The process begins with survey-level testing designed to answer the following questions:

1. Is the student fluent on basic facts?

2. Is the student accurate on basic facts?

3. Can the student carry out expected operations?

4. If the student is not at expected level, have you found any computation items which the student can work successfully?

Directions

Survey Facts Rate of response to basic facts is such a frequent explanation for other difficulties in math that it warrants attention at the survey level. Since most survey tests do not sample rate of response, you will need to add this test to your materials. For the purpose

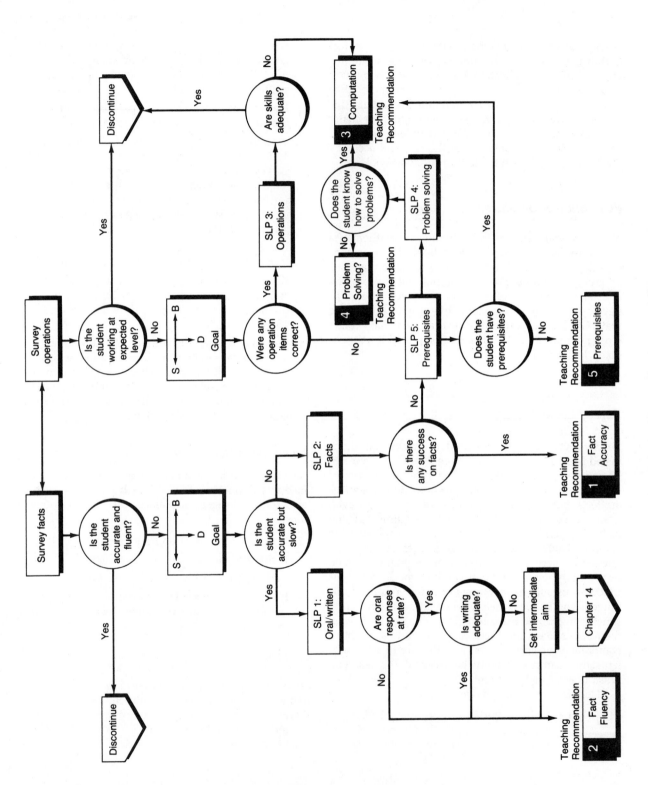

Exhibit 15.9   Decision making in computation.

Exhibit 15.10* Math Summary Checklist

Solve All Problems, Integrating Necessary Computation, Applications, and Problem-Solving Skills					Appropriate Curriculum Level	
					No Pass	Pass
Response	Identify	Produce				
Standard	Accuracy	Accuracy	Mastery	Automatic		
Problem Solving—Integrate Subskills						
Check work						
Estimate answer						
Work equation						
Set up equation						
Determine relevant information						
Determine correct operation/s						

Solve All Problems, Integrating Necessary Computation, Applications, and Problem-Solving Skills					Appropriate Curriculum Level	
					No Pass	Pass
Response	Identify	Produce				
Standard	Accuracy	Accuracy	Mastery	Automatic		
Applications—Integrate Subskills						
Measurement—Scaling						
Weight — Vocabulary						
Weight — Tools						
Weight — Content						
Volume — Vocabulary						
Volume — Tools						
Volume — Content						
Surface — Vocabulary						
Surface — Tools						
Surface — Content						
Linear — Vocabulary						
Linear — Tools						
Linear — Content						
Money — Vocabulary						
Money — Tools						
Money — Content						
Temperature — Vocabulary						
Temperature — Tools						
Temperature — Content						
Time — Vocabulary						
Time — Tools						
Time — Content						

(continued)

Exhibit 15.10*   **Math Summary Checklist (continued)**

				Solve All Problems, Integrating Necessary Computation, Applications, and Problem-Solving Skills					Appropriate Curriculum Level	
									No Pass	Pass
Response Type				Identify	Produce					
Standard				Accuracy	Accuracy	Mastery	Automatic			
Computation—Integrate Subskills										
+	−	×	÷	Operations—Rational Numbers						
				Ratios						
				Percents						
				Decimals						
				Fractions						
				Operations—Whole Numbers						
				÷						
				×						
				−						
				+						
				Basic Facts—Integrate Subskills						
				÷						
				×						
				−						
				+						

of this procedure, a "fact" is any addition or subtraction problem involving a number 0–10 added to or taken from a number 0–20. For multiplication a "fact" is any number 0–12 multiplied by any other number 0–12. For division, a "fact" is any number divided by 0–12 that yields an answer 0–12.

1. Select a basic fact test for each area the student is expected to know. Use tests 1–4 in the workbook.

2. For each fact test, say to the student: "I want you to work these items as quickly and as carefully as you can. Don't skip any problems unless you don't know how to do them. When you come to the end of a row, start at the next row. Keep working until I tell you to stop. Please, begin." Start your timing device and time the student for one minute. When the time is up, say "Stop." Repeat for each set of facts.

3. The answers and error-analysis grids are provided in Exhibit 15.11.

4. To establish rate per minute count the number of problems (you may want to count digits for more complex items, but problems is appropriate for basic facts) finished correctly and the number finished incorrectly. Next divide these totals by the time in minutes (in this case, 1). Omissions are not errors.

5. To determine accuracy divide the number of items worked correctly by the total number of items worked.

6. Compare the student's scores to the criteria suggested in Addition **Objective** 1m, Subtraction **Objective** 1m, Multiplication **Objective** 1m, and Division **Objective** 1m (Appendix C.1) or to a criterion you establish.

Interpretation Guidelines

Based on the accuracy and rate criteria in Appendix C.1, respond to the following computation questions.

Facts question 1: Is the student accurate and fluent on basic facts?

If YES, then discontinue testing facts (although you still need to administer survey tests for operations).

If NO, note the current level of accuracy and fluency and then, by comparing these to the criteria in

Exhibit 15.11   Fact Answers

Test 1: Addition Objective 1m

Practice Items:

7 +7 = 16	10 +2 = 12	3 +17 = 20	5 +5 = 10

												Digit count
16 +2 = 18	20 +0 = 20	7 +2 = 9	12 +6 = 18	9 +1 = 10	1 +8 = 9	2 +18 = 20	0 +10 = 10	15 +5 = 20	9 +7 = 16	3 +6 = 9	17 +1 = 18	(21) Facts 11–20
8 +4 = 12	11 +9 = 20	15 +4 = 19	1 +8 = 9	17 +2 = 19	8 +5 = 13	1 +6 = 7	3 +17 = 20	3 +3 = 6	4 +16 = 20	2 +5 = 7	10 +10 = 20	(41) Facts 0–10
8 +11 = 19	6 +9 = 15	14 +5 = 19	13 +7 = 20	2 +4 = 6	19 +0 = 19	1 +8 = 9	10 +6 = 16	4 +11 = 15	2 +7 = 9	14 +3 = 17	4 +9 = 9	(61) Facts 0–10
7 +13 = 20	0 +19 = 19	5 +1 = 6	0 +20 = 20	3 +17 = 20	4 +5 = 9	18 +1 = 19	5 +2 = 7	2 +3 = 5	12 +5 = 17	9 +0 = 9	1 +19 = 20	(80) Facts 0–20
8 +5 = 13	20 +0 = 20	3 +15 = 18	10 +10 = 20	1 +13 = 14	14 +5 = 19	8 +0 = 8	19 +1 = 20	4 +5 = 9	7 +2 = 9	12 +4 = 16	2 +9 = 11	(101) Facts 0–10
10 +10 = 20	5 +6 = 11	18 +2 = 20	6 +12 = 18	9 +1 = 10	16 +2 = 18	7 +11 = 18	4 +1 = 5	2 +17 = 19	6 +3 = 9	0 +9 = 9	14 +3 = 17	(122)
Facts 0–10	Facts 0–10	Facts 11–20	Facts 11–20	Facts 0–10	Facts 11–20	Facts 11–20	Facts 0–10	Facts 11–20	Facts 0–10	Facts 0–10	Facts 11–20	

Objective: Addition facts (0–20). Mastery CAP: 80 digits correct with zero errors.

Source: From K. W. Howell, S. H. Zucker & M. K. Morehead (1982) *Multilevel Academic Skills Inventory.* H & Z Publications, 6544 E. Meadowlark, Paradise Valley, Az 85253. Reprinted with permission.

(continued)

Appendix C.1, calculate the discrepancy and state the long term goal. Next answer question 2.

Facts question 2: Is the student accurate but slow?

If YES, then the student could be slow because she doesn't know the facts, or because she doesn't write quickly enough to display her knowledge. Employ Computation SLP 1.

If NO (the student is inaccurate), then employ Computation SLP 2.

Directions

The process for evaluating operations is also illustrated in Exhibit 15.9. Here is how it works:

1. Use tests 5–10 in the workbook, or select a test

Exhibit 15.11   Fact Answers (continued)

Test 2: Subtraction Objective 1m

Practice Items:

$$10 - 7 = 3 \qquad 17 - 8 = 9 \qquad 19 - 12 = 7 \qquad 9 - 2 = 7$$

12−10=*2*	2−2=*0*	19−5=*14*	6−5=*1*	16−3=*9*	3−6=*0*	13−1=*7*	1−1=*0*	20−9=*11*	10−8=*2*	15−9=*6*	4−1=*3*	11−8=*3*	0−0=*0*
7−3=*4*	17−12=*5*	10−9=*1*	15−4=*11*	9−8=*3*	13−2=*5*	5−13=*3*	19−1=*6*	8−3=*7*	14−5=*11*	7−5=*2*	13−11=*2*	6−5=*1*	14−9=*5*
17−14=*3*	1−0=*1*	20−8=*12*	0−0=*0*	18−11=*7*	9−2=*7*	20−10=*10*	4−4=*0*	12−10=*2*	2−1=*1*	20−16=*4*	3−2=*1*	15−13=*2*	8−4=*4*
3−1=*2*	18−10=*8*	9−2=*7*	13−3=*10*	5−2=*3*	11−10=*1*	7−2=*5*	15−12=*3*	10−6=*4*	17−5=*12*	7−7=*0*	12−8=*4*	1−1=*0*	19−12=*7*
12−8=*4*	2−0=*2*	16−12=*4*	3−0=*3*	16−4=*12*	4−3=*1*	14−3=*11*	0−0=*0*	18−10=*8*	5−5=*0*	11−7=*4*	6−0=*6*	16−9=*7*	8−3=*5*
4−1=*3*	15−3=*12*	0−0=*0*	20−12=*8*	8−4=*4*	17−6=*11*	2−1=*1*	18−13=*5*	9−6=*3*	19−7=*12*	6−2=*4*	14−3=*11*	0−0=*0*	11−1=*10*
16−9=*7*	5−3=*2*	13−2=*11*	10−0=*10*	18−2=*12*	9−3=*7*	15−3=*12*	7−1=*6*	12−2=*10*	6−3=*3*	11−0=*11*	5−5=*0*	17−2=*15*	2−0=*2*

Digit count (right column):

Digit count	Cumulative
0	Facts (16) 0–10
5	Facts (32) 11–20
4	Facts (48) 0–10
7	Facts (64) 11–20
5	Facts (80) 0–10
10	Facts (99) 11–20
2	Facts (120) 0–10

Column labels (bottom): Facts 11–20, Facts 0–10, Facts 11–20, Facts 0–10, Facts 11–20, Facts 0–10, Facts 11–20, Facts 0–10, Facts 11–20, Facts 0–10, Facts 11–20, Facts 0–10, Facts, 11–20

Objective: Subtraction facts (0–20). Mastery CAP: 80 digits correct with zero errors.

Source: From K. W. Howell, S. H. Zucker & M. K. Morehead (1982) *Multilevel Academic Skills Inventory.* H & Z Publications, 6544 E. Meadowlark, Paradise Valley, Az 85253. Reprinted with permission.

(continued)

(classwork) sampling a broad range of problems. The sample should include problem types on which the student has had instruction.

2. Say to the student: "Work each problem; take your time; show your work."

3. Score each item as correct or incorrect. In this case, count omissions as errors.

4. Answers to the problems on tests 5–10 are presented in Exhibit 15.12. Note that each item has two numbers in parentheses above it. The first of these numbers is the objective number and the second is the grade level at which this objective is routinely taught. The objective number always refers to the objectives for that operation (addition, fractions) found in Appendix C.1.

Exhibit 15.11 **Fact Answers (continued)**

Test 3: Multiplication Objective 1m

Practice Items:

4×3	3×7	9×8	5×6
12	21	72	30

1×6 = 6	5×8 = 40	8×9 = 72	2×2 = 4	4×7 = 28	0×3 = 0	1×1 = 1	7×0 = 0	6×4 = 24	8×5 = 40	9×10 = 90	7×7 = 49	
8×10 = 80	3×6 = 18	6×8 = 48	9×9 = 81	7×2 = 14	6×7 = 42	2×3 = 6	4×1 = 4	5×0 = 0	3×4 = 12	5×5 = 25	2×10 = 20	7s
3×5 = 15	1×10 = 10	4×6 = 24	7×8 = 56	3×9 = 27	6×2 = 12	5×7 = 35	9×3 = 27	6×1 = 6	4×0 = 0	9×4 = 36	3×5 = 15	10s
4×4 = 16	7×5 = 35	0×10 = 0	6×6 = 36	2×8 = 16	6×9 = 54	9×2 = 18	8×7 = 56	7×3 = 21	9×1 = 9	1×0 = 0	4×4 = 16	5s
6×0 = 0	5×4 = 20	6×5 = 30	5×10 = 50	7×6 = 42	3×8 = 24	1×9 = 9	5×2 = 10	2×7 = 14	8×3 = 24	5×1 = 5	0×0 = 0	4s
2×1 = 2	3×0 = 0	7×4 = 28	9×5 = 45	7×10 = 70	9×6 = 54	8×8 = 64	4×9 = 36	4×2 = 8	1×7 = 7	5×3 = 15	3×1 = 3	0s
0s	4s	5s	10s	6s	8s	9s	2s	7s	3s	1s	0s	

Objective: Multiplication facts (0–10). Mastery CAP: 80 digits correct with zero errors.

Source: From K. W. Howell, S. H. Zucker & M. K. Morehead (1982) *Multilevel Academic Skills Inventory.* H & Z Publications, 6544 E. Meadowlark, Paradise Valley, Az 85253. Reprinted with permission.

(continued)

5. Compare the items correct to expectancies for the student's current grade level by using the computation summary sheet shown in Exhibit 15.10*.

Interpretation Guidelines

Review your curriculum to determine what the student should know how to do at the curriculum levels we recommend (these are shown in Exhibit 15.12). Based on the student's performance, respond to the following questions.

Operations question 1: Can the student correctly work items at expected grade-level placement?

If YES, there isn't a problem (although you should administer items beyond the expected grade level to determine where to begin instruction).

If NO, use the student's expected performance on the test as a standard and then determine the discrepancy and goal. Next ask operations question 2.

Operations question 2: Were any operation items correct?

If YES, you have two choices. If you believe that you have obtained an adequate sample of the student's work, list objectives passed as indicators of the student's current level of performance. The objectives

Exhibit 15.11 Fact Answers (continued)

Test 4: Division Objective 1m

Practice Items: 2⟌4 = 2 3⟌12 = 4 6⟌24 = 4 8⟌16 = 2

5⟌25 = 5	4⟌36 = 9	7⟌49 = 7	6⟌48 = 8	2⟌2 = 1	8⟌0 = 0	9⟌9 = 1	5⟌0 = 0	1⟌1 = 1	Digit count (9)
3⟌30 = 10	5⟌45 = 9	4⟌4 = 1	7⟌63 = 9	6⟌60 = 10	2⟌8 = 4	8⟌64 = 8	9⟌54 = 6	5⟌30 = 6	(20)
1⟌9 = 9	3⟌27 = 9	5⟌35 = 7	4⟌20 = 5	7⟌56 = 8	6⟌54 = 9	2⟌6 = 3	8⟌40 = 5	9⟌81 = 9	5s (29)
10⟌90 = 9	1⟌10 = 10	3⟌21 = 7	5⟌40 = 8	4⟌16 = 4	7⟌42 = 6	6⟌6 = 1	2⟌10 = 5	8⟌16 = 2	9s (39)
9⟌27 = 3	10⟌50 = 5	1⟌2 = 2	3⟌15 = 5	5⟌20 = 4	4⟌40 = 10	7⟌35 = 5	6⟌0 = 0	2⟌14 = 7	8s (49)
8⟌24 = 3	9⟌18 = 2	10⟌30 = 3	1⟌4 = 4	3⟌9 = 3	5⟌15 = 3	4⟌32 = 8	7⟌21 = 3	6⟌6 = 1	2s (58)
2⟌16 = 8	8⟌48 = 6	9⟌36 = 4	10⟌40 = 4	1⟌3 = 3	3⟌18 = 6	5⟌10 = 2	4⟌24 = 6	7⟌28 = 4	6s (67)
6⟌18 = 3	2⟌18 = 9	8⟌56 = 7	9⟌63 = 7	10⟌80 = 8	1⟌6 = 6	3⟌24 = 8	5⟌5 = 1	4⟌28 = 7	7s (76)
7⟌14 = 2	6⟌24 = 4	2⟌20 = 10	8⟌32 = 4	9⟌45 = 5	10⟌70 = 7	1⟌5 = 5	3⟌12 = 4	5⟌50 = 10	4s (87)
4⟌8 = 2	7⟌7 = 1	6⟌30 = 5	2⟌0 = 0	8⟌72 = 9	9⟌90 = 10	10⟌20 = 2	1⟌8 = 8	3⟌6 = 2	5s (96)
7s	6s	2s	8s	9s	10s	1s	3s		

Objective: Division facts (0–10). Mastery CAP: 80 digits correct with zero errors.

Source: From K. W. Howell, S. H. Zucker & M. K. Morehead (1982) *Multilevel Academic Skills Inventory.* H & Z Publications, 6544 E. Meadowlark, Paradise Valley, Az 85253. Reprinted with permission.

(continued)

corresponding to items the student has missed should be listed on the student's teaching plan. Only list objectives the student is expected to know. If you lack confidence in the survey results, employ math SLP 3 to confirm what skills the student needs to be taught. It may be important to do this.

If NO, employ Math SLPs 4 and 5.

Survey-Level Application

The process of testing application is presented in Exhibit 15.13. Questions:

Exhibit 15.12   Operations Answers

Test 5: Addition Survey Test

1. (1,1)	2. (1,1)	3. (1,1)	4. (2,1)	5. (2,1)

$$\begin{array}{r} 8 \\ +7 \\ \hline 15 \end{array} \qquad \begin{array}{r} 13 \\ +\ 6 \\ \hline 19 \end{array} \qquad \begin{array}{r} 5 \\ +6 \\ \hline 11 \end{array} \qquad \begin{array}{r} 1 \\ +0 \\ \hline 1 \end{array} \qquad \begin{array}{r} 0 \\ +3 \\ \hline 3 \end{array}$$

6. (3,2)	7. (3,2)	8. (4,2)	9. (4,2)	10. (5,2)

$$\begin{array}{r} 7 \\ 2 \\ +2 \\ \hline 11 \end{array} \qquad \begin{array}{r} 9 \\ 3 \\ +4 \\ \hline 16 \end{array} \qquad \begin{array}{r} 64 \\ +\ 2 \\ \hline 66 \end{array} \qquad \begin{array}{r} 43 \\ +\ 5 \\ \hline 48 \end{array} \qquad \begin{array}{r} 32 \\ +\ 8 \\ \hline 40 \end{array}$$

11. (5,2)	12. (6,2)	13. (6,2)	14. (6,2)	15. (7,3)

$$\begin{array}{r} 47 \\ +\ 9 \\ \hline 56 \end{array} \qquad \begin{array}{r} 31 \\ +24 \\ \hline 55 \end{array} \qquad \begin{array}{r} 70 \\ +19 \\ \hline 89 \end{array} \qquad \begin{array}{r} 22 \\ +53 \\ \hline 75 \end{array} \qquad \begin{array}{r} 18 \\ +\ 96 \\ \hline 114 \end{array}$$

16. (7,3)	17. (7,3)	18. (8,3)	19. (8,4)	20. (8,4)

$$\begin{array}{r} 95 \\ +25 \\ \hline 120 \end{array} \quad \begin{array}{r} 48 \\ +37 \\ \hline 85 \end{array} \quad \begin{array}{r} 569 \\ 201 \\ +877 \\ \hline 1647 \end{array} \quad \begin{array}{r} 4020 \\ +\ 689 \\ \hline 4709 \end{array} \quad \begin{array}{r} 283 \\ 21 \\ +2764 \\ \hline 3068 \end{array}$$

Test 6: Subtraction Survey Test

1. (1,1)	2. (1,1)	3. (1,1)	4. (1,1)	5. (1,1)

$$\begin{array}{r} 3 \\ -2 \\ \hline 1 \end{array} \qquad \begin{array}{r} 16 \\ -\ 7 \\ \hline 9 \end{array} \qquad \begin{array}{r} 10 \\ -\ 4 \\ \hline 6 \end{array} \qquad \begin{array}{r} 14 \\ -\ 5 \\ \hline 9 \end{array} \qquad \begin{array}{r} 19 \\ -\ 2 \\ \hline 17 \end{array}$$

6. (2,2)	7. (3,2)	8. (3,2)	9. (3,2)	10. (4,2)

$$\begin{array}{r} 68 \\ -\ 5 \\ \hline 63 \end{array} \qquad \begin{array}{r} 50 \\ -10 \\ \hline 40 \end{array} \qquad \begin{array}{r} 40 \\ -30 \\ \hline 10 \end{array} \qquad \begin{array}{r} 60 \\ -60 \\ \hline 0 \end{array} \qquad \begin{array}{r} 80 \\ -\ 5 \\ \hline 75 \end{array}$$

11. (4,2)	12. (4,2)	13. (5,2)	14. (5,2)	15. (5,2)

$$\begin{array}{r} 23 \\ -\ 6 \\ \hline 17 \end{array} \qquad \begin{array}{r} 63 \\ -\ 9 \\ \hline 54 \end{array} \qquad \begin{array}{r} 93 \\ -61 \\ \hline 32 \end{array} \qquad \begin{array}{r} 58 \\ -23 \\ \hline 35 \end{array} \qquad \begin{array}{r} 46 \\ -13 \\ \hline 33 \end{array}$$

16. (6,3)	17. (6,3)	18. (7,4)	19. (7,4)	20. (7,4)

$$\begin{array}{r} 53 \\ -29 \\ \hline 24 \end{array} \qquad \begin{array}{r} 64 \\ -27 \\ \hline 37 \end{array} \qquad \begin{array}{r} 8942 \\ -5961 \\ \hline 2981 \end{array} \qquad \begin{array}{r} 400 \\ -165 \\ \hline 235 \end{array} \qquad \begin{array}{r} 5906 \\ -\ 248 \\ \hline 5658 \end{array}$$

Source: From K. W. Howell, S. H. Zucker & M. K. Morehead (1982) *Multilevel Academic Skills Inventory.* H & Z Publications, 6544 E. Meadowlark, Paradise Valley, AZ 85253. Reprinted with permission.

(continued)

Exhibit 15.12   *Operations Answers (continued)*

Test 7: Multiplication Survey Test

1.(1,4)

$$2 \times 6 = 12$$

2.(1,4)

$$9 \times 5 = 45$$

3.(1,4)

$$8 \times 3 = 24$$

4.(2,4)

$$64 \times 7 = 448$$

5.(2,4)

$$24 \times 3 = 72$$

6.(2,4)

$$91 \times 1 = 91$$

7.(3,4)

$$18 \times 9 = 162$$

8.(4,4)

$$22 \times 86 = 1892$$

9.(4,4)

$$85 \times 63 = 5355$$

10.(5,5)

$$194 \times 10 = 1940$$

11.(5,5)

$$3 \times 1000 = 3000$$

12.(5,5)

$$100 \times 74 = 7400$$

13.(6,4)

$$102 \times 40 = 4080$$

14.(6,4)

$$40 \times 31 = 1240$$

15.(6,5)

$$7005 \times 26 = 182130$$

16.(7,4)

$$87 \times 25 = 2175$$

17.(7,4)

$$215 \times 48 = 10320$$

18.(7,5)

$$5684 \times 39 = 221676$$

19.(8,8)

$$5^2 = 25$$

20.(8,8)

$$12^2 = 144$$

Test 8: Division Survey Test

1.(1,4)

$2\overline{)4}$ = 2

2.(1,4)

$7\overline{)56}$ = 8

3.(1,4)

$9\overline{)54}$ = 6

4.(1,4)

$10\overline{)90}$ = 9

5.(1,4)

$8\overline{)32}$ = 4

6.(2,4)

$3\overline{)72}$ = 24

7.(2,4)

$5\overline{)80}$ = 16

8.(2,4)

$7\overline{)91}$ = 13

9.(3,4)

$5\overline{)23}$ = 4 r 3 (.6)

10.(3,4)

$9\overline{)37}$ = 4 r 1 (.11)

11.(4,4)

$7\overline{)169}$ = 24 r 1 (.14)

12.(4,5)

$58\overline{)1209}$ = 20 r 49 (.84)

13.(5,5)

$100\overline{)4200}$ = 42

14.(5,5)

$10\overline{)1260}$ = 126

15.(5,5)

$1\overline{)48}$ = 48

16.(6,5)

$8\overline{)8500}$ = 1062 r 4 (.5)

17.(6,5)

$31\overline{)1307}$ = 42 r 5 (.16)

18.(6,5)

$15\overline{)306}$ = 20 r 6 (.4)

19.(7,8)

$\sqrt{4}$ = 2

20.(7,8)

$\sqrt{121}$ = 11

Source: From K. W. Howell, S. H. Zucker & M. K. Morehead (1982) *Multilevel Academic Skills Inventory.* H & Z Publications, 6544 E. Meadowlark, Paradise Valley, AZ 85253. Reprinted with permission.

(continued)

Exhibit 15.12 ***Operations Answers (continued)***

Test 9: Fractions Survey Test

1. (4,5)
$$1 = \frac{10}{10}$$

2. (8,5)
$$\frac{2}{8} = \frac{1}{4}$$

3. (9,5)
$$\frac{7}{3} = 2\frac{1}{3}$$

4. (13,5)
$$\frac{1}{8} + \frac{3}{8} = \frac{1}{2}$$

5. (14,6)
$$14\frac{8}{9} + 5\frac{5}{9} = 20\frac{4}{9}$$

6. (16,6)
$$\frac{7}{12} + \frac{1}{3} = \frac{11}{12}$$

7. (17,6)
$$\frac{3}{13} + \frac{1}{3} = \frac{22}{39}$$

8. (17,6)
$$\frac{3}{4} - \frac{2}{11} = \frac{25}{44}$$

9. (18,6)
$$\begin{array}{r} 1\frac{7}{10} \\ +2\frac{5}{6} \\ \hline 4\frac{8}{15} \end{array}$$

10. (18,6)
$$\begin{array}{r} 4\frac{2}{7} \\ +6\frac{3}{5} \\ \hline 10\frac{31}{35} \end{array}$$

11. (19,6)
$$\frac{5}{8} \times \frac{3}{4} = \frac{15}{32}$$

12. (19,6)
$$\frac{2}{3} \times \frac{1}{6} = \frac{1}{9}$$

13. (19,6)
$$\frac{3}{14} \times \frac{1}{1} = \frac{3}{14}$$

14. (20,6)
$$12\frac{3}{8} \times 4\frac{5}{6} = 59\frac{13}{16}$$

15. (20,6)
$$4\frac{1}{3} \times 7\frac{1}{2} = 32\frac{1}{2}$$

16. (22,6)
$$\frac{2}{5} \div \frac{4}{9} = \frac{9}{10}$$

17. (22,6)
$$\frac{3}{4} \div \frac{5}{7} = 1\frac{1}{20}$$

18. (23,6)
$$11 \div \frac{1}{2} = 22$$

19. (23,6)
$$4 \div \frac{1}{7} = 28$$

20. (24,6)
$$8\frac{5}{8} \div 1\frac{1}{6} = 7\frac{11}{28}$$

21. (24,6)
$$7\frac{1}{3} \div 2\frac{3}{4} = 2\frac{2}{3}$$

Test 10: Decimals, Ratios, Percents Survey Test

1. (3,7)
$$\frac{4}{9} = .444$$

2. (33,7)
$$\frac{5}{8} = .625$$

3. (4,8)
Convert to %
$$.7 = 70\%$$

4. (4,8)
Convert to %
$$.016 = 1.6\%$$

5. (5,8)
Convert to fraction
$$40\% = \frac{2}{5}$$

6. (5,8)
Convert to fraction
$$26\% = \frac{13}{50}$$

7. (6,8)
Convert to %
$$\frac{2}{8} = 25\%$$

8. (6,8)
Convert to %
$$\frac{3}{5} = 60\%$$

9. (7,7)
$$\begin{array}{r} 90.5 \\ -1.68 \\ \hline 88.82 \end{array}$$

10. (7,7)
$$\begin{array}{r} 813 \\ -13.9 \\ \hline 799.1 \end{array}$$

11. (7,7)
$$\begin{array}{r} 6.021 \\ +51.30 \\ \hline 57.321 \end{array}$$

12. (8,7)
$$\begin{array}{r} 16.2 \\ \times\ .40 \\ \hline 6.48 \end{array}$$

13. (8,7)
$$\begin{array}{r} .042 \\ \times .306 \\ \hline .012852 \end{array}$$

14. (8,7)
$$\begin{array}{r} 2.96 \\ \times\ .06 \\ \hline .1776 \end{array}$$

15. (9,7)
$$2.01\overline{)\,.603}^{\,.3}$$

16. (9,7)
$$1.2\overline{)\,.72}^{\,.6}$$

17. (10,8)
Round to the nearest hundredth
$$.1694 = .169$$

18. (10,8)
Round to the nearest tenth
$$.5096 = .51$$

19. (11,8)
Complete ratio
$$1:3 = 3:9$$

20. (11,8)
Complete ratio
$$2:8 = 4:16$$

Source: From K. W. Howell, S. H. Zucker & M. K. Morehead (1982) *Multilevel Academic Skills Inventory*. H & Z Publications, 6544 E. Meadowlark, Paradise Valley, AZ 85253. Reprinted with permission.

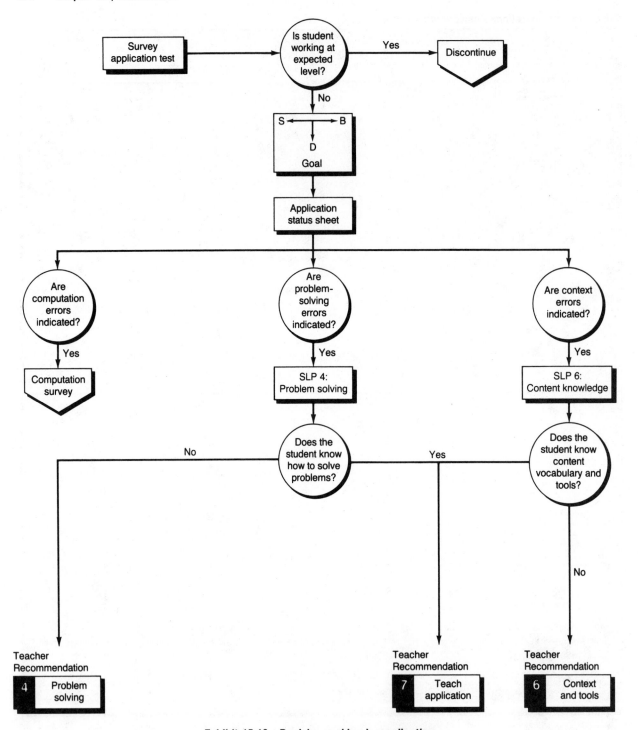

Exhibit 15.13   Decision making in application.

Exhibit 15.14*   Application Survey Answer Sheet

Content	"Select" Items				"Apply" Items			
	Easy		Hard		Easy		Hard	
	Item	Answer	Item	Answer	Item	Answer	Item	Answer
Problem solving	1	b	6	d	11	c	16	a
	2	d	7	a	12	d	17	c
	3	c	8	b	13	a	18	a
	4	a	9	d	14	c	19	b
	5	d	10	a	15	d	20	d
Money	21	d	22	b	23	a	24	c
Time & temp	25/26	b	27	b	28	b	29	c
Metric measure	30	a	31	a	32	c	33	c
Customary meas.	34	a	35	a	36	c	37	c
Geometry I	38	b	39	d	40	b	41	d
Geometry II	42	d	43	b	44	c	45	c

Source: From K. W. Howell, S. H. Zucker & M. K. Morehead (1982) *Multilevel Academic Skills Inventory*. H & Z Publications, 6544 E. Meadowlark, Paradise Valley, Az 85253. Reprinted with permission.

1. Is the student's application performance within curriculum-level expectations?
2. Does the student apply computation skills?
3. Does the student solve problems accurately?
4. Does the student know the content of time, temperature, money, and measurement?

▽ **Directions**

1. Use test 11 in the workbook or select/construct a test sampling a range of problem types including: problems that match recognized categories of application content; problems that require several steps; and problems that require multiple operations. Refer to Appendix C.1 for a list of application objectives.

2. This test is long and elaborate so use good sense giving it. Don't tire the student or require her to attempt problems which you know she hasn't the skill to complete. If she is very young, or unskilled, you may just skip the survey completely and go on to the specific procedures.

   Items 1–10, and some later items, ask the student to select the way a problem should be worked. When starting these items, say "One of these choices shows how to solve the problem. Read the problem out loud and circle the choice that shows you how to work the problem." If she has never been asked to "select procedures

for a solution," then demonstrate how to work them.

3. If the student cannot read, you will have to read the test to her (Terry, 1992). Have her work all of the problems if possible. Allow as much time as needed.

   Score the problems using the answers found in Exhibit 15.14* by circling the number of any item missed. Record the results on the math summary sheet in Exhibit 15.10.*

Interpretation Guidelines

The purpose of the application survey is to direct additional functional testing. The test items are keyed to content, problem-solving objectives, and computation objectives. These can be considered prerequisites of the application survey items. This prerequisite information is listed under each item in the Application Survey Error Analysis in Appendix C.3. For example, item 10 looks like this on the Error Analysis Table:

10. Addition 6a, Subtraction 7a
    Decimals, Ratios, Percents 4a, 7a
    a. Correct answer
    b. Problem Solving 3a
    c. Problem Solving 3a, 5i
    d. Problem Solving 5i

This item requires the student to add, subtract, and use percentages. Choice "a" is the correct answer. If the

Exhibit 15.15*   Applications Content Test

Time

Grade	Questions	Answers	Score
3	1. One minute has how many seconds?	60	1 0
3	2. One hour has how many minutes?	60	1 0
2	3. One day has how many hours?	24	1 0
1	4. One week has how many days?	7	1 0
4	5. One month has how many weeks?	4	1 0
1	6. One year has how many months?	12	1 0
4	7. One decade has how many years?	10	1 0
4	8. One century has how many decades?	10	1 0
4	9. One year has how many days?	365	1 0
4	10. One year has how many weeks?	52	1 0
		Total	

Money

Grade	Questions	Answers	Score
1	1. How many pennies make a nickel?	5	1 0
1	2. How many pennies make a dime?	10	1 0
2	3. How many dimes are in a quarter?	2	1 0
3	4. How many dimes are in $1?	10	1 0
3	5. How many quarters are in $1?	4	1 0
2	6. A quarter plus a dime are equal to how many pennies (cents)?	35	1 0
3	7. A half-dollar is worth how many dimes?	5	1 0
3	8. Which is worth more? Three $1 bills or one $5 bill?	one $5 bill	1 0
		Total	

Geometry

Grade	Target Words	Acceptable Responses	Score
3	1. perimeter	the distance around the outside edge	1 0
3	2. area	surface measurement	1 0
3	3. square units	what you get when you multiply the length times the width	1 0
3	4. cubic units	what you get when you multiply the length times the width times the height (depth)	1 0
3	5. volume	capacity; how much something holds; space inside	1 0
5	6. circumference	the distance around a circle	1 0
		Total	

Measurement–Customary Units

Grade	Target Questions	Answers	Score
4	1. How many ounces are in a pound?	16	1 0
4	2. How many pounds are in a ton?	2,000	1 0
4	3. How many cups are in 1 pint?	2	1 0
4	4. How many pints are in 1 quart?	2	1 0
4	5. How many quarts are in 1 gallon?	4	1 0
4	6. How many inches are in 1 foot?	12	1 0
4	7. How many inches are in 1 yard?	36	1 0
4	8. How many feet are in 1 yard?	3	1 0
4	9. How many feet are in 1 mile?	5,280	1 0
		Total	

Measurement–Metric Units

Grade	Target Questions	Answers	Score
4	1. What does *milli* mean?	thousandths	1 0
4	2. What does *deci* mean?	tenths	1 0
4	3. What does *centi* mean?	hundredths	1 0
4	4. What does *deca* mean?	ten	1 0
4	5. What does *hecto* mean?	hundred	1 0
4	6. What does *kilo* mean?	thousand	1 0
		Total	

Measurement–Vocabulary

Grade	Target Words	Acceptable Responses	Score
1	1. heavy	having weight	1 0
1	2. heavier	having more weight	1 0
1	3. heaviest	having the most weight	1 0
1	4. light	having little weight	1 0
1	5. lighter	having less weight	1 0
1	6. lightest	having the least weight	1 0
1	7. weight	how heavy	1 0
1	8. full	contains the maximum	1 0
1	9. fuller	contains more	1 0
1	10. fullest	contains the most	1 0
1	11. empty	contains nothing	1 0
1	12. emptier	contains less	1 0
1	13. emptiest	contains the least	1 0
1	14. more	a greater amount	1 0
1	15. less	not as much	1 0
1	16. height	tallness; how tall something is; how far up	1 0
2	17. width	how far across; how broad something is	1 0
2	18. depth	how far down; distance from front to back	1 0
1	19. length	how long something is	1 0
1	20. distance	amount of space between two things	1 0
		Total	

Scoring Summary

Subtest	Total Correct		Total Possible		Percent Correct
Time	_____	÷	_____	=	_____
Money	_____	÷	_____	=	_____
Geometry	_____	÷	_____	=	_____
Measurement–Vocabulary	_____	÷	_____	=	_____
Measurement–Customary Units	_____	÷	_____	=	_____
Measurement–Metric Units	_____	÷	_____	=	_____

From K. W. Howell, S. H. Zucker, and M. K. Morehead (1982), *Multilevel Academic Skills Inventory.* H. & Z Publications, 6544 E. Meadowlark, Paradise Valley, AZ 85253. Reprinted with permission.

student selects another choice, her mistake may be the result of the error type indicated. That is, a choice of "c" indicates an error in problem-solving skills 3a and/or 5i. Therefore, specific-level tests for 3a and 5i should be given to find out more about the student's skills in those areas. Student responses can be analyzed by item difficulty and by content. A rough estimate of computational skill can also be noted.

The steps for summarizing are as follows:

1. Score the application survey.
2. Circle each item no-passed on Exhibit 15.14*.
3. Total the item-type columns.
4. Total the content rows.
5. Use the Application Survey Error Analysis in Appendix C.3 to decide which specific subtest may need to be given.

A major problem with application is that, because it combines computation and content, it accumulates all of the variability in sequencing found in both of those domains. Therefore, it is not possible for us to give exact information about the grade level at which all students should work a particular problem. The only solution to this dilemma is to go through the objectives found in Appendix C.1 and Appendix C.3 to mark those items on the survey test the student should know how to work.

Answer the following questions:

Application question 1: Is the student working at about the expected level?

If YES, then discontinue or test at the next higher level in curriculum to determine where to begin instruction.

If NO, then answer application questions 2, 3 and 4.

Application question 2: Look at the analysis in Appendix C.3. Are computation errors indicated?

If YES, then go to computation and follow the process in Exhibit 15.9.*

Application question 3: Look at the analysis in Appendix C.3. Are problem-solving errors indicated?

If YES, then employ Math SLP 4.

Application question 4: Look at the analysis in Appendix C.3. Are content errors indicated?

If YES, then give Math SLP 6.

Specific-Level Testing

In this section we explain the use of six specific-level procedures. The procedures are to be employed in response to concerns raised within the interpretation guidelines at the survey level. Therefore, it is important that you consult the survey material before beginning these tests. If you don't do that, the SLPs won't make a lot of sense. Each specific-level procedure has been designed to answer one of the following questions:

1. Is the student's rate impeded by handwriting?

   Math SLP 1: Oral Response and Handwriting

2. Is the student accurate at basic facts?

   Math SLP 2: Accuracy on Basic Facts

3. Does the student have adequate computation skills for adding, subtracting, multiplying, and dividing whole numbers, decimals, ratios, percentage, and fractions?

   Math SLP 3: Operations

4. Does the student demonstrate adequate problem-solving skill?

   Math SLP 4: Problem Solving

5. Does the student have prerequisite skills and concepts?

   Math SLP 5: Prerequisite Test

6. Does the student know about content and tools?

   Math SLP 6: Content Knowledge

Math SLP 1: Checking Oral Response and Handwriting

Suppose you have tested a third-grade student and found that she accurately works 22 addition fact problems in a minute. The CAP for fluency is 40. There are three obvious assumed causes for a student's failure to meet fluency on a written basic facts test:

1. She is slow at adding.
2. She is slow at writing digits.
3. She is slow at adding *and* slow at writing digits.

It isn't possible to determine if assumed cause 3 is correct until assumed causes 1 and 2 have been checked. This is accomplished by having the student write digits and work problems aloud.

▽ Directions: Oral Response

1. Administer basic-facts tests 1–4 (assuming the student is expected to know all four). Have the student say the answers rather than write them (flash cards are appropriate but a probe sheet is the best stimulus).

2. Say "Point to each problem and tell me the answer. Work as fast but as carefully as you can. Begin."

3. Time the student for 60 seconds and say "Thank you."

4. Note corrects and errors per minute. The CAP for both oral and written facts is 40 correct, 0 errors per minute. Record results.

▽ Directions: Handwriting

1. Administer a writing-digits or a copying-digits test.

2. Say "Write/copy from 1 to 100 as quickly and carefully as you can. Please begin."

3. Time the student for 60 seconds. Say "Thank you."

4. Score the sample by counting the number of *digits* written.

5. Record the results.

∿ Interpretation Guidelines

Question A: Are the student's oral responses at rate?

　　If YES, then go to question B.

　　If NO, then teach fluency using Teaching Recommendation 2.

○ Objectives

Division 1m, Multiplication 1m, Subtraction 1m, or Addition 1m.

Question B: Can the student write fast enough to demonstrate math-fact fluency (criteria for writing digits is 100 per minute starting late in the second grade)?

　　If YES, then the student is accurate and slow in spite of sufficient writing skill. Teach fact fluency (Teaching Recommendation 2).

Objectives

Division 1m, Multiplication 1m, Subtraction 1m, or Addition 1m.

If NO, then you will want to go to Chapter 14 to find out about handwriting. However, that doesn't mean you should stop working on math. What you need to do next is set an intermediate aim. The next paragraphs explain how to do that.

"Writing digits" is a "tool movement" or "basic movement cycle" (BMC), which means that other skills (in this case, working written math) depend upon it (White & Haring, 1982). The relationship of BMCs to larger skills has been expressed in this formula:

$$\frac{\text{Task mastery rate} \times \text{Current BMC rate}}{\text{BMC mastery rate}} = \frac{\text{Intermediate}}{\text{aim}}$$

If the kid writes 75 digits a minute, you can compute her maximum addition rate by using the formula shown here:

$$\text{Mastery rate for addition facts} = \frac{40 \text{ problems per}}{\text{minute}}$$

$$\text{BMC rate for writes-digits} = \frac{100 \text{ digits per}}{\text{minute}}$$

$$\text{Current writes-digits rate} = \frac{75 \text{ digits per}}{\text{minute}}$$

$$\frac{40 \times 75}{100} = 30 \text{ problems per minute}$$

The formula tells us that the student should respond at a rate of 30 problems per minute given her slow handwriting rate. However, she only completed 22. In this case you can set an "intermediate aim" for improving addition without an increase in digit writing. This student is slow at writing digits (CAP = 100; student = 75) and is also slow at basic facts (CAP = 40). However, according to the formula, she has adequate writing skills to work 30 problems per minute right now. Therefore 30 can be used as an intermediate aim to specify a math expectation between her current level of performance and the final objective of 40 problems per minute. Ultimately of course, both handwriting and math skills should be taken to the recommended CAP. Setting an intermediate aim is *not* the same as lowering the final standard for slow-writing students.

Obviously, in cases where there are physical restrictions (for example, a student has no fingers with which to hold a pencil), it is necessary to use an alternative response mode (have the student say the answers).

Note: If the student is having trouble with *both* accuracy on facts and writing digits (i.e. fact rate is below intermediate aim) then teach the student to write digits while using Teaching Recommendation 2 to take the student to her intermediate aim. *Do not* delay math instruction while building handwriting fluency.

Math SLP 2: Accuracy on Basic Facts

Directions

1. Return to tests 1–4 in the workbook and read-minister them without an emphasis on fluency.

2. Have the student complete at least 50% of the items on each appropriate fact probe (if the student does very poorly, discontinue). This is to allow you to use the error-analysis grids. Say to the student: "Take your time and write the answer to each problem. Work carefully."

3. Score the responses. Compare the responses to standards you have established, or use ours (100%). Summarize error patterns.

4. Record the results on the math summary sheet.

Interpretation Guidelines

Question: Does the student correctly work any basic facts?

If YES, then go to Teaching Recommendation 1 (fact accuracy).

Objectives:

Division 1a, Multiplication 1a, Subtraction 1a, or Addition 1a.

If NO, go to Math SLP 5.

Math SLP 3: Checking Operations

You arrived at this SLP because the student missed items on a survey-level operations test for whole numbers, decimals, ratios, percentage, or fractions. The problem with such tests is that they collect a relatively limited sample of behavior. Therefore, you may wish to confirm the problem and to collect additional work

to allow for error analysis and to see if the student has acquired correct strategies for working operations.

Directions

1. Return to the survey computation tests and recognize the objectives represented by the items that were missed. Select or construct a test or series of tests sampling those objectives (to construct a test, write ten items like the ones missed at the survey level).

2. Administer the tests, encouraging the student to show all work. Several testing sessions may be required. Tests can be given during regularly scheduled math classes.

3. Score the tests and note error types.

Interpretation Guidelines

Question: Does the student have adequate computation skills for adding, subtracting, multiplying, and dividing whole numbers, decimals, ratios, percentages, and fractions?

If YES, then discontinue, or check skills at the next higher curriculum level.

If NO, begin to teach the specific operations the student failed, using Teaching Recommendation 3. *You should also give both Math SLPs 4 and 5 and check the prerequisites for each objective.* The prerequisites for each objective are indicated in Appendix C.1.

Objectives

Select objectives from Appendix C.1 by using the item cross-referencing on tests 5–11.

Math SLP 4: Problem-Solving Strategy

Note: Both Math SLPs 4 and 5 are interviews. The only difference between them is the content they address. Therefore it may be convenient simply to do them both at the same time.

Directions

1. Return to the tests you gave in Math SLP 3 and use them to conduct an interview.

2. Say to the student: "I want to ask you how you worked some of the problems." Then use the relevant questions from Exhibit 15.6. This sort of exercise will be new to most students—so be

patient. Also be aware that a student's poor language skills may confound your results. Ask the student to describe what she does when she works a problem.

3. Depending on the clarity of the student's explanation, you may need to select or construct a test to sample each of the following problem-solving skills:
   - knows which operations to use
   - recognizes relevant, irrelevant, or missing information
   - knows how to set up equations
   - knows how to estimate answers
   - knows how to use algorithms.

Exhibit 15.2 (items 29–35) shows formats for these skills. Depending on the student's skill level, you need to systematically check each problem-solving skill across each operation ($+$, $-$, $\times$, and $\div$).

Interpretation Guidelines

Compare the student's explanations or work to task requirements (how the problems should be done) to determine if she has an adequate knowledge of problem solving. (Remember, taping a paper tube to the hand to make an additional finger probably does not meet the requirement for efficiency and generalization inherent in good strategy use. Also statements like "I will remember" do not qualify as adequate recall strategies [see Chapter 17].)

Question: Does the student know the problem-solving strategy?

If YES, then teach application or operations using Teaching Recommendations 3 or 7.

If NO, then use Teaching Recommendation 5.

Objectives:
- Problem-solving 1a–7a in Appendix C.2.

Math SLP 5: Prerequisite Skills and Basic Concepts

Directions

1. Make a copy of Exhibit 15.2 and mark the concepts and prerequisites appropriate to the problems the student missed on the survey test or in Math SLP 3.

2. Using the results of Math SLPs 2 and 3, point to an item or write one (for example, $3 + 2 = $). Say to the student: " Tell me how you would figure out the answer to this problem." Next, say: "Tell me how you are going to remember $3 + 2 = 5$."

3. Script or tape-record the student's response.

4. Examine the student's written or oral responses for evidence that she understands applicable concepts and/or prerequisites from Exhibit 15.2. Mark the status of each prerequisite. Note if the student seems unaware of the material, if she has it wrong, or if she has it right.

5. Be sure to ask additional questions about those items the student may not have used or may have used incorrectly.

Interpretation Guidelines
Question. Are all prerequisites marked YES?

If YES, then begin teaching the operations of concern, using Teaching Recommendation 3.

If NO, then teach the prerequisites the student is missing.

Math SLP 6: Content Knowledge

Directions

1. Select or construct an interview or test to sample the student's knowledge of vocabulary, tools, and content for the material of concern (time, temperature, money, measurement [linear, surface, volume, weight]). Use the objectives in Appendix C.1 and the summary categories in Exhibit 15.10* as guides. (Be aware that many employers place the greatest emphasis on good measurement skills.) An example test is shown in Exhibit 15.15*.

You may need to construct an instrument that will sample equivalent units or specific algorithms. Have the student state equivalent units ("There are _____ inches in a foot"; "There are _____ feet in a yard"; "There are _____ centimeters in a meter") and explain algorithms ("The area of a triangle is equal to _____ the base times the height"; "The area of a circle is equal to _____ "). Many such tests already exist in math textbooks. It would be well worth your time to search out some of them.

Here is an example for tool knowledge: In linear measurement you need to evaluate a student's skill with rulers, tape measures, yardsticks, meter sticks, and so on. Evaluate the student's use of these tools by having her do things with them. Don't just ask questions.

2. Administer the test. If you have already noted computation problems (Math SLPs 2 and 3) allow the student to use a calculator while working on items involving the use of tools.

3. Score responses and summarize the results on the math summary sheet.

Interpretation Guidelines

Question: Does the student know content, tools, and vocabulary?

If YES, then teach the student to apply this knowledge using Teaching Recommendation 7.

If NO, then teach content knowledge, tools, and vocabulary. Use Teaching Recommendation 6.

Objectives:

• Select from Application Objectives in Appendix C.1.

Teaching Recommendations

Before we go on to the specific Teaching Recommendations, there is one question about math instruction that needs to be answered: "Is it OK for the student to use a calculator?" The answer is yes (Horton, Lovitt & White, 1992).

Recommendation 1: Teach Accuracy on Basic Facts

If you have been directed here, you have a student who is not accurate on basic arithmetic facts. There are two approaches to teaching facts: (a) By rote (as a series of separate numerical sentences learned in a basic stimulus/response format—like flash cards), or (b) through the instruction of underlying strategies (Christensen & Cooper, 1991). Because the student is inaccurate, you should teach the strategies until the student is accurate and then to use Teaching Recommendation 2 to build fluency.

When teaching facts, it is important to impress on the student the need to follow the strategy (Mercer & Miller, 1992). Do this by asking questions about the use of the strategy itself (Case, Harris & Graham, 1992). Here is an example for the problem $4 + 6 = ?$

QUESTION: "What kind of problem is this? Look at the sign."

RESPONSE: "Addition."

QUESTION: "What do we know about the answers to addition problems?"

RESPONSE: "They are bigger than the numbers in the problem." (This assumes you aren't into negative numbers yet.)

QUESTION: "How do you solve this problem?"

RESPONSE: "I start with one number and then count on as many times as the other number tells me to."

QUESTION: "What number will you start with?"

RESPONSE: "Six."

QUESTION: "Why?"

RESPONSE: "I don't have to count as many times."

QUESTION: "Good. Now solve the problem."

RESPONSE: "$6 + 4$ means $6 + 1 + 1 + 1 + 1 = 10$."

QUESTION: "Can you tell me the problem and the answer?"

RESPONSE: "$6 + 4 = 10$."

QUESTION: "Good. You followed the steps for adding."

In some cases teachers will separate facts into subdomains like 1–5 and 6–10. If you have done that, and the student becomes accurate at the first domain, begin fluency instruction with those items while continuing to build accuracy with those that remain. Teach the strategies for subtraction and addition (or division and multiplication) at the same time.

Recommendation 2: Teach Fluency on Basic Facts

As we noted earlier, there are at least three explanations for accurate but slow performance on basic facts: the student does not know the facts at the automatic level, the student writes slowly, or the student does not know facts *and* is a slow writer. The only way to pinpoint the source of the slow rate (as explained in SLP 1) is to show that the student does know basic facts or is not a slow writer. The simplest way to do this is to have her say (oral response) the answers to the facts. If the student can accurately say 40 or more answers per minute, rule out knowledge of facts and target writing fluency as an objective. If the student cannot say answers fluently, ask her to write the numerals 1 to 99 from memory as quickly as possible. If the student writes fewer than 100 digits in a minute, then writing fluency or number recall may not be sufficient to demonstrate fact competence. Speed of number recall can be checked by having the student count out loud. Writing fluency is discussed in Chapter 14.

Handwriting

If assessments indicate that the student simply writes slowly, then set an intermediate aim for fluency on facts while you work on increasing her writing fluency. Expect the student's rate on basic facts to be about two-thirds the rate on writing numerals. For example, a child who can write numerals at a rate of 45 numerals per minute should have a temporary criterion of about 30 facts per minute.

Slow writers with no physical condition prohibiting writing should generally be taught fluency. Writing slowly can limit the amount of work a student can produce and may contribute to difficulty in completing tasks. Slow writing may also impede acquisition of more complex skills if the student attends to handwriting instead of the critical mathematical attributes of problems. It is important to build writing rate; however, *never put off mathematics instruction while waiting for handwriting fluency to increase.*

Lessons designed for building handwriting fluency use brief, intense practice sessions in which the student is encouraged to write faster while maintaining accuracy. Such fluency-building routines can be incorporated into daily lessons, and students can be taught to time each other for one minute on a free writing task or a copying task. Often several very short (10-second) timings on dictated random numbers prove to be more beneficial than one long timing. After the timing, the students can check their accuracy and rate. It is very important to teach students strategies for self-monitoring (Frank & Brown, 1992). They should also record or chart their own progress.

Facts

Lessons designed to build fluency on facts are typically short (5–10 minutes) and use rapidly paced drill over material on which the student is at least 90% accurate. This is often accomplished with flash cards, computers, or timed practice sheets. (If you use a computer make sure that it is sensitive to the time it takes a student to respond, and that the fluency levels it requires are compatible with the CAP you use.)

During such lessons, the student is reinforced for rapid responding and daily improvement in fluency. Errors are typically viewed as rate-induced and are ignored to the extent that error correction procedures are not used (feedback may be given after the practice session, however). Peer teaching groups are especially effective and time-efficient. Peers can use cards that contain the problem on both sides, without the answer, so that both students must work each fact.

Fluency instruction is intended to make the student automatic at using a skill—which means that the student knows the skill so well she can recall the fact whenever necessary. This means the student must practice under different conditions including problems presented orally, in horizontal and vertical written formats, and ultimately on practice sheets with facts drawn from all operations (addition, subtraction, multiplication, and division mixed together). One particularly effective device for generalizing fluency instruction is to select facts that appear in a few higher-level problems. The student can then be rehearsed over this limited group of facts several times until she reaches fluency. Once that happens, the student is then allowed to work the larger problems.

Recommendation 3: Teach Computation

Unlike reading, computation skills have a relatively clear, highly progressive succession of complexity. Recognizing the subskills of a target task will make instruction in that task far more efficient. This is why the objectives in Appendix C.1 are organized in a descending sequence and cross-referenced to other skills.

There are more materials available to teach computation than any other math domain, so we aren't going to present any particular techniques in this section. However, it is our opinion that these methods often fail because they are applied to skills the student is not prepared to learn. Our fundamental recommendation for teaching computation is to directly teach subskills and then move up or down the hierarchy as warranted by the student's performance. This requires that the teacher cross-reference the skills to instructional techniques. We believe that the best reference for teaching math currently available is a text called *Direct Instruction Mathematics* by Silbert, Carnine and Stein (1990). Therefore, we are supplying information in Appendix C.1 that references computation skills to the pages in that book that describe how to teach key objectives. (This cross-referencing was prepared in part by Mark Jewell at Western Washington University.)

We'd also like to note another excellent presentation on teaching arithmetic to students with learning problems. It is an article by Cawley and Parmar (1992) and can be found in the references.

Recommendation 4: Teach Problem Solving

Students who are not accurate on facts or operations often need to develop a set of computational problem-solving strategies (Case et al., 1992). These strategies may be task specific, such as the algorithms for adding or subtracting mixed numbers, or they may be general. Task-specific strategies apply only to a small domain of tasks, while general strategies may apply across several broad domains. The task-specific strategy for adding or subtracting mixed numbers is: "Recognize the problem type; find the common denominator; find the answer; decide if the answer must be converted; convert if necessary." The general strategy for mathematics is to select the operation; recognize the unknown quantity; recognize relevant and irrelevant information; set up the necessary equation(s); estimate the answer; follow the task-specific strategy; and correct the work.

While it is difficult to separate problem-solving skills from other math skills, it is important to try to determine where problem-solving skills break down. For example, two frequent causes of failure to solve application problems correctly are (1) the failure to distinguish irrelevant from relevant information, and (2) failure to estimate answers.

Once you have identified the missing (or erroneous) problem-solving component, teach the student to use the correct one *within the context of real problems*. This often means deemphasizing the production of answers by asking questions about the use of the problem-solving strategy itself. (An example of this technique is included in Teaching Recommendation 1.) View problems as opportunities to practice or teach strategy use, not opportunities to find answers. This means focusing on explanations, questions, and feedback about the use of the problem-solving strategy. The following routines should help.

Verbal Mediation Begin demonstrating the strategy to the student by describing it aloud as you show how to work problems. Next, have the student practice saying the strategy with you as you guide her through doing problems herself. Next, ask the student to work the problem while saying the strategy aloud without you. Finally, teach the student to say the strategy to herself before beginning to work on a problem.

Questions Questioning can be an especially powerful device for teaching problem-solving strategies. Lead questions, described in detail by Stowitschek, Stowitschek, Hendrickson, and Day (1984), are used to guide a student into strategy use by focusing on one or more of the strategic elements of the task before asking the student to actually work the task. Here is an example for the problem $47 + 28$.

Strategy	Question	Desired response
Select operation	"What kind of problem is this?"	"Addition."
Set up operation	"Where will you start adding?"	"Seven plus 8."
Relevant vs. irrelevent information	"What does the fact that $7 + 8 =$ more than 10 mean?"	"I have to regroup" [or "carry"].
Follow task-specific strategy	"If $7 + 8$ is 15, where will you put the 5 ones?"	Student indicates the correct place.
	"Where will you put 1 ten?"	Student indicates the correct place.

This kind of questioning recognizes that a problem requires a student to make many procedural decisions, and not to simply write one answer.

Select Procedure Sometimes it is effective to have a student select the correct equation for a problem rather than actually work the problem. This focuses her attention on the strategy, deemphasizes the answer, and requires her to think through the problem from several possible directions.

For example, "Joy has 13 bicycles to fix. Four are

red. Jennifer brings her ten more. She fixes two each day. What procedure would you use to find out how many days it will take her to fix all the bicycles?"

a.   13
     $\times 10$ then 130/3

b.   13   17
     $+\ 4$ then $+10$ then 27/2

c.   13
     $+10$ then   23/2

d.   13/2 then   10/2

Corrections   Questions can also be used to correct strategy errors without immediately giving away the answer. This shows the student that she can reason through the problem independently. An ideal sequence presented by Stowitscheck and others works this way:

1. Demonstrate the strategy.

2. Use lead questions or open questions (ask the student to work on the whole item).

3. When errors occur, change the open question to a multiple-choice question.

4. If an error still occurs, change the multiple-choice question to a restricted-alternative question.

5. If an error still occurs, repeat the demonstration and start over.

For example, for the problem 8×6:

Device	Teacher	Student response
Open question	Shows flashcard of 6 $\times$ 8.	"Fourteen."
Feedback and multiple choice	"The answer is not 14. Do you have to add or multiply in this problem?"	"Add."
Feedback and restricted alternative	"We don't add, so what do we have to do?"	"I don't know."
Demonstrate	Repeats demonstration with emphasis on operation sign.	

Feedback.   Because you are teaching the student how to arrive at an answer, and not the answer itself, feedback should be directed at problem solving. Often a student can arrive at a correct answer by using an incorrect strategy (guessing, or working the problem backward). If you give feedback or praise in this case, you run the risk of inadvertently reinforcing the wrong way to solve problems. To prevent this, refer to the correct strategy when giving feedback. For example, "Good for you. You must have paid attention to the sign because you multiplied" (added, subtracted, etc.).

Recommendation 5: Teach Prerequisites

As noted in the description of Teaching Recommendation 3, the objectives in Appendix C.1 and Appendix C.2 are arranged in a sequence. This means that many of the lower-numbered objectives in any operation may be prerequisites for those with higher numbers. However, Appendix C.1 also includes a list of prerequisites after each computation and application objective. When a student is failing to carry out an objective, you need to consult this list and teach the indicated subskills. We will illustrate this process using addition objective 1a (addition facts).

The prerequisites for addition objective 1a are: addition 1i, prerequisite 5m, prerequisite 9i, prerequisite 7i, prerequisite 21a, and prerequisite 12m. These prerequisites for addition facts include knowledge of numerals, counting skills, and operation-distinct concepts. Because addition can be thought of as counting forward (and subtraction as counting backward), prerequisite 12m—rote counting—is important.

If a student is not ready to learn facts because she is missing prerequisite 12m skills, try teaching her to count by rote (forward and backward) from one number to another. Use directions such as "Count forward (or backward) from _____ to _____. What number are you going to start on? What number are you going to stop on? Begin." For example:

"Count forward from 3 to 9."
"Count forward from 46 to 57."
"Count forward from 77 to 86."
"Count backward from 6 to 3."
"Count backward from 34 to 28."
"Count backward from 54 to 45."

Also, teach the student to supply previous or next numbers in the counting sequence. This can be done by writing random numbers on a sheet and placing blanks either before or after them. Tell her to fill in the blanks as quickly as possible.

Once the student can count, and recognizes numbers (prerequisite 5m), teach addition and subtraction through the use of objects (like blocks) or pictures of objects. Then teach her to transfer these skills to written problems that are presented in standard form. At this point you would also substitute operation signs for the verbal directions to "add" or to "count forward" (prerequisite objective 21a).

Just because you may have targeted a prerequisite skill for instruction, do not assume the skill should be taught in isolation. Often the most effective way to teach things like counting and operation signs is within the context of real problems.

Recommendation 6: Teach Application Content, Vocabulary and Tools

Difficulties in applying mathematics skills in application content are sometimes based on inadequate knowledge of the content rather than any lack of proficiency in computation or problem solving. Thus, application content should often be targeted for direct instruction. The list of applications skills in Appendixes C.1 & C.3 includes content sequences for time and temperature, money, measurement of length, surface, volume, and weight (both metric and customary). From this exhibit you can see the magnitude of the task involved in teaching content-specific information. Content-specific information is to applications and problem-solving what prior knowledge is to reading comprehension.

If it appears that the student needs to be taught this material, then instruction should be preceded by a test to determine which things the student needs to learn. Such pre-tests may be found in many of the more structured application programs that accompany, or are included in, some math programs. Just as prob-

lem solving and other prerequisites are often best taught within the context of computation, application and problem solving should always be presented together.

Recommendation 7: Teach Application Strategies

If a student has arrived at this recommendation she has all the necessary prior knowledge to solve application problems but doesn't know how to combine this knowledge. In other words, she needs to be taught application. Because there are an unlimited number of tasks to which mathematics knowledge can be applied, this recommendation can only be stated in the simplest of terms: decide what you want to teach and teach it using the principles of strategy instruction outlined in Exhibit 8.4. (don't forget to demonstrate both behaviors and thought processes).

Summary

Our goal has been to help you identify what to teach a student in mathematics. Chapter 15 began by discussing math. Next it described survey-level procedures, provided some examples of survey material, and listed likely causes for failure at the survey level. We also discussed error analysis, reviewed specific-level procedures, and linked problems to instructional recommendations. In the process we have tried to illustrate the application of a task-analytical model to math. We have also emphasized strategic behavior for two reasons: First, a task-analytical model permits analysis of cognitive behavior; second, math instruction in the absence of strategy instruction has little utility.

Chapter 16 / Social Skills

Every normal human being is constantly making judgments about good and bad, better and worse . . . These judgments of good and bad, better and worse, are not only subjects of reflection or conversation, they are also absolutely necessary in any process of decision. A decision essentially involves a choice among different images of the future that we conceive to be within our power to achieve.

—K.E. Boulding (1985)

While estimates vary, it is generally agreed that, at some point in their schooling, something in the neighborhood of half of all students encounter major problems getting along with themselves or others. Sometimes these problems are so intense and intractable that the student may end up receiving a special program or mental health service. In other cases, the problems seem fairly minor. However, even comparatively lightweight problems for an individual can represent major problems for schools. Larson (1989) has concluded that in a typical junior high of 2000 students as many as 14,681 classroom removals for problem behavior can occur in a year. At that rate, a conservative allowance of 15 minutes of class/teacher time for each disruption yields a total of 3670 hours of lost teaching.

Beyond the disruption to schools and the heartache for staff, behavioral/emotional difficulties exact an incredible toll from troubled students (Allen, 1992). As a group they often have fewer friends, are estranged from family, are sick more often, make less money, end up in jail, and actually *die* earlier. Moreover, in most cases, they endure sadness and miss joy. They become hopeless (Clarizio & Payette, 1990). This particular effect seems all the more tragic when those who suffer are children. As Seligman puts it " . . . the notion of potential, without the notion of optimism, has very little meaning" (p 154).

Chapters 16 and 17 deal with content that is often left out of classroom-oriented evaluation texts: social and task-related skills. Yet both of these precincts have a direct relationship to topics presented in each of the preceding chapters. Let's begin illustrating that relationship by making the point that the distinction between academic and social skill is fairly arbitrary. In spite of the fact that methods for the two domains are often presented in separate courses, the authors believe that the principles of learning and teaching apply equally. Academic behaviors and social skills both respond to the same sorts of interventions. The critical distinction between the two is not found in the topography of the behaviors or the nature of their instruction, but in the minds of the teachers and researchers who work with them (Kauffman & Wong, 1991). We can briefly encapsulate the problem by stating that many teachers believe they are hired to "teach" academic behaviors and to "control" social-behaviors (Nichols, 1992). As a result, they develop curriculum, plan lessons, and schedule instructional time for academics, but not for social skills.

Time is seldom set aside to teach students how to behave socially; instead, teachers expect "good" social skill and react to "bad" social skill. In some ways, social skill is like oral language, in that students are expected to be proficient when they enter school (see Chapter 12).

Some Groundwork

In this chapter we will assume you already know:

1. that social skill is learned and determined, in part, by prior experience

2. that it is influenced by the context (situation) in which the individual is behaving

3. that acceptable behavior in one culture may not be acceptable in another (and that teachers should respect cultural diversity)

4. that behavior can be changed through the application of various interventions, including those that fall under the heading of "behavior management."

Throughout this chapter we will use terms like *inappropriate* and *appropriate*. The authors recognize that these terms are relative and subjective, so we won't even try to define them (but—as a teacher we know pointed out—"You know it when you see it"). *Maladaptive behavior* refers to behavior that interferes with the social, academic, or physical growth of the student or his peers. *Overt* behaviors are those requiring muscular movement, such as standing up or speaking. *Covert* behaviors are those involving cognitive activity, such as thoughts and feelings. Overt behaviors should be described in terms that are not open to interpretation and are easily understood by people who are not familiar with the student or his behavior. For this reason, all statements regarding the student's overt behavior are put to the stranger test (a test of reliability) (see Chapter 3, pp. 40-41). The process of writing a behavioral statement that passes the stranger test is referred to as *pinpointing*, and the resulting statement is called a *pinpoint*.

While inappropriate behavior is called maladaptive, appropriate, or positive, behavior is referred to as the *target*. Target behavior is the behavior the teacher wants the student to engage in after instruction is finished (because engaging in that behavior will promote the social, academic, and physical growth of the student and his peers). A target pinpoint is really nothing more than an objective. Because social skills are seldom described in task-analytic terms, we will often use the label *prerequisite* throughout this discussion. Prerequisites are the essential skills, knowledge, beliefs, expectations, and/or perceptions that a student must have to engage in a target pinpoint. *Type 1 prerequisites* consist of skill and knowledge. *Type 2 prerequisites* consist of beliefs, expectations, and perceptions.

Control vs. Education

Many teaching interventions designed to change children's social skills simply don't work. There are at least two explanations for this phenomenon. The first is that the intervention used was not properly designed, in that it didn't incorporate efforts to make sure that the change would maintain and generalize. The second is that the selection of the pinpoint (the behavior to be changed) was incorrect. If the wrong behavior is selected, any intervention is useless. Just as

in academic areas, we must use great care when deciding what to teach about social skills.

As you recall, a central component of any evaluative effort is comparison: to evaluate is to compare. Therefore, it is important to consider to what the student (or his behavior) is being compared. When one evaluates academics, the standard of comparison is a pre-existing set of learning outcomes or academic objectives. In social skills, this pre-specified set of learning outcomes does not exist because there is not a widely accepted social-skill curriculum. Obviously, curriculum-based evaluation is hard to do without a curriculum. Without a curriculum, comparisons (and consequently, evaluations) get sloppy.

The operational standard for maladaptive behavior in most classrooms is "whatever irritates the teacher." If all teachers were equally tolerant, this wouldn't be a problem. They aren't (Wong, Kauffman & Lloyd, 1991). When Walker and Rankin (1983) gave a group of teachers a list of maladaptive behaviors and asked them to note which ones they would not accept in their classroom, one teacher marked 51 as unacceptable while another marked 8.

In addition to confusion introduced by the tolerance of different teachers for a given behavior, there is also evidence of different levels of tolerance for the behavior of different "types" of students. Brantlinger (1991), for example, found indications that low-income students were more apt to receive punishments than high-income students. Of particular interest in that study was the finding that only high-income students seemed to become "teacher pets." Among other advantages, these students were told to fix less-than-adequate academic work, whereas low-income students were not. This variability in teacher tolerance introduces tremendous confusion into the educational system's efforts to deal with social-skill training. (It was also found that high-income students would periodically push other high-income students into low-income students to get them contaminated with "cooties." However, low-income students never violated the border between incomes by pushing their low-income peers in the other direction.)

Given findings like these, it appears that teachers, as a group, are as subject to the undermining effects of bias and stereotyping (see Chapter 1, p. 15) as anyone else (Algozzine, Herr & Eaves, 1976). This particular line of teacher research is not all that pleasant to review, and it can get even worse. For example, Peterson, Wonderlich,

Reaven and Mullins (1987) found that the teachers in their study responded to depressed children with rejection—a reaction that would likely increase the depression. An additional finding in that study is even more disturbing. The researchers also found that, when it was explained that a student might be depressed because of stress (for example, resulting from an injury, or the death of a pet), the teachers were still *less* accepting of the child. In other words, instead of deciding that the depression was understandable and that the child was deserving of attention, the teachers apparently viewed the child as doubly unattractive because she had two problems: depression *and* stress.

Because few school programs have articulated a set of objectives for social skills, interventions in this domain are almost always reactive. This means that no work is done in social skills until a student does something adequately disrupting to alarm a teacher. The weaknesses in this system stem from the knowledge that: (a) all teachers do not have the same personal standards, (b) all classrooms do not require the same social skills, (c) the behavioral requirements of classrooms are frequently quite different from the requirements of the everyday world, (d) reaction is seldom instructional (as it lacks focus, explanation, demonstration, and feedback on appropriate behavior) and (e) nondisruptive but personally debilitating problems (such as sadness) are not addressed. Consequently, controlling the student in one class doesn't guarantee his adjustment in another class, or in the community outside of the schools. Therefore, an exclusive focus on "situational control" is not educationally legitimate (Nichols, 1992).

External control is something others do to bring a person into alignment with the requirements of a current situation. Control is imposed and is effective only as long as the outside pressure is present, or perceived to be present (Evans, Evans, Gable & Kehlhem, 1991; Nichols, 1992). While education also begins as an external intervention, its purpose is to teach the skills a person needs to remain in control of himself and advance toward his objectives without violating socially imposed restrictions or consuming an inordinate amount of community resources.

It is easy for teachers and administrators to confuse control and education, particularly considering that control of the student behavior is a legitimate prerequisite for instruction. However, while the focus of education should always be beyond the walls of the classroom (Ensminger & Dangel, 1992), it is probably superhuman

to keep sight of this principle when dealing with certain behaviors. (Dr. Howell in particular can testify to these difficulties, having once been knocked unconscious by a student wielding a certain piece of classroom equipment. Based on this experience he now recommends that plastic—not metal—wastebaskets be used in all classrooms.) Still, educators must face the fact that in the Walker and Rankin (1983) study mentioned earlier, the authors, who were trying to develop a scale for recognizing potential mainstreaming sites for students with behavioral difficulties, found yet another indicator of the priority teachers often place on control. When the researchers asked classroom teachers to rank-order a list of problematic behaviors, the largest number responded that "poor attendance" was the *least* problematic, being ranked lower than all others (including profanity, nervous tics, and wearing a brace). It appears from these results that many of the teachers in the study would rather have a kid completely miss instruction than to have him there while being disruptive.

There are at least two other problems that come with a preoccupation with control. The first is that it tends to make the teacher reactive. This means that, in a very real way, the student sets the social agenda of the classroom while the teacher is forced into a role of following his lead. While that is not necessarily bad, it can be if the student is leading things in a injurious direction. (It is interesting to note that even the most resolute advocates of "child-centered" instruction do not extend that philosophy to classroom behavior.) The second problem is that a control orientation causes the teacher (or administrator) to focus on decreasing (getting rid of) behaviors. This promotes the use of punitive, and ultimately ineffective, interventions (Evans et al., 1991; Knitzer, Steinberg & Fleisch, 1990). Also, in our view, it destroys the very nature of the legitimate student/teacher relationship. Teaching is giving, it isn't taking away.

As educators, we really only have two options: We can either spend the rest of our lives with the students or we can teach them to control themselves. Given the first option, teaching self-control sounds like a good idea.

Teaching Social Skills

To promote self-control, teachers must first plan for generalization by seeing that every lesson in social skills (as well as academics) leads the student out of

Exhibit 16.1   Social Behavior Content Areas

1. Language
2. Relaxation
3. Self-monitoring/Evaluation
4. Problem solving
5. Recognition of target thoughts and behaviors
6. Knowledge of cognitive/behavioral change techniques
7. Decision making
8. Judgment
9. Interaction skills

the classroom and into the world (Clement-Heist, Siegel & Gaylord-Ross, 1992). Second, teachers must teach the student the skills necessary to adjust successfully to any new situation (to discover how he should behave if he wishes to stay, and how he can get out if he wishes to leave). This means that the student must be taught how to analyze each setting, and discover the critical aspects of that setting that tell how to behave. Next the student must be taught to use good judgment (see Chapter 1).

Socially effective individuals can do all of the things listed above. Somehow they've learned to find the cues in the environment and use their judgment to either select behaviors consistent with those cues, or avoid places where they can't adjust. The behavior-disordered individual hasn't learned these things.

Teaching social skills, particularly those involving the metacognitive operations listed in the last paragraph, is not easy (Webber, Anderson & Otey, 1991; Kauffman & Wong, 1991). To begin with, it is time consuming. However, several decades of teacher effectiveness and time-on-task literature have demonstrated that more time in the school day (roughly 55% of it) is spent managing students than is spent teaching them (Doyle, 1986). Consequently the argument that one does not have time for social-skills training is not persuasive; the time is already being spent.

Of perhaps greater concern is the knowledge that effective instruction in metacognitive and social skills require tremendous work. Our students will have already learned, through experience, a set of social

skills. That means we have to get them to abandon, at least in some situations, their existing skills.

In order to promote adaptive social skills, a teacher must teach adaptive social perception and problem-solving skills. This requires the use of instructional techniques that actively involve the student in reflection, hypotheses testing, and validation (see Chapter 2) (McDaniel & Schlager, 1990). Often the goal of this instruction is to teach the student to understand that the validation of social "truth" does not necessarily come through personal experience. That is because what one experiences in a social context is not completely personal. As Brehmer (1986) puts it, "the guarantee of validity is *not* in experience itself" (p. 706).

Social-Skills Curriculum

Some efforts, usually found in the form of commercially prepared programs, have been made to define a social-skills curriculum (Goldstein, 1988; Larson, 1989a, 1989b). Content domains that frequently appear in these programs are listed in Exhibit 16.1. These are the general areas in which students probably should be skilled if they are to behave appropriately across settings. Language is listed first because a large proportion of the cues that tell us how to behave in any situation are linguistic.

Another content area commonly included in social skills curriculum is relaxation. People who are considered successful can relax in stressful situations. This skill at relaxation allows them to function better. In addition, people can be taught to recognize when they are stressed and to respond by relaxing (Kaplan, 1990).

Self-monitoring/evaluation (see Chapter 17) is the skill to track one's own behavior. If you have self-monitoring skills, you are in a good position to begin to control yourself. Teachers often complain that they don't have time to take data on students; a good solution to that problem is to teach them to take data on themselves. Self-monitoring will not automatically change behavior, but it is a prerequisite for self-initiated change.

Judgment and decision making are probably the pivotal domains for a social-skills curriculum. While problem-solving and thinking-skills training has been widely discussed (Derry & Murphy, 1986), some main points need to be summarized. Students who have problems in social skill don't solve problems well (Schumaker, Pederson, Hazel, & Meyer, 1983). Given problems, they generate fewer solutions (meaning they literally have less freedom to act); given solutions, they pick those that are ineffective and sometimes dangerous (often picking options with which they are familiar over those that are more effective).

While many people imagine disruptive students to be clever and cunning adversaries, the truth is that students with behavior problems are often confined within a very limited set of behavioral options because they automatically select inappropriate responses from the very narrow range of cues with which they are familiar. Their skill at looking beyond personal experiences is so poor that it prevents them from pushing aside the first options they recall (the inappropriate ones they have practiced so often in the past) so that they can recognize more adaptive responses.

In addition to language, relaxation, and decision making, students need to be aware of behavioral and cognitive change techniques if they are to control their own behavior. They need to know a few simple principles of reinforcement, punishment, extinction, and positive self-talk, in order to use these techniques on themselves. Once students have intervention skills, they need to recognize target thoughts, feelings, and behaviors that need to be changed. This includes recognizing what is appropriate and what is not appropriate, given different situations.

The top domains listed in Exhibit 16.1 all contain content relevant to general social competence. The final category, Interaction Skills, contains particular behaviors associated with appropriate interpersonal relationships. These may range from basic (making eye contact) to complex (expressing opinions in large groups). For the most part, this is the domain covered by existing, published, social-skills training programs. Unfortunately, these programs are often so focused on classroom control that they present few lessons on the common interpersonal challenges of everyday life (we have yet to see a lesson on how to tell the difference between *advertisement* and *advice*). Additionally, some of these basal programs seem to reflect the habits and traditions of higher socioeconomic groups.

The Special Case of Social Judgment

The content listed in Exhibit 16.1 is probably distributed evenly across factual, strategic, and conceptual dimensions (see page 38). However, the domain of judgment is principally conceptual in nature. As you will recall, concepts are learned by encountering examples and nonexamples (as in Chapter 3). In the case of most academic tasks, the attributes that distinguish examples from nonexamples are easily distinguished, clearly defined, widely agreed upon, and fixed. This is not the case with social judgment.

The information about judgment in Chapter 1 and the information about conceptual curriculum in Chapter 3 is not completely descriptive of the social-judgment domain. This is because social concepts do not have the fixed attributes of squares (squares always have four sides regardless of the context in which they occur). As a result mere experience with examples of the concept will not always allow the student to deduce the critical attributes of social concepts.

In order to learn adaptive social judgment, a student must learn through experience *and* instruction (Brehmer, 1986; Goldstein, 1988). This instruction occurs most productively when pertinent experiences are publicly (overtly) interpreted for the student by exemplars (socially competent individuals). Let's see if we can state that more clearly:

- Encountering events involving social judgment, while necessary, will not automatically teach "appropriate" social judgment. In fact, such experiences may actually teach inappropriate judgment. That's because the "social" aspect of an event isn't in the event, it's in the social context.

- Additionally, the students we are talking about in this chapter are often not sufficiently skilled at analysis, or knowledgeable about social context, to deduce (figure out on their own) the defining attributes of "socially appropriate."

- As a result, while they may understand that there is something to learn from a particular experience, they don't know what it is. So, without guidance, they simply interpret the new experience in terms of their existing knowledge. They get better at using bad judgment.

- Therefore, these students need instruction that teaches them to see beyond their current understanding of an event (actually to ignore their previous experiences), and to adopt socially adaptive interpretations of experience.

- In order for this to happen, the student must "see" the interpretations that socially competent individuals bring to experiences. They must value what they see. And they must practice it.

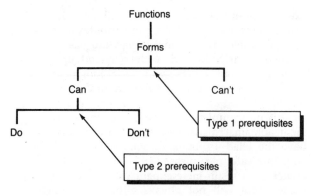

Exhibit 16.2   The basic model for evaluating social behavior.

• In short, the students need socially competent mentors who will tell them what to do and see to it that they practice until they get it right.

A Model of Behavior

If there were a widely accepted social-skill curriculum, then evaluators could compare students to the objectives of that curriculum (Epstein, Patton, Palloway & Foley, 1992). Without a curriculum, they must compare the student to their own standards or to various models of behavior. Many such models exist. To coordinate the material in this chapter, we have come up with our own nifty model (Exhibit 16.2). This model isn't very complex, and is not even unprecedented, but it seems useful. According to the model, there are many "forms" of behavior, and these forms are used to accomplish different "functions." Functions are easiest to conceptualize as the things we want to accomplish (avoid hassles, gain notoriety, watch a movie, or make a friend). The function of a behavior, therefore, is its purpose; the form is the way a person goes about trying to accomplish the purpose (Janney & Meyer, 1989; O'Neil et al., 1989).

There may be many possible forms of behavior that can be used in order to meet a function. Similarly, the same behavior may be used for many different functions. For example, a student who wants to avoid a task at which he knows he will fail could start a commotion to get thrown out of class or ask the teacher for permission to skip the lesson. Depending on the circumstances, either of these behaviors might accomplish the function of avoiding failure. It is entirely possible, therefore, for a student to experience success by starting commotions.

It is extremely important, if you intend to apply this model, that you understand that the functions of inappropriate behavior are *exactly* the same as the functions of appropriate behavior. The so-called behavior-disordered student is, therefore, trying to get exactly the same things a "behavior-ordered" person is trying to get. He is simply going about it in a socially unacceptable way. A list of functions developed by Neel (1984) is presented in Exhibit 16.3.

Forms

Let's ignore the function of behavior for a page or two and talk about forms. As seen in Exhibit 16.2, the forms (things that people do) can be divided into two categories, those forms the student cannot use and those he can. Next, the forms the kid *can* use are divided into two subcategories—those that he does and those that he doesn't. (We admit it's simplistic.) According to the model in Exhibit 16.2, a student may be using an inappropriate form because he actually *can't* use the appropriate form, or *isn't* using the appropriate form. These are two very different conditions. (In a way, it sounds as if we're saying that there are two types of students in classrooms—one type who can't behave appropriately, and another who is *electing* not to do so. We aren't. The same student may have both problems.)

You are currently reading a book (this one). If you are a student, you probably have two functions for this reading behavior: to learn, and to pass tests. Regardless of your purpose, there are many forms which your reading may take. Some of you are reading this chapter 10 minutes before the test (gotcha!) and others are reading it weeks ahead of time. As you read, some of you are seated in chairs, others on couches, and some are probably in bed or on the floor. None of you are sitting on the ceiling, because you can't. The environment (gravity) prohibits you from sitting on the ceiling.

When we say that a student *can't* do the appropriate thing, we mean that he lacks the skills to overcome the environmental influences that militate against it. We are not saying that the student has some sort of permanent incapacity, such as brain damage, that prohibits learning the skills.

Exhibit 16.3   Social Functions

Function	Description	Example Skills
1. Initiate/gain entry	Behavior that allows a person to gain access to interaction: either to initiate an interaction, to begin an event/exchange, or to enter one already underway.	1. Finding someone to talk to 2. Greeting others 3. Offering assistance 4. Asking for help 5. Asking for permission 6. Asking for some thing or action 7. Starting a conversation 8. Joining in 9. Giving instructions
2. Maintain interaction	Behavior that allows the interaction, activity and/or event to continue.	1. Answering 2. Helping others 3. Organizing play 4. Inviting others 5. Playing informally 6. Conversing 7. Listening 8. Convincing others 9. Responding to persuasion
3. Follow rules/regulations	Adhere to minimal "rules" of an activity or context, follow routines of given situation; generally implies serial order and/or branching to alternative series to select appropriate response.	1. Listening to teacher 2. Following teacher's verbal directions 3. Reading and following written directions 4. Following school, community rules 5. Accepting consequences 6. Following peer directions 7. Following rules when authority is absent 8. Avoiding trouble
4. Reinforce others/display affection	Provide others with feedback which is rewarding to them.	1. Smiling 2. Saying thank you 3. Saying something nice about what someone did 4. Saying something nice about how someone looks 5. Giving a general compliment 6. Receiving a compliment 7. Understanding the feelings of others 8. Consoling others when they have made a mistake or lost 9. Expressing satisfaction 10. Receiving affection

(continued)

Exhibit 16.3 Social Functions (continued)

Function	Description	Example Skills
5. Influence others/punish/ extinguish/reward	Provide others with feedback which indicates that their response was inappropriate, unpleasant, etc. and that you want them to stop that behavior.	1. Telling someone that you want to do something 2. Telling someone that you are mad without hurting them 3. Telling someone what you don't like (constructive criticism) 4. Ignoring a tease or other verbal remark 5. Ignoring or leaving when someone tries to hurt you (if you can) 6. Exploring the other person's point of view and expressing differences as you see them 7. Suggesting an alternate action the other person could take to make you less angry
6. Attend to relevant cues	Behaviors which accompany any social skills, are critical to the particular situation, and are included in any appropriate response.	1. Good grooming 2. Body posturing 3. Eye contact 4. Using right voice 5. Taking turns 6. Touching the right way
7. Provide information/describe	Behavior which shares information, feelings, etc., with others.	1. Answering questions 2. Showing something 3. Introducing yourself 4. Expressing an interest in the surroundings 5. Introducing other people 6. Telling about something not shared with listener 7. Expressing feelings
8. Indicate preference	Behavior which allows person to make a choice/decision from among alternatives available or presented by others.	1. Stating your preference 2. Choosing an alternative 3. Setting a goal 4. Arranging problems by importance 5. Participating in a decision 6. Deciding when given a choice 7. Determining the value before deciding to do something 8. Resisting peer pressure 9. Negotiating 10. Standing up for yourself and others 11. Convincing others

(continued)

Exhibit 16.3 **Social Functions** (continued)

Function	Description	Example Skills
9. Cope with negative situations	Behavior to generate and implement alternative strategies to continue an interaction or complete a task or select an alternative interaction when presented with a negative situation or consequence.	1. Dealing with interruptions 2. Finding an alternate activity when permission has been denied 3. Developing acceptable activities when bored 4. Seeking help when something goes wrong 5. Responding to embarrassment 6. Generating alternatives when excluded or left out 7. Dealing with fearful situations or events 8. Interpreting and evaluating contradictory messages
10. Dealing with anger	Behavior that receives, deflects and resolves angry situations without harming either the receiver or sender.	1. Receiving a complaint 2. Answering a complaint 3. Receiving an accusation 4. Apologizing 5. Defusing a hostile situation 6. Responding to an attack or fight
11. Leave—take exit	Behavior to terminate or withdraw from an interaction situation, cease participation in an activity when appropriate, desired, etc.	1. Moving to next activity at the end of a task 2. Leaving at the end of a positive social interaction 3. Leaving when an interaction/task is not complete 4. Leaving when an interaction/task is negative
12. Problem Solving	Behavior that is used to generate, evaluate and implement solutions to impasses or obstructions to goals.	1. Gathering information 2. Generating trial alternatives 3. Evaluating trial alternatives 4. Implementing (test) alternatives 5. Re-evaluating and modifying alternatives 6. Planning long-term goals 7. Accepting abilities and limitations

Source: "Teaching Social Routines to Behaviorally Disordered Youth," by R. S. Neal. In J. K. Grosenick, E. McGinnis, S. L. Huntze and C. R. Smith (Eds.), *Social/Affective Interventions in Behavioral Disorders.* Copyright © 1984 by Department of Public Instruction, Des Moines, IA.

When we say that a student *doesn't* do the appropriate thing, we mean that he has selected (from among the things he can do) the wrong form. Now we have to be careful here, because some of you may think this means the student has consciously, and with intent to irritate adults, selected an inappropriate way to behave. While this is sometimes true (in which case the student is reacting to you as much as you are reacting to him), more often *selecting* an inappropriate behavior is not the same as *deciding* to behave inappropriately.

People select most behaviors automatically

(Kirsch, 1985). If you recall the discussion of automaticity (Chapter 2), it said that automatic responses occur without the use of working (conscious) memory. So here's the question. When you started to read this chapter, did you say this to yourself: "Well, I'd rather not stand while I read, so I guess I'll lean, sit, or lie down. Research shows that those who lie down to study (particularly in bed) learn less—so I'll sit. I could sit on the floor or in a chair or on the couch. I never sit in 'that' chair, because that's where I throw my stuff when I walk in at night. The couch is OK but gets more like a bed the longer I sit in it. So I'll pick the floor. In fact I'll pick the floor next to the window so I get the best light and can see if anyone more interesting than this book is walking by."

While each of you had many options from which to choose (many places to sit while reading this passage), we doubt that you recall choosing where to sit. You did choose, but it was not the kind of rational and considered choice you might employ when selecting an investment or a new job. Just as you are not aware of all of the choices you make, kids with behavior problems are largely unaware of the ones they make and how they make them. (Incidentally, because they are unaware of the tactic they use to select the behavior, merely giving them feedback that their choices are wrong is not apt to alter the selections they make. That's because feedback about the quality of a choice doesn't say anything about how a better choice can be made.)

Can vs. Can't Problems

A student in this condition cannot engage in a behavior because (a) he doesn't have the skills to do so, or (b) something in the environment is inhibiting him. If either case is true, the evaluator has found an example of missing Type 1 prerequisites, because he has found a student who currently does not have the skill or knowledge to carry out an appropriate form of behavior.

Do vs. Don't Problems

In the model (Exhibit 16.2), the student who can do a behavior must still select whether or not to do it. The selection depends upon Type 2 prerequisites such as beliefs, expectations, and perceptions (selective attention—see Chapter 2). Let's go back to the discussion of choosing a place to sit. When you walk into a bank to apply for a loan, you still don't sit on the ceiling,

because that form of sitting is unavailable. You can sit on the floor, but you don't sit there because your perceptions of the situation, and your desire to get the loan, tell you that form is a bad idea.

Selections are based upon covert catalysts such as preferences, interests, perceptions, expectations, fears, and desires. All of these, which are learned through experience, combine with other prior knowledge to shape the selection tactic that the student uses to pick responses. When people have options, they select one and don't select the others according to what they're thinking at the time. These thoughts, as well as the way people go about changing and working with what they know, reside within prior knowledge—they are learned (see Chapter 2). Because different people have different learning histories, they have different ideas and beliefs about the world. As a result, they select different forms of behavior. If for some reason our thinking changes, then we make different selections.

To evaluate selection tactics, evaluators must work within the domain of covert behaviors. This is considerably more difficult, and chancy, than working with the overt explanations associated with Type 1 prerequisites.

The Contextual Analysis of Behavior

One way to find Type 1 and Type 2 prerequisites is to use applied behavior analysis (ABA) (Wolery et al., 1989). With this system, we attempt to specify the geographic antecedents and consequences of behaviors. The assumption behind ABA is that behavior is affected by context. That means that an understanding of the environment is necessary. This is particularly true within "high-impact environments" (Bower, 1972) such as the school and family.

Behavior is interactive. It takes place between the individual and the situation. So if you want to evaluate social skill, you can't just attend to the individual. You must also attend to the social environment. For example, suppose Ellen has the problem "hitting peers." How is her geographic environment supporting this undesirable behavior? To answer this question, the evaluator conducts an applied behavioral analysis by observing Ellen and then writing down what is seen in the format shown in Exhibit 16.4.

Imagine that in observing Ellen you find that she

Exhibit 16.4   Applied Behavioral Analysis of Ellen's Hitting Behavior

Antecedents S^1	Behavior R	Consequences S^2
a. Classroom b. Free time c. Morning d. Low structure e. Peers give negative comments	Ellen hits peer	a. Peer runs away b. Negative comments stop c. Teacher puts Ellen in time out

hits (a) in the classroom, (b) during free time, (c) in the mornings, (d) when there's low structure, and (e) when her peers are saying negative things about her. Next you look around to see what happens after she hits somebody and you find that (a) the peer runs away, (b) the negative comments stop, and (c) the teacher puts Ellen in "time out" (removes her from the classroom). If the behavior is maintaining (Ellen is continuing to hit peers), it is assumed that the antecedents and consequences are in balance.

Sometimes the environment may actually prohibit appropriate behavior. As a general rule, the criterion for appropriate social skill (unlike academic skills) is not the median of successful students. In North Amer-

Social behavior is interactive. To evaluate social skill, you must attend to both the individual and the social environment.

*Exhibit 16.5
Carl's "talk
out" behavior
decreasing to
the ecological
floor.*

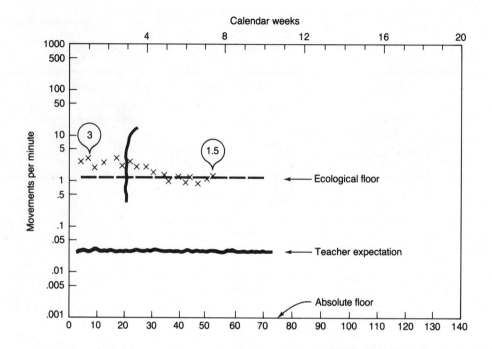

ican culture, the social criterion is the norm. Consequently, a teacher should not expect any student to exhibit a form of social behavior that isn't like the class average. (We are not suggesting that all students should behave in the same way. We are simply stating that it is unrealistic for teachers to expect them to do otherwise.)

The environmental frequency of a behavior places ecological boundaries, called the *ceiling* and *floor,* on that behavior. These may not be at the same level as the teacher's expectation. For example, imagine a student named Carl. Carl originally talks out in class three times per minute. The absolute floor for this behavior would be zero times per minute. The teacher expects Carl to talk out no more than .03 times per minute. Excluding Carl's behavior and that of another student with the same pinpoint, "talk-outs" occur in the classroom 1.5 times a minute. These levels are shown in Exhibit 16.5.

As you can see in Exhibit 16.5, Carl's behavior has moved toward the teacher's expectation but has not passed the ecological floor. For this behavior, or any other social skill, the ecological floor is as far as the change should go. At this point (.03 on the chart),

the environment actually begins to work against the behavior change. A teacher can cause the student to go beyond the ecological floor by calling upon increasingly powerful interventions, yet consider what incidental lessons he would be teaching. First, he would be teaching the student to deviate from his peers—which is often the behavior-disordered student's biggest problem in the first place. Second, he would be teaching the student to disregard the primary environmental cue defining appropriate behavior—the behavior of others. Therefore, he would be decreasing the likelihood of his intervention's generalizing to any other setting. If the "normal" student gets out of his seat six times in a period it is not unreasonable to expect the special education/remedial student to do likewise.

Atypical behavior, even if it is changing in the direction in which we are most comfortable, is still abnormal. If a teacher wants Carl to conform to his expectations, he should first move Carl to the class average, and then move the whole class to a preferred level. This level should be determined through careful observations of target settings, and not through teacher presumption alone.

ABA, and the sort of functional skill assessment advocated throughout the academic chapters of this text, can be used to determine if the student lacks Type 1 prerequisites and therefore "can't" engage in a necessary behavior. If he can't behave appropriately because he lacks the skills needed to deal with his environment, obviously the teacher should teach him these skills. But what about the student who can behave appropriately but doesn't? According to the model in Exhibit 16.2, we must also consider those factors that lead students to select inappropriate things to do. This requires a move away from the conventional consideration of the environment represented by ABA.

The Need to Consider Coverts

Some students know what to do and have the necessary skills to do it, but still misbehave because their judgment and belief systems (which comprise the selection tactics) encourage them to pick maladaptive forms of behavior. These students may automatically reject attempts at communication, distrust representatives of authority, and accept without question the opinions of those who enjoy status in their peer group. Anxiety, fear, anger, or just plain confusion may influence their selection of behaviors. Such students need to learn new selection tactics before they can realistically be expected to engage in the targeted forms of behavior that teachers select for them. To teach these tactics, we must evaluate the student to determine which Type 2 prerequisites need to be developed.

In the *operant* or *behavioral* camp, behaviors are viewed as the result of stimuli in the environment. A behavior learned in the presence of one set of stimuli may not occur as often in a setting where these stimuli are absent. Therefore, the best way to explain either the presence or absence of a behavior is to analyze the environment. This was illustrated with the ABA example of Ellen in Exhibit 16.4. This procedure makes sense if kids respond directly to the environment.

There is major evidence, however, that humans don't respond directly to the environment—or at least to what we usually think of as the environment. That evidence is the fact that all kids don't act the same way in the same class. They don't, because neither kids nor adults respond to the environment itself but to their cognitive representations of the environment (Ma-

honey, 1977; Moos, 1973). Stated another way, people don't behave according to what is going on, but according to what they think is going on. These thoughts and feelings are the result of the interpreter's explanations of environmental stimuli (see Chapter 2), perceptions, expectations, and beliefs are stored in memory. Because people have learned different things and their behavior is partially the result of their learning, they behave in different ways.

Take a second look at Ellen. Exhibit 16.4 is reproduced in Exhibit 16.6a. In Exhibit 16.6b an additional component, a thought, has been added to the analysis. This is an example of applied cognitive-behavior analysis. Applied cognitive-behavior analysis is not limited to an examination of the geographic environment of the student. The cognitive-behavior analysis shows us that Ellen believes that inactivity in the presence of insults is the sign of a sissy (we think she probably learned that from Carl). Since she thinks a sissy is something bad, Ellen doesn't remain inactive—she pummels her peers. If she had the belief "sticks and stones may break my bones, but words will never hurt me," she might select a different response to the situation.

Ellen's beliefs comprise part of the selection tactic by which she chooses what to do. If this idea (that prior learning cultivates beliefs, expectations, and perceptions that in turn determine behavior) is correct, it follows that efforts to change behavior should include efforts to change what the student thinks. Obviously, these efforts would have to be preceded by an evaluation of the student's cognitive environment.

Cognitive-Behavior Analysis

We are working on the premise that every student has a selection tactic that he applies to make choices from available responses in the environment (Tversky & Kahneman, 1973). This selection tactic is obviously not "real" in any physical or stable sense (that is, we cannot strain or bruise our selection tactic). Social judgment is the functional manifestation of the lessons, prejudices, interests, fears, and desires the student has acquired through experience. There are at least four labels applied to the cognitive behavior that comprise the selection tactic. They are *attention* or perception, *expectation*, *belief*, and *cognitive set*. While the authors don't maintain that these four are in any way indepen-

Exhibit 16.6   Two Kinds of Analysis

(a) Applied Behavior Analysis of Ellen's Hitting Behavior

Antecedents S^1	Behavior R	Consequences S^2
1. Classroom 2. Free time 3. Morning 4. Low structure 5. Peers give negative comments	Ellen hits peer	1. Peer runs away 2. Negative comments stop 3. Teacher puts Ellen in time out

(b) Applied Cognitive-Behavioral Analysis of Ellen's Hitting Behavior

Antecedents S^1	Behavior R	Consequences S^2
1. Classroom 2. Free time 3. Morning 4. Low structure 5. Peers give negative comments	Ellen thinks: "If I let them talk to me that way I'm a sissy." Ellen hits peer	1. Peer runs away 2. Negative comments stop 3. Teacher puts Ellen in time out

dent of each other or have any absolute reality, the terms themselves are useful for clarifying the cognitive-behavioral approach to evaluation.

Attention

Attention functions as a template between awareness and the outside world. It protects short-term memory by allowing people to notice only those things that prior experience has taught are worth consciousness—and to disregard those they have been taught to ignore. But what if these lessons have led to a fraudulent outcome?

To select an option, a student must first attend to it. But many students have learned to ignore some options, while others are so busy attending to one thing that they don't even see others. One explanation for this can be found in the so-called availability heuristic (Tversky & Kahneman, 1973).

According to the availability paradigm, people are most apt to select options that are easy for them to recall. This ease of recall is thought to be a function of experience. If in the past a person has experienced one type of option frequently (or dramatically), then that is the type of option he will most easily recall. If the student has not developed good social judgment, it is also the type of option he will be most apt to select. Aggressive behavior is a good example of this. If a student has seen force applied frequently or dramatically to solve problems, then he is best prepared to recognize (perceive) forceful solutions to problems. When he experiences a new situation he may search for options. However, because of his specially trained attention, he only recognizes those involving force. Because he fails to "see" nonforceful options, he has fewer choices to make and therefore less freedom to act.

Recognition of options is a Type 2 prerequisite skill that can be taught. Because the absence of the skill may cause a student to be unable to select appropriate behaviors, it must be considered in any functional social-behavior evaluation.

*Exhibit 16.7
The cognitive-
behavior
model.*

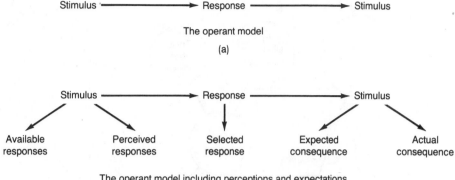

Stimulus ⟶ Response ⟶ Stimulus

The operant model

(a)

The operant model including perceptions and expectations

(b)

Expectations

If a student decides to work for candy, he carries out the work in the expectation that the candy will be received. This expectation is the result of experiences in which candy was actually received after work. When a teacher follows a response with a pleasant stimulus, the probability of the response recurring is linked to the student's expectation that more responses will lead to additional pleasant stimuli.

If we take the strict operant model (Exhibit 16.7a) and insert perceptions and expectations, the model looks like Exhibit 16.7b. This amended model (Exhibit 16.7b) says that behavior will be chosen from among the perceived available responses. The selection will also be based upon the expected consequences that go with choosing any of the perceived responses (Rotter, 1982).

Beliefs

A belief is an idea an individual takes as fact. What a person believes is as real to him as what he is seeing and hearing at any given moment. Beliefs have been raised to factual status by the experiences of the individual. These experiences were themselves affected by perceptions and expectations, so of course it isn't possible to clearly distinguish beliefs from perceptions and expectations. However, a belief can be viewed as a rule the person applies to all situations. A delinquent may believe, for example, that "cops can't be trusted" and hold that belief at all times. To others, that belief may seem appropriate in some situations and inappropriate in others. Prejudices are examples of beliefs.

They are acquired through unbefitting learning and can be diminished by teaching other incompatible beliefs.

Cognitive Set

Beliefs, expectations, and perceptions do not exist in isolation or function separately. Like all prior knowledge they are dumped into long-term memory to be retrieved through the activation of recall strategies, which are themselves reposed within executive control (see Chapter 2). The storage and recall of large knowledge structures is thought to be controlled, in part, by the individual's use of *schema* (see pp. 22 and 218). Cognitive sets are most conveniently conceptualized as schema. They are the webs, or nets, that tie together separate nodes of information. A schematic map of the cognitive set called "learned helplessness" is illustrated in Exhibit 16.8.

According to schema theory, once a sufficient number of the information nodes comprising a schema have been activated, the executive control function will recall the complete net of information, not the isolated nodes. This has the effect of making all available information about the topic immediately available to short-term memory. As a result, the student's thinking is flooded by the information that comprises the set. Schema activation allows for highly efficient access to large bodies of information by eliminating the executive's need to search out each separate bit (node) of information.

Unfortunately, with the efficiency of schema activation comes a certain danger. That danger is that the

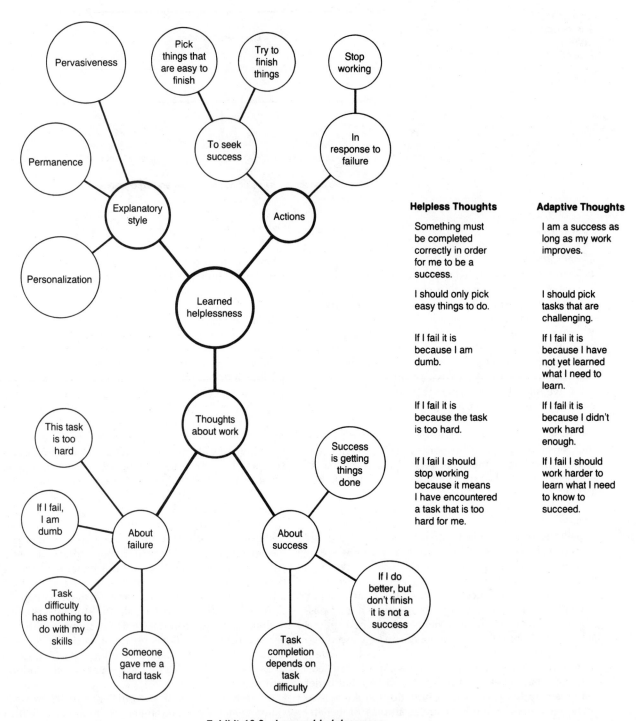

Helpless Thoughts

Something must be completed correctly in order for me to be a success.

I should only pick easy things to do.

If I fail it is because I am dumb.

If I fail it is because the task is too hard.

If I fail I should stop working because it means I have encountered a task that is too hard for me.

Adaptive Thoughts

I am a success as long as my work improves.

I should pick tasks that are challenging.

If I fail it is because I have not yet learned what I need to learn.

If I fail it is because I didn't work hard enough.

If I fail I should work harder to learn what I need to know to succeed.

Exhibit 16.8   Learned helplessness.

schema, which is composed of old information, may not be totally applicable to the current situation. Nodes that are in the net, but are unrelated to the immediate situation, get recalled along with all the others. That is apparently why, when you are upset about the death of a family member, you may suddenly start thinking about the loss of a childhood pet.

While we imagine that learning theorists would probably balk at the analogy, we are presenting cognitive sets as "habits" of thinking that are invoked under a familiar geographic *or cognitive* context. (Once these habits are developed they are hard to break because, like all other habits, they have their gratifying sides.) So here is what happens. When a student, we'll call him Dean, hears the teacher say "It looks like you are having trouble with your spelling" the following nodes are stimulated: Teacher, Classroom, Spelling, and Trouble. In Dean's case, prior learning has tied each of these nodes into a cognitive set, or schema. Unfortunately for Dean there are some other nodes in that set: Failure, Helplessness, and Task Difficulty. Therefore, when the teacher says "It looks like you are having trouble with your spelling," Dean thinks "It looks like I am *failing* because I am *helpless* when it comes to *tasks that are this hard.*" This may have two effects. First, Dean may stop working on his spelling, and second, he may begin to use the cognitive set (thinking pattern) of a helpless person (Winne & Marx, 1989).

While we have avoided most of the popular theories of mental health in this chapter, there is one construct that is so obviously related to classroom success that we have to bring it up. It is the idea of "learned helplessness" (Seligman, 1990; Dweck, 1986). Students who have developed learned helplessness have established habits of thought, relative to school, that cause them to stop working when they experience difficulty. This idea, which is the exact opposite of "When the going gets tough, the tough get going," translates into something like "When the going gets tough, it means I can't do anything about it so I might just as well quit."

Learned helplessness is (we guess this is sort of redundant) *learned* (Dweck, 1986). Therefore, it can be corrected just as other patterns of maladaptive behavior and thought can be corrected, through instruction (Seligman, 1990). This will be addressed again in Chapter 17 under the heading of Motivation. For now it is sufficient to be aware that cognitive sets, pertaining to habits of thought and work, may become acti-

vated. In all cases, the activation of these schema allows for the more efficient recall of prior learning. Unfortunately, in some cases, this allows more efficient recall of nonadaptive thoughts. The thoughts that come with nonadaptive cognitive sets encourage the student to ignore the current tasks and to act only on the basis of ineffective prior knowledge. Therefore, during the assessment of Type 2 prerequisites, an evaluator must try to identify those cognitive sets that interfere with appropriate social behavior.

Caution No. 1

Frankly, we have some concern about presenting this cognitive material. There are three reasons for this concern: uncertainty about its practicality, the risk of diluting the curriculum, and fear of misapplication. Special education has a long, unfortunate history of misplaced faith in ideas about the unseen. We have spent decades directing teachings at the hypothesized cognitive or perceptual characteristics of kids (see Chapter 2). Frequently our pursuit of the "psycholinguistic," "psychobehavioral," "psychomedical," and "psychoeducational" has led us far from the skills we have an ethical responsibility to teach. Why do it again by suggesting that teachers consider the cognitive strategies by which kids select behaviors? One answer is that most teachers, most of the time, are already directing their attention to the covert behaviors of students. While "education" has many meanings, it certainly implies an effort to teach students to believe, to expect, and to perceive things differently than those who are uneducated. We accept this when the task is long division; it is harder to accept when the topic is making friends, abortion, sexual orientation, or religion.

In Chapter 12 we presented an argument for respecting the first language of students and the culture from which that language evolved. Those arguments, about the value of diversity and the need to honor a student's heritage, certainly apply to domains like social skills, friendship, and religion (Eitzen, 1992). However, the call for respect in the language chapter was easy to make because different languages are clearly linked to different groups of people. Therefore, respect for Roberto's use of Spanish isn't tied to Roberto alone, but to the culture to which he belongs. But what about Roberto's *own* ideas? According to Coles (1990), it is a mistake to assume that students come to us without well-developed beliefs about topics like religion, ethics, and morality.

We believe that a teacher's responsibility is to increase the student's behavioral options along with his control over these options. The objective, therefore, is not to purge the student of "inappropriate thoughts" but to build a potentially useful repertoire of beliefs and perceptions along with the judgment to control and update them (Forness, 1992). If carried out with adequate reflection and honest adherence to that objective, our efforts should result in students who are better at being themselves—not students who are the way we happen to want them to be.

The student's current set of covert responses have been learned and have a reinforcement history. Because they may be quite appropriate in a nonschool setting, effective efforts to remove them could get the youth into trouble. (The idea that "words can never hurt me" may be fine for chemistry class but dead wrong in a particular home.) It would be nice to provide you with some closure relative to these issues, but we can't.

Evaluating Social Skills

The entire social-skill evaluation procedure is illustrated by the flowchart in Exhibit 16.9. It begins by carefully defining the form and function of the student's maladaptive behavior. Once the function of the problem behavior has been identified, the evaluator selects an appropriate form, or forms, that will accomplish that same function. This is called the target pinpoint. Data is then collected in order to determine the discrepancy between the student's expected level of performance and actual behavior. The goals of instruction are then stated.

The assumed-cause phase of evaluation begins with the evaluator's recognizing the prerequisites of the target pinpoint. During this task analysis, all of the Type 1 and Type 2 prerequisites essential to the successful completion of the target pinpoint are identified. Typically, these are listed on a status sheet. Suspected missing prerequisites are treated as assumed causes and highlighted for specific-level testing.

The final stages of the evaluation are validating and decision making. Validating begins when the evaluator selects and administers probes to determine which of the prerequisites the student lacks and therefore needs to be taught. The results of this specific-level testing are then combined with the product of the

status sheet and used to decide what to teach the student.

The complete evaluation results in the following products:

A. An exact description of the maladaptive behaviors.

B. An exact description of the target behaviors.

C. A comparison of the student's current level of performance on both the target and maladaptive behaviors to a standard.

D. A summary of the discrepancy between the student's performance and the standard.

E. A goal, or goals, describing in measurable terms the change in student behavior needed to remove the discrepancy.

F. A list of agents (antecedents or consequences) in the geographic/physical environment that prompt the maladaptive behavior or inhibit the target behavior.

G. A list of agents in the cognitive environment that prompt the maladaptive behavior or inhibit the target behavior.

H. Short-term instructional objectives describing a sequence of learnings to take the student from his current level of performance to his goals.

A Note on Pinpointing

In order to conduct a social-skills evaluation, it is necessary that you know how to measure social behavior (see Chapter 6). Therefore we want to spend some time describing how to pinpoint target and maladaptive behaviors. Pinpointing is the process of describing forms of behavior in measurable/observable terms. For example, if Pam makes negative statements about herself, they can be counted. Some people may think that Pam has "poor self-concept," but this is open to interpretation. To describe a student's maladaptive behavior as lazy, bad, disobedient, or disrespectful is not functional, because different people will put these labels on different groups of behaviors.

Specificity is particularly important for the target behavior. It is important because one cannot analyze anything operationally that is not clearly defined. One needs statements describing exactly what the student will do, or look like, when the target has been reached.

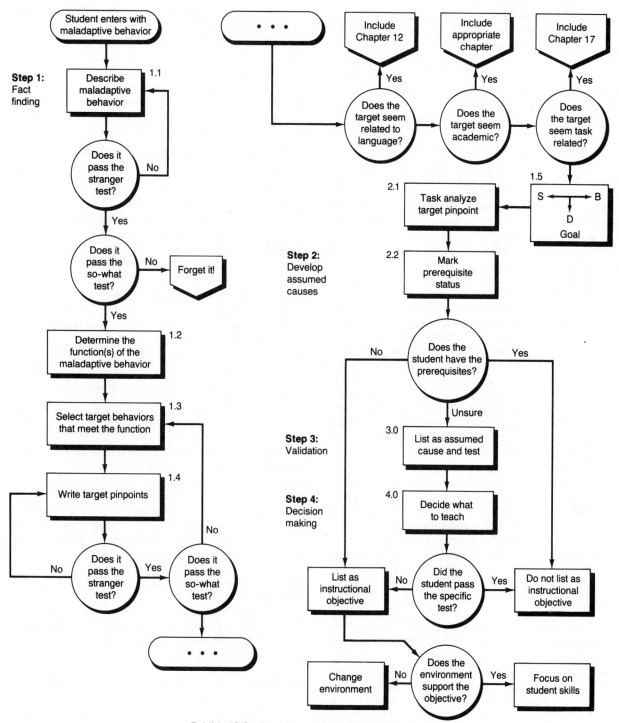

Exhibit 16.9 Decision making for social behavior.

If you pay attention to the following rules, you should have no trouble pinpointing maladaptive and target behaviors. First, try to use verbs instead of adjectives. Words like "hits," "smiles," "cries," and "talks" convey more meaning than "rough," "happy," "sad," or "motor-mouth." Second, avoid adverbs and adverbial phrases. For example, "talks *more*," "hits *hard*," "smiles *appropriately*," and "laughs *at the wrong time*." The secret here is to substitute, or include, the measurement rule you will use to define the adverb. This produces statements like "talks *4 times an hour*." Third, stay away from value judgments. Don't use constructs such as "lazy," "dumb," "generous," "considerate," or "conscientious." And finally, if you must use adverbs or make value judgments, then at least try to clarify them by supplying examples. Exhibit 16.10 provides instances and noninstances of maladaptive and target pinpoints.

Once you have stated the target and maladaptive behaviors in measurable terms, get everyone involved with the student—including the student—together. Sit back in your chairs. Relax. Then read over the pinpoints and ask "So what?" Is this behavior *really* worth the time and attention of a teacher and a student? If it isn't, forget it. (We also recommend asking yourself if the pinpoint falls into the domain of control or instruction. If it is only a control problem, then you should be aware that the time and effort you spend bending the student to the constraints of the current setting will most likely be of no benefit to him after the school day has ended.)

One additional point needs to be made about target pinpoints. They should always be statements of what you want the student to do, not what you want the student to stop doing. In other words "Ralph will not touch other people's possessions without permission" is *not* an acceptable target. "Ralph will ask permission before touching other people's possessions" is acceptable because it specifies what Ralph will do.

Measuring

Once the behaviors (target and maladaptive) have been specified, they need to be measured. Whenever possible, we recommend that you do this through direct observation of the target and maladaptive pinpoints. If direct observation is not possible, then we recommend that you use a structured interview to question individuals who have seen the behavior.

Tips on conducting an observation were provided in Chapters 5 and 6. It is best to collect data as unobtrusively as possible. If you are the teacher it is not a good idea to collect the data, as you may be a pivotal factor in the student's environment. In this case, design the observation system and then get an aide or another teacher to exchange some time to collect the data you need. Some general points about observation deserve to be repeated:

1. It is better to observe a behavior for several short periods than for one long one.

2. It is important to report the circumstances under which the observation occurs.

3. Use the median score from at least 3 days of observation as your best estimate of the kid's current status (obviously, if the maladaptive behavior is dangerous, you will not wait 3 days to start instruction).

4. If the pinpoints never occur, then you will need to prompt them by testing. In this case the tests may come in forms like role-playing, questioning, or student interviews.

5. If the problem requires you to collect data on the interactions of another teacher with the student, be aware of the potential for misunderstanding. Explain what you are doing and why you are doing it. In addition, as in every other case, observe and respect the canon of confidentiality.

Once you have collected data on the student's use of the target and maladaptive behaviors, examine them in terms of a standard. As you are about to learn, the standard for social skill is the class average as determined through the collection of data on ecological boundaries. If the student's behavior is no different from that of others in the environment, select a new pinpoint or devise a group intervention.

Techniques for Testing Type 2 Prerequisites

Type 2 prerequisites (coverts) present particular measurement problems. They also require the evaluator to utilize many procedures not typically associated with assessment. Some of these are explained here.

Questions   Often the simplest way to find out what someone is thinking is to ask. How reliable is it to simply ask? Up to a point it is safe to assume that any

Exhibit 16.10   *Instances and Noninstances of Maladaptive and Target Pinpoints*

Maladaptive Pinpoints	
Instances	**Noninstances**
1. Makes inaudible statements.	1. Is aggressive.
2. Makes self-deprecating remarks (e.g., "I'm dumb," "I'm stupid," "I'm a retard").	2. Is off task.
3. Plays with younger children during recess.	3. Is immature.
4. Hits peers without physical provocation.	4. Calls out inappropriately.
5. Answers do not include content of teacher's questions.	5. Is anxious.
6. Repeats questions he has already asked.	6. Cannot accept criticism.
7. Says "I don't have to" or "I don't want to" when given a direction.	7. Is immature.
8. Calls out without raising hand.	8. Uses back talk.
9. Does not complete assignments by due date.	9. Is tardy.
10. Is not in seat when late bell rings.	10. Is dirty.

Target Pinpoints Instances	
Instances	**Noninstances**
1. Speaks in a voice audible to all parts of the room.	1. Is considerate of others. [What does "considerate" mean?]
2. Lists ten good things about himself in one minute.	2. Is on task. [Open to interpretation]
3. Plays with children his own age during recess.	3. Is mature. [Construct]
4. Sits next to peers and talks to them.	4. Requests permission to speak appropriately. [What does "appropriately" mean?]
5. Answers include content of teacher's question.	5. Is mellow/calm. [Compared to what?]
6. Asks the same question only once.	6. Accepts punishment. [Open to interpretation.]
7. Complies with direction first time given.	7. Exercises self-control.
8. Raises hand and waits to be called.	8. Speaks respectfully.
9. Completes 100% of work by due dates.	9. Arrives when he should.
10. Is in seat before late bell rings.	10. Has good hygiene.

test can be made more reliable by adding a few more items (though this won't necessarily affect its validity). This means that if you observe a behavior 20 times you become more confident than if you observe it only once. Therefore, if you need to ask questions of a student, ask them several times in a variety of settings and circumstances. If the student tends to give consis-

tent responses, you may take this as evidence of reliability. If the responses are inconsistent, you don't know if the student is changing or if the question is poor. Either way you need to do additional testing.

There are several types of questioning techniques you can use (Stowitschek et al., 1984), and you may switch from one to another according to the responses you get. Let's go through these types using item 11 from Exhibit 16.18, p. 392:

Knows consequences of engaging in the target behavior.

Open Question.   This is the least constraining form of question. To use it, ask something like "What will happen to you if you get to class on time?" Because correct answers could include everything from "I'd feel good" to "Whatever the teacher wants to happen," you must be prepared to interpret the responses or to seek clarification of them.

A modification of the open-question approach is the use of story starters, much like the ones presented in Chapter 13. For example, "John is downtown at night and has lost his money. List as many ways as you can think of for him to call his friends." (If in this case the student cannot supply solutions to hypothetical problems, or if all of his solutions are unrealistic or illegal, his problem could be in the solutions he attends to, rather than in his skill at carrying them out.)

Multiple Choice.   This type limits possible responses to the choices supplied.

   "If you get to class on time, will you . . .
      (a) get sent to the office?
      (b) get to come to class?
      (c) get to take an extra two weeks off this summer?
      (d) get out of work?"

The choices may be presented verbally or in the form of cartoons/pictures. The complexity of the item can be increased or decreased by altering either the number or wording of the alternatives. One disadvantage of multiple-choice questioning is that it doesn't allow responses that are not supplied.

Restricted Alternatives.   If a student typically selects a certain alternative, then you can rule that one out by removing it from competition.

   "If you get to class on time you will not get out of work; what will you get?"

Role-Playing   Role-playing may or may not involve the student being evaluated. Sometimes you can use peers to role-play scenes, much as you would present cartoons, for the student to analyze. At other times you may ask the student to play a part in a hypothetical situation so that you can see how knowledgeable the student seems to be. Often, initial attempts at role-playing fail because students are uncomfortable with it. Therefore, you may need to use it routinely if you are going to use it at all. When using role-playing, keep the directions specific and the scenes short. Also be sure to specify the sort of behavior expected; for example, "Show me how I want students to arrive at class." To find out more about role-playing, refer to Goldstein (1988).

Cue Sorts   Cue-sort techniques (Stephenson, 1980) are particularly useful for Type 2, student-centered (odd-numbered items in Exhibit 16.18*, p. 392) prerequisite tests. To use a cue sort, give the student several terms, cartoons, or pictures, each on a separate card. These cards should include the content in which you are interested and a range of plausible distractors (if you are interested in the consequence "get to come to class," you would include options like "get extra points" or "go to the office").

Once the student has the cards, then you ask him to sort them according to some categorical system. For example, "Put the cards in two piles—one for what might happen if you come to class on time and one for what might happen if you are late." You then score the responses by noting how well the sorting matches the actual consequences.

Cue sorts are uniquely suited for gaining insight into a student's beliefs and perceptions. For example, you can give a student a stack of cards with various behaviors on them and ask him to put the behaviors in order according to those his teacher would find *least* acceptable. Next, ask him to order the same cards according to his own idea of acceptability, and then again according to what he thinks his best friend would find acceptable. Differences in the sortings reflect the student's beliefs about the behaviors as well as his perceptions of his teacher and his friend.

A sample cue sort is shown in Exhibit 16.11. The student was first asked to sort the ten words according to "What you like to do" and "What your teacher likes you to do." Next the teacher was asked to sort the cards in terms of what he wanted the student to do. Some conflicts in perceptions are apparent.

Structured Interviews   Like cue sorts, structured interviews are reserved for Type 2 prerequisites. The

Exhibit 16.11   A Sample Cue Sort

Kid's Sorting		Teacher's Sorting
What do you like to do?	What does the teacher want you to do in class?	What do you want the kid to do in class?
play	be quiet	learn
be happy	be serious	be happy
mess around	work	think
laugh	think	work
learn	learn	be serious
talk	talk	be quiet
think	laugh	talk
work	mess around	laugh
be quiet	be happy	play
be serious	play	mess around

purpose of the structured interview is to get the student to talk within a given framework, or scaffold (see Chapter 17, p. 405). If this scaffold is carefully structured, the things the student says can be used to draw inferences about covert thoughts/feelings. As always, it is important to note that these inferences may not always be correct and that generalizations from overt behavior (in this case, talk) to covert behavior (thought or feeling) should always be treated with some caution. However, if an evaluator asks a student "What is 6×8?" and the student says "48," few of us would question the inference that "the student knows how to multiply" even though the inference is based on verbal behavior. That's because the inference is supported by the structure supplied by the rules of the multiplication problem itself. If a similar scaffold can be developed for social skill, inferences here would also be easier to defend.

Exhibit 16.2 presented the model that has been used throughout this chapter to structure our discussion of social skill. Having a model of this kind helps you (and the authors) to organize and clarify thinking. This is the basic idea behind a structured interview. Students are given support they can understand so that they can organize and articulate their thoughts. Here are two scaffolds that are easy to explain and use with most students.

ABC   The ABC procedure is based on a therapeutic device developed by Ellis (1971) and elaborated on by Kaplan (1990). *A* stands for antecedents, *B* for beliefs, and *C* for consequences (this is another way of stating the stimulus-response-stimulus model). If B includes thoughts and C includes feelings, then a chain can be set up that sounds like this: stimuli (A) are interpreted through beliefs (B) to produce feelings (C). This model asserts that how you feel is controlled by what you think. In Exhibit 16.12, two individuals are presented with the same antecedent stimuli—the requirement that they attend a meeting. Joe thinks "I won't get my important other work done," so he feels frustrated and resentful about the requirement. Ken thinks "This is a good excuse to put off some work," so he feels relieved and cheerful.

The ABC model can be used to get insight into the relationship between a student's thoughts and feelings in this way. First you set up a situation. For example, let's say you tell the student "You get to school without your notebook, and a friend tells you there is to be a big biology test today." Then you give him two clearly different thoughts: (a) "There's no way I can pass without my notes—I'm in trouble!" and (b) "I wrote my notes, so even if I don't have them with me I can remember what is in them—I'll make it!." Next, you ask him to describe how he might feel when thinking each thought (Exhibit 16.13). This takes a lit-

Exhibit 16.12   ABC's

Antecedent	Belief	Consequence
Both individuals have work to do but their boss has called them and told them to attend a meeting	Joe: "I won't get my important work done" Ken: "This is a good excuse to put off this work"	Joe feels bad Ken feels good

tle practice, even for older, articulate students, so you shouldn't expect too much immediately in the way of revealing responses. Also you have to remember that there aren't a lot of feelings to list. Therefore, students may supply the same responses for very different stimuli. A "first date" or a "run-over pet" might both lead a perfectly well-adjusted child to say "I feel sick to my stomach."

After the student seems to have the idea of matching feelings to thoughts, you can reverse the exercise and give situations (A) and feelings (C). Now the student must come up with thoughts (B). For example: "You are walking out of the school in the afternoon; you feel nervous and uneasy; what might you be thinking?"

We've already alluded to one problem with the ABC model. The model as we've presented it assumes that stimuli in the environment cause thoughts which, in turn, spark feelings. However, there are an infinite number of environmental stimuli producing a finite number of thoughts that lead to comparatively few expressions of feelings. Consequently, any number of stimuli may evoke the same thought, and any number of thoughts can lead to the same feeling. The linear relationship between environment, thought, and feeling is not predictable (in fact, we don't even believe it is real). However, remember that we are not present-ing the model as a factual representation of the human psyche, but as a convenient scaffold for conducting a structured interview.

Control/Investment   The control/investment scaffold is shown in Exhibit 16.14. This model is particularly effective when presented to a group of students. The two circles represent the student's perceived control and perceived investment in a situation. The model is presented like this: "In any situation, we each have some investment and some control. For example, when we go to a hospital for surgery, we have tremendous investment in what the surgeon will do to us, but once we're asleep we have no control over what will be done. To the degree that our investment exceeds our control (is disproportionate to it), we experience anxiety."

Once again, we are not implying that this simple model enjoys the status of biblical truth. It does, however, provide a scaffold of common experience that may allow us to gain some information about the way the student exercises social judgment. Many of us suffer from inflated investment. It is the result of the anxiety-producing habit of adding tangential factors to an otherwise clear-cut decision. This practice can turn a trip to the grocery store into a life-and-death venture.

Exhibit 16.13   Thoughts and Feelings

A	B	C
Left biology notes at home	I'm in trouble! I'll make it!	Bad, worried, upset Good, concerned but hopeful

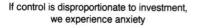

If control is disproportionate to investment,
we experience anxiety

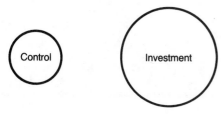

Exhibit 16.14   Control/investment scaffold.

Have you ever started to go to the store, then realized that you have no cash? If the banks are closed and you're afraid to cash a check without knowing your balance, and you've messed up your bank book, the anxiety you start feeling is greater than the bag of tortilla chips you were going to buy deserves. That's because you've inflated the trip to the store into a confrontation with your budget.

The other side of inflated investment is inadequate or incorrectly perceived control. Often it seems people will allow an anxiety-producing situation to go on indefinitely, when acquiring a few simple skills would help them control the situation. This is true of people who fear mechanics but don't learn about cars, or who bounce checks but won't organize a bookkeeping system.

Evaluators can build this scaffold by using examples the student can understand (the more you know about spelling the less you fear spelling tests). Once a student understands the model, one can begin to use it to assess his cognition. This is done by asking him to identify the things that are most important to him. Next, ask him to estimate the extent to which he can affect (control) these important things. If there is a discrepancy between the value he puts on something and the control he has (or thinks he has) over it, this discrepancy can be resolved two ways; either he must deflate his investment or expand his control.

How much control a person has over a situation depends, in part, on his skills and knowledge. Therefore, if it appears that the student lacks control, a Type 1 evaluation is called for. If it turns out that he has needlessly inflated his investment or overestimated his control, then the evaluator should try to recognize the beliefs leading to the inflation. Often this can be accomplished by asking the student to tell what he thinks is the worst (or best) thing that can happen to him in the circumstances being discussed (this can be facilitated by using multiple-choice or restricted-alternative questions).

Social Behavior CAP

It is as necessary to establish criteria for social behaviors as it is for academic behaviors. However, while the topic of CAP is largely dealt with in the portion of the workbook that supplements Chapter 3, we are going to talk about social-behavior criteria now. That is because the appropriateness of social behavior varies with the situation. Therefore, absolute criteria cannot be established.

The best approach to CAP for social behavior is ecological (Moos, 1973; and Tversky & Kahneman, 1973). The ecological model says that a student should be expected to engage in those behaviors that are (a) available in his environment, (b) acceptable to others in the environment, and/or (c) commonly occurring in the environment. What this means is that kids will act like those around them act (just as do adults).

Lack of criteria has always been a problem when evaluating social behavior. To evaluate, one must compare. In the ecological model, a student's behavior is compared to the environment by asking "Is this behavior acceptable in this context . . . ?" In order to find out it is necessary to attend to the environment and not just to the student (Sabornie, 1991).

One useful way to establish a social-behavior standard is to collect an *ecological baseline*. Suppose you think a student (Ed) is "out of seat" too often. You could set up an observation form like the one in Exhibit 16.15. With this form, behavior samples are taken on a student and a *random* peer. This means that for each interval you observe another student in the class along with Ed. The selection must be random; therefore, devise a system for picking the other student *before* the signal goes off. Collect the data for three days and summarize by recording the median score.

Let's suppose that you collect this data and find that the median "out of seat" for Ed is 7 and that it is only 4 for Ed's peers. This makes the standard 4, Ed's current level of performance 7, and the discrepancy −3. The goal for Ed, therefore, is to decrease his behavior by a factor of 1.75—or 3 per observation.

Exhibit 16.15   A Device for Collecting an Ecological Baseline

		Hour 1					Total		Hour 2					Total
Target student ED	+	0	0	0	+	+	3	0	0	0	0	+	+	4
Random peer	+	0	+	+	+	0	2	0	+	+	+	0	+	2

+ = In seat
0 = Out of seat

Target's Total _7_
Peer's Total _4_

An Example Evaluation

Back in Chapter 6 (p. 115), a social-behavior evaluation for 7-year-old Jay was presented in order to illustrate the use of status sheets. Jay was evaluated because, according to his teacher, he was "always hurting somebody." Based on observations, a maladaptive pinpoint (hits peers) was selected along with a target of socially acceptable physical interactions (touching without inflicting pain). You may want to look back at that example before reading on.

Once the target and maladaptive pinpoints had been defined, Ms. Witter observed Jay during recess and lunch activities using interval sampling. These

observations, summarized in Exhibit 16.16, show that Jay was hurting peers (the maladaptive pinpoint) a median of 3.2 times per observation each day. At the same time, his current level of acceptable physical interactions was almost four times lower than the standard. This information was converted, through the S-B-D comparison, into an annual goal.

Given the findings and goal specified in Exhibit 16.16, the teachers set about detailing the skill deficits that accounted for Jay's problem. The result of that activity, as explained in Chapter 6 and illustrated in Exhibit 6.15, is the list of objectives shown in Exhibit 16.16. These objectives were developed to move Jay from his current level of performance to the goal.

Exhibit 16.16   A Summary of Jay's Survey-Level Observations

	Target Behaviors	Maladaptive Behaviors
Standard	16.9	.8
Behavior (current level of performance)	4.2	3.2
Discrepancy	+12.3	−2.4

Goal: Jay will increase socially acceptable physical interactions to 16, while decreasing hitting to less than once a day.

Objective 1: Given examples of physical interactions (in the form of cartoons, photographs and role playing) Jay will correctly label the examples as "appropriate" or "inappropriate" with 100% accuracy.

Objective 2: When asked to provide examples of appropriate physical interactions, Jay will respond by describing and/or demonstrating an action which meets the criteria of the target pinpoint.

Objective 3: When cued that he has just engaged in an inappropriate physical interaction, Jay will supply an alternative appropriate physical action. He will do this within 10 seconds and with 100% accuracy.

A Note on "Mental Illness"

This book is about teaching. Therefore we cover material that we think teachers should address within their classrooms. That was true in the computation chapter and it is true in this chapter on social skills. However, unlike computation, there are professionals besides teachers who work with social behavior.

It is difficult to determine when a student's care should be shared with nonschool members of the mental health profession (Morse, 1992) and it has been difficult for a long time (Grave, 1944). When students say or do things that you simply can't understand, even if these things aren't disruptive, you should refer the student to a qualified professional. This is particularly true when the student is considering, or participating in, either violent or suicidal behavior. It is also true when the student has been abused. Such a referral *does not*, however, signal the end of your responsibility to the student. Frankly, expert pecking orders aside, there is no reason to assume that a referral will automatically lead the student to someone who is sufficiently skilled to provide him with the help he needs. The truth is, for an unconscionably large population of children in the United States, mental health services are not available. In these cases you may be the only game in town.

Obviously, mental illness is always a concern when social-behavior problems exist. (We don't know what "mental illness" means. We just decided to use the term to catch your attention.) So when you make a referral, be sure it is to an *effective* professional. (Develop a list of at least three good ones in the community, so you can make referrals without advocating a particular person.)

One indication of a mental health professional's quality will be that person's willingness (given the requisite of parental permission) to obtain data from, and share data with, the school. You should be particularly concerned about anyone who attempts to address problems that present themselves in school without routinely, and *directly*, contacting the school to monitor the effects of that treatment. This is especially true when the intervention involves the use of medications.

Evaluation Procedures

The questions to ask when you evaluate a social skill are:

1. What is the student doing (what is the *form* of the behavior)?

2. What is he trying to get/avoid with this form of behavior (what is the function)?

3. Is he behaving inappropriately because he can't use an appropriate form of behavior (is missing Type 1 prerequisites)?

4. Is the student behaving inappropriately because he has selected the wrong form (is missing Type 2 prerequisites)?

The answers to these questions will lead to instructional objectives. The answers are obtained by following the process that was illustrated in Exhibit 16.9. While this process approximates the survey/specific model used throughout the book, we are breaking it into finer steps because of the complexity of this content.

Step 1: Survey-Level/Fact Finding

Directions

1.1 *Describe maladaptive pinpoint*

   a. If another person has referred the student, explain the idea of maladaptive and target behaviors to them and show them the examples from each category presented in Exhibit 16.10.

   b. Define the maladaptive behavior in objective and measurable terms.

   c. Apply the stranger test by asking if someone who is unfamiliar with this student can, upon reading your pinpoint, recognize and count occurrences of the behavior. You may want to confirm your conclusion by asking someone to really do it.

   d. Apply the "So-what?" test by asking if the behavior you have pinpointed truly addresses the student's needs. Remember that classroom control, unless it is sought in order to assure a functional and therapeutic environment, is not a *legitimate* aim for individual students. It should be handled through classroom management (as described in Appendix B.1.2).

Exhibit 16.17*   "Function" Form

Identify the "Function" of the Undesirable Behavior(s). (WhatConsequences Maintain the Behavior(s)?)

Think of each of the behaviors listed and define the function(s) you believe the behavior serves for the person (i.e., what does he/she get and/or *avoid* by doing the behavior?)

	Behavior	What Does He/She Get	What Does He/She Avoid
1.			
2.			
3.			
4.			
5.			
6.			
7.			
8.			
9.			
10.			

Source: Functional Analysis: A Practical Assessment Guide, by R. E. O'Neill, R. H. Horner, R. W. Albin, K. T. Storey, and J. Sprague. Copyright © 1989 by University of Oregon. Reprinted by permission.

Interpretation Guidelines

If the maladaptive behavior does not meet the so-what test, forget it or return to step 1.1.

1.2 *Determine the function(s) of the maladaptive behavior*

a. Use the sheet developed by O'Neil et al., (1989) and shown in Exhibit 16.17*.

b. In order to fill out the sheet, interview people who are familiar with the student. You may want to fill out several in order to recognize patterns.

c. Examine the exhibit for "Themes" that consistently seem to underpin the student's maladaptive behavior. A list of possible functions was presented in Exhibit 16.3. Remember, it should be assumed that the functions of inappropriate behaviors are the same as those of appropriate behaviors.

d. Write down the function.

1.3 *Select target behaviors that meet the function*

a. Ask yourself how other students in the same situation achieve the function. This is the pool of behavior from which you will select the target.

b. Do not select behaviors that seem particularly at odds with what you know about the student's temperament, beliefs, or culture.

c. Select several target behaviors. This will allow the student to follow alternative paths to his goal. It will also allow you to "shape" the desired behavior by moving the student through a sequence of successive approximations of the goal (Kaplan, 1990; Wolery et al., 1989).

1.4 *Write target pinpoints*

a. Repeat procedures b, c, and d under step 1.1.

Interpretation Guidelines

If the target pinpoints do not meet the so-what test, stop the evaluation or return to step 1.3.

If the target does pass the so-what test, it still may not fall exclusively within the domain of social skills (as we have defined them for these procedures). Therefore, you will want to ask each of the following questions.

Question 1: Does the target pinpoint seem related to language?

If YES, particularly if the student seems to be having interpersonal problems, include a language screening in your evaluation by going to Chapter 12.

Question 2: Does the target pinpoint seem related to an academic skill problem?

If YES, particularly if the student is not complying with instruction, or the problems occur during lessons, include a screening in the topical areas involved. Go to the appropriate Chapter (10–15).

Question 3: Does the problem seem to be task-related?

If YES, particularly if the student is failing to display knowledge or complete assignments, go to Chapter 17.

1.5 *Specify goal*

    a. Using the ecological observation procedure explained earlier (Exhibit 16.15), determine the standard for the target and maladaptive behaviors in the setting. At the same time, you need to determine the student's current level of performance on these behaviors.

    b. Using the S-B-D worksheet found in the workbook, compare the standard to the student's behavior in order to recognize the discrepancy. State the discrepancy in absolute or ratio terms (see Appendix A).

    c. Write a goal specifying the long-term (annual) improvement you expect to produce. The goal must specify a reduction in the discrepancy.

Step 2: Developing Assumed Causes

In the task-analytical model, a maladaptive behavior is assumed to occur because something is keeping the target behavior from replacing it. Therefore the operational question is not "Why is the kid screwing up?" but "Why isn't the kid doing it right?" As with any other task, it is assumed that the student is failing at social tasks because of a missing prior knowledge.

Obviously, social-skill tasks vary from one another as much as academic tasks. "Asking for assistance" may be as different from "arriving on time" as "multiply fractions" is from "summarize paragraph." However, most social skills do share the common set of prerequisites illustrated in the status sheet found in Exhibit 16.18*. This list is based in part on the work of Kaplan (1990). The list contains two categories of items: the first category is defined by the content of the items (Type 1 and Type 2 prerequisites); the second category is defined by the focus of the item (the student or the

environment). On the status sheet, the first 22 items relate to Type 1 content and items 23 and 34 relate to Type 2 content. Even-numbered items pertain to the student's skills while odd-numbered items relate to the environment.

Directions

2.1 *Task-analyze target pinpoint*

    a. Using Exhibit 16.18*, decide if the generic prerequisites listed there apply. If they don't, cross them out. If there are other prerequisites, add them to the list. Don't forget environmental prerequisites.

2.2 *Determine the status of the prerequisites*

    a. Using Exhibit 16.18*, get everyone together who knows the student and mark the status of each prerequisite. Remember that an environmental prerequisite may be yes for one setting but no for another. If people report situational differences, record this information, because it will be important for decision making.

    b. Decide which prerequisites the student does or does not have. Also note those about which you are unsure.

Interpretation Guidelines

Question 1: Does the student have the prerequisite?

If YES, then the skill does not require instruction. List it under the student's current level of performance.

If NO, then the skill needs to be taught. See the teaching recommendations for guidance.

If UNSURE, then specific-level testing is required. Read the next section.

Question 2: Were items 31 or 33 marked NO or UNSURE?

If YES, be sure to include the thinking error summary, Exhibit 16.20*, in your testing.

Step 3: Specific-Level/Validation

Once a target behavior has been properly identified and several prerequisites for it have been specified, additional specific-level testing may be necessary to validate the rating or to test causes listed as "un-

Exhibit 16.18*   Social Skills Status Sheet

Directions:

1. Only use this status sheet after:
   - the maladaptive behavior(s) has been specified
   - the function of behavior has been specified
   - the target behavior(s) has been specified
2. The sheet should be filled out through collaboration with people who know the student.
3. Each question should be answered.

If a student does not engage in the target behavior, ask yourself if . . .

Type 1 (Do Behaviors)	Status (Yes—No—Unsure)	
	Odd Items	Even Items
1. . . . the student can discriminate the target and maladaptive behaviors from each other and from other behaviors.	_____	
2. . . . target and maladaptive behaviors are clearly and consistently labeled and reviewed.		_____
3. . . . the student can monitor his own behavior well enough to know when he is engaging in the target or maladaptive behavior.	_____	
4. . . . the student is encouraged to reflect on his behavior and is praised for self-corrections and/or early recognition of problems.		_____
5. . . . the student can monitor the environment well enough to recognize events that should prompt the target behavior or inhibit the maladaptive behavior.	_____	
6. . . . cause and effect relationships between events in the environment and the student's behavior are clearly explained and reviewed.		_____
7. . . . the student knows what behavior is expected of him.	_____	
8. . . . expectations are clearly explained and/or demonstrated to the student (they are also frequently reviewed).		_____
9. . . . the student has the skills/knowledge to engage in the target behavior successfully.	_____	
10. . . . the student is taught how to engage in the target behavior.		_____
11. . . . the student knows the consequences of engaging in the target behavior.	_____	
12. . . . the student is taught the consequences of engaging in the target behavior.		_____
13. . . . the student knows the consequences of engaging in the maladaptive behavior.	_____	
14. . . . the student is taught the consequences of engaging in the maladaptive behavior.		_____
15. . . . the student understands that his behaviors cause certain consequences.	_____	
16. . . . the reasons for the reactions of others to the student's behavior are explained.		_____
17. . . . there are no corporal factors which militate against the target behavior and/or promote the maladaptive behavior (e.g., allergies or seizures).	_____	
18. . . . there are environmental factors which promote the target behavior and/or militate against the maladaptive behavior.		_____
18.1 . . . examples of the target behaviors are commonly found in the student's environment.		
18.2 . . . appropriate instruction occurs in the student's classroom.		
18.3 . . . appropriate management techniques are used in the classroom.		
19. . . . the student generates solutions to problems that include the target behavior.	_____	
20. . . . the student is taught to solve problems.		_____
21. . . . the student knows that a target behavior may become maladaptive, and that maladaptive behaviors may become targets, depending on the situation/context in which the student is functioning.	_____	
22. . . . the situational cues promoting various behaviors are identified and adequately taught to the student, along with skills for analyzing new situations.		_____

If a student does not engage in the target behavior ask yourself if . . .

Type 2 (Select Behaviors)	Status (Yes—No—Unsure)	
	Odd Items	Even Items
23. . . . the student considers the consequences of engaging in the target behavior to be rewarding.	_____	
24. . . . the advantages of the target behavior are taught for the student.		_____
25. . . . the student considers the consequences of engaging in the maladaptive behavior to be aversive.	_____	
26. . . . the disadvantages of the maladaptive behavior are taught to the student.		_____
27. . . . the student values the target behavior more than the maladaptive behavior.	_____	

(continued)

Exhibit 16.18*   *Social Skills Status Sheet (continued)*

Type 2 (Select Behaviors)	Status (Yes—No—Unsure)	
	Odd Items	Even Items
28. . . . the student is taught to consider how the target and maladaptive behaviors fit within the student's belief system.		_____
29. . . . the student holds beliefs which are compatible with the target behavior and incompatible with the maladaptive behavior.	_____	
30. . . . the student is taught to develop beliefs through the active application of hypothesis formation, hypothesis testing, and reflection. This instruction must include public thinking by an exemplar and stress the need for beliefs to be ''valid.''		_____
31. . . . the student maintains an adaptive explanatory style when attributing the causes of events.	_____	
32. . . . the student is taught to avoid permanent and persuasive attributions to external causes and/or internal abilities.		_____
33. . . . the student avoids errors in thinking when developing and employing belief systems.	_____	
34. . . . the student is taught to avoid errors in cognition, irrational thoughts and a helpless cognitive set.		_____

sure.'' This usually means developing specific probes, as few ''knows the consequences of engaging in the target behavior'' tests already exist. Exhibit 16.19 provides brief descriptions of specific-level tests for each of the common student prerequisites (the odd-numbered items) found in Exhibit 16.18*. Most of these involve the use of direct questions or structured interviews, although role-playing and cue sorts may also be used. The even-numbered (environmental) prerequisites must be assessed by observations within the classroom (see Chapter 17, p. 413).

3.0 *List as assumed cause and test*

The validation step (step 3) often requires considerable time and effort, especially if the process was begun without a clearly defined set of pinpoints. Validation is also complicated if the assumed causes developed in step 2 did not conform to the rules for this activity presented in Chapter 7 (p. 140). While we are listing problems, the validating step is also complicated by the general absence of functional measurement tools for social-skill prerequisites. However, once this step has been completed you should have developed a clear understanding of the student's knowledge and skills, as well as an understanding of the interaction between the student and his environment (don't forget those even-numbered items in Exhibit 16.18—they are the key to future instruction).

a. Beginning with a list of prerequisites like the one in Exhibit 16.18, note those marked ''unsure'' and select or develop a test for each one.

b. If the prerequisite is odd-numbered, it is a student requirement. Refer to the examples provided in Exhibit 16.19 to see how this sort of prerequisite might be examined. Note that these ''tests'' are usually nothing more than brief exercises or interviews.

c. If student prerequisites 31 or 33 are marked either NO or UNSURE, fill out the *thinking error summary* found in Exhibit 16.20*. The form in Exhibit 16.20* is designed to help you recognize patterns of student talk during the testing. Each of these error types will be discussed shortly under the heading *Teaching Recommendations* and the subheading *''for missing Type 2 student prerequisites.''* If this is your first time through the chapter, you may want to read that material now.

d. If the prerequisite is environmental (even-numbered), refer to the procedures for recording interactions and taking spot observations (see Chapter 6, p. 113). Refer also to Exhibits 8.1–8.4, and the *TIES* descriptors to which these exhibits are cross-referenced. The complete list of *TIES* descriptors is presented in Appendix B.2. The process by which we evaluate the instructional environment is explained in Chapter 17.

Exhibit 16.19   Example Tests

Prerequisites Type 1 (Do Behaviors)	Specific-Level Probes
1. . . . the student can discriminate the target and maladaptive behaviors from each other and from other behaviors.	Give the student a list of behaviors, a series of pictures, or role-playing examples and ask him to indicate the target and maladaptive behavior.
3. . . . the student can monitor his own behavior well enough to know when he is engaging in the target or maladaptive behavior.	Ask the student to record his own behavior or to think back and state whether or not he engaged in two specific behaviors.
5. . . . the student can monitor the environment well enough to recognize events that should prompt the target behavior or inhibit the maladaptive behavior.	Ask the student how he can tell what to do or give the student statements of the behavior and various scenes (through pictures, descriptions, or role playing) and ask him to match scenes to behaviors.
7. . . . the student knows what behavior is expected.	Ask him. Say, ''What do I want you to do?'' or ''What should you be doing?'' If the student is unable to produce the desired response, give some choices and ask him to identify which one is correct. Say, ''Should you be in your seat, or should you be out of your seat?'' Use cue sorts.
9. . . . the student has the skills/knowledge to engage in the behavior successfully.	Conduct an assessment using criterion-referenced measures to check necessary skills. Task analyze the behavior first if it is fairly complex.
11. . . . the student knows the consequences of engaging in the target behavior.	Ask him. Say, ''What happens to you when you . . . ?'' If he is unable to produce the desired response, give some choices and ask him to identify which one is correct. Say, ''Do you get to go to recess?'' or ''Do you get to read?''
13. . . . the student knows the consequences of engaging in the maladaptive behavior.	Ask him. Say, ''What happens to you when you . . . ?'' If he is unable to produce the desired response, give some choices and ask him to identify which one is correct. Say, ''Do you miss recess?'' or ''Do you have to stay after school?''
15. . . . the student understands why his behaviors cause certain consequences.	Ask the student to explain the reactions of others to his behaviors. Note if he attributes these reactions to the beliefs and preferences of others, or if he simply knows what the reactions will be.
17. . . . there are corporal factors (e.g., allergies or seizures) that prohibit the target behavior or mandate the maladaptive behavior.	Look for any evidence of personal or environmental factors that might trigger the maladaptive behavior or prevent the student from engaging in the target behavior.
19. . . . the student generates solutions to problems that include the target behavior.	Supply the student with various restatements of the problem, involving other people. Ask, ''What could they do to get what they want?'' Use a forced-choice questioning format, e.g., ''Which would you rather have (*the problem solved*) or (*the resource required to solve it*)?

(continued)

Exhibit 16.19   Example Tests (continued)

Prerequisites Type 1 (Do Behaviors)	Specific-Level Probes
21. . . . the student knows that the target behavior may become maladaptive, and that the maladaptive behaviors may become targets, depending on the situation.	Supply a picture or role-play of a situation and several behavioral options. Ask the student to select the best, or worst, behavior. Note if the student adjusts his answers according to the situation.

Prerequisites Type 2 (Select Behaviors)	Specific-Level Probes
23. . . . the student considers the consequences of engaging in the target behavior rewarding.	Give him a list of rewards including ones you have used in the past and are presently using with him and ask him to sort them according to value (which he likes the most to the least). Use the ABC technique to determining thoughts about receiving various rewards.
25. . . . the student considers the consequences of engaging in the maladaptive behavior to be aversive (or less rewarding than engaging in the target behavior).	Give him a list of punishers, including ones you have used in the past and are presently using with him, and ask him to sort them according to value (which he finds the most aversive to the least). Use the ABC technique to determine thoughts about receiving various punishers.

Prerequisites Type 1 (Do Behaviors)	Specific-Level Probes
27. . . . the student values the target behavior more than the maladaptive behavior.	Give him a list of behaviors (including the target behavior) and have him sort them according to their importance to him. If he cannot complete this type of exercise, ask a series of restricted alternative questions such as, "Which would you rather do, work by yourself or with a group?"
29. . . . the student holds beliefs that promote the target behavior and are incompatible with the maladaptive behavior.	Use the control investment technique or other forms of structured interview.
31. . . . the student maintains an adaptive explanatory style when explaining the causes of events.	Use the *Thinking Error Summary* in Exhibit 16.20*.
33. . . . the student avoids errors in thinking when developing and employing belief systems.	Use the *Thinking Error Summary* in Exhibit 16.20*.

Step 4: Decision Making

Score Interpretation

There are no established standards for these procedures and frankly, given the fact that educators are still battling over how to measure academic achievement, we think you ought to be fairly cynical about any recommended scoring technique for social skills—particularly for Type 2 prerequisites. In the cases of goal setting and environmental assessment, we recommend the use of frequency data whenever possible.

Exhibit 16.20*   Thinking Error Summary

Directions:

1. During interviews or specific level testing for Type 2 prerequisites make a list of statements which seem to reflect errors in thinking.
2. Rate the errors under both the Explanatory Style and Cognitive Error categories.
3. Under the Explanatory style heading review the list of statements and select those which seem to relate to a positive or negative experience. Also list "absolute" statements.
4. You may categorize the same error under more than one heading.

Explanatory Style

List statements and mark the appropriate descriptors.

	Negative	Performance Oriented	Permanent	Pervasive	Personal
a.	☐	☐	☐	☐	☐
b.	☐	☐	☐	☐	☐
c.	☐	☐	☐	☐	☐
d.	☐	☐	☐	☐	☐

Cognitive Errors

List statements and mark the appropriate descriptors.

a.

b.

c.

d.

Errors in Problem Solving	Irrational Thoughts	Helpless Cognitive Set
☐ Lack of knowledge ☐ Stereotyping ☐ Failure to define problem ☐ Defining problem too narrowly ☐ Lack of perspective ☐ Fear ☐ Premature resolution ☐ Insensitivity to probabilities ☐ Sample size ☐ Misconceptions of chance ☐ Unwarranted confidence ☐ Selective or incomplete search ☐ Mistaking correlation for cause ☐ Lack of supportive environment	☐ I must be good at everything I do and it's terrible if I'm not. ☐ Everybody I meet must like me and it's awful if they don't. ☐ If people do things to me that I don't like, they must be rotten. ☐ You can't trust (anyone over thirty). ☐ When things don't go my way, it's awful. ☐ Everyone should treat me fairly and it's awful if they don't. ☐ I have no control over what happens to me in my life. ☐ I shouldn't have to wait for anything I want. ☐ When something bad happens to me, I should [think about it all the time]. ☐ Anyone who walks away from a fight is a punk. ☐ I must be stupid if I make mistakes. ☐ I always have to win and it's terrible if I don't. ☐ People should not have to do anything they don't want to do. ☐ School is dumb. You don't need to go to school.	☐ Something must be completed correctly in order for me to be a success. ☐ I should only pick easy things to do. ☐ If I fail it is because I am dumb. ☐ If I fail it is because the task is too hard. ☐ If I fail I should stop working because it means I have encountered a task that is too hard for me.

∿ *Qualitative Interpretation*

Using the results on both the status sheet in Exhibit 16.18* and the testing in step 3.0, ask yourself (or anyone else involved) the following question.

Question: During your analysis of prerequisites marked NO or UNSURE, were any of the following problems identified:

    Missing Type 1 student prerequisites?

    Missing Type 1 environment prerequisites?

    Missing Type 2 student prerequisites?

    Missing Type 2 environment prerequisites?

If YES, follow the teaching recommendations for the problem you found.

If NO, there are three possible explanations: (a) you missed something and need to start over, (b) you did everything right but we missed something so you need to get additional direction, or (c) the student does not have the sort of problem these procedures were developed to address. Go back to the three questions in the flowchart (Exhibit 16.9) that precede action 1.5. Consider the possibility that the difficulty may actually be academic in nature, language-based, or task-related. Task-related problems are dealt with in the next chapter.

Teaching Recommendations

Before getting too heavily into specific recommendations, we are compelled to point out that the general topic of behavioral change is simply too large to approach in the span of this chapter. That is why there are classes on behavior management and texts that tell how to use it. Two texts we highly recommend are Wolery et. al. (1989) and Kaplan (1990). The Kaplan text in particular places a heavy emphasis on effective applications of cognitive instruction (Reid & Stone, 1991). Excellent recommendations can also be found in Stoner, Shinn, and Walker (1991), as well as journals like *Beyond Behavior, Behavioral Disorders*, and *Remedial and Special Education*.

Objectives

For Missing Type 1 Student Prerequisites Convert any missing Type 1 *student* prerequisite (odd-numbered items) into an instructional objective. For example: Item 11 on Exhibit 16.18* states "If the student does not engage in a target behavior, ask yourself if the student knows the consequences of engaging in the target behavior." If a student's status on this prerequisite is marked NO, then the following **Objective** is appropriate:

"The student will demonstrate that he {knows the consequences of engaging in the target behavior} by listing the consequences in response to a question. CAP: 100%."

Note that the content of this example objective, the part placed in brackets, is taken directly from the Exhibit 16.18* status sheet. This means that Exhibit 16.18* can be used to generate objectives for the social-skill domain. Measurement procedures for these objectives are found in Exhibit 16.19.

Teaching Check the environmental prerequisites in the next paragraph for instructional recommendations. If you believe that all of the environmental prerequisites have been met (they are marked YES on Exhibit 16.18*), the student needs direct instruction on the missing prerequisites. Because this content is largely strategic and conceptual, consult Exhibits 8.3 and 8.4 for guidance. You may also want to refer to Appendix B.2.2.

For Missing Type 1 Environment Prerequisites Convert any missing Type 1 *environment* prerequisite (even-numbered items) into an instructional recommendation.

For example: Item 12 on Exhibit 16.18* states "If the student does not engage in the target behavior, ask yourself if the student is taught the consequences of engaging in the target behavior." If the answer to this question was NO, then it should be converted into a teaching recommendation (the teacher will explain, demonstrate, and provide practice on the skills required for the student to list the consequences of engaging in the target behavior).

For Missing Type 2 Student Prerequisites The objectives you list will depend on the evaluation procedures you used. If you only had to fill out the status sheet, you can convert any missing Type 2 *student* prerequisite (odd-numbered items) into an instructional objective. For example: Item 31 on Exhibit 16.18* states "If the student does not engage in a target behavior, ask yourself if the student maintains an adaptive explanatory style when attributing the causes of events." If a student's status on this prerequisite is marked NO, then the following **Objective** is appropriate:

"When experiencing difficulty in a social situation the student will {maintain an adaptive explanatory style} by attributing the problem to either a lack of effort, or to missing prior knowledge of the skills needed for success. CAP: {based on context}."

Note that the content of this example objective, the part placed in brackets, is taken directly from the Exhibit 16.18* status sheet. This means that Exhibit 16.18* can be used to generate objectives and Exhibit 16.19 can be used to develop measurement techniques.

Additional Analysis. If prerequisites 31 or 33 were questionable, you should have employed the thinking error summary in Exhibit 16.20*. If you found patterns to the student's statements, you are now in the position to generate more specific objectives and select more specific instructional methods. The goal of the thinking error summary is to recognize thoughts that indicate either a maladaptive explanatory style or cognitive errors. Each of these possibilities will now be explained, and example objectives will be provided to link these explanations to teaching.

Maladaptive Explanatory Style   In general, it is believed that successful students attribute their successes and their failures to their own efforts. Unsuccessful students tend to attribute events to either external factors (luck, task difficulty, the teacher), or to unalterable internal variables such as intelligence (see Chapter 2, p. 25). Whereas everyone makes statements that could be considered maladaptive, there are certain qualitative indicators of particularly debilitating thought processes. While the exact topic of these statements is generally unimportant, Dweck (1986) has noted that students who define success in terms of performance ("I got a high score on the test") are at greater risk than those who define success in terms of learning ("I did better on the test than I did before"). Additionally, Seligman (1990) states that the most maladaptive explanatory style is indicated by statements that are permanent, pervasive, and personal. For example, in the statement "I can't keep friends. No one likes me and no one ever will" the words *ever will* imply that the problem is permanent. In that same statement *No one* describes a pervasive problem and *I can't* makes the problem personal.

Objectives developed to change a student's explanatory style typically specify the use of attributions considered to be adaptive. For example:

- To correct the frequent use of *performance*-oriented statements, the goal/**Objective** might include "The student will seek out feedback relative to improvement, rather than current standing, following the completion of an assignment."

- To correct permanent or pervasive attributions, a goal/**Objective** might contain "Upon experiencing difficulty at {insert a relevant social skill or situation} the student will attribute the problem to a cause that is under his control and task-specific."

Errors in Problem Solving   Remember, students with social-skill problems want the same things anyone else wants and they make the same kinds of mistakes trying to get them (they just make the mistakes more often or more spectacularly). In Chapter 1, a series of threats to good judgment were listed for teachers. This same list applies equally to students. While each of the

threats are listed in Exhibit 16.20*, you will need to turn back to pages 10–16 for their explanation. If this seems to be a domain of concern, then you will want to teach problem solving. Here is an example **Objective:**

"Given {problems relevant to the student}, he will generate solutions in a manner that is consistent with {the instructional program used to teach him problem solving}. These solutions will not reflect any of the major threats to judgment listed in Exhibit 16.20*."

Problem-solving interventions may be general or specific. If the student seems to have only one particular block to effective problem solving (Fitzgerald, 1989), you may choose to go after it directly. For example, if the student seems to always produce the same solutions, regardless of the problem, these responses could be the result of a belief that overshadows his current perceptions about what is going on. Such inflexible beliefs often limit the student's options because they mask them. The stereotyped "delinquent" beliefs that authority is bad and that force is the most effective solution to conflict are the easiest for teachers to spot. That's because these beliefs lead kids into aversive contact with the teacher. Nevertheless, other beliefs such as "I should be taken care of" or "The others are better than I" are just as common and show up frequently in ABC exchanges. Here is an example **Objective** for stereotypic problem solving {material in brackets should be worded to match the student's individual needs}:

"The student will demonstrate flexible thinking by supplying multiple solutions to problems and interpretations of events (including empathetic descriptions of peers). These problems and events will include {items drawn from situations which are personally relevant to the student}. The number and form of the responses the student supplies will be {consistent with the instructional program used to teach the skill}."

If the student seems to have a more general difficulty with problem solving, we recommend the unit on that topic in *The Prepared Curriculum* by Goldstein (1988).

Irrational Thoughts   Some irrational thoughts are quite common and easily recognized. Kaplan (1990) has listed a variety of beliefs that will influence a student's social competence, including:

1. I must be good at everything I do.

2. Everyone should treat me fairly.

3. Anyone who walks away from a fight is a punk.

4. School is dumb.

The rest of Kaplan's list is included in Exhibit 16.20*. If the student expresses these beliefs, you need to convert them into adaptive target beliefs ("Everyone should treat me fairly" is converted to "No one gets fair treatment all of the time") and these targets should be taught.

Example Objective 1: "Given {lists of rational and irrational statements, including statements commonly made by the student}, the student will label them accurately. CAP: 100%."

Example Objective 2: "Given lists of {irrational statements}, the student will supply a rational counter-thought for each. CAP: 100%."

Example Objective 3: "The student will decrease spontaneous use of irrational statements and increase the use of rational statements {relative to his current frequency}."

When attempting to work with irrational statements, keep in mind that the actual stated expression often is **not** the focus of this intervention. That focus is the irrational belief that we assume generated the statement (although it may also be true that if you tell yourself something long enough you will believe it). Therefore, the intervention must be directed at the thought. In other words, don't just tell the student to stop making the statement—teach the student rational thinking skills. Some excellent procedures for doing this are found in Kaplan (1990).

Sometimes it also seems that irrational statements are the product of communicative confusion. For example, statements that seem to have little relationship to the situation, thought, or feeling supplied may be the result of:

• Lack of knowledge

• Misinterpretation

• Personal agenda (socially competent individuals do not insist on turning every conversation to a topic about which they are particularly concerned)

If out-of-context statements, as well as those that seem irrational, seem to be a problem for the student, use this **Example Objective** (material in brackets will vary with student):

"Given {commonly encountered social situations}

the student will analyze and interpret the context in accordance with the material learned through {a selected social-skills program} and will decrease the use of {out-of-context statements} to the level of {peers in the target setting}."

For teaching recommendations relative to out-of-context statements, consult the literature on pragmatics (see Chapter 12) and analysis of sociolinguistic context. A good place to start is with Paget and Galant (1991).

Cognitive Set   Exhibit 16.20* also contains a list of indicators that may cause you to believe the student has developed a cognitive set that is interfering with decision making and tending to limit the student's interpretation of current situations. The helpless cognitive set was mapped in Exhibit 16.8, and that exhibit also lists a sequence of counter-thoughts for nonadaptive student statements. Here are some **Objectives** for that domain:

Example Objective 1: "When given {samples of relevant actions, explanations, and thoughts about work}, the student will correctly sort these into "helpless" and "adaptive" categories. CAP: 100%".

Example Objective 2: "When given {samples of relevant actions, explanations, and thoughts about work}, the student will supply adaptive actions, explanations or counter-thoughts with 100% accuracy at a rate of {determine rate from successful peers} per minute."

Example Objective 3: "Upon encountering failure {on tasks at the correct level of difficulty}, the student will persevere {longer than on previous attempts}."

Example Objective 4: "When given a choice of tasks, the student will select those that are at the correct level of difficulty and challenging, over those that are personally easy. CAP: {set from successful peers}."

Cognitive sets, such as learned helplessness, are so entrenched that they usually require a concerted multiple-disciplinary approach to teaching. This is the sort of effort that is associated with individual "therapy" (although we don't mean to imply that learned helplessness constitutes a mental illness) and involves participants from the home and school. However, it is possible to approach the problem even when cooperation with the home is not feasible. This is because cognitive sets often are situation-specific, meaning that the student may feel pessimistic at recess and optimistic in class (Michael, Denny, Ireland-Galman & Michael, 1987).

If the presenting problem occurs at school, and a mental health professional is going to attempt to solve it, you need to be aware that its correction will almost certainly need to include a variety of school personnel. Therefore we do not recommend seeking the services of any mental health professional who does not have a good record of communicating and working with teachers. We also strongly recommend that the student's therapy follow an educative path in accordance with the so-called cognitive-behavioral techniques of authors like Kaplan (1990), Goldstein (1988), and Larson (1989b). Lovitt also presents some specific techniques for attribution retraining in his 1991 text *Preventing School Dropouts*.

There are things that individual teachers can do to counter a nonadaptive motivational set *and* there are things they can do to help students learn adaptive sets. The following quote from Dweck (1986) nicely summarizes this research:

> The motivational research is clear in indicating that continued success on personally easy tasks (or even on difficult tasks within a performance framework) is ineffective in producing stable confidence, challenge-seeking, and persistence. Indeed, such procedures have sometimes been found to backfire by producing lower confidence in ability. *Rather, the procedures that bring about more adaptive motivational patterns are the ones that incorporate challenge, and even failure, within a learning-oriented context and that explicitly address underlying motivational mediators.*" (p. 1046)

For Missing Type 2 Environmental Prerequisites

Convert any missing Type 2 *environment* prerequisite (even-numbered items) into an instructional recommendation.

For example: Item 32 on Exhibit 16.18* states "If the student does not engage in the target behavior, ask yourself if the student is taught to avoid permanent and pervasive attributions to external causes or internal abilities." If the answer to this question was NO, then it should be converted into a teaching recommendation (the student will be taught to list the consequences of engaging in the target behavior). Often the most effective instruction in the highly conceptual domain of social skills comes about through modeling by exemplars (see Chapters 4 and 8).

Caution No. 2: A Note on Type 2 Interventions

The authors have already discussed some concerns about evaluating cognitive behaviors. We have used the techniques just presented, but we have no personally generated data to show that they are better or worse than procedures you could make up yourself. For that matter, we have no personally generated data to show that they are better than doing nothing (that is why this chapter is filled with references). Sometimes, when working with a student, an obviously unrealistic expectation or inaccurate perception will pop out through one of the Type 2 techniques. In these cases, it seems clear that the inappropriate expectation/perception should be changed. Often the best change technique is to promote (through teaching and demonstration) cognitive behaviors that are incompatible with the inappropriate ones.

Cognitive changes are not always monumental readjustments of personal philosophy. More often they are simple corrections of an inaccurate expectation. A teacher friend of ours (Karna Nelson) used the process in this chapter with a teacher who had a troublesome new student. After being given assignments, the kid frequently just put them away saying "I'll do it tomorrow." The teacher was puzzled. When Karna task-analyzed "immediately begins work," the prerequisite "thinks work should be done immediately" emerged. As a test, the teacher asked "How long do you think you have to do an assignment?" to which the student replied "A week." Baffled, the teacher asked "Why do you think that?" and the kid explained "In my last school we had contracts, and it didn't matter when we worked as long as the contract was met in a week." This simple explanation took the two teachers some time to find, but they didn't find it at all until they sat down and analyzed the target behavior. The intervention took only a few minutes and involved explaining the differences between the new class and the old one. In this case, the student was behaving inappropriately, not because of complex missing skills, entrenched religious beliefs, or mysterious emotional peculiarities. Instead, he was behaving inappropriately because he held the unfortunately "irrational" expectation that two classroom teachers would have the same rules. If he lacked anything, it was the skills necessary to determine the rules of the new setting.

We're going to leave the topic of social behavior with a final thought. For any academic, social, or cognitive behavior, once you have selected a pinpoint and started an intervention, you must monitor the effect of the intervention. When dealing with cognitive pinpoints, poor teachers and therapists will often persist with an intervention that conforms to their idea of mental health but does not produce healthy change in the client. Sometimes this persistence will even produce damage. If a teacher cannot document positive change in the client, then it's time for the teacher to change. (Incidentally, that is the same recommendation we make regarding the use of drug therapy to address learning or behavior problems). Additionally, if a private mental health professional is working on a school-related problem and hasn't developed a mechanism for collecting data in the schools, you shouldn't cooperate with the treatment until he does.

As for the validity of cognitive procedures, reread the cautions expressed earlier. Each of these techniques is derived from the application of logic to the often less-than-logical domain of social behavior. Therein lies the ultimate uncertainty of the system. A very wise psychiatrist once advised the authors that logic can be applied successfully only to human-made things. To apply these techniques, one must assume that the perceptions, expectations, and beliefs of students are human-made in the sense that they have been learned during past social interactions. This assumption remains, and will remain, unproven. Therefore, attempts to alter selection tactics oblige us to adhere to the highest ethical standards and to proceed with caution.

Since we are dispensing cautions, here is one final thing to consider. The title of this chapter is "Social Behavior." Just as we must consider the students' behavior within the context of social environment, we must consider the impact our interventions may have on that environment. Some popular approaches to personal problems, many of which we admit grow out of the same rationale provided in this chapter, seem to us to be "technique-ish" at best and harmful at worst. Kaminer (1992) has nicely summarized this concern in observations on what she has termed the "cult of victimization."

The packaging of conventional wisdom about personality development, spirituality, family life, success, and gender roles as self-help reconciles American ideals of choice and individualism with the reality of majority rule and a hunger to belong. Eager for rules on how to be an individual, Americans consume millions of self-help books every year, choosing from an array of experts as wide as the array of TV dinners. (p. 163)

What are the political implications of a mass movement that counsels surrender of will and submission to a higher power describing almost everyone as hapless victims of familial abuse? What are the implications of a tradition that tells us all problems can be readily solved, in a few simple steps—a tradition in which order and obedience to technique are virtues and respect for complexities, uncertainties, and existential unease are signs of failure, if not sin? (p. 152)

Summary

This chapter has been different from those that preceded it because it deals with the global domain of social skill. Some of the major points presented were:

- Social skill and academic behavior are not that different.
- Efforts to develop social skills curriculum are needed.
- Social skills should be taught and not controlled.
- Attempts to deal with social skills must address covert as well as overt behaviors.

In addition to these points, we covered a variety of specific procedures and provided some examples. We intentionally omitted extensive discussions of data collection, observation, and charting from this chapter not because we think they are unimportant, but because we think they are important for academics as well as social skills. Throughout the chapter we attempted to illustrate the application of a curriculum-based, task-analytical approach to social skills and to caution against its misapplication.

Chapter 17 / Task-Related Skills

To be successful you don't need to work harder—you need to work smarter.

—Popular wisdom

Most of the students receiving support services have one thing in common: they were referred by a classroom teacher (Ysseldyke et al., 1983). As explained at the first of this text, teachers begin to look for help when they encounter a student with needs beyond the range they can accommodate (see Chapter 1). This doesn't just mean the teacher thinks the student needs help; it also means the teacher doesn't think she can supply that help without assistance. This perception is not based on achievement alone. It is often based on opinions about how the student responds to instruction. Problematic responses to instruction may include disruptive behavior, failure to complete assignments, or the poor use of "task-related" behavior (Lloyd & Loper, 1986).

Students use task-related behaviors to acquire and display knowledge in the classroom. For example, if a student completes a computation test, the answers represent the knowledge she was supposed to have acquired in the math class. However, her final test score may also reflect how well she studied for the test; if she even remembered there was going to be a test; how neatly she wrote out the answers; where she wrote her name; and, how well she anticipated what items the teacher would supply. All of those are examples of task-related skills.

In the past a student who was referred, and who qualified for support services, typically received this support outside of the general education class. This is no longer the case. Today we have collaborative models, teacher assistance teams, pre-referral interventions, and all sorts of other mechanisms to support students in general education. The aim of these mechanisms is to increase the range of student skills a classroom teacher can accommodate in order to decrease the number of students who need to leave that teacher's room. Often this means teaching academic or social skills. However, it may also mean teaching the task-related skills teachers expect students to employ.

Task-related behaviors embody a wide range of skills that teachers believe enable school success (Ellis & Lentz, 1990; Gresham & Reschly, 1986; Larson & Gerber, 1987; Lloyd & Loper, 1986). These include: following directions, completing tasks, attending, accepting authority, having an adaptive attitude about work, and maintaining beliefs about the value of tasks.

Task-Related Knowledge

Exhibit 17.1* is a status sheet for task-related skills. It lists the content that will be treated in this chapter. Two broad domains of knowledge influence how successfully students learn new material: topical knowledge and supporting knowledge. In this chapter, supporting knowledge will be broken into four other categories: knowledge of the instructional environment; study and test-taking skills; problem solving; and basic learning strategies. These various subdivisions have been developed to facilitate our explanation of the evaluation and decision-making process. In actuality they are highly interdependent.

Topical Knowledge

Topical knowledge is probably the best single predictor of success in a given lesson. A student attempting to learn multiplication who cannot currently add, for example, will have trouble. In a very real sense this sort of knowledge isn't really task-related, it *is* the task.

Chapters 10–16 of this text dealt with topical knowledge from the domains of literacy and social skills. These domains were selected because they are pivotal to success in so many endeavors and, as a result, are the source of so many referrals for support. However, there are other domains of knowledge in which students may be deficient. These include the

Exhibit 17.1*   Status Sheet for Task Related Knowledge

Directions:
1. Use this status sheet with a group of people who work with the student.
2. Carefully describe the settings and tasks on which the status designations are based.
3. Give an overall designation for each of the principle skill areas by marking the appropriate box.
4. Check or circle all those descriptors which seem to apply to the student or setting.
5. Employ the indicated SLPs.

Part A: Topical Knowledge

	Y N ?	Additional Testing
The Student Has Required Prior Knowledge:	□ □ □	SLP 1&2

Descriptors:
   Has taken prerequisite classes
   Received acceptable grades in prerequisite classes
   Understands text and presentations
   Knows topical vocabulary
   Is familiar with related topics

Part B: Support Knowledge

B.1 Instructional Environment

	Y N ?	Additional Testing
The Student Has the Skill and Knowledge Needed to Learn in this Setting:	□ □ □	SLP 3

Descriptors:
   Instructional presentation OK
   Classroom environment OK
   Teaching expectations OK
   Cognitive emphasis OK
   Motivational strategies OK
   Relevant practice OK
   Academic engaged time OK
   Informal feedback OK
   Adaptive instruction OK
   Progress evaluation OK
   Instructional planning OK
   Checks for student understanding OK

B.2 Study and Test-Taking Skills

	Y N ?	Additional Testing
Study and test-taking skills are adequate:		SLP 4
Before class:	□ □ □	

Descriptors:
   arrives on time
   enters in a pleasant manner
   brings materials to class
   gets ready for learning

| *During class:* | □ □ □ | |

Descriptors:
   follows classroom rules
   listens carefully
   works during class
   asks for assistance
   moves quickly to new activity

| *After class:* | □ □ □ | |

Descriptors:
   takes materials home
   completes homework
   brings homework back

| *Organization:* | □ □ □ | |

Descriptors:
   organization of materials (e.g., use of notebook or folders) OK
   organization of time (e.g., use of calendar, scheduling work) OK
   organization of content on paper (e.g., heading, margins) OK

	Y N ?	Additional Testing
Gaining information:	□ □ □	SLP 4

Descriptors:
   reading expository material OK
   reading narrative material OK
   gaining information from verbal presentations (lectures, demonstrations) OK

| *Demonstrating knowledge or skills:* | □ □ □ | |

Descriptors:
   completing daily assignments OK
   answering written questions OK
   writing narrative and expository products OK
   preparing for and taking tests OK

B.3 Problem Solving and Self-Monitoring

	Y N ?	Additional Testing
The Student's Problem Solving/Self-Monitoring Is Adequate:		SLP 5
The student recognizes problems:	□ □ □	

Descriptors:
   identifies goals
   identifies obstacles
   recognizes types of problems
   anticipates problems

| *The student recognizes types of problems:* | □ □ □ | |

Descriptors:
   identifies open system
   identifies closed system

| *The student recognizes solution:* | □ □ □ | |

Descriptors:
   generates options
   considers resources
   anticipates outcomes
   selects solutions

| *The student plans:* | □ □ □ | |

Descriptors:
   thinks before acting
   explains what will happen
   has intermediate goals
   allocates time

| *The student works:* | □ □ □ | |

Descriptors:
   follows plan
   follows schedule

| *The student monitors and adjusts work:* | □ □ □ | |

Descriptors:
   self-monitors
   recognizes errors
   uses "means-end" analysis
   changes with feedback

B.4 Basic Strategies

	Y N ?	Additional Testing
The student uses selective attention:	□ □ □	SLP 6

Descriptors:
   focuses on relevant cues
   ignores irrelevant cues
   uses effective techniques to focus and maintain attention

| *The student uses recall/memory:* | □ □ □ | SLP 6 |

Descriptors:
   recalls information
   uses effective techniques to store and recall material

| *The student uses motivation:* | □ □ □ | SLP 6 |

Descriptors:
   perseveres in the face of difficulty
   perceives value of task
   maintains an adaptive explanatory style (i.e. is not "learned helplessness")
   indicates feelings of control
   uses effective techniques to maintain motivation

various subjects in science, social studies, the arts, and humanities that are covered in greater depth as students advance through school.

Obviously the total range of topics students are expected to learn exceeds the capacity of this text. However, while it isn't possible to provide information about evaluation in each of these areas, it is possible to present formats for developing your own evaluation tools. These formats were illustrated most clearly in Chapters 10 and 15 and will be explained again shortly.

Supporting Knowledge

The role of supporting knowledge in learning is commonly illustrated through the metaphor of scaffolding (Gaffney & Anderson, 1991). The scaffolds with which most of us are familiar are the temporary structures assembled to support workers as they construct buildings. These are usually formed from prefabricated metal tubes and wooden planks so that they can be easily assembled, moved, and removed during the building process. Learning scaffolds work the same way. Here is an illustration.

Suppose you are about to get on an airplane for a flight out of town. While waiting for the flight you sit staring out the window at low clouds, fog, and drizzle. Given that it is hard for you to see the airplane, let alone the runway, you start worrying about the flight. Just as the worrying increases it is sharply aggravated when a woman dressed as a pilot walks up to the window, looks outside, and says "What an awful day!"

"Are you a pilot?" you ask.

"Yes," the woman replies, "I'm about to go to Phoenix."

"That's my flight," you say.

"Oh, good—then I'll be your captain. My name is Stewart." You shake hands.

"So, Captain Stewart," you venture, "I was sort of wondering. How can you find Phoenix when you can't see the end of the runway? And for that matter, how can you avoid hitting the flight coming *from* Phoenix when they can't see you?"

Captain Stewart smiles, as she has been trained to do, and explains.

"We do it the same way you drove to the terminal. We follow roads and make sure we are in the correct lanes. The difference is that these roads are defined by a navigational network. The roads (we call them air-

ways) are laid out all across the nation. For example, on part of our trip we will follow a route called "Vector 562" to Prescott then turn right onto V 105-257 and follow it to Phoenix. We have a map—just like a road map—that shows us all the airways and tells us how to get from one to another. We even have traffic signals, speed limits, and one-way streets to keep us from running into each other. The only real difference is that we also have assigned altitudes, speeds, and distances from each other."

As Captain Stewart turns to leave you notice that you feel less concerned about the flight (you also notice that airline captains always say "we" instead of "I"). This sense of relief might not have been as great if the captain had told you exactly the same thing in these words.

"We have to go IFR. I filed a flight plan, but because we'll be under positive control there's no telling where we'll get sent, or at what altitude. I expect that the trip will take us outbound on the 119-degree radial from 112.0 down V 562 to Drake, then 145 degrees from 114.1 to Rio Salado, the Papago NDB and a back course ILS. We'll assume center is guaranteeing separation."

The second explanation presupposes you know about instrument flight, whereas the first explanation allows you to gain understanding by temporarily using what you know about driving and road maps to explain the trip. This is called scaffolding (Palincsar, 1986). Essentially, Captain Stewart was assisting you as you constructed an understanding of the trip. This was done by assembling the temporary road-map metaphor (the scaffold) and using it to bridge the gaps in your existing understanding of the topic of flight.

Now consider this. Just as the second explanation would have confused you (assuming you aren't a pilot), the first explanation would have confused a person who had never experienced driving or road maps. That is because such a person, a young child or a citizen of a remote society, would not have been able to construct the scaffold even with Captain Stewart's assistance. Such a person would not have the prefabricated scaffolding materials—the supporting knowledge.

Special and remedial students, because they are deficient in literacy strategies and/or enabling skills, miss much of what is taught in schools. Consequently they may end up not being able to read *and* not knowing the stuff one learns about in books. As they move into higher and higher grades, the lack of general knowledge compounds until a student may literally not know enough to learn. (Because this is more apt to occur for those subjects acquired in school, the same student may seem "streetwise" and "intelligent" outside of school while appearing "stupid" and "slow" in class.)

The distinction between "topical knowledge" and "supporting knowledge" is fairly arbitrary, in that the same information could fit into either category (the road-map reference would be topical in a driver's ed class). In this chapter we will describe four kinds of support knowledge.

Knowledge of the Instructional Environment

Considerable information about the delivery of instruction was presented in Chapters 4 and 8. Considerable information about testing was given in Chapters 5, 6, and 7. However, we recognize that all teachers don't present the same way. Therefore, special/remedial teachers can't afford to prepare students with only one approach to studying and one approach to test taking. They must teach students skills for classroom success that will generalize across content and teachers. They must teach *students* to "individualize" for teachers.

In order to prepare students to adapt to a particular instructional environment, it is necessary to evaluate that environment in terms of its unique demands. This process will be conducted using the materials in Chapter 8 and Appendix B.

Study and Test-Taking Skills

Study and test-taking skills, like learning strategies and topical knowledge, influence how much students learn (Ellis & Lenz, 1990; Truesdell & Abramson, 1992). Study skills are those things that allow the student to make use of instruction. Test-taking skills are those things that allow a student to display what she has learned (Antes, 1989). Their application also tends to be *very* context- and task-specific. This means that the skills apply differently to each form of instruction and testing. As you can imagine, if one teacher lectures and gives multiple-choice tests while another assigns readings and gives essay exams, some students may do better in one class than in the other.

Exhibit 17.1* also listed content for study skills and test taking. The content was drawn from the work of

Archer and Gleason (1989). However, much of it is consistent with skill sequences produced by the Kansas Institute for Learning Disabilities (Schumaker, Nolan & Deshler, 1985). That institute, which was originally charged with investigating exemplary practices for junior and senior high-school students, attempted to define differences between study demands at early and later grades. The investigators concluded that, in later grades, students were expected to:

1. Work independently with little feedback
2. Gain information from grade-level texts
3. Gain information from lectures and discussions
4. Demonstrate command of knowledge through tests
5. Express themselves in writing

It is possible to build content sequences that are consistent with the direction taken by the Kansas Institute. Some of these tend to be metacognitive in nature, and focus on things like the student's awareness of task difficulty and of her own competence (Anderson et al., 1988), while others tend to emphasize task demands and specific classroom requirements (Archer & Gleason, 1989; Gleason, Colvin & Archer, 1991; Gresham & Reschly, 1986; Marx & Walsh, 1988). The content listed under study and test-taking skills in Exhibit 17.1* reflects the latter orientation.

Problem Solving and Self-Monitoring

Because problem solving and self-monitoring are so topic-specific, many procedures for evaluating them have been placed in the topical chapters (see Chapter 10, p. 214). Still, numerous researchers have noted that students who experience academic or social skill difficulties in school are poor at solving problems (Ellis & Lenz, 1990; Paris & Winograd, 1990). The theme and content of problem solving have been mentioned many times throughout this text.

We believe there is a set of general problem-solving steps which, when followed correctly, can help students succeed in most areas. While this problem-solving and self-monitoring strategy, which is outlined in Exhibit 17.1,* does not take the place of task-specific strategies, it can provide students with a plan for dealing with problems wherever they occur.

Note that the first two steps in the problem-solv-

Most students with remedial and special classifications are served in general education classrooms where all students need to follow directions, complete tasks, pay attention, accept authority, and maintain a positive attitude about learning without assistance.

ing sequence listed in Exhibit 17.1* are recognition and identification of problem type. Problem recognition is particularly important as it relates to self-monitoring, and this is an area in which mildly disabled students, as a group, experience difficulty (Lloyd, Landrum & Hallahan, 1991).

Identification of problem type is critical, as some problems are solved differently than others. As a result, all subsequent steps are carried out differently depending on the type of problem. Two types of problems are generally recognized: "open system" and "closed system" problems (McCagg & Dansereau, 1991). Closed-system problems, which tend to have distinct and predictable boundaries, are solved through task-specific strategies called algorithms (computation or location or phone numbers). Open-system problems have vague boundaries (selection of a friend or recognizing when to apologize) and are approached through general procedures called *heuristics.*

When rating a student's problem solving, you must consider the situation in which she is working. "Recognizing when an assignment is complete" could

involve distinct boundaries in one teacher's classroom and vague boundaries in another teacher's classroom. Therefore the same problem can be open or closed depending on the context in which it occurs.

Basic Learning Strategies

Learning strategies include the phenomena we recognize as self-monitoring, problem solving, attention, memory, and motivation. Therefore, this discussion will draw heavily from content presented in Chapter 2. If you haven't read that chapter, or need to be refreshed relative to its content, it would be a good idea to do that right now.

Things like attention, memory and motivation exist within executive control (see Chapter 2). They are complex and interactive sets of skills and strategies that predispose students to recognize relevant cues effectively, recall prior learning, and persevere in the face of failure. They are not, and cannot be, separated. Additionally, they cannot be detached from the various tasks that demand their use. This means that "attention" does not exist without something to which one can attend. It is appropriate, therefore, to say "The student does not attend to initial sounds." It is not appropriate to say "The student does not attend." No one, regardless of the impression conveyed by terms like "attention deficit disorder," lacks attention. Similarly, no one lacks memory or motivation. However, many students fail to focus on specific cues, recall information about certain topics, and persevere in the face of failure.

While there is evidence that students with learning problems are often deficient in basic learning skills, it is important to recognize that the content of basic strategies is far removed from the curriculum students are expected to learn. It is also very difficult to assess in any instructionally relevant fashion. That is why we are putting it at the bottom of Exhibit 17.1*, and of the flowchart presented in Exhibit 17.2. In most cases we believe that it is easier to build attention, memory and motivation through effective instruction than to attempt to isolate these very dynamic aspects of learning.

Evaluating Task-Related Behavior

The topics found on the task-related status sheet in Exhibit 17.1* do not, for the most part, appear within school curriculum guides. They cut across all content, ages, and conditions and are sometimes known as the "hidden" curriculum. These are the things all students are *expected* to know before arriving in class. Consequently few teachers directly teach these skills. Similarly this content has been generally ignored by evaluators. It is unlikely that any of you have ever heard someone say "Dolores *attends* at the fourth-grade, third-month level" or "Sam scored at the 27th percentile in *completing daily assignments*." That's because traditional evaluation procedures and devices are not designed, or intended, for the assessment of task-related behavior. In fact, most evaluators and teachers scrupulously try to avoid making lessons and measures that are sensitive to it.

A reading test score that reflects too much "careful listening" will be considered invalid. Similarly, a teacher who spends as much time preparing students to receive information as she does delivering information may be accused of "spoon feeding" the class. Like language and social skills, many educators do not think it is their job to teach task-related skills. At the same time, many of them will grade on things like

"organization" or "effort." When this happens, curriculum alignment is lost.

Today more and more special and remedial educators believe that task-related behaviors are the only legitimate curriculum for support services in the upper grades. To these educators, the task-related domain represents the only really special curriculum element. That is because, while both general-education and support teachers may address the domains of reading, mathematics, and language, only special/remedial teachers have commonly taken a hands-on approach to teaching task-related content.

Evaluation Procedures

Survey-Level Procedures

The process of evaluation for task-related skills is presented in Exhibit 17.2. The first question in the exhibit asks if "the student is failing to learn from classroom instruction." You would answer YES if the student isn't making expected progress in a particular class. Problems with task-related skills are indicated when a student fails to work efficiently, learn effectively, or to display knowledge adequately. If that is the case, your first action is carefully to define both the setting and the topic. This step is necessary because of the situational variability in instruction and the varying demands different topics place on prior knowledge. Don't merely state that the student is having trouble in social studies; try to identify the exact topics and activities that are problematic.

Directions

1. Carefully define the topic and setting of failure. Select topics and activities in which the student is having trouble. Define the settings according to the precept of the stranger test (see Chapter 16, p. 389). Be sure that you know exactly where, when, and under which conditions the student is experiencing difficulty. During this definition process, be sure to include the nature of the tasks (interactive/independent, long/short, directions clear or ambiguous), the composition of the work groups (large/small, skill-grouped or

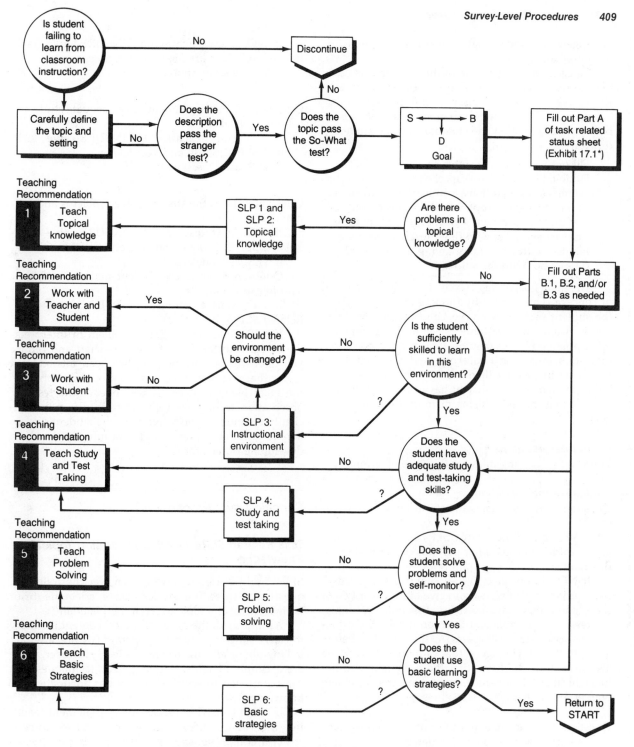

Exhibit 17.2*   *Decision making for task-related skills.*

heterogeneous) and format of instruction (generative/supplantive).

Consider the importance of the topic that is causing the student trouble by applying the so-what test. Remember that priorities may need to be established (see Chapter 7). Attempt to draw clear distinctions between tasks that do and do not cause the student difficulty.

2. Fill out part A of the status sheet presented in Exhibit 17.1.* (If you suspect that the student has extensive complications, you may want to fill out as much as you can of the whole sheet—but follow the interpretation sequence.) To fill out the status sheet, meet with other teachers who are familiar with the student and, if at all possible, fill one out with the student.

The main goal of this exercise is to narrow the field of concern. This is done by forming an opinion about the student's success within each of the primary categories listed on the status sheet and marking the appropriate box. This opinion should be based on the indicators under each category, and the confidence you have in judging them. If you are unsure of an indicator, remember that you have the ''?'' option. A student may have problems in more than one category.

~ Score Interpretation

There are no scoring rules for this type of summary.

~ Qualitative Interpretation

Question 1: Are problems in topical knowledge indicated?

If YES, give Task-Related SLPs 1 and 2. You may also want to interpret other portions of status sheet at this time.

If NO, fill out parts B.1, B.2, and B.3 as needed. Because it may be necessary to give only one or two of these parts, they have been listed in order of utility. Therefore, we recommend that you pursue the explanations associated with parts A, B.1, and B.2 before going to B.3. Having given that caution, however, we also need to remind you that these domains are not hierachical and that a student may have trouble in any one, or all, of them.

Question 2: Is the student sufficiently skilled to learn in this particular classroom environment?

If NO, start teaching. If UNSURE, give Task-Related SLP 3: Instructional Environment.

If YES, ask Question 3.

Question 3: Does the student have adequate study and test-taking skills?

If NO, start teaching. If UNSURE, give Task-Related SLP 4: Study and Test-taking.

If YES, ask Question 4.

Question 4: Does the student solve problems and self-monitor?

If NO, start teaching. If UNSURE, give Task-Related SLP 5: Problem Solving and Self-Monitoring.

If YES, ask Question 5.

Question 5: Does the student make use of basic learning strategies?

If NO, start teaching. If UNSURE, give Task-Related SLP 6: Basic Strategies.

If YES, then you've got a problem in interpretation. Return to the first of the flow chart and retrace your steps to be sure nothing has been missed. If it seems that you have followed the procedure correctly, the most likely problem is that one of the testing/observation techniques we've described is not sufficiently comprehensive to pinpoint the student's problem. Return to Chapters 6 and 7 for information about developing other probes.

Specific-Level Procedures

Task-Related SLPs 1 and 2: Evaluating Topical Knowledge

SLPs 1 and 2 are employed to answer the following question: ''Does the student have adequate prior knowledge of the topic to learn the material?''

As indicated, the range of topical content is simply too large for comprehensive coverage (we are, after all, talking about *all* human knowledge). However, there are a couple of fairly simple generic techniques that can be applied to see if a student has adequate prior knowledge.

If a text is used to teach, or to supplement teaching, then material from the text can be used to construct a comprehension measure that is sensitive to prior knowledge. This will be explained in SLP 1. If a text is not used, or even if it is, SLP 2 can be used to investigate the student's prior knowledge of lecture material. Employ both of these procedures.

SLP 1: Text Comprehension

▽ **Directions**

1. Select three passages of at least 250 words from that portion of the text which the student will be expected to read next.

2. Using these passages, develop either maze or cloze tests as explained in Chapter 10 (p. 193). The use of maze is probably superior in this case, as the items generated by blanking out every fifth word can be used as a bank of topic-related distractors. Words from all three passages may be used for the distractor pool.

3. Administer and score the tests as explained in Chapter 10.

Score Interpretation

Using the median score of the three passages, apply the following criteria.

Maze: 80% = pass
Cloze: 40% = pass

Qualitative Interpretation

If the student clearly passed the maze or cloze tests, it can be assumed that she has adequate prior knowledge to handle this portion of the text. (You may wish to repeat the process whenever new topics are introduced.)

If the student clearly did not pass the passages, the most likely explanation for the failure, as maze and cloze both rely on the redundancy of text wording, is that the student is missing topic-specific vocabulary. In this case your objective will be to teach the topical vocabulary. See Teaching Recommendation 1.

If the student's score is close to the criteria (60–80% for maze, 25–40% for cloze) you may want to doublecheck your findings by using Comprehension SLP 4 from Chapter 10.

SLP 2: Background Information

▽ **Directions**

1. Select three passages, or lessons, that the student is about to read or be taught. Carefully analyze these current lessons and identify examples of prerequisite knowledge in the categories of key vocabulary and main ideas. In highly organized topical domains, and with highly structured texts or teachers, this is fairly easy. If the material is not well-organized, try to find tests used in preceding units or classes.

2. To check key vocabulary, make up or use a test like the one shown in Exhibit 17.3. This test, along with others in math/science, social studies, language/music and everyday living, is found in the workbook. They were developed by selecting terms from the glossaries of published materials (see Chapter 6).

3. To test main ideas, provide the student with a precise summary statement describing the upcoming lesson or passage. For example, "You are about to read a set of passages dealing with the types, sources, and uses of energy." Then ask the student to tell you what she already knows about the topic and—this is important—what she expects to find in the passages (or lectures) when she reads (or hears) them.

4. Score the student's reaction to your question by checking off those terms or ideas you identified in step 1. This procedure is simply a modification of Comprehension SLPs 2 and 5 from Chapter 10.

Score Interpretation

For vocabulary, assuming the terms are critical, the criteria is 100%.

For main ideas, apply the scoring rules for Retell, found in Chapter 10 on page 204.

Qualitative interpretation

Question 1: Did the student correctly use a sufficient range of terminology?

If YES, go to the next question.

If NO, combine this information with the findings from SLP 1 to develop a list of topic-specific vocabulary. Teach this vocabulary using Teaching Recommendation 1. However, before you start teaching, we

Exhibit 17.3   A Technical Vocabulary Test

1. Abyss
   (a) infected cyst
   (b) bottomless pit
   (c) road equipment
2. Axis
   (a) being able to reach something
   (b) to keep changing one's mind
   (c) straight line about which things revolve
3. Condense
   (a) to make more compact
   (b) change from solid to liquid
   (c) a general agreement
4. Epicenter
   (a) part of a continuing story
   (b) earth's surface above the center of an earthquake
   (c) inside concentric circle of a geometric form
5. Diatom
   (a) unicellular algae
   (b) four-sided figure
   (c) combination of proton and electron
6. Saturation
   (a) holding up to ridicule
   (b) make a strong promise
   (c) maximum concentration
7. Solstice
   (a) point of greatest distance from sun
   (b) point of closest distance from sun
   (c) electromagnetic switch
8. Species
   (a) one of a kind
   (b) biological classification below genus
   (c) a scale of values
9. Blood pressure
   (a) pressure exerted by the blood
   (b) pressure at which the veins burst
   (c) hemoglobin count
10. Convex
    (a) curved in
    (b) curved out
    (c) violent shaking

11. Pasteurization
    (a) soft, pale colors
    (b) branching out from the center
    (c) partial sterilization by heat
12. Reflex
    (a) related to the subject of the sentence
    (b) type of blood vessel
    (c) an inborn act
13. Algorithm
    (a) step-by-step procedure
    (b) letters representing numbers
    (c) musical composition
14. Arc
    (a) a scenic representation
    (b) line from center of circle to perimeter
    (c) curved line between two points
15. Ellipse
    (a) partial blocking of the sun
    (b) a glowing fragment
    (c) oval shape
16. Equilateral
    (a) having all angles equal
    (b) having all sides equal
    (c) many sided figure
17. Exponent
    (a) symbol indicating power of a number
    (b) an integral part
    (c) a structural form
18. Median
    (a) average score
    (b) fortune teller
    (c) middle score
19. Pi
    (a) 6.28
    (b) 3.14
    (c) 1/2 of 3.14
20. Rational number
    (a) number used only in equations
    (b) divisible a finite number of times
    (c) computer related

Source: K. W. Howell, S. H. Zucker, and M. K. Morehead (1982), *Multilevel Academic Skills Inventory.* H & Z Publications, 6544 E. Meadowlark, Paradise Valley, AZ 85253. Reprinted with permission.

highly recommend that you employ Language SLP 6 from Chapter 12 to the word list you have identified.

Question 2: Did the student include the main ideas you had identified?

If YES, assume the student has adequate prior knowledge but be prepared to repeat this process on other topics.

If NO, repeat the process on material that should have been taught in earlier lessons. This is done in an attempt to locate the student's current level of knowledge regarding the topic. Once a level of adequate functioning has been located, you should begin instruction at that level using Teaching Recommendation 2.

Task-Related SLP 3: Instructional Environment

This procedure is used to answer the question "Does the student have the skills required to learn in this environment?" In order to employ SLP 3, it is necessary to gain information about the sort of instruction employed in the setting where the kid is failing. This may be accomplished, if you aren't the teacher, by interviewing the teacher or by going into the class to observe. If you are the teacher, a self-evaluation is possible, but we recommend getting someone else to come in and observe.

Appendix B.2 contains descriptors of effective instruction that have been categorized according to the schema presented in Chapter 8. These descriptors are drawn directly from the *TIES* developed by Ysseldyke and Christenson (1987), and they are cross-referenced to the original *TIES* components. The twelve *TIES* components are each summarized in Appendix B.1. You might want to take a look at all of Appendix B now.

There are four ways to link a class observation to the descriptors in Appendix B:

1. Read the component descriptors in B.1 and, using them as a holistic standard (an exemplar), judge the quality of the environment. This is the fastest option.

2. Using the descriptors in Appendix B.2 as a check sheet, rate the instructional environment. Then use Exhibit 8.1 as a summary form to record the results.

3. Buy the *TIES* and use it. This should produce the most accurate information, as the procedures have been standardized, observation techniques clarified, and student interviews included.

4. Combine 2 and 3 by using the *TIES* to collect the data and then converting the results (using the cross-reference in Appendix B.2) to the model of instruction in Exhibit 8.1. The use of Exhibit 8.1 has the advantage of producing results which are

conceptually keyed to the presentation of instruction in this text.

With SLP 3 you are trying to decide if the student needs to be taught to adapt to the class environment or if the environment should be changed to accommodate the kid. In most cases, both of these alternatives make sense. Students must learn to get information in a wide range of settings. However, if the class environment does not illustrate the sort of characteristics that have been shown to facilitate learning, obviously that could have something to do with your student's failure to learn.

The absence of clear criteria is a major problem with decision making in this area. The general descriptions in Appendix B.1 provide an image of exemplary practice, but there may be teachers who produce excellent learning while being weak in one or more components. This is because the teaching components are compensatory and an instructor can make up for weaknesses by excelling in another component. However there remains the possibility that your student needs the particular emphasis provided by the weak component. Then the instruction needs to be modified.

Directions

1. Read the material on conducting observations found in Chapters 6, 7 and 16.

2. Conduct and summarize an evaluation of the instructional environment using one of the four options just listed.

Score Interpretation

There aren't any scoring conventions for this procedure.

Qualitative Interpretation

Note potential weaknesses in the instructional environment then ask this question: "Should I focus on changing the environment, or teaching the student how to get along in it?" (Consider that the second option, teaching the student, may distract from instruction on the skills the student needs to learn. Additionally, if the instructional environment is atypical, the student will not receive any general benefit from the lesson.)

If you decide to work with the student, use Teaching Recommendation 2. If you decide to work with the

Exhibit 17.4*   Checklist for Study/Test Taking and Problem Solving/Self-Monitoring

Directions:
1. Designate skills passed in each column.
2. Start on the left and move right if skill is not passed.

	Know		Apply	
	Recognize	Explain	With prompts	Spontaneously
B.2 Study and Test Taking/SLP 4				
Before Class:				
arrive on time				
enter in a pleasant manner				
bring materials to class				
get ready for learning				
During Class:				
follow classroom rules				
listen carefully				
work during class				
ask for assistance				
move quickly to new activity				
After Class:				
take materials home				
complete homework				
bring homework back				
Organization:				
organization of materials (e.g., use of notebook or folders)				
organization of time (e.g., use of calendar, scheduling work)				
organization of content on paper (e.g., heading, margins)				
Gaining information:				
reading expository material				
reading narrative material				
gaining information from verbal presentations (lectures, demonstrations)				
Demonstrating Knowledge or Skills:				
completing daily assignments				
answering written questions				
writing narrative and expository products				
preparing for and taking tests				
B.3 Problem Solving/SLP 5				
Recognize Problem				
Identify Problem Type:				
open system				
closed system				
identify or develop solutions				
Select Solutions:				
consider resources				
anticipate outcomes				
plan				
carry out plan				
monitor and adjust work				

teacher (or yourself, if you are the teacher) focus on improving skills in those components that seem weak. There are a variety of training materials available that complement the descriptors in Appendix B.

Task-Related SLP 4: Study Skills and Test-Taking Skills

Study and test-taking skills were outlined in part B.2 of Exhibit 17.1*. Each of these skills are most appropriately examined through observation and interview techniques like the ones described in Chapter 16. Because they can be expected to occur with varying levels of success within different teaching environments, it is important to clearly define the situations in which you observe the student.

Directions

1. Review the status sheet in Exhibit 17.1* and note the categories under B.2 in which the student seems to be having trouble.

2. Using the Checklist in Exhibit 17.4*, begin at the righthand side and observe for the spontaneous use of each strategy. You may need to provide opportunities for this use to occur. If it does not occur spontaneously, provide assistance in the form of prompts or instruction to see if you can get the student to employ the strategy. On the checklist, be sure to note the kind of assistance you provide.

3. If the use of a particular strategy cannot be observed, ask the student to explain it. If the student can't do that, see if she can identify examples of the use by other students or through role playing.

Score Interpretation

There are no established scoring rules for this process.

Qualitative Interpretation

The student should spontaneously employ each of the study skills and test-taking skills listed in Exhibit 17.1* and 17.4*. If that doesn't happen, she should be taught to do so by starting at the level of current functioning and specifying objectives across the know/apply axis of 17.4*. For example, the "during class" content was used to produce the following sequence of **Objectives:**

4. The student will spontaneously move quickly to a new activity when the teacher signals to the class that it is time. CAP: 90%.

3. Given the support of additional prompts and/or signals indicating the need, the student will move quickly to a new activity. CAP: 100%.

2. When asked, the student will explain the process of moving quickly to a new activity. The explanation will conform to the material the student has been taught regarding classroom transitions. CAP: 100%.

1. When shown items representing examples and nonexamples of students moving quickly to a new activity, the student will correctly categorize the items. CAP: 100%.

These sorts of objectives can be addressed with Teaching Recommendation 3.

Task-Related SLP 5: Problem Solving and Self-Monitoring

This SLP is exactly like SLP 4. Problem solving and self-monitoring skills were outlined in part B.3 of Exhibit 17.1*. Each of these skills are most appropriately examined through observation and interview techniques and can be expected to occur with varying levels of success within different teaching environments (Lloyd et al., 1991).

▽ Directions

1. Review the status sheet in Exhibit 17.1* and note the categories under B.3 in which the student seems to be having trouble.

2. Using the checklist in Exhibit 17.4*, begin at the righthand side and observe for the spontaneous use of each strategy. You may need to provide opportunities for this use to occur. If it does not occur spontaneously, then provide assistance in the form of prompts or instruction to see if you can get the student to employ the strategy. On the checklist, be sure to note the kind of assistance you provide.

3. If the use of a particular strategy cannot be observed, ask the student to explain it. If the stu-

dent can't do that see if she can identify examples of the use by other students or in role playing.

Score Interpretation

There are no established scoring rules for this process.

Qualitative Interpretation

The student should spontaneously employ each of the skills listed in Exhibit 17.1* and 17.4*. If that doesn't happen, she should be taught to do so by starting at the level of current functioning and specifying objectives across the know/apply axis. For example, the problem-solving content was used to produce the following sequence of **Objectives:**

4. "The student will spontaneously recognize problems which have the potential of interfering with work. This recognition will be indicated by a labeling statement ("Oops, I think I've got a problem") or the onset of efforts at problem resolution/avoidance. CAP: 85%."

3. "Given the support of prompts and/or signals indicating the existence of a problem, the student will recognize the problem. Recognition will be indicated by labeling or another problem recognition response. CAP: 100%."

2. "When asked, the student will explain the process of problem recognition. The explanation will conform to the {material which the student has been taught regarding problem solving}. CAP: 100%."

1. "When shown items representing examples and nonexamples of problem recognition, the student will correctly categorize the items. CAP: 100%."

Problem solving can be taught using Teaching Recommendation 4.

Task-Related SLP 6: Basic Learning Strategies

Specific-Level Testing of Learning Strategies

While many tests of "attention," "self-concept," and "memory" exist, they often have little if any classroom utility. The nature of these constructs simply prohibits the production of any single test that is aligned with all of the various demands of individual tasks and classes. Yet everyone knows that basic learning strategies are important for classroom success.

The problem is that, in order to have a measure of attention that is relevant to reading, for example, it has to have reading content on it. This is because attention to reading cues can be unrelated to attention to computation cues. Similarly, attention to Dr. Howard's lectures may require different skills than attention to Dr. Bigelow's lectures. Attention is context-dependent. The secret to evaluating basic strategies, therefore, does not lie in the development of attention tests. It lies in the development of academic tests highly sensitive to learning. In case you don't recognize where this is going, we're talking about assisted assessment (see Chapter 5, pp. 88-89).

In Chapter 10, Comprehension SLP 1, we told you the way to find out if a student isn't self-monitoring is to provide monitoring assistance to the student and observe its effect. That procedure involved first taking a sample of oral reading. Next the evaluator took a second sample collected in conjunction with systematic feedback (table tapping) about reading accuracy. The score from the first sample became a personal (idiosyncratic) standard (see Chapter 5, p. 83), commonly called a baseline, while the second score was used to illustrate the effect of the assistance. If the feedback (self-monitoring assistance) caused a change in scores, it documented the impact that level of assistance had on the student. This is the format the authors recommend using whenever hypotheses about basic learning strategies are developed. (This process could also be used to assess a student's status in study and test-taking skills; however we don't necessarily recommend it in that domain because it is easier to simply observe for the student's use of those skills.)

Assisted assessment involves repeated measures taken across time to reflect the impact of various levels of assistance. The repeated measures must employ learning-sensitive curriculum-based samples. In order to aid interpretation, the assistance should be provided within a defined sequence so that conclusions about its impact can be formed (Duran, 1988).

The sequence of assistance we suggest for basic learning strategies is illustrated in Exhibit 17.5*. There are four levels of assistance: prompts, directions, practice, and lessons. *Prompts* are used to activate skills the student has already learned. They are conveniently thought of as reminders. *Directions* are explicit calls for the use of a skill. *Practice* is designed to promote profi-

Exhibit 17.5*   *Basic Learning Strategies and a Sequence of Assistance*

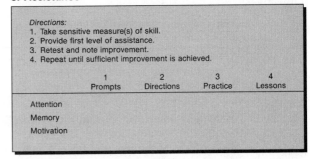

ciency on existing skills. Practice is carried out using the procedures outlined in the Appendix Exhibit B.2.5. *Lessons* are designed to teach a skill that is currently unknown. They include all of the actions related to the presentation of new material outlined in Appendix Exhibit B.2.2.

Exhibit 17.6 provides brief examples of teacher actions that might be employed at each level of assistance to promote attention, memory, and motivation. These examples are drawn from the recommendations found in Exhibits 17.7–17.9. To understand these actions you may need to review material in Chapters 2, 8, and 16. The material on adaptive motivational patterns in Chapter 16 is particularly relevant (see Chapter 16, pp. 377-379).

Directions

1. Select a relevant instructional objective.

2. Assess the student's status on the objective using tests, observations, or assignments. These *must* yield scores that are sensitive to instruction (terms read per minute, or words written to answer a question, rather than grade-equivalence scores). Refer to the monitoring procedures recommended in the topical chapters (10–17) of this text, and to the accompanying workbook, for advice about monitoring.

3. Provide assistance by using the techniques, or teaching the skills, presented for the first level of assistance (prompts). A digest of sample teacher actions for each basic strategy domain can be found in Exhibits 17.7–17.9.

4. Repeat the test or assignment given in Step 2 and note any improvement. Be aware that, as you

Exhibit 17.6   Basic Learning Strategies and a Sequence of Assistance

	1 Prompt	2 Direction	3 Practice	4 Lesson
Attention	Use novelty to change and surprise.	Direct the student to stop and think before working.	Have the student identify critical attributes at rate.	Explain and demonstrate ways of recognizing critical attributes.
Memory	Tell the student to preview the lesson and link it to previous lessons.	Tell the student to use a technique like note taking, or a key word strategy.	Teach skills to high levels of proficiency if the student must recall them.	Help students develop realistic ideas about their memory skill—teach them to recognize difficult material.
Motivation	Be personally interested in, and enthusiastic about, the task.	Relate the task to its context.	Place greater value on overcoming a problem than on initial success. Show the student evidence of her progress.	Teach tasks in the context of higher level tasks. Explain that success is the result of student effort.

move toward higher levels of assistance (levels 3 and 4), more sessions may be needed to produce an effect great enough to actually influence post-teaching scores. Summarize the effect of assistance by recording pre- and post-assistance scores on Exhibit 17.5*.

5. Repeat steps 1–4 until all levels of assistance have been given, or passing in performance has been noted.

∾ Score Interpretation

There are no scoring rules for this procedure. However, the scoring rules and interpretation guidelines for the targeted tasks found in the topical chapter covering that task should be applied. Also, the techniques for data display and analysis presented in the workbook that accompanies this text should be employed to recognize and illustrate trends in progress resulting from the assistance.

∾ Qualitative Interpretation

Attempt to map out the level of assistance required to assure success using Exhibit 17.5*. Refer to Teaching Recommendation 3.

Teaching Recommendations

Teaching Recommendation 1: Build Topic-Specific Vocabulary

Techniques for teaching vocabulary are covered in both Chapters 10 and 12. Some of the references in this text that apply to vocabulary instruction are Rauenbusch and Bereiter (1991), Graves (1986), and portions of Lovitt, (1991). *Preventing School Dropouts*. Austin, TX. Note: ISBN #0-89079-454-5. Rauenbusch and Bereiter's procedure for teaching technical terminology is presented in Exhibit 17.10.

Another particularly interesting approach to vocabulary instruction comes in the form of a computer program called *Think Fast* developed by Parsons (1992). *Think Fast* is a highly flexible program based on the principle of flashcard instruction. However, it allows the teacher to design in a variety of instructional options and data summaries. For more information about the program, you'll have to contact the author at: Counselling Services, University of Victoria, Victoria, BC, V8W 2Y2, Canada.

Exhibit 17.7   Attention

To have students attend a teacher must: Secure attention, direct attention, and teach attention skills.

Before saying, "The student has an attention problem," ask yourself if you have consistently employed the following teacher actions to promote attention:

Function	Action	Example/explanation
1. *Secure attention*	Use novelty, change, and surprise in your teaching.	Make lessons "worth" attending to by providing a rich classroom environment.
2. *Secure attention*	Make lesson meaningful.	Relate the lesson to the student's prior knowledge.
3. *Secure attention*	Use routines.	Employ uniform presentation techniques for all lessons. This will accentuate new content, and draw attention to the task— not your presentation.
4. *Secure attention*	Provide labels for the things you want the student to attend to and use these consistently.	"Look at the *operation sign.*" "What does the *operation sign* require?" "Does the *operation sign* require addition or subtraction?" "If the *operation sign* doesn't require addition, what does it require?"
5. *Secure attention*	Do not pause between cues and the presentation of material. If you say "pay attention" and then pause, the student is allowed to attend to something you don't want. This promotes attention errors.	Say, "Look at the corners." *Immediately* show the shapes to be attended to.
6. *Secure attention*	Do *not* try to remove distractions.	Be aware of distractions and teach student to ignore them.
7. *Direct attention*	Always be aware of the relevant attributes of a task.	Relevant attributes define the concept. For example, in "decoding" the relevant attributes are letter shape and combination—not letter size, style, color or position on a page.
8. *Direct attention*	Modify the relevant attributes to highlight distinctive features of the task.	If a student ignores the presence of a silent *e*—accentuate it by making it a different color.
9. *Direct attention*	If the relevant attributes are modified, the modification must eventually be faded to avoid over-attention to it.	To teach triangle and square, the corners are exaggerated and the exaggeration faded.

(continued)

Exhibit 17.7   Attention (continued)

10. *Direct attention*   Relevant attributes can be presented first and irrelevant attributes gradually introduced once the others have been learned.

To teach the concept "over" present several clear-cut instances first

before gradually introducing irrelevant attributes.

or nonexamples

11. *Direct attention*   Simplify the presentation of a task.

Pick one distinctive feature of the task to highlight—do not invent excess clues as they will detract from each other. For example, A is better than B.

12. *Direct attention*   During initial instruction separate easily confused items.

Do not present soft C and S in the lesson.

13. *Direct attention*   If errors occur present confused material in pairs and teach by directly contrasting the critical attributes.

"Look at the b and d. How are they the same? How are they different?"

14. *Direct attention*   Place importance on working the problem—as well as producing the answer. Don't emphasize isolated facts, but the processes which lead to problem solution.

Wrong. "Show me you know the answer to 17 + 5 = .
Better. "Show me that you know how to work addition problems—here is one: 17 + 5 = ."

15. *Direct attention*   Use lead questions prior to the main question to focus attention on the problem-solving process and relevant attributes.

Introduction: "Here is a shape I want you to name."
Lead Questions: "How many sides does it have?" "How many corners does it have?"
Main Question: "What is the shape?"

(continued)

Exhibit 17.7   Attention (continued)

16. *Teach attention skills*	Explain what attention means and that it *is* under the student's control.	Do not say "I know you have trouble attending." Do say "Let me show you what to attend to."
17. *Teach attention skills*	Direct students to stop and think before they go to work.	"Here is a problem. I want you to think about doing it—and then begin on my signal."
18. *Teach attention skills*	View "Attention problems" as failures to plan before taking action.	Teach students to use a "reflective," rather than an "impulsive" style of problem-solving.
19. *Teach attention skills*	Never convey the message that a quick, thoughtless response is better than no response at all.	"I always want you to work carefully. I want you to work these problems as quickly *and* as carefully as you can."
20. *Teach attention skills*	Utilize verbal mediation. Teach the student to repeat general strategies for problem solving. These may be repeated aloud at first and gradually faded. The strategies should deal with selective attention.	Teacher: "Here is a division problem. How do you solve *any* problem?" Student (aloud or to self): "First I stop and think. I look at the problem and think about the directions. I decide what to do. I decide how to do it. I go to work. I correct the way I work. I check my answer."
21. *Teach attention skills*	Utilize verbal mediation as explained above, but use task-specific strategies.	Teacher: "Here is a shape I want you to name. How do you name shapes?" Student: "I ask myself these questions. Are there corners? If there are, how many? Are these sides? If so, how many? Are the sides straight?"
22. *Teach attention skills*	Do not make general references to attention. Tell the student what you want him to attend to.	*Wrong.* "Pay attention to your work." *Right.* "Look at this problem and notice the operation sign."

Teaching Recommendation 2: Teach Prerequisite Content

While an intervention (Teaching Recommendation 1) is available for topical vocabulary, we can only provide general recommendations in this text for students who lack the fundamental knowledge to approach lessons on a particular topic. Missing prerequisite knowledge, particularly that knowledge which we think of as conceptual and procedural, can only be supplied by repeating earlier lessons using instruction tailored to the student's individual needs. Chapter 8 provides an extensive summary of effective instruction.

Teaching Recommendation 3: Study and Test-Taking Skills

While the evidence about general problem solving training isn't in yet, the results of specific study-skill interventions are clearly positive (Ellis & Lenz, 1990; Gleason, 1988). This research has clarified the study demands placed on students (Calhoun & Beattie, 1987), contrasted the approaches to studying used by different learners (Wade et al., 1990), and documented the effectiveness of various approaches to study-skill instruction in a variety of areas (Carnine, 1992; Gleason et al., 1991; Peterson, 1992).

There is one caution regarding study-skill instruction that we want to pass on. Given that different tasks place different demands on learners (Marx & Walsh, 1988), teachers must be aware that some study skills, even when taught effectively, may not help students deal with particular forms of instruction. This means that a student may learn the study strategies but find no place to use them (note also the cautions regarding the placement of the strategies in the curriculum found in Chapter 3). Make sure the approaches to studying you decide to teach are appropriate to the

Exhibit 17.8 Memory

To have students remember, a teacher must: promote storage, promote recall and teach memory skills.

Before saying "The student has a memory deficit," ask yourself if you have consistently employed the following teacher actions to promote memory.

Function	Action	Example/explanation
1. *Promote storage*	Tell students before lesson what they are to learn about and remember.	State objectives for the lesson or give the students a pretest. Use advanced organizers or provide the student with a topical outline, abstract, visual representation, or overview of the presentation they are about to be given.
2. *Promote storage*	Summarize and review the main points after a lesson.	"The main thing we learned about today was mammals. Be sure to remember that they are warm blooded."
3. *Promote storage*	Link current lessons to previous lessons.	"Today we will learn more about mammals. Remember that we have already learned that mammals have hair and give birth to live young."
4. *Promote storage*	Label and emphasize critical attributes of the concepts to be taught.	During the mammal lecture the teacher writes "warm blooded," "live young," and "hair" on the board.
5. *Promote storage*	It is better to teach a series of small specific lessons than to teach one large lesson.	*Wrong:* "How to get help in an emergency." *Better:* "How to recognize an emergency." "How to contact someone." "How to say you need help."
6. *Promote storage and recall*	Utilize location and time cues to label lessons for students who do not benefit from word labels.	Always teach the same lesson at the same time in the same location in the room.
7. *Promote storage*	Confirm that the student is attending to the material that you want them to remember.	Teacher: "The important thing to remember about mammals is that they are warm blooded. What is the thing to remember?" Student: "That mammals are warm blooded."
8. *Promote storage and recall*	Supply strategies for recalling information along with the information.	"This animal is a *platypus*. You can remember its name because it sounds like "plate" and see the nose of a platypus looks like a plate."
9. *Promote storage and recall*	Label a series of lessons so that information provided in the sequence can be easily tied together by the student. This will facilitate the consistent storage of related information.	"We are still in our unit on *mammals*" "our next *mammal* lesson will cover reproduction.'

(continued)

Exhibit 17.8   Memory (continued)

10. *Promotes storage and recall*	Encourage student to clump or cluster sematically related bits of information. This limits the total number of elements which must be recalled.	Tree, red, green, carrot, hammer, blue, saw, nail, and apple. "See this series of names?" To remember it you should start by remembering "plants," "tools," and "colors" trees hammer red carrot saw green apple nail blue
11. *Promotes storage and recall*	Provide the student with background about the context, source, or logical derivation of the information to be remembered. This increases the number of potential, and yet related, linkages the student can draw between the new information and previously stored information.	"We are studying mammals because they are one type of animal and in Biology we learn about the same groups of living things that scientists talk about."
12. *Promote recall*	Provide practice on the responses targeted for recall. Often, we overemphasize the stimulus students must attend to (e.g., letters) but not the responses they must make (sounds).	Teacher: "Say the word 'cat'." Student: "Cat." Teacher: "Good, say 'cat' every time I clap my hands." (Claps three times.) Student: "Cat, cat, cat." Teacher: Showing the word *cat* "This is what the word 'cat' looks like. When you see this, what will you say?" Student: "Cat."

13. *Promote recall*	Teach skills to high proficiency levels—including high rates of responding.	"Oral passage reading
		  140c 7 errors per minute."
		"Addition facts 0–20
		  40c 0 errors per minute."
		"List elements in human body—100% accuracy."

14. *Teaching memory skills*	Help students develop realistic ideas about their memory skills. They must be able to recognize material that is difficult to remember if they will be expected to select powerful strategies to remember the material.	"I want you to remember all of the elements in the human body. Will you be able to just remember them or should we devise a plan to help you remember?" Or "Which will be the hardest to remember? The capitals of all the states or the capitals of the states in the Northwest?"
15. *Teach memory skills*	Teach students to use keyword strategies.	"When you have a word like platypus ask yourself what it sounds like. Can you hear another word, or a rhyme, in platypus?"
16. *Teach memory skills*	Teach the student to use (a) elaboration, (b) organization, and (c) mnemonic strategies.	(a) Highlight important parts of a test. (b) take notes (c) "When you write remember the 'cops' are after you: Capitalize, Overall appearance, Punctuate and Spell."
17. *Teach memory skills*	Teach the student to review previous lessons.	"What should you do before today's lesson?"

(continued)

Exhibit 17.9 Motivation

To motivate students a teacher must: supply meaning, raise perceived value, convey a sense of control, promote feelings of success, and alter consequences.

Before saying "The student isn't motivated," ask if you have consistently employed the following teacher actions to promote motivation.

Function	Action	Example/explanation
1. *Supply meaning*	Be sure the students focus on what they are learning about *not* what they are doing.	When asked "Why are you working on that?" A student should say "To learn the capitals of states" *not* "to get it done by recess."
2. *Supply meaning*	Relate task to its context.	"If we learn to add we will be able to find information with numbers and keep score at games."
3. *Supply meaning*	Relate task to higher level tasks.	"Learning addition will help us when we multiply."
4. *Supply meaning*	Teach tasks in the context of a higher level task.	"Here is a long division problem. I will work all of the parts except the subtraction facts —you do those."
5 *Supply meaning*	Focus on using the meaning of the task to help complete the task.	"If this is an addition problem, the answer must be larger than the numbers with which we start.
6. *Raise perceived value*	Link task to a task the student is already interested in.	Learning to add and subtract will help us keep score at ball games."
7. *Raise perceived value*	As a teacher, be personally interested and enthusiastic about the task.	"I'm glad there is time for math. I enjoy learning about and working with numbers."
8. *Raise perceived value*	As a teacher, place a priority on the task.	"I'd like to talk about last night's TV show, but this is math class so math is more important now." Also: collect and grade assignments promptly to indicate that you value them.
9. *Raise perceived value*	Never lower the value of a task by using it as busy work, or a punishment.	*Do not* say: "You must stay in from recess and work addition problems because you were out of your seat."
10. *Convey a sense of control*	Always make it clear that successes or failures are the result of the student's effort—that they can control the outcome of their work.	"Good, *you* finished the work and *you* got it all right because *you* worked hard and cared about your work." or "*You* missed these items so *you* will need to work harder and more carefully on these problems next time."
11. *Convey a sense of control*	Do *not* link successes or failures on tasks to things the student can't control.	*Do not* say "Don't worry about missing those problems, you are just having a bad day." or "This word is a real stinker—it's OK to miss the hard ones sometimes." or "It's hard for you to read because you have a learning disability."

(continued)

Exhibit 17.9   Motivation (continued)

12.	*Promote feelings of success*	Show the student evidence of their progress.	Utilize a chart to show how much the student has improved as a result of their work.
13.	*Promote feelings of success*	Treat errors as opportunities to learn.	When reviewing an assignment, *don't say* "Let's count up your mistakes." *Do say:* "Let's find out which items we get to learn about next."
14.	*Promote feelings of success*	Place greater value on overcoming an error/problem than on initial success.	"You showed me how to do four problems correctly. Usually I give you 1 point for each problem, but here is one you have missed before. I'm giving you 2 points for it because you have improved so much."
15.	*Alter consequences*	Pair completion of the task with something the student likes to do.	"If you finish your math, I'll let you sit near a friend of your choice tomorrow."
16.	*Alter consequences*	Change the type of reinforcer (or back-up reinforcer) you are using.	From "good work" to "nice going" or from tangible to social.
17.	*Alter consequences*	Change the schedule of reinforcement (increase or decrease ratio).	From 1 reinforcer for every 5 correct problems to 1 on an average of every 10 problems.

places where your student is going to work. Be particularly aware that those tactics that seem useful in the special/remedial classroom may not work in some regular settings. Also be aware that, if the study skill procedures are too complex, they may actually take longer to teach than the learning they are meant to expedite.

Study and Test-Taking Skills

Antes, R.L. (1989). *Preparing students for taking tests: Fastback 291.* Bloomington, IN: Phi Delta Kappa. (*Note:* Available from ERIC ED 314-491 or publisher ISBN# 0-873567-291.)

Archer, A.L. & Gleason, M. M. (1989). *Skills for school success.* North Billerica, MA: Curriculum Associates.

Ellis, E.S. & Lenz, B.K. (1990). Techniques for mediating content-area learning: Issues and research. *Focus on Exceptional Children, 22*(9), 1–16.

Gleason, M.M., Colvin, G., & Archer, A. L. (1991). Interventions for improving study skills. In G. Stoner, M.R. Shinn and H.M. Walker (Eds.), *Interventions for achievement and behavior problems.* Silver Springs, MD: National Association of School Psychologists.

McNamara, T.C. (1990). Training students to take bet-

ter control of their learning by framing questions in multiple-choice format. Paper presented at the Annual Meeting of the American Educational Research Association, April 16–20. (Note: Available from ERIC ED 318–754.)

Missouri University Instructional Materials Laboratory. (1990). *Study Skills.* Columbia, MO: Author. (*Note:* Available from ERIC ED 321-232.) (This is a list of 20 resources and annotated coverage of 65 books, kits, and software programs for study skills.)

Schumaker, J.B., Deshler, D.D. & Knight, P.C. (1991). Teaching routines for content areas at the secondary level. In G. Stoner, M.R. Shinn, and H.M. Walker (Eds.), *Interventions for achievement and behavior problems.* Silver Springs, MD: National Association of School Psychologists.

Teaching Recommendation 4: Problem Solving

Instruction in general problem solving is becoming more common (Larson, 1989a) however there is little consensus about how to go about it (McKeachie, 1987a; Sweller, 1990). The two primary sources we recommend for classroom-specific guidance are Larson

Exhibit 17.10   Procedure for Learning New Terminology

Procedures	Prompts (on cue cards)
Establish a provisional macrostructure (i.e., scaffold)	Take 60 seconds to skim the passage to see what the author has to say

When a problematic word is encountered. . . .

evaluate the importance of the problematic word	Is the word critical to the meaning?

If no, then proceed to next word.
If yes, then select from these strategies:

summarizing	sum up what you know so far
reading ahead	read ahead to see if it will help
backtracking	go back to where it starts to get confusing
identify word type	think of what kind of word it is likely to be

When a tentative identification of the word is made, then . . .

critically evaluate the constructed word for internal consistency and compatibility with prior knowledge and common sense	does it fit with what you know so far?

Source: "Making Reading More Difficult: A Degraded Text Microworld for Teaching Reading Comprehension Strategies," by F. Rauenbusch, and C. Bereiter, 1991, *Cognition and Instruction*, 8, (2), p. 190. Reprinted by permission.

(1989b) and Goldstein (1988). The Goldstein source is most applicable to social skills.

Any successful approach to problem solving must include elements of problem recognition, problem analysis, resource analysis, planning, and monitoring. These functions may be addressed in classroom settings; however, they must also ultimately be transported out of the classroom. One way to do this initially is to use "routine" language and steps for each function regardless of the setting (Bulgren, Schumaker & Deshler, 1988). For example, the words *choose* and *plan* can be used to consistently debrief errors as follows:

"What happened?"

"What did you *choose* to do?"

"What happened because of your *choice*?"

"What else might you have *chosen* to do?"

"If you had *chosen* to do that, what do you think would have happened?"

"It looks to me as if you need a *plan* for solving this sort of problem in the future."

"How do you *plan* on recognizing this sort of problem in the future?"

"What is your *plan* for *choosing* the best things to do?"

There are many sequences like this one. Some of them have three steps while others may have a dozen. In our review we were unable to find compelling evidence that any of the various schemes were more or less effective. We have concluded, however, that none of them will work unless they are taught in ways that promote generalization.

The sort of problem analysis just illustrated can be applied across many situations and tasks. However, it isn't sufficient for the student to simply recognize problems and plans, she must also use them in order to solve problems in a variety of settings. This means that the problem-solving skills must be raised to automaticity through extensive practice and ongoing maintenance procedures.

Many of the techniques currently available to teachers in the form of published programs do not provide sufficient depth for this sort of learning. Using these programs, teachers often have students repeat rules, but seldom have them carry out the rules in actual practice. This problem of generalization is a major concern.

Here are some useful resource materials:

Goldstein, A.P. (1988). *The Prepare Curriculum*. Champaign, IL: Research Press. (*Note:* ISBN#0-87822-295-2.)

Larson, K.A. (1989). Task-related and interpersonal problem-solving training for increasing school success in high-risk young adolescents. *Remedial and Special Education*, 10(5), 32–42.

Teaching Recommendation 5: Basic Learning Strategies

First read the material on learning strategies in Chapters 2 and 8. Then review the results listed in Exhibit 17.5* to try and find the level of assistance the student requires on this task. Once these levels have been recognized, incorporate the instructional recommendations briefly outlined in Exhibits 17.7–17.9.

It is logical to wonder why, if the suggestions for assistance at each level in Exhibit 17.5* are any good, we wouldn't simply go to level 4 in all cases. Good question!

To answer the question, we remind you of the topic of this chapter—task-related skills. We are not trying to find out what the student does or doesn't know about a particular task. Nor are we trying to decide how to teach her a particular task. In this chapter we are trying to map the student's sophistication at learning. For basic learning strategies, this is done by establishing, if possible, the student's position along the sequence of assistance in Exhibit 17.5*. Objectives can then be specified leading from that position toward independent functioning. For example, if the student required lessons on memory skills in order to learn the chemical elements in the human body, her sequence of learning **Objectives** might look like this:

1. "Given assistance in the form of memory strategy lessons, the student will correctly list {insert new content}."

2. "Given assistance in the form of practice on memory strategies, the student will correctly list {insert new content}."

3. "Given assistance in the form of explicit directions to use memory strategies, the student will correctly list {insert new content}."

4. "Given assistance in the form of prompts for use of memory strategies, the student will correctly list {insert new content}."

5. "Given a list of {insert new content}, the student will learn the content without teacher assistance related to memory strategies, and will list the content accurately."

If you aren't trying to move the student toward independent use of basic learning strategies, and really want the student to learn something right away, employ *all* levels of assistance.

For additional information on basic learning strategies in the classroom see:

Lovitt, T.C. (1991). *Preventing School Dropouts*. Austin, TX: Pro-Ed. *Note:* ISBN #0-89079-454-5.

DuPaul, G.J., Stoner, G., Putman, D. & Tilly, W. D. (1991). Interventions for attention problems. In G. Stoner, M. Shinn, and H. Walker (Eds.), *Interventions for achievement and behavioral problems* (pp. 685–714). Silver Springs, MD: National Association of School Psychologists.

Summary

This chapter has covered task-related knowledge by referring to several extremely broad categories of information. These categories ranged from basic learning strategies to note taking. We believe this is an important chapter and hope that its position in the text does not somehow lead you to conclude that it isn't. It may very well be that support in this domain will have greater cumulative benefits than instruction in more "academic" content.

While we are mentioning the end of things, we'd like to note that this is the last chapter in the text. It has been a long trip and we hope a useful one for you. In thanking you all for your attention we leave you with the following ending from a junior-high student's writing sample:

"The End—See you later—Hasta la Vista, Baby—bye—That's it, folks, Elvis has left the building."

Appendix A / Survival Statistics

The following discussion deals with measurement content, including some statistics. The computational steps for each statistic will be presented along with an example. Practice exercises will also be made available so that you can follow the computational steps yourself. If this content is new to you (or old but painful), we encourage you to try these practice computations, as doing so will clarify our discussion.

Normative Standards and Scores

Scores

The terms *obtained* or *raw score* refer to the count derived directly from a test/observation. They are derived by assigning points to particular behaviors or products of the student. These raw scores may need to be translated or modified in order to make them more meaningful. Suppose you are taking a class during which you are given an exam. Later you ask the instructor how you did on the test and she replies "You got a score of 23." How do you feel? Without knowing how many points were possible, how others did on the test, or the grading scale, your only choice is to feel confused. Scores are nothing more than numerical recapitulations of behavior, and information about behavior without a standard is meaningless.

In order to derive meaning from scores, we must find ways to contrast the scores to standards. The standards most educators use are the normative, behavioral, and idiographic.

An NRT score derives meaning from reference to the norming sample. In order to make the raw score meaningful on an NRT, it must be placed within the context of the norming population. Visually this can be accomplished by presenting the scores of the entire population as a frequency distribution (Exhibit A.1) or as a curve (Exhibit A.2).

How good was a score of 23? Well, when we look at the frequency distribution, or the curve of class scores, we can see that a score of 23 is quite low com-pared to the scores obtained by most of the other students. The score of 23 now has meaning because we have referenced the score to the norming population.

In Exhibit A.1, the group's scores were first summarized according to the way they distributed from highest to lowest. A mark for each student obtaining a score was made next to it, giving an overall impression of how the class did on the test. If you got a score of 23, it seems you did poorly on the test compared to the other students. It is important to remember that we have no information about your actual knowledge— we only know that you scored lower than most other students. We are able to make this observation because we have placed your score within the norming sample's distribution.

Normal Distributions. Normative evaluation is conceptually linked to the idea of a normal distribution, sometimes called a *normal* or *bell-shaped curve*. The assumption underlying this idea is that the probability of a high score's occurring is the same as that of a low score's occurring. For example, suppose that ten people were asked to flip a coin ten times. The number of heads for the group might be summarized as in Exhibit A.3. Hardly anyone would be expected to get all heads or all tails. The probability of flipping a head is the same as flipping a tail, so most people would be expected to get about 50% heads or tails. As the number of people flipping coins increased, the distribution of heads should begin to take on the appearance of Exhibit A.4. Ultimately, if enough people flip enough coins, the picture of the number of heads obtained will approximate what is known as a normal curve. Exhibit A.5 shows a normal curve. The normal curve is an idealized prototype for many of the statistical operations employed in educational measurement. It occurs more commonly in statistics than it does in human behavior.

Pictured frequency distributions, like the one in Exhibit A.1, can be helpful for illustrating the performance of classes or other small groups, but they get unwieldy when applied to whole schools or school districts. Because it is often inconvenient to

Exhibit A.1   Frequency Distribution

Raw scores	Students obtaining score
30	/
29	/
28	//
27	////
26	///
25	///////
24	////
→ 23	///
22	//
21	/
20	/
19	/
18	
17	
16	
15	

A teacher does this when he reports that a student has scored "above average" or "below average." When making such statements, the teacher is simply halving the distribution (at the mean, as shown in Exhibit A.5) and reporting which half the student is in. Procedures of this type are simple and seem to convey some meaning, but obviously students who are below average do not all have the same score. Because small score differences may be meaningful, a finer subdivision of the distribution is necessary. Such a subdivision is derived from calculations that make use of the various parameters that describe distributions of scores.

The Center.   The *mean* $\bar{x}$ is one parameter used to describe the center of a distribution. The mean is known as a measure of central tendency. It is the best predictor of how any individual will behave on an NRT. As illustrated in Exhibit A.6, the scores in two distributions may differ from each other by having different means. If the average score of one group is 3.78 and the average score of another is 4.32, then the two groups have behaved differently on the test used. When reading research articles, you may have come across a reference to the "*t*-test," which is a procedure used to determine if differences in group means are statistically significant.

The mean is the average of the total of all scores (Σx). It is calculated by adding all the scores together and dividing by the number of scores. Other indicators of central tendency include the median (middle score) and the mode (most frequently occurring score).

Practice Computation

Computing the Mean

$$\text{Mean} = \frac{\text{Sum of the scores}}{\text{Number of scores}} = \frac{\Sigma x}{N} = \bar{x}$$

Drama Test (maximum score 30)

construct visual displays, statistical procedures are used to accomplish the same function. They do this by translating raw scores into a different type of score that conveys information about both the student's behavior and its relationship to the behavior of the students in the norm sample. It is this process of converting the raw score into a useful form that gives us most of the statistical content taught in evaluation texts.

It is possible to label portions of a distribution and to report the portion in which a student's score falls. This allows us to know where the student is within the context of the prototypical normal sample.

2 3 4 5 6 7 8 9 10 11 12 13 14 15 16 17 18 19 20 21 22 23 24 25 26 27 28 29 30

Exhibit A.2   A score curve

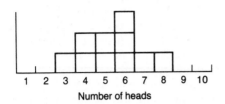

Exhibit A.3   **Ten flips of a coin**

Students	Raw Scores		
1.	25	Step 1.	List the scores in any order, but list each student's score.
2.	25		
3.	24		
4.	23		
5.	22	Step 2.	Add up the scores. Sum = 288.
6.	22		
7.	22		
8.	21	Step 3.	Divide the sum of the scores by the total number of scores.
9.	20		
10.	18		
11.	18		
12.	18		288/15 = 19.2.
13.	15		Conclusion: The mean is 19.2.
14.	9		
15.	6		
	288		

Now, find the mean for the following geology test scores and check your answer in Exhibit A.10.

Students	Raw Scores	Students	Raw Scores
1.	50	11.	28
2.	45	12.	28
3.	42	13.	24
4.	39	14.	23
5.	38	15.	21
6.	30	16.	20
7.	30	17.	15
8.	29	18.	10
9.	29	19.	10
10.	29	20.	9

The Width. The mean, median, and mode are all indicators of the center of a distribution and can be used to cut the distribution into two halves. A distribution of scores can also be segmented according to its variability. This is usually accomplished by calcu-

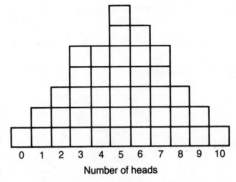

Exhibit A.4   **Forty flips of a coin**

lating the *standard deviation* (SD) of the distribution. This procedure allows us to recognize the degree to which the scores in a distribution cluster around, or deviate from, the center. If the scores are tightly clustered, as are the scores of Group A in Exhibit A.7, then a *raw* score of 18 indicates test behavior that is extremely different from the behavior of others taking the test. The score of 18 is said to be at the extreme lower end of the group's variability. However, the same score for Group B, while still below average, is well within the group of scores. This means 18 is not as deviant for Group B as for Group A. In Exhibit A.7 both groups of 30 students who took the same test had the same average performance, but their variability was different. This could be the result of any number of factors including the instruction they have received.

In order to make comparisons more sensitive, we slice the distribution into smaller and smaller pieces. By using *variability* as a parameter, we can report where a student's score falls in the distribution with greater accuracy. For example, a student who is two

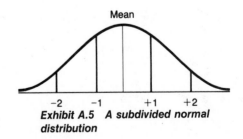

Exhibit A.5   **A subdivided normal distribution**

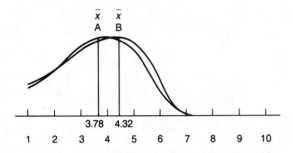

x̄   x̄
A   B

3.78 4.32

1 2 3 4 5 6 7 8 9 10

Exhibit A.6   A comparison of two different groups

	Raw Scores	Scores Squared		
1.	25	625	Step 1.	List the scores in any order, but list each student's score.
2.	25	625		
3.	24	576		
4.	23	529	Step 2.	Add up the scores. Sum = 288.
5.	22	484		
6.	22	484	Step 3.	Square each score in a list next to the student's score.
7.	22	484		
8.	21	441		
9.	20	400	Step 4.	Add up all the squared scores. Sum of the squares = 5962.
10.	18	324		
11.	18	324		
12.	18	324		
13.	15	225	Step 5.	Square the sum of the scores calculated in Step 2. 288 = 82,944.
14.	9	81		
15.	6	36		
	288	5962		

Step 6. Divide the number derived in Step 5 by the number of students. 82,944/15 = 5529.6.

Step 7. Subtract the number derived in Step 6 from the number derived in Step 4. 5962 − 5529.6 = 432.4.

Step 8. Divide the number derived in Step 7 by the number of students minus one.

$$\frac{432.4}{15 - 1} = \frac{432.4}{14}$$
$$= 30.89.$$

Step 9. Find the square root of the number derived in Step 8. $\sqrt{30.89} = 5.56$.

Conclusion: The standard deviation is 5.56.

standard deviations below the mean has scored relatively lower than a student who is only one standard deviation below the mean. In a normal curve (the ideal distribution illustrated in Exhibit A.5), 68% of all scores fall within +1 and −1 standard deviation (SD) of the mean; 95% fall within +2 and −2.

The standard deviation describes a group's variability. If all students taking a test made the same score on the test, there would be no variability. The more the students deviate (spread out) around the mean, the more variability there is in their scores. The significance of differences in variability between two groups is typically judged with an "F-test." The formula and computational steps for calculating the standard deviation appear below. As you do the steps note that squaring scores, as required by the formula, tends to place greater weight on extremely high and low scores. (Incidentally, if you are uncertain how to calculate square roots let us clarify that process for you—you press the "square root" button on your calculator).

Practice Computation

Computing the Standard Deviation

$$SD = \sqrt{\frac{\text{Sum of squared scores} - \dfrac{\text{Sum of scores squared}}{\text{Number of scores}}}{\text{Number of scores} - 1}}$$

$$= \sqrt{\frac{\Sigma x^2 - \dfrac{(\Sigma x)^2}{N}}{N - 1}}$$

Drama Test (maximum score 30)

Now, calculate the standard deviation for the geology test scores and check your answer with Exhibit A.10.

Students	Raw Scores
1.	50
2.	45
3.	42
4.	39
5.	38
6.	30
7.	30
8.	29
9.	29
10.	29
11.	28
12.	28
13.	24
14.	23
15.	21
16.	20
17.	15
18.	10
19.	10
20.	9

Exhibit A.7   The Variability of Two Distributions

Standard Scores

By using the mean and standard deviation of the distribution, a standard score can be devised for each raw score. This conversion of raw scores to a more easily interpreted form aids our use of normed test results. Standard scores are useful for comparing a student's relative performance on two different tests that may have been given to two different norming populations (and would therefore have different means and standard deviations).

z and T.   Standard scores include percentiles, z-scores, T-scores, stanines, and others. While a raw score of 11 may be high on one distribution and low on another, a standard score of 11 always labels the same portion of every distribution. A T-score of 50, for example, is always the average score of any distribution. Therefore we know, without looking at the distribution, that a T-score of 70 is further above average than a T-score of 51, regardless of the raw score obtained. Standard scores provide greater precision because they use the standard deviation to slice the distributions into fractions. In fact, the number of slices is only limited by the decimals a person wants to allow in their scores (and even these can be removed with T-scores).

Two common types of standard scores are the z-

score and T-score. They report where the student is in the distribution with reference to both the mean and standard deviation. The z-score is calculated by subtracting the mean score ($\bar{x}$) from the student's score (x) and then dividing the results by the standard deviation. In Exhibit A.8 we see that Ed's history test score was 8, so Ed's z-score is -1.41.

$$z = \frac{x - \bar{x}}{SD} = \frac{8 - 12.9}{3.48} = -1.41$$

The T-score is essentially the same as the z-score, except the result is multiplied by 10, 100, or 1000 to clear the decimal, and added to 50 to get rid of any negative numbers. The formula for calculating T-scores is:

$$T = 10 \left(\frac{x - \bar{x}}{SD} \right) + 50$$

So Ed's T-score is:

$$T = 10 \left(\frac{8 - 12.9}{3.48} \right) + 50 = 36$$

Calculating standard scores may seem like a lot of work, but they have some advantages. Converting the scores on two different normed tests to standard scores enables an evaluator to compare a student's performance in the two areas. For example, suppose Ed took a

Exhibit A.8   History Test T- and z-Scores

Raw Score	z-score	T-score
(x)	$z = \dfrac{x - \bar{x}}{SD}$	$T = 10\left(\dfrac{x - \bar{x}}{SD}\right) + 50$
20	2.04	70
17	1.18	62
16	.89	59
16	.89	59
15	.60	56
15	.60	56
14	.32	53
14	.32	53
14	.32	53
13	.03	50
12	− .26	47
12	− .26	47
11	− .55	45
11	− .55	45
10	− .83	42
10	− .83	42
Ed = 8	−1.41	36
4	−2.56	24
Sum = 232	$\bar{x} = 12.9$ SD = 3.48	

biology test the same day he took the history test. And then suppose that for some reason his teacher wished to determine in which course Ed was doing the best (in relation to the other students). On the history test Ed got a raw score of 8 and on the biology test he got a raw score of 15. However, there were 75 problems on the biology test and only 25 on the history test. On which test did he get the best score? By converting the two test scores to standard scores, it is possible to take into

Exhibit A.9   Ed's Standard Scores

	History Test (25 items)	Biology Test (75 items)
Ed's score (x)	8	15
mean ($\bar{x}$)	12.9	52.7
SD	3.48	14.5
z-score	− 1.4	− 2.6
T-score	36	24

account the mean and standard deviation for each test and therefore to compare Ed's scores (Exhibit A.9). The results indicate that Ed did best on the history test. But remember that his score on either normative test is related only to the performance of the other students. That Ed got a better standard score on the history test doesn't mean he knows more history than biology. To make that conclusion one would have to know about the reliability and validity of the test, as well as the characteristics of the other students who took it.

Practice Computation

Translating Raw Scores into z-Scores

$$z = \frac{x - \bar{x}}{SD}$$

Drama Test (maximum score 30)

	Raw Scores	z-Scores
1.	25	1
2.	25	1
3.	24	.06
4.	23	.7
5.	22	.5
6.	22	.5
7.	22	.5
8.	21	.3
9.	20	.1
10.	18	− .2
11.	18	− .2
12.	18	− .2
13.	15	− .8
14.	9	−1.8
15.	6	−2.4
	288	

Step 1. List the raw scores in any order, but list each score.

Step 2. Compute the mean. $288 \div 15 = 19.2$.

Step 3. Compute the standard.

$$\sqrt{\frac{5962 - \dfrac{82,944}{15}}{15 - 1}} = 5.56$$

Step 4. Subtract the mean computed in Step 2 from a raw score. For example, $25 - 19.2 = 5.8$.

Step 5. Divide the number derived in Step 4 by the number computed in Step 3. $5.8/5.56 = 1.04$.

Conclusion: The raw score 25 is equal to z-score 1.04.

Step 6. Repeat the process for each raw score.

Exhibit A.10

Summary of drama test scores (maximum score 30)				
Raw Scores	z-Scores	T-Scores	Percentile	Percentage
1. 25	1	60	97	83
2. 25	1	60	97	83
3. 24	.9	59	87	80
4. 23	.7	57	80	77
5. 22	.5	55	67	73
6. 22	.5	55	67	73
7. 22	.5	55	67	73
8. 21	.3	53	53	70
9. 20	.1	51	46	67
Mean ---	---	---	---	---
10. 18	− .2	48	33	60
11. 18	− .2	48	33	60
12. 18	− .2	48	33	60
13. 15	− .8	42	20	50
14. 9	− 1.8	32	13	30
15. 6	− 2.4	26	6	20
Sum = 288	Mean = 19 .2		SD = 5 .56	

Summary of geology test scores (maximum score 50)				
Raw Scores	z-Scores	T-Scores	Percentile	Percentage
1. 50	2	70	100	100
2. 45	1.5	65	95	90
3. 42	1.3	63	90	84
4. 39	1	60	85	78
5. 38	.9	59	80	76
6. 30	.2	52	72.5	60
7. 30	.2	52	72.5	60
8. 29	.1	51	60	58
9. 29	.1	51	60	58
10. 29	.1	51	60	58
11. 28	0	50	47.5	56
12. 28	0	50	47.5	56
13. 24	− .3	47	40	48
14. 23	− .4	46	35	46
15. 21	− .6	44	30	42
16. 20	− .6	44	25	40
17. 15	− 1	40	20	30
18. 10	− 1.5	35	12.5	20
19. 10	− 1.5	35	12.5	20
20. 9	− 1.6	34	5	18
Sum = 549	Mean = 27.45		SD = 11 .53	

Now translate the raw scores on the geology test into z-scores and check your results in Exhibit A.10.

Geology Test Scores

Students	Raw Scores	Students	Raw Scores
1.	50	11.	28
2.	45	12.	28
3.	42	13.	24
4.	39	14.	23
5.	38	15.	21
6.	30	16.	20
7.	30	17.	15
8.	29	18.	10
9.	29	19.	10
10.	29	20.	9

Translating z-Scores to T-Scores

$$T = 10 \left(\frac{x - \bar{x}}{SD} \right) + 50$$

Drama Test (maximum score 30)

	Raw Scores	z-Scores	T-Scores		
1.	25	1.0	60	Step 1.	List the raw scores in any order, but list each score.
2.	25	1.0	60		
3.	24	.9	59		
4.	23	.7	57		
5.	22	.5	55	Step 2.	Translate the raw scores to z-scores.
6.	22	.5	55		
7.	22	.5	55		
8.	21	.3	53		
9.	20	.1	51	Step 3.	Multiply the z-score by 10. (.5)10 = 5.
10.	18	− .2	48		
11.	18	− .2	48		
12.	18	− .2	48	Step 4.	Add 50 to the score derived in Step 3. 5 + 50 = 55.
13.	15	− .8	42		
14.	9	−1.8	32		
15.	6	−2.4	26		

Conclusion: The z-score .5 is equal to the T-score 55.

Step 5. Repeat the process for each z-score.

Now, translate the z-

Step 5 (continued): scores on the geology test into T-scores and check your results in Exhibit A.10.

Geology Test Scores

Students	Raw Scores	Students	Raw Scores
1.	50	11.	28
2.	45	12.	28
3.	42	13.	24
4.	39	14.	23
5.	38	15.	21
6.	30	16.	20
7.	30	17.	15
8.	29	18.	10
9.	29	19.	10
10.	29	20.	9

Percentile. Two other ways of reporting scores are percentages and percentiles. The two are different but often confused. The percentile tells how a student scored in relation to other students, and so it is used to report NRT results. The percentile (%ile) is not as useful as z- and T-scores for describing a student's position in a distribution, because the mean and standard deviation are not used to calculate it. Percentiles are determined in two ways. Sometimes, they are determined by rank ordering the students and finding out what percentage of the total number of students scored the same as, or lower than, the student in whom you are interested.

Rounded percentiles can be obtained by segmenting the entire range of scores into 100 slices. In the example of the history test (Exhibit A.8), there are 18 scores, so each slice covers .18 of a score (18/100 = .18) and each score has 5.6 slices in it. Because the top score of 20 is at the hundredth percentile, the next score (17) has a rounded percentile of 94 (100/5.6 = 94.4) and the next score of 16 has a rounded percentile of 89 (94.4/5.6 = 88.8).

Translating the Scores to Percentiles

Drama Test (maximum score 30)

	Raw score	Percentile	Percentile score	Rounded percentile
1.	25	100	96.7	97
2.	25	93.3	96.7	97
3.	24	86.6	86.6	87
4.	23	79.9	79.9	80
5.	22	73.2	66.5	67
6.	22	73.2	66.5	67
7.	22	73.2	66.5	67
8.	21	53.1	53.1	53
9.	20	46.4	46.4	46
10.	18	39.7	33	33
11.	18	39.7	33	33
12.	18	39.7	33	33
13.	15	19.6	19.6	20
14.	9	12.9	12.9	13
15.	6	6.2	6.2	6

Step 1. List the scores in order from largest to smallest. List all scores.

Step 2. Divide 100 by the number of scores. 100/15 = 6.67.

Step 3. Round off the number in Step 2 to one decimal. 6.67 = 6.7.

Step 4. Assign a value of 100 to the first score on the list. The first 25 score would have a value of 100.

Step 5. Subtract the number obtained in Step 3 from 100 and assign it to the second number on the list.

Score	Percentile
25	100
25	93.3
24	86.6

Continue subtracting down the entire list.

Step 6. When several scores are the same, average their percentiles together. The result is rounded to the nearest tenth and becomes the percentile score. For example, since the first two raw scores are 25, their percentiles (100 + 93.3) are averaged to 96.7. This becomes the percentile score.

Score	Percentile	Percentile score
25	100	96.7
25	93.3	96.7

Step 7.   Round off the percentile score from Step 6.

Score	Percentile	Percentile score	Rounded percentile
25	100	96.7	97
25	93.3	96.7	97

Conclusion: A student who scored 25 on the drama test is at the 97th percentile.

Now translate the raw scores on the geology test into percentiles and check your results in Exhibit A.10.

Geology Test Scores

Students	Raw Scores	Students	Raw Scores
1.	50	11.	28
2.	45	12.	28
3.	42	13.	24
4.	39	14.	23
5.	38	15.	21
6.	30	16.	20
7.	30	17.	15
8.	29	18.	10
9.	29	19.	10
10.	29	20.	9

Grade Equivalence Scores

Anyone who has ever listened to the reading of two students who both scored at the same grade level on a reading test is probably already suspicious of the term *grade level.* Most kids are in the grade they are in because of age, not specific skills. And age may have little or nothing to do with skill acquisition. Therefore, it seems ridiculous to use a term such as grade level to describe a student's academic skills. But it is done all the time.

Grade level is a normative idea based on the average performance of various sample populations. As they are currently determined and *scaled*, grade equivalence scores can only be used for normative comparison. The application of these is limited by the sample on which they are based; the other limitations inherent in all normative comparisons, and the imposition of a 10-month fixed scale of growth.

If Bridget scores at the sixth-grade level on a test, then she is scoring at the 50th percentile of the sixth-graders in the original sample. (Outlandish as it may sound, it is possible that none of the students in that sample could do a sixth-grade assignment, because the NRT scores tell us nothing about a stu-

Exhibit A.11   Grade-Level Scores

	Todd	Nancy
ate	x	x
they	x	-
house	-	x
originally	x	-
interpretation	-	x
nevertheless	-	-
	3	3

"They originally ate at the cafe."

dent's actual functioning.) Those sixth-graders and Bridget may have nothing else in common at all. Perhaps the greatest injustice done to remedial students is to treat them as if they were in the grade to which their grade equivalent scores correspond. A ninth-grade student who scores at the first-grade level doesn't learn like a first-grader, care about what first-graders care about, or even read in the same way.

Here is an oversimplified example (Exhibit A.11). Suppose the following list of words make up a reading test. Each word is given a score of one point. Todd and Nancy take the test and the teacher records the words they get wrong with an X. The average score for a first-graders is 1, second-grader 2, and so forth. In this case both Todd and Nancy would be considered third-grade readers because they both got a score of three. Armed with this knowledge their teacher might then place them in a third-grade book containing the sentence "They originally ate at the cafe." As you can see from the original test results in Exhibit A.11, even with the same test score, Todd and Nancy would read the sentence differently.

Another problem with grade equivalent scores is the matter of *scales*. Learning does not necessarily occur as an equal-interval scale, although grade equivalent scores treat it as if it does. The amount of math a student learns between the second grade and the third grade is not the same amount as she learns between the eleventh and twelfth grades. Similarly, the third-grade reading level is not half as difficult as the sixth-grade reading level. In fact, for some basic reading and math skills, the student is not exposed to any really new material after about the fourth grade, making the amount of decoding and computation covered each year progressively less. Because of this, saying a student decodes at the tenth-grade level in reading is like saying that a student is at the second-grade level in high school economics. It doesn't make sense because high-school economics isn't even taught in the second grade. Yet many popular achievement tests provide norms for primary content all the way into high school.

A final problem with grade equivalence scores is the way they are presented by test publishers. Many tests that are designed for and normed on students of a limited age span report grade equivalences higher or lower than the norming sample. In other words, a test designed for use on students in grades 6, 7, 8, and 9 may only be normed on students in those grades. Yet, the test manuals may report grade equivalence scores for the test which range from first to twelfth grade. Those equivalence scores that are not based on actual norms are projected through a process called *interpolation*, which is not the same as norming. The frequency with which grade equivalence scores are used to pick programs for students or to evaluate programming is probably due to their apparent simplicity. It is definitely not due to their validity.

Criterion-Referenced Test Scores

Criterion-referenced tests/observations are used to determine a student's performance relative to a behavioral standard, or criterion for acceptable performance.

Designing CRTs involves two steps. First, a behavioral objective is written, including a statement of the behavior that the students will use to indicate their learning and by what criterion they will use it. Second, the materials necessary for the student to exhibit the behavior are assembled. The criterion given in the objective is the behavioral standard that will be used to make decisions about the status of the student. We call that standard *CAP* (criterion for acceptable performance).

Because the criterion-referenced probe is based upon a behavioral objective, the raw score on the test can be read as a behavioral statement. As long as the conditions and behavior specified in the objective are relevant, the raw score does not require conversion or translation to be meaningful. For example, if an objective says "Given a sheet of mixed addition and subtraction facts (0–20), the student will write the answers at a rate of 40 correct with 0 errors" and the student writes 20 problems, then the raw score of 20 is all that is needed to see that she has not reached the criterion. As long as the teacher knows that writing answers is relevant and that the criterion (40 correct, 0 errors) is relevant, the raw score is relevant.

The meaning of a normative standard is based on the power of the argument that students should behave like other students. The meaning of a behavioral standard must be based on the power of evidence showing that it is relevant and functional. The teacher's belief in the criterion must be supported by more than personal opinion (see Chapter 6). The criteria statements found in objectives typically specify either levels of rate or accuracy.

The percentage score is one way to report a student's accuracy. A percentage is the obtained score, divided by the total possible score. In Exhibit A.9, Ed scored 8 out of 25 points on his history test, so he was accurate on 32% of the items and wrong on 68% of them ($8/25 = .32(100) = 32\%$).

Computing Percentages

Drama Test (maximum score 30)

Raw Score	Percentage		
1. 25	83	Step 1.	List the raw scores.
2. 25	83	Step 2.	Divide each raw score
3. 24	80		by the total possible
4. 23	77		score. $25/30 = .83 =$
5. 22	73		83%.
6. 22	73		Conclusion: A student
7. 22	73		who scores 25 out of
8. 21	70		30 has received 83%.
9. 20	67		
10. 18	60		
11. 18	60		
12. 18	60		
13. 15	50		
14. 9	30		
15. 6	20		

Now translate the raw scores on the geology test into percentages and check your results in Exhibit A.10.

Geology Test Scores

Students   Raw Scores

1.	50
2.	45
3.	42
4.	39
5.	38
6.	30
7.	30
8.	29
9.	29
10.	29
11.	28
12.	28
13.	24
14.	23
15.	21
16.	20
17.	15
18.	10
19.	10
20.	9

Rate data is used to summarize accuracy and fluency. Rate was discussed in some detail in Chapter 6. It is an important, although often ignored, dimension of proficiency. Rate is defined as behavior divided by time. To calculate rate, count the behavior and then divide it by the number of minutes during which the behavior occurred. For example, if Nancy reads 25 pages in one hour, her rate is $25/60 = .42$ pages per minute. It is customary to use minutes, regardless of the measurement interval, when calculating rate. This convention allows for behaviors counted during different intervals to be reduced to a standard matrix. Therefore, a 1-hour timing becomes 60 minutes and a 30-second timing becomes .5 minutes.

By counting the number correct and the number incorrect, you capture both the fluency and the accuracy of a student's work. If Nancy does 17 addition problems correctly and 5 incorrectly in 30 seconds, her rates are $17/.5 = 34$ per minute correct and $5/.5 = 10$ per minute incorrect.

Summarizing Results

Discrepancies

The original model of evaluation was $S \underset{D}{\overset{\longleftrightarrow}{}} B$. The previous discussions of scores and standards have dealt with the derivation of the B (the behavior) and the S (the standard). Ultimately, however, the essence of evaluation is the comparison of the standard and behavior to find a discrepancy. In order to be useful in decision making, a summary should supply information about both the direction and magnitude of the discrepancy. This helps us judge its significance. It is the magnitude of the discrepancy (how far from the standard one is) and its direction from the standard (above or below it) that determines the decisions we make. For example, if the standard for reading is the class average of 50 and a student (Tom) scored 45, we know the direction of his discrepancy is down (negative) and the magnitude is 5.

CRT Discrepancies.   Raw scores on normed tests take on different meanings according to the norming populations to which they are compared. Similarly, the differences in criteria found in objectives make the raw scores on criterion-referenced tests take on different meanings. While the raw score on a CRT does represent a defined unit of behavior, the implications that score has for decision making are not always clear. To determine educational significance a teacher must ask "How much teaching is needed to remove the discrepancy?"

The discrepancy between actual and expected behavior is what we are supposed to correct through teaching. A small discrepancy signals the need for a small change in behavior, and therefore less teaching, than a large discrepancy.

Criterion-referenced probes are designed to describe accurately the student's behavior relevant to task-specific standards (as opposed to norms). The discrepancy between the standard and the student's performance can be described in absolute or ratio terms. An *absolute discrepancy* is determined by subtracting the smaller of the two numbers from the larger.

Standard		Performance		Absolute discrepancy
75	−	60	=	−15

Performance		Standard		Absolute discrepancy
75	−	60	=	+15

Exhibit A.12   Discrepancy Ratios for Several Behaviors

Summary of Alvin's Current Level of Performance						
	Decoding CVC + e words	Math Facts 0–9 +	−	×	÷	Talks Out In Class
CAP	70	50	50	50	50	.03
Student performance	35	50	45	32	27	.2
Absolute discrepancy	+35	0	+ 5	+18	+23	− .17
Discrepancy ratio	× 2	× 1	× 1.1	× 1.6	× 1.9	÷6.7

A *ratio discrepancy* is determined by dividing the larger of the two by the smaller. For decision making, ratio discrepancies are superior to absolute ones.

Standard		Performance		Ratio discrepancy
75	/	60	=	×1.25
Performance		Standard		Ratio discrepancy
75	/	60	=	÷1.25

Discrepancy ratios (Deno & Mirkin, 1977) are a good way to summarize the current performance (or progress) of a student in different areas so priorities for instruction can be set. The discrepancy ratio is the criterion-reference equivalent of a standard score (z-score, *T*-score, percentile). It allows you to compare the student's behavior on different objectives in order to decide in which she needs the most help.

The steps to determine the ratio are simple:

1. Establish the standard.
2. Measure the performance.
3. Divide the larger of the two by the smaller to find the magnitude.
4. Indicate the direction of the discrepancy: "×" meaning the behavior must increase; "÷" meaning it must decrease.

The standard is CAP. Performance is the student's current functioning as determined through direct observation or testing.

Exhibit A.12 shows Alvin's performance and CAP for several skills. The discrepancy ratio has been calculated for each of these skills. Alvin is farthest behind in "talks out" because the magnitude of the discrepancy for that behavior shows that he needs to alter his behavior by a factor of 6.7.

The direction of change needed to remove the discrepancy is placed in front of the number. For a behavior you wish to *increase*, the ratio should be preceded by a plus sign (+) or times sign (×). For a behavior you want to *decrease*, the ratio is preceded by a subtract sign (−) or divide sign (÷). The times sign means the current performance must be increased by the proportion shown in order to rectify the discrepancy. In Exhibit A.12, Alvin's CVC + *e* behavior is currently 35 words per minute. If it increases (is multiplied) by a factor of 2, it will be at 70 and there will be no discrepancy. Ralph's "talks out" behavior occurs .2 times per minute (an average of once every 5 minutes). The average level of talking out in his class is .03 times per minute. His talks-out behavior must decrease (divide) by a factor of 6.7 in order to meet the standard. Therefore it is labeled ÷ 6.7.

Appendix B / Teaching Actions From TIES/ Cross-Reference to Chapter 8

1. Descriptors of TIES Components (Ysseldyke & Christenson, 1987)

TIES Descriptors for Component 1

Instructional Presentation

Instructional Presentation, a primary component of effective instruction, includes factors related to lesson development, clarity of directions, and checking for student understanding. *Lesson Development* refers to the presence of an adequate overview; the manner in which the lesson is explained, structured, and sequenced; the variety and richness of teaching examples; the clarity with which the lesson content is presented; the adequacy of guided practice opportunities and degree of teacher-student interaction; the kind of feedback used; and the appropriateness of task directions; kind and amount of examples used; and degree to which task directions are repeated. *Checking for Student Understanding* refers to the method used to check the student's understanding, the timing of the checking, the degree to which cues and prompts (error correction procedures) are used to promote accurate responses, and the way in which the teacher interprets student inattentiveness. Refer to Appendix B.2 for a listing of the *TIES* indicators that define effective teaching for this component.

TIES Descriptors for Component 2

Classroom Environment

An effective classroom environment is influenced by the extent to which classroom management procedures reduce disciplinary concerns; the extent to which instructional routines maximize productive use of time in the classroom; and the affective tone or climate in the classroom. *Classroom Management* refers to the kind of rules established to maintain appropriate behavior; how the rules are communicated; the system word to maintain appropriate behavior; and the emphasis placed on student

accountability. *Productive Time-Use* refers to the extent to which noninstructional routines are established and class time is used to increase academic activities. *Class Climate* refers to the extent to which the classroom atmosphere is characterized by cooperation, a pleasant atmosphere, and acceptance of individual differences. Refer to Appendix B.2 for a listing of the *TIES* indicators that define effective teaching for this component.

TIES Descriptors for Component 3

Teacher Expectations

Establishing high, yet realistic, expectations for student performance, including task completion, quality of work, and use of time in the classroom, is an important characteristic of effective instruction. *Teacher Expectations* refers to the kind of expectations set for student performance; the communication of the expectations; and the extent to which the student understands the expectations. Refer to Appendix B.2 for a listing of the *TIES* indicators that define effective teaching for this component.

TIES Descriptors for Component 4

Cognitive Emphasis

Effective instruction emphasizes the development of thinking skills. *Cognitive Emphasis* refers to the extent to which varied lessons are planned for the purpose of teaching recall, reasoning, evaluating, and application skills; the extent to which thinking skills necessary to accurately complete a task or master a skill are modeled for the student; and the extent to which learning strategies are directly taught. Refer to Appendix B.2 for a listing of the *TIES* indicators that define effective teaching for this component.

TIES Descriptors for Component 5

Motivational Strategies

Encouraging student motivation is an important component of effective instruction. Teachers understand the importance of motivation for learning and consequently use varied techniques to increase student motivation. *Motivational Strategies* refers to the enthusiasm with which the lesson is presented; the extent to which the lesson is interesting and varied; the kind of motivational strategy (extrinsic vs. intrinsic orientation) used; and the student's sense of self-efficacy. Refer to Appendix B.2 for a listing of the *TIES* indicators that define effective teaching for this component.

TIES Descriptors for Component 6

Relevant Practice

Students spend approximately 70% of their school day engaged in seatwork practice activities. In order for this time to be effective in promoting positive academic outcomes for a student, the student must engage in relevant practice. Relevant Practice includes the amount of practice opportunity on relevant tasks with appropriate instructional materials. *Practice Opportunity* refers to the amount and kind of practice. *Task Relevance* refers to the extent to which the practice activities are related to the lesson presented and are important for attaining the instructional goal in addition to the student's success rate. *Instructional Material* refers to the academic and affective appropriateness of the assigned materials for the target student to attain the instructional goal. Refer to Appendix B.2 for a listing of the *TIES* indicators that define effective teaching for this component.

TIES Descriptors for Component 7

Academic Engaged Time

In order to achieve optimally, students must be engaged and actively involved in completing academic tasks and responding to oral and written questions. Both the amount of opportunity to engage in academic work and the rate of student engaged time during completion of the work influence achievement levels. *Student Involvement* refers to the opportunities the student has to respond and the extent to which the student actively participates in academic activities. Contextual factors may influence student involvement. *Maintenance of Student Engagement* refers to the extent to which varied teacher behaviors or systems are used to facilitate time on task. Refer to Appendix B.2 for a listing of the *TIES* indicators that define effective teaching for this component.

TIES Descriptors for Component 8

Informed Feedback

Informed Feedback includes feedback and alternative, corrective procedures. The provision of specific, informative feedback and corrective procedures is a necessary step in successfully instructing students. *Feedback* refers to several characteristics of effective feedback, the type of feedback, and the student's understanding of the feedback. *Corrective Procedures* refers to the kind of alternative teaching strategies employed, the amount of supervised practice and monitoring provided, and the extent to which student accountability is stressed. Refer to Appendix B.2 for a listing of the *TIES* indicators that define effective teaching for this component.

TIES Descriptors for Component 9

Adaptive Instruction

Instruction needs to be modified to accommodate individual needs and differences. *Adaptive Instruction* refers to the extent to which there is a systematic effort to modify instruction, the options available for modifying instruction, and the degree to which the effectiveness of the modifications is communicated to the student. Refer to Appendix B.2 for a listing of the *TIES* indicators that define effective teaching for this component.

TIES Descriptors for Component 10

Progress Evaluation

Effective instruction includes continuous monitoring and systematic follow-up planning for a student. *Monitoring Student Progress* refers to the kind of student performance data collected, the frequency with which the student's performance is monitored, and the system used for record keeping and communicating to the student. Contextual factors may influence the amount of monitoring for an individual student. *Follow-Up Planning* refers to the basis for making subsequent instructional decisions for a student and the extent to which reviews are planned systematically. Refer to Appendix B.2 for a listing of the *TIES* indicators that define effective teaching for this component.

TIES Descriptors for Component 11

Instructional Planning

Systematic Instructional Planning includes two functions: diagnosis and prescription. *Instructional Diagno-sis* refers to the extent to which student characteristics (e.g., skill level, motivation), task characteristics (e.g., sequence, cognitive demands) and classroom characteristics (e.g., instructional groupings, materials) have been accurately assessed. *Instructional Prescription* refers to the match between the student's instructional needs and instruction delivered. Student success rate and amount of content covered characterize the degree of task appropriateness for a student. Several factors influence the extent to which instructional planning is optimal for a student's academic progress. Refer to Appendix B.2 for a listing of the *TIES* indicators that define effective teaching for this component.

TIES Descriptors for Component 12

Student Understanding

Student Understanding refers to the accuracy with which the student understands the instructional goal and interprets task directions and the processes needed to complete the assignment. Refer to Appendix B.2 for a listing of the *TIES* indicators that define effective teaching for this component.

2.   Cross-Reference of TIES Indicators of Effective Instruction to Teacher Actions in Exhibit 8.1

Exhibit B.2.1   Prepare for Instruction

TIES Reference		Indicators of Effective Preparation
Component 2, Classroom Management, Item 1	1.	A small number of important rules (e.g., talking, out of seat) are selected and reinforced.
Component 2, Classroom Management, Item 2	2.	Expected behavior in the classroom is communicated through discussion of rules and routines.
Component 2, Classroom Management, Item 3	3.	Behavior that will and will not be tolerated is clearly communicated to the student.
Component 2, Classroom Management, Item 4	4.	Both examples and nonexamples of rules and procedures are used.
Component 2, Classroom Management, Item 5	5.	Classroom rules and routines are introduced at the beginning of the year.
Component 2, Classroom Management, Item 15	6.	There is a system to involve the student in the management of his or her behavior.
Component 2, Productive Time Use, Item 1	7.	The instructional routines for time use, nonacademic class business (e.g., bathroom breaks) are understood and followed.
Component 2, Productive Time Use, Item 2	8.	The physical space of the classroom is well-organized.
Component 2, Productive Time Use, Item 3	9.	The student has easy access to high-use materials and supplies.
Component 2, Productive Time Use, Item 4	10.	The student knows what to do when finished with assigned work.
Component 2, Productive Time Use, Item 5	11.	The student knows how to get help when needed.
Component 2, Productive Time Use, Item 6	12.	There is a sufficient amount of time allocated to instruction in the content area.
Component 2, Productive Time Use, Item 7	13.	There is a task-oriented, academic focus in the classroom.
Component 2, Productive Time Use, Item 8	14.	The lessons, including necessary materials and teaching aids, are prepared in advance.
Component 2, Productive Time Use, Item 11	15.	Lessons begin and end on time.
Component 2, Productive Time Use, Item 12	16.	Transitions are short and brief.
Component 2, Productive Time Use, Item 13	17.	The student is given a warning for transitions between lessons.
Component 2, Productive Time Use, Item 14	18.	Disruptions or interruptions are infrequent and held to a minimum.

Exhibit B.2.1, *continued*

TIES Reference	Indicators of Effective Preparation
Component 2, Productive Time Use, Item 15	19. Expectations about use of class time are communicated clearly to the student.
Component 2, Class Climate, Item 1	20. The classroom is a pleasant, friendly, happy environment (one in which the student is not obviously uncomfortable).
Component 2, Class Climate, Item 2	21. The classroom is supportive and accepting of individual differences.
Component 2, Class Climate, Item 4	22. The student's opinions and concerns about the classroom are encouraged and valued.
Component 2, Class Climate, Item 5	23. The classroom is characterized by a cooperative rather than a competitive atmosphere.
Component 2, Class Climate, Item 7	24. The student is expected to respond and participate in the classroom.
Component 3, Teacher Expectations, Item 9	25. The student understands the teacher's expectations for neatness.
Component 3, Teacher Expectations, Item 10	26. The student understands the teacher's expectations for accuracy.
Component 5, Motivational Strategies, Item 12	27. The student believes he or she can do the assignment.
Component 5, Motivational Strategies, Item 13	28. Lesson content is relevant to the interests and background of the student (i.e., highlights student's personal experience).
Component 5, Motivational Strategies, Item 14	29. Tasks are at the student's appropriate instructional level.
Component 5, Motivational Strategies, Item 15	30. Student-teacher interactions are positive, encouraging, and emphasize the importance of student effort.
Component 6, Practice Opportunity, Item 5	31. There is an established system for the student to get help when needed.
Component 6, Task Relevance, Item 1	32. The instructional scope and sequence is specified clearly.
Component 6, Task Relevance, Item 4	33. Practice activities are related directly to the student's instructional goal.
Component 7, Student Involvement, Item 10	34. The student is expected to be an active and involved learner.
Component 7, Student Involvement, Item 12	35. Class size does not interfere with the amount of oral student responses needed for student progress.
Component 7, Student Involvement, Item 13	36. Class composition does not interfere with the amount of teacher-student interaction needed for the student.
Component 7, Maintenance of Student Engagement, Item 11	37. There is a system or procedure for the student to follow if he or she finishes early.
Component 7, Maintenance of Student Engagement, Item 12	38. Alternative academic options for the unengaged student exist.
Component 8, Feedback, Item 11	39. An appropriate rationale for the kind of feedback provided the student is present.
Component 8, Adaptive Instruction, Item 1	40. There is a systematic effort to adapt instruction so that the student can experience success.

Exhibit B.2.1, *continued*

TIES Reference	Indicators of Effective Preparation
Component 9, Adaptive Instruction, Item 2	41. The teacher is knowledgeable about different instructional modifications for teaching the student.
Component 9, Adaptive Instruction, Item 3	42. The teacher is knowledgeable about many ways for dealing with student behavior or affective concerns.
Component 9, Adaptive Instruction, Item 4	43. Varied options for modifying the curriculum are available.
Component 9, Adaptive Instruction, Item 5	44. The teacher is willing to use alternative methods, materials, or goals for the student.
Component 10, Follow-Up Planning, Item 1	45. Predetermined criteria for mastery for the student exists.
Component 10, Follow-Up Planning, Item 2	46. Student performance data are used regularly to make instructional decisions for the student.
Component 10, Follow-Up on Planning, Item 3	47. Progress through the curriculum depends on mastery of instructional objective.
Component 10, Follow-Up Planning, Item 4	48. Review and maintenance activities are planned systematically (daily, weekly, monthly).
Component 10, Follow-Up Planning, Item 8	49. The student is held accountable for the quality of his or her work and use of class time.
Component 11, Instructional Diagnosis, Item 6	50. There is a logical sequence to instruction.
Component 11, Instructional Diagnosis, Item 7	51. The steps involved in completing the classroom task are identified accurately through task analysis or similar procedures.
Component 11, Instructional Diagnosis, Item 8	52. Prerequisite skills needed to perform the task have been considered and accurately identified.
Component 11, Instructional Diagnosis, Item 10	53. Contextual variables (e.g., instructional groupings, interactions with other students, availability of materials, and kinds of tasks) have been considered.
Component 11, Instructional Prescription, Item 1	54. The student's instructional needs (e.g., strengths, weakness, skill level, prior learning) are considered when assigning tasks.
Component 11, Instructional Prescription, Item 2	55. Appropriate instructional goals/objectives are established on the basis of the student's instructional needs.
Component 11, Instructional Prescription, Item 3	56. The instructional process is guided by the objective or goal to be achieved rather than workbook pages to be completed.
Component 11, Instructional Prescription, Item 4	57. The priority of each goal/objective is determined.
Component 11, Instructional Prescription, Item 5	58. The instructional sequence for achieving the goals/objectives is planned.
Component 11, Instructional Prescription, Item 6	59. Instructional goals/objectives for the student are specific and described in measurable ways.
Component 11, Instructional Prescription, Item 7	60. Appropriate standards are established for satisfactory performance. Or it is clear how the student is to demonstrate mastery of the goal/objective.
Component 11, Instructional Prescription, Item 8	61. There is flexibility in choosing instructional materials/methods for the student.

Exhibit B.2.1, continued

TIES Reference	Indicators of Effective Preparation
Component 11, Instructional Prescription, Item 9	62. Instructional planning is not limited by strict adherence to district curriculum objectives or textbooks/materials.
Component 11, Instructional Prescription, Item 10	63. The student's interest or preference for learning materials is considered in planning instruction.
Component 11, Instructional Prescription, Item 11	64. There is flexible use of grouping structures to accommodate the student's instructional needs.
Component 11, Instructional Prescription, Item 12	65. Assignments are appropriately paced by the teacher.
Component 11, Instructional Prescription, Item 13	66. Different lessons are planned to accomplish varied goals (e.g., instruct, practice, generalize, review).
Component 11, Instructional Prescription, Item 16	67. The student's success rate on assigned tasks is predicted with reasonable accuracy (e.g., 75 to 90%).
Component 11, Instructional Prescription, Item 18	68. Potential problems or difficulties for the student on assigned tasks are anticipated by the teacher.

Exhibit B.2.2   Deliver Information

TIES Reference	Indicators of Effective Delivery
Component 1, Lesson Development, Item 1	1. Prerequisite skills, previous lessons, or prior knowledge are reviewed prior to teaching new content.
Component 1, Lesson Development, Item 2	2. Background information is provided to assist student understanding and interest and is relevant to the student's experience.
Component 1, Lesson Development, Item 3	3. An overview of lessons (what is to be learned, how it is to be learned, why it is important) is provided.
Component 1, Lesson Development, Item 4	4. The student's attention is focused during lesson presentation.
Component 1, Lesson Development, Item 5	5. The student's attention is maintained during lesson presentation.
Component 1, Lesson Development, Item 6	6. Modeling and teacher demonstration are used when appropriate to skills/content being taught.
Component 1, Lesson Development, Item 7	7. Concrete examples are used in the instructional lesson.
Component 1, Lesson Development, Item 8	8. There is a high degree of teacher-directed instruction on skills/content being presented.
Component 1, Lesson Development, Item 9	9. The necessary parts or distinctive features of new skills/concepts are specified clearly by the teacher.
Component 1, Lesson Development, Item 10	10. A sufficient amount of detail/information is provided in the instructional presentation.
Component 1, Lesson Development, Item 11	11. The key terms/ideas to be learned are clearly and directly taught.

Exhibit B.2.2, continued

TIES Reference	Indicators of Effective Delivery
Component 1, Lesson Development, Item 12	12. The lesson explanation is presented in an organized, step-by-step manner.
Component 1, Lesson Development, Item 13	13. A variety of teaching materials and strategies are used to explain the skill/content.
Component 1, Lesson Development, Item 18	14. The instructional pace is appropriate for the student's skill level and attention span.
Component 1, Clarity of Directions, Item 1	15. The student's attention is gained before task directions are given.
Component 1, Clarity of Directions, Item 2	16. Procedures for completing the task are specified clearly.
Component 1, Clarity of Directions, Item 3	17. Task directions are logically sequenced.
Component 1, Clarity of Directions, Item 4	18. The appropriate number of directions are given at one time.
Component 1, Clarity of Directions, Item 5	19. Directions are of a reasonable and appropriate length.
Component 1, Clarity of Directions, Item 6	20. Vocabulary in the directions is understood by or clarified for the student.
Component 1, Clarity of Directions, Item 7	21. Directions are given in both an oral and a written format.
Component 1, Clarity of Directions, Item 8	22. Example of the steps the student must follow is provided through modeling.
Component 2, Classroom Management, Item 6	23. The teacher continuously keeps good eye contact on the student.
Component 2, Classroom Management, Item 10	24. Reminders about expected behavior are given in advance of an activity (e.g., transition, field trip, assembly).
Component 2, Productive Time Use, Item 9	25. The pace of instructional lessons is brisk, well-organized, and directed by the teacher.
Component 2, Productive Time Use, Item 10	26. Directions are clear, simple, sequential, and often written on the board.
Component 3, Teacher Expectations, Item 3	27. The student understands the consequences of not achieving the expected standards of performance.
Component 3, Teacher Expectations, Item 4	28. Objectives or goals for the instructional lesson are communicated clearly.
Component 3, Teacher Expectations, Item 5	29. Desired or expected standards of performance are communicated clearly.
Component 3, Teacher Expectations, Item 8	30. The student understands the teacher's expectations for task completion.
Component 4, Cognitive Emphasis, Item 1	31. The lesson purpose is clear and understandable to the student.
Component 4, Cognitive Emphasis, Item 2	32. Steps for mastering an objective are specified clearly.

Exhibit B.2.2, continued

TIES Reference	Indicators of Effective Delivery
Component 4, Cognitive Emphasis, Item 3	33. The lesson purpose is identified in terms of thinking skills (e.g., memorizing, reasoning, concluding, evaluating) required for completion.
Component 4, Cognitive Emphasis, Item 4	34. Lesson explanation emphasizes a step-by-step description of the process to follow to solve the problem.
Component 4, Cognitive Emphasis, Item 5	35. The teacher models how to think through the steps involved in solving the problem (e.g., the mental operations involved).
Component 4, Cognitive Emphasis, Item 8	36. Appropriate learning strategies (e.g., how to memorize, how to study) are taught.
Component 5, Motivational Strategies, Item 1	37. The lesson is presented with enthusiasm.
Component 5, Motivational Strategies, Item 2	38. Teacher interest for the lesson content is communicated clearly.
Component 5, Motivational Strategies, Item 3	39. The instructional routine or presentation is varied.
Component 5, Motivational Strategies, Item 6	40. The rationale for the lesson is communicated and reinforced for the student.
Component 5, Motivational Strategies, Item 7	41. The value of learning is emphasized in addition to task completion.
Component 7, Maintenance of Student Engagement, Item 1	42. The student's attention is gained or focused during instruction.
Component 7, Maintenance Student Engagement, Item 2	43. The student's attention is maintained during instruction.
Component 9, Adaptive Instruction, Item 11	44. The student is informed of his or her instructional needs.
Component 10, Monitoring Student Progress, Item 11	45. The student understands both his or her current level of performance and the desired level of performance (e.g., instructional goal).
Component 10, Follow-Up Planning, Item 4	46. Review of content/skills is provided.
Component 10, Follow-Up Planning, Item 6	47. A sufficient amount of review for the student is provided.

Exhibit B.2.3 Ask Questions

TIES Reference	Indicators of Effective Questioning
Component 1, Lesson Development, Item 15	1. Various cuing and prompting techniques are used to elicit accurate responses from the student.
Component 1, Checking for Student Understanding, Item 1	2. Questions are frequently asked to check or test student understanding.
Component 1, Checking for Student Understanding, Item 2	3. The student is asked to demonstrate his or her understanding by explaining the process used to solve problems.

Exhibit B.2.3, continued

TIES Reference	Indicators of Effective Questioning
Component 2, Class Climate, Item 8	4. Cues and prompts are used to assist accuracy and frequency of the student's responses.
Component 3, Teacher Expectations, Item 1	5. The student is called on in the room and expected to answer (i.e., prompts and cues are provided to assist the student's responses).
Component 4, Cognitive Emphasis, Item 6	6. The student is asked to explain the process involved in solving problems or completing the work.
Component 7, Maintenance of Student Engagement, Item 7	7. Varied questioning techniques to engage the student are used.
Component 10, Monitoring Student Progress, Item 5	8. The teacher frequently asks the student questions to assess his or her understanding.
Component 10, Monitoring Student Progress, Item 14	9. Homework is checked, graded, and reviewed with the student.

Exhibit B.2.4   Respond to Efforts

TIES Reference	Indicators of Effective Responding
Component 1, Clarity of Directions, Item 9	1. Directions are repeated and stressed at difficult points.
Component 2, Classroom Management, Item 8	2. Noncompliance or disruptive behavior is handled immediately.
Component 2, Classroom Management, Item 9	3. Inappropriate behavior is used as an opportunity to reteach or reinforce behavioral expectations.
Component 2, Classroom Management, Item 11	4. Nonverbal signals are used to redirect the student while teaching other students.
Component 2, Classroom Management, Item 12	5. Praise is specific and administered contingently.
Component 5, Motivational Strategies, Item 8	6. Goal-setting techniques and procedures are used to direct student motivation and to provide feedback.
Component 5, Motivational Strategies, Item 9	7. Student involvement and choice are used in developing motivation and self-directedness (e.g., contingency contracting, opportunities for self-evaluation, self-monitoring, and charting).
Component 5, Motivational Strategies, Item 10	8. Reward systems and social reinforcers (external orientation) are effective.
Component 5, Motivational Strategies, Item 9	9. The student understands the consequences of not completing work accurately.
Component 6, Practice Opportunity, Item 4	10. Prompts, cues, or modeling (i.e., error correction procedures) are used rather than calling on another student to provide the answer.
Component 7, Student Involvement, Item 9	11. The teacher probes for correct responses from the student rather than moving on to another student or simply providing answers for the student.
Component 7, Maintenance of Student Engagement, Item 5	12. The student is directed to another activity when finished early but merely waiting.

Exhibit B.2.4, continued

TIES Reference	Indicators of Effective Responding
Component 7, Maintenance of Student Engagement, Item 8	13. The teacher circulates among students during seatwork assignments to check work and assist the target student.
Component 8, Feedback, Item 2	14. Feedback about performance is provided within a reasonable period of time (i.e., before beginning a new lesson).
Component 8, Feedback, Item 3	15. Feedback is provided about the student's behavior.
Component 8, Feedback, Item 4	16. Feedback informs the student about which answers are correct or incorrect.
Component 8, Feedback, Item 5	17. Feedback informs the student why answers are correct or incorrect.
Component 8, Feedback, Item 6	18. Feedback provides enough information for the student to make the necessary corrections.
Component 8, Feedback Item 7	19. Feedback if frequent enough to motivate the student and provide necessary corrections.
Component 8, Feedback, Item 8	20. Feedback is provided in a way that encourages the student to try again.
Component 8, Feedback, Item 9	21. Process feedback (i.e., prompts and cues to assist student response) rather than terminal feedback (i.e., answer given) is provided.
Component 8, Feedback, Item 10	22. Task-specific praise about the student's academic work is provided.
Component 8, Feedback, Item 12	23. The student knows which skills are mastered and which need additional review.
Component 8, Corrective Procedures, Item 1	24. Re-explanation is provided (not simply providing student with correct answer) when the student is confused or makes mistakes.
Component 8, Corrective Procedures, Item 2	25. Specific suggestions to correct student errors are provided.
Component 8, Corrective Procedures, Item 3	26. Varied alternative teaching methods to reteach and correct the student's confusion or mistakes are used.
Component 8, Corrective Procedures, Item 4	27. After correction of errors, the student has an immediate chance to practice the procedure or execute the task correctly.
Component 8, Corrective Procedures, Item 6	28. The student receives correction or assistance before errors are practiced over and over.
Component 8, Corrective Procedures, Item 7	29. Prompts and cues to increase the student's accuracy of response are used.
Component 8, Corrective Procedures, Item 9	30. The student is required to correct mistakes.
Component 9, Adaptive Instruction, Item 6	31. Different materials, alternative teaching strategies, increased practice opportunities, or alternative group placements are considered when a student fails to master an objective.
Component 9, Adaptive Instruction, Item 7	32. Lesson pace is adjusted to variations in the student's rate of mastery.
Component 9, Adaptive Instruction, Item 9	33. Tasks are modified until the student is no longer making errors or making only infrequent, careless mistakes.
Component 10, Follow-Up Planning, Item 7	34. Student errors trigger the need for corrective or adaptive instructional procedures.
Component 11, Instructional Prescription, Item 20	35. Tasks are modified as needed in order to ensure an appropriate success rate for the student.

Exhibit B.2.4, continued

TIES Reference	Indicators of Effective Responding
Component 12, Student Understanding, Item 9	36. The student is aware of his or her lack of understanding or confusion with the assigned work.
Component 12, Student Understanding, Item 10	37. The student knows specific strategies to employ himself or herself in completing the assigned work.

Exhibit B.2.5   Use Activities

TIES Reference	Indicators of Effective Activity Use
Component 1, Lesson Development, Item 14	1. Substantive teacher-student interaction (e.g., ask/answer questions, repeat directions, provide feedback) occurs.
Component 1, Lesson Development, Item 16	2. Guided practice opportunities are provided.
Component 1, Lesson Development, Item 17	3. Opportunities are provided for the student to explain the process or procedures.
Component 1, Clarity of Directions, Item 10	4. The student begins work after all directions have been provided.
Component 1, Checking for Student Understanding, Item 4	5. The student has had an opportunity to demonstrate his or her ability to perform the skill before beginning independent seatwork activities.
Component 1, Checking for Student Understanding, Item 9	6. The student understands how to get assistance when confused.
Component 3, Teacher Expectations, Item 2	7. The student is expected to be an active and involved learner.
Component 3, Teacher Expectations, Item 6	8. The teacher's expectations about use of time in the classroom are communicated clearly.
Component 4, Cognitive Emphasis, Item 7	9. The teacher asks the student to "think aloud" while working the problem in order to identify problem areas.
Component 5, Motivational Strategies, Item 4	10. Interesting and age-appropriate materials and assignments are used.
Component 5, Motivational Strategies, Item 5	11. Assignments are varied to heighten student interest.
Component 6, Practice Opportunity, Item 1	12. Sufficient opportunity for practice of skills/content exists.
Component 6, Practice Opportunity, Item 2	13. Practice opportunities are provided until the student makes only infrequent, careless mistakes.
Component 6, Practice Opportunity, Item 6	14. The student asks for assistance when needed.
Component 6, Practice Opportunity, Item 7	15. Homework is regularly assigned, checked and reviewed with the student.
Component 6, Practice Opportunity, Item 9	16. Assigned tasks are designed to include drill work, practice, generalization, and application opportunities.

Exhibit B.2.5, continued

TIES Reference	Indicators of Effective Activity Use
Component 6, Practice Opportunity, Item 10	17. Drill work and repeated practice are used to reinforce skills and build student accuracy.
Component 6, Practice Opportunity, Item 11	18. Speed work is provided to achieve automaticity of basic skills.
Component 6, Practice Opportunity, Item 12	19. Varied materials and different applications of the skill taught are used to assist generalization.
Component 6, Task Relevance, Item 4	20. Practice activities (assigned tasks) are at the appropriate instructional level for the student.
Component 6, Task Relevance, Item 5	21. Task directions contain sufficient detail so that the student understands what to do during practice.
Component 6, Task Relevance, Item 7	22. Practice activities are related directly to the lesson presentation explained and demonstrated by the teacher.
Component 6, Task Relevance, Item 8	23. Activities are important for student learning and, consequently, are not simply busy work.
Component 6, Task Relevance, Item 9	24. The student's engaged time is high during seatwork practice.
Component 6, Task Relevance, Item 11	25. The student is able to complete assigned tasks independently during practice. If so, the student's success rate is between 90 and 100%.
Component 6, Instructional Material, Item 3	26. Format of assigned materials is easy to understand, clear, and uncluttered.
Component 6, Instructional Material, Item 4	27. The student can read and understand written directions on the assigned materials.
Component 6, Instructional Material, Item 5	28. There is ample writing space for the student.
Component 6, Instructional Material, Item 6	29. The student is assigned the right amount of work.
Component 6, Instructional Material, Item 7	30. Varied instructional materials are used (e.g., workbook, tapes, films, peer interaction).
Component 6, Instructional Material, Item 8	31. Necessary modifications for successful completion of assignments are made (e.g., length reduced, concrete aids, cues provided).
Component 6, Instructional Material, Item 9	32. Materials are age-appropriate, interesting, and visually appealing.
Component 6, Instructional Material, Item 10	33. Instructional materials provide ample practice and reinforcement of skills to be mastered.
Component 6, Instructional Material, Item 13	34. Requirements for successful completion of independent assignments are at the appropriate level for the student (e.g., cognitive processing demands, number of steps/skills involved).
Component 7, Student Involvement, Item 7	35. Many opportunities for the student to respond exist.
Component 7, Student Involvement, Item 8	36. The student has an equal opportunity to respond when compared with classmates.
Component 7, Student Involvement, Item 15	37. Seatwork tasks promote active academic student responding (e.g., tutoring, peers, aides, computers).

Exhibit B.2.5, continued

TIES Reference	Indicators of Effective Activity Use
Component 8, Corrective Procedures, Item 5	38. Practice opportunities are provided until the student makes only infrequent, careless mistakes.
Component 10, Monitoring Student Progress, Item 12	39. Opportunities for the student to self-evaluate his or her work exist.
Component 10, Monitoring Student Progress, Item 13	40. Opportunities to review seatwork assignments are provided.
Component 11, Instructional Prescription, Item 16	41. The student's success rate on assigned tasks is carefully monitored. * Success rate is moderately high on new tasks (e.g., 70 to 85%). * Success rate is high on independent practice activities (e.g., 90 to 100%).
Component 11, Instructional Prescription, Item 17	42. The ratio of known material is appropriate (90 to 100% for independent work, 70 to 75% for instruction).
Component 12, Student Understanding, Item 5	43. The student demonstrates understanding of the task before beginning or within the first few minutes of independent practice opportunities.
Component 12, Student Understanding, Item 6	44. The student's success rate is moderately high (e.g., 75%) during initial instruction.
Component 12, Student Understanding, Item 7	45. The student's success rate is high during independent practice activities (e.g., 90 to 100%).

Exhibit B.2.6   Evaluate

TIES Reference	Indicators of Effective Evaluation
Component 1, Checking for Student Understanding, Item 3	1. The student's understanding of task directions is checked before beginning independent seatwork activities.
Component 1, Checking for Student Understanding, Item 5	2. Initial problems are checked within the first 10 minutes of independent seatwork activities.
Component 1, Checking for Student Understanding, Item 6	3. There is frequent monitoring of the student's success rate on assigned activities.
Component 1, Checking for Student Understanding, Item 8	4. The student's errors are used to reteach skills or re-explain procedures.
Component 1, Checking for Student Understanding, Item 10	5. Student engagement and attention are monitored as indicators of the student's item understanding.
Component 2, Classroom Management, Item 7	6. The student's compliance with rules is continuously monitored.
Component 2, Classroom Management, Item 13	7. The student understands the consequences of misbehavior.
Component 2, Classroom Management, Item 14	8. The student understands the classroom rules and routines.
Component 3, Teacher Expectations, Item 7	9. The student understands how to demonstrate mastery of the instructional goals.

Exhibit B.2.6, continued

TIES Reference	Indicators of Effective Evaluation
Component 3, Teacher Expectations, Item 11	10. The student is held accountable for correcting and completing unfinished work.
Component 5, Motivational Strategies, Item 11	11. Individual instructional conferences are held regularly with the student.
Component 5, Motivational Strategies, Item 16	12. The student has been asked his or her preference for how to learn the skill/content.
Component 5, Motivational Strategies, Item 17	13. The student's success rate is carefully monitored.
Component 5, Motivational Strategies, Item 18	14. The student is held accountable for completion of quality work.
Component 6, Practice Opportunity, Item 3	15. Student performance is carefully monitored by the teacher during seatwork (e.g., frequent checking, circulating among students).
Component 6, Practice Opportunity, Item 8	16. A minimal level of competence is ensured before a homework assignment is given.
Component 6, Task Relevance, Item 2	17. The student is placed appropriately within the instructional sequence.
Component 6, Task Relevance, Item 3	18. The student has acquired the necessary prerequisite skills to complete the task successfully.
Component 6, Task Relevance, Item 10	19. During the beginning stage of practice on a new skill, the student's performance is checked by the teacher. The student's success rate is 70% or better.
Component 6, Task Relevance, Item 12	20. The teacher's measure of student achievement reflects the material the student has been taught.
Component 6, Instructional Material, Item 1	21. The student can read the assigned curriculum materials.
Component 6, Instructional Material, Item 2	22. Assigned materials are at the appropriate skill level for the student.
Component 7, Student Involvement, Item 1	23. The student maintains eye contact and follows the lesson presentation and class discussion.
Component 7, Student Involvement, Item 2	24. The student participates in the lesson presentation (e.g., asks/answers questions; engages in teacher-student discussion).
Component 7, Student Involvement, Item 3	25. The student is involved in the large group via choral responses, direct questioning, and substantive interaction.
Component 7, Student Involvement, Item 4	26. The student begins, attends, and completes assigned work.
Component 7, Student Involvement, Item 5	27. The student spends little time sitting and waiting.
Component 7, Student Involvement, Item 6	28. The student returns to work promptly after a break.
Component 7, Student Involvement, Item 11	29. The student understands the lesson content.
Component 7, Maintenance of Student Engagement, Item 3	30. Student understanding of the assigned task is checked when the student is unengaged.

Exhibit B.2.6, continued

TIES Reference	Indicators of Effective Evaluation
Component 7, Maintenance of Student Engagement, Item 4	31. The teacher scans the class and the student engaged in learning activities.
Component 7, Maintenance of Student Engagement, Item 9	32. The teacher checks work, discusses, reviews, and provides corrective feedback to the student.
Component 7, Maintenance of Student Engagement, Item 10	33. Student performance is monitored to ensure an appropriate success rate.
Component 8, Feedback, Item 1	34. Student performance is monitored continuously.
Component 8, Corrective Procedures, Item 8	35. Student performance is monitored closely in order to prescribe activities to correct errors.
Component 9, Adaptive Instruction, Item 8	36. During monitoring the teacher continuously diagnoses errors and prescribes activities to correct incorrect responses.
Component 9, Adaptive Instruction, Item 10	37. Effectiveness of the alternative interventions is monitored.
Component 9, Adaptive Instruction, Item 12	38. The student is held accountable for his or her performance and quality of work.
Component 10, Monitoring Student Progress, Item 1	39. The teacher circulates among students during seatwork activities to provide assistance and to check work.
Component 10, Monitoring Student Progress, Item 2	40. The student's success rate is monitored regularly by the teacher.
Component 10, Monitoring Student Progress, Item 3	41. The student's engaged time is monitored carefully by the teacher.
Component 10, Monitoring Student Progress, Item 4	42. Student progress is monitored through both error analysis on daily work and unit tests.
Component 10, Monitoring Student Progress, Item 6	43. Direct and frequent evaluation (curriculum-based) of student progress toward mastery of objectives is used.
Component 10, Monitoring Student Progress, Item 7	44. There are enough evaluation items to measure student progress accurately.
Component 10, Monitoring Student Progress, Item 8	45. Student progress is monitored regularly to make adjustments in teaching strategies that better meet the needs of the student.
Component 10, Monitoring Student Progress, Item 9	46. Records of student progress are maintained.
Component 11, Instructional Diagnosis, Item 1	47. The student's level of skill development (i.e., entry level skills) is assessed accurately.
Component 11, Instructional Diagnosis, Item 2	48. The student's academic strengths and weaknesses are identified accurately.
Component 11, Instructional Diagnosis, Item 3	49. The student's behavioral strengths and weaknesses are identified accurately.
Component 11, Instructional Diagnosis, Item 4	50. The student's instructional needs in affective areas (i.e., attitude, self-concept) are identified accurately.
Component 11, Instructional Diagnosis, Item 5	51. The student's appropriate instructional level is identified.
Component 11, Instructional Diagnosis, Item 11	52. The gap between the student's actual and desired levels of performance is stated clearly.

Exhibit B.2.6, continued

TIES Reference	Indicators of Effective Evaluation
Component 11, Instructional Prescription, Item 19	53. Diagnostic teaching is used to ensure a successful instructional match.
Component 12, Student Understanding, Item 1	54. The student explains the purpose of the lesson.
Component 12, Student Understanding, Item 2	55. The student explains accurately the task directions (e.g., page numbers).
Component 12, Student Understanding, Item 3	56. The student explains accurately how to do problems/assignments (e.g., articulate the steps; processes to follow).
Component 12, Student Understanding, Item 4	57. The student understands the consequences of inferior quality work.
Component 12, Student Understanding, Item 8	58. The student's performance is monitored to ensure an appropriate success rate.

Appendix C / Specifications for Mathematics

This appendix contains a comprehensive list of computation and application objectives. It has three parts:

C.1 Objectives for computation and application.

C.2 A system for analyzing the results of survey level computation tests.

C.3 A system for analyzing the results of survey level application tests.

C.1 Objectives

These objectives are presented by operation (e.g., addition, subtraction), and content (e.g., time, measurement). The objectives with the smallest numbers are taught first. In some cases there will be multiple objectives for the same operation. If an objective has the letter **m** attached to it, it is a mastery objective specifying rate criteria. If the objective has the letter **a**, it is an accuracy objective. Both **a** and **m** objectives require the student to produce correct answers. Objectives with an **i** require identification of the correct answer. The **i** objectives always have accuracy criteria; **i** objectives are easiest and **m** objectives are hardest.

Computation objectives which appear in **bold face** are included in the analysis grid found in Appendix C.2.

Computation Objectives

Content	Number	Objective (Mastery CAP is in rate per minute)
Prerequisites		
Reading Number Words	23a	Read numbers in word form. Accuracy Cap 100%
Vocabulary	22a	Demonstrate a knowledge of computational vocabulary. Accuracy CAP 100%.
Symbols	21a	Demonstrate a knowledge of computational notation. Accuracy CAP 100%.
Place Value	20a	Demonstrate a knowledge of expanded notation (0–9, 0–20, 0–100). Accuracy CAP 100%.
Sets	19a	Intersect numerical sets. Accuracy CAP 100%.
Counting	18a	Skip count. Accuracy CAP 100%.
Rounding	17a	Round numbers to nearest ten's and/or hundred's place. Accuracy CAP 100%.
Place Value	16a	Supply the value of zero in multidigit numbers up to 1000. Accuracy CAP 100%.
Place Value	15a	Supply the number of 1000s, 100s, 10s, and/or 1s in a multidigit number. Accuracy CAP 100%.
Place Value	15i	Identify the digit holding the place of 1000s, 100s, 10s, and/or 1s in multidigit numbers. Accuracy CAP 100%.
Writing Digits	14m	Write digits (1–100). Mastery CAP: 100 correct with zero errors.
Writing Digits	14a	Write digits (1–100). Accuracy CAP 100%.
Counting	13m	Arrange three numbers in sequence (0–10, 10 or greater). Mastery CAP: 50 correct with zero errors.

Computation Objectives, continued

Content	Number	Objective (Mastery CAP is in rate per minute)
Counting	**13a**	Arrange three numbers in sequence (0–10, 10 or greater). Accuracy CAP 100%.
Counting	**12m**	Rote count (forward and backward from one number to another). Mastery CAP: 100 correct with zero errors.
Counting	**12a**	Rote count (forward and backward from one number to another). Accuracy CAP 100%.
Counting	**11m**	Supply previous or next number. Mastery CAP: 100 correct with zero errors.
Counting	**11a**	Supply previous or next number. Accuracy CAP 100%.
Sets	**10i**	Identify remainder of separation of sets. Accuracy CAP 100%.
Sets	**9i**	Identify sum of union sets (0–20). Accuracy CAP 100%.
Sets	**8a**	Count the elements in subsets. Accuracy CAP 100%.
Sets	**7i**	Match sets to numbers. Accuracy CAP 100%.
Sets	**6m**	Count the elements in sets. Mastery CAP: 50 elements counted with zero errors.
Sets	**6a**	Count the elements in sets. Accuracy CAP 100%.
Reading Numbers	**5m**	Read numbers (0–10, 10 or greater) from probe sheet. Mastery CAP: 100 numbers correct with zero errors.
Reading Numbers	**5a**	Read numbers (0–10, 10 or greater) from untimed probe sheet. Accuracy CAP 100%.
Reading Numbers	**5i**	Identify numbers (0–10, 10 or greater). Accuracy CAP 100%.
Counting	**4m**	Recite numbers (0–10, 10 or greater). Mastery CAP: 100 correct with zero errors.
Counting	**4a**	Recite numbers (0–10, 10 or greater). Accuracy CAP 100%.
Sets	**3a**	Identify equal and unequal sets. Accuracy CAP 100%.
Sets	**2a**	Identify which sets have the most (least). Accuracy CAP 100%.
Counting	**1a**	Indicate one-to-one correspondence between figures. Accuracy CAP 100%.
Addition		
	9p	Placement Test. Add mixed addition problems. Accuracy CAP 100%.
Regrouping and No Regrouping	**8a**	**Add two or more addends with two or more digits with or without regrouping. Accuracy CAP 100%.**
Regrouping and No Regrouping	**7a**	**Add two two-digit addends with or without regrouping. Accuracy CAP 100%.**
No Regrouping	**6a**	**Add two two-digit addends without regrouping. Accuracy CAP 100%.**
Regrouping	**5m**	**Add one-digit addend to two-digit addend with regrouping. Mastery CAP: 70 digits correct with zero errors.**
Regrouping	**5a**	**Add one-digit addend to two-digit addend with regrouping. Accuracy CAP 100%.**
No Regrouping	**4a**	**Add one-digit addend to two-digit addend without regrouping. Accuracy CAP 100%.**

Computation Objectives, *continued*

Content	Number	Objective (Mastery CAP is in rate per minute)
No Regrouping	3a	**Add three or more one-digit addends in a column. Accuracy CAP 100%.**
Zero	2a	**Add zero or 1 to one-digit addend. Accuracy CAP 100%.**
Facts	1m	**Addition facts (0–20). Mastery CAP: 80 digits correct with zero errors.**
Facts	1a	**Addition facts (0–20). Accuracy CAP 100%.**
Facts	1i	Identify answers to addition facts (0–20). Accuracy CAP 100%.
Subtraction		
	8p	Placement test. Subtract mixed subtraction problems. Accuracy CAP 100%.
Regrouping and No Regrouping	7a	**Subtract a two- or more-digit number from a three- or more-digit number with or without regrouping. Accuracy CAP 100%.**
Regrouping	6m	**Subtract a two-digit number from a two-digit number with regrouping. Mastery CAP: 40 digits correct with zero errors.**
Regrouping	6a	**Subtract a two-digit number from a two-digit number with regrouping. Accuracy CAP 100%.**
No Regrouping	5a	Subtract a two-digit number from a two-digit number without regrouping. Accuracy CAP 100%.
Regrouping	4m	**Subtract a one-digit number from a two-digit number with regrouping. Mastery CAP: 60 digits correct with zero errors.**
Regrouping	4a	**Subtract a one-digit number from a two-digit number with regrouping. Accuracy CAP 100%.**
Zero	3a	**Subtract a two-digit number ending in zero from a two-digit number ending in zero. Accuracy CAP 100%.**
No Regrouping	2m	**Subtract a one-digit number from a two-digit number without regrouping. Mastery CAP: 70 digits correct with zero errors.**
No Regrouping	2a	**Subtract a one-digit number from a two-digit number without regrouping. Accuracy CAP 100%.**
No Regrouping	2i	Identify answers to problems in which a one-digit number is subtracted from a two-digit number without regrouping. Accuracy CAP 100%.
Facts	1m	**Subtraction facts (0–20). Mastery CAP: 80 digits correct with zero errors.**
Facts	1a	**Subtraction facts (0–20). Accuracy CA 100%.**
Facts	1i	Identify answers to subtraction facts (0–20). Accuracy CAP 100%.
Multiplication		
	9p	Placement Test. Multiply mixed multiplication problems. Accuracy CAP 100%.
Squaring	8m	**Produce squares of numbers (0–12). Mastery CAP: 40 digits correct with zero errors.**
Squaring	8a	**Produce squares of numbers (0–12). Accuracy CAP 100%.**
Squaring	8i	Identify squares of numbers (0–12). Accuracy CAP 100%.
Regrouping and No Regrouping	7a	**Multiply a number containing two or more digits by another number containing two or more digits with or without regrouping. Accuracy CAP 100%.**

Computation Objectives, continued

Content	Number	Objective (Mastery CAP is in rate per minute)
Place Value	**6a**	**Multiply multidigit problems with zeros as place holders. Accuracy CAP 100%.**
Place Value	**5a**	**Multiply by 1, 10, 100, 1000. Accuracy CAP 100%.**
Regrouping and No Regrouping	**4m**	**Multiply a two-digit number by a two-digit number with or without regrouping. Mastery CAP: 40 digits correct with zero errors.**
Regrouping and No Regrouping	**4a**	**Multiply a two-digit number by a two-digit number with or without regrouping. Accuracy CAP 100%.**
Regrouping	**3m**	**Multiply a two-digit number by a one-digit number with regrouping. Mastery CAP: 30 digits correct with zero errors.**
Regrouping	**3a**	**Multiply a two-digit number by a one-digit number with regrouping. Accuracy CAP 100%.**
No Regrouping	**2m**	**Multiply a two-digit number by a one-digit number without regrouping. Mastery CAP: 40 digits correct with zero errors.**
No Regrouping	**2a**	**Multiply a two-digit number by a one-digit number without regrouping. Accuracy CAP 100%.**
Facts	1m	Multiplication facts (0–10). Mastery CAP: 80 digits correct with zero errors.
Facts	**1a**	**Multiplication facts (0–10). Accuracy CAP 100%.**
Facts	1i	Identify answers to multiplication facts (0–10). Accuracy CAP 100%.
Division		
	8p	Placement test. Divide mixed division problems. Accuracy CAP 100%.
Square Root	**7m**	**Produce the square root of a number in which the answer is 0–12. Mastery CAP: 40 digits correct with zero errors.**
Square Root	**7a**	**Produce the square root of a number in which the answer is 0–12. Accuracy CAP 100%.**
Square Root	7i	Identify the square root of a number in which the answer is 0–12. Accuracy CAP 100%.
Place Value	**6a**	**Divide a two- or more-digit number with zero as a place holder to get answers with or without remainders. Accuracy CAP 100%.**
Place Value	**5a**	**Divide a two- or more-digit number by 1, 10, 100, 1000 to get answers without decimals. Accuracy CAP 100%.**
Remainder and No Remainder	**4a**	**Divide a two- or more-digit number by a one- or two-digit number to get to an answer with or without a remainder. Accuracy CAP 100%.**
Remainder	**3m**	**Divide a two-digit number by a one-digit number to get a one- or two-digit answer with a remainder. Mastery CAP: 40 digits correct with zero errors.**
Remainder	**3a**	**Divide a two-digit number by a one-digit number to get a one- or two-digit answer with a remainder. Accuracy CAP 100%.**
No Remainder	**2m**	**Divide a two-digit number by a one-digit number to get a two-digit answer without a remainder. Mastery CAP: 40 digits correct with zero errors.**
No Remainder	**2a**	**Divide a two-digit number by a one-digit number to get a two-digit answer without a remainder. Accuarcy CAP 100%.**

Computation Objectives, continued

Content	Number	Objective (Mastery CAP is in rate per minute)
Facts	**1m**	**Division facts (0–10). Mastery CAP: 80 digits correct with zero errors.**
Facts	**1a**	**Division facts (0–10). Accuracy CAP 100%.**
Facts	1i	Identify answers to division facts (0–10). Accuracy CAP 100%.
Fractions Objectives		
	25p	Placement test. Produce answers to mixed fraction problems. Accuracy CAP 100%.
Dividing	24a	Divide a mixed number by another mixed number with conversion. Accuracy CAP 100%.
Dividing	23a	Divide whole numbers by fractions. Accuracy CAP 100%.
Dividing	22a	Divide fractions with conversion. Accuracy CAP 100%.
Dividing	21a	Divide fractions with cancellation. Accuracy CAP 100%.
Multiplying	20a	Multiply two mixed numbers with conversion. Accuracy CAP 100%.
Multiplying	19a	Multiply fractions with conversion to simplest form. Accuracy CAP 100%.
Adding and Subtracting	18a	Add and subtract mixed numbers without common factors between uncommon denominators (conversion required). Accuracy CAP 100%.
Adding and Subtracting	17a	Add and subtract fractions without common factors between uncommon denominators (conversion required). Accuracy CAP 100%.
Adding and Subtracting	16a	Add and subtract fractions with common factors between uncommon denominators (conversion required). Accuracy CAP 100%.
Adding and Subtracting	15a	Add and subtract fractions with common factors between uncommon denominators (no conversion required). Accuracy CAP 100%.
Adding and Subtracting	14a	Add and subtract mixed numbers with common denominators (conversion required). Accuracy CAP 100%.
Adding and Subtracting	13a	Add and subtract fractions with common denominators (conversion required). Accuracy CAP 100%.
Adding and Subtracting	12a	Add and subtract mixed numbers with common denominators (no conversion required). Accuracy CAP 100%.
Adding and Subtracting	11a	Add and subtract fractions with common denominators (no conversion required). Accuracy CAP 100%.
Converting	10a	Convert (rename) mixed numbers into improper fractions. Accuracy CAP 100%.
Converting	9a	Convert (rename) an improper fraction to a whole or a mixed number. Accuracy CAP 100%.
Converting	8a	Convert (rename) fractions to simplest form. Accuracy CAP 100%.
Equivalence	7a	Produce equivalent fractions. Accuracy CAP 100%.
Least Common Denominator	6a	Produce the least common denominator of two simple fractions. Accuracy CAP 100%.
Least Common Denominator	6i	Identify the least common denominator of two simple fractions. Accuracy CAP 100%.
Sets	5a	Locate intersection of denominator sets. Accuracy CAP 100%.
Equivalence	4a	Produce fractions equal to 1. Accuracy CAP 100%.

Computation Objectives, continued

Content	Number	Objective (Mastery CAP is in rate per minute)
Sets	**3i**	Identify fractions (simplest form) by matching them to subdivided objects. Accuracy CAP 100%.
Reading Fractions	**2a**	Read fractions. Accuracy CAP 100%.
Sets	**1a**	Subdivide sets and/or objects. Accuracy CAP 100%.
Decimals, Ratios, and Percents		
	12p	Placement test. Answer mixed decimal, ratio, and percent problems. Accuracy CAP 100%.
Ratio	**11a**	Complete ratio sentences. Accuracy CAP 100%.
Rounding	**10a**	Round decimals to nearest tenth, hundredth, and thousandth. Accuracy CAP 100%.
Computing Decimals	**9a**	Divide decimals having one to four decimal places. Accuracy CAP 100%.
Computing Decimals	**8a**	Multiply decimals having one to four decimal places. Accuracy CAP 100%.
Computing Decimals	**7a**	Add and subtract decimals having one to four decimal places. Accuracy CAP 100%.
Converting	**6m**	Convert a fraction to a percent. Mastery CAP 100%.
Converting	**6a**	Convert a fraction to a percent. Mastery CAP 100%.
Converting	**5m**	Convert a percent to a fraction. Mastery CAP 100%.
Converting	**5a**	Convert a percent to a fraction. Accuracy CAP 100%.
Converting	**4a**	Convert a decimal to a percent. Accuracy CAP 100%.
Converting	**3a**	Convert a fraction to a decimal. Accuracy CAP 100%.
Reading Fractions and Percents	**2a**	Read fractions and percents. Accuracy CAP 100%.
Reading Place Value	**1a**	Read decimals in tenths, hundreths, and thousandths. Accuracy CAP 100%.
Time and Temperature		
Knowledge	**10a**	Name the seasons. Accuracy CAP 100%.
Knowledge	**9a**	Know Fahrenheit or Celsius temperature units. Accuracy CAP 100%.
Knowledge	**8a**	Name the months of the year. Accuracy CAP 100%.
Knowledge	**7a**	Name the days of the week. Accuracy CAP 100%.
Knowledge	**6a**	Know equivalent units: seconds, minutes, hours, days, weeks, months, years, decades, centuries. Accuracy CAP 100%.
Tools	**5a**	Read temperatures. Accuracy CAP 100%.
Tools	**4a**	Use a calendar. Accuracy CAP 100%.
Tools	**3a**	Tell time. Accuracy CAP 100%.
Tools	**2a**	Describe uses of time-and-temperature tools: clock, watch, calendar, thermometer. Accuracy CAP 100%.
Tools	**1a**	Name clock, watch, calendar, thermometer. Accuracy CAP 100%.
Money		
Knowledge	**11a**	Enter credit and debit in checkbook record and balance. Accuracy 100%.

Computation Objectives, continued

Content	Number	Objective (Mastery CAP is in rate per minute)
Knowledge	**10a**	Write checks for bills. Accuracy CAP 100%.
Knowledge	**9a**	Determine the change due for purchases costing more than $1 and less than $20. Accuracy CAP 100%.
Knowledge	**8a**	Determine the change due, using the fewest possible coins, for purchases costing less than $1. Accuracy CAP 100%.
Knowledge	**7a**	Know symbols for money. Accuracy CAP 100%.
Knowledge	**7i**	Identify symbols for money. Accuracy CAP 100%.
Knowledge	**6a**	Know values of coins and currency. Accuracy CAP 100%.
Knowledge	**5a**	Know names of coins and currency. Accuracy CAP 100%.
Tools	**4a**	Use four-operation calculator to solve knowledge problems. Accuracy CAP 100%.
Vocabulary	**3a**	Know budget vocabulary. Accuracy CAP 100%.
Vocabulary	**2a**	Know banking vocabulary. Accuracy CAP 100%.
Vocabulary	**1a**	Know money vocabulary. Accuracy CAP 100%.

Geometry: Plane and Solid

Content	Number	Objective (Mastery CAP is in rate per minute)
Knowledge	**7a**	Produce formulas for calculating the volume of a cube, a rectangular prism, a cone, and a cylinder. Accuracy CAP 100%.
Knowledge	**7i**	Identify formulas for calculating the volume of a cube, a rectangular prism, a cone, and a cylinder. Accuracy CAP 100%.
Knowledge	**6a**	Produce formulas for calculating the area of a square, a rectangle, a triangle, and a circle. Accuracy CAP 100%.
Knowledge	**6i**	Identify formulas for calculating the area of a square, a rectangle, a triangle, and a circle. Accuracy CAP 100%.
Knowledge	**5a**	Produce formulas for calculating the perimeter of a polygon, a square, a rectangle, and a circle. Accuracy CAP 100%.
Knowledge	**5i**	Identify formulas for calculating the perimeter of a polygon, a square, a rectangle, and a circle. Accuracy CAP 100%.
Vocabulary	**4a**	Produce formula vocabulary meanings: perimeter, surface area, square units, cubic units, volume, circumference. Accuracy CAP 100%.
Vocabulary	**3a**	Produce dimensions vocabulary meanings: length, width, height, diameter, radius, degree, base. Accuracy CAP 100%.
Vocabulary	**3i**	Identify dimensions vocabulary meanings: length, width, height, diameter, radius, degree, base. Accuracy CAP 100%.
Vocabulary	**2a**	Produce elements-of-shapes vocabulary meanings: line, line segment, ray, angle, arc, point. Accuracy CAP 100%.
Vocabulary	**2i**	Identify elements-of-shapes vocabulary meanings: line, line segment, ray, angle, arc, point. Accuracy CAP 100%.
Vocabulary	**1a**	Produce geometric-shapes vocabulary meanings: circle, square, rectangle, triangle, trapezoid, parallelogram, pentagon, hexagon, octagon, cone, cylinder, oval. Accuracy CAP 100%.

Computation Objectives, continued

Content	Number	Objective (Mastery CAP is in rate per minute)
Vocabulary	1i	Identify geometric-shapes vocabulary meanings: circle, square, rectangle, triangle, trapezoid, parallelogram, pentagon, hexagon, octagon, cone, cylinder, oval. Accuracy CAP 100%.

Metric Measurement: Linear, Weight, and Capacity

Knowledge	11a	Produce abbreviations for weight units: gram, kilogram, centigram, decigram, decagram, milligram, hectogram. Accuracy CAP 100%.
Knowledge	10a	Produce abbreviations for capacity units: centiliter, milliliter, deciliter, hectoliter, decaliter, liter. Accuracy CAP 100%.
Knowledge	9a	Produce abbreviations for linear units: millimeter, kilometer, hectometer, centimeter, decameter, decimeter, meter. Accuracy CAP 100%.
Knowledge	8a	Produce meanings of metric prefixes: milli, centi, deci, deca, hecto, kilo. Accuracy CAP 100%.
Tools	7a	Use measuring tools to measure to nearest correct unit: millimeter, centimeter. Accuracy CAP 100%.
Tools	6i	Match linear tool to task: ruler, meter stick, tape measure, degree protractor, and rolling meter counter. Accuracy CAP 100%.
Tools	5i	Identify capacity tool for task: milliliter, liter. Accuracy CAP 100%.
Tools	4i	Identify weight tool for task: variety of scales. Accuracy CAP 100%.
Vocabulary	3a	Produce meaning of key vocabulary for weight measurement: heavy, heavier, heaviest, light, lighter, lightest, weight. Accuracy CAP 100%.
Vocabulary	3i	Identify meaning of key vocabulary for weight measurement: heavy, heavier, light, lighter. Accuracy CAP 100%.
Vocabulary	2a	Produce meaning of key vocabulary for liquid and dry measurement: full, fuller, fullest, empty, emptier, emptiest, more, less. Accuracy CAP 100%.
Vocabulary	2i	Identify meaning of key vocabulary for liquid and dry measurement: full, fuller, fullest, empty, more, less. Accuracy CAP 100%.
Vocabulary	1a	Produce meaning of key vocabulary for linear measurement: height, width, depth, length, long, longer, longest, short, shorter, shortest, deep, deeper, deepest, high, higher, highest, tall, taller, tallest, narrow, narrower, narrowest, wide, wider, widest, shallow, distance. Accuracy CAP 100%.
Vocabulary	1i	Identify meaning of key vocabulary for linear measurement: long, longer, longest, shorter, deepest, taller, narrow, wider. Accuracy CAP 100%.

Customary Measurement: Linear, Weight, and Capacity

Knowledge	13a	Produce abbreviations for weight units: ounces, pounds, tons. Accuracy CAP 100%.
Knowledge	12a	Produce abbreviations for capacity units: teaspoon, cup, pint, quart, gallon. Accuracy CAP 100%.
Knowledge	11a	Produce abbreviations for linear units: inch, foot, yard. Accuracy CAP 100%.
Knowledge	10a	Produce weight unit equivalents: ounces, pounds, tons. Accuracy CAP 100%.
Knowledge	9a	Produce capacity unit equivalents: teaspoons, tablespoons, cups, pints, quarts, and gallons. Accuracy CAP 100%.

Computation Objectives, continued

Content	Number	Objective (Mastery CAP is in rate per minute)
Knowledge	8a	Produce linear unit equivalents: inches, feet, yards, miles. Accuracy CAP 100%.
Tools	7a	Measure to nearest correct unit (⅛ in., ¼ in., ½ in., foot, yard), using the following tools: ruler, yardstick, degree protractor, tape measure, and rolling yard measure. Accuracy CAP 100%.
Tools	6i	Match linear tool to task: ruler, yardstick, degree protractor, rolling yard measure, tape measure. Accuracy CAP 100%.
Tools	5i	Match capacity tool to task: teaspoon, tablespoon, cup, pint, quart, and gallon. Accuracy CAP 100%.
Tools	4i	Match weight tool to task: ounces, pounds, tons. Accuracy CAP 100%.
Vocabulary	3a	Produce meaning of key vocabulary for weight measurement: heavy, heavier, heaviest, light, lighter, lightest weight. Accuracy CAP 100%.
Vocabulary	3i	Identify meaning of key vocabulary for weight measurement: heavy, heavier, light, lighter. Accuracy CAP 100%.
Vocabulary	2a	Produce meaning of key vocabulary for liquid and dry measurement: full, fuller, fullest, empty, emptier, emptiest, more, less. Accuracy CAP 100%.
Vocabulary	2i	Identify meaning of key vocabulary for liquid and dry measurement: full, fuller, fullest, empty, more, less. Accuracy CAP 100%.
Vocabulary	1a	Produce meaning of key vocabulary for linear measurement: height, width, depth, length, long, longer, longest, short, shorter, shortest, deep, deeper, deepest, high, higher, highest, tall, taller, tallest, narrow, narrower, narrowest, wide, wider, widest, shallow, distance. Accuracy CAP 100%.
Vocabulary	1i	Identify meaning of key vocabulary for linear measurement: long, longer, longest, shorter, deepest, taller, narrow, wider. Accuracy CAP 100%.

Problem Solving

Content	Number	Objective (Mastery CAP is in rate per minute)
Apply Knowledge	7a	Check solution to problems using functional algorithm. Accuracy CAP 100%.
Apply Knowledge	6a	Estimate correct answer to word problems. Accuracy CAP 100%.
Apply Knowledge	5i	Identify correct equation to solve word problems. Accuracy CAP 100%.
Apply Knowledge	4a	Recognize missing information in word problems. Accuracy CAP 100%.
Apply Knowledge	3a	Recognize essential and non-essential information in word problems. Accuracy CAP 100%.
Apply Knowledge	2a	Restate word problems in own words. Accuracy CAP 100%.
Vocabulary	1a	Match operation name to key vocabulary words and phrases. Accuracy CAP 100%.

C.2 Computation Analysis

Appendix C.2 contains a list of all computation items appearing on the survey tests found in your workbook and illustrated in Exhibit 15.12*. Next to the item numbers you will find the objective for that item, a list of subskills, and page references to instructional recommendations found within the text *Direct Instruction Mathematics* (Silbert, Carnine & Stein, 1990).

The prerequisite column in this grid contains the objective numbers of subskills selected in conformity with the standards set down in the "Rules for Developing Assumed Causes" in Exhibit 7.5*. When a student fails an item on the survey test, these prerequisites should be checked. The prerequisites in the table are those most likely to lead to instructionally relevant teaching decisions.

The basic assumption of the task analysis model is that any task is composed of a task strategy and a set of essential subtasks. If a student cannot complete a task, it is assumed that she lacks an essential subskill or cannot carry out the strategy. Strategies are the procedures by which the subtasks are combined to produce the task. In mathematics these strategies are referred to as algorithms, although the term *strategy* should connote more than a series of operational steps. Strategies are the organizational devices that teachers teach to students so they can pull operational knowledge and subtask knowledge together for task completion. No matter how good the instruction is, a student cannot carry out a strategy if he cannot carry out the subtasks that the strategy is to combine. Similarly, a student who can carry out all essential subtasks in isolation must know the strategy for organizing them in order to succeed at a task. An evaluator first needs to find out if a student can do a task. Next, he/she needs to check the student's use of subtasks and strategies. Here are the closest subtasks for Fraction Objective 20a:

"Multiply two mixed numerals on an untimed probe sheet with 100% accuracy."

Task-Specific Subskills

A. Multiplying fractions with conversion to simplest form (Fraction Objective 19a)

B. Multiplication facts (Multiplication Objective 1m)

C. Converting mixed numbers into mixed numbers with improper fractions (Fraction Objective 10a)

D. Producing the least common denominator of two simple fractions (Fraction Objective 6a)

If a student cannot pass objective 20a, then the evaluator should check the subskills of 20a, beginning with those listed. If the student passes the subskills, the assumption is that he cannot use the strategy. If a teacher is teaching at the correct level of difficulty, she has verified subskill adequacy and is teaching strategies.

Computation Analysis

Survey Test Item	Full Objective	Prerequisites from Appendix C.1	DI page #
Addition			
1–3	1a. Addition facts (0–20), accuracy CAP 100%.	add 1i, pre 5m, pre 9i, p 7i, p 21a, r 12m	108–118 138–149
	1m. Addition facts (0–20), mastery CAP 80 digits correct with zero errors.	add 1a, pre 14m, pre 9i, pre 7i, pre 12m	
4–5	2a. Add zero or _____ to one-digit addend, accuracy CAP 100%.	add 1m, add 1a, add 9i, pre 7i	108
6–7	3a. Add three or more one-digit addends in a column, accuracy CAP 100%.	add 2a, add 1m	149–150
8–9	4a. Add one-digit addend to two-digit addend without regrouping, accuracy CAP 100%.	3a, Add 2a 1m	149–150

Computation Analysis, continued

Survey Test Item	Full Objective	Prerequisites from Appendix C.1	DI page #
10–11	5a. Add one-digit addend to two-digit addend with regrouping, accuracy CAP 100%.	3a add 1m 1a 2a	150–152
10–11	5m. Add one-digit addend to two-digit addend with regrouping, mastery CAP is 70 digits correct with zero errors.	add 5a, add 4a, add 3a, add 1m	150–154
12–14	6a. Add two-digit addends without regrouping, accuracy CAP 100%.	add 4a, add 3a, add 1m	149–150
15–17	7a. Add two-digit addends with or without regrouping, accuracy CAP 100%.	add 6a, add 5m, add 1m	149–154
18–20	8a. Add two or more addends with three or more digits with or without regrouping, accuracy CAP 100%.	add 7a, add 6a, add 5m, add 1m	154–155
Subtraction			
1–5	1a. Subtraction facts (0–20), accuracy CAP 100%.	subtraction 1i prereq. 14m prereq. 10i	109 171–172
	1m. Subtraction facts (0–20), mastery CAP is 80 digits correct with zero errors.	subtraction 1a prereq. 10i prereq. 7i	
6	2a. Subtract a one-digit number from a two-digit number without regrouping, accuracy CAP 100%.	subtraction 2i subtraction 1m	149, 173
	2m. Subtract a one-digit number from a two-digit number without regrouping, mastery CAP is 70 digits correct with zero errors.	subtraction 2a subtraction 1m	
7–9	3a. Subtract a two-digit number ending in zero from a two-digit number ending in zero, accuracy CAP 100%.	subtraction 2m subtraction 1m	173
10–12	4a. Subtract a one-digit number from a two-digit number with regrouping.	subtraction 2m subtraction 1m	173–174
	4m. Subtract a one-digit number from a two-digit number with regrouping, mastery CAP is 60 digits correct with zero errors.	subtraction 4a subtraction 3a subtraction 2m subtraction 1m	
13–15	5a. Subtract a two-digit number from a two-digit number without regrouping, accuracy CAP 100%.	subtraction 2m subtraction 1m	173
16–17	6a. Subtract a two-digit number from a two-digit number with regrouping, accuracy CAP 100%.	subtraction 5a subtraction 4m subtraction 1m	173–175

Computation Analysis, continued

Survey Test Item	Full Objective	Prerequisites from Appendix C.1	DI page #
	6m. Subtract a two-digit number from a two-digit number with regrouping, mastery CAP is 40 digits correct with zero errors.	subtraction 6a subtraction 5a subtraction 4m subtraction 1m	
18–20	7a. Subtract a two-or-more digit number from a three-or-more digit number with or without regrouping, accuracy CAP 100%.	subtraction 6m subtraction 6a subtraction 5a subtraction 4m	178–179
Multiplication			
1–3	1a. Multiplication facts (0–10), accuracy CAP 100%.	division 1a multiplication 1i addition 1a prerequisite 18a	109, 120 193–202
	1m. Multiplication facts (0–10), mastery CAP is 80 digits correct with zero errors.	multiplication 1a division 1m addition 1m	
4–5	2a. Multiply a two-digit number by a one-digit number without regrouping, accuracy CAP 100%.	multiplication 1m and 1a division 1m addition 1m	203–204
	2m. Multiply a two-digit number by a one-digit number without regrouping, mastery CAP 40 digits correct with zero errors.	multiplication 2a multiplication 1m	
6–7	3a. Multiply a two-digit number by a one-digit number with regrouping, accuracy CAP 100%.	multiplication 2m multiplication 1m	203–205
	3m. Multiply a two-digit number by a one-digit number with regrouping, mastery CAP 30 digits correct with zero errors.	multiplication 3a multiplication 2m multiplication 1m	
8–9	4a. Multiply a two-digit number by a two-digit number with or without regrouping, accuracy CAP 100%.	multiplication 3m multiplication 2m multiplication 1m	206–207
	4m. Multiply a two-digit number by a two-digit number with or without regrouping, mastery CAP 40 digits correct with zero errors.	multiplication 4a multiplication 3m multiplication 1m	
10–12	5a. Multiply by 1, 10, 100, 1000, accuracy CAP 100%.	division 5a multiplication 4m multiplication 1m	203
13–15	6a. Multiply multi-digit problems with zeros as placeholders, accuracy CAP 100%.	division 6a multiplication 5a multiplication 5m multiplication 1m	202–204
16–18	7a. Multiply a number containing two or	multiplication 6a	202, 206, 211

Computation Analysis, continued

Survey Test Item	Full Objective	Prerequisites from Appendix C.1	DI page #
	more digits by another containing two or more digits with or without regrouping, accuracy CAP 100%.	multiplication 4m multiplication 3m multiplication 1m	
19–20	8a. Produce squares of numbers (0–12), accuracy CAP 100%.	division 7a multiplication 8i multiplication 1m	not in DI
	8m. Produce squares of numbers (0–12), mastery CAP 40 digits correct with zero errors.	division 7m multiplication 8a multiplication 1m	
Division			
1–5	1a. Division facts (0–10), accuracy CAP 100%.	division 1i multiplication 1a subtraction 1a	121, 129 222
	1m. Division facts (0–10), mastery CAP 80 digits correct with zero errors.	division 1a multiplication 1m subtraction 1m	
6–8	2a. Divide a two-digit number by a one-digit number to get a two-digit answer without a remainder, accuracy CAP 100%.	division 1m multiplication 1m subtraction 1m	222
	2m. Divide a two-digit number by a one-digit number to get a two-digit answer without a remainder, mastery CAP 40 digits correct with zero errors.	division 2a division 1m	
9–10	3a. Divide a two-digit number by a one-digit number to get a one- or two-digit answer with a remainder, accuracy CAP 100%.	division 2m division 1m	222–226
	3m. Divide a two-digit number by a one-digit number to get a one- or two-digit answer with a remainder, mastery CAP 40 digits correct.	division 3a division 2m division 1m	
11–12	4a. Divide a two-or-more-digit number to get an answer with or without a remainder, accuracy CAP 100%.	multiplication 4a division 3m division 1m prerequisite 17a	231–237
13–15	5a. Divide a two-or-more-digit number by 1, 10, 100, 1000 to get answers without decimals, accuracy CAP 100%.	multiplication 5a division 3m division 1m prerequisite 17a	
16–18	6a. Divide a two-or-more-digit number with zero as a place holder to get answers with or without remainders, accuracy CAP 100%.	division 4a division 3m division 1m prerequisite 16a prerequisite 17a	232

Computation Analysis, continued

Survey Test Item	Full Objective	Prerequisites from Appendix C.1	DI page #
19–20	7a. Produce the square root of a number in which the answer is 0–12, accuracy CAP 100%.	multiplication 8a division 7i division 1m	not in DI
	7m. Produce the square root of a number in which the answer is 0–12, mastery CAP 40 digits correct with zero errors.	multiplication 8m division 7a division 1m	

C.3 Application Error Analysis

Application Survey Error Analysis

Select: The items below sample the student's skill in identifying/selecting the correct operation.

Apply: The items below sample the student's skill in applying the correct operation and computing the answer correctly.

Easy Problem Solving

1. Addition 1m
   a. Problem Solving 5i, 1a, Prerequisite 21a
   b. Correct answer
   c. Problem Solving 5i
   d. Problem Solving 5i

2. Subtraction 4m
   a. Problem Solving 5i, 1a
   b. Problem Solving 5i, 1a
   c. Problem Solving 5i, 1a
   d. Correct answer

3. Multiplication 1m
   a. Problem Solving 5i
   b. Problem Solving 5i
   c. Correct answer
   d. Problem Solving 5i

4. Division 6a
   a. Correct answer
   b. Problem Solving 5i, 6a
   c. Problem Solving 5i, 6a
   d. Problem Solving 5i, 6a

5. Decimals, Ratios, Percents 8a, 4a
   a. Problem Solving 5i, 6a, Decimals, Ratios, Percents 7a
   b. Problem Solving 5i, 6a
   c. Problem Solving 5i, 6a
   d. Correct answer

Hard Problem Solving

6. Addition 1m
   a. Prerequisite 23a
   b. Problem Solving 5i
   c. Problem Solving 5i, Prerequisite 23a
   d. Correct answer

7. Subtraction 4m
   a. Correct answer
   b. Problem Solving 5i
   c. Problem Solving 3a, 5i
   d. Problem Solving 3a

8. Multiplication 1m, Subtraction 1m, Division 1m
   a. Problem Solving 5i
   b. Correct answer
   c. Problem Solving 5i
   d. Problem Solving 3a, Prerequisite 23a

9. Subtraction 3a, Addition 6a, Division 1m
   a. Problem Solving 5i
   b. Prerequisite 23a
   c. Problem Solving 5i
   d. Correct answer

10. Addition 6a, Subtraction 7a, Decimals, Ratios, Percents 4a, 7a
    a. Correct answer
    b. Problem Solving 3a
    c. Problem Solving 3a, 5i
    d. Problem Solving 5i

Easy Problem Solving

11. Addition 1m
    a. Problem Solving 7a
    b. Problem Solving 5i, 6a
    c. Correct answer
    d. Problem Solving 5i, 6a

12. Subtraction 4m
    a. Problem Solving 5i
    b. Problem Solving 5i, 6a
    c. Problem Solving 5i, 6a
    d. Correct answer

13. Multiplication 2m
    a. Correct answer
    b. Problem Solving 5i
    c. Problem Solving 5i
    d. Problem Solving 5i, 6a

14. Division 4a
    a. Problem Solving 5i
    b. Problem Solving 5i
    c. Correct answer
    d. Problem Solving 5i

15. Fractions 20a
    a. Problem Solving 5i, 6a
    b. Problem Solving 5i, 6a
    c. Problem Solving 5i
    d. Correct answer

Hard Problem Solving

16. Addition 1m
    a. Correct answer
    b. Prerequisite 23a
    c. Problem Solving 5i
    d. Problem Solving 5i

17. Subtraction 3a, Division 1m
    a. Problem Solving 3a, 6a
    b. Problem Solving 3a, 5i
    c. Correct answer
    d. Problem Solving 5i

18. Multiplication 1m, Subtraction 1m
    a. Correct answer
    b. Problem Solving 5i
    c. Problem Solving 5i
    d. Problem Solving 3a, 6a

19. Addition 8a, Multiplication 6a, Division 6a
    a. Problem Solving 5a
    b. Correct answer
    c. Problem Solving 5i
    d. Problem Solving 5i, 6a

20. Decimals, Ratios, Percents, 5a, 6a, 8a
    a. Problem Solving 5i, 3a
    b. Problem Solving 5i, 6a, 3a
    c. Problem Solving 5i, 6a, 3a
    d. Correct answer

Application Survey Error Analysis, continued

Select: The items below sample the student's skill in identifying/selecting the correct operation.

Apply: The items below sample the student's skill in applying the correct operation and computing the answer correctly.

| Easy Problem Solving | Hard Problem Solving | Easy Problem Solving | Hard Problem Solving |

Money

21. Decimals, Ratios, Percents 8a
    a. Problem Solving 5i
    b. Problem Solving 5i
    c. Decimals, Ratios, Percents 7a
    d. Correct answer

22. Decimals, Ratios, Percents 7a, 8a
    a. Problem Solving 5i, Prerequisite 23a
    b. Correct answer
    c. Problem Solving 5i
    d. Problem Solving 5i

23. Subtraction 5a
    a. Correct answer
    b. Problem Solving 6a, 7a
    c. Problem Solving 5i, 6a
    d. Problem Solving 5i, 6a

24. Fractions 20a, Decimals, Ratios, Percents 8a
    a. Problem Solving 5i
    b. Problem Solving 5i
    c. Correct answer
    d. Decimals, Ratios, Percents 9a, Problem Solving 6a

Time and Temperature

25/26.
    Subtraction 6m
    a. Problem Solving 5i
    b. Correct answer
    c. Problem Solving 5i
    d. Problem Solving 5i

27. Subtraction 1m, Multiplication 2m, Addition 4a
    a. Problem Solving 5i
    b. Correct answer
    c. Problem Solving 5i
    d. Time & Temperature 6a

28. Addition 8a
    a. Problem Solving 5i
    b. Correct answer
    c. Time and Temperature 3a
    d. Problem Solving 7a

29. Addition 8a
    a. Problem Solving 3a, Time & Temperature 6a
    b. Problem Solving 7a, Time & Temperature 6a
    c. Correct answer
    d. Problem Solving 3a

Metric Measurement

30. Multiplication 3m
    a. Correct answer
    b. Problem Solving 5i
    c. Problem Solving 5i
    d. Problem Solving 5i

31. Addition 8a, Multiplication 5a, Subtraction 7a
    a. Correct answer
    b. Problem Solving 5i, Metric Measurement 11a, 8a
    c. Problem Solving 5i, Metric Measurement 11a, 8a
    d. Problem Solving 5i, Metric Measurement 11a, 8a

32. Division 2m
    a. Problem Solving 5i
    b. Problem Solving 5i
    c. Correct answer
    d. Problem Solving 5i

33. Addition 8a, Multiplication 5a, Subtraction 7a
    a. Problem Solving 5i, Metric Measurement 10a, 8a
    b. Problem Solving 5i, Metric Measurement 10a, 8a
    c. Correct answer
    d. Metric Measurement 10a, 8a

Application Survey Error Analysis, continued

Select: The items below sample the student's skill in identifying/selecting the correct operation.

Apply: The items below sample the student's skill in applying the correct operation and computing the answer correctly.

Easy Problem Solving	**Hard Problem Solving**	**Easy Problem Solving**	**Hard Problem Solving**

Customary Measurement

34. Multiplication 3m
  a. Correct answer
  b. Problem Solving 5i
  c. Problem Solving 5i
  d. Problem Solving 3a, 4a
	35. Addition 8a, Multiplication 4a, Subtraction 7a
	  a. Correct answer
	  b. Problem Solving 5i, Customary Measurement 11a, 13a
	  c. Problem Solving 5i, Customary Measurement 11a, 13a
	  d. Problem Solving 5i, Customary Measurement 11a, 13a
		36. Division 2a
		  a. Problem Solving 5i
		  b. Problem Solving 5i
		  c. Correct answer
		  d. Problem Solving 5i
			37. Addition 1m, Multiplication 1m, Subtraction 1m
			  a. Problem Solving 5i, Customary Measurement 12a
			  b. Problem Solving 5i, Customary Measurement 12a
			  c. Correct answer
			  d. Customary Measurement 12a

Geometry I

38. Addition 4a
  a. Problem Solving 5i, Geometry 5a
  b. Correct answer
  c. Problem Solving 5i, Geometry 5a
  d. Problem Solving 5i, Geometry 5a
	39. Multiplication 4m, Division 4a
	  a. Problem Solving 5i, 3a, Geometry 6a
	  b. Problem Solving 5i, 3a, Geometry 6a
	  c. Problem Solving 5i, Geometry 6a
	  d. Correct answer
		40. Multiplication 1m
		  a. Problem Solving 5i, Geometry 6a
		  b. Correct answer
		  c. Problem Solving 5i, Geometry 6a
		  d. Problem Solving 5i, Geometry 6a
			41. Addition 1m
			  a. Problem Solving 5i, Geometry 5a
			  b. Problem Solving 5i, Geometry 5a
			  c. Problem Solving 5i
			  d. Correct answer

Geometry II

42. Multiplication 7a, 6a
  a. Problem Solving 5i
  b. Problem Solving 5i, Geometry 7a
  c. Problem Solving 5i, Geometry 7a
  d. Correct answer
	43. Fractions 20a, Multiplication 7a, 6a, 5a
	  a. Problem Solving 3a, 5i, Geometry 6a
	  b. Correct answer
	  c. Problem Solving 3a, 5i, Geometry 6a
	  d. Problem Solving 3a, 5i, Geometry 6a
		44. Decimals, Ratios, Percents 8a
		  a. Problem Solving 5i, Geometry 5a
		  b. Problem Solving 5i, Geometry 5a
		  c. Correct answer
		  d. Decimals, Ratios, Percents 8a
			45. Decimals, Ratios, Percents 8a, Multiplication 8m, Fractions 22a
			  a. Problem Solving 5i, Geometry 7a
			  b. Problem Solving 5i, Geometry 7a
			  c. Correct answer
			  d. Problem Solving 5i, Geometry 7a

The use of this table is explained in chapter 15 on page 351.

Problem Solving Answer Key and Error Analysis Grid

| Item | Operations | Correct Response | Error Categories | | | Item | Operations | Correct Response | Error Categories | | Total Correct by Operation |
			Select Wrong Operation	Set up Equation Incorrectly	Select Irrelevant Information				Inadequate Estimation	Analysis Required to Identify Errors	
1.	$+$	a	cd	b		11.	$+$	a	d	bc	/2
2.	$-$	d	cb	a		12.	$-$	d	c	ab	/2
3.	$\times$	b	ad	c		13.	$\times$	d	c	ab	/2
4.	$+$	a	dc	b		14.	$\div$	c	a	bd	/2
5.	$\frac{n}{n}-$	c	ad	b		15.	$\frac{n}{n}\times$	b	d	ca	/2
	Subtotal						Subtotal				/10
6.	$++$	a	d	b	c	16.	$++$	c	b	ad	/2
7.	$-+$	d	c	b	a	17.	$-+$	d	b	ac	/2
8.	$\times +$	c	b	a	d	18.	$\times -$	b	d	ac	/2
9.	$+\div$	c	a	d	b	19.	$\times \div$	c	a	bd	/2
10.	$\% +-\times$	b	c	a	d	20.	$\% \times +\div$	c	d	ba	/2
	Subtotal						Subtotal				/10
	Total	/10					Total	/10			/20

Glossary

Ability See *Potential*.

Ability Training Treatment that attempts to change cognitive or perceptual characteristics of the student. See *Aptitude Treatment Interaction*.

Acoustically similar Sounding almost like (b/p/d/t, f/v, k/p/g) (Carnine & Silbert, 1979, p. 75).

Active participation The time a student is actually involved in a lesson. It does *not* refer to passive activities such as waiting for a turn or for help. Active participation may be covert or overt. Covert participation refers to thinking about the *objective*; overt participation refers to doing something pertaining to the objective. The higher the active participation on an objective, the higher the learning.

Active reading Use and integration of a variety of skills and information sources to derive meaning from text. Active readers use relevant prior knowledge, decoding skills, language knowledge, and context to understand what they read. They monitor their own understanding and problem solve when they fail to understand.

Aim An objective expressed in terms of CAP and a target date.

Alterable variables In this text the only things that are referred to as alterable are those student characteristics that teachers can change through instruction. Alterable variables, therefore, include the student's skills, knowledge, and use of *executive control* strategies. See *Unalterable variables*.

Annual goal The expected outcome of one year's instruction. Annual goals for special education students are set in the *IEP* meeting.

Aphasic The term is misused in special ed to refer to almost any language disability, including those which are general (no language) or specific (inability to recall and use names). Aphasia is usually reserved for those cases of language disability associated with *neurological* damage.

Aptitude Treatment Interaction (ATI) The belief that individuals with certain abilities will behave dif-ferently in certain treatments than individuals who lack the abilities. Efforts to use ability measures to select treatments are commonplace and generally ineffective.

Assertiveness As used in popular psychology, assertiveness refers to the strong but nonaggressive declaration of opinion or need. In this context, being assertive is a positive and healthy activity. It does not mean being pushy.

Assisted assessment Assisted assessment involves the development of a sequence of instructional interventions that are systematically employed in combination with *formative evaluation* to recognize the degree of support a student must have in order to succeed on a *task*.

Assumed cause Hypothesized explanations for student failure. Different assumed causes may be developed by different evaluators resulting in different conclusions. In this text assumed causes are *curriculum-based* and deal exclusively with the student's *prior knowledge*.

Attributes Characteristics of a person or thing.

Authentic assessment Evaluation that makes use of real-life tasks rather than contrived test items.

Automaticity An accurate response performed at a high rate with distractions present. Automatic responses are often thought to occur without use of short-term memory. Automaticity is generally considered to be the highest level of proficiency.

Awareness of print Knowledge of the concepts and conventions of reading.

Basic learning strategies *Strategies* applied to the fundamental *information-processing* functions of attention, memory, and motivation.

Basic skills Sometimes referred to as *tool skills*, basic skills include elementary reading, mathematics, and communication tasks. They are the skills one must use repeatedly in order to carry out complex tasks.

Behavior In a classical sense, behavior refers to some kind of muscular activity or movement. However, in this text, there are two categories of behavior: overt and covert. Overt behavior involves movement that can be detected and confirmed reliably by observers without the use of specialized equipment. Covert behavior may be self-reported or detected by inference from overt behaviors (such as biofeedback recordings or psychological test scores). Covert behaviors include thoughts and feelings.

When special educators use the term *behavior*, they are often referring exclusively to social behavior, as in the explanation "She has a behavior problem." This gives the erroneous impression that *academic* and *social behaviors* are somehow different when, in fact, both respond to the same learning processes.

Behavior Disordered (BD) A label applied to individuals who engage in any of a variety of inappropriate or deviant behaviors. The term *behavior disordered* has gained wide acceptance as an alternative to *emotionally disturbed*. Many special educators are uncomfortable with the speculation and inference necessary to work with so-called emotions, and prefer the accent that behavior disorders places on observable or overt behaviors.

The term is used almost exclusively to describe social, addictive, or idiosyncratic behaviors. It is almost never used to describe academic, physical, or language disorders.

Behavior modification While the term could apply to any effort to change any behavior, it is used almost exclusively to describe the use of contingency management programs arranged by educators to address specific student behaviors. See *Contingency*.

Behavioral model See *Medical model*.

Best-fit line A line drawn through a set of data that best represents both the central tendency of the data and changes in data pattern.

Blending A decoding strategy in which the reader isolates letter and/or cluster sounds within words and combines them to say the word (in the word *sister*, a student would isolate sss, iii, sss, and combine to say *sis*, etc.).

Bottom up Instruction that begins with *subskills* and works toward increasingly complex objectives.

Bound morphograph Unit of meaning that cannot stand alone (affixes like re, de, ing, and er do not stand alone).

Calibrate To adjust the size of a task. Calibration involves slicing tasks into smaller ones, or combining them to others to produce more complex ones.

CAP See *Criteria*.

Categorical funding Money made available by federal or state governments for use with certain "types" of students. Categorical funding policies necessitate the time-consuming, expensive, and sometimes damaging process of *labeling*.

CEC See *Council for Exceptional Children*.

'Celeration A general term for changes (acceleration or deceleration) in behavior. On a graph it may be represented by a line drawn through the data.

Cerebral Palsy (CP) A condition of the central nervous system (brain), usually occurring prior to birth, that affects muscular coordination and strength, but not *necessarily* intelligence.

Child-study team A group mandated by federal law composed of a student's teacher and parents, an administrator, and an evaluator (usually a psychologist). The team's purpose is to determine the need for special education services. In some districts, this group also writes the *IEP*, although a separate meeting is suggested for this purpose. The meeting is often called a *staffing*. When appropriate, the student may also attend the meeting.

Classification The evaluative process of labeling or naming things in order to facilitate communication and understanding. In special education the term may refer to a label placed on a student (MR, or LD).

Cloze A procedure used to sample reading comprehension. The student is asked to fill in the blanks in a passage where every *n*th word has been deleted. Students who understand what they read are able to make good guesses about what the omitted word should be (in a book, words _____ defined in a glossary). Cloze is also a procedure used with oral language to check language comprehension.

Cluster Group of letters that can be sounded together to make one sound (in sister, *sis* is a cluster of letters that can be sounded together).

Code emphasis An approach to reading instruction that focuses on skills for decoding words. See *Decoding*.

Cognition Activity of the mind—thinking.

Compensatory The capability of one skill to balance the effect of another skill that is weaker.

Comprehension See *Reading comprehension*.

Comprehension monitoring   Self-checking for understanding during reading (students might say to themselves "What does this mean? Do I need to reread, should I slow down?")

Comprehensive evaluation   The evaluation required by *PL 94-142* and *IDEA* prior to a *child-study team* meeting. It typically includes estimates of skill and ability along with a *developmental* history and behavioral observations.

Computation operations   Rote skills, procedures, and concepts students use to (1) add, (2) subtract, (3) multiply, (4) divide, and (5) calculate fractions, decimals, ratios, and percents.

Concept analysis   Process through which defining characteristics are identified. Defining characteristics include critical and noncritical attributes (in the letter *b* the critical attributes are its shape and orientation. Noncritical attributes include size and typeface).

Consolidated   A term used to refer to groups of objectives that share common strategic or conceptual characteristics.

Constructive   A type of instruction through which the teacher actively arranges the environment to increase the probability that a student will *generate* knowledge. The teacher does not directly supply the targeted information because it is believed that the student's learning experience will be qualitatively superior if she extracts the information on her own. See *Generative.*

Context   The circumstances, either physical or cognitive, in which something exists.

Contingency   The arrangement between a behavior and its consequences. The contingency is the thing that links a behavior to the stimulus that follows it. It is the expectation that the contingency will function that raises (in the case of an expected reward) or lowers (in the case of an expected punisher) the probability of someone doing something.

Correlation   The relationship between two measures of student behavior (not necessarily a causative relationship).

Correlation coefficient   A fraction falling between +1 and −1, usually labeled *r*. The significance of the correlation depends on many things such as the size and composition of the population used to obtain it. The seriousness of the decision being made should be the primary determinant of any ideal level. However, levels above .85 are usually demanded for measures used to make treatment decisions for individuals.

Council for Exceptional Children (CEC)   The largest organization of special educators. The council has state branches and a large national structure. Its annual conventions have been attended by as many as 10,000 people. The organization promotes several publications and lobbies on behalf of special education at the state and national level. The address of CEC is 1920 Association Drive, Reston, Virginia 22091.

Covert behavior   Unseen behavior such as thinking/feeling.

Criteria (Criteria for Acceptable Performance, or CAP)   The standards in an *objective.* The criteria tell how well (accurately, frequently, or to what quality) a behavior should be carried out by a student who has finished instruction on a task.

Criterion-referenced testing   Evaluation that compares an individual's behavior to a performance standard or criterion.

Critical effect   The result of a *behavior.*

Critical thinking skills   Sometimes referred to as problem-solving skills, they are largely ill-defined. Critical thinking skills are supposed to be needed when working tasks which require inference, synthesis, or creative solutions. Teachers often refer to critical thinking skills as those that exceed rote recall or literal understanding. Their use implies the active application of *strategies* for solution, understanding, or memory. Individuals with these skills are supposedly better prepared to control their own learning and to achieve more sophisticated understanding of content.

Current level of performance   Sometimes thought of as the "instructional" level, this is the position of the student's skills within the curriculum. The current level is mapped out by identifying both skills the student does not have and those he has acquired.

Curriculum   The content and behaviors (*objectives*) taught in a class. It is not synonymous with the published materials used in a class, or the teacher's approach to delivery of instruction.

Curriculum level   The grade at which an objective is typically taught. The term is not synonymous with "grade level," which is a *normative* concept referring to the average test score of students at a grade level.

Data-based program modification (DBPM) An evaluative system that summarizes changes in performance over time through direct and daily measurement of behaviors. DBPM refers directly to a behavioral teaching procedure based on *repeated measures* of the *objective* behavior, charting, and standardized instruction. It is used in general to describe a variety of *formative evaluation* (data-based program modification) systems.

The basic idea of DBPM is that *trends* in objective learning can be summarized, and the trends of learning under different instructional conditions can be interpreted in order to select the most efficient instruction.

Data decision rules The use of empirically validated guidelines (rules) that can be used to aid in the interpretation of *data.* The rules are linked to patterns of data and are employed at some fixed interval (often every two weeks).

Date-determined 'celeration 'Celeration calculated by a line drawn from the student's data to the intersection of an aim rate and aim date.

Day lines Vertical lines on a chart.

Decision making In education this refers to the *labeling* or teaching of students. Teaching decisions deal with the selection of objectives and the delivery of instruction.

Decoding The sounding and blending of letters and words. Decoding and comprehension are the two primary subdivisions of reading. "Translating printed words into a representation similar to oral language, e.g., reading 'I am hot' for the words *I am hot*" (Carnine & Silbert, 1979, p. 30).

Decoding rules A rule that when applied should assist a reader in figuring out a word (when a word ends in "e," the vowel says its name and the "e" is silent. Mope. "O" says its name and "e" is silent).

Development The result of aging in a particular environment. It is not the same as maturation, which is simply aging. Two people of the same age may develop differently because of the different environments in which they have lived (or their different interpretations of the same environment).

Diagnosis In special education, diagnosis may have any of several meanings. It may refer to a statement of the student's physical or psychological status, or it may refer to the category of handicapping condition into which the student is placed. Diagnosis may also refer to a statement of what and how the student should be taught. The three definitions do not necessarily relate to each other.

Direct evaluation Evaluation that measures the performance of students in the materials that they are using or on the tasks they are learning. Direct evaluation is not possible without curriculum-test alignment.

Direct instruction The term originally referred to instruction limited to content (concepts, skills, discriminations) that is linked in a causative way to an *objective.* In that sense, direct instruction involved teaching only the target *task* or its immediate *subtasks.*

Direct instruction has also come to mean the use of various behavioral techniques during instruction. These include the consistent use of scripts, prompts, cues, *correction procedures*, and teacher responses.

A third definition emphasizes the relationship of tasks to each other and emphasizes concept analysis and curriculum design.

Disability The condition in which a person's functioning, relative to some *criteria*, is inferior. Disabilities are said to reside within the person and may have no consequences unless the person enters an environment that will only accommodate higher levels of function. In that case the person becomes *"handicapped"* by the nonsupportive environment.

Discrepancy Difference. A discrepancy may be either positive (above expectation) or negative (below expectation). Recognition of important discrepancies is fundamental to identification of annual goals and short-term objectives.

Discrimination Recognizing how things are different.

Domain A set of skills or ideas defined by some sort of unifying boundaries or common rules. See *Consolidated.*

Down syndrome A genetic condition associated with mental retardation. The syndrome accounts for a tremendous proportion of those considered to be mentally retarded for whom a known pathology exists.

DSM The *Diagnostic and Statistical Manual of Mental Disorders* is put out by the American Psychiatric Association.

Dumbing down The process, usually applied to reading texts, of reducing complexity in an effort to facilitate student use.

Dynamic data   Data that describe progress over a period of time. See *Formative evaluation*.

Dyslexia   Dyslexia is used to describe individuals who have difficulty dealing with symbols. In special ed, it is associated very closely with *learning disabilities* and nonreading. Originally a medical/psychological term, its transition into education resulted in tremendous overuse. Today it is not particularly useful.

Efficacy   In social service and particularly special education, this term refers to the "goodness" of a program. If the program is effective and cost-efficient, it has efficacy.

Eligibility decisions   Decisions that determine whether or not a student qualifies for a particular program. Eligibility decisions often seem to be unrelated to student need. See *Labeling* and *Categorical funding*.

Emotional disturbance (ED)   See *Behavior disordered*. Sometimes called Emotional Handicap (EH).

Enabling skill   The skills needed to employ a *strategy*.

Envelope   Best-fit lines drawn to incorporate the range of responding or variability in data.

EPS   Errors per symbol in handwriting. The average number of errors in a sample of handwriting.

Error analysis   The investigation of errors in order to recognize patterns of missing factual, conceptual, or strategic knowledge.

Error correction   A strategy employed to increase a student's accuracy.

Evaluation   The process by which investigators come to understand things and by which they attach relative value to things. Evaluation cannot take place without comparison of behavior to a standard.

Examples   In *concept analysis* examples are positive instances of the concept.

Exemplar   A product, or person, used as a benchmark of quality. Exemplars are selected to illustrate expected outcomes and are particularly important when using *holistic* measurement and *generative* instruction.

Expected level   The level of curriculum or proficiency at which a student is supposed to be working. It is the level at which general education students of the same age work.

F-A-C-T (Sheet)   Used to summarize a task analytical evaluation. It has columns for Fact/Assumed Cause/Test.

Fatigue point   The point at which a reduction in physical stamina is reflected in a skill (tired hand, poor handwriting).

Feedback   Feedback comes after a student has done something. It is the information that tells him if what he did was wrong or right. Whereas this information may also be reinforcing and even instructional, *reinforcement*, correction and feedback are not necessarily the same.

Fidelity   The degree to which a task or test item corresponds to real life. See *Authentic assessment*.

Fluency   Fluency is a proficiency dimension defined by the rate of student response. (See *Mastery*.) Reading fluency can be used to indicate comprehension. Fluency may also refer to the type of instruction used to raise a student from accuracy to mastery.

Form   The observable expression of a *behavior*. See *Function*.

Formative evaluation   Evaluation that occurs as skills are being developed. Formative data is called "dynamic" because it shows movement. See *Progress data*.

Formats   The arrangement or style of a test or test item. Example formats include multiple-choice, production, and fluency.

Free morphograph   Unit of meaning that can stand alone; a word (courage, male, tent).

Frequency data   The number of times a behavior occurs during a time interval (usually minutes).

Frequent evaluation   Ongoing or continual assessment (daily if at all possible).

Function   The goal of a *behavior*. See *Form*.

Generalization   A skill learned in one environment or under one condition is used under new conditions or in a new environment.

Generalize   In a special education, this term is usually used in a behavioral sense. A behavior is said to generalize if it transfers (switches) from one situation (set of stimuli) to another. Special students are often characterized as those who do not generalize—meaning that they learn to do something for one teacher in one class but can't do it anywhere else.

Generalization is harder if the two settings in question are very different. This is why special evaluation procedures should be similar to classrooms if their results are to be generalized to instruction. (Classrooms should be similar to the real world.)

Generative Instruction in which the student induces, or generates, the outcome. See *Constructive*.

Geographic environment The physical *context* in which a *behavior* occurs.

Handicap A debilitating condition imposed on a person by a hostile and/or nonsupportive environment. See *Disability*.

Hands-off instruction Instruction in which the teacher is nondirective and may even be inactive.

Hands-on instruction Instruction in which the teacher is actively involved in promoting a targeted outcome. See *Supplantive* and *Direct instruction*.

Handwriting Penmanship skills necessary to write letters and digits.

Holistic In evaluation this term refers to comparisons and judgments based on consideration of an entire behavior or product, rather than on an analysis of its components.

Hyperactive The term refers to abnormally frequent movement. It also is used to describe highly distractible or inattentive behavior. The term is associated with *learning disabilities* and has been widely misused. Today it has little descriptive power.

IDEA The Individual with Disabilities Education Act of 1990 (PL 101-476) reauthorized the intent and procedures of *PL 94-142*.

Idiosyncratic A type of *standard* which is used to determine if a student's skills have improved relative to her previous performance. Unlike *norms* or *CAP*, the idiosyncratic standard compares the student to herself and is useful for determining *progress* or change in student's performance over time. *Progress data* is not necessarily positive, as a student can "progress" away from an expected outcome.

IEP (Individual Education Plan) The control component of *PL 94-142* and *IDEA,* the plan is required for all special-ed students and contains a complete outline of the services they are provided. The IEP contains annual goals, specific short-term *objectives*, statements of current educational performance, statements describing the resources to be used to meet the goals and objectives, and dates for initiation and review of the program.

The IEP is written in conjunction with parents, teachers, the school administration and, in some cases, the student. Any party who disagrees with the plan may appeal it to a review board or to the courts. The plan is not a contract for service. See *Child-study team*.

Individualized instruction Making decisions about student instruction on a one-to-one basis. Individualized instruction implies tailored lessons on specifically selected objectives. It does not mean one-to-one instruction. (A teacher may employ individualized instruction by deciding to teach a student in a group.)

Information processing The activity of a person's mind.

Instructional aim An *objective* that also includes an expected date of completion.

Interactive process Activity which functions through the relating of multiple variables. Interactive processes are *compensatory*, as they may be successfully applied even when one of the variables is failing by adjusting for the failing skill with another.

Intermediate aim A reference point on the way to an aim. For example, if the aim (criteria) is to have a student be 100% accurate in six weeks, an intermediate aim could be to have him 50% accurate in three weeks.

Interpreter The function of *information processing* that attributes and explains events for the mind. This component within the information-processing model explains and attributes data. These explanations vary among people because the interpretations are based on categories of prior knowledge that develop differently according to a person's personal history.

Interrogative A question.

IQ The "Intelligence Quotient" is conceptualized as a summary of student *potential*. Under old psychology it was assumed that intelligence was fixed, therefore tests designed to measure it were constructed to be insensitive to instruction. While current theories of learning have de-emphasized the role of fixed *potential,* the score on IQ tests remain *unalterable*.

Judgment The set of knowledge and beliefs that focuses attention and leads to decisions. Good judgment increases the probability of successful decision making. Good judgment is learned.

Labeling A classification process. Not useful in treatment.

Language sample   The recorded transcription of oral communication. Often used in survey-level assessment of language.

Learning   Relatively permanent modifications in thought or behavior that result from environmental events (instruction) but not from things like pathology, maturation, or fatigue. Learning is operationally defined (indicated by) a change in behavior over time.

Learning disabled   The single most frequently redefined term in special education, *learning disabled* usually refers to someone who doesn't learn when no one can tell why. The explanations for this failure range from brain damage to bad teaching. Learning disabilities represent the largest (in terms of clients) category of educational disability. It is a mild designation and is definitionally linked to the lack of curricular progress in school.

Learning mode (modality, channel)   Mode or modality refers to the medium of presentation. It could be useful to refer to lecture, tutoring, or self-instruction; however, in education it tends to relate to so-called stimulus-response categories. The categories are sometimes called *channels*, particularly by those who believe in *process deficits* and remediation.

The common styles referred to by teachers are the auditory and visual channels. Some educators believe that learners have stable styles, and attempt to make use of these preferences during instruction. This idea has questionable utility. Learning is more clearly influenced by the structure, organization, presentation, and grouping practices of the teacher.

Least restrictive environment   A term from *PL 94-142* and *IDEA*, it refers to the placement of students. Given two equally productive settings, the student should be placed in the one which is "least restrictive." This means the placement most like the placement to which the treatment is to generalize (usually the regular classroom).

Literacy   The concept of literacy includes attributes of communication, planning, and accommodation of context. In this text the term is not necessarily associated with the rules of communication, but with *social competence*.

Maintenance   Continued mastery of a skill after instruction has ended.

Mastery   See *rate* and *fluency*. Mastery is a proficiency dimension. Mastery criteria go beyond accuracy in that they require the student to work correctly and quickly. Rate statements, usually in terms of a rate per minute, are used in mastery objectives. Percent statements are used in accuracy objectives.

Mastery learning   The idea that learning is accelerated if the student is instructed to sufficient proficiency on prerequisite skills. See *Prior knowledge*.

Maze   A procedure used to check reading comprehension. Students are asked to select correct words in passages in which words have been omitted. Like *cloze*, every *n*th word is omitted. Unlike cloze, the correct word and several incorrect words are presented above or below the blank where the word was omitted (In a book, words _____ defined in a glossary).   is, are, phonemes

Mean   The average score; a measure of central tendency.

Measurement   The assignment of numerals to objects or events according to rules (Campbell, 1940).

Median   The middlemost score; a measure of central tendency.

Medical model   The medical model assumes that causes of behavior problems reside within the client—that is to say, *the client* is sick. In contrast, the so-called behavioral model used in most social services assumes that behavior grows out of the interaction of the person and the environment. In the medical model, therapy is directed at the internal "cause" of the problem (surgery and medication are examples of this treatment). Teachers do not administer that kind of treatment. They attempt to alter people's behavior by manipulating the environment through instruction.

Metacognitive   The student's awareness of and control over her own thinking.

Minimal competency   The idea that students must reach a certain level of proficiency prior to graduation from a program or grade level.

Minimum 'celeration   The minimal amount of change considered acceptable; calculated by comparing current progress rate to the aim rate.

Mode   The most frequent score; a measure of central tendency.

Morphograph   Smallest unit of meaning in the English language (*born* is a morphograph, it has meaning; *orn* is not a morphograph, it does not have meaning; *ed* is morphograph, it has meaning; *e* is not).

Morphology Rule system for combining units of meaning to make words. We can add *ed* to *talk* to indicate that someone spoke in the past.

Narrative log A written record of comments.

Neurological (neurologically impaired) The neurological system comprises the brain and nerves. People who have injured their brains or nerves may have trouble with behavior or learning; however, not all problem learners have damaged neurological systems.

Nonexamples Illustrations that do not demonstrate the attributes of a given concept. A porcupine would be a nonexample of something soft.

Norm Scores generated from the behavior of a group.

Objective Objectives are statements of the expected behavioral outcomes that will result from instruction. They contain behavioral descriptors, conditions for the behavior, content descriptions, and *criteria*.

Off task A general term implying that the student isn't doing what he or she is supposed to be doing. A student could be "off" one task by being "on" another. The appropriate task is usually defined by the observer or teacher.

On task See *off task.*

Pace Pace has two meanings. It may refer to the actual speed of presentation or to the speed of movement from one *objective* to another. Speed of presentation includes the rate at which the teacher talks or uses other instructional techniques. Additionally, a class in which the students master and move to new objectives quickly may be called a fast-paced classroom.

Paraphrasing A procedure used to sample reading comprehension. Students read a passage and tell what was read in their own words. Specific criteria for judging the adequacy of a student's paraphrase have been developed by Schumaker, Denton, and Deshler (1984).

Peer tutoring The use of students to deliver instruction to other students.

Percentage Number correct divided by the total possible correct.

Performance A measure of behavior taken on one occasion.

Personal See *Idiosyncratic.*

Phoneme The smallest sound unit that can distinguish one utterance from another.

Phonemic segmentation Isolating sounds within a word (e.g., man—mmm aaa nnn). A subtask of blending. See *Blending.*

Phonetic generalizations Rules about the way combinations of letters are sounded.

Phonetic misspelling Misspelling of a word that can be read (ordr for order).

Phonetic segmentation Isolating and/or sequencing sounds within a word (man—mmm aaa nnn). A subtask of blending. See *Blending.*

Phonics Sound symbol relationships in words. See *Decoding.*

Pinpoint A measurement target that has been identified in behavioral terms. An *objective.*

Potential The hypothesized limit of a person's learning. Because potential is not an *alterable variable* its measurement is of little value to teachers. Deciding that a student's failure is due to a lack of potential is a major block to effective problem solving.

Portfolio assessment Measurement of skills and knowledge displayed in examples of daily assignments rather than tests.

Practice There are two elements of practice. The first is deciding what operation (*strategy*) to employ, and the second is carrying out the operation. For example, if students are given a math problem, they must decide what kind of problem it is and they must work it. Most teachers only have students "practice" by doing things (the second element) and do not allow sufficient practice at deciding what to do. For example, an arithmetic worksheet composed of only one problem type does not allow the student to practice problem type discriminations.

Pragmatics A term that refers to the purposes or functions of language (a purpose of communication may be to inform or control).

Pre-service teachers Teachers in training, practicum, or student teaching who have not yet been employed as teachers.

Prior knowledge The best single predictor of learning success. Prior knowledge is what a person knows about a *task*, or its prerequisites, before the lesson begins. When an evaluator summarizes a student's *current level of performance* she is reporting the student's relevant prior knowledge.

Probe   A criterion-referenced test or observation.

Problem solving   See *Strategy* and *Critical thinking skills*.

Process of written communication   There are at least four components—planning, transcribing, reviewing, and revising.

Process remediation (process deficit)   In this sense, a process is an unlearned sequence of activity leading to a product. This activity takes place within the individual at an unconscious level and is not directed by the person. If a person who is poked in the finger with a needle withdraws the finger and says "ouch," a process of the kind we are discussing has taken place. It is assumed that learning takes place through certain *neurological,* psychological, perceptual, and learning processes and that if one of these processes is damaged (or impaired), learning will not take place. Process remediation is directed at repairing or developing a process as opposed to teaching a particular lesson.

These learning processes are hypothetical and their remediation is based on theories of learning. Different theories produce different processes and different remediation activities. Process remediation directed at various so-called learning modalities was very popular in special ed during the 1960s and early 1970s. The theoretical basis and remedial utility of process remediation remains invalidated.

Proficiency   Criterion level necessary for student to satisfactorily perform next skill in skill sequence.

Prognosis   Prediction.

Progress data   Information obtained by taking repeated measures of a behavior across time. Progress data is typically used in *formative evaluation* and in conjunction with *data decision rules*.

Pseudo-reading   Asking a student to engage in such reading-related behaviors as turning pages or sounding nonsense words.

Psychoeducational evaluation   Assessment of processing abilities (also referred to as psychomedical evaluation).

Public   Observable. During *strategy* instruction a teacher should make his thought processes public.

Public Law 94-142   The public law mentioned here is PL 94-142, which is explained in the introduction to almost every special-ed text written since 1974. *PL* stands for public law; *94* refers to the Ninety-Fourth Congress, and *142* means it was the one hundred forty-second law that Congress passed.

PL 94-142 says students with disabilities should be given an education. Beyond that it is difficult to say what it means because of the various regulations it has spawned and court decisions it has led to. Special educators have probably erred by overstating the impact of the law to secure resources and respect for the field. It may have been better to say "it is correct and practical to educate the disabled" rather than to say "it is the law." Laws can disappear through funding cuts, legislation, or litigation. PL 94-142 was extended by *IDEA*.

Purpose of written communication   Why we write; the functions of written language (expressive, poetic, transactive).

Qualitative interpretation   The aspect of *behavior* analysis that is not predicated on the quantitative examination of scores. For example, if two teams are playing basketball and one gets 112 points while the other gets 113, the difference of a single point is not statistically significant and probably does not represent any real difference in team performance. But qualitatively, the team with 113 feels a lot better.

Rate   The number of responses divided by the time the behavior is observed. Rate is a form of data, or behavior summary, which takes into account the frequency with which a behavior occurs and the length of time during which it occurs (usually in minutes). The formula for rate is count $\div$ time. Other types of data include accuracy (percent), duration and intensity. See *Criteria*.

Raw score   The number of responses.

Reacting   The way a person responds to what she has read. A more behavioral way to refer to *reading comprehension*.

Reading   An interactive process in which the reader brings what he knows about the world to the printed page. What is known is used to construct meaning from what is written. See *Reading comprehension*.

Reading comprehension   Understanding text. Students combine what they know with what is printed to construct meaning. It occurs as a student reads. Students draw upon decoding skills, vocabulary knowledge, language and prior knowledge to make sense of what is written.

Reading method   An instructional approach, not a program that is a published series.

Reading program   A published series rather than a method.

Reductionist   An approach to curriculum development that involves the recognition of elements of the *task* to be taught. See *Task analysis.*

Referral   A teacher's request for additional resources when dealing with a particular student. Referral is the one thing that all special education students have in common.

Reflective reading   The active use of *reading comprehension* strategies and *metacognition* while reading.

Reformulate   To incorporate information into one's own knowledge base. Students reformulate during peer tutoring and cooperative learning as well as when asked to explain an idea in their own words.

Reliability   How consistently a test measures the same thing. The *Stranger Test.*

Remedial   A term applied to *curriculum* and occasionally to the students placed in that curriculum. Remedial instruction presents students with curriculum that typical students received at a younger age. It usually follows the same sequence but at a later time.

Repeated measure   A test or observation that is given the same way over time in order to note trends in learning. See *Slope* and *Data-based program modification.*

Resource (instruction or room)   Resource programs are designed to supplement regular class instruction, not to substitute for it. In a typical resource program, a student leaves the regular class for an hour a day for concentrated tutoring in areas of curricular weakness; therefore, the students in resource programs have two or more teachers, and it is necessary for the special-ed resource room teacher to communicate and schedule with the other teachers. Often the scheduling and communication/consultation role of the resource teacher requires more time and energy than instruction.

Response type   The way a student is expected to display knowledge during a test or observation. For example, the student may say the answer, write it, or act it out.

Retelling   A procedure used to sample reading comprehension. A student reads a passage and says what he read. Unlike paraphrasing, where a student must use their own words, a student may simply restate what he read.

Routines   Commonly employed procedures learned and used to accomplish trivial tasks. Routines free our *short-term memory* so we can attend to important things.

Scaffolding   The process of using a student's understanding of one topic to support learning of new information. The scaffold functions as a bridge between the *prior knowledge* from which it is constructed and the content of the new lesson.

Schema   A pattern of knowledge composed of several bits of information linked by a unifying theme. According to learning theory, information is stored in long-term memory within these schemata, and once activated by addressing a critical combination of the nodes, an entire schema can be recalled. When this happens the information-processing system has immediate access to all of the stored information. Recall by theme is therefore much more efficient than recall by a single stimulus. This is why efforts by the teacher to *consolidate* information by concept or strategy results in superior storage and recall.

Self-monitoring   The critical prerequisite for all problem solving is recognition that one has a problem. Effective learners constantly monitor their performance and their learning just as effective teachers are always aware of the status of their students.

Semantics   A term that refers to the study of meaning within language. It includes (1) meaning of single words and word combinations, (2) multiple meaning of words, (3) figurative language, and (4) the influence of content and structure on language.

Semantic maturity   Skill in selecting individual words for a particular message.

Sentence types:

   Complex sentence   A complete idea that includes one independent (Kim writes well . . .) and one dependent clause (when she plans, reviews, and revises her work).

   Compound sentence   Two complete ideas joined by a connecting word (Kim composes music and she enjoys playing the piano).

   Compound run-on sentence   More than two complete ideas joined by a connecting word (Eddie runs fast and Eddie drives fast and Eddie talks fast and Eddie likes cars).

   Sentence fragment   Incomplete idea (My grandchildren are . . .).

Simple sentence   Complete idea that consists of a single subject and a single predicate (Eddie runs fast. *Eddie* is the subject and *runs fast* is the predicate).

Sentence verification   A procedure used to sample reading comprehension. A multiple-choice format is used in which students select a sentence that means the same as an original sentence from the passage. Incorrect sentences may include similar sentence structure or similar vocabulary.

Short-term memory   Working memory. The function within the *information processing* model that allows for conscious attention to a task. Short-term memory is very limited.

Situational behavior   Behavior triggered by specific environmental conditions.

Slope (trend)   *Slope* refers to the slope of the student's learning as seen on a chart, with time on one axis and content or skill on the other. Slope is another term for progress, trends, or learning. The student with the greatest positive slope is progressing the fastest and learning the most. He is covering the most content in the least amount of time.

Social behavior   Social behavior includes those things that are done in response to, or in consideration of, others. It includes almost everything except self-stimulating behavior and addiction (although these may have social components, also). For some reason, social behavior is usually separated from *academic* behavior during teacher training.

Social competence   Using the skills required to advance both personal and community agendas without interfering with others, and without expending an inordinate amount of resources.

Sociolinguistic rules   Cultural guidelines for communication. Knowledge of what can be said, to whom, and in what context.

Sound analogy strategy   Refers to strategy where a student uses known sounds to decode new words (If I can decode *rich*, I can use that information to decode a similar word *which*.) This is sometimes referred to as a rhyming strategy.

Speech   Mechanical aspects of language (phonology, voice, and fluency).

Staffing   See *Child-study team*.

Standard error of measurement   A boundary of confidence that can be placed around a test score. Stan-dard error is calculated from the standard deviation and reliability of the test.

Standardization of criterion-referenced tests   Process of testing age-mates who possess the skill to establish criteria.

Standards   Expectations. See *Criteria*.

Status sheet   A list of the skills a student needs in order to succeed at a *task*. The list is typically developed through a *task analysis*, and the sheet is used to summarize what is known about the student's proficiency on each skill. Status sheets are usually employed in place of *survey-level testing* or during the development of *assumed causes* for a student's problem.

Story map   A technique used to assist readers in understanding what they read. Often a map is a diagram that illustrates how events are sequenced, how ideas are related, and what aspects of characters are important. It is a graphic representation of events and concepts in a story.

Strategy   A learned (although not necessarily consciously employed) procedure for dealing with a situation or problem. The term refers to any of a variety of activities employed to aid one's own attention, memory, academic production, or social competence. See *Task*.

Static data   Data that describe performance at only one time.

Structured instruction   See *Direct instruction*.

Subskill   See *Task analysis*.

Subtask   An essential component of a task that, when mastered, enables the learner to successfully perform the task.

Summarizing   Summarizing is one way a student can react to print. Summarizing can be taught and involves the development of a statement that relates the central message of a passage without redundancy or trivial information.

Summative evaluation   Evaluation that takes place at the end of a unit or section of instruction. Summative and formative evaluation can be contrasted like this: summative evaluation takes place at the end of a lesson or project and tells the evaluator what has happened. Formative evaluation takes place during the lesson or project and tells the evaluator what is happening. Summative evaluation "sums up" the activity.

It is after the fact, like end-of-the-year testing. Formative evaluation is ongoing, and yields information that can be used to modify the program prior to its termination.

Supplantive An approach to teaching through which the teacher actively adds to the student's knowledge through *direct instruction.* Supplantive instruction is *hands-on instruction.*

Syntactic interference The influence of the syntax of one language or dialect on another language or dialect.

Syntax Rule system that governs the order of words in a sentence.

Syntax maturity Skill in combining words to convey a message.

Task Any behavior, or set of behaviors.

Task (task analysis) The things we teach are sometimes called concepts or tasks. It is hard to separate these clearly. Superficially, a task is a thing and a concept is an idea; however, we only know the concept has been learned if the task can be completed and, if designed properly, the task can't be completed without knowing the concept. Therefore, a task could be just about anything.

Before a task can be dealt with, it must be made "behavioral" by stating it in the form of a performance *objective.* Several objectives form a *curriculum.*

In education, the objective is typically called a task. All tasks are composed of two things—essential subtasks and a task *strategy.* Essential subtasks are simply the other tasks a person *must* be able to complete in order to complete the main task. In a cumulative sense, a task is "harder" than its subtasks (although an individual subtask may have taken longer to learn). A subtask is essential if the task cannot be done without it.

A task may have several subtasks (the number depends on how finely the task is calibrated). The task strategy is the procedure by which these subtasks are combined to produce the task. If a student is skilled at all essential subtasks but does not know the strategy needed to combine them, he cannot do the task.

Effective teacher decision making is guided by task analysis. Task analysis is the process of clarifying the task, recognizing its essential subtasks, recognizing the task strategy, and sequencing the elements for instruction. Teachers use task analysis to avoid attempting to teach things students cannot learn (due to a missing subtask) or things they already know.

Task analysis The process of isolating, sequencing, and describing the essential components of a task.

Task related Skills that allow a student to succeed at learning a *task* which are not specific to that task. Task-related skills include note taking, listening, studying, and test taking.

Teacher action Things teachers can do. Effective teachers engage in different sets of teacher actions than do *pre-service* and ineffective teachers. See *Teacher thought processes.*

Teacher expectation What the teacher thinks the student will learn. High teacher expectations are related to high student learning.

Teacher thought processes Effective teachers think differently than teachers who are not effective. It is these different thoughts that cause them to use different *teacher actions.* The categories of teacher thought that seem related to effectiveness are: thoughts about the *task;* thoughts about instruction; thoughts about the student; and thoughts about the nature of learning. See *Teacher expectations.*

Test format The way the test stimuli are presented (multiple choice, fill in the blank, matching, etc.).

Testing A process to determine how a child functions in reality by asking him to perform a selected sample of behaviors.

Text structure The organization of written material; the way ideas are interrelated to convey a message. Some text structure interferes with a reader's comprehension while other text structure facilitates comprehension. Headings, transition statements, alerting statements, and summaries are often used by writers to organize a message so that it is easily understood.

Text variables The features of written material that contribute to or interfere with a reader's comprehension. Text variables include organizers such as headings, introductory comments, and summary statements. They also include vocabulary complexity and sentence length. See *Text structure.*

Therapy *Control* is what you do to accommodate the clients in the institution. It is the process by which you work to get the students to conform to the situation they are in. *Therapy* is what you do to prepare clients for situations outside of the institution. It goes beyond the rules and considerations of the moment. Therapy is analogous to teaching someone how to do something, while control is like doing it for him. Control is necessary for therapy to take place, but it is not sufficient.

TIES *The Instructional Environment Scale* is a device used to assess teaching environments. It serves as the basis for content listed in Appendix B.

Tool skills Skills that are essential subtasks of many *basic skills*. For example, "saying sounds" is a tool skill necessary for all oral language tasks, and "writing digits" is a tool necessary to write out a phone number or balance a checkbook.

Top down Instruction that focuses on the total task in the presumption that the student will learn the subtasks through deduction. See *Bottom up* and *Generative*.

Topical knowledge Knowledge of a curricular domain. In this text the term refers to material presented in Chapters 10–17.

Treatment modality See *Learning mode*.

Trend See *Slope*.

Trial A trial is a single stimulus-response presentation. In arithmetic, each problem on a worksheet is a trial. In language training, each request for an object is a trial. A trial has a clear beginning (teacher direction) and ending (student response).

T-unit A group of words which can stand alone and make sense. T-units are used in analysis of sentence complexity. The number of units which can stand alone within a sentence is one indicator of sentence complexity.

Unalterable variables Conditions of a student that cannot be altered within a reasonable time through the act of teaching. See *Alterable variables*.

Validity How well a test describes reality. Does the test measure what it's supposed to measure? The *So-What Test*.

Variable A characteristic, trait, skill, or condition of the student.

Verbal mediator Once the students are able to verbalize the procedure, they are able to literally "talk" their way through a situation to its solution. In the literature this is sometimes called *verbal mediation*.

Visually similar Look alike (b/d/p/q/g, m/n/u/h, v/w, n/r) (Carnine & Silbert, 1979, p. 73).

Working memory See *Short-term memory*.

Writing mechanics Grammar, punctuation, capitalization, handwriting, and spelling.

Writing-process approach A teaching focus that emphasizes writing as a communication act. Proponents suggest that currently there is too much emphasis on skill instruction and not enough on planning, transcribing, reviewing, and revising.

Written communication Written language, written expression.

References

Adams, J.L. (1979). *Conceptual Blockbusting* (2nd Ed.). San Francisco: W.H. Freeman.

Adams, M.J. (1990). *Beginning to Read: Thinking and Learning About Print*. Urbana-Champaign, IL: University of Illinois, Center for the Study of Reading.

Adams, M.J. (1991). "Beginning to Read": A critique by literacy professionals and a response by Marilyn Jager Adams. *Reading Teacher, 44*(6), 370–95.

Algozzine, B., Herr, D., & Eaves, R. (1976). Modification of biases held by teacher trainees toward the disturbingness of child behaviors. *Journal of Educational Research, 69*, 261–64.

Algozzine, B., O'Shea, D.J., Crews, W.B., & Stoddard, K. (1987). Analysis of mathematics competence of learning disabled adolescents. *The Journal of Special Education, 21*(2), 97–107.

Algozzine, B., & Ysseldyke, J.E. (1992). *Strategies and Tactics for Effective Instruction*. Longmont, CO: Sopris West.

Allen, R. (1992). Asking the experts: Students' view on delinquency. *Beyond Behavior, 3*(2), 12–19.

Allington, R.L. (1983). The reading instruction provided readers of differing reading abilities. *The Elementary School Journal, 83*, 548–59.

Allington, R.L. (1984). Oral Reading. In P.D. Pearson (Ed.), *Handbook of Reading Research*. White Plains, NY: Longman.

Allington, R.L. (1990). Children who find learning to read difficult: School responses to diversity. In E.H. Hiebert (Ed.), *Literacy for a Diverse Society: Perspectives, Programs, and Policies*. Palmer Press.

American Speech and Hearing Association. (1986). Personal comunication from the Director of the Professional Practices Division. Tempe, AZ: C.A. Kamara.

Anania, J. (1983). The influence of instructional conditions on student learning and achievement. *Evaluation in Education, 7*, 1–92.

Anderson, L.M. (1982). *Student responses to seatwork: Implications for the study of students' cognitive process-ing* (Research Series No. 102). East Lansing: Michigan State University, IRT Publications.

Anderson, L.M. (1984). The environment of instruction: The function of seatwork in a commercially developed curriculum. In G.G. Duffy, L.R. Roehler, & J. Mason (Eds.), *Comprehension Instruction: Perspectives and Suggestions* (pp. 93–103). New York: Longman.

Anderson, L.M. (1985). What are students doing when they do all that seatwork? In C. W. Fisher & D. C. Berliner (Eds.), *Perspectives on Instructional Time* (pp. 189–202). New York: Longman.

Anderson, L.M., Brubaker, N.L., Alleman-Brooks, J., & Duffy, G. (1985). A qualitative study of seatwork in first-grade classrooms. *The Elementary School Journal, 86*, 123–40.

Anderson, L.M., Stevens, D.D., Prawat, R.S., & Nickerson, J. (1988). Classroom task environments and student's task-related beliefs. *The Elementary School Journal, 88*, 281–95.

Anderson, R.C., & Armbruster, B. (1984). Content area textbooks. In R. C. Anderson, J. Osborn, & R. Tierney (Eds.), *Learning to Read in American Schools* (pp. 217–26). Hillsdale, NJ: Erlbaum.

Anderson, R.C., Osborn, J., & Tierney, R. (1984). *Learning to Read in American Schools: Basal Readers and Content Texts*. Hillsdale, NJ: Erlbaum.

Anderson, R.C., & Pearson, P.D. (1984). A schema-theoretic view of basic processes in reading comprehension. In D. Pearson, R. Barr, M. Kamil & P. Mosenthal (Eds.), *Handbook of Reading Research*. New York: Longman.

Andrews, J.F., & Mason J.M. (1991). Strategy use among deaf and hearing readers. *Exceptional Children, 57*, 536–45.

Antes, R.L. (1989). *Preparing Students for Taking Tests. Fastback 291*. Bloomington, IN: Phi Delta Kappa Educational Foundation.

Applebee, A.N. (1981). *Writing in the Secondary Schools*. Urbana, IL: National Council of Teachers of English.

Archer, A., & Gleason, M. (1989). *Skills for School Success*. North Billerica, MA: Curriculum Associates.

Arends, R.I. (1991). Translating research into practice: The effects of various forms of training and clinical experiences on preservice students' knowledge, skill and reflectiveness. *Journal of Teacher Education, 42*(1), 52–65.

Arkes, H. R., & Hammond, K. R. (Eds.). (1986). *Judgement and Decision Making: An Interdisciplinary Reader*. New York: Cambridge University Press.

Armbruster, B. (1984a). The problem of "inconsiderate text." In G. G. Duffy, L. R. Roewhler, & J. Mason (Eds.), *Comprehension Instruction Perspectives and Suggestions*. New York: Longman.

Armbruster, B. (1984b). Commentary. In R. J. Tierney & M. Leys (Eds.), *What Is the Value of Connecting Reading and Writing?* Reading Education Report No. 55. Urbana-Champaign, IL: University of Illinois.

Arter, J.A., & Jenkins, J.R. (1979). Differential diagnosis prescriptive teaching: A critical appraisal. *Review of Educational Research, 49*, 517–55.

Ashlock, R.B. (1990). *Error Patterns in Computation: A semi-programmed approach* (5th ed.). Columbus, OH: Merrill.

Assink, E.M.H., Kattenberg, G., & Wortmann, C. (1992). *Reading ability and the use of sublexical units in word identification*. Paper presented at the annual meeting of the American Educational Association, San Francisco, CA.

Baker, L., & Brown, A. (1984). Metacognitive skills and reading. In P.D. Pearson (Ed.), *The Handbook of Reading Research* (pp. 363–64). New York: Longman.

Baker, J.M., & Zigmond, N. (1990). Are regular education classes equipped to accommodate students with learning disabilities? *Exceptional Children, 56*(6), 515–26.

Baldauf, R.B. (1982). The effects of guessing and item dependence on the reliability and validity of recognition based cloze tests. *Educational and Psychological Measurement, 42*, 855–67.

Ball, E.W., & Blachman, B.A. (1991). Does phoneme awareness training in kindergarten make a difference in early word recognition and developmental spelling? *Reading Research Quarterly, 26*(1), 49–66.

Banbury, M.M., & Hebert, C.R. (1992). Do you see what I mean? Body language in classroom interactions. *The Council for Exceptional Children, 24*(2), 34–39.

Baroody, A.J., & Hume, J. (1991). Meaningful mathematics instruction: The case of fractions. *Remedial and Special Education, 12*(3), 54–68.

Barrett, M., Huisinigh, R., Jorgensen, C., & Zachman, L. (1983). *Teaching vocabulary, Volume 1, Grades K–4*. Moline, IL: LinguiSystems, Inc.

Barton, J.A. (1988). Problem-solving strategies in learning disabled and normal boys: Developmental and instructional effects. *Journal of Educational Psychology, 80*, 184–91.

Bateman, B.D. (1971). *Essentials for Teaching*. Sioux Falls, SD: Dimension.

Beaugrande, R. de. (1984). *Text Production: Toward a Science of Composition*. Norwood, NJ: Ablex.

Beck, I.L., McKeown, M.G., & McCaslin, E.S. (1983). Vocabulary development: All contexts are not created equal. *The Elementary School Journal, 83*, 178–81.

Beck, I.L., Perfetti, C.A., & McKeown, M.G. (1982). Effects of long-term vocabulary instruction on lexical access and reading comprehension. *Journal of Educational Psychology, 74*, 506–21.

Bennett, N., & Desforges, C. (1988). Matching classroom tasks to students' attainments. *The Elementary School Journal, 88*, 221–34.

Bennett, S.N., Roth, E., & Dunn, R. (1987). Task processes in mixed and single age classes. *Education, 15*, 43–50.

Bensoussan, M., & Ramraz, R. (1984). Testing EFL reading comprehension using a multiple-choice rational cloze. *The Modern Language Journal, 68*, 230–39.

Bereiter, C., & Scardamalia, M. (1984). Learning about writing from reading. *Written Communication, 1*, 163–188.

Berk, R.A. (1979). The relative merits of item transformations and the cloze procedure for the measurement of reading comprehension. *The Reading Teacher, 11*, 129–38.

Berk, R.A. (1980). A consumers' guide to criterion-referenced test reliability. *Journal of Educational Measurement, 17*, 323–49.

Berk, R.A. (1986). A consumers' guide to setting performance standards on criterion-referenced rests. *Review of Educational Research, 17*, 137–172.

Berliner, D.C. (1984). The half-full glass: A review of research on teaching. In P. L. Hosford (Ed.), *Using What We Know About Teaching*. Alexandria, VA: Association for Supervision and Curriculum Development.

Berliner, D. (1986). In pursuit of the expert pedagogue. *Educational Researcher, 15,* 5–13.

Berliner, D. (1987, January). *Effective classroom teaching*. Paper presented at the fourth annual School Effectiveness Workshop, Phoenix, AZ.

Berliner, D. (1989). *The place of process-product research in developing the agenda for research on teacher thinking*. Paper presented at the meetings of the American Educational Research Association, Boston, MA.

Berry, V. (1992). Communication priorities and strategies for the mainstreamed child with hearing loss. *Volta Review, 94*(1), 29–36.

Biemiller, A. (1978). Relationships between oral reading rates for letters, words, and simple text in the development of reading achievement. *Reading Research Quarterly, 13,* 223–53.

Bisanz, G.L., Das, J.P., Varnhagen, C.K., & Henderson, H.R. (1992). Structural components of reading time and recall for sentences in narratives: Exploring changes with age and reading ability. *Journal of Educational Psychology, 84*(1), 103–14.

Bishop, G. (1992). Personal communication. Tigard, OR.

Bitter, G.G., Englehart, J.M., & Weibe, J. (1977). *One Step at a Time*. St. Paul, MN: EMC Corp.

Bloom, B.S. (1976). *Human Characteristics and School Learning*. New York: McGraw-Hill.

Bloom, B.S. (1980). The new direction in education research: Alterable variables. *Phi Delta Kappan, 61,* 382–85.

Bloom, B.S., Madaus, G.F., & Hastings, J.T. (1981). *Evaluation to Improve Learning*. New York: McGraw-Hill.

Borg, W.R. (1980). Time and school learning. In C. Denham & A. Liberman (Eds.), *Time to Learn*. Washington, DC: National Institute of Learning.

Borko, H., Livingston, C., & Shavelson, R.J. (1990). Teachers' thinking about instruction. *Remedial and Special Education, 11*(6), 40–49.

Borkowski, J.G., Estrada, M.T., Milstead, M., and Hale, C.A. (1989). General problem-solving skills: Relations between metacognition and strategic processing. *Journal of the Council for Learning Disabilities, 12*(1), 57–70.

Boorstin, D.J. (1983). *The Discoverers*. New York: Random House.

Boulding, K. (1972). The schooling industry as a possible pathological section of the American economy. *Review of Educational Research, 42,* 129–43.

Bowen, E. (1984, December 3). A debate over dumbing down. *Time, 124,* 68.

Bower, E.M. (1972). Education as a humanizing process and its relationship to other humanizing processes. In S.E. Golann and C. Eisdorfer (Eds.), *Handbook of Community Mental Health*. Englewood Cliffs, NJ: Prentice-Hall.

Bracht, G.H. (1970). Experimental factors relating to aptitude treatment interactions. *Review of Educational Research, 40,* 627–45.

Brantlinger, E. (1991). Social class distinctions in adolescents' reports of problems and punishment in school. *Behavioral Disorders, 17*(1), 36–46.

Braun, C., Rennie, B.J., & Gordon, C.J. (1987). An examination of contexts for reading assessment. *Journal of Educational Research, 80*(5), 283–89.

Brehmer, B. (1986). In one word: Not from experience. In H. R. Arkes and K. R. Hammond (Eds.), *Judgement and Decision Making*. New York: Cambridge University Press.

Bridge, C.A., & Hiebert, E.H. (1985). A comparison of classroom teachers' perceptions of their writing instruction and textbook recommendations on writing practices. *The Elementary School Journal, 86,* 155–72.

Brigance, A.H. (1983). *Brigance Diagnostic Comprehensive Inventory of Basic Skills*. North Billerica, MA: Curriculum Associates.

Britton, J. (1978). The composing processes and the functions of writing. In C.R. Cooper & L. Odell (Eds.), *Research on Composing: Points of Departure* (pp. 13–28). Urbana, IL: National Council of Teachers of English.

Brokowski, J.G., & Muthurkrishna, N. (1992). Moving metacognition into the classroom: "Working models" and effective strategy teaching. In M. Pressley, K.R. Harris & J.T. Guthrie (Eds.), *Academic Competence and Literacy in Schools*. San Diego: Academic Press.

Brown, A.L. (1987). Metacognition, executive control, self-regulation and other even more mysterious mechanisms. In R.H. Kluwe and F.E. Weinert (Eds.), *Metacognition, Motivation and Learning*. Hillsdale, NJ: Erlbaum.

Brown, A.L., & Bryant, B.R. (1984). Critical reviews of three individually administered achievement tests. *Remedial and Special Education, 5,* 53–60.

Bulgren, J., Schumaker, J.B., & Deshler, D.D. (1988). Effectiveness of a concept teaching routine in enhancing the performance of LD students in secondary-level mainstream classes. *Learning Research Quarterly, 11,* 3–17.

Byrne, B., & Fielding-Barnes, R. (1988). Phoneme awareness and letter knowledge in the child's acquisition of the alphabetic principle. *Journal of Educational Psychology, 31*(3), 313–21.

Cadwell, J., & Jenkins, J. (1986). Teacher's judgements about their students: The effect of cognitive simplification strategies on the rating process. *American Educational Research Journal, 23,* 460–75.

Calfee, R. & Drum, P. (1986). Research on teaching reading. In M.C. Wittrock (Ed.), *Handbook of Research on Teaching* (3rd ed.) (pp. 804–49). New York: Macmillan.

California Department of Education. Division of Education Services & Personnel Management Services. (1991). *Current and Future Challenges.* Sacramento: California Youth Authority.

California Mathematics Assessment Advisory Committee. (1990). *Guidelines for the mathematics portfolio: Working paper.* Sacramento: California assessment program, California State Department of Education.

Campbell, N.R. (1940). *Final report, Committee of the British Association for Advancement of Science on the problem of measurement.* London: British Association.

Campione, J.C., & Brown, A.L. (1985). *Dynamic Assessment: One Approach and Some Initial Data* (Tech. Report No. 361). Urbana: University of Illinois, Center for the Study of Reading.

Carbo, M. (1992). Giving unequal learners an equal chance: A reply to a biased critique of learning styles. *Remedial and Special Education, 13*(1), 19–29.

Carnine, D.W. (1983). Direct instruction: In search of instructional solutions for educational problems. In D. Carnine, D. Elkind, A.D. Hendrickson, D. Meichenbaum, R.L. Seiben, & F. Smith (Eds.), *Interdis-*

ciplinary Voices in Learning Disabilities and Remedial Education (pp. 1–66). Austin, TX: Pro-Ed.

Carnine, D.W. (1990). New research on the brain: Implications for instruction. *Phi Delta Kappan, 71,* 372–77.

Carnine, D.W (1992). Introduction. In D. Carnine & E. J. Kameenui (Eds.), *Higher-Order Thinking: Designing Curriculum for Mainstreamed Students* (pp. 1–22). Austin, TX: Pro-Ed.

Carnine, D., Silbert, J., & Kameenui, E. (1990). *Direct Instruction Reading.* Columbus, OH: Merrill.

Carpenter, T.P., Matthews, W., Lindquist, M.M., & Silver, E.A. (1984). Achievement in mathematics: Results from the national assessment. *The Elementary School Journal, 84,* 485–95.

Carter, J., & Sugai, G. (1989). Survey on prereferral practices: Responses from state departments of education. *Exceptional Children, 55,* 298–302.

Carter, K., Cushing, K., Sabers, D., Stein, P., & Berliner, D.C. (1988). Expert-novice differences in perceiving and processing visual classroom information. *Journal of Teacher Education, 39,* 25–31.

Carver, R.P. (1983). Is reading rate constant or flexible? *Reading Research Quarterly, 18,* 190–215.

Case, L.P., Harris, D.R., & Graham, S. (1992). Improving the mathematical problem-solving skills of students with learning disabilities: Self-regulated strategy development. *The Journal of Special Education, 26*(1), 1–19.

Cataldo, S., & Ellis, N. (1988). Interactions in the development of spelling, reading and phonological skills. *Journal of Research Reading, 2*(2), 86–109.

Cawley, J.F., Baker-Kroczynski, S., & Urban, A. (1992). Seeking excellence in mathematics education for students with mild disabilities. *Teaching Exceptional Children, 24*(2), 40–43.

Cawley, J.F., & Parmar, R.S. (1992). Arithmetic programming for students with disabilities: An alternative. *Remedial and Special Education, 13*(3), 6–18.

Chi, M.T.H., & Glaser, R. (1985). Problem-solving ability. In R.J. Sternberg (Ed.), *Human Abilities: An Information-Processing Approach.* New York: W.H Freeman.

Chow, S.H. (1981). *A Study of Academic Learning Time for Mainstream Learning-Disabled Students.* Final report.

San Francisco, CA: Far West Laboratory for Educational Research and Development.

Christensen, C.A., & Cooper, T.J. (1991). The effectiveness of instruction in cognitive strategies in developing proficiency in single digit addition. *Cognition and Instruction, 8*(4), 363–71.

Christenson, S.L., Ysseldyke, J.E., and Thurlow, M.L. (1989). Critical instructional factors for students with mild handicaps: An integrative review. *Remedial and Special Education, 10*(5), 21–31.

Clarizio, H.F., & Payette, K. (1990). A survey of school psychologists' perspectives and practices with childhood depression. *Psychology in the Schools, 27*, 57–63.

Clark, C.M. (1987). The carrol model. In M.J. Dunkin (Ed.), *The International Encyclopedia of Teaching and Teacher Education.* Oxford: Pergamon.

Clark, C.M., & Peterson, P.L. (1986). Teachers' thought processes. In M.C. Wittrock (Ed.), *Handbook of Research on Teaching* (3rd ed.) (pp. 255–96). New York: Macmillan.

Clay, M.M. (1985). *Reading: The Patterning of Complex Behaviour* (2nd ed.) (pp. 200–204). Auckland, New Zealand: Heinemann.

Clement-Heist, K., Siegel, S., & Gaylord-Ross, R. (1992). Simulated and *in situ* vocational social skills training for youths with learning disabilities. *Exceptional Children, 58*(4), 336–45.

Cognition and Technology Group at Vanderbilt University. (1990). Anchored instruction and its relationship to situated cognition. *Educational Researcher, 19*(3), 2–10.

Cognition and Technology Group at Vanderbilt University. (1991, May). Technology and design of generative learning environments. *Educational Technology,* 34–40.

Cohen, A.S. (1987). Instructional allignment: Searching for a Magic Bullet. *Educational Researcher, 57*, 16–20.

Cole, L. (1956). Reflections on the teaching of handwriting. *Elementary School Journal, 57*, 95–99.

Coles, R. (1990). *Spiritual Life of Children.* Boston, MA: Houghton Mifflin.

Cromwell, R.L., Blashfield, R.K., & Strauss, J.S. (1975). Criteria for classification systems. In N. Hobbs (Ed.), *Issues in the Classification of Children.* San Francisco: Jossey-Bass.

Cronbach, L.J. (1957). The two disciplines of scientific psychology. *American Psychologist, 12*, 671–84.

Cummins, D.D. (1991). Children's interpretations of arithmetic word problems. *Cognition and Instruction, 8*(3), 261–89.

Cummins, J. (1986). Empowering minority students: A framework for interaction. *Harvard Educational Review, 56*, 18–36.

Cunningham, A.E., & Stanovich, K.E. (1990). Assessing print exposure and orthographic processing skill in children: A quick measure of reading experience. *Journal of Educational Psychology, 82*(4), 733–40.

Cziko, G.A. (1983). Commentary: Another response to Shannahan, Kamil, and Tobin: Further reasons to keep the cloze case open. *Reading Research Quarterly, 18,* 361–65.

Daiute, C., & Kruidenier, J. (1985). A self-questioning strategy to increase young writers' revising processes. *Applied Psycholinguistics, 6*(3), 307–318.

Daneman, M., & Stainton, M. (1991). Phonological recoding in silent reading. *Journal of Experimental Psychology: Learning, Memory, and Cognition, 17*(4), 618–32.

Davies, I.K. (1973). *Competency-Based Learning: Technology, Management and Design.* New York: McGraw-Hill.

Day, J.D. (1980). *Teaching Summarization Skills.* Unpublished doctorial dissertation, University of Illinois.

de Bettencourt, L. (1987). Strategy training: A need for clarification. *Exceptional Children, 54*(1), 24–30.

De Corte, E., Lodewijks, H., Parmentier, R., & Span, P. (Eds). (1987). *Learning and Instruction. European Research in an International Context* (Vol. 1). Oxford, England: Leuven University Press and Pergamon Press.

Deno, E. (1971). Some reflections on the use and interpretation of tests for teachers. *Focus on Exceptional Children, 2*, 1–11.

Deno, S. L. (1989). Curriculum-based measurement and alternative special education services: Fundamental and direct relationship. In M.R. Shinn (Ed.), *Curriculum-Based Measurement: Assessing Special Children* (pp. 1–17). New York: Guilford.

Deno, S.L., & Espin, C.A. (1991). Evaluation strategies

for preventing and remediating basic skill deficits. In G. Stoner, M. Shinn, & H. Walker (Eds.), *Interventions for Achievement and Behavior Problems* (pp 79–97). Silver Springs, MD: National Association of School Psychologists.

Deno, S.L., & Mirkin, P.K. (1977). *Data-Based Program Modification: A Manual*. Reston, VA: The Council for Exceptional Children.

Department of Education Task Force on Selected LEP Shortages (1991). *Remedying the Shortage of Teachers for Limited-English-Proficiency-Students*. Sacramento: California Department of Education.

Derry, S.J., & Murphy, D.A. (1986). Designing systems that train learning ability: From theory to practice. *Review of Educational Research, 56*, 1–39.

DeSanti, R.J., & Sullivan, V.G. (1984). Inter-rater reliability of the cloze reading inventory as a qualitative measure of reading comprehension. *Reading Psychology: An International Quarterly, 5*, 203–208.

Deshler, D. (1985). Strategies workshop presented to teachers in the Kyrene School District, Tempe, Arizona.

Diana v. State Board of Education. Civil Action No. C-70 37RFP (N.D. Cal. January 7, 1970 and June 18, 1973).

Dick, W., & Hagerty, N. (1971). *Topics in Measurement: Reliability and Validity*. New York: McGraw-Hill.

Dixon, R., & Carnine, D. (1992). A response to Heshusius' "Curriculum-based assessment and direct instruction: Critical reflections on fundamental assumptions." *Exceptional Children, 58*(5), 461–63.

Dixon, R., Englemann, S., & Olen, L. (1981). *Spelling Mastery: A Direct-Instruction Series*. Chicago, IL: Science Research.

Dole, J.A., Duffy, G.G., Roehler, L.R., & Pearson, P.D. (1991). Moving from the old to the new: Research on reading comprehension instruction. *Review of Educational Research, 61*(2), 239–64.

Doyle, W. (1983). Academic work. *Review of Educational Research, 53*, 159–99.

Doyle, W. (1986). Classroom organization and management. In M.C. Wittrock (Ed.), *Handbook of Research on Teaching* (3rd ed.) (pp. 392–31). New York: Macmillan.

Doyle, W., & Carter, K. (1987). Choosing the means of instruction. In V. Richardson-Koehler (Ed.), *Education Handbook*. White Plains, NY: Longman.

Du Charme, C., Earl, J., & Poplin, M.S. (1989). The author model: The constructivist view of the writing process. *Learning Disability Quarterly, 12*(3), 237–42.

Duffy, G.G. (1990). *Reading in the Middle School* (2nd Ed.). Newark, DE: International Reading Association.

Dunn, R. (1983). Learning style and its relation to exceptionality at both ends of the spectrum. *Exceptional Children, 49*, 496–506.

Dunn, R., Dunn, K., & Price, G.E. (1981). Learning styles: Research vs. opinion. *Phi Delta Kappan, 62*, 645–46.

Dunston, P.J. (1992). A critique of graphic organizer research. *Reading Research Instruction, 32*(2), 57–65.

DuPaul, G.J., Stoner, G., Putnam, D., & Tilly, W.D. (1991). Interventions for attention problems. In G. Stoner, M. Shinn, & H. Walker (Eds.), *Interventions for Achievement and Behavioral Problems* (pp. 685–714). Silver Springs, MD: National Association of School Psychologists.

Duran, R.P. (1988). Learning and assisted performance. In B.Z. Presseisen (Ed.), *At-Risk Students and Thinking*. Washington, D.C: National Education Association.

Durkin, D. (1990). *Matching Classroom Instruction with Reading Abilities: An Unmet Need* (Tech. Report No. 499). Urbana-Champaign: University of Illinois, Center for the Study of Reading.

Dweck, C. (1986). Motivational processes affecting learning. *American Psychologist, 41*(10), 1040–48.

Eaton, M.D. (1978). Data decisions and evaluation. In N.G. Haring, T.C. Lovitt, M.D. Eaton, and C.L. Hanson, *The Fourth R: Research in the Classroom*. Columbus, OH: Merrill.

Eckhoff, B. (1983). How reading affects children's writing. *Language Arts, 60*, 607–616.

Edwards, P.A., Beasley, K., & Thompson, J. (1991). Teachers in transition: Accomodating reading curriculum to cultural diversity. *The Reading Teacher, 44*, 436–37.

Edwards, W.J., & Newman. R.J. (1986). Multiattribute evaluation. In H.R. Arkes & K.R. Hammond (Eds.), *Judgement and Decision Making: An Interdisciplinary Reader*. New York: Cambridge University Press.

Eeds, M.A. (1985). Bookwords: Using a beginning word list of high frequency words from children's literature K–3. *The Reading Teacher, 38,* 418–23.

Ehri, L.C., & Sweet, J. (1991). Fingerpoint reading of memorized text: What enables beginners to process the print? *Reading Research Quarterly, 26*(4), 442–62.

Ehri, L.C., & Wilce, L.C. (1985). Movement into reading: Is the first stage of the printed word learning visual or phonetic? *Reading Research Quarterly, 20,* 163–79.

Eisenhart, M.A., & Cutts, K. (1991). Social and cultural influences on students' access to school knowledge. In E. Hiebert (Ed.), *Literacy for a Diverse Society: Perspectives, Programs and Policies.* New York: Teachers College Press.

Eisner, E.W. (1982). *Cognition and curriculum.* New York: Longman.

Eitzen, S.D. (1992). Problem students: The sociocultural roots. *Phi Delta Kappan, 73*(73), 584–90.

Elley, W.B. (1989). Vocabulary acquisition from listening to stories. *Reading Research Quarterly, 24*(2), 174–87.

Elliott, S.N. (1986). Children's ratings of the acceptability of classroom interventions for misbehavior: Findings and methodological considerations. *Journal of School Psychology, 24,* 23–35.

Ellis, A. (Ed.). (1971). *Growth Through Reason: Verbatim Cases in Rational-Emotive Therapy.* Palo Alto, CA: Science and Behavior.

Ellis, E.S., & Lenz, B.K. (1990). Techniques for mediating content-area learning: Issues and research. *Focus on Exceptional Children, 22*(9), 1–15.

Engle, R.W., Nations, J.K. & Cantor, J. (1990). Is "working memory capacity" just another name for word knowledge? *Journal of Educational Psychology, 82,* 799–804.

Englemann, S., & Carnine, D. (1982). *Theory of Instruction.* New York: Irvington.

Englemann, S., Carnine, D., & Steely, D.G. (1992). Making connections in mathematics. In D. Carnine & E.J. Kameenui (Eds.), *Higher-Order Thinking: Designing Curriculum for Mainstreamed Students* (pp. 75–106). Austin, TX: Pro-Ed.

Englert, C.S. (1984). Measuring teacher effectiveness from the teacher's point of view. *Focus on Exceptional Children, 17*(2), 1–15.

Englert, C.S. (1987). *The Nature of Writing Instruction in Regular and Special Education Clasrooms.* Paper presented at the international convention of the Council for Exceptional Children, Chicago.

Englert, C.S. (1992). Writing instruction from a sociocultural perspective: The holistic, dialogic, and social enterprise of writing. *Journal of Learning Disabilities, 25*(3), 153–72.

Englert, C.S., Raphael, T.E., Anderson, L.M., Anthony, H.M., & Stevens, D.D. (1991). Making strategies and self-talk visible: Writing instruction in regular and special education classrooms. *American Education Research Journal, 28,* 337–72.

English, F.W. (1987). *Curriculum Management for Schools, Colleges, Business* (pp. 157–80). Springfield, IL: Charles C Thomas.

English, F.W. (1988). Writing the audit. In *Curriculum Auditing.* Lancaster, PA: Technomic Publishing.

Enright, B.E. (1983). *Enright Diagnostic Inventory of Basic Arithmetic Skills.* North Billerica, MA: Curriculum Associates.

Ensminger, E., & Dangel, H.L. (1992). The Foxfire pedagogy: A confluence of best practices for special education. *Focus on Exceptional Children, 24*(7), 1–16.

Epstein, M.C., Patton, J.R., Polloway, E.A., & Foley, R. (1992). Educational services for students with behavior disorders: A review of individualized education programs. *Teacher Education and Special Education, 15*(1), 41–48.

Evans, W.H., Evans, S.S., Gable, R.A., & Kehlhem, M.A. (1991). Assertive discipline and behavior disorders: Is this a marriage made in heaven? *Beyond Behavior, 2,* 13–16.

Everston, C., Anderson, C., & Anderson, L., & Brophy, J. (1980). Relationships between classroom behaviors and student out-comes in junior high mathematics and English classes. *American Educational Research Journal, 17,* 43–60.

Evoy, A. (1992). Personal communication. Vancouver, BC.

Farr, R.C. (1969). *Reading: What Can Be Measured?* Newark, DE: International Reading Association Research Fund.

Fernald, G. M. (1943). *Remedial Techniques in Basic School Subjects*. New York: McGraw-Hill.

Feuerstein R. (1980). *Instrumental Enrichment: An Intervention Program for Cognitive Modifiability*. Baltimore, MD: University Park Press.

Fisher, C., Berliner, D., Filby, N., Marliave, R., Cahen, L., & Dishaw, M. (1980). Teaching behaviors, academic learning time, and student achievement. In C. Denham & A. Liberman (Eds.), *Time to Learn*. Washington, DC: National Institute of Learning.

Fisher, C.W., & Hiebert, E.H. (1990). Characteristics of tasks in two approaches to literacy instruction. *The Elementary School Journal*, *91*(1), 3–18.

Fitzgerald, F.S. (1989). In J.E. Russo & Schoemaker (Eds.), *Decision Traps*. New York: Doubleday.

Flood J., & Lapp, D. (1989). Reporting reading progress: Comparison portfolio for parents. *Reading Teacher*, *42*(7), 508–515.

Flower, L.S., & Hayes, J.R. (1990). The dynamics of composing: Making plans and juggling constraints. In L.W. Gregg & E.R. Steinberg (Eds.), *Cognitive Process in Writing* (pp. 31–50). Hillsdale, NJ: Erlbaum.

Forness, S.R. (1992). Broadening the cultural perspective in exclusion of youth with social maladjustment: First invited reaction to the Maag and Howell paper. *Remedial and Special Education*, *13*(1), 55–59.

Frank, A.R., & Brown, D. (1992). Self-monitoring strategies in arithmetic. *The Council for Exceptional Children*, *24*(2), 52–53.

Frederiksen, N. (1962). Proficiency tests for training evaluation. In R. Glaser (Ed.), *Training Research and Education*. Pittsburgh: University of Pittsburgh Press.

Frederiksen, N. (1984). Implications of cognitive theory for instruction in problem solving. *Review of Educational Research*, *54*, 363–407.

Frederiksen, N. (1986). Toward a broader concept of human intelligence. *American Psychologist*, *41*, 445–52.

Freeman, D.J., Kuhs, T.M., Porter, A.C., Floden, R.E., Schmidt, W.H.I., & Schuille, J.R. (1983). Do textbooks and tests define a national curriculum in elementary school mathematics? *The Elementary School Journal*, *83*, 501–513.

Fuchs, D., Fuchs, L.S., Benowitz, S., & Barringer, K. (1987). Norm-referenced tests: Are they valid for use with handicapped students? *Exceptional Children*, *54*, 263–71.

Fuchs, D., Fuchs, L.S., Dailey, A.M., & Power, M.H. (1985). The effect of examiner's personal familiarity and professional experience on handicapped children's test performance. *Journal of Educational Research*, *78*, 141–46.

Fuchs, L.S. (1992). Enhancing instructional programming and student achievement with curriculum-based measurement. In J. Kramer (Ed.), *Curriculum-Based Assessment: Examining Old Problems—Evaluating New Solutions*. Hillsdale, NJ: Erlbaum.

Fuchs, L.S., & Deno, S.L. (1991). Paradigmatic Distinctions between instructionally relevant measurement models. *Exceptional Children*, *57*, 488–500.

Fuchs, L.S., Deno, S.L., & Mirkin, P.K. (1985). Database program modification: A continuous evaluation system with computer software to facilitate instruction. *Journal of Special Education*, *6*, 50–57.

Fuchs, L.S., & Fuchs, D. (1986). Linking assessment to instructional interventions: An overview. *School Psychology Review*, *15*(3), 318–23.

Fuchs, L.S., & Fuchs, D. (1987). The relation between methods of graphing student performance data and achievement: A meta-analysis. *Journal of Special Education Technology*, *8*(3), 5–10.

Fuchs, L.S., & Fuchs, D. (1992). Identifying a measure for monitoring student reading progress. *School Psychology Review*, *21*, 45–58.

Fuchs, L.S., Fuchs, D., & Hamlett, C.L. (1989). Computers and curriculum-based measurement: Effects of teacher feedback systems. *School Psychology Review*, *18*, 112–29.

Fuchs, L.S., Fuchs, D., Hamlett, C.L., & Ferguson, C. (1992). Effects of expert system consultation within curriculum-based measurement using a reading maze task. *Exceptional Children*, *58*(5), 436–50.

Fuchs, L.S., Fuchs, D., & Maxwell, L. (1988). The validity of informal reading comprehension measures. *Remedial and Special Education*, *9*(2), 20–28.

Fuson, K.C. (1990). Conceptual structures for multiunit numbers: Implications for learning and teaching multi-digit addition, subtraction, and place value. *Cognition and Instruction*, *7*(4), 343–403.

Gaffney, J.S. (1991). Reading recovery: Widening the

scope of prevention for children at risk of reading failure. In K. Wood and B. Algozzine (Eds.), *Teaching Reading to High-Risk Learners: A Multidisciplinary Perspective*.

Gaffney, J.S., & Anderson, R.C. (1991). Two-tiered scaffolding: Congruent processes of teaching and learning. In E.H. Hiebert (Ed.), *Literacy for a Diverse Society: Perspectives, Programs and Policies*. New York: Teachers College Press.

Gajria, M., & Salvia, J. (1992). The effects of summarization instruction on text comprehension of students with learning disabilities. *Exceptional Children, 58*(6), 508–516.

Galagan, J.E. (1985). Psychoeducational testing: Turn out the lights, the party's over. *Exceptional Children, 52*, 288–299.

Gambrell, L.B., & Chasen, S.P. (1991). Explicit story structure instruction and the narrative writing of fourth- and fifth-grade below-average readers. *Reading Research and Instruction, 31*(1), 54–62.

Garner, R. (1992). Learning from school texts. *Educational Pscyhologist, 27*(1), 53–63.

Gazzaniga, M.S. (1989). Organization of the human brain. *Science, 24* 947–52.

Gerber, A., & Bryen, D.N. (1981). *Language and Learning Disabilities*. Baltimore, MD: University Park.

Gerber, M.M. (1987). Application of cognitive-behavioral training methods to teaching basic skills to mildly handicapped elementary school students. In M.C. Wang, M.C. Reynolds, & H.J. Walberg (Eds.), *Handbook of Special Education: Research and Practice* (Vol. 1). (pp. 167–86). New York: Pergamon.

Gersten, R. (1990). Enemies real and imagined: Implications of "teachers' thinking about instruction" for collaboration between special and general education. *Remedial and Special Education, 11*(6), 50–53.

Gersten, R. (1992). Passion and precision: Response to "Curriculum-based assessment and direct instruction: Critical reflections on fundamental assumptions. *Exceptional Children, 58*(5), 464–66.

Gersten, R., Woodward, J., & Darch, C. (1986). Direct instruction: A research-based approach to curriculum design and teaching. *Exceptional Children, 53*, 17–31.

Gettinger, M. (1989). Effects of maximizing time spent and minimizing time needed for learning on pupil achievement. *American Educational Research Journal, 26*(1), 73–91.

Geva, E., & Tierney, R.J. (1984). *Text Engineering: The Influence of Manipulated Compare/Contrast Selections*. Paper presented at the American Educational Research Association annual meeting, New Orleans.

Giek, K.A. (1992). Monitoring student progress through efficient record keeping. *Teaching Exceptional Children, 24*(3), 22–27.

Gilbert (1978). *Human Competence*. New York: McGraw-Hill.

Gillespie, C. (1991). Questions about student-generated questions. *The Journal of Reading, 34*, 250–57.

Glass, G.G. (1971). Perceptual conditioning for decoding: Rationale and method. In B.B. Bateman (Ed.), *Learning Disorders* (Vol. 4). Seattle, WA: Special Child Publications.

Glass, G.V. (1974a, May). *Excellence: A Paradox*. Speech presented at the second annual meeting of the Pacific Northwest Research and Evaluation Conference sponsored by the Washington Educational Research Association, Seattle, WA.

Glass, G.V. (1974b). Teacher effectiveness. In H.J. Walberg (Ed.), *Evaluating Educational Performance*. Berkeley, CA: McCutchan.

Glass, G.V. (1983). Effectiveness of special education. *Policy Studies Review, 2*, 65–78.

Gleason, M.M. (1988). Teaching study strategies. *Teaching Exceptional Children*, 52–57.

Gleason, M.M., Carnine, D., & Vala, N. (1991). Cumulative versus rapid introduction of new information. *Exceptional Children, 57*(4), 353–59.

Gleason, M.M., Colvin, G., & Archer, A.L. (1991). Interventions for improving study skills. In G. Stoner, M. Shinn, & H. Walker (Eds.), *Interventions for Achievement and Behavior Problems* (pp. 130–167). Silver Springs, MD: National Association of School Psychologists.

Goldstein, A.P. (1988). *The Prepare Curriculum*. Champaign, IL: Research Press.

Good, T.L., & Brophy, J.R. (1986). School effects. In M.C. Wittrock (Ed.), *Handbook of Research on Teaching* (3rd ed.). New York: Macmillan.

Graham, S., & Harris, K.R. (1988). Instructional recommendations for teaching writing to exceptional students. *Exceptional Children, 54,* 506–512.

Graham, S., MacArthur, C., Schwartz, S., & Page-Voth, V. (1992). Improving the compositions of students with learning disabilities using a strategy involving product and process goal setting. *Exceptional Children, 58*(4), 322–34.

Grave, C.E. (1944). The psychotherapeutic value of a remedial education program. *The Nervous Child, 3,* 343–49.

Graves, M.F. (1986). Vocabulary learning and instruction. In E. Z. RothKopf (Ed.), *Review of Educational Research,* (Vol. 13) (pp. 49–89). Washington D.C: American Educational Research Association.

Graves, M.F., Prenn, M.C., Earle, J., Thompson, M., Johnson, V., & Slater, W.H. (1991). Commentary: Improving instructional text: Some lessons learned. *Reading Research Quarterly, 26*(2), 110–22.

Greenburg, D. (1984). The 1984 annual report to Congress: Are we better off? *Exceptional Children, 51,* 203–208.

Greene, S.B., McKoon, G., & Ratcliff, R. (1992). Pronoun resolution and discourse models. *Journal of Experimental Psychology: Learning, Memory, and Cognition, 18*(2), 266–83.

Greenwood, C.R. (1991). Longitudinal analysis of time, engagement and achievement in at-risk versus non-risk students. *Exceptional Children, 57,* 521–35.

Gresham, F.M., & Reschly, D.J. (1986). Social skill deficits and low peer acceptance of mainstreamed learning disabled children. *Learning Disabilities Quarterly, 9,* 23–32.

Griffith, P.L., & Olson, M.W. (1992). Phonemic awareness helps beginning readers break the code. *The Reading Teacher, 45*(7), 516–23.

Gronlund, N.E. (1973). *Preparing Criterion-Referenced Tests for Classroom Instruction.* New York: Macmillan.

Grossen, B., & Carnine, D. (1991). Strategies for maximizing reading success in the regular classroom. In G. Stoner, M. Shinn, & H. Walker (Eds.), *Interventions for Achievement and Behavioral Problems* (pp. 333–356). Silver Springs, MD: National Association of School Psychologists.

Grossen, B., & Carnine, D. (1992). Translating research on text structure into classroom practice. *Teaching Exceptional Children, 24*(4), 48–53.

Gruenewald, L.J., & Pollak, S.A. (1990). *Language interaction in curriculum and instruction* (2nd Ed.). Austin, TX: Pro-Ed.

Guthrie, J.T. (1973). Reading comprehension and syntactic responses in good and poor readers. *Journal of Educational Psychology, 65,* 294–99.

Guthrie, J.T., Britten, T., & Baker, K.G. (1991). Roles of document structure, cognitive strategy, and awareness of searching for information. *Reading Research Quarterly, 26*(3), 300–324.

Hall, T., & Tindal, G. (1991). *The Portfolio Concept with Applications in Curriculum-Based Measurement.* Resource Consultant training program (Research Report No. 13). Eugene: University of Oregon.

Hallahan, D.P., & Kauffman, J.M. (1986). *Exceptional Children* (3rd ed.). Englewood Cliffs, NJ: Prentice-Hall.

Hambleton, R.K., & Novik, M. (1973). Toward an integration of theory and method for criterion-referenced tests. *Journal of Educational Measurement, 10,* 159–70.

Hansen, C. (1978). Story retelling used with average and learning disabled readers as a measure of reading comprehension. *Learning Disability Quarterly, 1,* 65.

Haring, N.G., & Eaton, M.D. (1978). Systematic instructional procedures: An instructional hierarchy. In N.G. Haring, T.C. Lovitt, M.D., Eaton, & C.L. Hansen (Eds.), *The Fourth R: Research in the Classroom* (pp. 23–40). Columbus, OH: Merrill.

Haring, N.G., Liberty, K.A., & White, O.R. (1980). Field Initiated Research Studies of Phases of Learning and Facilitating Instructional Events for the Severely/Profoundly Handicapped. (Available from the U.S. Office of Special Education, Project No. 413CH60397A, Grant No. G007500593.)

Harris, K.C. (1991). An expanded view on consultation competencies for educators serving culturally and linguistically exceptional students. *Teacher Education and Special Education, 14*(1), 25–29.

Harris, K.R.J., & Pressley, M. (1991). The nature of cognitive strategy instruction. *Exceptional Children, 57,* 392–404.

Hasbrouck, J.E., & Tindal, G. (1992). Curriculum-based oral reading fluency norms for students in grades two through five. *Exceptional Children, 24*(3), 41–44.

Haskell, D.W., Foorman, B.R., & Swank, P.R. (1992). Effects of three orthographic/phonological units on first-grade reading. *Remedial and Special Education, 13*(2), 40–49.

Haynes, M.C., & Jenkins, J.R. (1986). Reading instruction in special education resource rooms. *American Educational Research Journal, 23*, 161–90.

Hemingway, Z., Hemingway, P., Hutchinson, N.L., & Kuhns N.A. (1987). Effects of student characteristics on teachers' decisions and teachers' awareness of these effects. (British Columbia), *Journal of Special Education, 11*, 313–26.

Herbert, C.H. (1979). *Basic inventory of natural language.* San Bernardino, CA: CHEC Point Systems.

Herrmann, B.A. (1988). Two approaches for helping poor readers become more strategic. *Reading Teacher, 42*(1), 24–28.

Heshusius, L. (1991). Curriculum-based assessment and direct instruction: Critical reflections on fundamental assumptions. *Exceptional Children, 57*(4), 315–28.

Heward, W.L., Heron, T.E., Gardner, R., & Prayzer, R. (1991). Two strategies for improving students' writing skills. In G. Stoner, M. Shinn, & H. Walker (Eds.), *Interventions for Achievement and Behavioral Problems* (pp. 379–98). Silver Springs, MD: National Association of School Psychologists.

Hiebert, E.H. (1991). *Literacy for a Diverse Society.* New York: Teachers College Press.

Hildreth, G. (1964). Manuscript writing after sixty years. In V.D. Anderson et al. (Eds.), *Readings in the Language Arts.* New York: Macmillan.

Hirumi, A., & Bowers, D.R. (1991). Enhancing motivation and acquistion of coordinate concepts by using concept trees. *Journal of Educational Research, 84*, 273–79.

Hobson v. Hanson, 269F, Supp. 401. (Washington, D.C. 1967).

Hoffer, K. (1983). Assessment and instruction of reading skills: Results with Mexican-American students. *Learning Disability Quarterly, 6*, 458–67.

Hofmeister, A. (1975). Integrating criterion-referenced testing and instruction. In W. Hively & M. Reynolds (Eds.), *Domain-Referenced Testing in Special Education*

(pp. 77–87). Reston, VA: Council for Exceptional Children.

Holbrook, A.P. (1990). Handwriting legibility. In H.J. Walberg and G.D. Heartel (Eds.), *The International Encyclopedia of Educational Evaluation* (pp. 146–55). New York: Pergamon.

Holdaway, D. (1979). *The Foundations of Literacy.* Sidney, Australia: Ashton Scholastic.

Hoogeveen, R.R., Birkhoff, A.E., Smeets, P.M., Lancioni, G.E., & Boelens, H.H. (1989). Establishing phonemic segmentation in moderately retarded children. *Remedial and Special Education, 10*(3), 47–53.

Hoover, J.J., & Collier, C. (1991). Meeting the needs of culturally and linguistically diverse exceptional learners: Prereferral to mainstreaming. *Teacher Education and Special Education, 14*(1), 30–36.

Hopkins, K.D., Stanley, J.C., & Hopkins, B.R. (1990). *Educational and Psychological Measurement and Evaluation* (7th Ed.). Englewood Cliffs, NJ: Prentice-Hall.

Hopper, R., & Naremore, R.C. (1978). *Children's Speech: A Practical Introduction to Communication Development* (2nd ed.). New York: Harper & Row.

Horner, R.H., Albin, R.W.J., & O'Neil, R.E. (1991). Supporting students with severe intellectual disabilities and severe challenging behaviors. In G. Stoner, M.R. Shinn and H.M. Walker (Eds.), *Interventions for Achievement and Behavior Problems* (pp. 269–87). Silver Springs, MD: National Association of School Psychologists.

Horton, S.V., Lovitt, T.C., & White, O.R. (1992). Teaching mathematics to adolescents classified as educable mentally handicapped: Using calculators to remove the computation onus. *Remedial and Special Education, 13*(3), 36–61.

Hosseini, J., & Ferrell, W.R. (1982). Measuring metacognition in reading by detectability of cloze accuracy. *Journal of Reading Behavior, 14*, 263–74.

Howell, K.W. (1983). Task analysis and the characteristics of tasks. *Journal of Special Education Technology, 5*, 5–14.

Howell, K.W. (1986). Direct assessment of academic performance. *School Psychology Review, 15*(3), 324–35.

Howell, K.W. (1991). Curriculum-based evaluation: What you think is what you get. *Diagnostique, 16*(4), 193–203.

Howell, K.W., & Kaplan, J.S. (1978). Monitoring the behavior of peer tutors. *Exceptional Children, 45,* 135–37.

Howell, K.W., Kaplan, J.S., & O'Connell, C.Y. (1979). *Evaluating Exceptional Children: A Task Analysis.* Columbus, OH: Merrill.

Howell, K.W., & Lorson-Howell, K. (1990). What's the hurry? Fluency in the classroom. *Teaching Exceptional Children, 22*(3), 20–23.

Howell, K.W., & McCollum-Gahley, J. (1986). Monitoring instruction. *Teaching Exceptional Children, 19,* 47–49.

Howell, K.W., Zucker, S.H., & Morehead, M.K. (1982). *Multilevel Academic Skills Inventory: Math.* Columbus, OH: Merrill.

Howell, K.W., Zucker, S.H., & Morehead, M.K. (1985). *MAST: Multilevel Academic Survey Test.* Austin, TX: Psychological Corporation.

Howell, S.C., & Barnhart, R.S. (1992). Teaching word problem solving at the primary level. *Teaching Exceptional Children, 24*(2), 44–46.

Hunt, K.W. (1965). *Grammatical Structures Written at Three Grade Levels.* NCTE Research Report No. 3. Urbana, IL: National Council of Teachers of English (ERIC Document Reproduction Service #ED113735).

Huot, B. (1990). The literature of direct writing assessment: Major concerns and prevailing trends. *Review of Educational Research, 60*(2), 237–64.

Idol, L., & West, J.F. (1987). Consultation in Special Education (Part II: Training and Practice). *Journal of Learning Disabilities, 20,* 474–94.

Iglesias, A. (1985). Communication in the home and classroom: Match or mismatch? *Topics in Language Disorders, 6,* 29–41.

Isaacson, S. (1985). Assessing written language. In C. S. Simon (Ed.), *Communication Skills and Classroom Success: Assessment Methodologies for Language–Learning Disabled Students.* San Diego, CA: College Hill.

Isaacson, S. (1989a). Role of secretary vs. author: Resolving the conflict in writing instruction. *Learning Disability Quarterly, 12*(3), 209–217.

Isaacson, S. (1989b). Confused dichotomies: A response to Du Charme, Earl, and Poplin. *Learning Disability Quarterly, 12*(3), 243–47.

Isaacson, S. (1990). Written language. In P.J. Schloss, M.A. Smith, & C.N. Schloss (Eds.), *Instructional Methods for Secondary Students with Learning and Behavior Problems* (pp. 202–28). Boston: Allyn & Bacon.

Isaacson, S.L. (1992). Volleyball and other analogies: A response to Englert. *Journal of Learning Disabilities, 25*(3), 173–77.

Ivarie, J.J. (1986). Effects of Proficiency Rates on Later Performance of a Recall and Writing Behavior. *Remedial and Special Education, 7,* 25–30.

James, S.L. (1990). *Normal Language Acquisition.* Austin, TX: Pro-Ed.

Janney, R., & Meyer, L. (1989). *An Educative Approach to Behavior Problems.* Syracuse, NY: Child-Centered Inservice Training and Technical Assistance Network.

Jenkins, J.R., & Dixon, R. (1983). Vocabulary learning. *Contemporary Educational Psychology, 8,* 237–60.

Jenkins, J.R., & Jenkins, L.M. (1988). *Cross-Age and Peer Tutoring: Help for Children with Learning Problems.* Reston, VA: The Council for Exceptional Children.

Jenkins, J.R., & Leicester, N. (1992). Specialized instruction within general education: A case study of one elementary school. *Exceptional Children, 58,* 555–63.

Jenkins, J.R., & Pany, D.D. (1978). Standardized achievement tests: How useful for special education? *Exceptional Children, 44,* 448–53.

Jenkins, J.R., Pious, L., & Jewell, M. (1990). Special Education and the regular education initiative: Basic assumptions. *Exceptional Children, 56,* 479–91.

Johnson, D.D. (1983). *Three Sound Strategies for Vocabulary Development.* Ginn Occasional Papers: Writings in reading and language arts, Number 8. Columbus, OH: Ginn.

Johnson, D.D., & Baumann, J.F. (1984). Word identification. In P. D. Pearson (Ed.), *Handbook of Reading Research,* Part 3. New York: Longman.

Johnson, L. J., & Pugach, M.C. (1991). Peer collaboration: Accommodating students with mild learning and behavioral problems. *Exceptional Children, 57,* 454–61.

Johnson, M. (1967). Definitions and models in curriculum theory. *Educational Theory, 7,* 127–40.

Juel, C. (1985). Support for the theory of phonemic awareness as a predictor in literacy acquisition. Paper presented at the National Reading Conference, New Orleans, Louisiana.

Kaplan, J. (1990). *Beyond Behavior Modification* (2nd Ed.). Austin, TX: Pro-Ed.

Kaplan, J.S. (1972). *A Comparison of the Effects of Giving versus Receiving Instruction on the the Oral Reading of Low Achievers.* Unpublished doctoral dissertation, University of Oregon.

Katzell, R.A. & Thompson, D.E. (1990). Work motivation: Theory and practice. *American Psychologist, 45,* 144–53.

Kauffman, J.M. (1989). The regular education initiative as Reagan-Bush education policy: A trickle-down theory of education of the hard to teach. *Journal of Special Education, 23,* 256–78.

Kauffman, J.M., & Wong, K.L. (1991). Effective teachers of students with behavioral disorders: Are generic teaching skills enough? *Behavior Disorders, 16,* 225–37.

Kavale, K. (1981). Functions of the Illinois Test of Psycholinguistic Abilities (ITPA): Are they trainable? *Exceptional Children, 47,* 496–510.

Kavale, K.A., & Forness, S.R. (1987). Substance over style: Assessing the efficacy of modality testing and teaching. *Exceptional Children, 54,* 228–39.

Kawakami, A.J., & Hupei Au, K. (1986). Encouraging reading and language development in cultural minority children. *Topics in Language Disorders, 6,* 71–80.

Keel, M.C., & Gast, D.L. (1992). Small-group instruction for students with learning disabilities: Observational and incidental learning. *Exceptional Children, 58*(4), 357–67.

Kintsch, W., & Greene, E. (1978). The role of culture-specific schematics in the comprehension and recall of stories. *Discourse Processes, 1,* 1–13.

Kirsch, I. (1985). Response expectancy as a determinant of experience and behavior. *American Psychologist, 40,* 1189–1202.

Klare, G.R. (1984). *The Measurement of Readability* (pp. 681–744). Ames, IA: Iowa State University Press.

Kletzien, S.B. (1991). Strategy use by good and poor comprehenders reading expository text of differing levels. *Reading Research Quarterly, 26*(1), 67–86.

Knitzer, J., Steinber, Z., & Fleisch, B. (1990). *At the School House Door: An Examination of Programs and Policies for Children with Behavioral and Emotional Problems.* New York: Bank Street College of Education.

Korzybski, A. (1948). *Science and Sanity: An Introduction to Non-Aristotelian Systems and General Semantics* (3rd ed.). Lakeville, CN: Institute of General Semantics.

Kotovsky, K., & Simon, H.A. (1990). What makes some problems really hard: Explorations in the problem space of difficulty. *Cognitive Psychology, 22*(2), 43–83.

Kulik, J.A., Kulik, C.C., & Bangert-Drowns, R.L. (1990). Is there better evidence on mastery learning? A response to Slavin. *Review of Educational Research, 60*(2), 303–307.

Labov, W. (1969). The logic of nonstandard English. In J. E. Alates (Ed.), *Monograph Series on Language and Linguistics,* No. 22. Washington, DC: Georgetown University Press.

Lakin, K.C. (1983). A response to Gene V. Glass. *Policy Studies Review, 2,* 233–39.

Landfried, S.E. (1989). "Enabling" undermines responsibility in students. *Educational Leadership,* 79–83.

Langer, J.A. (1991). Literacy and schooling: A sociocognitive perspective. In E.H. Hiebert (Ed.), *Literacy for a Diverse Society* (pp. 9–27). New York: Teachers College Press.

Larry P. v. Riles, 495 F. supp 926 (N.D. CAL 1979) aff'd, 83–84 EHLR 555–304 (CAG 1984).

Larson, K.A. (1989a). Problem-solving training and parole adjustment in high-risk young adult offenders. *The Yearbook of Correctional Education,* 279–299.

Larson, K.A. (1989b). Task-related and interpersonal problem-solving training for increasing school success in high-risk young adolescents. *Remedial and Special Education, 10*(5), 32–42.

Larson, K.A., & Gerber, M.M. (1987). Effects of social metacognitive training for enhancing overt behavior in learning disabled and low achieving delinquents. *Exceptional Children, 54*(3), 201–211.

Lawlor, J. (1983). Sentence combining: A sequence for instruction. *Elementary School Journal, 84*(1), 53–62.

Leader, C.A. (1983). The talent for judgment. *Proceedings.* 49–53.

Leinhardt, G., & Greeno, J.C. (1986). The cognitive skill of teaching. *Journal of Educational Psychology, 78,* 75–95.

Liberman, I.Y., & Shankweiler, D. (1985). Phonology

and the problems of learning to read and write. *Remedial and Special Education, 6*, 8–17.

Liberty, K.A., Haring, N.G., & White, O.R. (1980). Rules for data-based strategy decisions in instructional programs: Current research and instructional implications. In W. Sailor, B. Wilcox, and L. Brown (Eds.), *Methods of Instruction for Severely Handicapped Students*. Baltimore, MD: Paul H. Brookes.

Livingston C., & Borko, H. (1990). High school mathematics review lessons: Expert-novice distinctions. *Journal for Research in Mathematics Education, 21*, 372–87.

Lloyd, J.W. (1984). How shall we individualize instruction—Or should we? *Remedial and Special Education, 5*, 7–15.

Lloyd, J.W., Crowley, E.P., Kohler, F.W., & Strain, P.S. (1988). Redefining the applied research agenda: Cooperative learning, prereferral, teacher consultation, and peer mediated intervention. *Journal of Learning Disabilities, 21*, 43–52.

Lloyd, J.W., Landrum, T.J., & Hallahan, D.P. (1991). Self-monitoring applications for classroom intervention. In G. Stoner, M. Shinn, & H. Walker (Eds.), *Interventions for Achievement and Behavior Problems* (pp. 201–214). Silver Springs, MD: National Associations of School Psychologists.

Lloyd J.W., & Loper, A.B. (1986). Measurement and evaluation of task related learning behaviors: Attention to task and metacognition. *School Psychologist Review, 15*(3), 336–46.

Loban, W.D. (1963). *The Language of Elementary School Children*. NCTE Research Report No. 1. Urbana-Champaign, IL: National Council of Teachers of English.

Lovitt, T.C. (1973). *Applied behavior analysis techniques and curriculum research*. Report submitted to the National Institute of Education.

Lovitt, T.C. (1984). *Tactics for teaching*. Columbus, OH: Merrill.

Lovitt, T.C. (1991). *Preventing school dropouts*. Austin, TX: Pro-Ed.

Lovitt, T., & Horton, S.V. (1991). Adapting textbooks for mildly handicapped adolescents. In G. Stoner, M. Shinn, & H. Walker (Eds.), *Interventions for Achievement and Behavior Problems* (pp. 439–72). Silver Springs, MD: National Association of School Psychologists.

Lysynchuk, L.M., Pressley, M., & Vye, N.J. (1990). Reciprocal teaching improves standardized reading-comprehension performance in poor comprehenders. *The Elementary School Journal, 90*(5), 469–84.

Maag, J.W., & Howell, K.W. (1992). Special Education and the exclusion of youth with social maladjustments: A cultural organizational perspective. *Remedial and Special Education, 13*(1), 47–54.

MacGinitie, W.H. (1984). Readability as a solution adds to the problem. In R.C. Anderson, J. Osborn, & R. Tierney (Eds.), *Learning to Read in American Schools* (pp. 141–51). Hillsdale, NJ: Erlbaum.

Madden, M. (1991, January). *I have test scores. Now what?* Paper presented at curriculum-based assessment conference. Eugene: University of Oregon.

Maheady, L., Mallette, B., Harper, G.F., & Sacca, K. (1991). Heads together: A peer-mediated option for improving the academic achievement of heterogenous learning groups. *Remedial and Special Education, 12*(2), 25–33.

Mahoney, M.J. (1977). Reflections on the cognitive-learning trend in psychotherapy. *American Psychologist, 32*, 5–13.

Mandler, J.M., & Johnson, N.S. (1977). Remembrance of things passed: Story structure and recall. *Cognitive Psychology, 9*, 111–51.

Marge, M. (1972). The general problem of language disabilities in children. In J.V. Irwin & M. Marge (Eds.), *Principles of Childhood Language Disabilities*. New York: Appleton-Century-Crofts.

Margolis, H. (1987). *Patterns, Thinking, and Cognition*. Chicago: University of Chicago Press.

Marston, D. (1988). Measuring academic progress on IEPs: A comparison of graphing approaches. *Exceptional Children, 55*(1), 38–44.

Marston, D., & Magnusson, D. (1988). Curriculum-based measurement: District level implementation. In J. Graden, J. Zins, & M. Curtis (Eds.), *Alternative Educational Delivery Systems: Enhancing Instructional Options for All Students* (pp. 137–172). Washington, DC: National Association of School Psychologists.

Marston, D., Tindal, G., & Deno, S.L. (1984). Eligibility for learning disability services: A direct and repeated measurement approach. *Exceptional Children, 50*(6), 554–55.

Martens, B.K., & Witt, J.C. (1988). On the ecological validity of behavior modification. In J.C. Witt, S.N. Elliott, & F.M. Gresham (Eds.), *Handbook of Behavior Therapy and Education* (pp. 115–39). Plenum.

Martin Jr., B., & Carle, E. (1983). *Brown Bear, Brown Bear, What Do You See?* New York: Henry Holt.

Marx, R.W., & Walsh, J. (1988). Learning from academic tasks. *Elementary School Journal, 88* (3), 207–219.

Mason, J.M., Herman, P.A., & Au, K.A. (1990). *Children's Developing Knowledge of Words* (Tech. Report No. 513). Urbana-Champaign: University of Illinois, Center for the Study of Reading.

McCagg, E.C., & Dansereau, D.F. (1991). A convergent paradigm for examining knowledge mapping as a learning strategy. *Journal of Educational Research, 84*(6), 317–24.

McDaniel, M.A., & Schlager, (1990). Discovery learning and transfer of problem-solving skills. *Cognition and Instruction, 7*(2), 129–59.

McGee, L.M., & Lomax, R.G. (1990). On combining apples and oranges: A response to Stahl and Miller. *Review of Educational Research, 60*(1), 133–40.

McGill-Franzen, A., & Allington, R.L. (1991). The gridlock of low reading achievement: Perspectives on practice and policy. *Remedial and Special Education, 12,* 20–30.

McIntyre, D.J., Copenhaver, R.W., Byrd, D.M., & Norris, W.R. (1983). A study of engaged student behavior within classroom activities during mathematics class. *Journal of Educational Research, 27,* 55–59.

McKeachie, W.J. (1987a). Cognitive skills and their transfer: Discussion. *International Journal of Educational Research, 11*(6), 707–712.

McKeachie, W.J. (1987b). The new look in instructional psychology: Teaching strategies for learning and thinking. In E. De Corte, H. Lodewijks, R. Parmentier, & P. Span (Eds.), *Learning and Instruction: European Research in an International Context*: Vol. I. (pp. 443–456).

McKeown, M.G., & Curtis, M.E. (Eds.). (1987). *The Nature of Vocabulary Acquisition*. Hillsdale, NJ: Erlbaum.

McLain, K., & Victoria, M. (1991, November). *Effects of Two Comprehension-Monitoring Strategies on the Metacognitive Awareness and Reading Achievement of Third- and Fifth-Grade Students*. Paper presented at the annual meeting of the National Reading Conference, Miami, Florida.

Medina, J., & Neill, D.M. (1990). *Fallout from the Testing Explosion: How 100 Million Standardized Exams Undermine Equity and Excellence in America's Public Schools* (3rd ed., revised). ED318749.

Mercer, C.D., & Miller, S. P. (1992). Teaching students with learning problems in math to acquire, understand, and apply basic math facts. *Remedial and Special Education, 13*(3), 19–35.

Mercer, J.R. (1973). Crosscultural evaluation of exceptionality. *Focus on Exceptional Children, 5,* 8–15.

Mergendoller, J.R., Marchman, V.A., Mitman, A.L., & Parker, M.J. (1988). Task demands and accountability in middle-grade science classes. *The Elementary School Journal, 8,* 251–65.

Meyer, B., & Rice, G.E. (1984). The structure of text. In D. Pearson, R. Barr, M. Kamil, & P. Mosenthal (Eds.), *Handbook of Reading Research*. New York: Longman.

Michael, W., Denny, B., Ireland-Galman, M., & Michael, J.J. (1987). The factorial validity of a college-level form of an academic self-concept scale. *Educational Research Quarterly, 11*(1), 34–39.

Miller-Jones, D. (1989). Culture and testing. *American Psychologist, 44*(2), 360–66.

Moos, R.H. (1973). Conceptualizations of human environments. *American Psychologist, 28,* 652–55.

Morrow, L.M., & Smith, J.K. (1990). The effects of group size on interactive storybook reading. *Reading Research Quarterly, 25*(3), 213–31.

Morse, W. (1992). Mental health professionals and teachers: How do the twain meet? *Beyond Behavior, 3*(2), 21–23.

Muma, J. (1973). Language assessment: Some underlying assumptions. *ASHA, 15,* 331–38.

Muma, J.R. (1978). *Language Handbook—Concepts, Assessment, Intervention*. Englewood Cliffs, NJ: Prentice-Hall.

Murphy, J., Weill, M., & McGreal, T.L. (1986). The basic practice model of instruction. *The Elementary School Journal, 87,* 83–183.

Nagy, W. E. (1988). *Vocabulary Instruction and Reading Comprehension* (Tech. Report No. 431). Champaign, IL: Center for the Study of Reading.

Nagy, W., Anderson, R.C., Schommer, M., Scott, J.A., & Stallman, A.C. (1989). Morphological families in the internal lexicon. *Reading Research Quarterly, 24*(3), 262–82.

Nagy, W.E., & Scott, J.A. (1990). Word schemas: Expectations about the form and meaning of new words. *Cognition and Instruction, 7*, 105–157.

National Coalition of Advocates for Students (1985). *Barriers to Excellence: Our Children at Risk.* Boston, MA: NCAS.

Nelson, C.M., Rutherford, R.B., Center, D.B., & Walker, H.M. (1991). Do public schools have an obligation to serve troubled children and youth? *Exceptional Children, 57*, 406–416.

Nichols, P. (1992). The curriculum of control: Twelve reasons for it: Some arguments against it. *Beyond Behavior, 3*(2), 5–11.

Nolet, V., Tindal, G., & Howell, K.W. (1992). *Monograph No. 4: Teacher Assistance Team (TAT) Models.* Eugene: University of Oregon, Resource Training Program.

Northwest Regional Educational Laboratory. (1990). *Effective Schooling Practices: A Research Synthesis 1990 Update.* Portland, OR: Northwest Regional Educational Laboratory.

Nowacek, E.J. (1992). Professionals talk about teaching together: Interviews with five collaborating teachers. *Intervention in School and Clinic, 27*(5), 262–76.

Nowacek, E.J., McKinney, J.D., & Hallahan, D.P. (1990). Instructional behaviors of more and less effective regular and special educators. *Exceptional Children, 57*, 140–49.

O'Connor, R. (1992, April 20). Personal communication. Washington Research Institute.

Ogle, D.M. (1986). K-W-L: A teaching model that develops active reading of expository text. *The Reading Teacher, 36*, 564–70.

Ohlsson, S., & Rees, E. (1991). The function of conceptual understanding in the learning of arithmetic procedures. *Cognition and Instruction, 8*(2), 103–179.

Okyere, B.A., & Heron, T.E. (1991). Use of self-correction to improve spelling in regular education classrooms. In G. Stoner, M. Shinn, & H. Walker (Eds.), *Interventions for Achievement and Behavioral Problems* (pp. 399–414). Silver Springs, MD: National Association of School Psychologists.

O'Neil, R.E., Horner, R.H., Albin, R.W., Storey, K.T. & Sprague, J. (1989). *Functional Analysis: A Practical Assessment Guide.* Eugene: University of Oregon.

O'Sullivan, P.J., Ysseldyke, J., Christenson, S.L., & Thurlow, M.L. (1990). Mildly handicapped elementary students' opportunity to learn during reading instruction in mainstream and special education settings. *Reading Research Quarterly, 25*(2), 131–46.

Paget, K.D., & Galant, K. (1991). Promoting communication competence in pre-school children. In G. Stoner, M. Shinn, & H. Walker (Eds.), *Interventions for Achievement and Behavioral Problems* (pp. 289–304). Silver Springs, MD: National Association of School Psychologists.

Palincsar, A.S. (1986). The role of dialogue in providing scaffolded instruction. *Educational Psychologist, 21*, 73–98.

Palincsar, A.S. (1990). Reaction: Providing the context for intentional learning. *Remedial and Special Education, 11*(6), 36–39.

Palincsar, A.S., & Brown, A.L. (1984). Reciprocal teaching of comprehension-fostering and comprehension-monitoring activities. *Cognition and Instruction, 1*, 117–75.

Palincsar, A.S., & Brown, A.L. (1987). Advances in improving the cognitive performance of handicapped students. In M.C. Wang, M.C. Reynolds, and H.J. Walberg (Eds.), *Handbook of Special Education: Research and Practice.* New York: Pergamon.

Palincsar, A.S., & David, Y.M. (1992). Promoting literacy through classroom dialogue. In E. Hiebert (Ed.), *Literacy for a Diverse Society: Perspectives, Programs, and Policies.* New York: Teachers College Press.

Pany, D. (1987, January). *Phonemic Segmentation.* Paper presented at Regional Reading Conference, Phoenix, Arizona.

Paris, S.G., & Jacobs, J.E. (1984). The benefits of informed instruction for children's reading awareness and comprehension skills. *Child Development, 55*, 2083–93.

Paris, S.G., & Oka, E.R. (1989). Strategies for comprehending text and coping with reading difficulties. *Learning Disabilities Quarterly, 12*, 32–42.

Paris, S.G., & Winograd, P. (1990). Promoting metacognition and motivation of exceptional children. *Remedial and Special Education*, 11(6), 7–15.

Parker, R., Hasbrouck, J., & Tindal, G.J. (1991) The utility P.F. Caum's oral reading miscue categories, *Research Report RR5*. Eugene, OR: Resource Consultant Training Program, University of Oregon.

Parker, R., Hasbrouck, J., & Tindal, G. (1992–In press). The maze as a classroom-based reading measure: Construction methods, reliability, and validity. *The Journal of Special Education*.

Parker, R.I., Tindal, G., & Hasbrouck, J. (1991). Progress monitoring with objective measures of writing performance for students with mild disabilities. *Exceptional Children*, 58(1), 61–73.

Patching, W., Kameenui, E., Carnine, D., Gersten, R., & Colvin, G. (1983). Direct instruction in critical reading skills. *Reading Research Quarterly*, 18, 361–65.

Paulos, J.A. (1988). *Innumeracy: Mathematical Illiteracy and Its Consequences*. New York: Hill and Wang.

Pearson, D.P., Roehler, L.R., Dole, J.A., & Duffy, G.G. (1990). *Developing Expertise in Reading Comprehension: What Should Be Taught?* (Tech. Report No. 512). Urbana-Champaign: University of Illinois, Center for the Study of Reading.

Peterson, L., Wonderlich, S.A., Reaven, N.M., & Mullins, L.L. (1987). Adult educators' response to depression and stress in children. *Journal of Social and Clinical Psychology*, 5(1), 51–58.

Peterson, M., & Haines, L. (1992). Orthographic analogy training with kindergarten children: Effects on anology use, phonemic segmentation, and letter sound knowledge. *Journal of Reading Behavior*, 23(1), 109–127.

Peterson, P.L., Fennema, E., Carpenter, T.P., & Loef, M. (1989). Teachers' pedagogical content beliefs in mathematics. *Cognition and Instruction*, 6, 1–40.

Peterson, S.E. (1992). The cognition functions of underlining as a study technique. *Reading Research and Instruction*, 32(2), 49–56.

Petty, W.T., & Finn, P.J. (1981). Classroom teachers' reports on teaching written composition. In S. Haley-James (Ed.), *Perspectives on Writing in Grades 1–8* (pp. 19–33). Urbana, IL: National Council of Teachers of English.

Philips, S. (1970). Acquisition of roles in appropriate speech usage. *Monograph Series on Language and Linguistics, No. 23*. Washington, DC: Georgetown University Press.

Pianta, R.C. (1990). Widening the debate on educational reform: Prevention as a viable alternative. *Exceptional Children*, 56(4), 306–313.

Pikulski, J.J., & Pikulski, E.C. (1977). Cloze, maze, and teacher judgment. *The Reading Teacher*, 30, 776–70.

Polloway, E.A., & Smith, J.E. (1982). *Teaching Language Skills to Exceptional Learners*. Denver: Love.

Postman, N., & Weingartner, C. (1969). *Teaching as a Subversive Activity*. New York: Dell.

Powers, A.R., & Wilgus, S. (1983). Linguistic complexity in written language of hearing-impaired children. *Volta Review*, 85, 201–210.

Pressley, M., Ghatala, E.S., Woloshyn V., & Pirie, J. (1990). Sometimes adults miss main ideas and do not realize it: Confidence in responses to short answer and multiple-choice comprehension questions. *Reading Research Quarterly*, 25(3), 232–49.

Pressley, M., Harris, K.P., & Mark, M.B. (1992). But good strategy instructors are constructivists! *Educational Psychology Review*, 4(1), 3–31.

Pritchard, R. (1990). The effects of cultural schemata on reading processing strategies. *Reading Research Quarterly*, 25(4), 273–95.

Propst, I.K., & Baldauf, R.B. (1981). Psycholinguistic rationale for measuring beginning ESL reading with matching cloze tests. *RELC Journal*, 12, 85–89.

Pugach, M.C., & Johnson, L.J. (1988). Rethinking the relationship between consultation and collaborative problem solving. *Focus on Exceptional Children*, 21, 1–8.

Putnam, J.W., Rynders, J.E., Johnson, R.T., & Johnson, D.W. (1989). Collaborative skill instruction for promoting positive interactions between mentally handicapped and nonhandicapped children. *Exceptional Children*, 55(6), 550–57.

Quay, H.C. (1973). Assumptions, techniques and evaluative criteria. *Exceptional Children*, 40, 165–70.

Raphael, T.E., & Pearson, D.P. (1985). Increasing students' awareness of sources of information for answering questions. *American Research Journal*, 22, 217–35.

Rauenbusch, F., & Bereiter, C. (1991). Making reading more difficult: A degraded text microworld for teaching reading comprehension strategies. *Cognition and Instruction, 8*(2), 181–206.

Raymond, R.C. (1989). Teaching students to revise: Theories and practice. *Teaching English in the Two-Year College, 16*(1), 49–58.

Read, C., & Ruyter, L. (1985). Reading and spelling skills in adults of low literacy. *Remedial and Special Education, 6*, 53–60.

Reid, D.K., & Stone, C.A. (1991). Why is cognitive instruction effective? Underlying learning mechanisms. *Remedial and Special Education, 12*, 8–19.

Reid, S.K. (1992). *Cognition* (3rd Ed.). Pacific Grove, CA: Brooks/Cole.

Reif, L. (1990). Finding the value in evaluation: Self-assessment in a middle school classroom. *Educational Leadership, 47*(6), 24–29.

Reschly, D.J. (1991). The effects of placement litigation on psychological and educational classification. *Diagnostique, 17*(1), 6–20.

Reschly, D.J., Genshaft, J., & Binder, M.S. (1986). *The 1986 NASP Survey: Comparison of Practitioners, NASP Leadership, and University Faculty on Key Issues* (pp. 1–58). Silver Springs, MD: National Association of School Psychologists.

Reutzel, R. (1985). Story maps to improve comprehension. *The Reading Teacher, 38*, 400–404.

Reyes, M. (1990, April). *Comparison of L1 and L2 Pre and Post Writing Samples of Bilingual Students.* Paper presented at the annual meeting of the American Educational Research Association Conference, Boston, MA.

Reynolds, M.C., & Balow, B. (1972). Categories and variables in special education. *Exceptional Children, 38*, 357–66.

Reynolds, R.D., & Anderson, R.C. (1982). Influence of questions on the allocation of attention during reading. *Journal of Educational Psychology, 74*(5), 623–32.

Rich, S., & Pressley, M. (1990). Teacher acceptance of reading comprehension strategy instruction. *The Elementary School Journal, 91*(1), 43–64.

Rigney, J. W. (1980). Cognitive learning strategies and dualities in information processing. In R. Snow, P. A. Federico, & W. Motaguel (Eds.), *Aptitude, Learning and Instruction* (Vol. 1). Hillsdale, NJ: Erlbaum.

Roberts, G.H. (1968). The failure strategies of third-grade arithmetic pupils. *The Arithmetic Teacher, 15*, 442–46.

Robinson, V. (1992). Court lifts California ban on I.Q. tests for black students. *Counterpoint, 13*(1), 18.

Roden-Nord, M.K., & Shinn, M.R. (1991). The range of reading skills within and across the general education classroom. *The Journal of Special Education, 24*, 441–53.

Rogoff, B. (1978). Spot observation: An introduction and examination. *Quarterly Newsletter of the Institute for Comparative Human Development, 2*, 21–26.

Roid, G.H., & Haladyna, T.M. (1982). *A Technology for Test-Item Writing.* New York: Macmillan.

Roller, C.M. (1990). The interaction between knowledge and structure variables in the processing of expository prose. *Reading Research Quarterly, 25*(2), 79–89.

Rosenshine, B.V. (1983). Teaching functions in instructional programs. *Elementary School Journal, 83*, 335–52.

Rosenshine, B.V., & Stevens, R. (1986). Teaching functions. In M.C. Wittrock (Ed.), *Handbook on Research and Teaching* (3rd Ed.). New York: Macmillan.

Rotter, J.B. (1982). *The Development and Application of Social Learning Theory: Selected Papers.* New York: Praeger.

Rueda, R., Figueroa, R., Mercado, P., & Cardoza, D. (1985). *Performance of Hispanic Educable Mentally Retarded, Learning Disabled, and Nonclassified Students on the WISC-R, SOMPA, and S-KABC.* Final report: Handicapped-Minority Research Institute. Los Alamitos, CA: Southwest Regional Laboratory Educational Research and Development.

Rueda, R., Goldenberg, C., & Gallimore, R. (1993-in press). *A Manual for the Use of the Instructional Conversion Rating Scale.* National center on cultural diversity. Second language learning and center for applied linguistics. Santa Cruz, CA: University of California.

Ryder, R.J. (1991). The directed questioning activity for X subject matter text. *Journal of Reading, 34*, 606–612.

Sabers, D. (1992). Personal communication. Tucson, Arizona.

Sabers, D., Cushing, K.S., & Berliner, D.C. (1991). Differences among teachers in a task characterized by simultaneity, multidimensionality and immediacy. *American Educational Research Journal, 28*, 63–88.

Sabornie, E.J. (1991). Measuring and teaching social skills in the mainstream. In G. Stoner, M. Shinn, & H. Walker (Eds.), *Intervention for Achievment and Behavior Problems* (pp. 161–78). Silver Springs, MD: National Association of School Psychologists.

Salvia, J., & Hughes, C. (1990). *Curriculum-Based Assessment: Testing What Is Taught.* New York: Macmillan.

Samuels, J., & Kamil, M.L. (1984). Models of the reading process. In P.D. Pearson (Ed.), *Handbook of Reading Research* (pp. 185–224). New York: Longman.

Samuels, S.J. (1983). Diagnosing reading problems. *Topics in Learning and Learning Disabilities, 2,* 1–11.

Saville-Troike, M. (1976). *Foundation for Teachinq English as a Second Language: Theory and Method for Multi-Cultural Education.* Englewood Cliffs, NJ: Prentice-Hall.

Scardamalia, M., & Berieter, C. (1986). Research on written composition. In M.C. Wittrock (Ed.), *Handbook of Research on Teaching* (pp. 778–803). New York: Macmillan.

Schickedanz, J.A. (1990). The jury is still out on the effects of whole language and language experience approaches for beginning reading. *Review of Educational Research, 60*(1), 127–32.

Schloss, P.J., & Sedlak, R.A. (1982). Behavioral features of the mentally retarded adolescent: Implications for mainstream educators. *Psychology in the Schools, 19,* 98–105.

Schmitt, M.G. (1990). A questionaire to measure children's awareness of strategic reading processes. *The Reading Teacher, 43,* 454–61.

Schoenfeld, A.H. (1989). Teaching mathematical thinking and problem solving. In L.B. Resnick & L.E. Klopfer (Eds.), *Toward the Thinking Curriculum: Current Cognitive Research* (pp. 83–103). Alexandria, VA: ASCD Yearbook.

School Improvement Program. (1990). *Effective Schooling Practices: A Research Synthesis 1990 Update.* Portland, OR: Northwest Regional Educational Laboratory.

Schumaker, J.B., Denton, P.H., Deshler, D.D. (1984). *Learning Strategies Curriculum: The Paraphrasing Strategy.* Lawrence: University of Kansas.

Schumaker, J.B., Deshler, D.D., Alley, G.R., Warner, M.W., & Denton, P.H. (1982). Multipass: A learning strategy for improving reading comprehension. *Learning Disability Quarterly, 5,* 295–304.

Schumaker, J.B., Deshler, D.D., & McKnight, P.C. (1991). Teaching routines for content areas at the secondary level. In G. Stoner, M. Shinn, & H. Walker (Eds.), *Intervention for Achievement and Behavioral Problems* (pp. 473–494). Silver Springs, MD: National Association of School Psychologists.

Schumaker, J.B., Nolan, S.M., & Deshler, D.D. (1985). *Learning Strategies Curriculum: The Error-Monitoring Strategy.* Lawrence: University of Kansas.

Schumaker, J.B., Pederson, C.S., Hazel, J.S., & Meyer, E.L. (1983). Social skills curriculum for mildly handicapped adolescents: A review. *Focus on Exceptional Children, 4,* 1–16.

Self, H., Benning, A., Marston, D., & Magnusson, D. (1991). Cooperative teaching project: A model for students at risk. *Exceptional Children, 58,* 26–34.

Seligman, M.E.P. (1991). *Learned Optimism.* New York: Knopf.

Semmel, M.I., Abernathy, T.V., Butera, G., & Lesar, S. (1991). Teacher perceptions of the Regular Education Initiative. *Exceptional Children, 58,* 9–24.

Serapiglia, T. (1978). Comparison of the syntax and vocabulary of bilingual Spanish, Indian, and monolingual Anglo-American children. *Working Papers on Bilingualism, 16,* 75–91.

Serapiglia, T. (1992). Personal communication. Tempe, Arizona: Kyrene School District.

Shavelson, R.J. (1983). Review of research on teachers' pedagogical judgements, plans, and decisions. *Elementary School Journal, 83,* 392–413.

Shavelson, R.J., & Stern P. (1981). Research on teachers' pedagogical thoughts, judgements, decisions, and behavior. *Review of Educational Research, 51,* 455–98.

Shinn, M. R. (1989). *Curriculum-Based Measurement: Assessing Special Children.* New York: Guilford.

Shinn, M.R., Good III, R.H., Knutson, N., Tilly III, D.W., & Collins, V.L. (1992-In press). Curriculum-based measurement of reading fluency: A confirmatory analysis of its relationship to reading. *School Psychology Review.*

Shinn, M.R., Habedank, L., Rodden-Nord, K., & Knutson, N. (1993-in press). Using curriculum-based measurement to identify potential candidates for reintegration into general education. *The Journal of Special Education*.

Shinn, M.R., & Hubbard, D.D. (1992). Curriculum-based measurement and problem-solving assessment: Basic procedures and outcomes. *Focus on Exceptional Children, 24*(5), 1–20.

Showers, B. (1990). Aiming for superior classroom instruction for all children: A comprehensive staff development model. *Remedial and Special Education, 11*(3), 35–39.

Shriner, J., & Salvia, J. (1988). Chronic noncorrespondence between elementary math curricula and arithmetic tests. *Exceptional Children, 55*, 240–48.

Shuell, T.J. (1990). Phases of meaningful learning. *Review of Educational Research, 60*(4), 531–47.

Shulman, L.S. (1986). Paradigms and research programs in the study of teaching: A contemporary perspective. In M.C. Wittrock (Ed.), *Handbook of Research on Teaching* (3rd Ed.). New York: Macmillan.

Siegler, R.S. (1983). How knowledge influences learning. *American Scientist, 71*, 631–38.

Silbert, J., Carnine, D., & Stein, M. (1990). *Direct Instruction Mathematics* (2nd Ed.). Columbus, OH: Merrill.

Simmons, D.C., & Kameenui, E.J. (1989). Direct instruction of decoding skills and strategies. *LD Forum, 15*(1), 35–38.

Simmons, D.C., & Kameenui, E.J. (1990). The effect of task alternatives on vocabulary knowledge: A comparison of students with and without learning disabilities. *Journal of Learning Disabilities, 23*(5), 291–97.

Sindelar, P.T., & Stoddard, K. (1991). Teaching reading to mildly disabled students in regular classes. In G. Stoner, M. Shinn, & H. Walker (Eds.), *Interventions for Achievement and Behavior Problems* (pp. 357–79). Silver Springs, MD: National Association of School Psychologists.

Skrtic, T. (1991). The special education paradox: Equity as the way to excellence. *Harvard Educational Review, 61*(2), 148–206.

Smith, F. (1982). *Writing and the Writer*. New York: Holt, Rinehart & Winston.

Smith, P. L. (April 1992). *A Model for Selection from Supplantive and Generative Instructional Strategies for Problem-Solving Instruction*. Paper presented at the conference of the American Educational Research Association, San Francisco, CA.

Snider, V.E. (1992). Learning styles and learning to read. *Remedial and Special Education, 13*(1), 6–18.

Snow, R.E., & Lohman, D.F. (1984). Toward a theory of cognitive aptitude for learning from instruction. *Journal of Educational Psychology, 76*(3), 347–76.

Spaai, G.W., Ellermann, H.H., & Reitsma, P. (1991). Effects of segmented and whole-word sound feedback on learning to read single words. *Journal of Educational Research, 84*(4), 204–213.

Spache, G.D. (1940). Characteristic errors of good and poor spellers. *Journal of Educational Research, 34*, 182–89.

Spady, W.G. (1988). Organizing for results: The basis of authentic restructuring and reform. *Educational Leadership, 46*, 4–8.

Spiro, R.J., Coulson, R.C., Feltovich, P., & Anderson, D.K. (1988). *Cognitive Flexibility Theory: Advanced Knowledge Acquisition in Ill-Structured Domains* (Tech. Report No. 441). Urbana-Champaign: University of Illinois, Center for the Study of Reading.

Staats, A.W., Brewer, B.A., & Gross, M.C. (1970). Learning and cognitive development: Representative samples of cumulative-hierarchical learning and experimental longitudinal methods. *Monographs in the Society of Research in Child Develoment, 35*(8) (Serial No. 141).

Stahl, S.A. (1990). Riding the pendulum: A rejoinder to Schickedanz and McGee and Lomax. *Review of Educational Research, 60*(1), 141–51.

Stahl, S.A., Jacobson, M.G., Davis, C.E., & Davis, R.L. (1991). Prior knowledge and difficult vocabulary in the comprehension of unfamiliar text. *Reading Research Quarterly, 26*(1), 27–43.

Stahl, S.A. & Miller, P.D. (1989). Whole language and language experience approaches for beginning reading: A quantitative research synthesis. *Review of Educational Research, 59*, 87–116.

Stainback, S., Stainback, W., & Forest, M. (Eds.). (1989). *Education of All Students in the Mainstream of Regular Education*. Baltimore: Paul H. Brookes.

Stallman, A.C., & Pearson, D.P. (1990). *Formal Measures of Early Literacy* (Tech. Report No. 511). Urbana-

Champaign: University of Illinois, Center for the Study of Reading.

Stanovich, K.E. (1991). Discrepancy definitions of reading disability: Has intelligence led us astray? *Reading Research Quarterly, 26* (1), 7–29.

Starlin, C.M. (1982). *Iowa Monograph: On Reading and Writing*. Des Moine, IA: Department of Public Instruction.

Stenmark, J.K. (1989). *Assessment Alternatives in Mathematics*. Berkeley: California Mathematics Council, University of California.

Stephenson, W. (1980). Newton's fifth rule and Q methodology application to educational psychology. *American Psychologist, 35*, 882–89.

Sternberg, R.J. (1982). Reasoning, problem solving, and intelligence. In R.J. Sternberg (Ed.), *Handbook of Human Intelligence*. New York: Cambridge University Press.

Stevens, R.J., Madden, N.A., Slavin, R.E., & Farnish, A.M. (1987). Cooperative integrated reading and composition: Two field experiments. *Reading Research Quarterly, 22*, 433–54.

Stoner, G., Shinn, M., & Walker, H. (1991). *Interventions for Achievement and Behavioral Problems*. Silver Springs, MD: National Association of School Psychologists.

Stowitschek, J.J., Stowitschek, C.E., Hendrickson, J.M., & Day, R.M. (1984). *Direct Teaching Tactics for Exceptional Children*. Rockville, MD: Aspen.

Strickland, B., & Turnbull, A. (1990). *Developing and Implementing Individualized Education Programs* (3rd ed.). Columbus, OH: Merrill.

Strickland, D.S., & Morrow, L.M. (1990). Integrating the emergent literacy curriculum with themes. *Reading Teacher, 43*(8), 604–605.

Stump, C.S. (1991, October). Editing checklist for written expression. Presentation for the 13th International Conference on Learning Disabilities. Minneapolis, Minnesota.

Sulzer-Azaroff, B., & Mayer, R. (1991). *Behavior Analysis for Lasting Change*. New York: Holt, Rinehart & Winston.

Swanson, H.L. (1989). Strategy instruction: Overview of principles and procedures for effective use. *Learning Disability Quarterly, 12*, 3–14.

Sweller, J. (1990). On the limited evidence for the effectiveness of teaching general problem-solving strategies. *Journal for Research in Mathematics Education, 21*(5), 411–15.

Tallmadge, G.K., & Horst, D.P. (1974). *A procedural guide for validating achievement gains in educational projects*. Washington, DC: U.S. Department of Health, Education, and Welfare, Office of Education.

Tateyama-Sniezek, K.M. (1990). Cooperative learning: Does it improve the academic achievement of students with handicaps? *Exceptional Children, 56*(5), 425–37.

Teale, W.H. (1989). Developmentally appropriate assessment of reading and writing in the early childhood classroom. *The Elementary School Journal, 89*(2), 173–83.

Teddlie, C., Kirby, P.C., & Stringfield, S. (1989). Effective versus ineffective schools: Observable differences in the classroom. *American Journal of Education, 97*, 221–36.

Templin, M.C. (1957). *Certain Language Skills in Children: Their Development and Interrelationships*. Minneapolis: University of Minnesota Press.

Tennenbaum, H.A. (1983). Effects of oral reading rate and inflection on comprehension and its maintenance (doctoral dissertation, University of Florida). *Dissertation Abstracts International, 45*, 1086A.

Terry, P.W. (1992). The reading problem in arithmetic. *Educational Psychology, 84*(1), 70–75.

Tharp, R. (1989). Psychocultural variables and constant: Effects on teaching and learning in schools. *American Psychologist, 44*, 349–59.

Tharp, R., & Gallimore, R. (1989). Rousing schools to life. *American Education, 13*(2), 20–25.

Thiagarajan, S., Semmel, D.S., & Semmel, M.I. (1974). *Instructional Development for Training Teachers of Exceptional Children*. Bloomington, IN: Center for Innovation in Teaching the Handicapped.

Thistlethwaite, L.L. (1991). Summarizing: It's more than finding the main idea. *Intervention in School and Clinic, 27*, 25–30.

Thompson, L., & Majsterek, D.J. (1992, April 20). *Classroom Procedures for Increasing Phonological Awareness of Preschool Children: Justification and Preliminary Support*. Paper presented at the annual meeting of the

American Education Research Association, San Francisco, CA.

Thorndike, E.L. (1917). *Education: A First Book*. New York: Macmillan.

Thorndike, R.L., & Hagan, E. (1969). *Measurement and Evaluation in Psychology and Education* (3rd ed.). New York: Wiley.

Thornton, N.E., Bohlmeyer, E.M., Dickson, L.A., & Kulhavy, R.W. (1990). Spontaneous and imposed study tactics in learning prose. *Journal of Experimental Education, 58*(2), 111–24.

Tierney, R., & Leys, M. (1984). *What Is the Value of Connecting Reading and Writing?* (Reading Education Report #55). Urbana-Champaign: University of Illinois.

Tindal, G.A., & Hasbrouck, J. (1991). Analyzing student writing to develop instructional strategies. *Learning Disabilities Research & Practice, 6*, 237–45.

Tindal, G.A., & Marston, D.B. (1990). *Classroom-Based Assessment*. Columbus, OH: Merrill.

Tindal, G., & Parker, R. (1991). Identifying measures for evaluating written expression. *Learning Disabilities Research & Practice, 6*, 211–18.

Torgesen, J., & Kail, R.J. (1980). Memory processes in exceptional children. In B.K. Keogh (Ed.), *Advances in Special Education: Basic Constructs and Theoretical Orientations* (Vol. 1). Greenwich, CT: JAI Press.

Treiman, R. (1985). Onsets and rims as units of spoken syllabus: Evidence from children. *Journal of Experimental Child Psychology, 39*, 161–81.

Truesdell, L. A., Abramson, T. (1992). Academic behavior and grades of mainstreamed students with mild disabilities. *Exceptional Children, 58*(5), 392–98.

Tucker, J.A. (1985). Curriculum-based assessment: An introduction. *Exceptional Children, 52*, 199–204.

Tversky, A., & Kahneman, D. (1973). Availability: A heuristic for judging frequency and probability. *Cognitive Psychology, 5*, 207–232.

Tversky, A., & Kahneman, D. (1988). Judgement under uncertainty: Heuristics and biases. In H.R. Arkes & K.R. Hammond (Eds.), *Judgement and Decision Making*. New York: Cambridge University Press.

U.S. Department of Education, Office of Special Education. (1984). *Report of Handicapped Children Receiving Special Education and Related Services as Reported by State Agencies Under PL 94-142 and PL 89-313, School Year 1983-1984*. Washington, DC: U.S. Office of Education.

Ulman, J.D., & Rosenberg, M.S. (1986). Science and superstition in special education. *Exceptional Children, 52*, 459–60.

United States Department of Education. (1991). *Thirteenth Annual Report to Congress on the Implementation of the Education of the Handicapped Act (EHA)*. Washington, DC: Author.

Valdez, C. (1986, February). *Effectiveness of Bilingual Education as Related to Teacher Training*. Keynote address, Arizona Association for Bilingual Education, Tucson, Arizona.

Valencia, S. (1990). A portfolio approach to classroom reading assessment: The whys, whats, and hows (assessment). *Reading Teacher, 43*(4), 338–40.

Valencia, S., McGinley, W.L., & Pearson, D.P. (1992). Assessing literacy in the middle school. In G. Duffy (Ed.), *Reading in the Middle School* (2nd ed). Newark, DE: International Reading Association.

Valencia, S.W., Stallmann, A.C., Commeyras, M., Pearson, D.P., & Hartman, D.D. (1990). *Four Measures of Topical Knowledge: A Study of Construct Validity* (Tech. Report No. 501). Urbana-Champaign: University of Illinois, Center for the Study of Reading.

Valencia, S.W., & Wixson, K.K. (1991). Diagnostic teaching. *The Reading Teacher, 44*(6), 420–22.

Videen, J., Deno, S., & Marston, D. (1982). *Correct Word Sequences: A Valid Indicator of Proficiency in Written Expression* (Research Report No. 84). Minneapolis: University of Minnesota, Institute for Research of Learning Disabilities.

Vygotsky, L.S. (1978). In M. Cole, V. John-Steiner, S. Scribner, & E. Souberman (Eds.) *Mind in Society: The Development of Higher, Psychological Processes*. Cambridge, MA: Harvard University Press.

Wade, S.E., Trathen, W., & Schraw, G. (1990). An analysis of spontaneous study strategies. *Reading Research Quarterly, 25*(2), 147–66.

Wagner, R.K., & Sternberg, R.J. (1984). Alternative conceptions of intelligence and their implications for education. *Review of Educational Research, 54*, 179–223.

Walberg, H.J. (1988). Synthesis of research on time and learning. *Educational Leadership, 45*, 76–85.

Walker, H.M., & Rankin, R. (1983). Assessing the behavioral expectations and demand of less restrictive settings. *School Psychology Review, 12,* 274–84.

Wang, M.C., Haertel, G.D.,& Walberg, H.J. (1990). What influences learning? A content analysis of review literature. *Journal of Educational Research, 84,* 30–43.

Wang, M.C., & Peverly, S.T. (1987). The role of the learner: An individual difference variable in school learning and functioning. In M. C. Wang, M.C. Reynolds, and H. J. Walberg (Eds.). *Handbook of Special Education: Research and Practice,* (Vol.1). New York: Pergamon.

Warger, C.L. (1992). *Peer Tutoring: When Working Together Is Better Than Working Alone* (Research and Resources No. 30). ERIC/OSEP Special project. Reston, VA: The Council for Exceptional Children.

Waugh, R.P. (1975). The I.T.P.A.: Ballast or bonanza for the school psychologist? *Journal of School Psychology, 13,* 201–208.

Waugh, R.P. (1978). *Research for Teachers: Teaching Students to Comprehend.* A document. Portland, OR: Northwest Regional Educational Laboratory.

Webber, J., Anderson, T., & Otey, L. (1991). Teacher mindsets for surviving in BD classrooms. *Intervention in School and Clinic, 26*(5), 288–92.

Weed, K., Ryan, E.B., & Day, J. (1990). Metamemory and attributions as mediators of strategy use and recall. *Journal of Educational Psychology, 82*(4), 849–55.

Weinstein, C.E. & Mayer, R.E. (1983). The teaching of learning strategies. *Innovation Abstracts, 5*(32).

Welch, M. (1992). The PLEASE strategy: A metacognitive learning strategy for improving the paragraph writing of students with mild learning disabilities. *Learning Disability Quarterly, 15*(2), 119–28.

Wells, G. (1973). *Coding Manual of the Description of Child Speech.* Bristol, England: University of Bristol School of Education.

Wesson, C.L., King, R.P., & Deno, S.L. (1984). Direct and repeated measurement of student performance: If it's good for us, why don't we use it? *Learning Disability Quarterly, 7,* 45–48.

Westby, C. (1992). Whole language and learners with mild handicaps. *Focus on Exceptional Children, 24*(8), 1–16.

Westby, C.E., & Rouse, G.R. (1985). Culture in education and the instruction of language learning disabled students. *Topics in Language Disorders, 5,* 15–28.

White, O.R. (1986). Precision teaching—Precision learning. *Exceptional Children, 52,* 522–34.

White, O.R., & Haring, N.G. (1982). *Exceptional Teaching* (2nd ed.). Columbus, OH: Merrill.

Wiig, E.H., Freedman, E., & Secord, W. (1992). Developing words and concepts in the classroom: A holistic-thematic approach. *Intervention in School Clinic, 27*(5), 278–85.

Wiig, E.H., & Semel, E. (1984). *Language Assessment and Intervention for the Learninq Disabled* (2nd ed.). Columbus, OH: Merrill.

Williams, J.P. (1984). Phonemic analysis and how it relates to reading. *Annual Review of Learning Disabilities, 2,* 91–96.

Willis, G.W. (1985). Successive and simultaneous processing: A note on interpretation. *Journal of Psychoeducational Assessment, 4,* 343–46.

Winn, W. (1991). Learning from maps and diagrams. *Educational Psychology Review, 3*(3), 211–47.

Winne, P.H., & Marx, R.W. (1989). A cognitive-processing analysis of motivation within classroom tasks. In C. Ames & R. Ames (Eds.), *Research on Motivation in Education* (3rd ed.), pp. 223–58. San Diego: Academic Press.

Wittrock, M.C. (1991). Generative teaching of comprehension. *Elementary School Journal, 92,* 169–84.

Wolery, M., Bailey Jr., D.B., & Sugai, G.M. (1989). *Effective Teaching: Applied Behavior Analysis with Exceptional Students.* Boston: Allyn & Bacon.

Wolf, D.P. (1989). Portfolio assessment: Sampling student work. *Educational Leadership, 46,* 35–39.

Woloshyn, V.E., Pressley, M., & Schneider, W. (1992). Elaborative-interrogation and prior-knowledge effects on learning of facts. *Journal of Educational Pscychology, 84*(1), 115–23.

Wong, B.Y.L. (1991a). *Learning about learning disabilities.* San Diego: Academic Press.

Wong, B.Y.L. (1991b). The relevance of metacognition to learning disabilities. In B.Y.L. Wong (Ed.), *Learning About Learning Disabilities.* San Diego: Academic Press.

Wong, K.L.H., Kauffman, J.M. & Lloyd, J.W. (1991). Choices for integration: Selecting teachers for mainstreamed students with emotional and behavioral disorders. *Intervention in School and Clinic, 27*, 108–115.

Yavorsky, D.K. (1977). *Discrepancy Evaluation: A Practitioner's Guide*. Charlottesville, VA: University of Virginia, Evaluation Research Center.

Yopp, H.K. (1988). The validity and reliability of phonemic awareness tests. *Reading Research Quarterly, 23*, 159–77.

Yopp, H.K. (1992a). Developing phonemic awareness in young children. *The Reading Teacher, 45*(9), 696–703.

Yopp, H.K. (1992b). *A Longitudinal Study of Phonological Awareness and Its Relationship to Reading Achievement*. Paper presented at the annual meeting of the American Educational Research Association, San Francisco, CA.

Ysseldyke, J.E. (1987). The impact of screening and referral practices in early childhood special education: Policy consideration and research directions. *Journal of Special Education, 21*(2), 85–96.

Ysseldyke, J.E., Algozzine, B.J., & Thurlow, M.L. (Eds.). (1992). *Critical Issues in Special Education*. Dallas, TX: Houghton Mifflin.

Ysseldyke, J.E., & Christenson, S.L. (1987). *TIES: The Instructional Environment Scale*. Austin, TX: Pro-Ed.

Ysseldyke, J.E., Thurlow, M., Graden, J., Wesson, C., Algozzine, B., & Deno, S. (1983). Generalizations from five years of research on assessment and decision making: The University of Minnesota Institute. *Exceptional Education Quarterly, 4*(1), 75–93.

Ysseldyke, J.E., Thurlow, M.L., Mecklenburg, C., & Graden, J. (1984). Opportunity to learn for regular and special education students during reading instruction. *Remedial and Special Education, 5*, 29–37.

Zechmeister, E.B. & Johnson, J.E. (1992) *Critical Thinking: A Functional Approach*. Pacific Grove, CA: Brooks/Cole.

Zukav, G. (1979). *The Dancing Wu Li Masters*. New York: Bantam.

Name Index

Subject Index

Page numbers that appear in boldface refer to definitions of terms.